THE BEGINNINGS OF CHRISTIANITY

THE BEGINNINGS OF CHRISTIANITY

PART I
THE ACTS OF THE APOSTLES

EDITED BY

F. J. FOAKES JACKSON, D.D.

AND

KIRSOPP LAKE, D.D.

VOL. II
PROLEGOMENA II
CRITICISM

Wipf and Stock Publishers
EUGENE, OREGON

Wipf and Stock Publishers
199 West 8th Avenue, Suite 3
Eugene, Oregon 97401

The Beginnings of Christianity: The Acts of the Apostles
Volume II: Prolegomena II: Criticism
By Jackson, F.J. Foakes and Lake, Kirsopp
ISBN: 1-59244-070-3
Publication Date: October, 2002
Previously published by Macmillan and Co., 1922.

PREFACE

IN the preface to the former volume of this book we declared the general purpose of our undertaking to be the study and, so far as possible, the explanation of the Beginnings of Christianity. Before, however, attempting to reconstruct this history we believed it necessary to study Acts in the light of the results of modern criticism. Unfortunately some of our reviewers considered that we were already endeavouring fully to reconstruct the narrative. This was not our purpose, which was in fact to indicate the points necessary to a more detailed study of Acts and suitable as prolegomena. Later on we hope to return to the subject and reconsider the narrative of the life of Jesus, and the influence on the Church of his own teaching and of the teaching of others about him,—two subjects which are not identical though necessarily related.

In the present volume we have endeavoured to deal with the difficult questions of the composition and authorship of Acts and the history of their treatment by other critics. We greatly regret that the important works of Professor Zahn and Professor Loisy on the Acts did not reach us in time to be mentioned.

We have begun by dealing in the first part with the Greek and Jewish traditions of writing history, which must necessarily, by their points of affinity with Acts, modify our estimate of the book as a record of events; Professor de Zwaan has dealt with the language of Acts, and Mr. Clarke with its relation to the Septuagint; Professor Burkitt has discussed Luke's use of Mark, whilst we ourselves have treated the sources employed by the author of Acts and the light thrown by analysis on the history, purpose, and theology of the book. In the second part the topic is the question of authorship. Professor Cadbury has collected the chief *Testimonia Veterum*, and discussed their value; Mr. Emmet has stated the case for the identity of the author of Acts with the Luke who was the companion of Paul, and Professor Windisch has given the arguments in favour of the opposite view. The last part is devoted to two short statements by President McGiffert and Mr. Hunkin of the history of the criticism of Acts. We were very glad to be enabled, through the kind introduction of Professor Burkitt, to allow British scholars to be represented by one of themselves.

It remains for us to justify one of the appendices which to some of our readers may appear to have little connection with Acts. In modern historical work the psychological factor has attained a prominence which it did not formerly possess. It may, indeed, be prophesied that the writers of the future will be less occupied with the collection of material, its analysis and synthesis, than with the application of psychology to the established facts and to the problems raised. It is not within our purpose to offer an elaborate contribution to this important subject; but we have thought it well to illustrate the way in which the figures of history were soon invested with new characteristics, so that in the subsequent development of thought concerning them these new and relatively unhistorical features became more important than the original facts. How this could happen can only be explained by the psychology of authorship. In order to concentrate attention on two aspects of this fact, apart from the details of the history with which we are more immediately concerned, we have chosen two examples from ages remote from the first appearance of Christianity. Mr. Coulton has given the facts concerning the true Saint Francis of Assisi and the literary image which was subsequently created by Franciscan piety. There would never have been a Franciscan Order without the true Saint Francis, but what would have been its history had not the unhistorical image been created ? Our

PREFACE

second example is even more remote from Acts,—the story of Margaret Catchpole, which happened to be familiar to one of the editors. The extreme dissimilarity of this material from anything in the New Testament rendered it admirably adapted to focus attention on the points where comparison was important, —the complicated redaction of a simple narrative and its manipulation of non-literary sources which are happily still extant. It affords an example of how an intelligent and honest man endeavouring to make history out of imperfect material often makes it impossible to decide what actually happened, because the psychology of authorship impels him quite unconsciously to change problems into propositions. Similarly for the historian of the Church—not of the life of Jesus—the Fourth Gospel and the Jesus imagined by its author are more important than the Jesus of history portrayed in the Gospel of Mark; and probably the Paul of Acts is more important for the same purpose than the Paul of the Epistles.

In this way we have tried to prepare for a better understanding of the great history known as Acts. That it is history and that it is great we do not doubt, for great histories are evoked by great events. Herodotus had seen the liberation of Greece from the ever-present danger of Persian despotism, Thucydides had witnessed the rise of the Athenian democracy and its collapse before the disciplined, military aristocracy of Sparta, Josephus the terrible ruin of the theocratic state of Judah, while Eusebius had passed through the last and greatest persecution to witness the triumph of the Christian Church under Constantine. When a man with the historic instinct survives a great revolution in human affairs, he is irresistibly impelled not only to record his experiences, but to go backward into the past and investigate the causes of the catastrophe he has witnessed. Thus Herodotus surveys the ancient world and makes the nations pass in review before him till he is prepared to relate the main theme of his history; Thucydides begins with a description of ancient Athens and its manners and customs; Josephus recapitu-

Reasons for writing history.

lates the history of Israel to lead up to the outbreak of the final struggle with Rome; Eusebius sketches the course of Christian history from the first before he brings us to his own personal experiences of the martyrs of Palestine and to the conversion of the Emperor Constantine. As historians these writers take a comprehensive view, and so co-ordinate events as to make them lead up to their result.

Historians must be artists. Accuracy, firmness of judgment, impartiality, and many other qualities are virtues in a historian, but not always found. Lord Macaulay, for example, is rightly ranked by those most competent to judge among the greatest writers of history; yet who can read his magnificent story of the Revolution of 1688 and deny that it is the account of a partisan? His description of England in the seventeenth century will remain a monument of historical writing, but some statements have proved misleading and inaccurate. No one reading his description of the non-jurors can fail to recognise the bias of the writer against them, and further acquaintance with the subject reveals that he was completely out of sympathy with their aims and constitutionally incapable of appreciating their virtues. But these defects are compensated for by great learning and power of vivid description. It is true that some inaccuracies are unpardonable, as when the historian repeats on trust that which a little trouble would have enabled him to correct. There is a partiality which is even more worthy of condemnation, when persons, parties, or nations are wilfully misrepresented and misjudged, and a writer's bias makes him neglect or suppress evidence which would tell against his case; for the duty of the advocate is almost the crime of the writer of history. But it may be even a matter for commendation if a writer knows where to leave out cumbrous details which only obscure the effect of his picture, and where to heighten the impression he desires to create by a few vivid touches of his own. There is a Muse of History as of other arts, and he who serves her has the rights of an artist. He must throw his own personality into his work and endeavour to make his reader take a general view of events. He has to produce a picture rather than a ground plan or even a photograph, and he may, no more than the painter, be estimated by the mere size of his work. He may be a very poor artist although his canvas is immense, and great genius may be contained in the smallest of frames. Gibbon's greatness consists not in the vastness of his design, but in the ability with which he dealt with his subject. Indeed more skill and mastery of detail may be shown in the record of a day than in a description of a century. The true historic instinct manifests itself in the power to recognise what is important and interesting and to reject the trivial. Every one is familiar with writers who can search archives with amazing care, and produce a narrative as inconsequent as it is dull and tedious. But the genius of an historian is shown when in a few pages a man or a period stands out in unmistakable vividness.

But history means many things, and it is necessary to define what is implied in the term, or, at least, to recapitulate the different senses in which the word can be employed. Modern historians delight to attach to their work the epithet "scientific." They are sometimes ridiculed for so doing, but without reason. For all good work must be thus described. The word "science" is often connected with a certain dryness and meticulous accuracy, and to us the word is usually applied to those processes of thought which are popularly supposed to result in precise and well-defined conclusions. The scientific man, whether he be a mathematician or engaged in the pursuit of natural economic or even moral sciences, is supposed to argue from the seen to its causes or results to the exclusion of the imaginative faculties. Yet no one would repudiate such a definition more earnestly than the true scientist. He would point out that the imagination had its part in his severest studies, and that the only restraint he would place upon it is that he would not permit it to lead him to abandon the demonstrable path of truth based on accurate observation. And here the historian, and for that matter the theologian, is only anxious to claim to follow his example. Deal-

Scientific history.

ing as they often have to do with very uncertain factors, requiring undoubtedly a considerable exercise of the imagination, both desire to treat their materials with accuracy and impartiality. They are as liable to error as are their so-called "scientific" brethren, and when they see that they have erred they are as ready to abandon their position and to take up a fresh one. Those who do this, who work honestly and without unfair presuppositions, can truly claim that their work is scientific.

Modern criticism. In forming an ideal of what the "science" of history should be, as in every branch of human learning there is a constant advance and the science of one age becomes the obscurantism of the next. The older method differs from the new, in history as elsewhere in the treatment of sources. There was a common but by no means universal tendency in antiquity to receive the statements of earlier writers with little or no investigation. Historians accepted the authorities of the past much as for generations naturalists did the statements of Aristotle and Pliny the Elder. In our day the investigator tries to go behind his authority and to sift the evidence of his statements with all the information and ingenuity at his command. This may be described as a method in historical investigation which has only been fully adopted in comparatively recent days.

Political history. Science, strictly speaking, has no motive but a desire to record facts with exactitude. But those who write history almost invariably set about their task to prove something which they have at heart. Tacitus, for example, was a great historian, but he wrote as a politician. He had a theory to maintain, and desired to show that the best government for the Roman empire was that of the old aristocracy, guided, if necessary, by a virtuous prince. He saw in the century before his life-time a departure from the principle in the rule of a succession of tyrants who conciliated the proletariat. He deliberately ignored the undoubted benefits conferred on the empire by Tiberius, and throws over his latter days a darker cloak of infamy than the facts seem to justify. In this writer we have political history inferior to truly scientific history, but superior to the kind which must next be described.

A great deal which passes for history has been written with the object of pointing a moral or adorning a tale, the writer's aim being to edify rather than to inform. A familiar example of this is the book of Judges in the Old Testament. Chapters iii.-xvi. are arranged on a definite plan, each incident being recorded in order to emphasise the same lesson, that national sin brings punishment, and repentance deliverance. This method is common in the Old Testament. The interest of the reader is aroused by the story, and thus the moral is driven home. But this artifice is by no means confined to a portion of humanity, it pervades all literature, and was especially prevalent throughout the Roman world in the days of primitive Christianity. Whether the subject chosen was a nation or a society or an individual, the moral was the chief thing. Whatever may have been the methods of the writer of Acts, or the sources which he used, he was assuredly no exception. Acts is history, but history compiled with a purpose and with a moral. It is our hope to have contributed something in this volume to the better understanding of the method of its compilation, of the purpose with which it was written, and the moral it was intended to enforce.

Pragmatic history.

CONTENTS

I. THE COMPOSITION AND PURPOSE OF ACTS

	PAGE
INTRODUCTION	3
I. THE GREEK AND JEWISH TRADITIONS OF WRITING HISTORY. HENRY J. CADBURY AND THE EDITORS . . .	7
II. THE USE OF THE GREEK LANGUAGE IN ACTS. J. DE ZWAAN	30
III. THE USE OF THE SEPTUAGINT IN ACTS. W. K. L. CLARKE	66
IV. THE USE OF MARK IN THE GOSPEL ACCORDING TO LUKE. F. C. BURKITT	106
V. THE INTERNAL EVIDENCE OF ACTS. THE EDITORS .	121

II. THE IDENTITY OF THE EDITOR OF LUKE AND ACTS

INTRODUCTION. THE EDITORS	207
I. THE TRADITION. HENRY J. CADBURY . .	209
II. THE CASE FOR THE TRADITION. C. W. EMMET	265
III. THE CASE AGAINST THE TRADITION. H. WINDISCH	298
IV. SUBSIDIARY POINTS. HENRY J. CADBURY AND THE EDITORS	349

III. THE HISTORY OF CRITICISM

I. THE HISTORICAL CRITICISM OF ACTS IN GERMANY. A. C. McGIFFERT	363
II. BRITISH WORK ON THE ACTS. J. W. HUNKIN .	396

		PAGE
APPENDIX A—Two Literary Analogies.		
1. The Story of St. Francis of Assisi. G. G. Coulton		437
2. The Story of Margaret Catchpole. The Editors		464
APPENDIX B—Vestigia Christi. F. C. Burkitt		485
APPENDIX C—Commentary on the Preface of Luke. Henry J. Cadbury		489
INDEX		511

I
THE COMPOSITION AND PURPOSE OF ACTS

INTRODUCTION

IN the middle of the eighteenth century it was suggested that Moses had used two separate documents when he wrote the Book of Genesis. The important consequences of this view were only slowly recognised, and it was not till after more than a century that scholars realised that the Five Books of Moses and the Book of Joshua were composite and represented very different strands of thought and development. Those who tried to follow up this line were often the victims of outraged orthodoxy. Anglicanism repudiated Colenso, Presbyterianism Robertson Smith in Scotland, and Briggs and Henry Preserved Smith in America. Nevertheless the correctness of the Higher Criticism in its main conclusions was perforce recognised by all competent scholars throughout the world, and those who advocated its adoption are trusted and honoured as the safest exponents of modern orthodox Christianity. *[Higher Criticism and the O.T.]*

The controversy on the Old Testament was due to the fact that in their dealing with the Old Testament the Higher Critics turned from analysis to history. Not content with ingenious attempts to resolve the Hexateuch into its component parts, they applied the results they had arrived at to the elucidation of the history of Israel. It then appeared that the whole story had completely to be retold from a standpoint entirely different from that of the older writers. There was loss and gain in the process. Many cherished beliefs had to be given up, many interpretations useful for moralisation abandoned; but the historians and prophets of the ancient covenant appeared in a new light, and what had once been regarded as infallible, in ceasing to be so, became intelligible. *[Historical as well as analytical.]*

4 THE COMPOSITION AND PURPOSE OF ACTS

N.T. criticism hesitates to be historical.

New Testament criticism has hitherto, in English-speaking communities, been kept too much outside the sphere of historical research. There is general agreement, for example, that the Synoptic Gospels consist of allied documents, dependent partly on one another and partly on common sources now lost. The dependence of Matthew and Luke on Mark has been demonstrated and widely accepted; so that though the synoptic question still presents many problems to be solved, the main outlines of the work have been traced and agreed upon. Similarly much has been done to elucidate the travels of Paul, and the circumstances under which he wrote, but little or nothing to show how his development of theological and Christological thought is related to the analysis of the Gospels. We have the analogies to Driver's *Introduction to the Old Testament*, but not to Robertson Smith's *Old Testament in the Jewish Church*.

Need for the methods of O.T. criticism to be applied to the N.T.

Because so little has been done to push the matter of synoptic criticism to a logical conclusion, it is widely held that whereas the criticism of the Old Testament has overturned many traditional beliefs concerning it, that of the New only confirms its position. Even in Germany little has been done to place before the public the effect which the study of the synoptic problem has had on the history of the beginnings of the Christian religion. The three chief contributions, Bousset's *Kyrios Christos*, J. Weiss's *Urchristentum*, and W. Wrede's *Das Messias-Geheimniss* are technical works, comprehensible only to those who have mastered the details of the subject. What therefore is necessary in the future is to do for the New Testament what Robertson Smith did for the Old. Perceiving that the entire history of Israel had to be remodelled if the Graf-Wellhausen theory were accepted, in his *Old Testament in the Jewish Church* and his *Prophets of Israel* he placed before the English-speaking world the conclusion to which modern criticism had led.[1] In clear and

---

[1] To guard against misapprehension the Editors would disclaim any attempt to do this in the present work. Their aim is to provide material for it. Before we can try to "explain Christianity" it is well to ask what Christianity actually was in its earliest years.

INTRODUCTION 5

intelligible language he pointed out that a new era in Biblical history had dawned, and that every event in the progress of the Chosen People had to be viewed in its light. The translations into English of Wellhausen's and Kuenen's accounts of the religion and history of Israel made clear what Robertson Smith's lectures had suggested. Every one realised that the older histories, however brilliantly written, had been superseded; that the Hexateuch was the outcome of the early story of the nation, and not the basis on which every event after the death of Moses depended.

As soon as this had been done, and the general outlines of the history of Israel re-established, it was possible to go back and reconsider many of the details of criticism. The tentative analysis of documents could now be revised and corrected. So criticism and history went hand in hand. But the reconstruction of the earlier periods had to wait for the analysis of the later documents. The correct appreciation of the eighth century was not possible until the proper understanding of the reforms of Josiah and the Deuteronomic code had been reached.

Guided by this experience of the study of the Old Testament, similar progress in the New must begin by the critical study of Acts. Lightfoot's commentaries dealt adequately with the main problems of the Epistles, and the Synoptic question is as nearly solved as the problem of the Pentateuch was when Robertson Smith wrote. Acts is almost untouched. The essential step is its critical analysis, in the light of our knowledge of its background and of synoptic criticism. *Acts demands criticism on O.T. lines.*

The endeavour to discover the sources used by an author and the method which he follows in his composition can be made only in the light of knowledge of the plan usually followed by his contemporaries and, if possible, by himself in other writings. In the case of Acts this means a consideration of the methods followed by Jewish as well as by Greek writers of history. For though the writer was certainly a Greek he was *The method of analysis.*

also deeply imbued with the tradition of the Old Testament. It also calls for a consideration of his methods as revealed by his use of the Septuagint and of the Greek language, and by his treatment of the Markan material in the Gospel according to Luke. Only when this preliminary matter has been disposed of is it possible to analyse the internal evidence of Acts as to its sources, and plan with any proper criterion as to the relative probability of the suggestions made by this analysis.

The discussion of these topics has therefore been divided into the following chapters : (1) The Greek and Jewish Traditions of Writing History ; (2) the Use of the Greek Language in Acts ; (3) The Use of the Septuagint in Acts ; (4) The Use of Mark in the Gospel according to Luke ; (5) The Internal Evidence of Acts.

I

THE GREEK AND JEWISH TRADITIONS OF WRITING HISTORY

By HENRY J. CADBURY AND THE EDITORS

IN Josephus and Luke two streams of the writing of history converge. It may be said in general that the Greek and Roman method of composition is more varied and more artistic than the Jewish; but each needs a fairly full description, at least on the points which come prominently forward in the criticism of Luke and Acts. It is easiest to begin with the Greek tradition.

THE GREEK TRADITION

The tradition of Greek historiography begins with Herodotus and continues through the Hellenistic age to the contemporaries of Luke, both Greek and Roman. The methods of these Gentile writers have something in common with those of the Jewish chroniclers, but the Hellenistic writing of history is perhaps more self-conscious, more expressive of its principles, and offers a more considerable body of material from which to reconstruct the theory and practice of its composition.[1]

Greek traditional methods.

[1] For modern summaries see among others: E. Norden, *Antike Kunstprosa* (3rd edition), 1919; H. Peter, *Die geschichtliche Literatur über d. römische Kaiserzeit*, 1897; *Wahrheit und Kunst: Geschichtsschreibung und Plagiat im klassischen Altertum*, 1911; E. Stemplinger, *Das Plagiat in der griechischen Literatur*, 1912; P. Scheller, *De Hellenistica historiae conscribendae arte*, 1911; H. Liers, *Die Theorie der Geschichtsschreibung des Dionys von Halikarnass*, 1886 (with much reference to Polybius and Cicero); F. Halbfas, *Theorie und Praxis in der Geschichtsschreibung bei Dionys von Halikarnass*, 1910.

Discussion of other historians. These materials are not only derived from an intensive study and comparison of the writings of the historians, especially Thucydides, Diodorus Siculus, Tacitus, and Livy, but are supplemented by essays, prefaces, or long digressions discussing the general principles of historical composition. Thus Dionysius of Halicarnassus not only produced *Roman Antiquities* in twenty volumes; he also wrote several essays on literary criticism; while Polybius is constantly filling his pages with trenchant discussion of earlier and contemporary historiography. His principal complaint is against the rhetorical historians.[1] The rhetorical studies—even those of later date, and those composed in Latin—bear testimony to the traditional problems and principles of the historians, while satire contributes its share to the illumination of the subject in the *De historiae conscribendae arte* of Lucian.[2]

Use of material. The raw materials of history were very miscellaneous and scattered. Official archives are mentioned as sources of information, but less frequently quoted, and, though this does not necessarily follow from the absence of mention, were perhaps rarely used. Polybius lays stress on first-hand knowledge of places to be gained by travel, on participation so far as possible in affairs, and on personal contact with eyewitnesses where the author himself was not present. Thus he criticises Timaeus because he had no acquaintance with the localities which he was describing, or with military or naval matters, or with politics.[3] "It is difficult perhaps for a man to have been actually and literally engaged in everything, but in the most important

---

[1] Norden (*op. cit.* p. 82) selects as the most important criticisms made by Polybius the following passages; Book xii. (against Timaeus); xvi. 17, 9 f. (against Zeno of Rhodes); ii. 56 (against Phylarchus); i. 14 (against Philinus and Fabius).

[2] "Πῶς δεῖ ἱστορίαν συγγράφειν" is the Greek title of this essay, which professes to be divided between a statement of errors to be avoided and of methods to be followed; but in general it is a miscellaneous collection of excesses and abuses in both matter and style of historiography drawn from the contemporary "fever" for history-writing that resulted from the Parthian war.   [3] Polybius xii. 25 g, h.

GREEK AND JEWISH TRADITIONS

actions and most frequently occurring he must have been so." " For as historical events take place in many different localities and as it is impossible for the same man to be in several places at the same time, and also impossible for him to see with his own eyes all places in the world and observe their peculiarities, the only resource left is to ask questions of as many people as possible; to believe those who are worthy of credit; and to show critical sagacity in judging of their reports."[1]

The written materials of first value are the memoranda of eyewitnesses, whenever these are obtainable. In the case of campaigns or journeys, day-books or ὑπομνηματισμοί were kept by order of the king or official in charge and marked with his imprimatur.[2] Unofficial notes and diaries, reports of travellers, impressions of participants were all useful. All such raw materials, unedited and unarranged, bore in Greek the title ὑπομνήματα, and in Latin *commentarii*. Many such writings were written, in spite of the author's personal participation, in the third person, as in the well-known *commentarii* of Julius Caesar. But that others, including satirical and fictitious ὑπομνήματα, used the first person is only natural.[3]

Memoranda employed by historians.

The first task of the ancient historian was the discovery and collection of this raw material. This, if undertaken conscientiously, was an arduous task requiring years of time and a great deal of effort. But there were historians, as Polybius scornfully reminds us,[4] who wrote their histories by the easy method of the armchair. They knew nothing of the labours of true research,

Ancient view of research.

---

[1] Polybius xii. 4 c.
[2] On the ὑπομνηματισμοί see Wilcken, *Philologus*, liii. (1894), pp. 80-126.
[3] G. Misch, *Geschichte der Autobiographie*, i. 1907, mentions as written in the first person the memoirs of Ptolemy Euergetes II. in 24 books, and the *vita* of Augustus in 13 books, and from Jewish sources the *vita* of Josephus and the memoirs of Nehemiah. Purely fictitious " we "-tales may be illustrated from Lucian's *True History* and *Icaromenippus*. For other fictitious travel stories in the first person see E. Norden, *Agnostos Theos*, p. 313.
[4] xii. 25 e ἔνιοι δὲ τῶν δοκούντων εὐλόγως προσάγειν πρὸς τὴν ἱστορίαν, καθάπερ οἱ λογικοὶ τῶν ἰατρῶν ἐνδιατρίψαντες ταῖς βιβλιοθήκαις καὶ καθόλου τὴν ἐκ τῶν ὑπομνημάτων περιποιησάμενοι πολυπειρίαν πείθουσιν αὑτοὺς ὡς ὄντες ἱκανοὶ πρὸς τὴν ἐπιβολήν. Cf. also Lucian, *op. cit.* 37 καὶ τοίνυν καὶ ἡμῖν τοιοῦτός τις ὁ μαθητὴς

10   THE COMPOSITION AND PURPOSE OF ACTS

but relied principally upon the writings of others. Indeed for ancient history no other method was possible, and since the material was all collected by others, the historian need only compare authorities and arrange the material to suit his own purpose. This easier method seems to have been practised most, while the other was most praised. No moral stigma attached to the wholesale use of what earlier writers had supplied, and when this method was followed it was usual not to mention by name the authorities borrowed. Sometimes a general ἔνιοι or τινές betrays the use of a previous historian,[1] but authors are mentioned by name most often to point out their errors or emphasise the writer's disagreement with their statements.

Purposes of ancient historians. The purposes of ancient historians were varied. They are often discussed and compared in prefaces, as for instance is done by Dionysius of Halicarnassus and Josephus in both their *Antiquities*. Polybius declares his purpose is practical; the guidance of men, especially statesmen, by the lessons of history. " The study of history is in the truest sense an education, and a training for political life." [2] Sometimes the purpose is apologetic, or the history is intended to glorify the deeds of men and nations. But a predominant object was often to entertain or to interest [3] the reader. And this purpose had a considerable effect on the methods of the historian.

νῦν παραδεδόσθω. . . . οἷος καὶ πράγμασι χρήσασθαι ἄν . . . καὶ ὅλως οὐ τῶν κατοικιδίων τις οὐδ' οἷος πιστεύειν μόνον τοῖς ἀπαγγέλλουσι. In this passage κατοικιδίων is especially delightful; should it be translated " parlour patriots " ?

[1] See Stemplinger, *op. cit.* pp. 177 ff., 219. One example may suffice : Plutarch's *Coriolanus* does not anywhere mention Dionysius of Halicarnassus, the principal source, but in the σύγκρισις (2) Plutarch criticises Dionysius by name for holding a different view on a certain matter. In the Life itself (26) this same objectionable view is mentioned as being held by ἔνιοι.

[2] Polybius i. 1. Cf. iii. 4, v. 75, ix. 2, *et al.*

[3] Philo is not far from correctly hitting the conventional term when in contrast with the religious purpose of Moses' ἀρχαιολογία, he speaks of the usual purpose of historians as being ψυχαγωγῆσαι (*De vita Mosis*, ii. 8, p. 141 M). ψυχαγωγία is constantly used of Hellenistic histories : cf. 2 Macc. ii. 25 for another Jewish example.

GREEK AND JEWISH TRADITIONS 11

In the first place it did not require conscientious and discriminating emphasis of historical fact. The abstract search for truth of the modern historian was possibly understood in theory, but it was by no means the main object of ancient writers. Of course some historians were very credulous, and others exercised their judgment in avoiding extremely incredible stories. But the question of historicity was vigorously debated chiefly when some personal or national controversies were involved. The Greek law of restraint had a wholesome influence, and scorn is expressed for the very crude faith in local myths of other historians. Thus Polybius rejects [1] the fabulous tales of statues of Asia that are never touched by snow or rain, and the legend which even Theopompus records of sacred precincts in which no shadow is cast by the sun. Dionysius, however, while speaking very sceptically of certain myths,[2] does not hesitate to record the most extravagant legends of early Rome, fully aware that they are rejected by those who strictly exclude everything μυθῶδες from history.[3] But it must be constantly remembered that the modern criticism of sources, tests of historical probability, and insistence on first-hand evidence were not customary in antiquity even among those writers who in their criticism of others and in their conventional claims for their own work seem most nearly to have understood modern criteria.

Historical criticism of impossible tales.

Instead of accuracy the purpose of ancient historians tended to make the form the chief point of emphasis. As Herodian says,[4] τῆς μὲν ἀληθείας ἐν ταῖς ἀφηγήσεσιν ὠλιγώρησαν, οὐχ ἥκιστα δὲ ἐπεμελήθησαν φράσεώς τε καὶ εὐφωνίας. History is described as an art rather than as a science. Sometimes it is compared with poetry,[5] sometimes with the plastic arts. "One's whole thought must be," says Lucian,[6] "that the writer of history must be like Phidias or Praxiteles or Alcamenes or one

Importance of form.

---
[1] xvi. 12.   [2] De Thuc. 5. 6.
[3] Ant. i. 84. 1 ; ii. 61. 1. Cf. Lucian, op. cit. 60.   [4] i. 1. 1.
[5] Quintil. x. 1. 31. Cf. Norden, Antike Kunstprosa, pp. 91 ff.
[6] Op. cit. 51.

of the others. For they used not to make the gold or the silver or the ivory or other material, but it was at hand and was set before them in advance, supplied by the Elians, Athenians, or Argives, but they only moulded and sawed the ivory, and polished and glued and brought it into proportion and decked it with the gold, and this was their art—to arrange the material properly. Something of this sort, then, is the task of the historian,to set forth the deeds that have been done and to show them as clearly as possible."

Rhetorical form of composition.

The last and most important stage in the historian's task is the composition in rhetorical form of the material that he is using. Of course the ὑπομνήματα are bald, unadorned prose. They are therefore unfit for publication until they have been fitted out in rhetorical style. This contrast in style is constantly mentioned, and the rhetorical principles which history must follow are set forth in full. Plutarch [1] describes the memoirs of Aratus as written παρέργως καὶ ὑπὸ χεῖρα διὰ τῶν ἐπιτυχόντων ὀνομάτων. The same lack of rhetorical adornment was felt by Cicero for his own ὑπόμνημα,[2] and for the *commentarii* of Caesar.[3] Lucian [4] criticises one who published ὑπόμνημα τῶν γεγονότων γυμνὸν συναγαγὼν ἐν γραφῇ κομιδῇ πεζὸν καὶ χαμαιπετές, οἷον καὶ στρατιώτης ἄν τις τὰ καθ' ἡμέραν ἀπογραφόμενος συνέθηκεν ἢ τέκτων ἢ κάπηλός τις συμπερινοστῶν τῇ στρατιᾷ. For the real historian such material is the *corpus vile*, ὑπόμνημά τι or σῶμα ἀκαλλὲς ἔτι καὶ ἀδιάρθρωτον, to which he must bring the adornment of τάξις and λέξις, σχήματα and ῥυθμός.[5] History is close to oratory, and therefore its principles are the same.[6] Indeed an important part of history is the oratory it contains. In the speeches of

---

[1] *Aratus*, 3. [2] *Ad Att.* ii. 1. 1 f.
[3] *Brut.* 262. [4] *De hist. conscrib.* 16.
[5] Lucian, *op. cit.* 48 εἶτα ἐπιθεὶς τὴν τάξιν ἐπαγέτω τὸ κάλλος καὶ χρωννύτω τῇ λέξει καὶ σχηματιζέτω καὶ ῥυθμιζέτω.
[6] See Cicero, *De or.* ii. 15. 62. So he speaks (*De legibus*, i. 2. 5) of history as *opus unum oratorium maxime*, as Dionys. Hal. calls it (*De Thucyd.* 9) a ὑπόθεσις ῥητορική.

the actors the artist can more fully show his skill.¹ To suppose that the writers were trying to present the speeches as actually spoken, or that their readers thought so, is unfair to the morality of one and to the intelligence of the other. From Thucydides² downwards, speeches reported by the historians are confessedly pure imagination. They belong to the final literary stage. If they have any nucleus of fact behind them it would be the merest outline in the ὑπομνήματα.

Sometimes we can see the various stages of composition in the works of a single writer, when for some reason or other certain books of his history have come down to us only rough hewn without any flowing rhetorical style and without the illustrative adornment of speeches usual in the finished volumes. Thus it is believed that certain books of Thucydides³ which quote original records verbatim, have come from him without final editorial revision, while his last book is notably lacking in speeches. In the last eight books of Strabo the excerpts from his sources are given in their original form, but not elsewhere.

For this ultimate stage of composition it made little difference whether the historian was using the real documents and memoranda of research or merely the finished work of some predecessor. In either case he must make a new work, recasting all in his own style by the method of paraphrase. Verbatim copying of sources was not tolerated, for no matter how slavishly one followed the substance of his predecessor's narrative one must recast his style. And the speeches must be the writer's own. When Livy follows Polybius for the facts of his narrative he almost regularly makes a change in the occasion and form of his speeches. So Plutarch and Tacitus agree very closely in

Habit of recasting the style of material used.

---

¹ Dionysius, *De Thucyd.* 34 ἐν αἷς [δημηγορίαις] οἴονταί τινες τὴν ἄκραν τοῦ συγγραφέως εἶναι δύναμιν. Lucian, *De hist. conscrib.* 58 πλὴν ἐφεῖταί σοι τότε (*i.e.* when supplying appropriate speeches) καὶ ῥητορεῦσαι καὶ ἐπιδεῖξαι τὴν τῶν λόγων δεινότητα.
² Cf. Thucyd. i. 22.
³ *E.g.* iv., v., viii.

14 THE COMPOSITION AND PURPOSE OF ACTS

their account of Otho but give entirely different reports of his last address.[1] Josephus, who has occasion in his parallel works to deal twice with the same situation, puts two different speeches in the mouth of Herod.[2] The speech of Caesar to his soldiers in Dio Cassius [3] is very different from the brief address reported by Caesar himself [4] on the same occasion. When the actual speech had been published the historian usually mentions the fact as a reason for omitting any speech of his own.[5]

Rhetorical artificiality. It is not necessary to recount here the conventional rhetorical figures and devices which became the standards of the more elegant historians. There is something grotesque to modern eyes in the excesses of Dionysius. Even in antiquity the extreme artificiality of the historians aroused some protest. Polybius held himself free from many of the excesses which he scorned in others,[6] and some of his criticisms and claims were conven-

---

[1] Plut. 15; Tac. *Hist.* ii. 47.   [2] *B.J.* i. 19. 4; *Ant.* xv. 5. 3.
[3] 38. 36-46.   [4] *B.G.* i. 40.

[5] Sallust, *Catiline*, omits all Cicero's speeches against Catiline and explains (31): "tunc M. Tullius Cicero consul orationem habuit quam postea scriptam edidit." Tacitus significantly says of Seneca's published last words that he would omit transferring them to his pages in paraphrase (*Ann.* xv. 63 "quae in vulgus edita eius verbis invertere supersedeo ").

[6] Polybius uses among other phrases ὑπερβολὴ τερατείας. One of the abuses to which Polybius and others object is the excessive use of speeches. Timaeus as usual receives severest censure, because in his speeches " he has not written down the words actually used, nor the real drift of these speeches ; but, imagining how they ought to have been expressed, he enumerates all the arguments used, like a schoolboy declaiming on a set theme " (xii. 25 a). " Surely," he says again, " a historian should not aim at producing speeches which might have been delivered, nor study dramatic propriety in details like a writer of tragedy : but his function is above all to record with fidelity what was actually said or done, however commonplace it may be. For the purposes of history and of drama are not the same " (ii. 56). In a later passage (xxxvi. 1) he expresses very clearly his restraint—he does not reject giving the appropriate arguments on either side on some occasions, but this convenient practice should not be indulged in at every point. Although Dionysius joins in this protest (*Ad Pomp.* 3. 12) he is one of the worst offenders, the speeches amounting, according to Liers (*op. cit.* p. 14), to about one-third of his history. This is one of the faults removed by Plutarch when he uses Dionysius, as in the *Coriolanus* (see above). According to H. Peter (*Wahrheit und Kunst*, p. 356) there are more than four hundred speeches in the extant thirty-five books of Livy, while the speeches of Thucydides occupy one-fifth of his text (*ibid.* p. 120). The ratio just mentioned is also that of the book of Acts. Lack of proportion

tionally accepted by writers who did not follow his example. The habit of adopting the style of memoirs, and the emphasis laid on having been an eyewitness were valued as literary artifices. It is noteworthy that some unrevised memoirs and excerpts from earlier histories have survived, and these serve to illustrate the material on which much rhetorical history was based. It is thus possible to compare the more conventional finished product with the original.

It is interesting now to ask how far these Hellenistic principles affect the composition of the writings of Luke. The Christian author's Semitic and religious background do not guarantee him any exemption from the literary standards of his day. Josephus the Jew, his contemporary, is largely under the spell of these principles. He edits the unrhetorical records of the Bible, inserting long rhetorical speeches invented to suit his own tastes, and compiles an *Antiquities* of the Jews in twenty volumes to match the work of Dionysius of Halicarnassus. The author to Theophilus is perhaps not so Hellenised as Josephus, and yet he may have been a Gentile and no Jew. His prefaces and dedications at once suggest classification with the contemporary Hellenistic historians. With Mark in our hands we can frequently confront his work with the unpolished ὑπόμνημα which he paraphrases, corrects, and recasts in his own style. In Acts the elaborate, homogeneous and schematic speeches suggest, if not the rhetoric, at least the free composition of the speeches in Greek and Roman histories, while the " we-passages " raise the insoluble problem of the use, imitation, or incorporation of autoptic records or the participation of the author in the events which he records.

_{Lucan writing tested by the above.}

---

between the preface and the body of a work, the excesses of imitation and many other things satirised by Lucian in his essay are only exaggerations of the current stylistic frigidity, artificiality, and credulity of Hellenistic historians.

THE JEWISH TRADITION

Use of documents in biblical history.

The tradition of historical writing among the Jews is adequately represented, in a series of documents some of which overlap the others, in the Old Testament, in the Apocrypha, and in Josephus. In these each writer makes use of the material provided by his predecessor, and the beginning of the process is hidden ; for even the earliest of the books which have come down to us depend on sources no longer extant. The critical study of the earlier historical books has revealed that there were several documents employed in the composition of their history. To take 2 Samuel as a single example there is an allusion, as in Joshua, to a "book of Jasher," and lists of David's wives, ministers, and warriors obviously copied from possibly official sources. Poems and sayings are introduced to illuminate the narrative. Prayers, both in 2 Samuel and also in 1 Kings, are made by David and Solomon, obviously the free composition of the writer.

A little later there is an elaborate example of the employment of sources and the introduction of literary devices in the work of the Chronicler, including the books of Ezra and Nehemiah. Still later, in 1 Maccabees, there is opportunity for studying a later Jewish composition designedly written in biblical style. Of this the first chapters are specially important as resembling the historical style and religious tone of the prophetic writers. These deal with the story of the Syrian persecution, begun by Antiochus Epiphanes, and the career of Judas Maccabaeus. It is possible to check the correctness of what is here stated by using 2 Maccabees, an independent work. Finally, these historical books became the basis of the *Antiquities* of Josephus, who has treated them with a freedom which may supply a clue to other contemporary literary compositions. This freedom also appears in the translators of the Old Testament, who either had a text of the Old Testament different from ours or else felt themselves at liberty to adapt, rearrange, and expand

GREEK AND JEWISH TRADITIONS 17

or contract, to a greater degree than a modern would feel justified in doing. All this deserves attention in order to illustrate the standards to which translators and editors in early days conformed.

The interest in these books to a student of the New Testament lies in the fact that they not only throw much light on the literary methods of the Jews in the Exile and in the Persian and Greek periods, but that the problems they present are analogous, if not parallel, to those of the historical books of the New Testament, the Gospels, and Acts.

Literary methods of Chronicler.

The Chronicler, like the author of the Lucan books, used sources, some of which we have within the cover of the Bible, and adapted them to the object they had in view. No one can fail to notice how the narrative of Samuel and Kings is altered to suit the decidedly legalistic bias of the age. All that could detract from the high estimation in which David and Solomon were held is omitted, and much is added to the narrative with the object of edification. Throughout are inserted speeches and prayers, many of which appear to be the work of the author.

All the books of this series—Chronicles, Ezra, Nehemiah— are avowedly compilations. They refer to authorities and reproduce documents. In Chronicles no less than fifteen sources are enumerated;[1] in Ezra-Nehemiah registers, letters of Persian kings, decrees, etc. are introduced, and there are in addition personal memoirs, as has been shown, professedly written by Ezra and Nehemiah. But the Chronicler is no mere collector; he has a marked style of his own and gives to all the material he uses the impress of his personality.[2] A dry legalist he assuredly was not; for he possessed the power of telling a story vividly and dramatically. And here the "personal" sections in Ezra-

---

[1] Torrey, *Ezra Studies*, pp. 228-229.

[2] Dr. Torrey's chapter vii. in his *Ezra Studies* is peculiarly valuable. He is the first English-speaking scholar who has shown that Chronicles is an interesting study, as Dr. Cheyne was to indicate that it was important. Most commentators seem to have made the student believe that it is a very dull book.

18 THE COMPOSITION AND PURPOSE OF ACTS

Nehemiah are of special interest to the student of Acts. The same question arises, Are these sections written in the style of the author or not? In Chronicles, Ezra, and Nehemiah the answer, according to Dr. Torrey, appears to be decidedly in the affirmative. In the opinion of many the style is uniform throughout, and there is no variety when Ezra or Nehemiah is speaking in his own name.

Moreover, there are two Greek recensions of Ezra and there is a dispute as to which is the earlier; and the problem of translation from the Aramaic occurs in certain portions of the Greek Ezra (1 Esdras).

Summary of the Hebrew recension of Ezra.

The book of Ezra opens with a repetition of the last two verses of 2 Chronicles, only it gives the decree of Cyrus in somewhat fuller form.[1] The people make ready to go up to Jerusalem. Cyrus hands the treasures of the Temple to Mithredath, who delivers them to Sheshbazzar the leader of "those of the captivity" from Babylon to Jerusalem.[2] Then follows a list of people and priests who returned.[3] On their arrival Jeshua, the son of Jozadak, the high priest and Zerubbabel, the son of Shealtiel, set up the altar and lay the foundations of the Temple.[4]

Seeing the Jews commencing to build the Temple the "adversaries of Judah and Benjamin" ask leave to co-operate and are repelled by Zerubbabel.[5] Whereupon, "in the days of Artaxerxes" a letter is written "in the Syrian tongue" complaining of the Jews.[6] The letter states that if the city of Jerusalem is built and the gates set up the Jews will refuse to pay taxes or tribute. Nothing is said of the building of the Temple. The answer of the king prohibits the building of the city; and the work ceases till the second year of Darius.[7] Then the prophets Haggai and Zechariah urge that the Temple should be built[8]; and Tattenai, the governor, Shethar-boznai, and "his companions the Aphar-

---

[1] Ezra i. 1-4; 2 Chr. xxxvi. 22-23.
[2] Ezra i. 5-11.
[3] Ezra ii. 1-70.
[4] Ezra iii. 1-13.
[5] Ezra iv. 1-6.
[6] Ezra iv. 7-16.
[7] Ezra iv. 17-24, *esp.* 21 and 24.
[8] Ezra v. 1, vi. 14.

sachites" write to Darius informing him that the Jews are rebuilding the Temple and asking that search be made whether there was a decree of Cyrus allowing them to do so.[1] A roll is found at Achmetha in the palace, proving that Cyrus had ordered the Temple to be built and prescribing its dimensions.[2] Darius, accordingly, commands the rebuilding of the Temple, which was finished on the third day of Adar, in the sixth year of Darius, and was solemnly dedicated.[3]

In the next chapter Ezra, "a ready scribe in the law of Moses," goes up from Babylon to Jerusalem "in the seventh year of Artaxerxes." He takes with him a letter from Artaxerxes, giving him extensive powers to restore the worship at Jerusalem, and exempting the priests, Levites, and all Temple ministers from taxes.[4] Then, as abruptly as in Acts, a section in the first person is introduced, which continues for fifty-three verses.[5] The narrative in the third person is resumed as suddenly as it was abandoned, "Now when Ezra had prayed," etc.[6] The present book of Ezra closes as abruptly as the Gospel of Mark, with an unfinished sentence.[7]

Nehemiah is introduced like the prophets by a preface: "The words of Nehemiah the son of Hachaliah." His narrative is given in the first person and extends over seven chapters,[8] at the end of which is transcribed a genealogy "which I found registered" of those who had come up with Zerubbabel. This is virtually a repetition of the second chapter of Ezra.[9] Again, without warning, the third person appears in the story of Ezra the scribe[10] reading the Law and Nehemiah the governor exhorting the people not to be dismayed, but to keep the feast of Tabernacles. After the feast the people made a solemn covenant,

Summary of Nehemiah.

---

[1] Ezra v. 6-17.
[2] Ezra vi. 1-5, *esp.* 3-5.
[3] Ezra vi. 6-22.
[4] Ezra vii. 1-26, *esp.* 1, 6, 11, 24.
[5] Ezra vii. 27 to ix. 15.
[6] Ezra x. 1.
[7] Ezra x. 44; Mark xvi. 8.
[8] Neh. i.-vii. 5.
[9] Neh. vii. 6-73. Cf. Ezra ii. 1-70.
[10] Neh. viii. 1. Ezra is also called "the priest" in Ezra x. 10 where, as here (*v.* 2), the narrative is in the third person.

20   THE COMPOSITION AND PURPOSE OF ACTS

prefaced by a long confession of national sin by the Levites.¹ A list is given of those who subscribed, in which Ezra's name is conspicuously absent. In the substance of the covenant which follows the first person plural is employed.² A chapter and a half is devoted to a list of names;³ and then, quite abruptly, the account of the dedication of the Wall of Jerusalem is resumed. From this point to the end of the book Nehemiah is made to write partly in the first person.⁴

Summary of 1 Esdras.

Ezra appears in two forms in Greek. The version which represents the Hebrew, as we now have it, is that of Theodotion.⁵ But an earlier one was known to Josephus which is otherwise arranged, and differs from that of the Hebrew Ezra in many important particulars, and has significant additions. It begins with an account of Josiah's Passover, taken from the narrative of 2 Chronicles, and follows the Chronicler in describing the destruction of Jerusalem and the Captivity. It agrees with the Hebrew Ezra in giving the decree of Cyrus and the preparation for the Return.⁶ The vessels of the Temple were entrusted to Sheshbazzar, or, as the Greek has, Sanabassar, the governor of Judah, apparently a Persian official who cannot possibly be identified with Zerubbabel.⁷ Thus far the Hebrew and Greek Ezras agree; but now a large section of the Hebrew Ezra is omitted and placed elsewhere, nothing being as yet said of the erection of the altar or the offer of the "adversaries" to join in building the Temple.⁸ The letter to Artaxerxes and his reply stopping the work are virtually the same in both versions,

---

¹ Neh. ix. The prayer is in *vv*. 6-38.
² Neh x. 28-39.   ³ Neh. xi. 1-xii. 26.
⁴ Neh. xii. 27-xiii. 31. The verses in the first person are xii. 31, 38, 40 and xiii. 6-31.
⁵ It is not, however, quite certain what is the date. Theodotion himself is post-Christian, but there is some evidence which suggests that the text which he issued (or re-issued) is earlier.
⁶ 1 Esdras i. 1-ii. 14; Ezra i. 1-11. Cf. 2 Chron. xxvi. 22-23.
⁷ 1 Esdras ii. 15. In Ezra i. 8 "Sheshbazzar the prince of Judah" is perhaps identified with Zerubbabel, Ezra ii. 2, iii. 2. In 1 Esdras vi. 18, the holy vessels were delivered to Zerubbabel and Sanabassarus by Cyrus (evidently a gloss by an ignorant scribe).   ⁸ Ezra iv. 1-3.

GREEK AND JEWISH TRADITIONS 21

only 1 Esdras does not note that the letters were originally in Aramean.[1]

A long section follows in the Greek, which is not in the Hebrew, namely, the story of how Zerubbabel obtained leave from Darius to finish the Temple.[2] This is no mere interpolation, but reflects the writer's opinion that Zerubbabel was not the prince of the Return under Cyrus, but only made his appearance in the reign of Darius. The whole order of events is different from that in the Hebrew Ezra, as the following table will show:—

(1) Ezra i. Jews return from Babylon (Cyrus).	(1) 1 Esdras ii. 1-15. Cyrus and the Return.
(2) Ezra ii. Those who came back with Zerubbabel.	(2) 1 Esdras ii. 16-30. Correspondence with Artaxerxes; the work ordered to cease.
(3) Ezra iii. Setting up of the altar by Jeshua and Zerubbabel. Those who had seen the glory of the first house weep, etc.	(3) 1 Esdras iii. 1-v. 6. The feast of Darius. Zerubbabel obtains permission to rebuild Temple.
(4) Ezra iv. 1-3. The offer of the adversaries of Judah and Benjamin is repulsed.	(4) 1 Esdras v. 7-55. Those who came back with Zerubbabel.
(5) Ezra iv. 4-24. Correspondence with Artaxerxes; the work is ordered to cease.	(5) 1 Esdras v. 56-65. Laying the foundations. Those who had seen the old house weep, etc.
(6) Ezra v. 1-2. Haggai and Zechariah incite Zerubbabel and Jeshua to rebuild the Temple.	(6) 1 Esdras v. 66-73. The offer of the "adversaries" of Judah and Benjamin is repulsed.
(7) Ezra v. 3-vi. 12. Correspondence between the "adversaries" and Darius.	(7) 1 Esdras vi. 1-2. Haggai and Zechariah incite Zerubbabel and Jeshua to rebuild the Temple.
(8) Ezra vi. 13-22. Temple dedicated.	(8) 1 Esdras vi. 3-34. Correspondence between the "adversaries" and Darius.
	(9) 1 Esdras vii. 1-15. Temple dedicated.

Hebrew and Greek Ezra compared.

The rest of Ezra and 1 Esdras are similar; but at the end 1 Esdras reproduces Nehemiah viii. 1-12—the reading of the Law by Esdras "the chief priest."[3] Nehemiah does not appear at all on this occasion, and in the verse in which the name occurs in the Hebrew as "Nehemiah the Tirshatha" the Greek has

---
[1] Ezra iv. 7; 1 Esdras ii. 16.   [2] 1 Esdras iii. 1-v. 6.
[3] 1 Esdras ix. 38-55.

"Then spake Attharates to Esdras, the chief priest and reader."[1]

The relation of Ezra to 1 Esdras raises the problem whether 1 Esdras is not a translation of an early edition of the book of Ezra, which at a later date was replaced by the recension found in the Hebrew canon. If the additions and rearrangement are expansions of the Hebrew as we now have it, they throw an important light upon the methods of translators and the liberties they permitted themselves in producing their versions. This appears not only in 1 Esdras but elsewhere in the LXX., notably in Judges, in 1 Samuel (where the whole account of David and Goliath is re-edited and the inconsistencies in the Hebrew narrative removed by condensing the story), and in the book of Jeremiah. Either, therefore, translators allowed themselves great freedom in dealing with their material, or later editors of the Hebrew did so.

The difficulty of deciding as to whether a book or passage in the Greek Bible is translated from a Semitic language or not is revealed by the contrary decisions of the experts. The interpolated passage in 1 Esdras about the Three Youths [2] has been declared to be unmistakably Greek by some scholars, and equally clearly to be a translation from the Aramaic by others. As the same problem occurs in regard to the first half of Acts, similar methods have to be applied to the solution of both, and similar hesitation may be expected.

1 Maccabees.
The first book of Maccabees is an example of a narrative originally in Hebrew which has come down only in a Greek translation. The first part which concerns our purpose is the story of Judas Maccabaeus told with a markedly religious purpose. The thought is clearly that of the Old Testament. Yet its diction lacks that archaic restraint of the early canonical Scriptures, and is reminiscent of the last days of biblical composition; in its original form it may have been, perhaps, a forecast of the

---

[1] 1 Esdras ix. 49. Attharates is probably the same as Tirshatha (governor), but it appears that Nehemiah's name is deliberately omitted in this text.

[2] 1 Esdras iii. 1-v. 6.

GREEK AND JEWISH TRADITIONS 23

Hebrew of the Synagogue. Passing over the first chapter as introductory, the story may be said to begin with Mattathias and his sons in ch. ii. The narrative commences with a poetic lament over the fall of Israel. At the end of the same chapter, Mattathias makes a deathbed speech, in which he gives a summary of Israel's past like Stephen's in Acts vii. or Paul's in Acts xiii. 16-41.[1] A prayer is recorded as made by Judas and his company before attacking Gorgias which may be paralleled by that of the Apostles in Acts iv.[2] There is a tendency to omit important details, as, for example, what led to the estrangement between Judas and Nicanor,[3] and to introduce persons without explanation, like the Assidaeans, mentioned twice in 1 Maccabees.

It is interesting, further, to compare 1 Maccabees with the second book bearing that name as showing how the history can be checked by an independent document. It was customary to declare 2 Maccabees to be valueless in comparison with the earlier history; but a reaction against this judgment has set in, and a high value is now, in many quarters, set on the second book, which possesses an additional interest in being professedly based on a lost history by Jason of Cyrene.[4] The parallel chapters are 1 Macc. iii.-vii. and 2 Macc. viii.-xv. In both, Judas is supported by his four brothers; but in 1 Maccabees their names are Joannan, Simon, Eleazar, and Jonathan, and in 2 Maccabees Simon, Joseph, Jonathan, and Eleazar. Thus, as with the Twelve Apostles, the names and order differ in the enumeration. The first victory of Judas is related thus in the two books:—

2 Maccabees a parallel and independent narrative.

1 Maccabees.	2 Maccabees.
Judas wins renown by his irregular warfare against Syrians and apostates (iii. 1-9). Apollonius gathers a host and is defeated. Judas takes his sword and here-	viii. 1-7 virtually the same as 1 Macc. iii. 1-9. Philip (Governor of Jerusalem, 2 Macc. v. 22) sends for aid, and Nicanor is sent and with him Gorgias (9); with them mer-

---

[1] 1 Macc. ii. 49-70.   [2] 1 Macc. iii. 50-53.
[3] 1 Macc. vii. 29 f.   [4] 2 Macc. ii. 23.

24 THE COMPOSITION AND PURPOSE OF ACTS

after uses it (10-12). Seron attacks and is defeated at Bethhoron (13-24). Judas inspires awe (25-26). Antiochus Epiphanes leaves for Persia in quest of money, entrusting his kingdom to Lysias, who sends Ptolemy, Nicanor, and Gorgias against Judah (27-39). They encamp at Emmaus and the merchants come to buy the captive Israelite slaves. The Jews pray solemnly at Maspha (Mizpah) (40-60). Gorgias attempts a surprise; his army is utterly destroyed by Judas (iv. 1-25). Lysias comes in person and is defeated at Bethsura (26-35). Judas is now able to rededicate the temple (36-61) and to institute the feast.

chants come to buy the Jews as slaves. Nicanor proposes to pay tribute to Rome with the money collected (10, 11). Judas divides his troops between himself, Simon, Joseph, and Jonathan, appoints Eleazar to read the holy book, and attacks and routs Nicanor, who escapes to Antioch (12-29). Judas is also said to have attacked Bacchides and Timotheus, and to have killed Philarces, a great enemy of the Jews, and also Callisthenes. The next chapter (ix.) relates the death of Antiochus Epiphanes, which was followed in chapter x. by the rededication of the Temple and the institution of the feast.

The above comparison discovers difficulties not wholly dissimilar to those presented by the often-discussed discrepancies between Acts and Paul's statements in Galatians. From 2 Maccabees it might be inferred that Judas achieved one single success over Nicanor and was able to follow it up by the dedication of the Temple owing to the Syrian power being weakened by the death of Antiochus. But in the first book the dedication precedes the news that Antiochus was dead: and here the dates are carefully given, the dedication being in the hundred and forty-eighth, and the death of Antiochus in the hundred and forty-ninth year (165–164 B.C.). The same species of difficulty as to the Apostolic Council meets the student of Acts. There is no parallel for the differences in the names of the Syrian leaders in the two Maccabean books. The fact, however, that 2 Maccabees is avowedly an epitome from a larger history may explain the omission of the fuller details of the first book, and may also illustrate the brevity with which Acts treats the adventures of Paul in such a chapter as Acts xviii.

Josephus rewrites the O.T. history.

With the books of Maccabees ends the list of the canonical and deutero-canonical histories of the Jews, but the whole task was taken up once more by Josephus and rewritten for

GREEK AND JEWISH TRADITIONS

Greek readers. For the student of the New Testament, and especially of Acts, his methods are of primary importance, for though trained as a Jew he subsequently acquired a Greek education, as did probably the writer of Acts. Though the sources which he used for the later parts of his history are unknown or lost, for the earlier portion they are preserved in the Old Testament and Apocrypha. The historian may have little to learn from his retelling of the story, but the student of literary methods has no more valuable source of information.

Josephus was apparently acquainted with a text resembling 1 Esdras with the interpolations, and with our book of Nehemiah, and he evidently was better informed in general history, for he changes the names of the Persian kings which appear in the two Ezra documents, viz.: Cyrus [Ahasuerus], Artaxerxes, Darius,[1] and introduces the name of Cambyses. The Return from the Captivity is the subject of the eleventh book of the *Antiquities*, and Josephus's account is briefly:

Chapter I.—§ 1. Decree of Cyrus—obviously taken from the Bible. § 2. Cyrus acted upon a vision of *Isaiah*, whose prophecy he had studied; perhaps this is a piece of *Midrash* added by the historian. § 3. Restoration of the vessels—from the Bible; also a letter to Sisinnes and Sathrabuzanes from Cyrus, which in Ezra vi. 3-12 is given in connection with Darius's permission to build the Temple, but helps the story better in this place. *(Josephus's narrative, Antiq. xi.)*

Chapter II.—The Temple work is hindered after the death of Cyrus by the adversaries of Judah. Cambyses forbids the work, his name being substituted for that of Artaxerxes in the Ezra narrative.

Chapter III.—§ 1. Darius, whilst in a private station, had made a vow to God to restore the Temple; this is taken from the words of Zerubbabel to him in 1 Esdras iv. 45.[2] §§ 2-10. The story of the Three Youths and of Zerubbabel's obtaining leave

---

[1] Ezra iv. ff. 24. Ahasuerus is not in 1 Esdras; Josephus, *Antiq.* xi. 21 f.
[2] 1 Esdras iv. 45.

26   THE COMPOSITION AND PURPOSE OF ACTS

to go to Jerusalem and rebuild the Temple, virtually the same as in the long section peculiar to 1 Esdras.[1]

Chapter IV.—§§ 1-7 follow the arrangement of 1 Esdras and not that of Ezra in relating the opposition of the Cuthaeans or Samaritans, and the completion of the Temple under Darius.[2] § 8 relates the celebration of the Passover as in 1 Esdras, and § 9 is a section peculiar to Josephus about an embassy of Zerubbabel and three others to Darius.

Chapter V.—The story of Ezra's mission and his reforms in Jerusalem is continued, as it is in the two Ezra books; but the Persian King is here not Artaxerxes, but Xerxes the successor of Darius. In § 6, however, Nehemiah appears, and the narrative of the book of Nehemiah is related in the historian's own words down to the rebuilding of the Walls and the repeopling of Jerusalem.[3] "He left," says Josephus of Nehemiah, "the walls of Jerusalem an eternal memorial of himself. Now this was done in the days of Xerxes."

Chapter VI. gives the substance of the book of Esther, and places it in the days of Artaxerxes the son of Xerxes. From this it might be inferred that Josephus had other information which appeared sufficient for him to alter the narrative as he found it in the Greek of 1 Esdras. He knew, for instance, his Persian history more correctly. For some reason, or possibly because he had another text, Josephus says nothing of the reading of the Law by Ezra[4] or of Nehemiah's absence from Jerusalem or his return.[5] Nor does he mention Sanballat at the same time as Nehemiah, but places him a century later in the time of Alexander the Great, and in a different context.

Josephus and Maccabees.

As the story of the Maccabees is retold by Josephus, it is possible to see how one narrative can be checked by another, as Acts is by the Pauline letters. It is also interesting to observe how Josephus who wrote in Greek uses 1 Maccabees, originally

---

[1] 1 Esdras iii. 1-v. 6. It is thus evident that Josephus used 1 Esdras rather than the Hebrew Ezra.
[2] 1 Esdras v. 47-vii. 9, vii. 10-15.   [3] Josephus, *Antiq.* xi. 6-8.
[4] Neh. viii.; 1 Esdras ix. 42.   [5] Neh. xiii. 6.

written in Hebrew, as his method throws a light on the possible employment by the author of Acts of Aramaic sources or their translations.

Josephus follows 1 Maccabees—of 2 Maccabees he is ignorant —fairly closely, but here and there he adds to the narrative and occasionally makes a material alteration : a few examples will suffice to make this clear.

The speech of Mattathias on his deathbed, In 1 Macca- bees the patriotism is biblical. The dying priest exhorts his sons to be zealous for the law, and to give their lives for the covenant. He reminds them of Abraham, Joseph, Phineas, Joshua, Caleb, David, Elijah, the Three Children, and Daniel. Finally, he recommends them to take Simon as their counsellor and Judas as their leader in war. Josephus gives the speech a totally different aspect. He concludes with the advice about Simon and Judas ; but he makes Mattathias exhort his sons to preserve the customs of their country, and to recover the ancient form of government. Mattathias is represented as philosophising on the subject of immortality. "Your bodies," he remarks, " are mortal and subject to fate ; but they receive a sort of immortality by the remembrance of what actions they have done." Josephus obviously had the speech as given in Maccabees, but thought it unsuitable for his public.[1]

Speech of Mattathias.

The mention of the "Assidaeans" in 1 Maccabees evidently perplexed Josephus, and he decided to say nothing about them, either because he did not know who they were or because his readers would not understand. But he clearly had before him at least one passage mentioning them ; for, after relating the appointment of Alcimus as high priest, he says that " some of the people " relying on him, deserted Judas, and obeyed the orders of Bacchides, the Syrian governor, and were treacherously murdered.[2] With this may be compared " Luke's " treatment of the Herodians whom he found in his Marcan material, *e.g.* when the warning to beware of the " leaven of the Pharisees

The Assidaeans.

---

[1] 1 Macc. ii. 50-68 ; *Antiq.* xii. 6. 3.   [2] 1 Macc. vii. 13 ; *Antiq.* xii. 10. 2.

28   THE COMPOSITION AND PURPOSE OF ACTS

and the leaven of Herod " is changed into " the leaven of the Pharisees, which is hypocrisy." [1]

Dedication of the Temple. The rededication of the Temple after its profanation by Antiochus Epiphanes in 1 Maccabees is obviously copied by Josephus with a few significant variations.[2] The date, 25 Chislev in the 148th year, is given in both, only Josephus adds the name of the Macedonian month Apelleus and the Olympiad. He condenses the narrative by omitting some of the ritual details, but he adds that the annual feast then instituted was called the feast of lights. "I suppose because this liberty beyond our hopes appeared unto us; and that thence was the name given to the festival." [3]

Treaty with Rome. Josephus gives an abbreviated account of the negotiations between Judas and the Romans.[4] He omits the description of the Republic as it is given with a childlike simplicity and inaccuracy in Maccabees. The copy of the treaty with Rome is condensed and made far less difficult to understand; and Josephus adds a subscription saying that it was written by Eupolemus, son of John, and by Jason, the son of Eleazar, when Judas was high priest of the nation, and Simon his brother, general of the armies. Just before Josephus had remarked that the people had elected Judas high priest, whereas 1 Maccabees implies that the first of the family to hold the office was Jonathan.[5]

Additions in Josephus. Josephus sometimes either supplements or corrects 1 Maccabees. He relates an Embassy of the Samaritans to Antiochus Epiphanes, expressing their readiness to apostatise and to dedicate their temple on Gerizzim to Zeus Hellenius, quoting documents;[6] he gives the name of the officer slain by Mattathias as Apelles;[7] he acknowledges that Judas was defeated by Nicanor at Caphar Salama, whereas 1 Maccabees

---

[1] Luke xii. 1; cf. Mk. viii. 15.   [2] 1 Macc. iv. 42 ff.; *Antiq.* xii. 7. 6.
[3] *Antiq.* xii. 7. 7.   [4] 1 Macc. viii. 1-32 *passim*; *Antiq.* xii. 10. 6.
[5] *Antiq.* xii. 10. 6.; 1 Macc. x. 20. 21.   [6] *Antiq.* xii. 5. 5.
[7] *Antiq.* xii. 6. 2; 1 Macc. ii. 25.

certainly implies that there was a Jewish victory, though the concluding words καὶ ἔφυγον εἰς τὴν πόλιν Δαυείδ are ambiguous, and the context implies that it may have been the men of Judas.[1]

A comparison of Josephus with Greek and Jewish methods thus shows how in him the two streams of tradition flowed together. It remains for others to decide how far or when he was influenced by the one or the other.[2] The same is probably true of his great contemporary, the writer of Luke and Acts; here, too, the question is still unsettled, and the editors of this book are anxious to state as emphatically as possible their conviction that much more can be done by considering how far Luke was Greek and how far Jewish in his methods of writing. The foundation of all wisdom on this subject must be a consideration of the use made by Luke of the Septuagint, of the Gospel of Mark, and of the Greek language in general.

[1] 1 Macc. vii. 31, 32; *Antiq.* xii. 10. 4.
[2] The Editors regret that Laqueur's work on this subject reached them too late to be used. See R. Laqueur, *Der jüdische Historiker Flavius Josephus*, Giessen, 1920.

II

THE USE OF THE GREEK LANGUAGE IN ACTS

By J. DE ZWAAN

The Greek κοινή. THE language of the New Testament is the Greek vernacular of the first century A.D. This fact is established by the study of Papyri and Inscriptions. The nature of this vernacular is not easily definable. It is uniform enough : Egypt does not yield the Copticisms which one would expect, and real Semitisms are extremely scarce. The difficulty lies in a peculiarity of the Greek language which cannot be completely paralleled from any living European tongue except perhaps from modern Greek itself. Then, as now, the language which was popularly spoken and even written differed widely from that used in literature. Compare, for instance, the translation of the preface of Luke into modern literary Greek, published by the Bible Society, with Pallis's version in the spoken language.

(Bible Society)

Ἐπειδὴ πολλοὶ ἐπεχείρησαν νὰ συντάξωσι διήγησιν περὶ τῶν μετὰ πληροφορίας βεβαιωμένων εἰς ἡμᾶς πραγμάτων, καθὼς παρέδοσαν εἰς ἡμᾶς οἱ ἀπ' ἀρχῆς γενόμενοι αὐτόπται καὶ ὑπηρέται τοῦ λόγου, ἐφάνη καὶ εἰς ἐμὲ εὔλογον, ὅστις διηρεύνησα πάντα ἐξ ἀρχῆς ἀκριβῶς, νὰ σοὶ γράψω κατὰ σειρὰν περὶ τούτων, κράτιστε Θεόφιλε· διὰ νὰ γνωρίσῃς τὴν βεβαιότητα τῶν πραγμάτων, περὶ τῶν ὁποίων κατηχήθης.

(Pallis's version)

Ἐπειδὴς πολλοὶ προσπάθησαν τὸ νὰ καταστρώσουν ἱστορία τῶν περιστατικῶν ποὺ μάθαμε, καθὼς μᾶς τὰ παράδωκαν ὅσοι εἶδαν ἀπὸ τὴν ἀρχὴ καὶ δούλεψαν τὸ λόγο, ἀποφάσισα κι' ἐγὼ—ποὺ ξέτασα ἀπὸ τὴν πηγή τους ὅλα σωστὰ —νὰ σ' τὰ γράψω μὲ τὴ σειρά, λαμπρότατε Θεόφιλε, γιὰ νὰ καταλάβεις τῶν λόγων ποὺ κατηχήθηκες τὴν ἀλήθια.

THE GREEK OF ACTS

To such a degree of difference the relative independence of the literary from the popular idiom has arrived in our days. In the first century the distance was smaller, but the problems remain the same for us. Both forms of speech have indeed always been living their own lives. Even Plato's *Dialogues* were not in purely colloquial Greek, though they were much nearer to it than what we see here. The first problem, therefore, is to estimate the distance between the two idioms as they existed in New Testament times. This would require an approximate knowledge of the normal literary and the normal popular language. With the literary idiom the difficulty is to decide at what point its archaising tendencies become illegitimate. With the popular idiom the difficulty is to find out the real laws of the living speech. Only extensive knowledge of the spoken language could warrant an opinion on these laws. One can easily see how difficult this is even in our days. Dealing with the literary language of to-day, an educated Greek with modern philological training would be the fit person to decide whether a given piece of literary prose was unduly archaising or not. A foreigner might perhaps obtain a sure knowledge of the real facts about the modern popular κοινή by living among the people and applying methodical research over all the field from Alexandria to the harbours of the Black Sea. His freedom from reminiscences from school-days would be an advantage, and make him perhaps a better observer of the actual state of the language. Only these methods would be really adequate, but it is impossible to apply them to New Testament times.

The situation is, moreover, embarrassed by some tenets of first century school-craft. Men were as a rule not taught to mould their literary style on the language as it was spoken by educated people, but the syntax, grammar, and even the *copia verborum* of a long-gone age were set up as a general standard. The development of the literary language was hampered by this, and whenever it followed the course of popular speech, it did so *Rules of composition.*

with a bad conscience.[1] From these preliminaries it becomes clear why—as Radermacher has put it [2]—" the Syntax of the 'common' Greek leaves much room for personal caprice and preference. . . . Its character, contrary to that of Attic Syntax, may be described as individualistic." This element of individual preference becomes evident in the different degrees in which real knowledge and even pedantry on the subject of the syntax of bygone days was assimilated and applied in practice, and, secondly, in the various ways in which the exigencies of clear periodical structure were discarded. Of course this does not apply to all authors. Those that stand nearest to the popular idiom are more consistent in following such usages as it had developed in its own course.

The origin of the κοινή. Moreover, the composite origin of the κοινή should be taken into account. Its main constituents seem to be Attic and Ionic speech. The influence, either small or great, of other dialects, especially of those of the North, is still disputed, but Schlageter's [3] studies of the Attic inscriptions abroad seem to have justified Thumb's [4] opinion that the κοινή in its nascent stage was formed by a dominant influence of Attic crossed by an Ionic counter-current.

[1] Polybius is the notable exception, but the Anti-Atticists were powerless in the schools. Galen, A.D. 130-200, has devoted to this disease of Atticism a treatise against τοὺς ἐπιτιμῶντας τοῖς σολοικίζουσι τῇ φωνῇ, but no Dante, Petrarch, or Boccaccio arose to break the old routine by high achievement in the literary use of the living speech. What remained hidden from their eyes Dante saw and expressed in the beginning of his *De vulgari eloquentia* : " The common speech is the more noble, because it was the first mankind made use of, because it is of service to the whole world . . . because, finally, it is natural to us, while the literary idiom enjoys rather an artificial existence." The labours of the Anti-Atticists were unfruitful, and the irony even of so great a man as Galen was lost : vi. 633. 4 (Kuhn) τοῦτο τὸ λάχανον [sc. τὴν κράμβην] οἱ τὴν ἐπίτριπτον ψευδοπαιδείαν ἀσκοῦντες ὀνομάζειν ἀξιοῦσι " ῥάφανον," ὥσπερ τοῖς πρὸ ἑξακοσίων ἐτῶν 'Αθηναίοις διαλεγομένων ἡμῶν, ἀλλ' οὐχὶ τοῖς νῦν ῾Ελλησιν, or vi. 584. 12 οὗτοι [sc. οἱ ἰατροί] γὰρ οἶδ' ὅτι τὴν μὲν 'Αθηναίων φωνὴν οὐδὲν ἡγοῦνται τιμιωτέραν τῆς τῶν ἄλλων ἀνθρώπων, ὑγιείαν δὲ σώματος ἀξιολογώτερόν τι εἶναι νομίζουσι πρᾶγμα, cf. Thumb, *Die griechische Sprache im Zeitalter des Hellenismus*, Strassburg, 1901, p. 253, to whom these facts are due.

[2] " Besonderheiten der Koine Syntax," *Wiener Studien*, 1909, pp. 1 sqq.

[3] Schlageter, *Der Wortschatz der ausserhalb Attikas gefundenen attischen Inschriften*, Strassburg, 1912.   [4] Thumb, *op. cit.* pp. 202-253.

THE GREEK OF ACTS   33

This Ionic element accounts for the so-called "poetical" words (*e.g.* μεσονύκτιον, Acts xvi. 25, xx. 7; Luke xi. 5; Mark xiii. 35),[1] and for many of the ἅπαξ εἰρημένα, the number of which is gradually being restricted by the continuous stream of new documents. Even the Christian meanings of some words have a less isolated appearance in this light, and appear to be natural to that freedom in using a living language which a fresh spiritual message must have.

With the writers of the New Testament, however, other influences also counted. The translation-Greek of the LXX. was already in the field as a sort of technical style. In these terms the Greek of Acts should be defined.

The first question in the case of Acts is how deep the influence of the literary idiom went, as education, literature, and fashion together were supporting it. This may be answered by a rapid survey.

Literary and vulgar elements in Acts.

The Papyri betray the obsolescence of the Optative in New Testament times. The more striking therefore would be the appearance of a use that was extinct there and not too frequent even in Attic : [2] πρὶν ἢ ὁ κατηγορούμενος κατὰ πρόσωπον ἔχοι . . . τόπον τε ἀπολογίας λάβοι (Acts xxv. 16), but the optative here is rather due to indirect discourse and not really to an erratic reminiscence of literary style. The Optatives after εἰ (xvii. 27, xxvii. 12, 39),[3] those which appear in indirect questions (v. 24, x. 17), and the Potential optatives (viii. 31, xvii. 18, xxvi. 29) are more scarce in the Papyri than in Acts. Peculiar to Acts and also literary is the use of ἄν after a final ὅπως and of ἔσεσθαι after μέλλειν (iii. 20, xv. 17, xi. 28 [xxiii. 30 HLP], xxiv. 15, xxvii. 10). So is the Future participle as a circumstantial equivalent to a final clause of purpose [4] in viii. 27, xxiv. 11, 17,

[1] Rutherford, *The New Phrynichus*, London, 1881, xxxvi. p. 126; cf. Acts xxvii. 27.
[2] Goodwin, *Syntax of Greek Moods and Tenses*, London, 1897, § 644, and Robertson, *Grammar of the Greek N.T.*, London, 1914, p. 970.
[3] Acts xxiv. 19 is *plus royaliste que le roi* : Attic either ἔχουσι or ἐάν τι ἔχωσι.
[4] Goodwin, *op. cit.* § 840, Burton, *N.T. Moods and Tenses*,[3] Edinburgh, 1898, § 442.

which might have been more often applied, *e.g.*, in x. 33, xv. 27, etc. If MS. authority were not so adverse, and the usage of Acts better fit to inspire confidence on such a point, one would like to follow the later MSS. in reading also ἀσπασόμενοι in Acts xxv. 13 to get rid of the vexed question of an aorist participle used of action subsequent to that of the principal verb.[1] This well marked lack of consistency in syntax and style must have been a fault in the eyes of contemporary judgment. Some well-balanced phrases do not sufficiently atone for it, *e.g.* Acts xxvi. 29 εὐξαίμην ἂν τῷ Θεῷ καὶ ἐν ὀλίγῳ καὶ ἐν μεγάλῳ οὐ μόνον σε ἀλλὰ καὶ [2] πάντας . . . γενέσθαι τοιούτους ὁποῖος καὶ ἐγώ . . . or Acts xv. 24-26, since the more literary expressions clash again and again with so-called vulgarisms. Even the modern reader cannot but feel the incongruity between such Attic forms as ἥγημαι (v. 2),[3] ἴσασι (v. 4), constructions like ἐγκαλεῖσθαι with περί,[4] isolated forms as ἀκριβεστάτη [5] (v. 5, true superlative), words like οὐρανόθεν, and the rest of chapter xxvi. It is vigorous [6] Greek, but it is not homogeneous. A bold beginning as : "Οθεν, βασιλεῦ Ἀγρίππα,[7] οὐκ ἐγενόμην ἀπειθὴς [8] τῇ οὐρανίῳ ὀπτασίᾳ [9] (v. 19 [10]) is in strange contrast with the

---

[1] Radermacher, *W. St.* xxxi. p. 11 : " Every personality in the world of letters stands by itself, and even with the best - educated authors one is never safe from surprises." Ἀσπασάμενοι is either subsequent or coincident action, cf. Burton, *N.T. Moods and Tenses*,[3] Edinburgh, 1898, §§ 142-145 ; Goodwin, *op. cit.* § 152 ; Blass-Debrunner, *Grammatik des neutestamentlichen Griechisch*,[4] Göttingen, 1913, § 339 ; Moulton, *Grammar of N.T. Greek*, Edinburgh, 1906, vol. i. pp. 132-133.

[2] Peculiar to the second part of Acts xix. 26, 27, xxi. 13, xxvi. 29, xxvii. 10.

[3] Perfect with present sense.

[4] Cf. πρός c. gen., "in the interest of," Acts xxvii. 34.

[5] Cf. ὡς τάχιστα, Acts xvii. 15.   [6] *Vss.* 7, 8 are very effective.

[7] The omission of ὦ is not un-Attic and frequent in the Papyri (ἡγεμὼν κύριε et sim.).

[8] A *litotes* of which Luke is fond (second part of Acts) and which he repeats in the same chapter : οὐ γὰρ . . . ἐν γωνίᾳ (Acts xxvi. 26). Οὐκ ὀλίγος xii. 18, xiv. 28, xv. 2, xvii. 4, 12, xix. 23, 24, xxvii. 20; οὐχ ὁ τυχών xix. 11, xxviii. 2; other expressions : i. 5, xiv. 17, xvii. 27, xx. 12, xxi. 39, xxvii. 19. The habit of returning to a phrase once used is again very obvious here.

[9] A 'Lucan' word, also 2 Cor. xii. 1.

[10] On v. 20 cf. Blass, *Acta Apostolorum, editio philologica*, Göttingen, 1895, p. 268, and Ramsay, *St. Paul the Traveller and the Roman Citizen*, London, 1905, p. 382.

changed style of ending (v. 22, 23): οὐδὲν ἐκτὸς λέγων ὧν τε οἱ προφῆται ἐλάλησαν μελλόντων [1] γίνεσθαι καὶ Μωϋσῆς, εἰ παθητὸς ὁ Χριστός, εἰ πρῶτος ἐξ ἀναστάσεως νεκρῶν φῶς μέλλει καταγγέλλειν τῷ τε λαῷ καὶ τοῖς ἔθνεσιν. The same may be observed in the vocabulary as a whole: θυμομαχεῖν (xii. 20), ὁμοθυμαδόν (ten times in Acts and Rom. xv. 6), πανοικί (xvi. 34), ναῦς (xxvii. 41),[2] νεανίας (vii. 58, xx. 9, xxiii. 17, xxiii. 22 peculiar to Acts, but also νεανίσκοι [ii. 17], v. 10 ; Luke vii. 14), local πρό (xii. 6, xiv. 13 [3]) instead of ἔμπροσθεν (x. 4, xviii. 17 ; Luke v. 19, vii. 27, x. 21, xii. 8 bis, xix. 27, xxi. 36), etc., contrasting with a host of less distinguished words and expressions. In some cases a striking effect is obtained either consciously or not just by the use of such uneven Greek.[4] The Ephesian 'town-clerk's' address opens (xix. 35) with a rhetorical question, mounts to pathos combined with literary elegance (καὶ γὰρ κινδυνεύομεν[5] ἐγκαλεῖσθαι στάσεως πέρι[6] τῆς σήμερον), followed by a sound genitive absolute (μηδενὸς αἰτίου ὑπάρχοντος). Then, suddenly, it dies away in the confused construction περὶ οὗ οὐ δυνησόμεθα ἀποδοῦναι λόγον περὶ τῆς συστροφῆς ταύτης. The dangerous word στάσεως once being pronounced, the embarrassment of this too rhetorical dignitary in his efforts to take it back brings again to the surface the associated περί —which had been so elegantly placed—the cumbersome style

[1] A laboured attraction. The last words καὶ Μωϋσῆς and the next verse sound very much like headlines from a book of Testimonies, added as an afterthought either by the author or by somebody else.

[2] Blass, op. cit. p. 19, thinks it not improbable that a reminiscence of Homer should be found here.

[3] But cf. Ramsay, The Church in the Roman Empire before A.D. 170,[8] London, 1914, pp. 51-52.

[4] Cf. C. B. Williams, The Participle in the Book of Acts, Chicago, 1909, pp. 32-33 on Acts xxi. 34.

[5] Again a 'Lucan' word: Lk. viii. 23, Acts xix. 27. Once (different) in Paul: 1 Cor. xv. 30.

[6] Field, Notes on the Translation of the N.T.,[2] Cambridge, 1899, p. 131 ; Blass, op. cit. p. 213 : Radermacher, Lietzmann's Handbuch zum N.T. i. 1, p. 99 [1] ; Blass-Debrunner, op. cit. § 178, prefer, against the usage of the author and on weak evidence (cf. Hort, The N.T. in the Original Greek, Introduction, Appendix, London, 1896, in loc.), a reading which makes the passage less striking.

36 THE COMPOSITION AND PURPOSE OF ACTS

reflecting all the while his disturbed state of mind. If freely invented this touch is a token of consummate skill in reaching the effect of ἔκπληξις [1] by a peculiar [2] but quite adequate means.

Illiterate sources. This uneven character of the Greek of Acts must be largely due to the illiterate documents which went into its composition. In some places, however, it looks even as if some additional information on "correct" usage were acquired during the work. In the Gospel, e.g., πλήν is used fifteen times and without exception as an adversative conjunction equalling "But," in Acts it is never so used, not even in passages of "lower" style.

The unity of authorship of Acts and Luke is, however, generally accepted on the strength of the apparent unity of style and syntax.[3] Even the "we" sections [4] correspond in phraseology [5] with the Gospel, and, conversely, the first chapters of Acts are in many significant details unmistakably "Lucan." [6]

Medical language. The question of traces of "medical" idiom in Luke has been quite changed by the appearance of Cadbury's *Style and Literary Method of Luke* (Harvard Theological Studies, vi.), 1920. By very painstaking methods the whole problem has been sifted out again, or rather for the first time, as Hobart,[7] even supplemented with the observations of Harnack [8] and Zahn,[9] cannot be com-

---

[1] Kroll, "Die Originalität Vergils," *Neue Jahrbb.* xxi., Leipzig, 1908, p. 521 [3], quotes Plut. *De glor. Ath.* iii. 347 a τῶν ἱστορικῶν κράτιστος ὁ τὴν διήγησιν ὥσπερ γραφὴν πάθεσι καὶ προσώποις εἰδωλοποιήσας, cf. the 'picturesque' element in Acts.

[2] *Ibid.* Longinus, *On the Sublime*, i. 4, xii. 5.

[3] Moulton, *op. cit.* p. 216 f., *e.g.* τοῦ + Inf. in Acts; C. B. Williams, *op. cit.* pp. 69, 72, participial usage; Hawkins, *Horae Synopticae*,[1] Oxford, 1899, p. 142 f., compound verbs. For the absolute genitives, see p. 42, n. 3.

[4] Acts xvi. 10-17, xx. (4), 5-16, xxi. 1-18, xxvii. 1-xxviii. 16.

[5] Hawkins, *op. cit.* pp. 148-154, 179 f.

[6] Harnack, *Die Apostelgeschichte*, Leipzig, 1908, p. 131 f.; *Lukas der Arzt*, Leipzig, 1906, pp. 19-85; Vogel, *Zur Charakteristik des Lukas nach Sprache und Stil*,[2] Leipzig, 1899, pp. 16-18.

[7] W. K. Hobart, *The Medical Language of St. Luke*, 1882.

[8] Harnack, *Lukas der Arzt*, Leipzig, 1906 = *Luke the Physician*, London, 1907.

[9] Zahn, *Einleitung in das N.T.*, Leipzig, 1906 [3] = *Introduction*, New York, 1909.

pared with the conscientious way in which the matter is handled here. Very significant is the statement on p. 38 f. : "The question may be . . . asked whether the gulf between New Testament Greek in general and Attic or Atticistic Greek is not being exaggerated . . . owing to our fresh knowledge of the vernacular Greek through the papyri. If so, the exaggeration is probably due to two factors, viz. the overrating of the purely imitative and classical elements in the so-called Atticists, and the underrating of the literary element in the vocabulary of the New Testament writers. I am inclined to revolt slightly also from the extreme view of Deissmann and Moulton, who minimise the Semitic or Biblical or Jewish element in the New Testament and ascribe such phenomena to the vernacular Greek of the time. I have already indicated that much of Luke's post-classical vocabulary appears to be due to a distinctly Jewish-Christian language. This is probably true even of his post-classical syntax. And still more allowance must be made if it is assumed that in some parts of his work he consciously imitates the LXX. or Mark." This view I should like to endorse, as will appear further in the discussion of the question of translation-Greek and Semiticising " sacred " prose.

The vocabulary of Luke and Acts is tested by Cadbury on pages 10-36 to determine Luke's literary standard by working out a parallel for A-E with the vocabulary in Schmid's *Atticismus* [1] for Dio Chrysostom, Lucian, Aristides, Aelian, and the younger Philostratus. Words frequent in Attic and later on are omitted as not characteristic. Five classes are formed, viz. :

The literary standard of Acts.

A. Common Attic, found in several writers.
B. Only or principally in one prose writer before Aristotle.
C. Absent in Attic prose, but found in poetry.
D. Post-classical prose, including Aristotle.
E. First occurrences in the work under investigation.

For A, B, C, D, E the results for Luke-Acts and for Acts

[1] Schmid, *Der Atticismus in seinen Hauptvertretern*, 1887-97.

alone are shown in the following table, the last column of which gives the percentage of the total of significant words.

Class.	Luke-Acts.	Acts.	Percentage.
A	137	90	29
B	27	13	6
C	87	50	18
D	202	119	42
E	22	15	5
	475	287	100

These results justify the statement quoted above : the post-classical element is larger than in Dio where it is 21 per cent, in Lucian 20 per cent, in Aristides 9 per cent, in Aelian 23 per cent, and in II. Philostratus 16 per cent, but deduction ought to be made for the necessary use of the vocabulary of "sacred prose" and for some flaws in Schmid's methods.

More interesting is the next chapter with its extensive notes on the alleged medical language of Luke, occupying pp. 39-50, 51-64, and followed by an excursus on medical terms in Lucian. Especially the excursus provides a counter proof, adequate portions of Lucian being substituted for Luke, which method apparently justifies the verdict (p. 71) : "There can be no doubt that such an investigation could produce a volume quite as large as Hobart's, and that the best examples selected from it would be found quite as cogent as those of Harnack, Moffatt, and Zahn to prove by his ' medical language ' that Lucian was a physician."

This result is reached by applying a test which has been strangely neglected in former investigations. Cadbury has formulated it on p. 50 : "Any sound argument . . . must not only show a considerable number of terms possibly or probably medical,[1] but must show that they are *more numerous and of*

[1] Cadbury also quotes from Galen's treatise "On the Natural Faculties" this unfavourable judgment on the use of technical terms by medical men : "We, however, for our part, are convinced that the chief merit of language is clearness, and we know that nothing detracts so much from this as do

more *frequent occurrence* than in other *writers of his time and degree of culture.* .... The evidence is cumulative, but it must also be comparative." Luke should be compared with " non-professional men, writing with the same culture as Luke and on similar subjects. If not, the argument of Hobart and the rest is useless." It may be questioned whether these conditions are adequately satisfied by the proof that Luke's medical examples are by no means more striking and abundant than those which could be collected from Josephus, Philo, Plutarch, or Lucian; but the case is really clinched by the lists on pp. 42-45, showing how overwhelming is the mass of LXX. parallels. Lucian may be " a fair parallel to Luke " or not, the evidence seems conclusive that Luke's style does not bear such traces of medical training and interest as could support an argument from professional style for " the beloved physician," as the author of the two books which tradition ascribes to him. He is even guilty of some passages which make it very doubtful whether he can have been a physician.[1] But as Cadbury observes on p. 51: " One cannot know to-day what an ancient physician would not have written." Even greater men among them than Luke have written down very strange things. Moreover, we should be on our guard not to overrate Luke's degree of culture. The medical profession was not then what it is now, slaves largely filling its ranks, and the public did not reserve the name of ἰατρός for a select few.

But the author's command of the popular κοινή is perfect. It is used to full advantage in Gamaliel's address (Acts v. 38), ἐὰν ᾖ (as their adversaries are supposing: *Subjunctive*) ἐξ ἀνθρώπων . . ., εἰ δὲ ἐκ Θεοῦ ἐστιν (reality) οὐ δυνήσεσθε κτλ.[2] Here the author betrays himself as composer of the speech as

Luke and the κοινή.

---

unfamiliar terms; accordingly we employ those terms which the bulk of people (οἱ πολλοί) are accustomed to use " (Brock's translation in the Loeb Classical Library, p. 3, quoted by Cadbury, *op. cit* p. 64, note 91).

[1] Cf. C. Clemen, in the *Theol. Rundschau*, x. (1907), p. 102, *e.g.* the use of λεπίδες in Acts ix. 18.

[2] Radermacher, *op. cit.* p. 144.

he unconsciously has stepped into the place of the person speaking.[1] Attention has also been drawn [2] to the accurate use of the tenses in Acts xv. 37. " Barnabas, with easy forgetfulness of risk, wishes συμπαραλαβεῖν Mark—Paul refuses συμπαραλαμβάνειν, to have with them day by day one who had shown himself unreliable." In Acts xxvi. " The A.V. commits Paul to the statement that he had actually forced weak Christians to renounce their Master. But the sudden abandonment of the Aorist used up to this point gives a strong grammatical argument for the alternative ἠνάγκαζον : ' I tried to force.' " Another typical instance is συνήλλασσεν (Acts vii. 26). The distinction between the Present and Aorist Imperatives is in full vigour : μὴ ποίει, to stop action in progress (Acts x. 15, xviii. 9, xx. 10) ; μὴ ποιήσῃς, to prevent action (vii. 60, ix. 38, xvi. 28, xxiii. 21). Good vernacular is the use of ὑπάρχειν in various constructions, which is very frequent in Luke and Acts, but altogether absent from Matthew, Mark, and John. Well known from the Papyri is also the pronounced preference for the Infinitive passive after verbs of commanding, etc. This is a decidedly unclassical use, but it may seem doubtful whether Acts v. 34, xvi. 22 are in conscious agreement with the classical rule. So with οὐ + Participle : the popular tendency was to construe all Infinitives and Participles with μή, but for a long time the feeling that οὐ was yet in all cases the right negation for statements of fact seems to have lingered. Literary influence in such cases (Acts vii. 5, xxvi. 22, xxviii. 17-19) is therefore a doubtful assumption. A general estimate of the author's style and preferences applied to each special case should guide our judgment here. For such an estimate a test

---

[1] E. Norden, *Antike Kunstprosa*,[2] Leipzig and Berlin, 1909, p. 482.

[2] By Moulton, *op. cit.* pp. 128 *sqq.* : " Luke the Greek physician, and as such, considering the education of medical men in those times, also a man of letters." This is, however, asserting too much. It is quite possible that "Luke was a freedman," but "a man of letters," is, after all, a rather high distinction. Slaves trained in literature and philosophy were no exception, but of course neither a current article. The sort of Greek Luke was trained in I should value—with Cadbury—rather high, but of his attainment I am inclined to think less favourably. At most it was rather unequal.

case is presented by Moulton's observation [1] on the Historic Present: "Josephus would use the tense as an imitator of the classics,[2] Mark as a man of the people ... while Luke would have Greek education enough to know that it was not common in cultured speech of his time, *but not enough to recall the encouragement of classical writers.*"

After the blurring of old usages, fresh distinctions arose: ὅστις, e.g., is used as a somewhat emphasised relative or in the sense which in English would be expressed by a demonstrative and a conjunction,[3] just as is also the *Article* with places that occur in the narrative signalled as "stations in the course of a journey [4] (Acts xvii. 1, xx. 13, xxi. 1-3, xxiii. 32), but xx. 14 sq. anarthrous," cf. Blass-Debrunner, *op. cit.* § 261 *sub.* 2. Peculiar is also ὁ ὤν [5] in the sense of ὁ ὀνομαζόμενος in v. 17, xiii. 1 [xiv. 13 D], and also in xxviii. 17.[6]

[1] Moulton, *op. cit.* pp. 120-121, quoting Hawkins, *op. cit.* pp. 113-119. The Historic Presents in Acts are thirteen in number, nine of them (Hawkins), eight (Moulton) or "possibly eleven " (Robertson, *Grammar*, p. 867) occurring in Luke.

[2] But Josephus had his " ghosts " (*C. Apion.* i. 9), who may have earned these laurels for him.

[3] Robertson, *Grammar*, p. 731, quotes the only instance of ὅ τι in indirect question, Acts ix. 6 λαληθήσεταί σοι ὅ τι σε δεῖ ποιεῖν rightly, as a mark of literary influence, the various reading τι being significant. Ὅσα or πάντα ὅσα, cf. ix. 16, would have done quite well.

[4] The general rule is that a place named as the end of a journey or of a distinct part of it is introduced *without the Article* (but xxviii. 14 τὴν 'Ρώμην, v. 16 regular). Movings from a place already mentioned—Jerusalem always excepted as constantly anarthrous, except v. 28, cf. Robertson, *Grammar*, p. 760— require the *Article* (xiii. 13-14, xviii. 1-21, 22, but faulty xxi. 7 ἀπὸ Τύρου). Places emphasised as stations—the text oftenest shows why—have the *Article*. xxi. 1 Cos and Rhodes (town distinct from the island ?); x. 8 turning-point from which they should return with Peter (in v. 5 merely destination ?), xiv. 21 Derbe, *end* of the journey; Lystra, etc., stations on the journey home, xvii. 1, xx. 6, 13-17, xxiii. 32-33. In xxi. 3 εἰς Τύρον, the vessel was unloaded, 8 εἰς Καισαρίαν, end of the voyage, xxviii. 12. In v. 14 εἰς τὴν 'Ρώμην = arrival at the boundary of the *ager Romanus*, but v. 16 εἰς 'Ρώμην end of the travel? end of the crossing, v. 13 of the coasting along Sicily, 13 [Ποτιόλους] end of the voyage. A mistake seems to lurk perhaps in xxvii. 3, εἰς Σιδῶνα : this is emphasised as a station by Paul's getting "leave to go unto his friends and refresh himself."

[5] Ramsay, *Church*, p. 52.

[6] Cf. p. 57 for the discussion of Torrey's suggestion to explain this as translation-Greek for *di 'īth*.

Increased acquaintance with the living vernacular has justified much that seemed unwarranted. A slight case is the omission of ὄντες in ἄσιτοι διατελεῖτε [1] (Acts xxvii. 33). The very free use of the partitive genitive would recall the Semitic constructions with *min*. The earliest κοινή, however, —which has left its traces on the pages of Xenophon— knew this construction, and the Papyri have preserved it in a large number of examples. Even more literary writers than Luke have sinned against the genitive absolute, the classical rule [2]

[1] *New Phrynichus*, ccxliv. p. 342 f.
[2] The genitive absolute in Acts:

Chapters	i.	ii.	iii.	iv.	v.	vi.	vii.	viii.	ix.	x.
Good	3	1	1	-	1	1	1	-	2	3
Dubious	-	-	-	1	-	-	1	-	-	-
Faulty	-	-	-	?	-	-	2	-	-	1
Total	3	1	1	3	1	1	4	-	2	4

Chapters	xi.	xii.	xiii.	xiv.	xv.	xvi.	xvii.	xviii.	xix.	xx.
Good	-	2	2	1	2	1	-	2	3	3
Dubious	-	-	1	-	-	-	-	-	1	-
Faulty	-	-	1	-	-	1	1	3	1	-
Total	-	2	4	1	2	2	1	5	5	3

Chapters	xxi.	xxii.	xxiii.	xxiv.	xxv.	xxvi.	xxvii.	xxviii.		
Good	3	1	4	3	6	2	10	5	(in total)	63
Dubious	2	-	-	3	1	1	1	-	,,	12
Faulty	2	1	-	1	2	-	-	2	,,	20
Total	7	2	4	7	9	3	11	7	,,	95

The genitive absolute in the 'We' Sections (and in the remaining parts of chaps. xvi., xx., etc.):

Chapters	xvi. 10-17.	Rest.	xx. 5-18.	Rest.	xxi. 1-18.	Rest.	xxvii. 1-xxviii. 16.	Rest.
Good	-	1	2	1	2	1	13	2
Dubious	-	-	-	-	1	1	1	-
Faulty	1	-	-	-	1	1	2	1
Total	1	1	2	1	4	3	16	3

The greater frequency after chapter xvii. is what we should expect. The figures are apparently in favour of the unity of authorship and the identity of the author of the 'we' sections and the rest of the narrative. Acts xxi. 10, 31, xxv. 17: *gen. abs.* without noun or pronoun in agreement, frequent in the Papyri, cf. Moulton, *op. cit.* p. 74. C. B. Williams, *op. cit.* pp. 31-32, seems to apply a different standard, discussing only as "loose constructions" Acts vii. 21, xxi. 17, 34, xxii. 17, xxv. 21. "There are a few other loose constructions of the genitive absolute in the book. But these few exceptions only emphasise the fact that the author of the book closely followed the rule to make the genitive absolute refer to a substantive not connected with the rest of the being no longer felt. The same applies to the *acc. c. inf.*; Luke has combined in one verse (Acts xxii. 17) a misuse of both which appears to be as hard a case as any in the Egyptian documents. The hinged construction of ὅτι and *acc. c. inf.* in chap. xxvii. 10 is, notwithstanding isolated classical instances, a symptom of degeneration by overgrowth of the constructions with the Infinitive. The indeclinable πλήρης [1] has early precedent and, in Acts, good MS. evidence. Taken from life and thoroughly vernacular is the dative in μηδὲν πράξῃς σεαυτῷ κακόν (Acts xvi. 28).[2]

Latinisms might be expected in popular Greek of the first century, and may serve as an introduction to the less clear case of Semitisms. The influence of the Latin construction of *iubere c. inf. pass.* may be seen in the deviations from classical usage in favour of infinitive-passive with verbs of commanding (Acts xxiii. 10 being an exception), but the tendency is easily explained by the clearer sense which this construction gave. Temporal πρό (Acts v. 36, xxi. 38) would be an almost self-evident Latinism but for Herodotus, Hippocrates, and epigraphical facts prior to any Latin influence. Very striking is *genua ponere* and τιθέναι τὰ γόνατα (Acts vii. 60, ix. 40, xx. 36, xxi. 5; Luke xxii. 41; Mark xv. 19), but unless a reason can be suggested for the imitation of just this expression, spontaneous parallelism may stand as an alternative. In forensic [3] surroundings Latinisms are of course natural: λαβόντες τὸ ἱκανόν [4] (Acts xvii. 9), ὄψεσθε αὐτοί (Acts xviii. 15), or ἀγοραῖοι ἄγονται (Acts xix. 38). A 'vulgar' Latinism is perhaps οὐ μετὰ πολλὰς ταύτας ἡμέρας (Acts i. 5), but it contains the only instance of the "Lucan" *litotes* in these first

Latinisms.

---

sentence." It is difficult to judge how 'connected' should be interpreted, but at least twelve more instances are to be added at all events to those mentioned by the author.

[1] Moulton, *op. cit.* p. 50.
[2] Attic double acc., cf. Radermacher, *op. cit.* p. 99.
[3] "Negative" Latinisms are possibly διετία (Acts xxiv. 27, xxviii. 30) and τριετία (xx. 31), corresponding to *biennium* and *triennium*.
[4] A favourite word with Luke: Matt. 3, Mark 3, Luke 10, Acts 19, Paul 6 occurrences.

44 THE COMPOSITION AND PURPOSE OF ACTS

chapters,[1] and this makes inadvertency a less probable explanation. It has also been claimed as an Aramaism by Torrey,[2] and so it will lead us up to the main question of the Greek of Acts, viz. the so-called Semitisms.

Semitisms. Semitism and Semiticising style are expressions which are much in need of sharp definition and closer scrutiny. Both purposes and some more besides will be served by a discussion of the valuable contribution which Torrey has made to this subject.

Torrey's theory. This question of Semitisms in Acts has obtained a new aspect by Torrey's *Composition and Date of Acts*. It is now bound up with the larger questions of unity of authorship and sources by the alleged demonstration of an Aramaic document extending from i. 1b–xv. 35, and translated by Luke. The remaining chapters he holds to have been written by the same writer but added as an afterthought. In order to make good this contention the difference in style between the translated documents and the rest of the book is emphasised. " It is not enough to speak of frequent Semitisms; the truth is that the language of all these fifteen chapters is translation-Greek through and through, generally preserving even the order of the words. In the remainder of the book, chapters xvi.–xxviii., the case is altogether different. Here there is no evidence of an underlying

---

[1] Somewhat similar is iv. 20 οὐ δυνάμεθα . . . μὴ λαλεῖν. But the first real litotes is οὐκ ὀλίγος xii. 18, cf. xiv. 28, xv. 2, xvii. 4, 12, xix. 23, 24, xxvii. 20. The first three instances are significant against the " 1 Acts " theory as compared with the modification proposed further down in this article. Other cases are οὐκ ἀμάρτυρον, xiv. 17 (again important from this point of view); οὐ μακράν, xvii. 27; οὐ τὰς τυχούσας, xix. 11, cf. xxviii. 2; οὐ μετρίως, xx. 12; οὐκ ἀσήμου πόλεως, xxi. 39; οὐκ . . . ἀπειθής, xxvi. 19; οὐ . . . ἐν γωνίᾳ, xxvi. 26.

[2] Torrey, *Composition and Date of Acts* (Harvard Theological Studies, i.), Cambridge, Mass., 1916, pp. 6, 24 claims this as a case of Jewish Aramaic on the strength of the redundant demonstrative ταύτας, cf. Dalman, *Gramm. des judisch-palästinischen Aramaisch*, Leipzig,[1] 1894,[2] 1905, pp. 113 ff. The *litotes*, however, is not the less Greek and Latin for this reason. That such a Lucanism should stand solitary in the beginning of the translation of an Aramaic source is not unnatural. The author or translator may have abandoned or postponed the idea of more thoroughly " Lucanising " the style of this document.

Semitic language. The few apparent Semitisms (καὶ ἰδού: ἐγένετο with infin.: τότε used in continuing a narrative: ἐνώπιον with genitive: ἐθέτο ἐν τῷ πνεύματι πορεύεσθαι: ἐκ μέσου [ἐν μέσῳ] αὐτῶν) are chargeable to the κοινή; though their presence may be due in part to the influence of the translation-Greek which Luke had so extensively read and written. In either case they are negligible" (pp. 7, 8).

This statement does not seem to be wholly accurate. To the "few apparent Semitisms"—taking the word in the less precise sense in which it was used here—an imposing array must be added. Between chapter xviii. and xxii. they are even thickly enough strewn to impart a distinct colour to the whole. Chapter xix. is especially characteristic from this point of view, as a rapid survey will show: (1) ἐγένετο δὲ ἐν τῷ τὸν Ἀπολλὼ εἶναι ἐν Κορίνθῳ (cf. *op. cit.* pp. 6 and 7, Acts iv. 30, viii. 6, ix. 3; but also xix. 1, xxii. 6, 17, xxviii. 8, 17) . . .; (5) ἐβαπτίσθησαν εἰς τὸ ὄνομα (cf. *op. cit.* p. 15, Acts iii. 16) . . .; (8) διαλεγόμενος καὶ πείθων (cf. *op. cit.* p. 36, Acts xi. 6; but also ἐλάλει καὶ ἐδίδασκεν, xviii. 25; and other instances in chapter xix. 2, 16, 18, 19) . . .; (9) ὡς δέ (cf. *op. cit.* p. 6 וכדי: καὶ ὡς, Acts i. 10, but also ὡς δέ v. 24, vii. 23, viii. 36, ix. 23, x. 7, 17, 25, xiii. 25, 29, xiv. 5; and in "2 Acts" 18 times) . . . ἐσκληρύνοντο καὶ ἠπείθουν (see above, v. 8) κακολογοῦντες τὴν ὁδόν (*op. cit.* p. 34; Acts ix. 2; but also xvi. 17, xviii. 25, 26, xix. 9, 23, xxii. 4, xxiv. 22) ἐνώπιον (pp. 6, 7; Acts vi. 5; cf. xix. 19, xxvii. 35) τοῦ πλήθους . . .; (11) δυνάμεις . . . ὁ θεὸς ἐποίει διὰ τῶν χείρων (*op. cit.* p. 6; Acts ii. 23; but also xvii. 25, xix. 11, 26, xxi. 11, xxiv. 7, xxviii. 17) Παύλου . . .; (15) ἀποκριθὲν δὲ τὸ πνεῦμα . . . εἶπεν αὐτοῖς (*op. cit.* p. 7; Acts xv. 3, v. 8, iii. 12. The very common Aramaic ענה ואמר . . . cf. Dan. iv. 27. The idiom is also Hebrew) . . .; (16) κατακυριεύσας . . . ἴσχυσεν κατ' αὐτῶν (see above) . . . ἐκφυγεῖν ἐκ τοῦ οἴκου ἐκείνου . . .; (17) τοῦτο δὲ ἐγένετο γνωστὸν (*op. cit.* p. 30; Acts iv. 16, ידיע, but also i. 19, ix. 42, xix. 17, xxviii. 22, ii. 14, iv. 16, xxviii. 28) πᾶσιν . . . τοῖς κατοικοῦσιν τὴν Ἔφεσον . . . ἐπέπεσεν φ. ἐπὶ πάντας . . .;

(18) ἤρχοντο ἐξομολογούμενοι καὶ ἀναγγέλλοντες (see above, v. 8) . . . ; (19) ἐνώπιον πάντων (see above, v. 9) . . . καὶ συνεψήφισαν . . . καὶ εὗρον (Semitic 3rd plural for passive) . . . ; (21) ὡς δὲ (see above, וכד) ἐπληρώθη ταῦτα (*op. cit.* pp. 28, 37 ; Acts ii. 1, but also xxiv. 27) ἔθετο . . . ἐν τῷ πνεύματι (p. 6, Acts v. 4, see above, p. 8 quoted) πορεύεσθαι . . . ; (23) περὶ τῆς ὁδοῦ (see further down) . . . ; (26) οἱ διὰ χειρῶν γενόμενοι (see above, v. 11) . . . ; (28) ἔκραζον λέγοντες (see above v. 8) . . . ; (34) φωνὴ ἐγένετο μία ἐκ πάντων . . . κράζοντες (reduced to Aramaic this would sound much better and the loose sequence would cause no trouble).

A perusal of these various and unequal cases of Semiticising Greek is perhaps sufficient to substantiate some doubts. Of course the style of the first half of Acts is decidedly more Semitic than that of the second. But it has also often been observed that within the limits of each of these halves of Acts the colouring itself is unequal. The usual explanation of the first fact was found in Luke's sense of *local colour*. The second fact, viz. the difference of *nuance* within each half of the book, is more difficult to explain consistently. Torrey has recourse to minimising these shades in both halves, making 1 Acts " translation-Greek through and through " and 2 Acts almost pure κοινή. Neither the one nor the other seems warranted by the facts. That this is so follows equally from some considerations on the methods which ought to be applied and is confirmed by the results obtained.

The test of reversion. The test of reversion means obviously that a given Greek phrase which sounds somewhat strange, goes easily into Aramaic. Now much κοινή, not even sounding strange even in the order of the words, has this quality. But strange-sounding Greek may be due not only to translation, but also to the influence of translation-Greek on original composition. In Luke's case it is evident that strict account must be kept of this influence. Moreover, this " Semiticising " style in writing original Greek prose was not invented by him and applied only for " *local colour,*" but it was the style of "*sacred prose.*" Not only some books of the LXX. but also the remains of the voluminous and widely read Apocalyptic writings confirm this. Early Christian literature in general is written in κοινή tinged with the influence of Semiticising Greek of both these types.[1] To distinguish between these types, viz. "sacred prose," if Semiticising strongly enough, and translation-Greek on the other hand is a matter of delicate handling. Mere reversion is obviously not always a sufficient test. To deal quite safely some rules must be laid down, among which these might be followed :—

I. Current Septuagintisms are to be eliminated.
II. Cases which can be closely paralleled from the Papyri should be ruled out.
III. The case for translation-Greek presupposing an underlying document written *either* in Aramaic *or* in Hebrew, Semitisms which are impossible in one of these languages occurring side by side with such as are only ascribable to the other are conclusive evidence for "sacred prose" and against translation-Greek.
IV. The frequency and clearness of the cases should be tabulated, and the factor of clearness have its test-value numerically expressed. In this way "stretches" of weak cases must appear which will enable us to assign a higher test-value to doubtful numbers which appear between strong cases.
V. In the case of "1 Acts" locutions occurring also in "2 Acts" should count as evidence for translation-Greek only if they occur in a "stretch" of strong cases.

There is a certain amount of personal equation in this. It is, however, safer to handle the matter in small doses than otherwise. If one wishes to decide between translation-Greek and Semiticising prose without such measures, the results cannot inspire lasting confidence. The criticisms in Dalman's *Worte*

[1] Cf. the quotation from Cadbury, above, p. 37.

48 THE COMPOSITION AND PURPOSE OF ACTS

Jesu are very instructive on the value of many alluring suggestions even by very competent Semitic and Greek scholars.

After all the question is mainly one of Greek. We have on the one hand the Papyri, etc., and on the other Jewish and Early Christian Greek. The first must answer the question: Is this usage legitimate or Semitic? The other must solve the difficulty whether a given locution is still possible in an original Semiticising composition or can only be explained as a result of translation. We may refine our methods as much as possible, but in the last instance the cases come on the scales of this balance.

Variations in 1 Acts. Taking the cases in "1 Acts" which are discussed, about 85, as a workable average, the fact of weak and strong "stretches" at once appears. This was to be expected as Guillemard's *Hebraisms in the New Testament*,[1] though utterly antiquated, yet possesses some test-value and gives about the same results, chapters, vi., xii., xiii., xiv. being weak.

Giving the results for no more than a provisory estimate, it appears that the case for i.-v. 16 and ix. 31–xi. 18 is strong, for vii. doubtful, owing to the difficulty of estimating the value of separate cases among the host of quotations of which the apology of Stephen is made up, while chapter xv. rests on one case, the other instances being doubtful.

The curious fact is that if, therefore, an Aramaic source or sources be assumed for these "stretches," they coincide with the rough average result of current source criticism. For that reason verses v. 16 and xi. 18 are put in, though by philological means such a sharp dividing line is not obtainable, not even between "1 Acts" and the other chapters. As a piece of weak evidence the cases in chapter xv. might be analysed.

Acts xv. xv. 3 προπεμφθέντες ἀπό is quoted by Torrey[2] as a case of the Aramaic מן to denote the agent with a passive verb,

---

[1] Guillemard, *Hebraisms*, etc., Cambridge, 1879.

[2] *Op. cit.* pp. 7 and 28. The various reading ὑπό often occurs, ἀπό being vulgar. Ἀπό has become the rule in modern Greek.

but cases of this usage from the Papyri and later Greek are available. Moreover, the same construction occurs in xx. 9.

xv. 4 παρεδέχθησαν ἀπὸ τῆς ἐκκλησίας should answer to מן עדתא, but ἀπεδέξαντο ἡμᾶς οἱ ἀδελφοί, xxi. 17, goes as well into Aramaic, and the passive construction may be paralleled.

xv. 4 ὅσα ὁ θεὸς ἐποίησεν μετ' αὐτῶν is paralleled in xiv. 27, but cf. Grinfield, *Nov. Test. Gr. ed. Hellenistica, I. ad loc.* for parallels from LXX.

xv. 7 ἀφ' ἡμερῶν ἀρχαίων ἐν ὑμῖν ἐξελέξατο ὁ θεὸς διὰ τοῦ στόματός μου ἀκοῦσαι, pp. 7, 21, 22, is a strong case for בָּחַר בְּ unless the omission of ἐν ὑμῖν by Peshitto and Sahidic should afterwards appear to be right, which is not very probable. The case of ἀρχαίων is not much bettered by reversion; Peter might think himself predestined of old just as well as the ὑμεῖς or ἡμεῖς he is addressing.

xv. 13 ἀπεκρίθη of James' beginning to speak, with parallels in iii. 12 and v. 8, corresponding to Aramaic and Hebrew ענה, may be paralleled from xix. 15 (see above) and there are a host of similar cases in the LXX. and some elsewhere.

xv. 18 γνωστὰ ἀπ' αἰῶνος is probably direct quotation.

xv. 23 οἱ πρεσβύτεροι ἀδελφοί, pp. 7, 39, is a case of exegesis. The difficulties may be wholly imaginary and "the elder brethren" the final solution. An adjective may quite well find its place before ἀδελφός, cases being extant in the Papyri.

xv. 28 πλὴν τούτων τῶν ἐπάναγκες may be set right in the way suggested by Torrey on p. 39, but also without need of any Aramaic whatever; cf. Moulton and Milligan, *Vocabulary*, Part iii., *sub voce*, and Cadbury, *op. cit.* p. 16, classing it as common Attic.

xv. 33 ἀπελύθησαν ἀπό, see note on xv. 3.

On xv. 16-18, pp. 38, 39, nothing can be founded. Here the question of *Books of Testimonies* comes in. It cannot be discarded, since headlines are quoted in xxvi. 23: εἰ παθητὸς ὁ Χριστός and εἰ πρῶτος ἐξ ἀναστάσεως νεκρῶν φῶς μέλλει καταγγέλλειν τῷ τε λαῷ καὶ τοῖς ἔθνεσιν. The interruption of

50 THE COMPOSITION AND PURPOSE OF ACTS

Festus shows that Paul had been pouring out a stream of such " proof texts " (xxvi. 24 τὰ πολλὰ . . . γράμματα) referring to Gospel history (xxvi. 26 οὐ γάρ ἐστιν ἐν γωνίᾳ πεπραγμένον τοῦτο) as their fulfilment.

Strong and weak examples of Torrey's theory. Stronger are the arguments for i. 6–v. 16 and ix. 31–xi. 18. In the first stretch, discarding all weaker ones, the decisive points appear to be :

i. 15, ii. 1, 44, 47 ἐπὶ τὸ αὐτό, but cf. Cadbury, *A.J.Th.*, July 1920.
i. 22 ἀρξάμενος ἀπό.
ii. 7 οὐχὶ ἰδού.
iii. 16 ἐστερέωσε τὸ ὄνομα for ὑγιῆ κατέστησεν (cf. below, pp. 141 f.).
iv. 12 τὸ δεδομένον ἐν ἀνθρώποις.
iv. 25 ὁ τοῦ πατρὸς ἡμῶν διὰ πνεύματος ἁγίου στόματος Δαυεὶδ παιδός σου εἰπών.

Perhaps συναλίζομενος, i. 4, should be added (p. 23).

In the second stretch the case seems to rest upon five instances :

ix. 31 οἰκοδομουμένη καὶ πορευομένη τῷ φ. τ. κ.
ix. 32 διὰ πάντων.
x. 15 οὐδέποτε . . . πᾶν κοινόν.
x. 30 ἀπὸ τετάρτης . . . ὥρας (all on p. 34) and ἀρξάμενος (on pp. 6, 23, 25, 36).

Many weaker examples are interspersed and several may be paralleled from " 2 Acts " :

i. 5 οὐ μετὰ πολλὰς ταύτας ἡμέρας may be paralleled from Aramaic, but also from Latin (see above, pp. 43 f.).
i. 10 καὶ ὡς, see above, and cf. xix. 9 ὡς δέ.
i. 10 καὶ ἰδού, cf. xvi. 1, xx. 22, 25, xxvii. 24.
ii. 1 ἐν τῷ συμπληροῦσθαι τὴν ἡμέραν τῆς πεντηκοστῆς, cf. xix. 21 (ἐπληρώθη ταῦτα), xxiv. 27 (διετίας δὲ πληρωθείσης).
ii. 22 ἀποδεδειγμένον ἀπό.
iv. 36 ἐπικληθεὶς ἀπό, see above xv. 3 προπεμφθέντες ἀπό and xv. 33 ἀπελύθησαν ἀπό.
ii. 23 διὰ χειρός (χειρῶν), cf. xvii. 25, xix. 11, 26 (see above); xxi. 11, xxiv. 7, xxviii. 17.
ii. 24 ὠδῖνες τοῦ θανάτου is to be read with a capital letter—Θανάτου, a personification of death, cf. Od. Sal. xlii. 15, Hos. xiii. 14, 1 Cor. xv. 55.

THE GREEK OF ACTS

ii. 33 ἐξέχεεν τοῦτο ὃ ... βλέπετε καὶ ἀκούετε, πνεύματος ἁγίου being the reference immediately preceding in the same sentence, cf. also ii. 17, 18, x. 45 and Grinfield *ad loc.*

iii. 2 ἐκ κοιλίας μητρὸς αὐτοῦ, cf. LXX.,

iii. 12 ἀπεκρίνατο and v. 8 ἀπεκρίθη, see above xix. 15, xv. 13.

iii. 16 τὸ ὄνομα, see above xix. 5 and the use of ὀνόματα (i. 15) = persons and parallels in Papyri and Modern Greek.

iii. 20 καιροὶ ἀναψύξεως ἀπὸ προσώπου τοῦ κυρίου sounds much like a quotation from some apocalyptic writing.

iii. 24 sounds very much like translation-Greek, though in other surroundings the case would not be stringent. For ὅσοι ἐλάλησαν καὶ κατήγγειλαν see above xix. 8, 9, 16, 18, 19.

iv. 16 γνωστὸν σημεῖον, see above xix. 17 for γνωστός, though σημεῖον is absent.

iv. 30 ἐν τῷ τὴν χεῖρα ἐκτείνειν σε for ἐκτ. τ. χ., cf. LXX. For similar constructions cf. xix. 1, xxii. 6, 17, xxviii. 8, 17.

v. 4 τί ὅτι ἔθου ἐν τῇ καρδίᾳ σου, cf. xix. 21 ἐν τῷ πνεύματι and cf. LXX. Hagg. ii. 18, Sirac. i. 28.

Besides those adduced above from chapter xix., instances of about the same doubtful value [1] might be quoted from " 2 Acts." The only difference is found in the absence of stringent cases for translation-Greek and the only occasional presence of patches of Semitic colour. They are, of course as different in value as those quoted above from Torrey, the rules laid down above again not being applied.

Semitisms in "2 Acts."

xv. 39 ἐγένετο δὲ παροξυσμός (rare in class., often in LXX.; the substantive in Deut. xxix. 28, Jer. xxxii. 37—the construction ἐγ. π. instead of παρωξύνθησαν [ἐπ' ἀλλήλους] absent in LXX.).

xv. 40 παραδοθεὶς τῇ χάριτι τοῦ κυρίου ὑπὸ (D ἀπὸ) τῶν ἀδελφῶν.

xvi. 1 καὶ ἰδού.

xvi. 2 ὃς ἐμαρτυρεῖτο, cf. xxii. 12.

xvi. 3 καὶ λαβὼν περιέτεμεν.

xvi. 4, 10 ὡς δέ.

xvi. 16, 17 ἐγένετο δὲ ... παιδίσκην ... ὑπαντῆσαι ἡμῖν, ἥτις ... αὕτη κατακολουθοῦσα ... ἔκραζεν λέγουσα ... ὁδὸν σωτηρίας.

xvi. 19 ἐξῆλθεν ἡ ἐλπίς.

---

[1] By chance Galatia is in Aramaic *Gallia* and not *Galatiqi* as, *e.g.*, *Gerariqi* (a district in Philistia). This prevents our solving the riddle (Acts xvi. 6, xviii. 23) τὴν Γαλατικὴν χώραν καὶ Φρυγίαν by retroversion, which otherwise would have furnished a splendid instance of fallacious proof!

xvi. 36 ἀπήγγειλεν ... τοὺς λόγους τούτους ... ὅτι ἀπέσταλκαν ... ἐξελθόντες πορεύεσθε ἐν εἰρήνῃ (cf. xv. 33).

xvi. 40 ἐξελθόντες δὲ ἀπὸ τ. φ. εἰσῆλθον πρὸς τὴν Λυδίαν καὶ ἰδόντες παρεκάλεσαν τοὺς ἀδελφοὺς καὶ ἐξῆλθαν.

xvii. 7 καὶ οὗτοι πάντες ἀπέναντι [usual meaning is, however, local over against] τῶν δογμάτων Καίσαρος πράσσουσι.

xvii. 13 ὡς δὲ ἔγνωσαν ... ὅτι ... κατηγγέλη ὑπὸ τοῦ Παύλου.

xvii. 14 εὐθέως δὲ τότε ... ἕως ἐπί (cf. ἕως εἰς in LXX.).

xvii. 16 παρωξύνετο τὸ πνεῦμα αὐτοῦ ἐν αὐτῷ.

xvii. 17 κατὰ πᾶσαν ἡμέραν.

xvii. 19 δυνάμεθα γνῶναι, cf. Syriac *meshkehinan lmeda*ᶜ : why not ἔξεστιν or the like?

xvii. 20 εἰσφέρεις εἰς τὰς ἀκοὰς ἡμῶν, cf. xi. 22 ἠκούσθη εἰς τὰ ὦτα, sounding much like a negative Semitism.

xvii. 25 ὑπὸ χειρῶν ἀνθρωπίνων.

xvii. 26 ἐποίησεν ἐξ ἑνὸς πᾶν ἔθνος ἀνθρώπων ... κατοικίας αὐτῶν.

xvii. 31 ἐν ἀνδρὶ ᾧ ὥρισεν, negative Semitism for בְּרַד.

xvii. 33 ἐξῆλθεν ἐκ μέσου αὐτῶν.

xviii. 2, 3 διὰ τὸ διατεταχέναι ... προσῆλθεν αὐτοῖς, καὶ διὰ τὸ ὁμότεχνον εἶναι ἔμενεν ... καὶ ἠργάζοντο, ἦσαν γὰρ ...

xviii. 4 κατὰ πᾶν σάββατον.

xviii. 5 ὡς δέ.

xviii. 6 τὸ αἷμα ὑμῶν ἐπὶ τὴν κεφαλὴν ὑμῶν.

xviii. 10 λάλει καὶ μὴ σιωπήσῃς ... οὐδεὶς ἐπιθήσεταί σοι τοῦ κακῶσαί σε διότι λαός ἐστί μοι πολὺς ἐν τῇ πόλει ταύτῃ.

xviii. 23 ποιήσας χρόνον ... ἐξῆλθεν διερχόμενος, cf. xviii. 21 τὴν ἑορτὴν ... ποιῆσαι εἰς Ἱεροσόλυμα.

xviii. 25 οὗτος ἦν κατηχημένος τὴν ὁδὸν τοῦ κυρίου ... ζέων τῷ πνεύματι ἐλάλει καὶ ἐδίδασκεν.

xviii. 26 οὗτός τε ἤρξατο παρρησιάζεσθαι.

xviii. 27 ἀποδέξασθαι αὐτόν.

In chapters xx.–xxviii. a few examples will suffice; for instance xx. 9 κατενεχθεὶς ἀπὸ τοῦ ὕπνου, and xx. 22, 25 καὶ νῦν ἰδού. In xx. 28 διὰ τοῦ αἵματος τοῦ ἰδίου would by means of retroversion yield *badma dileh* : *by his (own) blood*, implying that the *ruḥa dqudsha* had assumed flesh and blood in the person of Jesus. This would be quite interesting and remind one of Hermas and 2 Cor. iii. 17 ὁ δὲ κύριος τὸ πνεῦμά ἐστιν. Yet it would be mere quicksand to go on. The case is the more alluring by its Semiticising surroundings : xx. 29 λύκοι βαρεῖς

THE GREEK OF ACTS 53

... εἰσελεύσονται εἰς ὑμᾶς; xx. 30 ἐξ ὑμῶν αὐτῶν ἀναστήσονται ἄνδρες λαλοῦντες διεστραμμένα τοῦ ἀποσπᾶν τοὺς μαθητὰς ὀπίσω ἑαυτῶν. Even if the position of this passage did not exclude the thought of translation-Greek, the fact that βαρεῖς would represent a Hebrew word, the Aramaic using another root, not meaning " heavy," would be decisive against the theory. Translation-Greek cannot at the same time reflect Hebrew and Aramaic where these languages differ, this being just the distinguishing characteristic of Semiticising Greek or " sacred prose " (cf. the third rule above). In xxi. 5 ὅτε δὲ ἐγένετο ἐξαρτίσαι ἡμᾶς τὰς ἡμέρας could be an ashamed Semitism. The root מלא is represented by a more fashionable word than συμπληροῦσθαι. The surroundings are again favourable: xxi. 1 ὡς δὲ ἐγένετο ἀναχθῆναι ἡμᾶς ἀποσπασθέντας ἀπ' αὐτῶν and in verse 5 the next words ἐξελθόντες ἐπορευόμεθα, where only the participles blur the Semitic colouring. Further on we find xxi. 11, 12, 13 παραδώσουσιν εἰς χεῖρας ἐθνῶν. ὡς δὲ . . . παρεκαλοῦμεν . . . τοῦ μὴ ἀναβαίνειν αὐτὸν εἰς Ἰερουσαλήμ. τότε ἀπεκρίθη ὁ Παῦλος, and in xxi. 17 ἀπεδέξαντο ἡμᾶς οἱ ἀδελφοί.

Without proceeding any further it is evident that the notion " Semitism " must be sharply defined in order to avoid constant confusion between translation-Greek and " sacred prose " and several other misunderstandings. *What are Semitisms?*

It is but natural to call every deviation from legitimate κοινή in the direction of Semitic idiom a Semitism. Even in cases where no idiom occurs which cannot be justified thus, Greek may be said to be " Semiticising " when the crowding together of otherwise legitimate locutions stamps the passage as tinged with alien influence. In such a case one decided Aramaism may turn the scales for translation from Aramaic. With Hebraisms however distinct, the LXX. will often make the case remain doubtful.

To see clearly into this matter we should distinguish the cases which may occur. A man may either have (a) perfect or

(b) imperfect knowledge of Greek. We may call (a) a "Greek" and (b) for convenience a "Semite."

Now, either of these two may attempt four things: on the one hand (1) *translation* from a Semitic dialect into idiomatic or (2) into Semiticising Greek, or, on the other hand, (3) *original composition* in idiomatic Greek, or (4) in Semiticising Greek.

A "Greek" trying (3) will produce no "Semitisms," a "Semite" cannot fail to do so. The same holds good of (1), but only approximately, the underlying Semitic may still shine through by means of what Psichari calls [1] "negative Semitisms," that is, the use of locutions from a higher style, such as Attic, which would not naturally come in, but are preferred because they square with a peculiarity of the translated document.[2] We can, therefore, distinguish between "*positive*" and "*negative*" Semitisms and, what is more important perhaps, between "primary" and "secondary" ones.

<small>Primary Semitisms.</small> *Primary Semitisms* are those which a "Semite" commits in (1) or (3). He is, however, always in danger of betraying himself by this cause even in cases (2) and (4), since the one source of these primary or real Semitisms is his imperfect knowledge of natural Greek. The deviations, however, which a man with perfect knowledge in this regard—for these ends, therefore, a "Greek"—may let pass in cases (1), (2), or (4) have a *secondary* cause, secondary because they are due to an extraneous factor: the exigencies of the reader whom he is addressing, or of the documents he is translating. We have still left out of account the more or less perfect knowledge which this "Greek" author may have of the Semitic idiom in which his source was written. Yet with these preliminaries the question of Semitisms in Acts is perhaps clearly enough put.

Primary Semitisms, either positive or negative, seem to be

---

[1] "Essai sur le grec de la Septante," par Jean Psichari (Ψυχάρης), *Revue des études juives*, 1908, Avril.

[2] *E.g.* οὐκ + participle as an equivalent of Hebrew *lo*, or ἐν ὀνόματι regularly for *bᵉ shem*, while the more popular εἰς ὄνομα is reserved for the few occurrences of *lᵉ shem*.

wholly absent. Secondary Semitisms are especially frequent in the first fifteen chapters, but are still much in view in the second half of the book. These secondary Semitisms warrant the hypothesis of translation-Greek for i. 1b–v. 16, and so also for ix. 31–xi. 18. The documents translated were couched in Aramaic of a Southern dialect with which the translator was not sufficiently acquainted, being himself from the North.

In the case of chapters vii. and xv. it is difficult to decide between translation-Greek and mere Semiticising Greek. A slight presumption in favour of translation-Greek might be found in the possibility that the author himself acted as translator, but literal fidelity in translating is very common and Luke has set his stamp on every chapter of his books.

This possibility that Luke himself was a translator of Aramaic sources has been brought well within the range of discussion by the splendid observation of Torrey,[1] viz. that ἐπὶ τὸ αὐτό = lahda. This betrays a translator from the North, who was ignorant of the Judean meaning of lahda = σφόδρα.[2] Combined with the Eusebian tradition of Luke's Antiochene descent, the case for Luke seems to become a good deal stronger.

A discussion of the arguments for the unity of " 1 Acts " as a whole only partly falls within the scope of this chapter. An obvious difficulty is perhaps unduly neglected by Torrey on pp. 64 ff., viz. that this supposed Aramaic author of " 1 Acts " would have been a veritable âme sœur of Luke. If his Aramaic went so easily into a Greek that after all is decidedly Lucan, one might even turn the case the other way round and assume that Luke had written an Aramaic treatise (as Josephus did), embodying fragments of Aramaic of Southern provenance. The

Unity of " 1 Acts."

---

[1] Torrey, op. cit. pp. 10-14, but cf. Cadbury, A.J.Th., July 1920.

[2] On p. 37 Torrey treats xii. 20 θυμομαχῶν as a case for חרא, to be angry, which, however, is said to have been translated in such a way as to better agree with the Southern meaning of this root than with the Northern dialect. But in Cook's Glossary of Aramaic Inscr., Cambridge, 1898, p. 56, this root is quoted from Zenjirli with the meaning ' wrath.' As Torrey assigns xii. to his Aramaic document, a point which would tell against his position may be ruled out in this way.

problem of sources in "1 Acts" is not discarded by making Luke the translator of an Aramaic document: it seems merely to shift one step backwards. Moreover, the unity of "1 Acts" as "translation-Greek" from one end to the other does not appear to be proven by conclusive evidence.

A word or two might be added to complete the case. A dividing line has been drawn above at v. 16, and it is proposed that v. 17–ix. 30 (with the possible exception of chapter vii.) should be considered as not necessarily translated from Aramaic, but as being fully explicable as Semiticising Greek, the secondary Semitisms being due to the character of the available (written ?) traditions and to the scene of the narrative. The same applies to chapter xi. 19–xv. 36, with the possible exception of xv. 1-36.

On pp. 32, 33, however, Torrey discusses v. 17 : ἀναστὰς δὲ ὁ ἀρχιερεὺς καὶ πάντες οἱ σὺν αὐτῷ, ἡ οὖσα αἵρεσις τῶν Σαδδουκαίων. It is said that one does not "stand up" to be "filled with anger." The text itself, however, makes it necessary to refer ἀναστάς to ἐπέβαλον τὰς χεῖρας. If πλησθέντες ζήλου ἐπέβαλον had been written, not even Wellhausen or Preuschen would have ventured their "*unmöglich*." But the text is quite defensible as Semiticising Greek, and reminds one of Psalm vii. 7 ἀναστῆθι . . . ἐν ὀργῇ σου or ci. (cii.) 14 ἀναστὰς οἰκτειρήσεις . . . τὴν Σειών and of the constructions of the verb with εἰς, ἐπί, ἀντί, κατενώπιον with a hostile sense. The incongruity of ἀναστὰς . . . ἐπέβαλον is a *constructio ad sensum* quite easy in ordinary Greek and occurring often enough in the LXX. Perhaps Hebrew would better answer the purpose than Aramaic if an underlying document should be accepted. But ἡ οὖσα αἵρεσις is said to be (p. 33) a careful reproduction of an Aramaic locution or rather a Syriac expression which more closely equals the Greek οὐσία. Further, on xiii. 1 κατὰ τὴν οὖσαν ἐκκλησίαν (p. 37) Torrey says : "The Aramaic was probably simply (or אִיתֵיהּ) בְּעֶדְתָּא דִי אִית, no accompanying adverb being necessary, since it was made evident by the context. The commentators sometimes compare Rom. xiii. 1, also Acts xviii. 17, etc.; but these passages are not really parallel cases, since in them the participle, or its equivalent, is indispensable. Other passages in the Aramaic half of Acts where די אית seems to be rendered are xi. 22 and xiv. 13."

The use of *di ith*, however, without *tham* or *thamma* = there, appears to be at least as peculiar as ἡ οὖσα or ἥτις ἔστιν with ἐκεῖ left out. Moreover, this would not fit well in v. 17. In xi. 22 τῆς οὔσης ἐν Ἰερουσαλήμ no recourse to Aramaic is wanted, while xiv. 13 is a different case that should be compared with xxviii. 17 and v. 17. In these three cases ἡ οὖσα, ὁ ὤν, οἱ ὄντες clearly have the meaning "the so-called." This meaning must have developed from the regular use of the participle followed by some qualifying statements, *e.g.* (local), xvi. 3 ὄντας ἐν τοῖς τόποις ἐκείνοις, xxii. 5 τοὺς ἐκεῖσε ὄντας; (dignity), xxv. 23 τοῖς κατ' ἐξοχὴν οὖσι (but אB omit οὖσι), or xix. 35 νεωκόρον οὖσαν (which would give ἡ οὖσα νεωκόρος). In the last two cases the way in which usage has arisen is clear enough, cf. Armitage Robinson in Ramsay's *Church in the Roman Empire*, p. 52.[1] The case for v. 17 is therefore, to say the least, rather doubtful and, as it is the first of a series of weak cases, must be abandoned. This will appear from a rapid survey:

v. 28 παραγγελίᾳ παρηγγείλαμεν, cf. xxiii. 14, xxviii. 26.
v. 41 ἀπὸ προσώπου, LXX. and *e.g.* xxv. 16 (κατὰ πρόσωπον) or xvii. 26 (πᾶν τὸ πρ. τῆς γῆς). Neither usage is distinctly Aramaic.
vi. 5 ἐνώπιον παντὸς τοῦ πλήθους, cf. xix. 9, 19 (see above), and xxvii. 35.

Nothing distinctly Aramaic following, the case for v. 17 as representing translation-Greek and not an original Semiticising source or tradition cannot derive the support, which it is in need of, from the only side left for it.

In spite of its peculiar character chapter vii. ought not to be omitted. It is said that vii. 13 ἐν τῷ δευτέρῳ (cf. πάλιν ἐκ δευτέρου, x. 15, and ἐκ δευτέρου xi. 9) is Aramaic, but with ἐν τῷ δευτέρῳ one must supply in thought some word ending in -μός, equi-

---

[1] Cf. also Moulton, *Prol.* p. 228, and above, p. 41.

valent to ἀπαντήσει, as ἐγνωρίσθη is the next word and the story is treated as well known. Moreover, ἐκ δευτέρου has seven occurrences in the LXX. and occurs in the Papyri (Moulton and Milligan, Part II., s.v., giving one instance of A.D. 123). vii. 23 ἀνέβη ἐπὶ τὴν καρδίαν αὐτοῦ is not distinctly Aramaic and occurs, e.g., in LXX., Jer. iii. 16, xliv. 21, li. 50, Ezech. xxxviii. 10, Is. lxv. 16 ; and ἀνέβη φάσις τῷ χιλιάρχῳ, xxi. 31, reminds one just as much of the same Aramaic verb. In vii. 38 λόγια ζῶντα should not be pressed to render by mistranslation λόγια ζωῆς, much nearer and popular parallels being at hand, viz. the ὕδωρ ζῶν καὶ λαλοῦν, Ignatius *Ad Rom.* vii. 2, the ὕδωρ of Ezech. xlvii., which is also found in *Od. Sal.* vi., xi., xxx. Every student of modern Greek is reminded also of the ζωντανὸ νερό. The expression is no more surprising than ὁδὸς ζῶσα, Heb. x. 20, or 1 Pet. i. 23 διὰ λόγου ζῶντος θεοῦ καὶ μένοντος, or Heb. iv. 12, ζῶν γὰρ ὁ λόγος τοῦ θεοῦ κτλ. The case of vii. 52 Δίκαιος for the Messiah is covered by xxii. 14, and the quotations by the author on p. 33 ; vii. 53 εἰς διαταγὰς ἀγγέλων is a curious phrase, but not distinctly Aramaic and therefore open to explanation by LXX. and kindred usage.

Equally weak is chapter viii. There is not one tenable case for translation-Greek here or in chapter ix. up to verse 30. The instances are : viii. 6 ἐν τῷ ἀκούειν αὐτοὺς καὶ βλέπειν τὰ σημεῖα ἃ ἐποίει, cf. xix. 5 (see above), xxii. 6, 17, xxviii. 8, 17. The corrupt text of viii. 7 is rendered in an Aramaic (p. 34) that " would almost inevitably " result in this corruption. viii. 10 ἀπὸ μικροῦ ἕως μεγάλου is LXX. and even Greek ; the δύναμις ἡ καλουμένη μεγάλη is a matter of exegesis and κοινή. That the deity of Heaven, the great Lord of Heavens (בעל־שמין) should count in his court among other δυνάμεις also a " Grand Vizir," a " Lord of the Palace " (בעלובול), called the " Great One," is what should be expected. Why should not the Samaritans have their Michael as well as the Jews, or the Tarsians their Sandan ? For ix. 2 τῆς ὁδοῦ cf. above on ch. xix ; for ix. 3 ἐν δὲ τῷ πορεύεσθαι ἐγένετο see above ; ix. 22

THE GREEK OF ACTS 59

ἐνεδυναμοῦτο is not distinctly Aramaic, and occurs already in LXX., Judges vi. 34, Ps. li. 7.

For chapter xi. 19–xiv. 28 the average is not better; xi. 21 ἦν χεὶρ κυρίου μετ' αὐτῶν, cf. LXX. (e.g. 2 Sam. iii. 12); xi. 22 ἠκούσθη δὲ ὁ λόγος εἰς τὰ ὦτα τῆς ἐκκλησίας, cf. above xvii. 20 and LXX., Is. v. 9 ἠκούσθη γὰρ εἰς τὰ ὦτα κυρίου Σαβαὼθ ταῦτα and 1 Kings x. 6, Gen. xx. 8. Of course this phrase is not distinctly Aramaic. xi. 28 ἐφ' ὅλην τὴν οἰκουμένην cannot be a mistranslation (pp. 20, 21). A man not knowing that ארעא means γῆ (sc. γῆ Ἰσραήλ), γῆ in general, and οἰκουμένη, did not know enough Aramaic to translate at all. It is a conscious heightening of colour, a common case of the "laws" of the growth of legendary narrative. Benigni would call it "quantitative or proper megalosia."[1] xii. 3 προσέθετο συλλαβεῖν is a Hebraism which even Josephus's advisers have let slip through. xii. 10 ῥύμην μίαν is sound κοινή; xii. 11 προσδοκία is certainly sharper defined in Torrey's proposed equivalent and would be a distinct Aramaism, if the equation were necessary or supported by other strong cases. This not being the case, its inherent weakness is not taken away (pp. 36, 37). xii. 20 θυμομαχῶν (see above, p. 55, n. 2) is not stringently for either Aramaic or Hebrew and, moreover, cf. Plutarch, Demetr. 22, and θυμομαχία, exasperation, Polyaen. ii. 1. 19, ps.-Justin, 1184. B. xiii. 1 τὴν οὖσαν, see above; xiii. 11 καὶ νῦν ἰδού, and xxii. 22 ἄχρι τούτου, cf. LXX.; xiii. 12 ἐκπλησσόμενος ἐπί (p. 7) is good κοινή after verbs of emotion; xiii. 22 ἤγειρεν τὸν Δαυεὶδ αὐτοῖς εἰς βασιλέα, LXX. and κοινή; xiii. 24 πρὸ προσώπου τῆς εἰσόδου (pp. 7, 29, 37), nothing distinctly Aramaic, cf. Mal. iii. 1, 2; xiii. 25 ὡς δὲ ἐπλήρου Ἰωάνης τὸν δρόμον, cf. Jer. viii. 6 (διέλιπεν ὁ τρέχων ἀπὸ τοῦ δρόμου αὐτοῦ) and e.g. πληροῦν τὸν χορόν (Plato) or ἡ ὁδὸς πληροῖ ἐς τὸν ἀριθμὸν τοῦτον, Herodotus ii. 7. Compare, moreover, Moulton and Milligan, "Lexical Notes from the Papyri" in Expositor, 1910, ii. pp. 564 f., with instances from the κοινή beyond any suspicion of Aramaism.

[1] Cf. Van Gennep, La Formation des légendes, Paris, 1910, p. 293.

I cannot understand how in xiii. 25 οὐκ εἰμὶ ἐγώ after the question τί ἐμὲ ὑπονοεῖτε εἶναι should compel us to think of the Aramaic אנא אנא. That Blass has stamped τί as "*nicht erträglich*" is not final. It is quite sound vulgar Greek. Even if οὐκ εἰμὶ ἐγώ were rightly interpreted "I am not he," it does not cover *ana ana*. G. P. Wetter[1] has made the formula ἐγώ εἰμι the subject of special research and seems to have ascertained its currency as part of the theurgical vocabulary. As little distinctly Aramaic is xiv. 2 ἐκάκωσαν τὰς ψυχὰς τῶν ἐθνῶν, cf. xviii. 10, see above; xiv. 3 διδόντι σημεῖα καὶ τέρατα γίνεσθαι and μαρτυροῦντι ἐπὶ τῷ λόγῳ τῆς χάριτος αὐτοῦ, cf. LXX. and kindred literature; xiv. 8 χωλὸς ἐκ κοιλίας μητρὸς αὐτοῦ, cf. LXX.; xiv. 15 εὐαγγελιζόμενοι ἀπὸ τούτων τῶν ματαίων ἐπιστρέφειν ἐπὶ θεὸν ζῶντα is all LXX.; xiv. 17 is retroverted on p. 38 into ἐμπιπλῶν πάσης (*mikkol* = *min kol* being read as *mekal* = τροφή) εὐφροσύνης τὰς καρδίας αὐτῶν as "filling hearts with food" would be "no more Aramaic or Greek than it is English." But the text is by no means absurd; ἐμπιπλῶν τροφῆς καὶ εὐφροσύνης τὰς καρδίας has been telescoped from ἐμπιπλῶν τροφῆς τὴν ψυχήν, which is current in LXX., and ἐμπιπλῶν εὐφροσύνης τὴν καρδίαν, which is equally sound. There are astounding cases enough of ἐμπί(μ)πλημι used by the LXX. in a very strange way, which make the invocation of Aramaic on this place superfluous. Therefore, given the absence of distinct Aramaisms in this stretch, it is decidedly not allowable. For xiv. 27 ἀνήγγελλον ὅσα ἐποίησεν ὁ θεὸς μετ' αὐτῶν, cf. above, chapter xv. 4.

These necessary deductions made, Torrey's book has much furthered the question of Semitisms in Acts. It has provided some results which, as research will be pushed further with more refined methods, will perhaps be conclusively proven. If certainty is attained on the extent of the underlying Aramaic, and the result of these pages, that it extends over i. 1b–v. 16, ix. 31–xi. 18, perhaps also xii. and part of xv. should be confirmed and corrected by research, the gain for the criticism of Acts would

[1] See G. P.: son Wetter, *Der Sohn Gottes*, Göttingen, 1916.

not be small. Perhaps also the case for Luke as a translator of these Aramaic documents could be made more stringent, which would certainly increase the value of these results.

For the philology of Acts no more can be hoped than an increased value for some secondary Semitisms in those parts of the weak stretches, which may perhaps gain the support of some distinct Aramaisms that will stand criticism. Perhaps also some primary Semitism may be found which will strengthen the case for Luke. If it should be discovered in a chapter beyond xv., this would be conclusive, but I do not think either of these cases probable.

Without further reference to the investigations to which the theory of the composition and date of Acts formulated by Torrey must give rise, the subject is important enough to justify the discussion of some more isolated cases of secondary Semitisms.

The replacement of a predicative case by εἰς (e.g. Acts vii. 21, xiii. 22-47) might seem a not unnatural extension of the use of εἰς expressing destination, but it appears in Acts only in the sphere of LXX. diction. The Papyri and Inscriptions, moreover, disclaim this suspicion : [1] *C.I.G.* xiv. 607 εἰς ἴα σου, Πώμπιλλα, καὶ εἰς κρίνα βλαστήσειαν ὄστεα . . . , or *Philologus* vii. p. 82 στέφειν εἰς γυμνασίαρχον, Pap. Fay. 119 (A.D. 100) ἵνα μὴ εἰς ψωμίον γένηται. A somewhat out-of-place LXX.-ism in the second part of Acts (xxviii. 15) is justified in the same way.[2] Throughout Acts we observe the construction of ἐν τῷ + Inf. It is one of its characteristic phrases surely apt to provoke Semitic associations. But we learn from Krapp [3] that the articular Infinitive governed by a preposition is characteristic of historical style from the second century B.C. to the first A.D. This helps us to locate our author in time, and, as far as such a minor

---

[1] Quoted by Radermacher, *op. cit.* pp. 16, 100, 121; cf. Moulton, *op. cit.* p. 71.

[2] Moulton, *op. cit.* p. 14, refers to *Tebt. Pap.* 43 (ii. B.C.) and *B.U.* 362 (A.D. 215).

[3] *Der substantivierte Infinitiv*, Heidelberg, 1892, quoted by Radermacher, *op. cit.* p. 151.

62   THE COMPOSITION AND PURPOSE OF ACTS

point will bear the stress, also in the literary world.[1] The pleonastic demonstrative standing in apposition to a foregoing noun or, more often, to a participial or equivalent clause is plain vernacular, though not without classical precedent [2] and as natural to nearly every language as the so-called "pendant nominative" is (Acts ii. 23, iv. 10, vii. 35, xv. 17).[3] The frequent use of periphrastic forms, especially those which seem to correspond to an Aramaic Imperfect, has raised suspicion. As has been observed above, possible traces of a Semitic mind in the second half of Acts should deserve special attention, and so the Imperfects of εἶναι with the Present Participle in Acts xiv. 7, xvi. 12, xviii. 7, xix. 14, xxi. 3, xxii, 19 are important. In these instances, however, the periphrasis is not real. We might put a comma between the two parts without damaging the sense. In Acts xxi. 3 ἀπεφορτίζετο was impossible, and in the clearest case (xxii. 19), ἤμην φυλακίζων καὶ δέρων, we should remember that it occurs in a speech pronounced ἐν τῇ Ἑβραΐδι διαλέκτῳ. The Papyri, moreover, give analogous instances of periphrasis, and an occasional parallel is found even in the classics.[4] In other tenses it is amply justified by classical warrant or vernacular usage. Luke has not availed himself of the advantage which a judicious use of the shades of mean-

---

[1] Luke was consciously a historian, cf. Vogel, *op. cit.* pp. 12-13 (his use of the historical books of the LXX., especially 2 Macc., Judges, Samuel, cf. p. 54); Ramsay, *St. Paul*, *passim*; though, Norden, *Die antike Kunstprosa*, ii.², 1909, p. 481, disagrees: "Acts also is relatively isolated as a literary *genre*, but to the Hellenic taste it was much less of a foreign product than the Gospels, for though the wrong conception that it is to be classed as historiography is done with, yet already the title (of course chosen for this reason) must recall to the Hellenic mind its own once very voluminous literature of πράξεις."

[2] Simcox, *Language of the N.T.*, London, 1899, p. 66, quotes Xenophon, *Ages.* 4. 4 οἱ προῖκα εὖ πεπονθότες, οὗτοι ἀεὶ ἡδέως ὑπηρετοῦσι τῷ εὐεργέτῃ, cf. *Symp.* viii. 33. Of course the frequency of such a construction may exceed the limits of natural Greek.

[3] Acts vii. 40 is quoted by Moulton, *Prol.* p. 69, as a typical case in Acts, though it is a quotation from LXX., cf. also p. 225 and references there.

[4] Moulton, *op. cit.* p. 227, refers to Rutherford, *Cl. Rev.* xvii. p. 249, for Thucyd. iv. 54, Antiphon (Fr. M. iii. 67), Aristoph. *Ach.* 484. In classical Greek the construction imparts some emphasis.

THE GREEK OF ACTS 63

ing which this usage is capable of conveying might have offered.[1]

Luke's general attitude towards Semitic influence is therefore as hard to define as the extent to which he would or could have yielded to the opposite force, Atticism or, in general, literary fashion. We know that he could not possibly have succeeded as well as Josephus [2] in this direction. We guess that he would never have leaned to the other side so much as his sources must have done. A good test case of his attitude in this matter is again suggested by Moulton (*op. cit.* p. 16). Luke alone of New Testament writers has substituted in Acts, for the popular ἐγένετο ἦλθε and the unidiomatic phrase of translation-Greek ἐγένετο καὶ ἦλθε, a construction of ἐγένετο with the Infinitive. This construction is an improvement which is warranted by Papyrus evidence (*e.g.* ἐὰν γένηται c. *Inf.*), and yet it does not fail to recall [3] the sacred style. Such a fine sense in handling the language justifies us again in ascribing cruder expressions [4] to a dominant extraneous influence: the translated Aramaic of some of his sources or the exigencies of an existing more or less "technical" phraseology, the missionary style of Paul or of other less educated preachers.

Character of Luke's Semitisms.

The existence—within these limits—of something like a sort of "Christian Greek" is proved, *e.g.*, by the use of ὁδός as equivalent to our words "religion" or "Christianity," Acts ix. 2, xix. 9, 23, xxii. 4, xxiv. [14] 22, ὁδὸς σωτηρίας xvi. 17, ὁδὸς τοῦ Θεοῦ or κυρίου, xviii. 25, 26.[5] The absence of the current τυγχάνω constructions ("by chance," "to happen to") is perhaps

"Christian Greek."

---

[1] Acts xxv. 10 the Perfect Participle seems to add to the sense of duration; in xxvi. 26, however, this is evidently not the case.

[2] Thumb, *Die griechische Sprache im Zeitalter des Hellenismus*, Strassburg, 1901, pp. 125 f., quotes W. Schmidt, *Fleckeisens Jahrbb.* xx. pp. 514-517, for the one Semitism of which Josephus is guilty, viz. προστίθεσθαι c. *Inf.* It is found also once in Acts xii. 3, as has been observed above.

[3] Συνέβη was in the author's vocabulary if he preferred to leave τυγχάνω alone (Acts xxi. 35).

[4] *E.g.* εἰς διαταγὰς ἀγγέλων (Acts vii. 53) or τὸ γενόμενον ῥῆμα (x. 37), σωτηρία ἔν τινι or ὄνομα ἐν ᾧ δεῖ σωθῆναι ἡμᾶς (iv. 12), and many other cases.

[5] Cf. the remarks on this case above.

also significant. So certainly are the constructions of πιστεύω with ἐπί (Acts ix. 42, xi. 17, xvi. 31, xxii. 19) or εἰς (x. 43, xiv. 23, xix. 4) instead of the dative (v. 14, viii. 12, xvi. 34, xviii. 8, xxiv. 14, xxvi. 27), which correspond with our *to believe on* and *to believe in*. In the LXX. the prepositional construction is extremely rare,[1] though it may have been the starting-point. Even the dative is not used of simple trusting, but it carries a religious sense, God, an Apostle, or the Scriptures being the objects. Less markedly Christian is the construction of εὐαγγελίζεσθαι. In this case Phrynichus[2] preferred the dative to the accusative for the person addressed. The technical sense, "*to evangelise*," was, of course, favourable for the accusative, the dative being used only[3] when the message was already added in the accusative (viii. 35, xvii. 18). The LXX. did, of course, not yet know this technical sense, and the corresponding construction is therefore absent.

<small>Greek of Acts 'living.'</small>

The Greek of Acts—to summarise the case—is essentially living : it combines conflicting elements into a real unity. This unity, however, was residing ultimately in the mind of the author. It was natural for him—and this intention has guided him all along the way—to hold the upper side of the popular language. A sprinkling of more or less literary words and constructions bears witness to this tendency even in the first chapters, where it was restrained by the nature of his sources and by an adaptation of the style to the scene and the persons acting in it. There is also a generally recognised picturesqueness and dramatic power in his style and a movement in the narrative which makes it sometimes proceed by leaps and bounds. This is perhaps not only due to the individual character of the author, but it may have

---

[1] Is. xxviii. 16 ὁ πιστεύων ἐπ' αὐτῷ; Sap. Sol. xii. 2 πιστεύσωσιν ἐπί σε κύριε; Ps. lxxvii. 26 πιστεύω ἐν. Ps. lxxvii. 36 and Jer. xii. 6 are different in sense.

[2] Ed. Rutherford, ccxxxv. pp. 334 f.

[3] Double accusative in Acts xiii. 32, but here the accusative of the message is taken beforehand from the following clauses.

had even a deeper cause. The same is to be observed in Vergil,[1] and there it is signalised as marking Alexandrian influence. As a reaction against the compact uninterrupted narrative style, pathetic effects and an episodic composition, meant to give a dramatic movement to the whole, were preferred. Plutarch[2] appreciated these characteristics in history, and Luke seems to be in this stream. Yet on the whole his style must have been a serious drawback. It answered his purposes, being well adapted to the foreign scene and the exceptional subject, but, unless more narrative prose of this technique should come to light, we can but guess that he went far enough in the first half of his booklet. His personal style is seen in those speeches and narrative portions of the latter half, where he seems to have had a free hand, though even here he may have been under the restraining influence of his Christian readers, and that to a greater extent than we are able to detect. Yet he undoubtedly is the most Greek of New Testament writers,[3] perhaps also in this regard, that he has a fine sense of humour [4] and a certain reserve of power.

[1] Kroll, *op. cit.* pp. 521 ff., " He aims everywhere at dramatic and pathetic effects and abandons carelessly whatsoever is not serviceable to these ends. Ἔκπληξις is the clue to his plan : discarding all attractive prolixity it steadily mounts towards culminating points which always bear a strong character of sentiment . . . important preliminaries are often not sketched or only very briefly, *e.g.* we do not hear the end of Laocoön, and the union of Aeneas and Dido is merely alluded to and a part of Aeneas' wanderings is described with a lapidary conciseness which is quite foreign to the traditional style of epic poetry (*e.g.* bk. iii. 270 *sqq.*). This technique (viz. of the Alexandrian ἐπύλλιον which had won favour during Vergil's youth) is also recalled by the fact that the narrative does not proceed in an uninterrupted flow but confines itself from time to time to a sharply limited episode, partly even coincident with the limits of single books."

[2] See above, p. 36, n. 1.

[3] Hier. *Ep.* 20 "qui inter omnes evangelistas Graeci sermonis eruditissimus fuit, quippe ut medicus." We would not be as sure of this "quippe ut medicus" as St. Jerome seems to be. The attitude of Galen in the days of the Greek renaissance under Trajan and Hadrian points in the opposite direction.

[4] Cf. *e.g.* McLachlan, *St. Luke, the Man and his Work*, London, 1919.

III

THE USE OF THE SEPTUAGINT IN ACTS

By WILLIAM KEMP LOWTHER CLARKE

SYNOPSIS

I. VOCABULARY

A. The influence of the LXX. on the vocabulary of Acts as shown by an examination of (i.) the entire vocabulary, (ii.) peculiar words, (iii.) characteristic words and phrases.

B. Special affinities of Acts with the apocryphal books, especially: (i.) 2 and 3 Maccabees, (ii.) Tobit, (iii.) Judith, (iv.) Wisdom, (v.) the Pseudepigrapha.

C. The bearing of the LXX. on three important problems: (i.) The β-text, (ii.) Luke and Josephus, (iii.) Luke's medical language.

II. FORMAL QUOTATIONS

A. *Substantially LXX.*: (i.) Exact agreement, (ii.) close agreement.

B. *Substantial variation from LXX.*, due to (i.) loose citation, (ii.) substitution of a gloss, (iii.) adaptation to circumstances of fulfilment, (iv.) conflation, (v.) recensional causes, (vi.) translational causes.

III. INFORMAL QUOTATIONS, REMINISCENCES, AND ALLUSIONS

A. *In the speeches.*
    (i.) Confirmation of results of previous section.
    (ii.) Light on problem of sources of Acts.

B. *In the narrative.*
    (i.) List of passages where influence is possible or probable.
    (ii.) Conclusions.

Biblical Greek.

DR. HATCH in his *Essays in Biblical Greek* (1889) maintained the unity of Biblical Greek and the consequent unique importance of the Greek Old Testament as a guide to the interpretation of the New.[1] The movement of critical opinion during the ensuing quarter of a century has been a continued reaction from this position. Dr. T. K. Abbott (*Essays chiefly on the Original Texts of the Old and New Testaments*, 1891) discussed Hatch's work and concluded that the influence of the LXX. had been much exaggerated.[2] One verdict of his is worth recording, since it has been so strikingly confirmed by the course of events. "The number of instances in which the Septuagint alone vouches for the use of particular words, small comparatively as it is, would no doubt be considerably diminished if our knowledge of the current popular language was greater."[3] A fuller treatment of the subject was provided by Dr. H. A. A. Kennedy in his *Sources of New Testament Greek* (1895), the sub-title of which is *The Influence of the Septuagint on the Vocabulary of the New Testament*. His conclusion was that the light thrown by the LXX. on the New Testament is of considerable importance, but simply because the LXX. is "the only other record we possess of the current popular speech prevailing at the time."[4] On this showing the LXX. must by now have lost much of its importance, since the popular speech has become well known, thanks to the numerous discoveries of papyri in Egypt. The papyrologists, as was natural, have been inclined to emphasise the importance of their own contribution to New Testament research, and Professor Deissmann in *Bible Studies* (Eng. ed., 1901) minimised the significance of the LXX.[5] Probably the reaction has gone too far, and Dr. Milligan's caution was needed : "The denial of a distinctive 'Biblical' or 'New Testament Greek' is often too unqualified to-day owing to the recoil from the old position of treating it as essentially an isolated language, and the whole question of how far the Greek of the New Testament deviates

---

[1] See especially pp. 10-12.
[2] Pp. 67 ff.
[3] P. 87.
[4] P. 137.
[5] Pp. 64-70 ; cf. J. H. Moulton, *Grammar of New Testament Greek* (2nd ed., 1906), *passim*.

68   THE COMPOSITION AND PURPOSE OF ACTS

from the Κοινή requires a fuller discussion and statement than it has yet received."[1]

The LXX. The fact is that the LXX. was the Bible of Jews and Christians alike, and the primitive Church, conscious of being the new Israel of God, found a natural medium for self-expression in biblical phraseology. Of course Christian writers vary in the use they make of the LXX. The second Gospel shows few traces of its influence, the Lucan writings very many. Dr. Harnack, writing on the assumption that Luke was of Gentile parentage, remarks paradoxically: "We must also remember that St. Luke as a theologian, like all Gentile Christians, was more a man of the Old Testament than St. Paul, because he had never come to a real grip with the problem it presented."[2] It is hoped that the present chapter, devoted to an independent discussion of the problems of the relation of Acts to the LXX., will throw some light on the extent to which Luke was "a man of the Old Testament."

Some have maintained that the dependence of much of the New Testament, and especially the Lucan writings, on the LXX. is not to be confined to vocabulary and style. Dr. Selwyn, who represents such views in England, supposed that much of the Acts was deliberately composed on LXX. models.[3] Luke was a prophet and, as such, set himself to find fulfilments of the Old Testament scriptures in the everyday incidents of missionary travel. In the course of several books it was impossible that Dr. Selwyn should not point out a number of interesting parallels between the two Testaments; but much of his work seems to suffer from an excess of ingenuity. For instance, when the apostles entered Macedonia, they are supposed to have taken with them the book of Joshua or Jesus as a guide-book,

---

[1] *Selections from the Greek Papyri* (1910), p. xxx.
[2] *Luke the Physician*, p. 127.
[3] See *St. Luke the Prophet*, 1901, *The Oracles in the New Testament*, 1912. Cf. also *The Christian Prophets*, 1900, and some magazine articles. Some interesting suggestions on the same lines are to be found in Dr. E. A. Abbott's works.

THE USE OF THE SEPTUAGINT IN ACTS 69

and to have seen in the topography of Macedonia an almost exact correspondence with that of Canaan ; the founding of the church of Philippi was the spiritual antitype of the fall of Jericho, and so on.[1] But as there are few books of the Old Testament that have left less mark on the New Testament than Joshua,[2] the theory that it was considered highly significant by primitive Christian missionaries is improbable. Further, the conception of the Christian prophets as a new order of scribes, with their eyes glued to the letter of the Jewish Scriptures, seems curiously wide of the mark. Nevertheless, the theory that Luke's description of events is modelled in certain cases on Old Testament patterns needs a serious discussion, which will be given in the concluding section of this chapter.[3]

A. (i.) The influence of the LXX. on the language of the Acts *Vocabulary.* may be tested first by examining the entire vocabulary. An overwhelming proportion of the words used in Acts, 88 per cent, have already occurred in the LXX.[4] But the proportion is actually less than in the Gospels, the figures for which are Matthew 93 per cent, Mark 90 per cent, Lk. 92 per cent, John 93 per cent. The reason for this is clear. Luke's[5] vocabulary is much richer than that of the other evangelists. In the third Gospel more words[6] are employed than in the first ; and in the Acts the vocabulary is further increased by the use of terms

[1] *St. Luke the Prophet*, pp. 33-58. The above is a typical specimen of this author's method.

[2] According to Swete, *Int. to O.T. in Greek*, p. 383, there are no quotations from Joshua in the N.T.

[3] The materials of the following investigation were derived from an independent study of the concordances of Hatch-Redpath and Moulton-Geden ; other books used will be mentioned where necessary. The LXX. is understood to mean the books contained in Hatch-Redpath. The later Greek versions, and with them Theodotion's Daniel, are excluded, but both recensions of Tobit are included. Unless otherwise stated, Swete's text is implied and Westcott and Hort's text of the N.T. The choice of books to represent the LXX. is determined solely by the plan of Hatch-Redpath.

[4] Cadbury, *The Style and Literary Method of Luke*, p. 5, makes the figure 90 per cent for Luke and Acts together.

[5] Luke is used throughout for the *auctor ad Theophilum*, Lk. for the third Gospel.

[6] Some 300 more.

descriptive of the conditions of life in the first century of our era,[1] which could not be expected in the LXX.

Words peculiar to Acts.

(ii.) When we come to investigate the words peculiar to Acts, we must avail ourselves of the tables provided by Hawkins, *Horae Synopticae* (2nd ed.), pp. 198-207. Of 413 words peculiar to Acts (proper names, Aramaic words, and numerals being omitted), 261 occur in the LXX. Hawkins reckons 259; but ἀντοφθαλμεῖν and μετρίως should be added to his list of LXX. words. Out of 58 words that occur in Lk. and Acts but nowhere else in the New Testament, 51 are found in the LXX. (περιλάμπειν is not in the LXX.; the asterisk is omitted in Hawkins by a misprint [2]). The figures for all the books may be given in tabular form.

	Not in LXX.	In LXX.	Total of peculiar Words.	Percentage found in LXX.
Acts	152	261	413	63
Lk. + Acts	7	51	58	..
Lk.	73	188	261	72
Matt.	36	76	112	67
Mark	31	40	71	56

From this it is clear that Luke uses a large number of rare words which also occur in the LXX., but owing to the quantity of non-LXX. words also found in his vocabulary, the actual proportions are not far different from those that obtain in Matthew.

(iii.) Further proof of the exceptional extent to which Luke's style is influenced by the LXX. is given by a list of *characteristic*

---

[1] In making the above calculation the *pericope adulterae* and the ending of Mark were excluded, as also were proper names, Aramaic words, numerals, and adjectives derived from numerals. If all the readings given in the concordances are included, the proportions are altered only imperceptibly. There is, of course, a subjective element involved in the decision whether or not certain forms should be counted as separate words. The figures given cannot be checked with the aid of Moulton-Geden alone, as the signs of this concordance do not distinguish between words found in the LXX. and those that occur only in the later Greek versions.

[2] It appears in the 1st edition.

words and phrases in Acts. By this is meant that they occur at least five times in Acts, and also twice as often as in the rest of the New Testament, excluding Lk. They reach a total of 69. The following, 68 out of the 69, are found in the LXX., an asterisk following denoting those which occur at least twenty-five times, and may therefore be regarded as specially characteristic of the LXX.

Αἵρεσις, ἄνδρες ἀδελφοί, ἄν with opt.,* ἀνάγεσθαι="embark" (2 Macc. v. 9), ἀναιρεῖν,* ἀναλαμβάνειν* (eight times in Acts, four times in rest, excluding Mark xvi. 19), ἀναστάς or ἀναστάντες,* ἀποδέχεσθαι, ἀπολογεῖσθαι, ἀτενίζειν, βῆμα, βουλή,* γίγνεσθαι foll. by ἐπί with acc.,* γνωστός, διαλέγεσθαι, διάλεκτος, διασώζειν,* διατρίβειν, διαφθορά, διέρχεσθαι with acc.,* ἐᾶν,* ἐγκαλεῖν, ἔθος, εἶπεν δέ or εἶπαν δέ,* εἰσάγειν,* ἑκατοντάρχης or -ος, ἐλεημοσύνη,* ἐνθάδε, ἐξάγειν,* ἐξαποστέλλειν,* ἡ ἐπιοῦσα (ἡμέρα), ἐπιβαίνειν,* ἐπικαλεῖν with prop. noun,* ἐφιστάναι,* ζήτημα, Ἱερουσαλήμ,* κακοῦν,* καλούμενος with prop. noun, κατάγειν, καταντᾶν, κατέρχεσθαι, κελεύειν,* (ὁ) λόγος (τοῦ) κυρίου,* μεταπέμπεσθαι, νῆσος,* ξενίζειν, ὁμοθυμαδόν,* ὀνόματι, ὅραμα,* ὁρίζειν, παῖς applied to Christ (see Isa. lii. 13), παραγίνεσθαι,* παραχρῆμα, παρρησιάζεσθαι, πᾶς or ἅπας ὁ λαός,* τὰ περί, πιπλάναι,* πλῆθος,* πυνθάνεσθαι, σέβειν, διὰ στόματος, στρατηγός,* συνέδριον, τανῦν, τε,* ὑποστρέφειν, διὰ χειρός or χειρῶν,* χιλίαρχος. Sixty-eight in all, of which 33 are "characteristic" in the LXX. One word only, ἀνθύπατος, of those that are characteristic in the sense described above, does not occur in the LXX.; one phrase, ἐγένετο foll. by infin., has been omitted from the calculation owing to the difficulty of verification in the LXX.

For purposes of comparison the corresponding figures for Lk. are now given. The following words and phrases, occurring (a) at least five times in Lk. and also (b) at least twice as often in Lk. as in the rest of the New Testament excluding Acts,[1]

---

[1] See Hawkins, *op. cit.* pp. 15-23, where "characteristic" means occurring

are found in the LXX., those with asterisks being 'characteristic' in the sense of occurring at least twenty-five times.

'Αναστάς or ἀναστάντες,* ἀπὸ τοῦ νῦν, βρέφος, γίγνεσθαι foll. by ἐπί with acc.,* ἐγένετο foll. by καί,* ἐγένετο foll. by finite verb,* εἴη,* εἰπεῖν παραβολήν, εἶπεν δέ or εἶπαν δέ,* ἐν τῷ with infin.,* ἐπιδιδόναι, ἐπιστάτης, ἐφιστάναι,* ἰδοὺ γάρ, Ἱερουσαλήμ,* καλούμενος with names or appellations, κατακλίνειν, κοιλία = womb,* λέγειν παραβολήν, μνᾶ, νομικός, παραχρῆμα, πᾶς ὁ. or ἅπας ὁ λαός,* πρός used of speaking to,* συνέχειν,* τις with opt., τίς ἐξ ὑμῶν, τοῦ before infin.,* ὑποστρέφειν.

One phrase only, of those that satisfy the above requirements, ἐν μιᾷ τῶν, does not seem to be represented in the LXX.; of 29 found in the LXX. 14 are "characteristic."[1]

In the light of the statistics given in previous sections of entire vocabulary and peculiar words it would seem that Matthew was as much influenced by the LXX. as Luke and Acts; but such an impression is dispelled by an extract from Hawkins's list (pp. 4-8) showing the words and phrases characteristic of Matthew that occur in LXX., the same tests and marks as before being employed.

Ten occur in the LXX.—ἀναχωρεῖν, βρυγμός, γενηθήτω, ἔνδυμα, κλαυθμός, ῥηθέν, συλλέγειν,* τάλαντον, τάφος,* ὑποκριτής,* while 9 do not occur—ἀργύρια plur., βασιλεία τῶν οὐρανῶν, ζιζάνιον, ὄναρ, πατὴρ ὁ ἐν (τοῖς) οὐρανοῖς, πατὴρ ὁ οὐράνιος, συμβούλιον λαμβάνειν, συντέλεια τοῦ αἰῶνος, τί σοι or ὑμῖν δοκεῖ;[2] some of these prove little or nothing, but an examination of the figures as a whole, as given below in tabular form, shows a marked difference between the two writers in their relation to the LXX.[3]

---

at least four times in Lk., and also at least twice as often in Lk. as in Matthew and Mark together. The test here is made stricter in order to economise space.

[1] Ἐγένετο foll. by infin. is omitted as before.
[2] Ἰδού after gen. abs. is omitted owing to difficulty of verification.
[3] The above lists, though as full as possible, are not necessarily exhaustive.

	Characteristic Words and Phrases.	Occurring in LXX.	Characteristic in LXX.
Acts	69	68	33
Lk.	30	29	14
Matt.	19	10	3

B. The vocabulary of Luke, far more than that of the other evangelists, is akin to that of the Apocryphal books. Out of 261 words peculiar to Acts which occur in the LXX., 59 are found only in those books which have no Hebrew equivalent (Sirach being counted as such for this purpose). They are as follows : ἄγνωστος, ἀναδιδόναι, ἀνάκρισις, ἀνατρέφειν, ἄντικρυς (in Neh. xii. 8 א*AB omit) ἀντοφθαλμεῖν, ἀπασπάζεσθαι, ἀσκεῖν, ἀσμένως, ἄφιξις, βίωσις, δημόσιος, διάγνωσις, διανύειν, εἰστρέχειν, ἐκλαλεῖν, ἐκπληροῦν, ἐκπλήρωσις, ἐκτένεια, ἔξυπνος, ἐπιγίγνεσθαι, ἐπικουρία, ἐπισφαλής, ἐπιτροπή, ἔσθησις, εὔθυμος, ἱερόσυλος, καθημερινός, καταδίκη, κατασείειν, καταστέλλειν, μεστοῦσθαι, μετρίως, οὐρανόθεν, ὀχλεῖσθαι, πάντῃ, παραινεῖν, παράσημος, περιαστράπτειν, περιρηγνύναι, περιτρέπειν, πλοῦς, πρηνής, προσαπειλεῖσθαι, προσκλίνεσθαι, προτείνειν, προτρέπεσθαι, πυρά, ῥωννύσθαι, σκαφή, σκευή, συνδρομή, συνέπεσθαι, τεκμήριον, ὑπηρετεῖν, ὑποζωννύναι, φιλανθρώπως, φιλοφρόνως, φυλακίζειν, χλευάζειν.

Lukan vocabulary and the Apocrypha.

Compare the corresponding figures for the other books.[1]

Of 51 LXX. words peculiar to Lk. + Acts   3 are in Apocrypha only.
„ 188   „   „   „   Lk.   28   „   „   „
„ 76   „   „   „   Matt.   9   „   „   „
„ 40   „   „   „   Mark   5   „   „   „

The affinities extend to phrases as well as individual words, and suggest that Luke was familiar with some at least of the Apocryphal books.

The resemblance between the Greek of these books and that *2 and 3 Maccabees.*

[1] See Hawkins, pp. 198-207.

of the Lucan writings has been noticed ere now,[1] but the figures given here may prove of interest. Of 2061 words in 2 Maccabees 765 (or 37 per cent) recur in Acts, 737 (35 per cent) in Lk., 626 (30 per cent) in Matthew, 469 (22 per cent) in Hebrews. Of 1267 words in 3 Maccabees 561 (44 per cent) recur in Acts, 549 (43 per cent) in Lk., 441 (34 per cent) in Matthew, 356 (28 per cent) in Hebrews.[2] When allowance has been made on the one hand for the smaller extent of Hebrews, and on the other for the number of common words which must inevitably be found in every book, the degree of affinity evinced by Lk.-Acts and Hebrews towards 2 and 3 Maccabees seems substantially the same. The extent to which Luke's style resembles that of these books appears also from an examination of peculiar words.

In the whole Greek Bible two words occur only in 2 and 3 Maccabees and Matthew : διετής, χλαμύς. There are none confined to 2 and 3 Maccabees and Mark, whereas 9 words are found only in Lk. and 2 and 3 Maccabees—ἀγωνία (?), ἀντιβάλλειν, ἄτερ, αὐστηρός, ἐπικρίνειν, κλισία, περιάπτειν, πρεσβεία, συντυγχάνειν ; and no less than 27 only in Acts and 2 and 3 Maccabees—ἀνάκρισις, ἄντικρυς (in Neh. xii. 8 ℵ*AB omit), ἀσκεῖν, ἀσμένως, ἄφιξις, δημόσιος, διανύειν, εἰστρέχειν, ἐκπληροῦν, ἐκπλήρωσις, ἐπιτροπή, ἔσθησις, εὔθυμος, ἱερόσυλος, καταστέλλειν, μεστοῦσθαι, μετρίως, παραινεῖν, παράσημος, περιρηγνύναι, προσκλίνεσθαι, προτείνειν, ῥώννυσθαι, σκευή, συνέπεσθαι, ὑποζωννύναι, φιλανθρώπως.

These figures suggest that Luke may have read 2 and 3 Maccabees before writing Acts. In the case of 2 Maccabees the suggestion is highly probable. It was no doubt known to the author of Hebrews, who belonged to the same literary circles

---

[1] E.g. by Harnack, *Luke the Physician*, p. 105.

[2] These figures are given in good faith, but not more than approximate accuracy is claimed for them. The labour entailed by an effort after complete inerrancy seemed hardly worth the while. The method employed was to make out a list of words from the LXX. concordance, verifying in Swete wherever the reading seemed doubtful, and omitting proper names and numerals ; then to compare them with Moulton-Geden, counting *all* words given there as N.T. words. See Cadbury, *op. cit.* p. 7, for some similar investigations.

THE USE OF THE SEPTUAGINT IN ACTS 75

as Luke.[1] A number of phrases in Acts have no parallels in the whole Greek Bible except in 2 Maccabees. For example, διανοίγειν τὴν καρδίαν, Acts xvi. 14, 2 Macc. i. 4 ; περιρηγνύναι ἱμάτια or χιτῶνας, Acts xvi. 22, 2 Macc. iv. 38 ; τάσσεσθαι ἡμέραν, Acts xxviii. 23, 2 Macc. iii. 14, xiv. 21 (? Tobit v. 6) ; Acts xxiv. 3, πολλῆς εἰρήνης τυγχάνοντες . . . διὰ τῆς σῆς προνοίας, may be modelled on 2 Macc. iv. 6 ἄνευ βασιλικῆς προνοίας ἀδύνατον εἶναι τυχεῖν εἰρήνης. The courtly use of πρόνοια in reference to a ruler is the same in both passages, and τυγχάνειν εἰρήνης is not found elsewhere in the Greek Bible. But the most important instance is the description of the death of Herod, which seems to be dependent on 2 Maccabees in its use of traditional material to describe the death of a persecutor ; the parallels are best shown in two columns.[2]

Acts xii.	2 Macc. ix.
20. ἦν δὲ θυμομαχῶν.	4. ἐπαρθεὶς τῷ θυμῷ.
22. θεοῦ φωνή.	10. τὸν . . . τῶν οὐρανίων ἄστρων ἅπτεσθαι δοκοῦντα (cf. Isa. xiv. 13).
23. ἐπάταξεν αὐτὸν ἄγγελος κυρίου.	5. ὁ δὲ παντεπόπτης κύριος ὁ θεὸς τοῦ Ἰσραὴλ ἐπάταξεν αὐτὸν (cf. 2 Kings xix. 35.)

---

[1] E.g. Heb. xi. 34 f. = 2 Macc. viii. 24, vi. 19, 28 ; for other parallels see Moffatt, Int. to N.T. p. 32.

Clement of Alexandria deduced from the style of Hebrews that it was a Greek edition made by Luke of an original Hebrew letter of Paul (see Eus. H.E. vi. 14). The hypothesis has found supporters up to the present day, see Moffatt, Int. pp. 435 ff., for the arguments in its favour, and Hawkins, Horae Synopticae (2nd ed.), pp. 192 f., for lists of words common to the Lucan writings and the other Gospels on the one side, and Hebrews on the other. Moffatt's own conclusion is that " community of atmosphere is all that can fairly be postulated." According to Moulton Luke was " the only N.T. writer except the author of Hebrews to show any conscious attention to Greek ideas of style " (Grammar, p. 18). This fact might be considered sufficient in itself to account for the similarity of style, but it seems unlikely that the development of the church at this stage was so far advanced as to admit of two unconnected literary circles with the same atmosphere.

[2] These and all other parallels in this chapter are given for what they are worth ; probably recent criticism has exaggerated their value. Many apparent instances of borrowing are in reality examples of two writers making independent use of the common literary stock of the period.

76   THE COMPOSITION AND PURPOSE OF ACTS

    ἀνθ' ὧν οὐκ ἔδωκεν τὴν δόξαν   4. ὑπερηφάνως. 7. ὑπερηφανίας.
τῷ θεῷ.
καὶ γενόμενος σκωληκόβρωτος   9. ὥστε καὶ ἐκ τοῦ σώματος τοῦ
ἐξέψυξεν.   δυσσεβοῦς σκώληκας ἀναζεῖν.
     15. οἰωνοβρώτους.
xiii. 1. Μαναήν τε Ἡρῴδου . . .   29. παρεκομίζετο δὲ τὸ σῶμα Φί-
σύντροφος.   λιππος ὁ σύντροφος αὐτοῦ.

Most of these are resemblances of thought rather than language, and would hardly be worthy of attention, if it were not for the two striking linguistic parallels at the end. The σκωληκόβρωτος of Acts seems to be inspired by the οἰωνοβρώτους of Maccabees,[1] and we have a reference to the σύντροφος (here only in New Testament, very rare in LXX.) of the persecutor; but in a totally different connection.[2]

Tobit.   *Tobit* seems to have been known to Luke,[3] so traces in Acts are to be expected. The story of Paul's blindness reminds us of Tobit's similar affliction. λεπίδες (here only in New Testament), ix. 18, fell from Paul's eyes; cf. Tobit iii. 17, xi. 12, where λεπίζειν is used in the corresponding context. As the blind Paul needed men as χειραγωγοῦντες (not elsewhere in New Testament except xxii. 11), so the men of Nineveh were surprised to find Tobit ὑπὸ μηδενὸς χειραγωγούμενον (xi. 16 ‍א, elsewhere in LXX. only Judges xvi. 26 A).[4]

Judith.   *Judith* was known to the author of Hebrews,[5] possibly also to Luke. The speech of Stephen belongs to a fixed literary type,

    [1] I find I have been anticipated in this suggestion, see Selwyn, *Oracles in the N.T.* pp. 99-113.
    [2] It is noticeable that the authors of Acts and 2 Maccabees are both fond of introducing angels. Perhaps Luke may have dealt with his source, written or oral, for Acts xii. in the same way as the author of 2 Maccabees may be supposed to have treated Jason's narrative.
    [3] *E.g.* Lk. xv. 20 = Tobit xi. 9; see Simpson in Charles's *Apocrypha*, i. 199.
    [4] If the above suggestion is correct, Luke may have spoken of λεπίδες in allusion to the well-known story, and added ὡσεί as a kind of apology for the expression. This would answer the objection of Preuschen, who calls the word in this context "eine sehr unmedizinische volkstümliche Vorstellung."
    [5] Heb. xi. 34 παρεμβολὰς ἔκλιναν ἀλλοτρίων; cf. 1 Clem. 55 Ἰουδὶθ . . . ᾐτήσατο . . . ἐξελθεῖν εἰς τὴν παρεμβολὴν τῶν ἀλλοφύλων. The whole chapter is a commentary on the Hebrews passage; see R. Harris, *Side Lights on New Testament Research*, pp. 169, 170.

an early example of which is found in Jud. v. 5 ff. (apart from the original passage, Exod. i. 10, κατασοφίζεσθαι occurs in the Greek Bible only in Jud. v. 11, x. 19; Acts vii. 19). Jud. v. 20, 21 may be compared with Acts v. 38, 39; συνδρομή, apart from 3 Macc. iii. 8, comes in the Greek Bible only in Jud. x. 18 and Acts xxi. 30, in Judith with παρεμβολή, in Acts with παρεμβολή in the same context, xxi. 34; καθημερινός is found twice only in the Greek Bible, Jud. xii. 15 and Acts vi. 1, in similar contexts.

There is a probability that the description of Judas in i. 18, and especially the curious use of πρηνής (="swollen"?), was suggested by Wisd. iv. 19: καὶ ἔσονται μετὰ τοῦτο εἰς πτῶμα ἄτιμον καὶ εἰς ὕβριν ἐν νεκροῖς δι' αἰῶνος, ὅτι ῥήξει αὐτοὺς ἀφώνους πρηνεῖς, καὶ σαλεύσει αὐτοὺς ἐκ θεμελίων.[1]

Wisdom.

Certain affinities which exist between Acts and the Pseudepigrapha may be fitly discussed at this point. As might be expected, they are of secondary importance, since the eschatological motive, dominant in the Jewish Apocalypses, has left but faint traces in Acts. The data may be treated under three heads: (a) a parallel to the prison story of Acts xvi. from the *Testaments of the XII. Patriarchs*; (b) elements in the narrative of the speech and death of Stephen possibly derived from Jewish Apocalypses; (c) some other parallels. The references added in brackets are to Dr. Charles's edition of the *Apocrypha and Pseudepigrapha*, 1913.

Pseudepigrapha.

(a) Acts xvi.

23. πολλὰς δὲ ἐπιθέντες αὐτοῖς πληγὰς ἔβαλον εἰς φυλακήν, παραγγείλαντες τῷ δεσμοφύλακι ἀσφαλῶς τηρεῖν αὐτούς.

Testament of Joseph viii.[2] (Charles, ii. 349).

4. καὶ ἐλθὼν ὁ ἀνὴρ αὐτῆς ἔβαλέ με εἰς φυλακὴν ἐν τῷ αὐτοῦ οἴκῳ καὶ τῇ ἑξῆς μαστιγώσας ἐξέπεμψέ με εἰς τὴν τοῦ Φαραὼ εἱρκτήν.

---

[1] See F. H. Chase, *J.T.S.*, January 1912, and R. Harris, *Am. Journ. of Theol.*, January 1914.

[2] Dr. Charles's edition of the Greek text. Most of this section is taken from a note of mine in *J.T.S.*, xv. (1914) p. 599, with the permission of the editors.

24. ὃς παραγγελίαν τοιαύτην λαβὼν ἔβαλεν αὐτοὺς εἰς τὴν
ἐσωτέραν φυλακὴν καὶ τοὺς
πόδας ἠσφαλίσατο αὐτῶν εἰς
τὸ ξύλον.
25. κατὰ δὲ τὸ μεσονύκτιον Παῦλος
καὶ Σίλας προσευχόμενοι
ὕμνουν τὸν θεόν, ἐπηκροῶντο
δὲ αὐτῶν οἱ δέσμιοι.

5. καὶ ὡς ἤμην ἐν τοῖς δεσμοῖς, ἡ
Αἰγυπτία συνείχετο ἀπὸ τῆς
λύπης.

(a)
ἐλθοῦσα δὲ ἐπη-
κροᾶτό μου πῶς
ηὐχαρίστουν τῷ
Κυρίῳ καὶ ὕμνουν
ἐν οἴκῳ τοῦ σκότους
καὶ ἔχαιρον ἐν
ἱλαρᾷ φωνῇ δοξά-
ζων τὸν θεόν μου,
ὅτι διὰ προφάσεως
ἀπηλλάγην τῆς
Αἰγυπτίας.

(β)
καὶ ἐπηκροᾶτό μου
πῶς ὕμνουν Κύριον
ἐν οἴκῳ σκότους καὶ
ἐν ἱλαρᾷ φωνῇ
χαίρων ἐδόξαζον
τὸν θεὸν μόνον ὅτι
διὰ προφάσεως ἀπ-
ηλλάγην τῆς Αἰ-
γυπτίας.

ii. 3. τοῦ δεσμοφύλακος.

ix. 4. ἤκουσε τῆς φωνῆς μοῦ προσ-
ευχομένου.

29. αἰτήσας δὲ φῶτα εἰσεπήδησεν.

vii. 3. τότε οὖν εὐκαιρίαν λαβοῦσα
εἰσεπήδησε πρός με.

The two narratives have in common (i.) a beating; (ii.) a *double* casting into prison; (iii.) the mention of bonds; (iv.) the connecting of a house with the prison, see Acts xvi. 34; (v.) two words—δεσμοφύλαξ and ἐπακροᾶσθαι—which do not occur elsewhere in the Greek Bible, though ἀρχιδεσμοφύλαξ is found in Gen. xxxix.; and (vi.) one word—εἰσπηδᾶν—the only other occurrence of which in the Greek Bible is Amos v. 19. The effect is cumulative, and some literary connection between the two passages becomes highly probable.

(b) The following parallels to the story of Stephen are worthy of notice. I offer no opinion as to the extent to which Christian elements occur in these apocalyptic writings.

Acts vii.

36. οὗτος ἐξήγαγεν αὐτοὺς ποιήσας
τέρατα καὶ σημεῖα ἐν τῇ
Αἰγύπτῳ καὶ ἐν Ἐρυθρᾷ
Θαλάσσῃ καὶ ἐν τῇ ἐρήμῳ
ἔτη τεσσαράκοντα.

Ass. Mos. iii. 11 (Charles, ii. 417).

Moses . . . who suffered many things in Egypt and in the Red Sea and in the wilderness during forty years.[1]

---

[1] This combination of words does not occur in the LXX.

	Apoc. Mos. xxxiii. 2 (ii. 149).
55. ἀτενίσας εἰς τὸν οὐρανὸν εἶδεν δόξαν θεοῦ καὶ Ἰησοῦν ἑστῶτα ἐκ δεξιῶν τοῦ θεοῦ . . .	And she [Eve] gazed steadfastly into heaven, and beheld a chariot of light . . .
	Apoc. Mos. xlii. 8 (ii. 153).[1]
59, 60. τὸν Στέφανον ἐπικαλούμενον καὶ λέγοντα Κύριε Ἰησοῦ, δέξαι τὸ πνεῦμά μου . . . καὶ τοῦτο εἰπὼν ἐκοιμήθη.	But after she had prayed, she gazed heavenwards and groaned aloud and smote her breast and said : " God of all, receive my spirit," and straightway she delivered up her spirit to God.

In illustration of Acts vii. 38, τοῦ ἀγγέλου τοῦ λαλοῦντος αὐτῷ ἐν τῷ ὄρει Σινά, may be adduced Jub. i. 27, ii. 1 (Charles, ii. 13), where the angel talks with Moses on the mount, and the (later) preface to Apoc. Mos. (ii. 138), where the angel is identified as Michael.

(c) Acts i. 8 ἕως ἐσχάτου τῆς γῆς. Cf. Ps. Sol. viii. 16, where Pompey is described as τὸν ἀπ᾽ ἐσχάτου τῆς γῆς (ed. Ryle and James, Charles, ii. 641).

Acts i. 18 πρηνὴς γενόμενος ἐλάκησεν μέσος, καὶ ἐξεχύθη πάντα τὰ σπλάγχνα αὐτοῦ. Cf. The Story of Ahikar, viii. 38, Arabic (Charles, ii. 776). " And when Nadad heard that speech from his uncle Haiqâr, he swelled up immediately and became like a blown-out bladder. And his limbs swelled and his legs and his feet and his side, and he was torn and his belly burst asunder and his entrails were scattered, and he perished, and died. And his latter end was destruction and he went to hell." Cf. Acts i. 25 ; if πρηνής in i. 18 may be translated " swollen " (see p. 77) the resemblance becomes more striking.

Acts ii. 8 Πάρθοι καὶ Μῆδοι. Cf. 1 Enoch lvi. 5 (ii. 222), where the "Parthians and Medes" are " the chief nations in the league against Israel " (Charles, *The Book of Enoch*, 1912, *in loc.*).

Acts viii. 10 οὗτός ἐστιν ἡ Δύναμις τοῦ θεοῦ ἡ καλουμένη Μεγάλη. Cf. Jub. xl. 7 (ii. 71), where the Egyptians proclaim

[1] See Charles, ii. 126, where the editor apparently sees no Christian influence here.

before Joseph "'El, 'El wa 'Abîrĕr," rendered by Charles, "God, God, the Mighty One of God," and explained as "the title of a great magician."

C. There are three important questions which arise in connection with Acts, in each of which it is natural to ask what bearing, if any, the LXX. has on the problem: (i.) the "Western" or β-text, (ii.) Luke and Josephus, (iii.) the author's medical phraseology.

(i.) The β-text.

There are some 50 words [1] used in the Codex Bezae version of Acts, which do not occur elsewhere in the true text of Lk. or Acts, it being assumed for this purpose that the Westcott and Hort text is the true one.

Thirty-one of these are found in the LXX.: δειλινόν iii. 1, σφυρόν iii. 8, συνεκπορεύεσθαι iii. 11, βαρύνειν iii. 14, ἐνέργεια iv. 24, διάκρισις iv. 32, ἐγκλείειν v. 23, μιαίνειν v. 38, τύραννος v. 39, φυγαδεύειν vii. 29, διαλιμπάνειν viii. 24, xvii. 13, ἄμμος vii. 24, προσεγγίζειν x. 25, διασαφεῖν x. 25, βέλτιον x. 28, ἀκουστός xi. 1, ἐπιλάμπειν xii. 7, νύσσειν xii. 7, βαθμός xii. 10, ἐπιτυγχάνειν xiii. 29, ἐπιθύειν xiv. 13, ἐπισείειν xiv. 19, ἀποστερεῖν xvi. 19, ἀναμιμνήσκειν xvi. 35, ἀναίτιος xvi. 37, παριδεῖν xvii. 30, ἐντιθέναι xviii. 4, καταβοᾶν xviii. 13, ἐπιφέρειν xix. 12, ἐξορκίζειν xix. 14, ἐνάλλεσθαι xix. 16 ἄμφοδον xix. 28, πλεῖστος xix. 32, ἀνέρχεσθαι xxi. 11.

On the other hand, 19 do not occur in the LXX.: συνέδριος v. 35, ἐπιχείρησις xii. 3, τυχόν xii. 15, ἐξανοίγειν xii. 16, ἥδιστα xiii. 8, ἑτέρως xiii. 35, ἀνάλλεσθαι xiv. 10, μέγως xv. 4, συζήτησις xv. 7, ἐπικράζειν xvi. 39, διιστορεῖν xvii. 23, ἀπολαλεῖν xviii. 25, συγκατανεύειν xviii. 26, συντεχνίτης xix. 25, πεμπταῖος xx. 6, ὑπολάμπας xx. 8, ποταπῶς xx. 18, ὅμοσε xx. 19, καταφωνεῖν xxii. 24, προστείνειν xxii. 25.

Several words in the above lists are clearly scribal blunders, and it must be remembered that a corrupt text, such as Codex Bezae confessedly is, comes badly out of such an inquiry. How-

---

[1] These lists, though as full as I have been able to make them, are not necessarily exhaustive.

THE USE OF THE SEPTUAGINT IN ACTS

ever, the evidence, so far as it goes, does not suggest any marked difference between the a and β texts in their relation towards the LXX. In two instances the author of the Bezan gloss seems to use the Hellenistic Old Testament in exactly the way that has been shown above to be characteristic of Luke: Acts iv. 24 ἐπιγνόντες τὴν τοῦ θεοῦ ἐνέργειαν . . . καὶ εἶπον Δεσπότα κτλ. = 3 Macc. v. 28 τοῦτο δὲ ἦν ἐνέργεια τοῦ πάντα δεσποτεύοντος θεοῦ, cf. v. 12, 2 Macc. iii. 29, Wisd. vii. 26; and Acts viii. 24 ὃς πολλὰ κλαίων οὐ διελίμπανεν = Tob. x. 7 οὐ διελίμπανεν θρηνοῦσα.

The question of the influence of Josephus turns upon certain passages wherein Luke appears to have been influenced by Josephus. But the general resemblance of vocabulary and style between the two authors forms a subsidiary argument, which has been worked out in great detail by Krenkel, *Josephus und Lukas* (1894), pp. 289 ff. (ii.) Luke and Josephus.

He examines the 751 words [1] peculiar to the Lucan writings in the New Testament, and gives four tables of results. Out of the 751 (*a*) 309 are found in Lk.-Acts, LXX., and Josephus; (*b*) 87 in Lk.-Acts and LXX., but not in Josephus; (*c*) 178 in Lk.-Acts and Josephus, but not in LXX.; (*d*) 177 in Lk.-Acts, but neither in LXX. nor Josephus. He concludes that a writer who, on the one hand, shows his dependence on the LXX. so clearly, and, on the other, has more than twice as many peculiar words in common with Josephus as he has with the LXX., must have been influenced by the former in a greater degree than by the latter.[2]

Unfortunately Krenkel's work was written before the Oxford concordance to the LXX. was available, and considerable deductions must be made before his figures can be accepted. Of his third list no less than 78 words which are said to be absent from the LXX., are actually found there, or 83, counting doubtful

[1] Note that Hawkins makes 413 + 58 + 261 = 732 peculiar words, by a more careful scrutiny of doubtful readings; see above, p. 70.
[2] p. 331.

82 THE COMPOSITION AND PURPOSE OF ACTS

readings not found in Swete's text. Of these 74 come in those parts of the Greek Old Testament which have no Hebrew equivalent [1]: ἄγνωστος, ἀγωνία, αἴτιον (=αἰτία), ἀναδιδόναι, ἀναιδεία, ἀνάπηρος, ἀνατρέφειν, ἀνευρίσκειν, ἄντικρυς (with gen.), ἀποδέχεσθαι, ἀποψύχειν, ἀσκεῖν, ἀσμένως, ἄφιξις, δημόσιος, διάγνωσις, διανύειν, ἔγκυος, ἐθίζειν, εἰστρέχειν, ἐκλαλεῖν, ἐκτένεια, ἔξυπνος, ἐπιβοᾶν, ἐπιβουλή, ἐπιγίνεσθαι, ἐπικουρία, ἐπικρίνειν, ἐπισφαλής, ἐπιτροπή, εὐεργέτης, εὔθυμος, ἱερόσυλος, καθημερινός, καταδίκη, κατασείειν, καταστέλλειν, κλισία, λῆρος, λυσιτελεῖν, μετρίως, μόγις, οὐσία, ὀχλεῖν, παράδοξος, παραινεῖν, παράσημος, περιρηγνύναι, περιτρέπειν, πλοῦς, πρεσβεία, πρηνής, προσκλίνειν, προτείνειν, προτρέπεσθαι, ῥωννύσθαι, συμπαρεῖναι, συμφύειν, συνελαύνειν, συνέπεσθαι, συνοδεύειν, συντυγχάνειν, τεκμήριον, τελεσφορεῖν, ὑπηρετεῖν, ὑποβάλλειν, ὑποζωννύναι, ὑποκρίνεσθαι, ὑπονοεῖν, ὑποχωρεῖν, φιλανθρώπως, φιλονεικία, φιλοφρόνως, χλευάζειν.

Four actually occur in the rest of the LXX.—ἐκεῖσε, ῥιπτεῖν,[2] σύντροφος, σφυρόν—while βάτος, εὐπορία, προσαπειλεῖν, σκευή, συμπληροῦν are given in Hatch-Redpath, though absent from Swete.

In this way the non-LXX. peculiar Lucan words, which Luke has in common with Josephus, are brought down to about one hundred. A further reduction may be made for a few nautical terms, which could hardly be expected in the LXX., where the subject is practically unrepresented, and also for such words as ἀνθύπατος, σεβαστός, and others which are specially applicable to the conditions of the first century. The number of peculiarly Lucan words absent from the LXX. but found in Josephus thus becomes about equal to those which are in the LXX., but absent from Josephus, and this part of Krenkel's argument thus loses its force.

(iii.) Medical phraseology.

The argument in Hobart's *The Medical Language of St. Luke*, which even since the publication of Harnack's *Lukas der Arzt*

---
[1] See p. 73.
[2] See Thackeray, *Grammar of Old Testament Greek*, i. p. 244.

still remains the classic presentment of the theory that the language of Lk. and the Acts shows that the author had received a medical training, is twofold, being based on (a) the supposition that the narratives of healing disclose a special medical interest, and (b) the employment by Luke of a number of non-medical terms of frequent occurrence in medical books.

As regards the latter, if it can be shown that these words are found in the LXX., it is as legitimate to account for their presence by Luke's familiarity with the Greek Scriptures as by knowledge of medical literature.

The figures for Acts are as follows. Of the words claimed by Hobart as medical (of which 6 do not occur in Westcott and Hort), about 84 per cent are found in the LXX. (including 5 not given in Swete's text). Out of the 30 non-LXX. words, 4 may be disregarded—ἀνεύθετος, ὀχλοποιεῖν, σκωληκόβρωτος, συνθρύπτειν—since Hobart produces no parallels, only analogous formations, 2 occur in a nautical context in chapter xxvii., where it seems perverse to suppose any medical interest—κολυμβᾶν, ὑποτρέχειν—and 23 are given in Liddell & Scott's lexicon as used by authors of the classical and pre-classical periods: ἀκωλύτως, ἀνακαθίζειν, ἀποκατάστασις, ἀσιτία, ἄσιτος, ἀχλύς, διαπορεῖν, διαχειρίζεσθαι, δυσεντέριον, εἰσκαλεῖν, ἐπακροᾶσθαι, ἐπιδημεῖν, εὐπορεῖσθαι, καθάπτειν, κλινάριον, ὁδοιπορεῖν, ὀθόνη, ὁμότεχνος, παροτρύνειν, πίμπρασθαι, προσπηγνύναι, συγκινεῖν, συναλίζεσθαι. One word only remains, ἀνωτερικός, and it is hard to see why any writer should have described high ground by this term because he was familiar with its technical sense of "emetic."

This does not necessarily invalidate the argument, for Luke's choice of LXX. words may have been determined by his previous training, but it certainly makes a restatement of it desirable. In a few cases Luke seems to have used LXX. words, but in the vast majority of instances he employed such words as would have occurred to an educated Greek with Jewish connections.[1]

---

[1] See further, p. 68.

84   THE COMPOSITION AND PURPOSE OF ACTS

Turning to Hobart's argument from the use of technical medical language in narratives of healing, we find it hardly affected by any evidence drawn from the LXX. For this purpose examples from the LXX. are of no value unless they are taken from a more or less medical context. Harnack,[1] following Hobart, has given a list of passages in Acts where Luke seems to be using technical terms in describing disease. Very few of these can be paralleled from the LXX. at all. The following may be noted : ἐξέψυξεν xii. 23, cf. Ezek. xxi. 7 (12), ἀδύνατος xiv. 8, cf. Tob. ii. 10א, ὕπνῳ βαθεῖ xx. 9, cf. Sir. xxii. 7, καταπίπτειν xxviii. 6, cf. 4 Macc. iv. 11. However, these parallels are of little importance compared with the mass of evidence which Hobart has brought from medical writers. His argument is cumulative. Even one such phrase as that in xxviii. 8, πυρετοῖς καὶ δυσεντερίῳ συνεχόμενον, deserves attention ;[2] for here there are three usages without parallel in the LXX.—δυσεντερίῳ, the plural of πυρετός and συνέχεσθαι of disease.[3]

Formal quotations.

Actual quotations in the Acts from the Old Testament [4] must

[1] *Luke the Physician*, pp. 175-198.

[2] In the Gospel, Luke's alterations of the Marcan narrative in stories of miraculous healings give the best opportunity for investigating the problem. Harnack, *Luke the Physician*, pp. 182 ff., gives ten passages of this nature ; in four of these there is a possibility of Luke having been influenced by LXX. phraseology : (i.) Lk. iv. 35 = Mark i. 26, ῥίψαν substituted for σπαράξαν. σπαράσσειν comes 4 times in LXX., ῥίπτειν over 100 times, and is constantly used of casting a body on to the ground ; (ii.) Lk. iv. 39 = Mark i. 30 with ἐπιστὰς ἐπάνω αὐτῆς ἐπετίμησε τῷ πυρετῷ, in place of προσελθὼν ἤγειρεν αὐτὴν κρατήσας τῆς χειρός. Στῆναι ἐπάνω τινός is a LXX. phrase, e.g. Gen. xviii. 2, a passage perhaps familiar to Luke ; cf. Acts x. (see below, p. 103 note). There is no parallel to ἐπετίμησεν τῷ πυρετῷ in LXX., nor is one given by Hobart ; (iii.) Lk. v. 18 = Mark ii. 3. Luke substitutes παραλελυμένος (5 times in LXX.) for παραλυτικός (not in LXX.) ; (iv.) Lk. viii. 55 = Mark v. 42. Luke introduces καὶ ἐπέστρεψεν τὸ πνεῦμα αὐτῆς, a LXX. phrase ; see Judges xv. 19 (cf. also 1 Kg. xvii. 21).

[3] But it is joined with φόβῳ in Job iii. 24 and πικρίᾳ in Job x. 1.
The foregoing section was written in 1913-14. Prof. Cadbury's investigations mark a great advance (see pp. 349 ff.), and had I written later it would have been on somewhat different lines. The results of my studies are given without alteration as corroborating his main position.

[4] See Swete, *Int.* pp. 381-405 ; Dittmar, *Vetus Testamentum in Novo*,

now be discussed, informal quotations being reserved for the next section. If the actual quotations are defined as consisting of passages cited by καθὼς γέγραπται or other introductory formula, or the context of which makes it plain that a citation rather than mere allusion is intended, they appear to be 28 in number.[1] In places the criterion is somewhat subjective, especially in chap. vii. Where the passage is prefaced by a verb of saying, it has been treated as a formal quotation. All three divisions of the Old Testament—Law, Prophets and Writings—are amply represented, and some books are quoted, such as Amos and Joel, which have otherwise left little mark on the New Testament.

The citations may be divided into: A, those which are in exact or substantial agreement with the LXX.; B, those which show substantial variation. Here again it is difficult to draw the line, and there are one or two which might without impropriety be put in either class.[2]

A. Passages agreeing with the LXX. may be classed as showing (i.) exact agreement, (ii.) substantial agreement.

A. (i.) Exact Agreement between Acts and LXX.

Acts ii. 25-28. Psalms xv. 8-11.

25. Δαυεὶδ γὰρ λέγει εἰς αὐτόν·
προορώμην τὸν κύριον ἐνώπιόν μου διὰ παντός, ὅτι ἐκ δεξιῶν μού ἐστιν, ἵνα μὴ σαλευθῶ.
26. διὰ τοῦτο ηὐφράνθη μου ἡ καρδία καὶ ἠγαλλιάσατο ἡ

8. προωρώμην τὸν κύριον ἐνώπιόν μου διὰ παντός, ὅτι ἐκ δεξιῶν μού ἐστιν ἵνα μὴ σαλευθῶ.
9. διὰ τοῦτο ηὐφράνθη ἡ καρδία μου καὶ ἠγαλλιάσατο ἡ

---

pp. 130-169. In the earlier part of this article Swete's *Old Testament in Greek* has been used. Here, however, in writing out the text of the LXX. Tischendorf was followed. This was originally accidental, but it has been allowed to stand on the ground that Tischendorf's text is probably nearer than Swete's to the text current in the first century. It seemed unnecessary to burden the page with textual notes which will be added when called for at the appropriate places in the commentary.

[1] See Swete, *Int.* p. 382. On p. 388 a somewhat shorter list of citations is given.

[2] Textual variations will be treated in the commentary.

γλῶσσά μου, ἔτι δὲ καὶ ἡ σάρξ
μου κατασκηνώσει ἐπ' ἐλπίδι,

27. ὅτι οὐκ ἐνκαταλείψεις τὴν
ψυχήν μου εἰς ᾅδην οὐδὲ
δώσεις τὸν ὅσιόν σου ἰδεῖν
διαφθοράν.
28. ἐγνώρισάς μοι ὁδοὺς ζωῆς,
πληρώσεις με εὐφροσύνης
μετὰ τοῦ προσώπου σου.

Acts iv. 25, 26.

25. ὁ τοῦ πατρὸς ἡμῶν διὰ πνεύματος ἁγίου στόματος Δαυεὶδ παιδός σου εἰπών· ἵνα τί ἐφρύαξαν ἔθνη καὶ λαοὶ ἐμελέτησαν κενά;
26. παρέστησαν οἱ βασιλεῖς τῆς γῆς καὶ οἱ ἄρχοντες συνήχθησαν ἐπὶ τὸ αὐτὸ κατὰ τοῦ κυρίου καὶ κατὰ τοῦ χριστοῦ αὐτοῦ.

Acts vii. 27, 28.

27. ὁ δὲ ἀδικῶν τὸν πλησίον ἀπώσατο αὐτὸν εἰπών· τίς σε κατέστησεν ἄρχοντα καὶ δικαστὴν ἐφ' ἡμῶν;
28. μὴ ἀνελεῖν με σὺ θέλεις, ὃν τρόπον ἀνεῖλες ἐχθὲς τὸν Αἰγύπτιον;

Acts vii. 35.

τοῦτον τὸν Μωυσῆν, ὃν ἠρνήσαντο εἰπόντες· τίς σὲ κατέστησεν ἄρχοντα καὶ δικαστήν, τοῦτον ὁ θεὸς καὶ ἄρχοντα καὶ λυτρωτὴν ἀπέσταλκεν σὺν χειρὶ ἀγγέλου τοῦ ὀφθέντος αὐτῷ ἐν τῇ βάτῳ.

γλῶσσά μου, ἔτι δὲ καὶ ἡ
σάρξ μου κατασκηνώσει ἐπ'
ἐλπίδι.
10. ὅτι οὐκ ἐγκαταλείψεις τὴν
ψυχήν μου εἰς ᾅδην, οὐδὲ
δώσεις τὸν ὅσιόν σου ἰδεῖν
διαφθοράν.
11. ἐγνώρισάς μοι ὁδοὺς ζωῆς·
πληρώσεις με εὐφροσύνης
μετὰ τοῦ προσώπου σου,
τερπνότητες ἐν τῇ δεξιᾷ σου
εἰς τέλος.

Psalms ii. 1, 2.

1. ἵνα τί ἐφρύαξαν ἔθνη, καὶ λαοὶ ἐμελέτησαν κενά;
2. παρέστησαν οἱ βασιλεῖς τῆς γῆς καὶ οἱ ἄρχοντες συνήχθησαν ἐπὶ τὸ αὐτὸ κατὰ τοῦ κυρίου καὶ κατὰ τοῦ χριστοῦ αὐτοῦ.

Exodus ii. 13, 14.

13. λέγει τῷ ἀδικοῦντι· διὰ τί σὺ τύπτεις τὸν πλησίον;
14. ὁ δὲ εἶπε· τίς σε κατέστησεν ἄρχοντα καὶ δικαστὴν ἐφ' ἡμῶν; μὴ ἀνελεῖν με σὺ θέλεις ὃν τρόπον ἀνεῖλες χθὲς τὸν Αἰγύπτιον;

Exodus ii. 14.

ὁ δὲ εἶπε· τίς σε κατέστησεν ἄρχοντα καὶ δικαστὴν ἐφ' ἡμῶν; μὴ ἀνελεῖν με σὺ θέλεις ὃν τρόπον ἀνεῖλες χθὲς τὸν Αἰγύπτιον;

THE USE OF THE SEPTUAGINT IN ACTS 87

Acts xiii. 33.

ὡς καὶ ἐν τῷ ψαλμῷ γέγραπται
τῷ δευτέρῳ· υἱός μου εἶ σύ,
ἐγὼ σήμερον γεγέννηκά σε.

Psalms ii. 7.

κύριος εἶπε πρὸς μέ· υἱός μου
εἶ σύ, ἐγὼ σήμερον γεγέννηκά σε.

A. (ii). Substantial Agreement between Acts and LXX.

Acts i. 20.

γέγραπται γὰρ ἐν βίβλῳ
ψαλμῶν· γενηθήτω ἡ ἔπαυλις
αὐτοῦ ἔρημος καὶ μὴ ἔστω ὁ
κατοικῶν ἐν αὐτῇ, καί· τὴν
ἐπισκοπὴν αὐτοῦ λαβέτω
ἕτερος.

Psalms cviii. 8.

γενηθήτωσαν αἱ ἡμέραι αὐτοῦ
ὀλίγαι, καὶ τὴν ἐπισκοπὴν
αὐτοῦ λάβοι ἕτερος.

Acts ii. 34, 35.

34. οὐ γὰρ Δαυεὶδ ἀνέβη εἰς τοὺς
οὐρανούς, λέγει δὲ αὐτός·
εἶπεν κύριος τῷ κυρίῳ μου·
κάθου ἐκ δεξιῶν μου,
35. ἕως ἂν θῶ τοὺς ἐχθρούς σου
ὑποπόδιον τῶν ποδῶν σου.

Psalms cix. 1.

εἶπεν ὁ κύριος τῷ κυρίῳ μου·
κάθου ἐκ δεξιῶν μου ἕως ἂν
θῶ τοὺς ἐχθρούς σου ὑποπόδιον τῶν ποδῶν σου.

Acts vii. 37 (cf. iii. 22).

οὗτός ἐστιν ὁ Μωυσῆς ὁ εἴπας
τοῖς υἱοῖς Ἰσραήλ· προφήτην
ὑμῖν ἀναστήσει ὁ θεὸς ἐκ
τῶν ἀδελφῶν ὑμῶν ὡς ἐμέ.

Deut. xviii. 15.

προφήτην ἐκ τῶν ἀδελφῶν σου
ὡς ἐμὲ ἀναστήσει σοι κύριος
ὁ θεός σου, αὐτοῦ ἀκούσεσθε.

Acts vii. 40.

εἰπόντες τῷ Ἀαρών· ποίησον
ἡμῖν θεοὺς οἳ προπορεύσονται
ἡμῶν· ὁ γὰρ Μωυσῆς, οὗτος
ὃς ἐξήγαγεν ἡμᾶς ἐκ γῆς
Αἰγύπτου, οὐκ οἴδαμεν τί
ἐγένετο αὐτῷ.

Exod. xxxii. 23.

λέγουσι γάρ μοι· ποίησον ἡμῖν
θεοὺς οἳ προπορεύσονται
ἡμῶν. ὁ γὰρ Μωυσῆς οὗτος
ὁ ἄνθρωπος ὃς ἐξήγαγεν ἡμᾶς
ἐξ Αἰγύπτου, οὐκ οἴδαμεν τί
γέγονεν αὐτῷ.

Acts viii. 32, 33.

32. ἡ δὲ περιοχὴ τῆς γραφῆς ἣν
ἀνεγίνωσκεν ἦν αὕτη· ὡς
πρόβατον ἐπὶ σφαγὴν ἤχθη,

Isaiah liii. 7, 8.

ὡς πρόβατον ἐπὶ σφαγὴν ἤχθη,

καὶ ὡς ἀμνὸς ἐναντίον τοῦ κείροντος αὐτὸν ἄφωνος, οὕτως οὐκ ἀνοίγει τὸ στόμα αὐτοῦ.

καὶ ὡς ἀμνὸς ἐναντίον τοῦ κείροντος ἄφωνος, οὕτως οὐκ ἀνοίγει τὸ στόμα.

33. ἐν τῇ ταπεινώσει ἡ κρίσις αὐτοῦ ἤρθη· τὴν γενεὰν αὐτοῦ τίς διηγήσεται; ὅτι αἴρεται ἀπὸ τῆς γῆς ἡ ζωὴ αὐτοῦ.

8. ἐν τῇ ταπεινώσει ἡ κρίσις αὐτοῦ ἤρθη· τὴν γενεὰν αὐτοῦ τίς διηγήσεται; ὅτι αἴρεται ἀπὸ τῆς γῆς ἡ ζωὴ αὐτοῦ. . . .

Acts xiii. 35.

Psalms xv. 10.

διότι καὶ ἐν ἑτέρῳ λέγει· οὐ δώσεις τὸν ὅσιόν σου ἰδεῖν διαφθοράν.

ὅτι οὐκ ἐγκαταλείψεις τὴν ψυχήν μου εἰς ᾅδην, οὐδὲ δώσεις τὸν ὅσιόν σου ἰδεῖν διαφθοράν.

Acts xxviii. 26, 27.

Isaiah vi. 9, 10.

26. λέγων· πορεύθητι πρὸς τὸν λαὸν τοῦτον καὶ εἰπόν· ἀκοῇ ἀκούσετε καὶ οὐ μὴ συνῆτε, καὶ βλέποντες βλέψετε καὶ οὐ μὴ ἴδητε· ἐπαχύνθη γὰρ ἡ καρδία τοῦ λαοῦ τούτου,

καὶ εἶπε· πορεύθητι καὶ εἰπὸν τῷ λαῷ τούτῳ· ἀκοῇ ἀκούσετε καὶ οὐ μὴ συνῆτε, καὶ βλέποντες βλέψετε καὶ οὐ μὴ ἴδητε.

27. καὶ τοῖς ὠσὶν βαρέως ἤκουσαν, καὶ τοὺς ὀφθαλμοὺς αὐτῶν ἐκάμμυσαν· μή ποτε ἴδωσιν τοῖς ὀφθαλμοῖς καὶ τοῖς ὠσὶν ἀκούσωσιν καὶ τῇ καρδίᾳ συνῶσιν καὶ ἐπιστρέψωσιν, καὶ ἰάσομαι αὐτούς.

10. ἐπαχύνθη γὰρ ἡ καρδία τοῦ λαοῦ τούτου, καὶ τοῖς ὠσὶν αὐτῶν βαρέως ἤκουσαν, καὶ τοὺς ὀφθαλμοὺς ἐκάμμυσαν, μή ποτε ἴδωσι τοῖς ὀφθαλμοῖς, καὶ τοῖς ὠσὶν ἀκούσωσι, καὶ τῇ καρδίᾳ συνῶσι καὶ ἐπιστρέψωσι, καὶ ἰάσομαι αὐτούς

B. Free Versions of the LXX. in Acts.

Acts i. 20.

Psalms lxviii. 26.

γέγραπται γὰρ ἐν βίβλῳ ψαλμῶν· γενηθήτω ἡ ἔπαυλις αὐτοῦ ἔρημος καὶ μὴ ἔστω ὁ κατοικῶν ἐν αὐτῇ, καί· τὴν ἐπισκοπὴν αὐτοῦ λάβετω ἕτερος.

γενηθήτω ἡ ἔπαυλις αὐτῶν ἠρημωμένη, καὶ ἐν τοῖς σκηνώμασιν αὐτῶν μὴ ἔστω ὁ κατοικῶν.

Acts ii. 17-21.

Joel ii. 28-32.

17. καὶ ἔσται ἐν ταῖς ἐσχάταις ἡμέραις, λέγει ὁ θεός, ἐκχεῶ ἀπὸ τοῦ πνεύματός μου ἐπὶ

28. καὶ ἔσται μετὰ ταῦτα καὶ ἐκχεῶ ἀπὸ τοῦ πνεύματός μου ἐπὶ

πᾶσαν σάρκα, καὶ προφητεύσουσιν οἱ υἱοὶ ὑμῶν καὶ αἱ
θυγατέρες ὑμῶν, καὶ οἱ νεανίσκοι ὑμῶν ὁράσεις ὄψονται,
καὶ οἱ πρεσβύτεροι ὑμῶν
ἐνυπνίοις ἐνυπνιασθήσονται·
18. καί γε ἐπὶ τοὺς δούλους μου
καὶ ἐπὶ τὰς δούλας μου ἐν
ταῖς ἡμέραις ἐκείναις ἐκχεῶ
ἀπὸ τοῦ πνεύματός μου, καὶ
προφητεύσουσιν.
19. καὶ δώσω τέρατα ἐν τῷ οὐρανῷ
ἄνω καὶ σημεῖα ἐπὶ τῆς γῆς
κάτω, αἷμα καὶ πῦρ καὶ ἀτμίδα
καπνοῦ.
20. ὁ ἥλιος μεταστραφήσεται εἰς
σκότος καὶ ἡ σελήνη εἰς αἷμα,
πρὶν ἐλθεῖν ἡμέραν κυρίου
τὴν μεγάλην καὶ ἐπιφανῆ.
21. καὶ ἔσται πᾶς ὃς ἐὰν ἐπι-
καλέσηται τὸ ὄνομα κυρίου
σωθήσεται.

πᾶσαν σάρκα, καὶ προφητεύσουσιν οἱ υἱοὶ ὑμῶν καὶ αἱ
θυγατέρες ὑμῶν, καὶ οἱ πρεσβύτεροι ὑμῶν ἐνύπνια ἐνυπ-
νιασθήσονται, καὶ οἱ νεανίσκοι
ὑμῶν ὁράσεις ὄψονται·
29. καὶ ἐπὶ τοὺς δούλους μου καὶ
ἐπὶ τὰς δούλας ἐν ταῖς ἡμέραις
ἐκείναις ἐκχεῶ ἀπὸ τοῦ πνεύματός μου·
30. καὶ δώσω τέρατα ἐν οὐρανῷ,
καὶ ἐπὶ τῆς γῆς αἷμα καὶ πῦρ
καὶ ἀτμίδα καπνοῦ.
31. ὁ ἥλιος μεταστραφήσεται εἰς
σκότος καὶ ἡ σελήνη εἰς αἷμα
πρὶν ἐλθεῖν τὴν ἡμέραν κυρίου
τὴν μεγάλην καὶ ἐπιφανῆ.
32. καὶ ἔσται πᾶς ὃς ἐὰν ἐπι-
καλέσηται τὸ ὄνομα κυρίου
σωθήσεται.

Acts iii. 22, 23 (cf. vii. 37).

22. Μωυσῆς μὲν εἶπεν ὅτι προφήτην
ὑμῖν ἀναστήσει κύριος ὁ θεὸς
ἐκ τῶν ἀδελφῶν ὑμῶν ὡς
ἐμέ· αὐτοῦ ἀκούσεσθε κατὰ
πάντα ὅσα ἂν λαλήσῃ πρὸς
ὑμᾶς.
23. ἔσται δὲ πᾶσα ψυχὴ ἥτις ἂν
μὴ ἀκούσῃ τοῦ προφήτου
ἐκείνου ἐξολεθρευθήσεται ἐκ
τοῦ λαοῦ.

Deut. xviii. 15 ff.

15. προφήτην ἐκ τῶν ἀδελφῶν σου
ὡς ἐμὲ ἀναστήσει σοι κύριος
ὁ θεός σου, αὐτοῦ ἀκού-
σεσθε.
16. κατὰ πάντα ὅσα ᾐτήσω παρὰ
κυρίου . . .
19. καὶ ὁ ἄνθρωπος ὃς ἐὰν μὴ
ἀκούσῃ ὅσα ἂν λαλήσῃ ὁ
προφήτης ἐκεῖνος ἐπὶ τῷ
ὀνόματί μου, ἐγὼ ἐκδικήσω
ἐξ αὐτοῦ.

Lev. xxiii. 29.

πᾶσα ψυχὴ ἥτις μὴ ταπεινωθή-
σεται ἐν αὐτῇ τῇ ἡμέρᾳ ταύτῃ
ἐξολοθρευθήσεται ἐκ τοῦ λαοῦ
αὐτῆς.

Acts iii. 25.

ὑμεῖς ἐστὲ οἱ υἱοὶ τῶν προφητῶν καὶ τῆς διαθήκης ἧς
ὁ θεὸς διέθετο πρὸς τοὺς
πατέρας ὑμῶν, λέγων πρὸς
Ἀβραάμ· καὶ ἐν τῷ σπέρματί
σου εὐλογηθήσονται πᾶσαι
αἱ πατριαὶ τῆς γῆς.

Acts vii. 3.

καὶ εἶπεν πρὸς αὐτόν· ἔξελθε
ἐκ τῆς γῆς σου καὶ τῆς
συγγενείας σου, καὶ δεῦρο εἰς
τὴν γῆν ἣν ἄν σοι δείξω.

Acts vii. 6, 7.

6. ἐλάλησεν δὲ οὕτως ὁ θεὸς ὅτι
ἔσται τὸ σπέρμα αὐτοῦ πάροικον ἐν γῇ ἀλλοτρίᾳ, καὶ
δουλώσουσιν αὐτὸ καὶ κακώσουσιν ἔτη τετρακόσια·

7. καὶ τὸ ἔθνος ᾧ ἂν δουλεύσουσιν
κρινῶ ἐγώ, ὁ θεὸς εἶπεν, καὶ
μετὰ ταῦτα ἐξελεύσονται καὶ
λατρεύσουσίν μοι ἐν τῷ τόπῳ
τούτῳ.

Acts vii. 32.

ἐγὼ ὁ θεὸς τῶν πατέρων σου,
ὁ θεὸς Ἀβραὰμ καὶ Ἰσαὰκ
καὶ Ἰακώβ. ἔντρομος δὲ
γενόμενος Μωυσῆς οὐκ ἐτόλμα
κατανοῆσαι.

Acts vii. 33, 34.

33. εἶπεν δὲ αὐτῷ ὁ κύριος· λῦσον
τὸ ὑπόδημα τῶν ποδῶν σου,

Gen. xxii. 18.

καὶ ἐνευλογηθήσονται ἐν τῷ
σπέρματί σου πάντα τὰ ἔθνη
τῆς γῆς, ἀνθ' ὧν ὑπήκουσας
τῆς ἐμῆς φωνῆς.

Gen. xii. 1.

καὶ εἶπε κύριος τῷ Ἀβραμ·
ἔξελθε ἐκ τῆς γῆς σου καὶ ἐκ
τῆς συγγενείας σου καὶ ἐκ
τοῦ οἴκου τοῦ πατρός σου,
καὶ δεῦρο εἰς τὴν γῆν ἣν ἂν
σοι δείξω.

Gen. xv. 13, 14.

13. καὶ ἐρρέθη πρὸς Ἀβραμ·
γινώσκων γνώσῃ ὅτι πάροικον
ἔσται τὸ σπέρμα σου ἐν γῇ
οὐκ ἰδίᾳ, καὶ δουλώσουσιν
αὐτοὺς καὶ κακώσουσιν αὐτοὺς
καὶ ταπεινώσουσιν αὐτοὺς
τετρακόσια ἔτη.

14. τὸ δὲ ἔθνος ᾧ ἐὰν δουλεύσωσι
κρινῶ ἐγώ· μετὰ δὲ ταῦτα
ἐξελεύσονται ὧδε μετὰ ἀπο-
σκευῆς πολλῆς.

Exod. iii. 6.

καὶ εἶπεν· ἐγώ εἰμι ὁ θεὸς τοῦ
πατρός σου, θεὸς Ἀβραὰμ καὶ
θεὸς Ἰσαὰκ καὶ θεὸς Ἰακώβ.
ἀπέστρεψε δὲ Μωυσῆς τὸ
πρόσωπον αὐτοῦ· εὐλαβεῖτο
γὰρ κατεμβλέψαι ἐνώπιον τοῦ
θεοῦ.

Exod. iii. 5, 7-10.

5. ὁ δὲ εἶπε· μὴ ἐγγίσῃς ὧδε
λῦσαι τὸ ὑπόδημα ἐκ τῶν

THE USE OF THE SEPTUAGINT IN ACTS 91

ὁ γὰρ τόπος ἐφ' ᾧ ἕστηκας
γῆ ἁγία ἐστίν.

34. ἰδὼν εἶδον τὴν κάκωσιν τοῦ
λαοῦ μου τοῦ ἐν Αἰγύπτῳ,
καὶ τοῦ στεναγμοῦ αὐτοῦ
ἤκουσα, καὶ κατέβην ἐξελέσθαι αὐτούς· καὶ νῦν δεῦρο
ἀποστείλω σε εἰς Αἴγυπτον.

ποδῶν σου, ὁ γὰρ τόπος ἐν ᾧ
σὺ ἕστηκας γῆ ἁγία ἐστί....
7. εἶπε δὲ κύριος πρὸς Μωυσῆν·
ἰδὼν εἶδον τὴν κάκωσιν τοῦ
λαοῦ μου τοῦ ἐν Αἰγύπτῳ,
καὶ τῆς κραυγῆς αὐτῶν ἀκήκοα
ἀπὸ τῶν ἐργοδιωκτῶν· οἶδα
γὰρ τὴν ὀδύνην αὐτῶν,
8. καὶ κατέβην ἐξελέσθαι αὐτοὺς
ἐκ χειρὸς τῶν Αἰγυπτίων
καὶ ἐξαγαγεῖν αὐτοὺς ἐκ τῆς
γῆς ἐκείνης, καὶ εἰσαγαγεῖν
αὐτοὺς εἰς γῆν ἀγαθὴν καὶ
πολλήν,...
10. καὶ νῦν δεῦρο ἀποστείλω σε
πρὸς Φαραὼ βασιλέα Αἰ-
γύπτου, καὶ ἐξάξεις τὸν λαόν
μου τοὺς υἱοὺς Ἰσραὴλ ἐκ
γῆς Αἰγύπτου.

Acts vii. 42, 43.

42. ἔστρεψεν δὲ ὁ θεὸς καὶ παρέδωκεν αὐτοὺς λατρεύειν τῇ
στρατιᾷ τοῦ οὐρανοῦ, καθὼς
γέγραπται ἐν βίβλῳ τῶν
προφητῶν· μὴ σφάγια καὶ
θυσίας προσηνέγκατέ μοι ἔτη
τεσσεράκοντα ἐν τῇ ἐρήμῳ,
οἶκος Ἰσραήλ;
43. καὶ ἀνελάβετε τὴν σκηνὴν
τοῦ Μολὸχ καὶ τὸ ἄστρον
τοῦ θεοῦ Ῥομφά, τοὺς τύπους
οὓς ἐποιήσατε προσκυνεῖν
αὐτοῖς. καὶ μετοικιῶ ὑμᾶς
ἐπέκεινα Βαβυλῶνος.

Amos v. 25-27.

25. μὴ σφάγια καὶ θυσίας προσηνέγκατέ μοι, οἶκος Ἰσραήλ,
τεσσαράκοντα ἔτη ἐν τῇ
ἐρήμῳ;
26. καὶ ἀνελάβετε τὴν σκηνὴν τοῦ
Μολὸχ καὶ τὸ ἄστρον τοῦ θεοῦ
ὑμῶν Ῥαιφάν, τοὺς τύπους
αὐτῶν οὓς ἐποιήσατε ἑαυτοῖς·
27. καὶ μετοικιῶ ὑμᾶς ἐπέκεινα
Δαμασκοῦ, λέγει κύριος, ὁ θεὸς
ὁ παντοκράτωρ ὄνομα αὐτῷ.

Acts vii. 49, 50.

49. ὁ οὐρανός μοι θρόνος, καὶ ἡ γῆ
ὑποπόδιον τῶν ποδῶν μου·
ποῖον οἶκον οἰκοδομήσετέ μοι,
λέγει κύριος, ἢ τίς τόπος τῆς
καταπαύσεώς μου;

Isaiah lxvi. 1, 2.

οὕτως λέγει κύριος· ὁ οὐρανός
μου θρόνος, καὶ ἡ γῆ ὑπο-
πόδιον τῶν ποδῶν μου· ποῖον
οἶκον οἰκοδομήσετέ μοι; καὶ
ποῖος τόπος τῆς καταπαύσεώς
μου;

50. οὐχὶ ἡ χείρ μου ἐποίησεν ταῦτα πάντα;

2. πάντα γὰρ ταῦτα ἐποίησεν ἡ χείρ μου, καί ἐστιν ἐμὰ πάντα ταῦτα, λέγει κύριος . . .

Acts xiii. 22.

Psalms lxxxviii. 21.

καὶ μεταστήσας αὐτὸν ἤγειρεν τὸν Δαυεὶδ αὐτοῖς εἰς βασιλέα, ᾧ καὶ εἶπεν μαρτυρήσας· εὗρον Δαυεὶδ τὸν τοῦ Ἰεσσαί, ἄνδρα κατὰ τὴν καρδίαν μου, ὃς ποιήσει πάντα τὰ θελήματά μου.

εὗρον Δαυὶδ τὸν δοῦλόν μου, ἐν ἐλέει ἁγίῳ ἔχρισα αὐτόν.

Acts xiii. 34.

Isaiah lv. 3.

ὅτι δὲ ἀνέστησεν αὐτὸν ἐκ νεκρῶν μηκέτι μέλλοντα ὑποστρέφειν εἰς διαφθοράν, οὕτως εἴρηκεν ὅτι δώσω ὑμῖν τὰ ὅσια Δαυεὶδ τὰ πιστά.

. . . εἰσακούσατέ μου, καὶ ζήσεται ἐν ἀγαθοῖς ἡ ψυχὴ ὑμῶν, καὶ διαθήσομαι ὑμῖν διαθήκην αἰώνιον, τὰ ὅσια Δαυὶδ τὰ πιστά.

Acts xiii. 41.

Hab. i. 5.

ἴδετε, οἱ καταφρονηταί, καὶ θαυμάσατε καὶ ἀφανίσθητε, ὅτι ἔργον ἐργάζομαι ἐγὼ ἐν ταῖς ἡμέραις ὑμῶν, ἔργον ὃ οὐ μὴ πιστεύσητε ἐάν τις ἐκδιηγῆται ὑμῖν.

ἴδετε οἱ καταφρονηταὶ καὶ ἐπιβλέψατε, καὶ θαυμάσατε θαυμάσια καὶ ἀφανίσθητε· διότι ἔργον ἐγὼ ἐργάζομαι ἐν ταῖς ἡμέραις ὑμῶν ὃ οὐ μὴ πιστεύσητε ἐάν τις ἐκδιηγῆται.

Acts xiii. 47.

Isaiah xlix. 6.

οὕτω γὰρ ἐντέταλται ἡμῖν ὁ κύριος· τέθεικά σε εἰς φῶς ἐθνῶν τοῦ εἶναί σε εἰς σωτηρίαν ἕως ἐσχάτου τῆς γῆς.

. . . ἰδοὺ δέδωκά σε εἰς διαθήκην γένους, εἰς φῶς ἐθνῶν, τοῦ εἶναί σε εἰς σωτηρίαν ἕως ἐσχάτου τῆς γῆς.

Acts xv. 16-18.

Amos ix. 11, 12.

16. μετὰ ταῦτα ἀναστρέψω καὶ ἀνοικοδομήσω τὴν σκηνὴν Δαυεὶδ τὴν πεπτωκυῖαν, καὶ τὰ κατεστραμμένα αὐτῆς ἀνοικοδομήσω καὶ ἀνορθώσω αὐτήν,

11. ἐν τῇ ἡμέρᾳ ἐκείνῃ ἀναστήσω τὴν σκηνὴν Δαυὶδ τὴν πεπτωκυῖαν, καὶ ἀνοικοδομήσω τὰ πεπτωκότα αὐτῆς, καὶ τὰ κατεσκαμμένα αὐτῆς ἀναστήσω, καὶ ἀνοικοδομήσω αὐτὴν καθὼς αἱ ἡμέραι τοῦ αἰῶνος,

17. ὅπως ἂν ἐκζητήσωσιν οἱ κατά-

12. ὅπως ἐκζητήσωσιν οἱ κατά-

THE USE OF THE SEPTUAGINT IN ACTS 93

λοιποὶ τῶν ἀνθρώπων τὸν
κύριον, καὶ πάντα τὰ ἔθνη
ἐφ' οὓς ἐπικέκληται τὸ ὄνομά
μου ἐπ' αὐτούς,
18. λέγει κύριος ποιῶν ταῦτα
γνωστὰ ἀπ' αἰῶνος.

λοιποὶ τῶν ἀνθρώπων, καὶ
πάντα τὰ ἔθνη ἐφ' οὓς ἐπικέκληται τὸ ὄνομά μου ἐπ'
αὐτούς, λέγει κύριος ὁ ποιῶν
πάντα ταῦτα.

Acts xxiii. 5.

ἔφη τε ὁ Παῦλος· οὐκ ᾔδειν,
ἀδελφοί, ὅτι ἐστὶν ἀρχιερεύς·
γέγραπται γὰρ ὅτι ἄρχοντα
τοῦ λαοῦ σου οὐκ ἐρεῖς κακῶς.

Exod. xxii. 28.

θεοὺς οὐ κακολογήσεις, καὶ ἄρχοντα τοῦ λαοῦ σου οὐ κακῶς
ἐρεῖς.

It will be noticed that, with one exception, viii. 32, 33, the above quotations all occur in speeches, and all except three came in the first half of the book. It now becomes necessary to study the sixteen free quotations more closely, following the guidance of Dr. Swete, who thus distinguishes the causes which may have produced variations from the standard text of the LXX.: [1] "It may be due to (i.) loose citation, or to (ii.) the substitution of a gloss for the precise words which the writer professes to quote, or to (iii.) a desire to adapt a prophetic context to the circumstances under which it was thought to have been fulfilled, or to (iv.) the fusing together of passages drawn from different contexts. Of the variations which cannot be ascribed to one or other of these causes, some are (v.) recensional, whilst others are (vi.) translational, and imply an independent use of the original, whether by the Evangelist, or by the author of some collection of excerpts which he employed."

(i.) The following variations may be ascribed to free citation, natural in an age when modern aids to study were not available.[2] The last two clauses of ii. 17 are inverted; ἄνω and κάτω are inserted in ii. 19; vii. 3 is shortened by the substitution of καὶ δεῦρο for καὶ ἐκ τοῦ οἴκου τοῦ πατρός σου; in vii. 32 ὁ θεὸς Ἀβραὰμ καὶ Ἰσαὰκ καὶ Ἰακώβ is read for ὁ θεὸς Ἀ. καὶ θ. Ἰ. καὶ θ.

[1] *Int.* p. 394.
[2] See Sanday in *Oxford Studies in the Synoptic Problem*, pp 16-19.

'I. ;[1] in vii. 33, 34, Exod. iii. 5, 7-10 is shortened considerably, and εἰς Αἴγυπτον takes the place of πρὸς Φαραὼ βασιλέα Αἰγύπτου ; in vii. 50 οὐχὶ ἡ χείρ μου ἐποίησεν ταῦτα πάντα ; is read for πάντα γὰρ ταῦτα ἐποίησεν ἡ χείρ μου ; in xiii. 34 διαθήκην αἰώνιον is omitted and διαθήσομαι replaced by δώσω ; in xiii. 41, Hab. i. 5 is shortened and modified.

(ii.) There seem to be no clear cases of glosses made by the writer unless perhaps the change of ἑαυτοῖς into προσκυνεῖν αὐτοῖς in vii. 43.

(iii.) In i. 20 αὐτῶν of the LXX. is changed to αὐτοῦ to apply to Judas, and ἐν αὐτῇ then takes the place of ἐν τοῖς σκηνώμασιν αὐτῶν, which is no longer applicable. The repetition of καὶ προφητεύσουσι in ii. 18 makes the prophecy more appropriate to the events. In vii. 43 Βαβυλῶνος is put for Δαμασκοῦ to bring the quotation into accord with the history of the Jews ; while in xxiii. 5 ἄρχοντα is substituted for the less suitable ἄρχοντας, though the MSS. of the LXX. vary.

(iv.) The fusing of two or more passages plays an important part in the quotations of Acts. In ii. 17 the prophecy from Joel is introduced by ἐν ταῖς ἐσχάταις ἡμέραις, taken from Isa. ii. 2 ; iii. 22, 23 is a conflation of Deut. xviii. 15, 16, 19 and Lev. xxiii. 29 ; iii. 25 is a conflation of Gen. xxii. 18 with Gen. xii. 3, with possibly a reminiscence of Ps. xxi. 28 ; vii. 6, 7 is a conflation of Gen. xv. 13, 14 with Exod. ii. 22 and iii. 12 ; in vii. 34 we have τοῦ στεναγμοῦ αὐτοῦ ἤκουσα instead of τῆς κραυγῆς αὐτῶν ἀκήκοα, probably owing to the influence of Exod. ii. 24 ; a remarkable combination is found in xiii. 22, where Ps. lxxxix. 21, 1 Sam. xiii. 14, Isa. xliv. 28 make a composite quotation ;[2] while xv. 16-18 is a conflation of Amos ix. 11-12 with Jer. xii. 15.[3]

[1] Lk. xx. 37 has LXX. formula. Perhaps Exod. ii. 24b, τῆς διαθήκης αὐτοῦ τῆς πρὸς 'Α. καὶ 'Ι. καὶ 'Ι., has influenced Acts vii. 32, seeing that Exod. ii. 24 a has influenced vii. 34 ; see below, under section (iv.).

[2] See 1 Clem. xviii., where the first two passages are combined. It is generally supposed that Acts and 1 Clem. are both dependent on some collection of Messianic proof-texts. See R. Harris, *Exp.*, November 1906, " The Use of Testimonies in the early Christian Church " ; Moffatt, *Int.* pp. 23-25.

[3] Swete, p. 399.

THE USE OF THE SEPTUAGINT IN ACTS

(v.) The quotations in Acts show the usual New Testament tendency in that they follow the A text of the LXX. as against the B.[1] The subjoined list gives the readings in which Acts agrees with A; the B readings are added in brackets. For the sake of completeness we also give the minor variants in favour of the A text in the quotations already treated under A (ii.) above.

ii. 17 ἐνυπνίοις (ἐνύπνια), ii. 18 καί γε (καί), ἐπὶ τὰς δούλας μου (ἐπὶ τὰς δούλας), vii. 40 ἐκ γῆς Αἰγύπτου (ἐξ Αἰγύπτου), vii. 43 τοὺς τύπους (τοὺς τύπους αὐτῶν), vii. 49 μοι θρόνος (μου θρόνος), viii. 32 τοῦ κείροντος αὐτόν (τοῦ κείροντος), xiii. 41 ἐκδιηγῆται ὑμῖν (B om. ὑμῖν), xiii. 47 τέθεικά σε εἰς φῶς (δέδωκά σε εἰς διαθήκην γένους, εἰς φῶς) xv. 16 κατεστραμμένα with Αᵇ (κατεσκαμμένα), xv. 17 ὅπως ἂν (ὅπως), τὸν κύριον (B om.), xxiii. 5 οὐκ ἐρεῖς κακῶς (οὐ κακῶς ἐρεῖς). In vii. 49 Acts (except in B) agrees with Isa. lxvi. 1 B (ἡ δὲ γῆ) against A (καὶ ἡ γῆ).

(vi.) In one instance Acts seems at first sight to be nearer the Massoretic text than the LXX., namely, iii. 25 = Gen. xxii. 18, where LXX. renders Heb. כֹּל גּוֹיֵי הָאָרֶץ by πάντα τὰ ἔθνη, while Acts with its πᾶσαι αἱ πατριαὶ τῆς γῆς has הָאָרֶץ represented. But it is better to suppose that such passages as Gen. xii. 3, πᾶσαι αἱ φυλαὶ τῆς γῆς, or Ps. xxi. 28, πᾶσαι αἱ πατριαὶ τῶν ἐθνῶν, have influenced the quotation in Acts, than to assume that the writer has any acquaintance with the original Hebrew, or is making an independent translation from an Aramaic version of the speech.

A. *In the Speeches.*—The less direct references to the LXX. are so numerous that any attempt to point them out in detail must be reserved for the commentator. Many informal quotations and allusions are distinguished in Westcott and Hort's text by the employment of uncials, but even after their careful work gleanings remain for their successors. In the present connection the use of the Old Testament in the speeches of Acts, apart from formal citations, has a twofold interest, in that it (i.)

Informal quotations, reminiscences, and allusions.

[1] *Ibid.* p. 395.

96 THE COMPOSITION AND PURPOSE OF ACTS

confirms the results reached in the previous section, (ii.) throws light on the author's method of composition and the sources he may have had at his disposal.

(i.) It is clear from the loose manner in which the allusions are woven into the text that it would be hazardous to use them as a source from which to draw textual conclusions; but it is legitimate to use the evidence, such as it is, for the purpose of confirming the results already attained. The first three headings under which Dr. Swete accounts for variations from the standard text of the LXX. do not apply here. The fourth cause, conflation of different passages, is seen clearly at work. Thus Acts iii. 13 ὁ θεὸς 'Αβραὰμ καὶ 'Ισαὰκ καὶ 'Ιακώβ, ὁ θεὸς τῶν πατέρων ἡμῶν, ἐδόξασεν τὸν παῖδα αὐτοῦ, is formed from Exod. iii. 6 ἐγώ εἰμι ὁ θεὸς τοῦ πατρός σου, θεὸς 'Αβραὰμ καὶ θεὸς 'Ισαὰκ καὶ θεὸς 'Ιακώβ (cf. 1 Kg. xviii. 36)+Isa. lii. 13 ὁ παῖς μου . . . δοξασθήσεται. The following conflations among others are also worthy of attention: Acts ii. 24 λύσας τὰς ὠδῖνας τοῦ θανάτου=Ps. xvii. 5, etc. + Job xxxix. 2 (see below); vii. 5=Gen. xii. 7+xvii. 8+Deut. ii. 5; vii. 10=Gen. xxxix. 4, 21+xli. 40, 41+Ps. civ. 21; x. 35, 36=Ps. xiv. 2+cvi. 20+Isa. lii. 7.

Passing on to recensional variations, we note a few instances where the A text of the LXX. is followed against the B. If iv. 24 (cf. xiv. 15) is based on Exod. xx. 11, the addition of καὶ τὴν θάλασσαν agrees with A (and B[ab mg]) against B, but the phrase occurs also in Ps. cxlv. 6. In vii. 30 ἐν φλογὶ πυρός agrees with Exod. iii. 2 A, B having ἐν πυρὶ φλογός. The formation of the sentence in vii. 14, 15 leads to the conclusion that it is drawn from Deut. x. 22, where A gives the number that went down to Egypt as 75 (B gives 70, but cf. Gen. xlvi. 27, Exod. i. 5, which have 75). However, in xvii. 25 the phrase διδούς . . . πνοήν recalls the B text of Isa. xlii. 5 (where A has δοὺς πνοήν. The passage is known to the author of Acts, cf. xxvi. 17 with Isa. xlii. 7.) [1]

---

[1] In v. 10 the rare word ἐκψύχειν occurs—ἔπεσεν δὲ παραχρῆμα πρὸς τοὺς πόδας αὐτοῦ καὶ ἐξέψυξεν; cf. v. 4 and xii. 23. Possibly it may have been

Finally, there are three passages in which an independent translation is perhaps to be postulated.

1. The curious phrase λύσας τὰς ὠδῖνας τοῦ θανάτου occurs in ii. 24.[1] In the LXX., e.g. 2 Sam. xxii. 6, Ps. xvii. 5, cxiv. 3, ὠδῖνες θανάτου translates חֶבְלֵי מָוֶת (probably = " cords of death "). As λύσας suits the meaning "cords" better than "pains," it has been suggested that the phrase goes back to an independent knowledge of the Hebrew, or an Aramaic version of Peter's speech. But an explanation from the LXX. only will suffice, that the phrase is a conflation of ὠδῖνες θανάτου with Job xxxix. 2 ἠρίθμησας δὲ μῆνας αὐτῶν πλήρεις τοκετοῦ αὐτῶν, ὠδῖνας δὲ αὐτῶν ἔλυσας.

2. In ii. 30 = Ps. cxxxi. 11, Acts has ἐκ καρποῦ τῆς ὀσφύος αὐτοῦ καθίσαι ἐπὶ τὸν θρόνον αὐτοῦ, which is an independent version, diverging both from the Hebrew and Greek texts. While the possibility of the verse having come through the medium of Aramaic cannot be excluded, a free quotation from memory is a more likely explanation of the variation.

3. The well-known Messianic passage Ps. cxvii. 22 is quoted in iv. 11 in a unique form—οὗτός ἐστιν ὁ λίθος ὁ ἐξουθενηθεὶς ὑφ' ὑμῶν τῶν οἰκοδόμων, ὁ γενόμενος εἰς κεφαλὴν γωνίας. This is quite a different version from that of the LXX.—λίθον ὃν ἀπεδοκίμασαν οἱ οἰκοδομοῦντες, οὗτος ἐγενήθη εἰς κεφαλὴν γωνίας— which is repeated in Matt. xxi. 42; Mark xii. 10; Lk. xx. 17; 1 Pet. ii. 7; Barn. vi. 4. Now in Lk. xx. 17 the author follows Mark, whereas here he has an independent translation. The variation seems more than can be accounted for by a lapse of memory. It should be noted that the version of Acts is even further removed from the original Hebrew than is the LXX.; however ἐξουδενεῖν is used as well as ἀποδοκιμάζειν by the LXX. to translate מאס.

As these three passages all occur in the Petrine speeches of

---

suggested by its use in Judges iv. 21A καὶ ἐξέψυξεν, of Sisera's death. Cf. Judges v. 27 ἀνὰ μέσον τῶν ποδῶν αὐτῆς . . . ἔπεσεν.

[1] Also in Polyc. i. 2 in this form λύσας τὰς ὠδῖνας τοῦ ᾅδου.

the opening chapters, it is legitimate, though not necessary, to interpret the first two in the light of the conclusions reached with reference to the last, and to suppose that the source used by Luke is responsible for the peculiarities of the text. In this case the speeches in question are not simply the free compositions of the writer.[1]

(ii.) Two of the speeches of Acts require special treatment in regard to their use of the Old Testament. Stephen's speech at Jerusalem in chap. vii. and Paul's at Antioch in chap. xiii. are little more than centos of Old Testament quotations and allusions. They recall the past history of the Jews and are naturally couched in biblical language.[2]

Taking the speeches as a whole, there is a clear distinction between the first and second half of the Acts in respect to the influence of the Old Testament; in the later chapters it is far less marked. For example, Peter's speech to the people at Jerusalem in chap. iii. is full of Old Testament allusions, while Paul's Jerusalem speech in chap. xxii. has hardly any (Westcott and Hort give no uncials at all). The rule is not universally carried out; *e.g.* in the Areopagus speech, chap. xvii., delivered to an audience supposed to be unfamiliar with the Jewish Scriptures, there are a number of literary reminiscences—24 = Exod. xx. 11; 25 = Isa. xlii. 5; 26 = Deut. xxxii. 8 (?); 31 = Ps. ix. 8. Again, some of the utterances put into the mouth of Peter are simply strings of LXX. phrases. Two examples may be given:

---

[1] In xii. 11 ἐξαπέστειλεν ὁ κύριος τὸν ἄγγελον καὶ ἐξείλατό με ἐκ χειρὸς Ἡρώδου, there seems to be a reminiscence of Dan. Theod. iii. 95 ὃς ἀπέστειλεν τὸν ἄγγελον αὐτοῦ καὶ ἐξείλατο (LXX. ἔσωσε) τοὺς παῖδας αὐτοῦ. This is in keeping with the tendency of the N.T. quotations to support Theodotion against the LXX.; see Swete, *Int.* pp. 48, 395.

[2] In these two speeches there are a number of passages where Acts, agreeing with later Jewish tradition, has modified the O.T. records. Thus in vii. 2 the command comes to Abraham when still in Mesopotamia—Philo and the Samaritan Pentateuch have the same tradition; in vii. 16 Jacob and the patriarchs are buried at Sichem in Abraham's tomb (perhaps mere carelessness on the part of the writer); in vii. 23, 30 Moses is forty years old when he flees to Midian and spends forty years there; in xiii. 21 Saul's reign lasts forty years. For further "Midrashic elements" in Stephen's speech see the full note in *Encycl. Bibl.* 4791.

THE USE OF THE SEPTUAGINT IN ACTS

Acts viii.

21. οὐκ ἔστιν σοι μερὶς οὐδὲ κλῆρος ἐν τῷ λόγῳ τούτῳ, ἡ γὰρ καρδία σου οὐκ ἔστιν εὐθεῖα ἔναντι τοῦ θεοῦ.

22. μετανόησον οὖν ἀπὸ τῆς κακίας σου ταύτης, καὶ δεήθητι τοῦ κυρίου εἰ ἄρα ἀφεθήσεταί σοι ἡ ἐπίνοια τῆς καρδίας σου.

23. εἰς γὰρ χολὴν πικρίας καὶ σύνδεσμον ἀδικίας ὁρῶ σε ὄντα.

Deut. xii. 12.
οὐκ ἔστιν αὐτῷ μερὶς οὐδὲ κλῆρος . . ; cf. xiv. 28.

Ps. lxxvii. 37.
ἡ δὲ καρδία αὐτῶν οὐκ εὐθεῖα μετ' αὐτοῦ.

Jer. viii. 6.
οὐκ ἔστιν ἄνθρωπος ὁ μετανοῶν ἀπὸ τῆς κακίας αὐτοῦ.

Deut. xxix. 18.
ῥίζα ἄνω φύουσα ἐν χολῇ καὶ πικρίᾳ.

Isa. lviii. 6.
πάντα σύνδεσμον ἀδικίας.

In x. 14, xi. 8 we have a short version of Ezekiel's protest.

Acts x. 14.
ὁ δὲ Πέτρος εἶπεν· μηδαμῶς, κύριε, ὅτι οὐδέποτε ἔφαγον πᾶν κοινὸν καὶ ἀκάθαρτον.

Acts xi. 8.
εἶπον δέ· μηδαμῶς κύριε, ὅτι κοινὸν ἢ ἀκάθαρτον οὐδέποτε εἰσῆλθεν εἰς τὸ στόμα μου.

Ezek. iv. 14.
καὶ εἶπα· μηδαμῶς, κύριε θεὲ τοῦ Ἰσραήλ· εἰ ἡ ψυχή μου οὐ μεμίανται ἐν ἀκαθαρσίᾳ καὶ θνησιμαῖον καὶ θηριάλωτον οὐ βέβρωκα ἀπὸ γενέσεώς μου ἕως τοῦ νῦν, οὐδὲ εἰσελήλυθεν εἰς τὸ στόμα μου πᾶν κρέας ἕωλον.

There is a tendency to represent God or the risen Lord as speaking in an Old Testament manner. Thus in chap. xxvi. Paul's speech has practically no Old Testament affinities until he describes the words of the ascended Jesus.

Acts xxvi.

15. ἀνάστηθι καὶ στῆθι ἐπὶ τοὺς πόδας σου.

16. εἰς τοῦτο γὰρ ὤφθην σοι, προχειρίσασθαί σε ὑπηρέτην καὶ μάρτυρα ὧν τε εἶδές με ὧν τε ὀφθήσομαί σοι.

Ezek. ii. 1.
στῆθι ἐπὶ τοὺς πόδας σου.

17. ἐξαιρούμενός σε ἐκ τοῦ λαοῦ καὶ ἐκ τῶν ἐθνῶν, εἰς οὓς ἐγὼ ἀποστέλλω σε ἀνοῖξαι ὀφθαλμοὺς αὐτῶν.

18. τοῦ ἐπιστρέψαι ἀπὸ σκότους εἰς φῶς καὶ τῆς ἐξουσίας τοῦ Σατανᾶ ἐπὶ τὸν θεόν, τοῦ λαβεῖν αὐτοὺς ἄφεσιν ἁμαρτιῶν καὶ κλῆρον ἐν τοῖς ἡγιασμένοις πίστει τῇ εἰς ἐμέ.

Jer. i.
8. μετὰ σοῦ ἐγώ εἰμι τοῦ ἐξαιρεῖσθαί σε.
7. ὅτι πρὸς πάντας οὓς ἐὰν ἐξαποστείλω σε πορεύσῃ.

1 Chron. xvi. 35.
καὶ ἐξελοῦ ἡμᾶς ἐκ τῶν ἐθνῶν.

Isa. xlii. 7.
ἀνοῖξαι ὀφθαλμοὺς τυφλῶν.

16.
ποιήσω αὐτοῖς τὸ σκότος εἰς φῶς.

Deut. xxxiii. 3, 4.
πάντες οἱ ἡγιασμένοι ὑπὸ τὰς χεῖράς σου . . . κληρονομίαν συναγωγαῖς Ἰακώβ.

Compare also ix. 15 = Jer. i. 10, xviii. 9 = Gen. xxvi. 24.

Throughout the first part of the book the speeches have a decidedly Old Testament ring. That this is not so much the case in the second part may be due to the fact that the writer was relying less on his own powers of composition, and that he had at his disposal reminiscences, written or otherwise, of the actual words used.

B. *In the Narrative.*—The distinction between speeches and narrative must be carefully observed. As is well known, to compose speeches appropriate to the occasion and put them into the mouth of the various characters was a recognised practice among the historians of antiquity. The existence of a large amount of traditional Old Testament material in the speeches of Acts may likewise be conceded without prejudice to the literary honesty of our author. But such a latitude cannot be transferred without question to the narrative. If we find descriptions of events moulded to any serious extent on the LXX., the character of a conscientious historian claimed in the prologue to the Gospel is considerably impaired.

THE USE OF THE SEPTUAGINT IN ACTS 101

An instance will show what is meant. The story of the meeting of Philip with the Ethiopian eunuch seems *prima facie* to be a straightforward record of actual events. Yet it may be plausibly maintained that the narrative has been built up out of hints contained in Zephaniah and other parts of the Old Testament.

Acts viii.

26. ἀνάστηθι καὶ πορεύου κατὰ μεσημβρίαν ἐπὶ τὴν ὁδὸν τὴν καταβαίνουσαν ἀπὸ Ἰερουσαλὴμ εἰς Γάζαν, αὕτη ἐστὶν ἔρημος.

27. καὶ ἀναστὰς ἐπορεύθη καὶ ἰδοὺ ἀνὴρ Αἰθίοψ εὐνοῦχος δυνάστης Κανδάκης βασιλίσσης Αἰθιόπων, ὃς ἦν ἐπὶ πάσης τῆς γάζης αὐτῆς, [ὃς] ἐληλύθει προσκυνήσων εἰς Ἰερουσαλήμ.

39. πνεῦμα κυρίου ἥρπασεν τὸν Φίλιππον.

Zeph. ii. 4.
(= Hebrew קוּם לְךָ)
Ἄζωτος (cf. Acts viii. 40 Φίλιππος εὑρέθη εἰς Ἄζωτον) μεσημβρίας ἐκριφήσεται... Γάζα διηρπασμένη ἔσται.

Zeph. ii. 11, 12.
(= Hebrew וַיֵּלֶךְ הִנֵּה וְקָם)
καὶ προσκυνήσουσιν αὐτῷ ἕκαστος ἐκ τοῦ τόπου αὐτοῦ, πᾶσαι αἱ νῆσοι τῶν ἐθνῶν. καὶ ὑμεῖς, Αἰθίοπες, τραυματίαι ῥομφαίας μού ἐστε.

iii. 10.
ἐκ περάτων ποταμῶν Αἰθιοπίας προσδέξομαι ἐν διεσπαρμένοις μου, οἴσουσιν θυσίας μοι. Cf. Ps. lxvii. 32. Isa. lvi. 3.

iii. 4.
οἱ προφῆται αὐτῆς πνευματοφόροι. Cf. 1 Kg. xviii. 12, 2 Kg. ii. 16: Ezek. iii. 12; viii. 3.

Note the double meaning of γάζα, " Gaza " and " treasure"; also the possibility that εὐνοῦχος and δυνάστης represent the same Hebrew word, since LXX. translates סָרִים by both words, see Jer. xli. (xxxiv.) 19. The point at issue is, whether this is merely a natural colouring of the narrative by Old Testament language, or whether the facts themselves have been put together out of hints contained in the Old Testament. As the passage considered in isolation hardly warrants a definite conclusion, a list of passages is given where it is possible that similar influences may have been at work. Where the bare references are given, it must be taken as implying that the parallels seem of little importance. It will be understood that this list might be enlarged considerably.

i. 3 = Tob. xii. 19, see Simpson in Charles, *Apocrypha*, i. 234.
ii. 2 = Isa. xxix. 6.
ii. 4 = Isa. xxviii. 11, cf. 1 Cor. xiv. 21.
ii. 41 = Exod. xxxii. 28, see *Zeitschrift f. N.T. Wiss.* (1913), pp. 94-6.[1]
iii. 8 = Isa. xxxv. 6 : Leaping of the lame as a sign of the Messianic kingdom.
iv. 34 = Deut. xv. 4.
v. 2 = Jos. vii. 1.
viii. 26, 27 = Zeph. ii. 4, etc., see above.
viii. 39 = 1 Kg. xviii. 12, 2 Kg. ii. 16, Ezek. iii. 12, viii. 3, Zeph. iii. 4, Bel 36.
ix. 10-12 = 1 Sam. iii. 4, Isa. xlii. 6.
ix. 18 = Tob. xi. 12, see above, p. 76.
ix. 38 ff. = Num. xxii. 5-41.

The parallels here are worked out in detail by Krenkel, *Josephus und Lukas*, pp. 194-6. A specimen is given here with the similarities of language underlined.

x. 19, 20. εἶπεν τὸ πνεῦμα αὐτῷ ... ἀναστὰς ... καὶ πορεύου σὺν αὐτοῖς
x. 21. τίς ἡ αἰτία δι' ἣν πάρεστε;
x. 33. πάρεσμεν
xi. 14. Πέτρον, ὃς λαλήσει ῥήματα πρὸς σέ.

Num. xxii. 20. καὶ ἦλθεν ὁ θεὸς πρὸς Βαλαὰμ νυκτὸς καὶ εἶπεν αὐτῷ, εἰ καλέσαι σε πάρεισιν οἱ ἄνθρωποι οὗτοι, ἀναστὰς ἀκολούθησον αὐτοῖς· ἀλλὰ τὸ ῥῆμα ὃ ἐὰν λαλήσω πρὸς σέ, τοῦτο ποιήσεις.

---

[1] Three thousand were added to the Church in one day, just as 3000 members of the Church in the wilderness perished in one day. A faint vein of reminiscence of the story of Moses is possibly to be detected in Acts i.-vii. The story of Pentecost in Acts ii. is generally acknowledged to owe something to Jewish legends of the giving of the Law on Mount Sinai. The forty days in Acts i. 4 in connection with the Mount of Olives in i. 12 recall Moses' forty days in the mount, Exod. xxiv. 18. The apostles in Acts vi., like Moses in Exod. xviii., appoint helpers to share with them the burden of administration. Christ is depicted as the new Moses in Acts iii. 22, cf. vii. 35 ; see Heb. iii., where the comparison is made explicit.

The case for direct influence would be strengthened if the order of the passages in Acts corresponded in any way to that in Numbers, but on the contrary they are picked out arbitrarily from all parts of chaps. ix.-xi. in order to make the required parallels. It is probable that nothing more is demonstrated than that these chapters are composed in a strongly LXX. style.¹

ix. 40 = 2 Kg. iv. 35, cf. Tob. xi. 7. ἡ δὲ ἤνοιξεν τοὺς ὀφθαλμούς of Acts may be taken from καὶ ἤνοιξεν τὸ παιδάριον τοὺς ὀφθαλμούς of Kings. These are the only passages in the Greek Bible where ἀν. τ. ὀφθ. is used of a *man* opening his own eyes (but cf. Acts ix. 8). It is used of an opening by some one else, 2 Kg. vi. 20, Matt. xx. 33, John ix. 10 ff., x. 21, xi. 37, Acts xxvi. 18; also of God opening his eyes as in 2 Kg. xix. 16, Bar. ii. 17, Dan. ix. 18.

xii. 23   = 2 Kg. xix. 35, 2 Macc. ix. 5, 9, see above, p. 75.
xvi. 14, 16 = 1 Sam. xxviii. 7, 21, 23, see Selwyn, *St. Luke the Prophet*, pp. 50, 51.
xx. 10   = 2 Kg. iv. 34, 1 Kg. xvii. 23, see Selwyn, pp. 58 ff.

The parallels are by no means close, as will be seen by an examination of the passages.

The majority of these instances are of slight importance. In none is the resemblance so striking as in the verses of Zephaniah with which we started.

It appears from the foregoing that the LXX. has been an important factor in the composition of some of the speeches of Acts, but that its influence in moulding the narrative has been slight, except in chaps. viii.-xii. Now viii., ix. 31-43, x. 1-xi. 18, xii. form a well-defined section, which may be termed the Acts of Peter and Philip. There can be little doubt that Luke regarded these chapters as genuine history, but it may well

Conclusions.

---

¹ It is hard to see what purpose, except that of humour, is served when Krenkel adduces Num. xxii. 28 καὶ ἤνοιξεν ὁ θεὸς τὸ στόμα τῆς ὄνου, in illustration of Acts x. 34 ἀνοίξας δὲ Πέτρος τὸ στόμα. If veins of reminiscence are sought here, it is better to use Gen. xviii., where the parallels run consecutively; cf. Acts x. 17, 19, 23-25 with Gen. xviii. 2, 3-8, 16, xix. 2.

be that the tradition had been affected, even to the extent of remoulding, by certain passages of the LXX. before it was brought to his notice. Other ways in which Luke betrays the influence of the LXX. were discussed in the earlier part of the chapter. No very definite results were attained, but the investigators of other problems of Acts may find the facts as here stated useful as criteria by which to test the soundness of their own conclusions.[1]

[1] A complete treatment of the subject would include an extension of the inquiry to the third Gospel, which space forbids. All that can be attempted is to point out the probable results of such an investigation. It would probably be found that (i.) Luke's modifications of the Marcan narrative were sometimes dictated by a desire to make it accord more closely with (a) a well-known incident of the LXX. or (b) conventional methods of treating a story, and that (ii.) the narratives found in Lk. only are more dependent on conventional material than is the case with the special matter of the other Gospels. The following examples will illustrate these positions.

(i.) (a) In leaving the upper room and proceeding across the Kedron to the Mount of Olives, Christ is represented as consciously fulfilling prophecy (τὸ περὶ ἐμοῦ τέλος ἔχει, Lk. xxii. 37). The analogy with the experience of David, who went along the same path in his flight from Absalom, would strike any student of the Old Testament. Resemblances between the two histories occur in all four Gospels (cf. e.g. 2 Sam. xv. 14 ἀνάστητε καὶ φύγωμεν, with John xiv. 31 ἐγείρεσθε, ἄγωμεν ἐντεῦθεν), but by far the most striking parallels are found in the additions made by Luke. See Lk. xxii. 32 f., which seems to be modelled on 2 Sam. xv. 20 f.

Lk. xxii.	2 Sam. xv.
32. καὶ σύ ποτε ἐπιστρέψας στήρισον τοὺς ἀδελφούς σου.	20. ἐπιστρέφου καὶ ἐπίστρεψον τοὺς ἀδελφούς σου μετὰ σοῦ. . . .
33. ὁ δὲ εἶπεν αὐτῷ Κύριε, μετὰ σοῦ ἕτοιμός εἰμι καὶ εἰς φυλακὴν καὶ εἰς θάνατον πορεύεσθαι.	21. καὶ ἀπεκρίθη Ἐθὶ τῷ βασιλεῖ καὶ εἶπεν Ζῇ Κύριος καὶ ζῇ ὁ κύριός μου ὁ βασιλεύς, ὅτι εἰς τὸν τόπον οὗ ἐὰν ᾖ ὁ κύριός μου, καὶ ἐὰν εἰς θάνατον καὶ ἐὰν εἰς ζωήν, ὅτι ἐκεῖ ἔσται ὁ δοῦλός σου.

(b) Two details added by Luke to Mark's account of the end of the crucifixion (xxiii. 47 f., the " glorifying of God " and the return of the spectators to their homes) agree with the end of Enoch's life as described in 2 Enoch (Slavonic Enoch) lxvii. 1-3. " When Enoch had talked to the people, the Lord sent out darkness on to the earth, and there was darkness, and it covered those men standing and talking with Enoch, and they took Enoch up to the highest heaven, where the Lord is; and he received him and placed him before his face, and the darkness went off from the earth, and light came again. And the people saw and understood not how Enoch had been taken, and *glorified*

God, and found a roll in which was traced: 'the invisible God,' and *all went to their homes* " (Charles' translation*).

(ii.) Chaps. i. and ii. are, as is well known, saturated with LXX. words and phrases. For instance, the annunciations of the births of John and Jesus Christ are modelled on the annunciation of the birth of Samson in Judges xiii., as the transcribing of a few verses will show.

Lk. i.

11. ὤφθη δὲ αὐτῷ ἄγγελος Κυρίου . . .
13. εἶπεν δὲ πρὸς αὐτὸν ὁ ἄγγελος.
7. καὶ οὐκ ἦν αὐτοῖς τέκνον, καθότι ἦν ᾿Ελεισάβετ στεῖρα.
31. ἰδοὺ συλλήμψῃ . . . υἱόν.
15. καὶ οἶνον καὶ σίκερα οὐ μὴ πίῃ.
31. καὶ ἰδοὺ συλλήμψῃ ἐν γαστρὶ καὶ τέξῃ υἱόν.
15. καὶ πνεύματος ἁγίου πλησθήσεται ἔτι ἐκ κοιλίας μητρὸς αὐτοῦ.
31. καὶ καλέσεις τὸ ὄνομα αὐτοῦ ᾿Ιησοῦν.

cf. Matt. i. 21.

αὐτὸς γὰρ σώσει τὸν λαὸν αὐτοῦ ἀπὸ τῶν ἁμαρτιῶν αὐτῶν.

ii. 23.

Ναζωραῖος κληθήσεται.

Judges xiii.

3. καὶ ὤφθη ἄγγελος Κυρίου πρὸς τὴν γυναῖκα καὶ εἶπε πρὸς αὐτήν ᾿Ιδοὺ σὺ στεῖρα καὶ οὐ τέτοκας, καὶ συλλήμψῃ υἱόν.
4. καὶ νῦν φύλαξαι δὴ καὶ μὴ πίῃς οἶνον καὶ μέθυσμα, καὶ μὴ φάγῃς πᾶν ἀκάθαρτον.
5. ὅτι ἰδοὺ σὺ ἐν γαστρὶ ἔχεις καὶ τέξῃ υἱόν, καὶ σίδηρος ἐπὶ τὴν κεφαλὴν αὐτοῦ οὐκ ἀναβήσεται, ὅτι ναζὶρ θεοῦ ἔσται τὸ παιδάριον ἀπὸ τῆς κοιλίας· καὶ αὐτὸς ἄρξεται τοῦ σῶσαι τὸν ᾿Ισραὴλ ἐκ χειρὸς Φυλιστιίμ.

Again, in a characteristic Lukan parable, such as the Prodigal Son, free use is made of traditional material.

Lk. xv.

15. καὶ πορευθεὶς ἐκολλήθη ἑνὶ τῶν πολιτῶν τῆς χώρας ἐκείνης, καὶ ἔπεμψεν αὐτὸν εἰς τοὺς ἀγροὺς αὐτοῦ βόσκειν χοίρους.
18. ἀναστὰς πορεύσομαι πρὸς τὸν πατέρα μου καὶ ἐρῶ αὐτῷ· πάτερ, ἥμαρτον εἰς τὸν οὐρανὸν καὶ ἐνώπιόν σου,
19. οὐκέτι εἰμὶ ἄξιος κληθῆναι υἱός σου· ποίησόν με ὡς ἕνα τῶν μισθίων σου.
20. καὶ δραμὼν ἐπέπεσεν ἐπὶ τὸν τράχηλον αὐτοῦ.

Aḥiḳar viii.

34. Syr. (Charles, *Apoc.* ii. 775):
"Forgive me this my folly: and I will tend thy horses and feed thy pigs which are in thy house, and I shall be called evil."

24b. Arm. (Charles, *ibid.*): "Father, I have sinned unto thee, forgive me, and I will be to thee a slave henceforth for ever."

Tob. xi. 8.

καὶ προσδραμοῦσα ῎Αννα ἐπέπεσεν ἐπὶ τὸν τράχηλον τοῦ υἱοῦ αὐτῆς.

Cf. also Lk. xiii. 7-9 = Aḥiḳar Syr. viii. 35.

A note by H. St. J. Thackeray in *J.T.S.* xiv. (1913), pp. 389 ff., shows the kind of discoveries that still await investigators.

---

* See my note in *J.T.S.* xv. (1914), p. 597, from which, by permission of the editors, this paragraph is taken.

IV

THE USE OF MARK IN THE GOSPEL ACCORDING TO LUKE

By F. C. Burkitt

<small>Treatment of Mark's narrative in the third Gospel.</small>   In the following pages it is assumed that the author of the third Gospel used the Gospel of Mark practically in its extant form, and also that where he does thus follow Mark he had no other source available. The differences between 'Luke' and Mark in these parallel narratives are consequently regarded as due to the literary manner of the later writer, in a word, to his style and methods of writing history, not to fresh, independent information.

<small>Luke's other sources.</small>   In addition to Mark the Third Evangelist, no doubt, had other sources for many parts of his Gospel to which there are no Marcan parallels, sources such as the mysterious 'Q.' In the Acts, which is simply Volume II. to the Third Gospel, there must also have been 'sources' used, written or oral. But we do not possess them, and we cannot reconstruct them. We can, however, study in detail the way in which 'Luke' has treated Mark, and judge whether he treated it fairly or unfairly, with historical acumen, or unintelligently. Our aim will be to form some idea of the value of the rest of his work as a picture of the early days of Christianity.

<small>'Luke' and the Marcan order.</small>   One point may be noted at the beginning. We must beware of confounding the narrative of Mark with the actual course of events in the Ministry of Jesus. No doubt Mark is the best

source we have, the nearest both in time and information to the actual happenings. And I assume that for all the public life of Jesus, with the possible exception of the actual Passion, Luke's other sources gave him nothing like a detailed itinerary or connected story of our Lord's public career. Now Mark obviously offers us a very imperfect itinerary at the best. During the final sojourn in Jerusalem it does assume the nature of a diary, and indeed from x. 32 onwards I see no reason to doubt that it is written in strict chronological order. We may go back further and say that, after Peter's confession at Caesarea Philippi, the approaching visit to Jerusalem is held steadily in view. But from the beginning of the Gospel to Mark viii. 26 the impression I get is of a series of anecdotes, arranged only roughly in the order of time, or indeed in any order at all. The evidence may show that Luke was as dependent as we are upon Mark for his information about large sections of the Gospel narrative, but he had the same right as Loisy or Harnack, or any other modern writer, to rearrange the tale told by his authority into what he might consider to be a form essentially more true to the underlying reality.

A somewhat different question which may be asked is, how far 'Luke's' sources may be supposed to reappear intact, or essentially intact, in his own narrative ? In other words, how far could we reconstruct Mark out of Luke ? The answer must be that we can do very little. The Gospel of Luke is very far from being a "second edition of Mark, revised and enlarged," as I have elsewhere ventured to call the Gospel of Matthew.[1] Luke is a fresh historical work, in which the Marcan thread is often dropped, and the bits of Mark are ingeniously fitted into the Lucan scheme by alterations and omissions which would have made their original setting unrecognisable, were it not for the fact that the original is still extant. *St. Luke's free use of his source.*

To take the clearest instance, what information did 'Luke' possess about the final Visit to Jerusalem ? I leave out for the *(a) The visit to Jerusalem.*

[1] *Earliest Sources for the Life of Jesus*, p. 97.

present everything after the Last Supper. This Visit to Jerusalem was the most public period of the whole Ministry; in the words of Acts xxvi. 26: "The thing was not done in a corner." Here, therefore, an historical inquirer might be expected to amass new material. But as a matter of fact 'Luke' seems to have had little beyond the narrative of Mark. There is the story of Zacchaeus, the parable of the Pounds, the saying about Stones crying out, and the story of Christ weeping over Jerusalem. All the rest of Luke xix.-xxi. is a mere rewriting of Mark x. 32–xiii. It may be added that the opening section of Luke xxii. is directly taken from Mark xiv.: 'Luke' does not seem to have had any information about the policy of the Chief Priests or the 'betrayal' by Judas beyond what Mark tells us.

The treatment of Mark by Luke.

First let us ask how this section of Mark fares in the Lucan narrative. To begin with, the section of Mark occupies nearly nine pages in Westcott and Hort, while in Luke it occupies only eight pages, notwithstanding the fresh stories of Zacchaeus and the parable of the Pounds. Thus the Marcan narrative appears in Luke considerably curtailed.

What is more important is that the chronological links have been removed. The chronology of Holy Week rests on Mark, and Mark alone. It is from Mark that we infer that the entry into Jerusalem took place on "Palm Sunday," the cleansing of the Temple on the Monday in Holy Week, the vigorous disputes with Chief Priests and others in Jerusalem on the Tuesday, the Supper at the house of Simon the Leper on the Wednesday. All this reckoning by days disappears in Luke of set purpose. Jesus is 'teaching' daily in the Temple (Luke xix. 47); on "one of the days" he is asked about his authority (xx. 1), and in xxi. 7 ff. there is nothing to show that the great eschatological sayings were not spoken in the very courts of the Temple itself, with all Jerusalem listening. These sayings are nothing more than Luke's version of Mark xiii. 3-37, *i.e.* words spoken in private to four intimate friends outside the city on the Mount of Olives, at a moment when Jesus had apparently abandoned his public activity in Jerusalem.

Thus we have not merely to do with the dropping of a few dates : a considerably different historical picture is presented in Luke from that in Mark. In Mark, so it seems to the present writer, we can trace some real reminiscences of an eye-witness. There is no valid reason to question the accuracy of the reckoning by days. The entry into Jerusalem in Mark ends lamely with an afternoon visit to the Temple (Mark xi. 11), just as it may have done in " real life " ; the very curious story of the cursing of the fig tree is told in two sections, each of which is accompanied by details which, while they somewhat embarrass the miraculous effect (as compared with the way the tale is told in Matthew), yet at the same time suggest that the story is based on real recollections of a real incident. Further on in the story of the Great Commandment the answer of Jesus according to Mark begins with the recitation of the *Shema‘*, as the answer of a Jew should begin, and Jesus and the questioning Scribe part with friendly speeches.[1] All these things have something of the objective, almost pointless, quality of a spectator's reminiscences. They do not help on the drama, however valuable they may be to the modern investigator, whose desire is not to receive a mental impression from ancient writers, but to collect material for reconstructing the scenes for himself.

The corresponding narrative in 'Luke,' on the other hand, is admirably staged to produce an impression. The march of the great drama is not cut up into days. There is nothing left to indicate the length of Jesus' visit to Jerusalem. By day he remains in the Temple teaching, by night he used to stay outside the city by the Mount of Olives. Every day the 'people' assembled early in the Temple to hear Him (Luke xxi. 37, 38).

---

[1] The answer about the Great Commandment is given elsewhere by St. Luke, so he leaves out the whole of the section of Mark in which the story is told except a few words (Luke xx. 39, 40, taken from Mark xii. 32, 34*b*), which as they appear in the Third Gospel give no idea at all of the character of the tale from which they were extracted !

This goes far beyond Mark xii. 38a. One gets the impression not merely of sympathy from the Galilean crowd, but of dominance over the whole population of Jerusalem. According to Luke the entry of Jesus had been that of a monarch taking possession of his own. The followers of Jesus hail him as King (xix. 38). He weeps, indeed, at the sight of the City, for he knows the fate in store for it forty years later. But on his arrival he turns out the tradesmen at once from the Temple, and converts it into his place of instruction. There is no indecision or delay : the challenge to the rulers of Jerusalem is thrown down at once. And further, I venture to think it would have passed the analytical skill of our critics, if they had not the narrative of Mark before them, to discover that the Zacchaeus story was a later insertion into the main fabric, while the story of the blind man was not. Who would have guessed that the Weeping over Jerusalem (Luke xix. 42-44) was an insertion by the Evangelist into a narrative which did not originally contain it ? If we only knew of the story through the tale as Luke tells it, it is likely that *vv.* 42-44 would have been accepted as taken from the main source, and *vv.* 45, 46, which give the Cleansing of the Temple, would have been regarded as a secondary addition. And this would have been all the more plausible, because the allusion to the future siege would appear to be borne out by xxi. 24 (Jerusalem trodden down by Gentiles). We should not have known that xxi. 24 was only Luke's rationalising interpretation of the far vaguer Apocalyptic phrase about "the abomination of desolation," so that the only consistency is the consistency of the Evangelist's additions and alterations, not the consistency of his materials.

The fact is that 'Luke' is far too skilful and intelligent a writer to yield very much to cross-examination. He tells us what he wants to tell us with lucidity and charm, but you cannot get much more out of him than what he has chosen to say. It is the naïve, the clumsy, the stupid writers that let out what they try to suppress, and 'Luke' is neither clumsy nor stupid, and he certainly is not naïve.

But now let us turn to 'Luke's' tale, as it is in itself. What would have been the effect of his story of the Last Days in Jerusalem upon readers who had no other Gospel to compare with it? St. Luke wrote that Theophilus might know upon what the matters about which he had been instructed were based (περὶ ὧν κατηχήθης λόγων τὴν ἀσφάλειαν). No doubt these matters, λόγοι, were of the nature of doctrines and 'mysteries,' foundations of the Christian faith, such as are enumerated in Heb. vi. 1, 2, rather than tales about Jesus the Nazarene. The object of the Evangelist was not to compile a scientific historical memoir so much as to give a clear and readable account of the *origines* of the Christian 'Way,' an account which, in style and treatment, should be worthy of its noble subject. Such an aim includes general historical truth as apprehended by St. Luke, for the Birth, Career, Death, and Resurrection of the Lord had really happened; but it did not necessarily include meticulous accuracy of detail. To give the broad effects their proper values it is often necessary to suppress details which, in the opinion of the artist, are not significant.

Judged by this broader standpoint, what are we to say of the portion of Luke which we are considering? Surely it is a fine and well-proportioned story. 'Luke' takes the tales and sayings which he finds in his authority, and tells them in his own incomparable style. Much of Mark's wording remains, but here and there it is effectively paraphrased. A few additional sayings, one at least of great dramatic interest, are incorporated into the narrative, but so skilfully that no break is perceptible. We learn that Jesus entered the City accompanied by a festive procession of his disciples, that his first public act was to turn out the sellers from the Temple, that the grandees of Jerusalem were hostile, but did not know at first what to do in face of the popular interest. Jesus speaks openly in the Temple about John the Baptist, about God's martyred Messengers to those in authority, about questions of the Law, and against the self-seeking expounders of it. As we might expect, Luke does not fail to tell

The story in Luke.

the story of the Widow's Mite, before ending his narrative (as Mark had done before him) with an announcement of the impending woes and an exhortation to watch for the impending judgment.

In all this Luke has followed his source. He identifies the coming troubles with the Roman war and the Destruction of Jerusalem—a very questionable piece of exegesis—and he has altered the language of Mark almost in every verse. Moreover, as I have pointed out already, you cannot reconstruct from the narrative of Luke either a diary or an itinerary for the stay of Jesus in Jerusalem. But the general ethical and rhetorical effect of the whole is very much the same as the narrative in Mark. It is still the story of the Galilean Prophet coming up to the Holy City, and there discoursing about Jewish problems and coming into collision with the Jewish authorities. It is the same play restaged, not a fresh drama. And when we remember how differently St. Luke is able to arrange a narrative, as, for instance, the last visit of Paul to Jerusalem and his subsequent trial at Caesarea, we shall realise that here in the Gospel he has treated his source not only with freedom and skill, but also with intelligence and substantial fairness.

The speeches in Luke. Before leaving 'Luke's' account of our Lord at Jerusalem we may consider what light our investigation throws upon the old question of the historical value of the 'speeches' in Acts. The "eschatological discourse" given in Luke xxi. 7-36 is in many respects similar to the speeches in Acts. How would it appear to us if we were wholly dependent upon the text of Luke?

In the first place the unimpeachable witness of the Concordance shows the vocabulary of Luke xxi. 7-36 to be characteristically Lucan. The details are best left to a footnote, but the fact admits of no dispute.[1] The style is eminently Lucan : in addition

---

[1] Of the special Lucan peculiarities noticed by Sir John Hawkins there occur δὲ καί xxi. 16 (Hawkins, p. 37), εἶπεν παραβολήν, xxi. 29 (Hawk. 39), τίς with optative, xxi. 33 (Hawk. 46), τοῦ with inf., xxi. 22 (Hawk. 48). The following words are Lucan : ἀντειπεῖν, ἀπολογεῖσθαι, γονεῖς, δεῖσθαι, ἐπαίρειν, ἐφιστάναι, καιροί (pl.), κτᾶσθαι, λαός, ἡ οἰκουμένη, πλησθῆναι, προβάλλειν, πτοεῖσθαι, συγγενεῖς, φίλος. Further, προσδοκία, συνοχή, and στρατόπεδον

to those words and locutions enumerated in the footnote we may notice the phrase "set in your hearts," which is also found in Luke i. 66 and Acts v. 4. Still more striking is the fact that the words, "not a hair of your head shall perish," reappear in Acts xxvii. 34, in the midst of 'Luke's' account of Paul's shipwreck.

With these linguistic facts in our minds it would have been impossible not to give full weight to the suspicious circumstance that the siege of Jerusalem by hostile armies is foretold in so many words in v. 20: it would be fairly urged that it is unlikely that the words as they stand in that verse could have been what Jesus said. Finally, there is something improbable in the general situation as given in Luke. Was this discourse the sort of thing that all the people came early to hear in the Temple (xxi. 38)? And, when closely looked at, many of the verses, e.g. 12-19, are inappropriate to a public speech. Indeed, this very inappropriateness might have been made the excuse, among critics of a conservative and apologetic turn, for saving a few of the sayings as possibly based on tradition. But the rest would have seemed to be nothing more than a free composition by 'Luke.' We might have given him credit for remembering to supply an eschatological air to the discourse, but we should have regarded it as a mere literary effort, no more historical than the speech of Paul at Athens.

Well, but what are the facts? Of this speech, Luke xxi. 7-36, we do know the genesis. It is Luke's version of Mark xiii. 3-37. Let us now take Mark xiii. 3-37 and see how our theories fare. Some of what has been said in the preceding paragraphs remains. There *is* a large Lucan element in Luke xxi. 7-36, an element which belongs to the Evangelist and does not go back to the sayings of Jesus. Luke has rewritten the discourse throughout. For the most part this is a mere matter of style. After all, we are dealing with translations, with a rendering of

---

do not occur elsewhere in the N.T., but προσδοκᾳν and συνέχειν are characteristically Lucan, and Luke has a certain taste for military words.

the Lord's words into an alien literature. An impression of them was required, rather than a report, something, moreover, not too uncouth for Greek ears. And is not Luke xxi. 7-36 dignified and impressive? Note, too, how in v. 26 the evangelist emphasises the psychological element in the terrors to come rather than the mere signs in the material heavens. The special Lucan words and phrases noted above do turn out to be 'Luke's' words, not those of his source, but he has not altered the general tenor of what was in the source. Not all his alterations, indeed, are improvements, and not all his interpretations of his sources prove to be correct. This is notably the case with xxi. 20, the verse that so much too clearly indicates the siege of Jerusalem. But when we compare it with its immediate original, Mark xiii. 14, we see that, whatever else may be said of it, it is not a mere free composition by 'Luke.' It is 'Luke's' *interpretation* of the saying of Jesus about Daniel's "abomination of desolation," a saying which, as we read it in Mark, implies some general apocalyptic catastrophe rather than so mundane and secular an affair as a Roman campaign. However, this is not the place to discuss the older form of this traditional saying; my point is, that the Lucan form is, after all, based on tradition. The form which Luke gave it is, as we see, coloured by the events of A.D. 70, but the underlying substance of it is older.

More important still is the fact that the speech itself proves not to be 'Luke's' compilation. It may be, of course, that the speech in Mark xiii. is not, strictly speaking, historical; the discussion of this belongs to another inquiry and need not be pursued here. But we see it was known to 'Luke': the reason that an eschatological speech is put into our Lord's mouth in Luke xxi. is because 'Luke' found an eschatological speech of our Lord reported in Mark xiii. He has, indeed, suppressed the illuminating circumstance that this forecast of the future was spoken in private to a few intimate associates of Jesus, not declaimed in the Temple courts. But that circumstance, though of great importance to historical investigators, would have been of little interest to Theophilus : I daresay most Christian congregations, even at the present day, care very little whether Jesus spoke about the future to his disciples in the Temple or on the Mount of Olives.

However this may be, what concerns us here is not that Luke has changed so much, but that he has invented so little. It may indicate that the same has happened with some of the speeches in Acts. At the same time it warns us not to trust too closely to the times or the places in which these speeches in Acts are said to have been delivered, or to place any special reliance upon details of their phraseology. With Luke xxi. 7-36 in our minds we may indeed have greater confidence that Peter's great speech after Pentecost (Acts ii. 14-36) is not an invention of 'Luke,' but we must be prepared to keep before us the possibility that in the source from which Luke took it Peter spoke in private, and that the wording of the speech was quite different,—the wording, but not the general sense. For after all the chief point is, that the general tenor of Luke xxi. 7-36 and Mark xiii. 4-37 is one and the same. What does 'Luke' tell Theophilus that Jesus said about the future ? He tells him that Jesus said, "First of all, do not imagine that every calamity is the last. You will suffer grievously for my sake, but it will be given to you what to say : in the end your steadfastness will be rewarded. When evil comes, do not imagine the Holy Place will be inviolable : escape and hide while there is time, for inconceivable destruction will happen in heaven and earth ! But when things are at their worst, the Son of Man will come from heaven as Daniel foretold, and will gather his saints from their hiding-places. It is all as inevitable as the leaves on the fig-tree every summer, and it will surely come in this generation, though no one knows the exact moment. So watch ! Watch ! Keep yourselves on the alert, lest you be caught unprepared ! "

Is this a summary of the speech in Luke ? It would stand equally well for that in Mark. The length and detail of the common summary is a measure of the general faithfulness of

'Luke' to his sources, and of the confidence which we may reasonably place in his reports of speeches in his second volume.

<small>Luke's general method.</small> We must now return to our main thesis. What is true of 'Luke's' account of the final visit of Jesus to Jerusalem is generally true of all the rest of the Gospel. Surely we may confess, in the words I have already had occasion to use, that "in style and treatment it is worthy of its noble subject," and that the sketch which it gives of the Ministry of Jesus is characterised by "general historical truth." We read in the Third Gospel of the preaching of the Baptist and the Baptism of Jesus, followed by his retirement for a while into the desert. When he is ready (Luke iv. 13 f.) he returns to Galilee as a Herald of good tidings for the poor and the oppressed. He teaches his message in the synagogues, and we are given a specimen of his method, which serves as a sort of overture to the tale of the Ministry (iv. 16-30). Then follow anecdotes of wonderful deeds, the call of Peter and others, a collection of ethical counsels for disciples, sayings about the Baptist, sayings about forgiveness of sins. All this takes place while Jesus goes from place to place, accompanied by his twelve chosen associates and certain grateful women who have been healed by him, and in return support the itinerant Herald of the Kingdom of God (viii. 1-3). After this we read of a short visit over the Lake, of the feeding of 5000 men near Bethsaida, but otherwise there is no indication of absence from the towns and villages of Galilee. Jesus, however, knows well that the time for his "exodus" is at hand (ix. 31, 44, 51), and so he sets his face to go to Jerusalem. It is apparently a leisurely journey through cities and villages (xiii. 22). No itinerary of it can be constructed, except that it begins by going south through Samaritan country (ix. 52 f.), proceeds through Samaria and Galilee (xvii. 11), and so reaches Jericho (xviii. 35). Theophilus certainly possessed no atlas, and probably all Palestinian villages were much alike to him, if not to 'Luke' himself.[1]

[1] See Appendix B on *Vestigia Christi*.

I do not think 'Luke' intends us to follow the footsteps of Jesus and his companions. To do so would be to distract our eyes from the goal. *Respice finem* is all that these later notices of place signify. Chorazin, Bethsaida, Capernaum have not repented, soon it will be too late; the Son of Man must be handed over to the Gentiles; God will avenge His elect speedily, before the careless expect it, yet not till after some delay, and He is always ready to forgive those who repent. Something like this is the impression which these central chapters of the Third Gospel are meant to convey, and surely they do convey it with consummate art, with the simplicity that is the highest art. And much of this simplicity and directness of effect comes, no doubt, from the fact that Luke is not inventing, but simply retelling, without essential change, tales that are to a large extent founded on the reminiscences of those who had heard the Master. The result is a picture, a sketch, an impression, most admirable from the point of view from which it is taken. But it tells us little more than what is on the surface. It tells us what Luke wished to tell Theophilus, but very little of the nature of the sources from which Luke worked or of those features in the history which Luke did not think worth while to record.

One of the sources from which Luke worked was the Gospel of Mark. Luke iv. 31-44, v. 12-vi. 19, viii. 4-ix. 50, xviii. 15-43, and xix. 29-xxii. 14 corresponds to Mark i. 29-39, i. 40-iii. 19, iii. 31-ix. 50 (with gaps), x. 13-52, and xi. 1-xiv. 17 respectively. When this list is analysed it will be found that very little of Mark's material has been dropped, except the section Mark vi. 45-viii. 26, comprising disputes with Rabbis upon ' clean ' and ' unclean,' the long journey to the north outside the Holy Land, the second Feeding (of the 4000), and a couple of incidental anecdotes connected with these events. To the modern historian these things are important, but they add little to the sacred drama, and their omission is rather an artistic gain than a loss. Everything else omitted from Mark by Luke is either small in bulk or represented elsewhere in his Gospel from another source. We get, therefore,

Treatment of the Marcan source.

the impression that Luke tends to utilise his sources in full. Further, the material is given almost entirely in Mark's order; there are hardly any transpositions or regroupings of material, and that is all the more noteworthy, as many of the tales in the early part of Mark appear to have been thrown together almost haphazard. This adherence to the order of the source does not come from any theoretical objection to change, seeing that St. Luke places the scene of our Lord's rejection in 'Nazara' by his own townsfolk at the beginning of the public Ministry, contrary to historical probability but for what may be called literary effect. Yet in doing so he does not transpose the Marcan narrative; it would be more accurate to say that he drops the Marcan narrative when he comes to it (at the beginning of Luke ix.), for Luke iv. 16-30 is not based on Mark vi. 1-6, though it may owe something to Luke's acquaintance with those verses.

General conclusions.
The preceding sketch of the literary methods of the Third Evangelist has been undertaken not so much to appraise the value of his Gospel as to endeavour to find out what hopes the investigator of the beginnings of the Christian Church may have of "getting behind" the narrative of Acts and, what is still more important, of estimating with what degree of confidence we may trust the story there told.

One clear result is a demonstration of the difficulty, if not the impossibility, of "getting behind" Luke by a mere close consideration of what he chooses to tell us. There is a certain resemblance between the way the visit of Jesus to Jerusalem is told in Luke and the way the early history of the Church is told in Acts i.-xii. I have ventured elsewhere [1] to conjecture that both Gospel and Acts are here based on the earlier narrative of Mark. The chief difference to us on this hypothesis is that the Gospel chapters are based on the part of Mark's work which is extant, while Acts i.-xii. corresponds to the lost part of Mark that followed Mark xvi. 8. But from what has been said above

[1] *Earliest Sources*, pp. 79 f.

it is impossible to reconstruct the lost narrative of Mark from the text of Acts. The most we can do is to note the probability that such-and-such an episode is ultimately Marcan.[1] Further, we cannot reconstruct the chronology of Luke's source any more than we could reconstruct the chronology of Holy Week from Luke xix.-xxiii. And when we consider how indifferent Luke in his Gospel appears to be to the details of Palestinian topography—quite a contrast, it may be remarked in passing, to his intelligent interest in Asia Minor and Macedonia—we must renounce any hope of making anything consecutive or consistent in the wanderings of Peter and others as recorded in these early chapters of Acts. The story of Peter and Cornelius *may* be a tale rewritten by Luke and put for effect out of its chronological setting, just as Mark vi. 1-6 appears in Luke out of its chronological setting. We cannot guess at the relative proportion which the several events bore to each other in the source from the way they are told in Acts.

It may be remarked in passing that the vagueness as to place and time characteristic of Luke as compared with Mark is an argument for accepting the statements made by Paul about himself in Galatians and elsewhere, rather than for attempting to combine them with the *prima facie* meaning of the corresponding statements in Acts.

What reason, then, have we for trusting the narrative of the first twelve chapters of Acts? Or rather, what measure of credence ought we to give them? Roughly, this: we should give them much the same measure of credence that we give to the story of the visit of Jesus to Jerusalem as related in Luke, as compared with the story in Mark. It seems to me that this measure of credence may be compared with that which we give to Shakespeare's *Henry V.* as compared with Hall's *Chronicle*. Shakespeare's play is very much more than a work of fancy. If we knew nothing about the great Lancastrian except what we get from Shakespeare, we should still have a great deal of solid

[1] The clearest example is the story of Rhoda (Acts xii. 13 ff.).

information. We should know the outlines of the history and the heroic story of Agincourt. We should also have a not unhistorical picture of the character of the heroic king, drawn for us by a great literary genius. Something of this is what we have in the Lucan writings. In the Gospel we can partially control the author's tale, for we possess one of his sources. In the Acts we are almost entirely dependent on what he has chosen to tell us.

V

THE INTERNAL EVIDENCE OF ACTS

By The Editors

It may be well at this point to make a superficial comparison of Acts with the results of these investigations. It is clear that the writer was thoroughly impregnated with the Greek Old Testament; there is no good evidence that he was acquainted with the Hebrew original. He is able to use Greek like a Greek, and in this respect he is more Greek than Josephus, but he does not always write thus; sometimes, perhaps, owing to the influence of Aramaic originals which he translated, sometimes owing to his imitation of the Septuagint. But it is also obvious—and this is of great importance—that, at least in the Gospel, he was nearer to the old Jewish literary tradition than was Josephus. He does not, indeed, copy his sources with quite the same verbal fidelity as does the Chronicler, but he paraphrases and polishes far less than Greek custom would have demanded. Above all, in the Gospel he does not invent speeches. A purely Greek writer of history would have respected the facts of the life of Jesus, but would have freely invented speeches. Luke, on the contrary, respects the sayings of Jesus more than the narrative of events which lay before him. That is Jewish: to give teaching and law rather than the accurate and full narration of events is the ideal. But is this equally true of Acts? The question is all the more delicate, because it must be admitted that Luke had a special reason for respecting the speeches of Jesus: they had authority. It is a different matter with the speeches of the apostles, and though there is a presumption in favour of similarity of treatment, the possibility is open that the writer followed somewhat different plans in Acts and in the Gospel. We have not, however, in Acts any of the original documents used by the writer, and the questions of his sources and his plan of composition can only be carried further after a discussion of relatively modern researches into the internal evidence of the book itself.

The 'we' sections and twofold division of the book recognised.   The first period of the history of research on this subject began in 1793 when Königsmann published as his *Rectoralprogram* an essay on the Sources used by Luke in the Gospel and Acts. He did little more than call attention to the 'we' sources and drew from them the conclusion that the writer of these passages was not the author of the whole book, but had written a document which an editor had used. Following up this suggestion after many years increasingly elaborate attempts to deal with the problem were published between 1821 and 1847 by J. C. Riehm, Schleiermacher, Gfrörer, and Schwanbeck. All these attempts had certain characteristics in common. They recognised that the Acts could be divided at chapter xii. or at chapter xv., and in general they agreed in attributing these two parts to different writers, as a rule attaching greater value to the later chapters.

This distinction between the two parts of Acts and the probability that therein is represented a diversity of sources used by the editor is the permanent contribution of this period. In working out the details of further suggestions the scholars mentioned pursued various lines of thought, but none of them has really proved to be entirely sound.

Riehm.   Riehm [1] thought that Acts i.-xii. rested on a series of small essays discovered and used by the editor, but that xiii.-xxviii. rested on his own observation, or on other persons' verbal testimony, except for the speeches and the letters in Acts xv.

[1] *Dissertatio critico-theologica de fontibus Act. Apost.* 1821.

and xxiii., for which he had access to written reports or to written originals.

Gfrörer[1] thought that the compiler of Acts, writing about A.D. 90, used a collection of unhistorical legends arranged by a zealous Petrinist; this source covers Acts i.-xii., and only the speech of Stephen is of first-rate historical value. The remaining chapters of the book are a good historical document compiled by a companion of Paul. *[marginal note: Gfrörer.]*

Schleiermacher,[2] following up his well-known theory of the origin of the Gospels from a series of scattered essays which the Evangelist collected, thought that Acts had a similar origin. His work remains a valuable collection of the discrepancies, repetitions, etc., found in Acts, but he did not systematise his data or give precision to his theory. So far he was probably not wrong: it is easy to see considerable evidence in Acts for the use of earlier material and editorial work. Probably, however, it is impossible so to unravel the editor's work as to be able to determine the exact limits of his sources; and it is even harder to reconstruct their contents. *[marginal note: Schleiermacher.]*

Schwanbeck[3] tried to give definite form to the theory which Schleiermacher had more vaguely suggested. According to him the compiler of Acts had used (1) a biography of Peter (Acts i.-vi. 7, viii., xi. 1-18); (2) a biography of Barnabas (iv. 36 f., ix. 1-30, xi. 19-30, xiii., xiv., xv. 2-4); (3) a memorandum made by Silas (xv. 14, to the end of Acts); (4) special sources (*e.g.* the speech of Stephen vii., and xv. 3-13). *[marginal note: Schwanbeck.]*

Schwanbeck's work was the most minute and painstaking of all these publications, but his theory was so complex and hypothetical that a twofold reaction followed. The conservative critics pointed out that these theories were based on insufficient grounds, and, emphasising the essential unity of the book, clung to the view that it was therefore all equally credible and *[marginal note: Reactions against Schwanbeck: (a) Conservative.]*

---

[1] *Die heilige Sage*, 1838.
[2] *Einleitung in das N.T.*, 1845.
[3] *Ueber die Quellen der Apostelgeschichte*, 1847.

historical. Thus they contributed nothing to the elucidation of the problem; for, excited by their refutation of the untenable details of the schemes of the critics, they ignored the existence of the difficulties which had at least been recognised by their opponents, and, under cover of the confusion occasioned by the rout of the Liberals of the nineteenth century, succeeded in evading the consideration of the real problems of Acts.

(b) Radical. On the other hand, the radical theologians of the school of Tübingen were not more successful; like the conservatives they saw that Schwanbeck's structure was larger than his foundations justified, and that he had not been sufficiently attentive to the general unity of Acts. They therefore fastened upon this unity, and recognising, like all the liberal critics, that the opening chapters of Acts are largely legendary, deduced the conclusion that Acts as a whole is legendary. To them it appeared that any minute criticism of sources was unprofitable and unnecessary, and they passed on to develop their famous series of inquiries into the reason why Acts was written rather than into the method of its composition.

So the matter remained for many years. Schwanbeck's criticisms and reconstruction were not seriously improved, though efforts in the same direction never entirely ceased. The situation was summed up by E. Zeller, whose statement [1] of the whole question remains the classic summary of the position as it was in the middle of the nineteenth century.

Bernhard Weiss revives theory of written sources. A new period began in 1886. B. Weiss in his *Einleitung in das Neue Testament* revived the theory of the use of written sources in the earlier part of Acts. His lead was followed by other scholars, and between 1886 and 1897 a series of studies were published which when taken together formed a complete discussion of various possibilities. The close of this period may fairly be regarded as marked by the articles of A. Hilgenfeld in *Z.W.Th.*, 1895 and 1896. It is impossible to give a

---

[1] *Die Apostelgeschichte*, 1854, pp. 489 ff. (English translation, 1875-76, vol ii. pp. 291 ff.)

detailed account of this group of writings, which is admirably summarised by W. Heitmüller in the *Theologische Rundschau* for 1899, but certain points are noteworthy.

(1) An attempt was made (notably by Spitta) to abandon the obvious division of Acts into a Petrine and a Pauline half, by arguing that the source which contains the 'we' sections appears in the earlier part of the book, sometimes from Acts vi., sometimes even from the beginning of the book.

(2) Great emphasis was laid on the indications of doublets which by some critics, especially Spitta,[1] were carefully grouped, so that Acts was divided into two primitive documents, both of which had originally covered the same ground and were skilfully united by the final editor.

(3) Very little attention was paid to the language of Acts, and no serious interest was taken in the possibility of the use of Aramaic sources in the earlier chapters.

On the whole, it cannot be said that this period of activity in research was marked by the same ability as that displayed earlier in the nineteenth century. The critical insight of the writers seems inferior to that of their predecessors; much of their work was marked by a perverse ingenuity, and by a tendency to obscure the main problem in excessive detail. Thus their results have little permanent importance.

There has been no general interest shown recently in the analysis of Acts, but attempts have been made by J. Wellhausen, E. Schwartz, and A. von Harnack in Germany, and by C. C. Torrey in America.

Eduard Schwartz in the *Nachrichten* of the *Königliche Gesellschaft der Wissenschaften zu Göttingen, philologisch-historische Klasse*, 1907, pp. 263 ff., published a very valuable disquisition *Zur Chronologie des Paulus*. Its importance for the criticism of Acts is the argument that the chronological data involved in the death of Herod [2] and what followed show that the writer

Eduard Schwartz.

[1] *Die Apostelgeschichte, ihre Quellen und deren geschichtlicher Wert*, 1891
[2] Acts xii. 20.

has divided a single visit and a single journey into two separate visits to Jerusalem, each followed by a missionary journey, probably because he had two traditions of this series of incidents and did not recognise that they referred to the same events seen from different points of view.

J. Wellhausen. Julius Wellhausen in the *Nachrichten* of the *Königliche Gesellschaft der Wissenschaften zu Göttingen* for 1907, pp. 1 ff., independently of Schwartz, but in the same spirit, argued that chapter xv. is a misplaced doublet of the famine relief visit in chapter xi., and he also tried to distinguish the 'we' source of the shipwreck from the 'we' source of the 'second' missionary journey. He maintained that the passages in this story in which Paul is mentioned are interpolations, and that the original document had no reference to him.

A. von Harnack. More elaborate than the work of Schwartz, yet in some respects less profound, is A. von Harnack's *Apostelgeschichte*, 1908. It makes little or no allusion to the work of other investigators, and is extraordinarily fresh and interesting.

The general unity of Acts, Harnack thinks, is too great to permit any consistent use of linguistic tests, except the simple ones of Aramaic idiom, which he did not seriously consider. The test of logical connection between paragraphs had been pushed by earlier critics to an extent which would only be justifiable if man were an entirely logical being; he therefore fell back on general principles, and considered the contents of Acts in relation to the persons and places which are central in the narrative. This is in some ways a return to older methods, but Harnack lays more stress on places, whereas the older school chiefly considered persons.

Acts i.-xv. The starting-point of his inquiry is the evident bisection of Acts at xv. 35 or xvi. 5. The second part is, in his judgment, an obvious unit, which cannot be analysed into sources. But the first part is quite different. The opening chapters, Acts i. 1 to v. 1-16, are concerned chiefly with the history of Jerusalem; but at viii. 40 the centre changes to Caesarea and finally to

Antioch. Moreover, these changes are roughly coincident with the central positions of Peter, or of Peter and John, in the Jerusalem section, of Philip, or Peter and Philip, in the Caesarean section, and of Hellenistic Christians, notably Barnabas and Saul or Paul, in the Antiochene section. Working backwards a closer analysis shows that the Antiochene section most clearly contains xi. 19 ff., and that the οἱ μὲν οὖν διασπαρέντες of xi. 19 picks up the narrative of viii. 2-4, where the same phrase is found. But viii. 2-4 is the end of a long story about the Hellenistic Christians which begins in vi. 6. Thus we obtain an Antiochene source consisting of vi. 6–viii. 4 and xi. 19-24, and the same methods show that this source continues from xi. 25 to xi. 30, is resumed in xii. 25, and goes on to xv. 35.

A similar analysis is then applied to the remaining chapters of the earlier part. Acts viii. 5-40 and ix. 31–xi. 18 seem to belong to a source in which the interest is divided between Jerusalem and Caesarea, and xii. 1-24 is its natural continuation. This source may be called the Jerusalem-Caesarean source, and in this way the whole of Acts from vi. 1 to xv. 35, with the exception of ix. 1-30 (the conversion of Paul) is accounted for as belonging either to the Antiochene or the Jerusalem-Caesarean source.

The sections i. 1–v. 42 are obviously concerned with Jerusalem, and in some points seem to be connected closely with the Jerusalem-Caesarean source. Further analysis, however, shows that these chapters are composite, and contain two accounts which are largely parallel, and in some cases probably give two versions of the same account. By using this clue a series of doublets may be discovered, of which the one beginning in chapter ii. is obviously inferior to that in chapters iii. f., and Harnack calls the latter Jerusalem source A (Ja), and the former Jerusalem source B (Jb). He sees a continuation of Ja in v. 1-16 and of Jb in v. 17-42. He thinks that Ja may be identical with the Jerusalem-Caesarean source.

Acts i.-v. Ja and Jb.

Thus the complete analysis of the first part of Acts, according to the sources distinguished by Harnack, is as follows:

Ja (Jerusalem source *A*)	iii. 1–v. 16
Jb (Jerusalem source *B*)	ii. 1-47
	v. 17-42
Jc (Jerusalem-Caesarean source, perhaps Ja)	viii. 5-40
	ix. 31–xi. 18
	xii. 1-24
P. (Pauline source)	ix. 1-30
A. (Antiochene source)	vi. 1–viii. 4
	xi. 19-30
	xii. 25–xv. 35

Possible explanations. This analysis draws attention to undoubted facts of grouping. The question is the choice between two or three possible explanations. (1) Do these divisions in the narrative represent the use of different *sources*, in the sense of written documents; or (2) separate *traditions*, in the sense of definite blocks of information derived independently from separate places and persons but not necessarily written; or (3) are they merely due to the fact that the events really happened in this way? It is of course obvious that the tradition of events in Antioch, if it be true, necessarily goes back to Antioch, and similarly with the other sources. In this sense Harnack's proposition is self-evident. The problem is whether we can say more than this with any certainty. The reason for still maintaining a certain scepticism is that by common consent there is very little serious linguistic difference between the various sections of Acts i.-xv. Thus to base the investigation on the peculiarities of the narrative, apart from linguistic details seems to be a dangerous return to the methods of Schwanbeck or Spitta, from whose efforts the main lesson to be learnt is that the indications are too faint to justify any certainty of statement. So far, therefore, as this method is used to indicate a general outline, as it is by Harnack, it is attractive, but it cannot be carried out in detail.

Nevertheless the contributions of Wellhausen, Schwartz, and Harnack are quite different in tone and workmanship from the distressingly dull work which was produced in the 'nineties. They are marked by much more common sense and introduce broad historical questions. Many of their arguments are complementary, though there is a clear distinction between them, for Harnack attaches greater value and an earlier date to Acts than the others would probably allow.

C. C. Torrey's [1] contribution to the source criticism of Acts is of a different kind. He contends that Acts i.-xv. is the careful—even too careful—translation by the writer of the 'we' sections of an Aramaic document written by a Christian of Jerusalem. The primary evidence in support of this view is a series of passages in which obscure or impossible Greek becomes intelligible if translated, word for word, into Aramaic. This is corroborated by a number of smaller points, in which the Greek is more intelligible if it be regarded as a mistranslation. These vary in importance from those in which the Greek is extremely harsh if not impossible to those in which it would scarcely arouse criticism if found elsewhere, but deserves attention if the theory of an Aramaic original be conceded as otherwise probable.

This linguistic argument is the permanent contribution of his *Composition and Date of Acts*. The subject is discussed elsewhere, and it is only necessary here to say that so far as the evidence for an Aramaic original is concerned Torrey does not seem to be finally answered by his critics.

On the further point of the unity of this Aramaic original, and its meticulous translation by Luke, the case for a single source does not seem to be very strong, and the positive arguments of Harnack and Schwartz weigh down the scale, especially

[1] "The Composition and Date of Acts," in *Harvard Theological Studies*, i, 1916.

in view of the light thrown on the subject by the use made of Mark in the Third Gospel.

It remains to consider the problem afresh, gathering up the points which seem best to have endured criticism, passing over those which by common consent have proved ineffective, and adding such suggestions as these studies have produced.

<small>Written documents or oral traditions</small>

Few will deny that progress has been hindered by failure to distinguish adequately between the closely connected phenomena which form the basis of *Quellenkritik*. In any historical work it is probable that the writer has made use of more than one tradition; but these traditions may have been preserved orally, or in written documents, which may have originally existed in some other language, and have been accessible to him only through translations. It is plain that the use of traditions as distinguished from that of documents will be indicated by the existence of contradictions in statements of fact, and divergences both in forms of thought and methods of presentation, but not necessarily by any variation of style. If, therefore, really serious differences of language and style can be traced between different parts of a book, written sources, as distinct from traditions, may be postulated. The reverse of this argument, however, is not necessarily true, and unity of style does not necessarily prove the absence of documentary sources; for the final editor of the book, who put together the materials derived from various traditions and documents, may have re-written the whole in his own language. If so, it may be impossible to say whether written documents or merely oral traditions were used.

One further complication has to be considered. If an editor be using various documents in his own language, and not recasting them with great freedom, the probability is that the original style will betray itself, but if he be translating, the probability is considerable that he will use the same style throughout. This style will be so far coloured by the idiom of the original that those who are perfectly at home both in it and in the language into which it is translated will be able to see that they are dealing with translation and not an original composition; but they will not be able to decide whether the editor was translating one or several documents.

The question of the original language in which the sources of an early Christian document were written is always difficult. No doubt the earliest Christians spoke and thought in Aramaic: but did they produce any historical documents in it? The only test is that of style. The more practised a translator the less the idiom of the original language is perceptible; but probably no one can always cover his traces successfully. Moreover, human frailty provides the critic with a further occasional help. Any one who has tried to translate knows that it is fatiguing work, and that after a time the tired brain refuses to follow the argument of the writer: it is impossible to translate and study an author simultaneously. The result is an occasional mistranslation, due to taking the words in a plausible but wrong sense. This produces sometimes a meaningless passage, sometimes one which can be greatly improved by discovering what original it represents. Nor is this all. If any one of ordinary capacity tries to translate he will speedily become confused in his mind between the two languages, and, when sufficiently tired, will scarcely know which idiom he is using. The words, for instance, may be Greek, but the idiom Aramaic, and at times the translator will produce something quite unintelligible.[1]

This nice discrimination of style is in the end the only real proof of the use of a lost original source in another language. It can be applied by but a few scholars, and the rest are obliged to follow with humility. But this humility need not extend to the point of blind acceptance of opinion, or of

Style in translation.

---

[1] The same phenomenon occurs in talking two languages. One may spend an evening turning, almost with alternate sentences, from one to the other, and end by being able to use neither without error. It is merely a form of fatigue, and explains many " translation-phenomena."

an equally blind abandonment of the problem. In Torrey's hypothesis, for instance, Semitic scholars are unanimous in admitting his mastery of Aramaic: the point at issue is whether the Greek which he translates back into Aramaic is in some places inconceivable as an original composition, and in others unidiomatic. Knowledge of Hellenistic Greek, not of Aramaic, is required for this purpose, and many who do not know any Semitic language are qualified to discuss the point. Indeed, they are likely to be far better critics of the question than those Semitic scholars whose acquaintance with Greek is limited. After all, many things can be said similarly in two languages, and the man who knows Semitic idioms well, and Greek less intimately, is apt to find Semitic originals in every document which he touches, because he realises that some phrase or idiom would be perfectly good Semitic, and does not appreciate the fact that it is also perfectly good Greek.

Editorial additions. When the question of language and the general boundaries of sources has been settled, the most difficult problem of all remains, for it will sometimes be possible to detect short passages which have been put in by the editor in order to improve or elucidate a narrative. But it must be remembered that many critics have erred by assuming too easily that the editor always did his work badly, and that the original document which he was copying was invariably logical. There is not, however, really any decisive reason why it should always be the editor, and never the writer of the original, who is illogical.

Many of these points have been consistently overlooked by critics who have investigated Acts. They have not distinguished between criteria pointing to the use of written documents, and those indicating merely that an historian dealing with a large subject naturally used several traditions corresponding in the main to the localities with which he was concerned. They have been inclined either to overestimate the unity of style in the book or to exaggerate the divergencies of thought; and have been singularly blind to the generally Semitic idiom of the earlier chapters as compared with the much more purely Greek style of the later ones. They have either ignored entirely the traces of illogical connection, or have attributed them all—and much which was not really illogical—to the editor, and none of them to his sources. The truth seems to be that although there is a *prima facie* probability for the use of written sources in Acts, and especially for Aramaic sources in the earlier chapters, the writer wrote too well to allow us to distinguish with certainty either the boundaries of his sources or the extent of his own editorial work.

In the following paragraphs, therefore, no attempt will be made to distinguish minutely the work of the final redactor. This point can best be discussed in the pages of a commentary. But it is possible and necessary to bring together the existing evidence for the use of sources in Acts and to indicate the comparative probability—it is never more—of alternative theories. *Evidence of sources in Acts.*

The two treatises or λόγοι addressed to Theophilus, and generally known as the Gospel according to Luke and Acts, obviously form a single literary work. The critical questions concerned with them deal with the documents and traditions which may have been used by the author, and the way in which he put them together.

To solve these problems we have, apart from the probabilities established by the tradition of the writing of history among Greeks and Jews, and, above all, by the author's use of Mark in the Gospel, only two sources of information.

(1) The statement of the author in his preface at the beginning of Luke.

(2) The internal evidence given in Acts by linguistic indications and by seams which show that he has passed from one source (traditional or documentary) to another.

The opening verses of the Gospel and of Acts are often, but somewhat loosely, called Prefaces. Ancient writers, however, distinguished between three phrases which might with more or *Ancient Prefaces.*

less correctness be translated by Preface—προοίμιον, προγραφή, and προέκθεσις.[1]

The προοίμιον was the introduction at the beginning of a work explaining the writer's purpose. This naturally would come at the beginning of the first of a series of λόγοι or 'books'; and, as a rule, nowhere else.

The προγραφή and προέκθεσις were devices sometimes, but not always, adopted by historical writers to serve as signposts to their readers. They were especially used at the beginning of a λόγος in a work comprising many λόγοι to show the stage which had been reached in the narrative. The προγραφή differed from the προέκθεσις only because it was not an integral part of the text. This is clearly seen from Polybius, who says (xi. 1. 5):

... ἴσως δέ τινες ἐπιζητοῦσι πῶς ἡμεῖς οὐ προγραφὰς ἐν ταύτῃ τῇ βίβλῳ, καθάπερ οἱ πρὸ ἡμῶν, ἀλλὰ καὶ προεκθέσεις καθ' ἑκάστην ὀλυμπιάδα πεποιήκαμεν τῶν πράξεων. ἐγὼ δὲ κρίνω, χρήσιμον μὲν εἶναι τὸ τῶν προγραφῶν γένος ... θεωρῶν δὲ διὰ πολλὰς αἰτίας καὶ τὰς τυχούσας ὀλιγωρούμενον καὶ φθειρόμενον τὸ τῶν προγραφῶν γένος, οὕτως καὶ διὰ ταῦτα πρὸς τοῦτο τὸ μέρος κατηνέχθην· τῆς γὰρ προεκθέσεως οὐ μόνον ἰσοδυναμούσης τῇ προγραφῇ, ἀλλὰ καὶ πλεῖόν τι δυναμένης, ἅμα δὲ καὶ χώραν ἐχούσης ἀσφαλεστέραν διὰ τὸ συμπεπλέχθαι τῇ πραγματείᾳ, τούτῳ μᾶλλον ἐδοκιμάσαμεν χρῆσθαι μέρει κτλ. That is to say, "But perhaps some are asking why we are not using προγραφαί in this book like our predecessors, but have prefixed προεκθέσεις to each Olympiad. Now I consider that the usual kind of προγραφαί are useful, ... but noticing that for many ordinary reasons προγραφαί are treated lightly and are destroyed, I was induced to adopt my present procedure. For προεκθέσεις have the same

[1] The technical question of the literary use of προγραφαί and προέκθεσις is best discussed by R. Laqueur in his "Ephoros" in *Hermes* xlvi. (1911), pp. 161 ff. See also Th. Birt, *Das antike Buchwesen*, 1882, pp. 141 ff., 464 ff. The application of the facts to Acts is made—but rather perversely—by E. Norden, *Agnostos Theos*, 1913, pp. 311 ff. Some critical doubts as to the technical use of these phrases are expressed in Appendix C.

value as προγραφαί, indeed somewhat more, and, besides, they come in a safer place because they are an integral part of the text, so that we thought it best to make use of them."

It is clear that a προγραφή is a label with the table of contents attached to a λόγος, or (which is the same thing differently described) to a τόμος, while a προέκθεσις is a similar statement incorporated into the text. If properly drawn up it contained a statement of the subjects discussed in the previous λόγος, and of those which would be dealt with in the λόγος to which it was prefixed.

Not all writers made use of this device, but it was obviously useful and common. The customary form of προέκθεσις may be found in Polybius and Diodorus Siculus: it gives a short account of what has been dealt with in the preceding book, and a summary of what is to come. For instance, in Diodorus Siculus ii. 1 there is the following scheme. ἡ μὲν πρὸ ταύτης βίβλος . . . περιέχει τὰς κατ' Αἴγυπτον πράξεις, ἐν αἷς ὑπάρχει τὰ . . . μυθολογούμενα . . . καὶ τἆλλα τὰ . . . παραδοξολογούμενα . . . πρὸς δὲ τούτοις . . . ἑξῆς δὲ . . . ἔπειτα δὲ . . . ἔτι δὲ . . ., ἐν ταύτῃ δὲ ἀναγράψομεν τὰς κατὰ τὴν Ἀσίαν γενομένας πράξεις. The same type of construction can be found in other writers, especially in Polybius and in Josephus, *Antiq.* viii., xiii., xiv., xv.[1]

The important point is that the προέκθεσις summarised the contents of the previous λόγος in a long μέν clause and then in a corresponding δέ clause gave a shorter summary of the contents of the λόγος which is being opened.

Obviously the opening verses of Acts are a προέκθεσις, but the difficulty is that there is no δέ clause, which is needed grammatically to balance the sentence, and required by the general construction of a προέκθεσις to give the contents of the λόγος which is just beginning. Ed. Norden thinks that the δέ clause must once have been present, and believes that in the source of

Acts opens with a προέκθεσις.

---

[1] Elsewhere Josephus has a different method: ending one book with a μέν clause and beginning the next with a δέ clause.

Acts the text must have run τὸν μὲν πρῶτον λόγον . . . ἀνελήμφθη, νυνὶ δὲ τὰ συνεχῆ τούτοις ἅ τε αὐτὸς παρὼν εἶδον, ἅ τε παρ' ἄλλων ἀξιοπίστων ὄντων ἐπυθόμην συγγράψαι πειράσομαι μέχρι τῆς ἐπὶ τῆς Ῥώμης ἐπιδημίας τοῦ Παύλου. Had Acts been constructed properly, according to the rules of Hellenistic writing, the opening would doubtless have been so phrased, but there is no certainty that it was, and the preferable alternative is to recognise that here, as elsewhere, the writer is not completely skilful.

Thus taking the Lucan writings [1] as they stand we have a genuine προοίμιον to the whole work in Luke i. 1-4, and the beginning of an imperfect προέκθεσις to the second λόγος in Acts i. 1.

According to the προοίμιον the purpose of the λόγοι sent to Theophilus was to assure him of the certainty of the things in which he had been instructed. The author says that many attempts had been made to draw up (ἀνατάξασθαι) the narrative of the πραγμάτων πεπληροφορημένων among them, on the basis of the tradition of those who had been eye-witnesses and had taken part in them. The next phrase in his statement is obscure: ἔδοξε κἀμοὶ παρηκολουθηκότι ἄνωθεν πᾶσιν ἀκριβῶς καθεξῆς σοι γράψαι.[2] To what does πᾶσιν refer? It may mean either the events alluded to (πραγμάτων) or the previous writers (πολλοί). The latter seems to be indicated by the general balance of the paragraph, and, if so, the important point is the implication, slight but unmistakable, that the author himself had not been an

[1] What was the original title of the whole? The first λόγος certainly was not called τὸ εὐαγγέλιον κατὰ Λουκᾶν when it was sent to Theophilus: it required this title when it was detached from Acts, and became part of the 'fourfold gospel canon.' It is unfortunately easy to forget that Luke and Acts came in the New Testament as separate books. Is it possible that πράξεις (πράξεις τῶν ἀποστόλων is a late form) was originally the title of the whole? But against the view that the author himself gave the title πράξεις to the whole work or even (as Zahn has come lately to believe) to the second volume is the fact that in the text of his writings this noun and usually also the verb πράττω are used *in malam partem*.

[2] The use of these words is curious and technical. They are discussed in Appendix C.

αὐτόπτης or an ὑπερέτης τοῦ λόγου. Moreover, if on other grounds the theory be acceptable that the compiler of the whole is not identical with the author of the 'we' sections, the interest shown in the preface in the narrations of αὐτόπται explains why the compiler preserved the use of the first person. He desired to indicate that here at least he was using the narration of an αὐτόπτης.

The only method of discovering internal evidence in a book which, as its treatment of Mark shows, cannot be expected easily to reveal its composition by its style, is to consider the 'seams,' not of language but of narrative, which suggest that the editor has passed from one tradition to another. Of course such 'seams' do not in themselves prove the use of documentary sources: they only indicate that it is possible. Whether this possibility is probable or not will always remain a matter of judgment. It is, however, to be remembered that, in the case of a writer who is known to have been in the habit of using documentary sources, to regard this possibility as improbable is quite as much a 'subjective' act of individual judgment as it is to treat it as probable.[1] *The internal evidence of Acts.*

The first 'seam' which attracts attention is not in the Acts but in the Gospel. Its importance for the study of Acts is the light which it throws on the source or tradition used in the early chapters, and on the method of the editor. *Accounts of the Passion.*

In Luke two traditions are combined in the account of the Passion and Resurrection. One was undoubtedly documentary, for we still possess it in a separate form in the Gospel according to Mark. The other may have been written or oral; there is no decisive evidence. Throughout the last chapters of the Gospel though Luke uses the greater part of the Marcan narrative he

---

[1] The choice is not between 'subjective' and 'objective' criticism, but between 'subjective' criticism and ignorance. The problems are not invented by critics; they are internal in the books. We cannot advance knowledge without taking up a position of some kind.

prefers this second source, edited so as to fit into the other as his framework.

It has generally been held that Luke has freely changed the wording and meaning of Mark; and on the hypothesis that Matthew and Luke both used the Greek Mark, the evidence of a comparison between the three gospels supports the primary nature of Mark. The verbal differences between Mark and the Lucan version of Mark have, it is true, been explained by Professor Torrey as due to a separate translation made from an Aramaic Mark. This would render it impossible to appeal to Matthew as evidence that the existing gospel of Mark is verbally identical with the Marcan source of Matthew and Luke, and is not a later recession of it. But Torrey's theory on this point seems unnecessary. Even, however, if it be conceded, the historical evidence remains, and Mark's account is historically more probable than Luke's.

Luke's ingenuity in piecing traditions together.

Mark implies the departure of the disciples to Galilee, clearly intending to lead up to the Galilean tradition of the appearances of the Risen Jesus. 'Luke' prefers the contradictory tradition, which makes Jerusalem the centre of everything, leaving out all reference to Galilee. Whether written or oral this tradition can scarcely have originated anywhere except in Jerusalem. Luke has pieced this into the Marcan framework so skilfully that, but for the existence of the Gospel according to Mark, the composite character of his narrative could never have been so much as suspected. He did not abruptly stop using Mark and continue from another source, but wove the two together so that there is not so much a single seam as a prolonged splice.

Are the opening chapters of Acts the continuation of this tradition, or are they, like the closing chapters of the Gospel, produced by the interlacing and editing of various sources, written or oral? If the latter view be adopted, can we trace in Acts the continuation of Mark, as well as of the other source? Or does Acts represent a wholly new source?

THE INTERNAL EVIDENCE OF ACTS 139

Harnack's analysis of Acts i.-v. makes the further formulation of this complicated problem possible. Clearly Acts i. and ii., the account of the Ascension, the choice of Matthias, and the gift of the Spirit at Pentecost, can fairly be regarded as continuing the tradition of Jerusalem followed in Luke xxiv. Whether it is accurate is of course a different question; the Galilean narrative of Mark seems to prove that it is not; but it is a consecutive narrative, and there is no seam between it and the end of the gospel, except that which is provided by the division into two books, clearly due to the editor. It seems to be the tradition of a circle of Christians living in, or coming from, Jerusalem, who had attached themselves to Peter on his return to Jerusalem and had ignored or forgotten the Galilean tradition. *Acts i. continues Third Gospel.*

The questions then arise (1) whether this splice extended beyond chapter ii.; (2) whether (since Harnack doubts it) chapter i. as well as chapter ii. belongs to it; (3) whether it was written or oral, and, (4) if it were written, was it Aramaic or Greek? To answer the first of these questions demands a decision on the arguments of Harnack and Torrey. *Problems raised.*

Harnack's theory is based chiefly on the same phenomenon as assisted an earlier generation of scholars to a triumphant analysis of the Pentateuch. The five opening chapters of Acts, like the opening ones of Genesis, are marked by doublets: there are two accounts of the same events. The main incidents in Acts ii.-iv. can be described as follows: *Doublets in Acts i.-v.*

(1) The gift of the Spirit, Acts ii. 1-13 and also Acts iv. 31.
(2) A speech of Peter, Acts ii. 14-36 and also Acts iii. 12-26.
(3) A record of extraordinary conversions, Acts ii. 37-41 and also Acts iv. 4.
(4) The growth of communism, Acts ii. 42-47 and also Acts iv. 34-37.

This is similar to the doublets in the narrative of creation in Genesis. They are not indeed so impressive, for the events of creation can have taken place once, and only once, while Peter doubtless spoke often, great conversions may have often been made, and so far as the gift of the Spirit was regarded as a transient phenomenon of excitement, it could be repeated. But this cannot be said of the accounts of the growth of communism. An editor may easily admit by inadvertence summaries in similar language and of identical content from two sources; but he is very unlikely to treat a summary of his own in this way at an interval of two chapters.[1]

Acts ii. and iii.

This *prima facie* case for considering the possibility of two sources is confirmed by certain small points of language and thought, justifying the distinction of Acts ii. from Acts iii.

In Acts iii. f. Jesus is four times (iii. 13, 26; iv. 27, 30) described as a παῖς of God (though the phrase παῖς θεοῦ does not itself occur), but nowhere else in Acts is the phrase found: it is rare and usually liturgical in early documents. Moreover, Peter is usually accompanied by John; the importance of this is increased by the fact that John takes no part in the action of the narrative: he is mentioned, but does nothing.[2] There is also a slight but perceptible difference in doctrine between the two speeches of Peter. In ii. 38 Peter calls for repentance from his hearers and for baptism in the name of Jesus Christ which

[1] On the other hand the author is capable of repeating a summary derived from *one* written source as is shown by his treatment of Mark. See Cadbury, *Style and Literary Method of Luke*, p. 111.

[2] This peculiarity extends to Jc (viii. 14): this may mean that Ja and Jc are closely connected, or that the 'Peter' part of Acts viii. is a fragment of Ja and not originally connected with the 'Philip' part. But Peter and John are also mentioned in Luke xxii. 8 (not in Mark xiv. 13), so that if this combination is pressed as the sign of the Jerusalem source it must be extended to include the last days of Jesus. Such a Jerusalem source for Luke's passion narrative has been independently proposed by some scholars, *e.g.* Perry, *The Sources of Luke's Passion-Narrative*, 1920. The alternative explanation would be that the editor is responsible for the combination wherever it appears, since elsewhere he represents messengers in pairs (Luke vii. 18, not Matt. xi. 2; Luke x. 1, not Matt. x. 5, but cf. Mark vi. 7; Acts *passim*; even angels are in pairs, Luke xxiv. 4, not Mark xvi. 5; Acts i. 10) and since in Acts i. 13 he not only arranges the eleven in pairs but has the unique order, "Peter and John."

will obtain for them remission of their sins. In iii. 19 he calls for repentance to wipe out their sins, but baptism is not mentioned. Much stress cannot be laid on this point, for the references to baptism in chapter ii. may be and probably are redactorial. If, however, the views expressed in Vol. I. p. 340 be rejected, the case in favour of Harnack's analysis of sources is proportionately strengthened. In any case the theological difference between the two speeches is not confined to the question of baptism. In Acts iii. the return of Jesus is the main hope and message of the disciples : in Acts ii. this hope is in the background, if it be present at all, and the central place is given to the gift of the Spirit, and to obtain it for the Church is the main work of the ascended Jesus. This confirms the general impression, adequately represented in Catholic teaching, that the purpose of Acts ii. 1-13 is to describe the foundation of the Church as the Apostolic body which had then received and could henceforth transmit Power from on High, a theory of which Acts iii. is ignorant, for it regards the gift of the Spirit as a transient supernatural phenomenon, promised and given to the disciples in hours of need.

Without contending that these arguments completely prove Harnack's hypothesis they seem to render it probable, especially when it is remembered that the writer is known to have been in the habit of using and editing earlier documents.

Were either of these hypothetical sources in Aramaic ? It is here that Torrey's arguments have to be discussed. The collateral evidence of the facts known to us is against him. Whatever may have been the original language of Mark it must have been known to Luke in Greek, and the same is true of Q, if that be regarded as a single document. But the evidence contained in Acts itself seems convincing. It is impossible to discuss each example which he gives, together with Burkitt's adverse criticism ; they must be dealt with in the pages of the commentary. But two examples may be given.

The language of these sources.

(1) Acts iii. 16 καὶ τῇ πίστει τοῦ ὀνόματος αὐτοῦ τούτου

ὃν θεωρεῖτε καὶ οἴδατε ἐστερέωσεν τὸ ὄνομα αὐτοῦ, καὶ ἡ πίστις ἡ δι' αὐτοῦ ἔδωκεν αὐτῷ τὴν ὁλοκληρίαν ταύτην ἀπέναντι πάντων ὑμῶν. The impossibility of any satisfactory translation of this passage is notorious, but it is easily explained if it be translated into unpointed Aramaic: ובהימנתא די שמה להדן די חזין אנתון וידעין אנתון תקף שמה והימנתא די בה יהבה לה חלימות אדא קדם כלכון. The translator seems to have read in the middle of this sentence תְּקֵף שְׁמֵהּ = ἐστερέωσε τὸ ὄνομα αὐτοῦ, but what was meant was תְּקֵף שָׂמֵהּ = ὑγιῆ κατέστησεν αὐτόν,—a phrase idiomatic in all respects, and suiting its context perfectly, as the sentence runs on from that which precedes it, and the subject of ὑγιῆ κατέστησεν is ὁ θεός in v. 15. But the suggested mistake on the part of the translator is a very natural one, since he had before him the same letters (שמה) which he had immediately before correctly read as שְׁמֵהּ (his name), and it did not occur to him that in this place it should be read שָׂמֵהּ (put or made).

This seems convincing; by the consent of all those who have sufficient knowledge of the language the suggested Aramaic is easy in itself but liable to have been misread by a tired translator; it gives an admirable sense while the Greek is unintelligible as it stands.[1] Burkitt,[2] it is true, offers a rival suggestion. He thinks that it is possible to punctuate thus : τὸν δὲ ἀρχηγὸν τῆς ζωῆς ἀπεκτείνατε, ὃν ὁ θεὸς ἤγειρεν ἐκ νεκρῶν, οὗ ἡμεῖς μάρτυρές ἐσμεν καὶ τῇ πίστει τοῦ ὀνόματος αὐτοῦ· τοῦτον ὃν θεωρεῖτε καὶ οἴδατε ἐστερέωσε τὸ ὄνομα αὐτοῦ καὶ ἡ πίστις ἡ δι' αὐτοῦ ἔδωκεν αὐτῷ κτλ. But it seems improbable that any one who had just written οὗ as a genitive dependent on μάρτυς should write τῇ πίστει as a dative dependent on it, when he might so easily have written τῆς πίστεως.[3]

---

[1] It might be said that unintelligibility suggests textual corruption rather than the use of an intelligible Aramaic source, but few who have actually made translations would say this, and—one would have supposed—none who have corrected the efforts of others.

[2] *Journal of Theological Studies*, xx. (1919), 320 ff.

[3] The concordance does not reveal any instance of μάρτυς with a dative,—the genitive is the usual idiom. Nor does the use of τοῦτον here seem to be

THE INTERNAL EVIDENCE OF ACTS 143

(2) Similarly in Acts ii. 47 there is notorious difficulty in the phrase ὁ δὲ κύριος προσετίθει τοὺς σωζομένους καθ' ἡμέραν ἐπὶ τὸ αὐτό. The narrator in this passage is describing the growth of the community: "Day by day, continuing stedfastly with one accord in the temple, and breaking bread at home, they did take their food with gladness and singleness of heart, praising God and having favour with all the people." The verse which follows is natural enough except the last three words. What is the meaning of ἐπὶ τὸ αὐτό? It can only mean 'together' or 'in the same place' (cf. ii. 44 πάντες δὲ οἱ πιστεύσαντες ἦσαν ἐπὶ τὸ αὐτό κτλ.) and is constantly used in the LXX. as the translation of יַחַד and יַחְדָּו (cf. also Luke xvii. 35 and Acts i. 15, ii. 1, iv. 26). But in this passage this meaning is obviously inadmissible.

The ancient interpreters felt the difficulty and tried in various ways to overcome it. In the *Textus Receptus* ἐπὶ τὸ αὐτό is joined on to the next sentence, but the textual evidence is decisive against this reading, which is only important as evidence of the inability of early readers to explain the correct text. The paraphrastic text of D also tries to emend the difficulty by reading ... καθ' ἡμέραν ἐπὶ τὸ αὐτὸ ἐν τῇ ἐκκλησίᾳ. No modern commentator has so far succeeded in explaining the difficulty. But the problem is solved at once if ἐπὶ τὸ αὐτό be translated back into Aramaic by the adverbial compound לַחְדָּא (or לַחֲדָא), which has in the Judaean dialect of Aramaic the meaning 'greatly,' 'exceedingly.' This second sense is exactly what is needed instead of 'together,' and the probability that this is the true explanation of the difficulty is greatly increased by the fact that the word has this significance only in Judaean[1] Aramaic, and

---

parallel to the instances of a 'resumptive' τοῦτον which Burkitt quotes; it needs the καί before τῇ πίστει to make it natural. It should be noted that the Western text seems to have taken Burkitt's view and inserted ἐπί before τῇ πίστει in order to make it possible.

[1] Found in both Targums (cf. Onkelos, Gen. xii. 14) and in the late Christian Palestinian dialect; but not in Midrash or Talmud (cf. Dalman, *Grammatik*, s.v.).

might well be unknown to the editor of Acts, and that when it is used to modify a verb it is regularly placed at the end of the clause.

The full translation into Aramaic suggests another small point. The whole passage would run וּמָרְיָא מוֹסִף הֲוָא לְדִי חָיִין כָּל יוֹם לַחֲדָא. The preposition לְ in the fourth word (לְדִי) might signify either the dative or the direct object. Doubtless (if the original were really as suggested) it was intended for the dative, but, if the translator failed to recognise the peculiar Judaean meaning of לַחֲדָא, it was inevitable that he should render it with the Greek accusative. The meaning of the original source would be, "The Lord added greatly to the saved."[1]

Professor Burkitt is not convinced by this rendering, and prefers to follow out a suggestion made by Mr. Vazakas,[2] who noted that ἐπὶ τὸ αὐτό is often found in connection with meetings for worship, so that for instance when Ignatius says ὅταν γὰρ πυκνῶς ἐπὶ τὸ αὐτὸ γίνεσθε it means "when you go constantly to church." Surely both Mr. Vazakas and Professor Burkitt are confusing the connotation of the phrase with its actual denotation. No doubt it connotes—at least when combined with appropriate verbs—meetings for worship, but it denotes merely, "at the same place." Moreover, though the interpretation of a phrase may take connotation into account, the grammatical structure of a sentence rarely does. Professor Burkitt's rendering only just stops short of rendering ἐπὶ τὸ αὐτό as though it were a dative dependent on προσετίθει, and is obliged to treat προστιθέναι as though it were a synonym for συνάγειν. The Greek is in fact impossible, and cannot be explained except as due to a confusion of thought such as is common in translations.[3]

[1] It should be noted that attempts to refine on the meaning of the various present or aorist participles is negatory if Aramaic be presupposed. Any one who doubts this may be invited to translate into Aramaic the story of the theologian who, when asked if he were saved, replied that he wished first to know whether his questioner meant σεσωσμένος, σωθείς, or merely σωζόμενος.

[2] *Journal of Biblical Literature*, xxxvii. (1919), 105 ff.

[3] It might be said that this passage is a very undesirable one to use, inasmuch as, according to the view here taken, it comes exactly at the juncture

There are many other indications of an Aramaic source in these chapters, collected by Professor Torrey, which are less spectacular, but taken together seem to present an extremely strong case in favour of translation from Aramaic. Obviously, however, such evidence can prove nothing as to the extent or number of the documentary sources indicated. Thus Torrey's hypothesis so far as its linguistic side is concerned, and this is its strength, combines excellently with that of Harnack, and probably justifies the statement that all the facts are best covered by the supposition that Acts ii. represents one Aramaic source called B, and Acts iii. another, known as A.

It is now possible to discuss the extent of these two sources and their affiliation with others.

Does Acts i. belong to source *A* or source *B* ? Harnack is doubtful, but thinks that if it belongs to either it is to *B*. This is surely right : moreover the continuity between Acts i. and the special tradition of Jerusalem in ' Luke ' is so clear that it seems probable that source *B* is identified with this source in the Gospel. It is for the learned in Aramaic to consider whether there is any evidence of translation in these last chapters of ' Luke.' {Acts i.}

The recognition that Acts iii. introduces a new source and that it is probably a translation from the Aramaic raises new problems. If Acts iii. and iv. had been found in one book and Acts i. and ii. in another, there would be few to doubt that it was a variant tradition of the gift of the Spirit, with which it ends, and it would have been accepted as historically more probable.[1] But if so we have here an acephalous source. It assumes the presence of the apostles in Jerusalem : it does not {Acts iii.}

---

of the sources. But the general reason for this objection is that junctures are often covered by " connective tissue," and it is clear that here there is none. Acts ii. 47 is as much part of the Jerusalem *B* source as any part of the chapter, and ἐπὶ τὸ αὐτό belongs to it, so cannot, with our present text, go with the beginning of chapter iii.

[1] It is worth observation that it is noticeably nearer to the point of view represented by Mark xiii. 11, which seems to look forward to the gift of the Spirit mainly as an assistance to the disciples in time of persecution.

say how they came there. Can we guess at its antecedents, or find its sequel ?

Perhaps we can never even guess with profit at its antecedents. We cannot tell whether it really is a purely Jerusalem narrative, or belonged to the Galilean tradition, the beginning of which 'Luke' may have omitted as in the interests of the Jerusalem tradition he omitted or changed the end of Mark. Nevertheless, though the verdict of *non liquet* be inevitable, there will probably always be a few who will sometimes allow themselves to think that these chapters continue the Marcan narrative and that the John who accompanies Peter was, in the original form of the tradition, not the son of Zebedee, but that other John whom later tradition associated with Peter— John Mark.

Acts iv. f. The question of continuation is equally doubtful. Does iv. 36 ff., the story of Barnabas selling his property, belong to this tradition ? Does the story of Ananias and Sapphira which follows in v. 1-11 ? Or does the story of the apostles' miracles, arrest and release on the advice of Gamaliel in v. 17-42 ? Except in the last case there is no special reason for associating these with Acts i. and ii. rather than with iii. and iv., but it is probable that the second account of a hearing before the Sanhedrin is another variant of the incident described in iv. 1-23. If so the version in Acts v. 17-42 is clearly the inferior one, and belongs, as Harnack has seen, to the *B* source. It is one of the sections which has least claim to be history. To say nothing of the angelic interpositions to rescue "Peter and the Apostles," the knowledge shown of a speech by Gamaliel in the Sanhedrin, in which he appeals to events which had not yet happened, and dates them earlier than others which had taken place some twenty-five years before,[1] contrasts unfavourably with the story in Acts iv. 1-23, which has in it nothing to suggest that it is unhistorical.

---

[1] The insurrection of Theudas to which Gamaliel is made to refer took place in 44 A.D. and the census of Quirinius which is described as earlier was held in 6 A.D.

THE INTERNAL EVIDENCE OF ACTS 147

Thus, the probable analysis of chapters i. to v. would seem to divide the section into two sources which, following Harnack, may be called *A* and *B*. *A* contains Acts iii.-iv. 35. *B* contains Acts i.-ii. and v. 17-42. It is doubtful whether the remaining parts of chapters iv. and v. should be attributed to one source rather than to the other. Both these sources represent traditions belonging to Jerusalem, but *B* seems the continuation of the non-Galilean source used by Luke in the Gospel, and *A* may perhaps be connected with the Galilean tradition of Mark.

With chapter vi. a new section begins. The obvious facts and problems in it are : (1) Acts vi.-viii. ·3 describes a new factor in the history of the Church in Jerusalem—the growth of a Hellenistic as distinct from a Hebrew Christianity. This led to a more violent persecution and to the scattering of the Hellenistic Christians outside of Jerusalem. (2) Acts viii. 4-25 describes the evangelisation of Samaria first by Philip, then by Peter. (3) Acts viii. 26-40 and Acts ix. 31-x. 48 describe a missionary journey ending in Caesarea, undertaken first by Philip, then by Peter. (4) Acts xi. 19-26 describe the evangelisation of Antioch by the disciples of Stephen, by Barnabas, and by Paul, whom Barnabas selects as an assistant and fetches from Tarsus. It is clear that in a certain sense, therefore, we have here Samaritan, Caesarean, and Antiochian traditions. But there are several problems involved in their consideration. The story of Stephen's preaching, and the quarrel which arose among the Hellenistic Greeks among themselves, between Christian and Jewish factions, covers Acts vi. 8-viii. 3. Is this based on an Aramaic original, and does it come from Jerusalem or Antioch ?

Torrey claims that it is all part of the original Aramaic source, but his evidence here is much less satisfactory than before. None of the instances of mistranslation which he quotes comes from this section, and only two of the instances of Aramaic idiom.

Acts vi. ff.

Of these the more striking one is in Acts vii. 53, for εἰς διαταγὰς ἀγγέλων is almost hopeless in Greek, but represents easily enough an Aramaic לְפוּקְדָּנֵי מַלְאָכִין in which the לְ corresponds to 'by' or 'according to' (διά or κατά) rather than to the 'to' (εἰς) by which it is often rightly translated in other contexts. If it were not for this instance it might seem probable that Torrey's theory ought to be abandoned for this section, but, in face of it, it is only justifiable to say that the evidence is much weaker than elsewhere, and that the real strength of the case for Torrey's position is the sense—so hard to communicate—that the style is here the same as in Acts i.-v.

On the other hand, it has been held by many critics that the section is composite, and to analyse it was a favourite endeavour of the critics of the end of the nineteenth century. The real facts upon which many divergent theories were based are: (1) an apparent doublet in the account of the accusation brought against Stephen, so that the substance of vi. 9-11 is repeated in vi. 12-14.

Ἀνέστησαν δέ τινες τῶν ἐκ τῆς συναγωγῆς τῆς λεγομένης Λιβερτίνων καὶ Κυρηναίων καὶ Ἀλεξανδρέων καὶ τῶν ἀπὸ Κιλικίας καὶ Ἀσίας συνζητοῦντες τῷ Στεφάνῳ, καὶ οὐκ ἴσχυον ἀντιστῆναι τῇ σοφίᾳ καὶ τῷ πνεύματι ᾧ ἐλάλει. τότε ὑπέβαλον ἄνδρας λέγοντας ὅτι Ἀκηκόαμεν αὐτοῦ λαλοῦντος ῥήματα βλάσφημα εἰς Μωυσῆν καὶ τὸν θεόν.

Συνεκίνησάν τε τὸν λαὸν καὶ τοὺς πρεσβυτέρους καὶ τοὺς γραμματεῖς, καὶ ἐπιστάντες συνήρπασαν αὐτὸν καὶ ἤγαγον εἰς τὸ συνέδριον, ἔστησάν τε μάρτυρας ψευδεῖς λέγοντας Ὁ ἄνθρωπος οὗτος οὐ παύεται λαλῶν ῥήματα κατὰ τοῦ τόπου τοῦ ἁγίου [τούτου] καὶ τοῦ νόμου, ἀκηκόαμεν γὰρ αὐτοῦ λέγοντος ὅτι Ἰησοῦς ὁ Ναζωραῖος οὗτος καταλύσει τὸν τόπον τοῦτον καὶ ἀλλάξει τὰ ἔθη ἃ παρέδωκεν ἡμῖν Μωυσῆς.

(2) The same phenomenon appears in the conclusion of the

story: the stoning of Stephen is described twice, vii. 54-58a and vii. 58b-60.

Ἀκούοντες δὲ ταῦτα διεπρίοντο ταῖς καρδίαις αὐτῶν καὶ ἔβρυχον τοὺς ὀδόντας ἐπ' αὐτόν. ὑπάρχων δὲ πλήρης πνεύματος ἁγίου ἀτενίσας εἰς τὸν οὐρανὸν εἶδεν δόξαν θεοῦ καὶ Ἰησοῦν ἑστῶτα ἐκ δεξιῶν τοῦ θεοῦ, καὶ εἶπεν Ἰδοὺ θεωρῶ τοὺς οὐρανοὺς διηνοιγμένους καὶ τὸν υἱὸν τοῦ ἀνθρώπου ἐκ δεξιῶν ἑστῶτα τοῦ θεοῦ. κράξαντες δὲ φωνῇ μεγάλῃ συνέσχον τὰ ὦτα αὐτῶν, καὶ ὥρμησαν ὁμαθυμαδὸν ἐπ' αὐτόν, καὶ ἐκβαλόντες ἔξω τῆς πόλεως ἐλιθοβόλουν.	Καὶ οἱ μάρτυρες ἀπέθεντο τὰ ἱμάτια αὐτῶν παρὰ τοὺς πόδας νεανίου καλουμένου Σαύλου. καὶ ἐλιθοβόλουν τὸν Στέφανον ἐπικαλούμενον καὶ λέγοντα Κύριε Ἰησοῦ, δέξαι τὸ πνεῦμά μου· θεὶς δὲ τὰ γόνατα ἔκραξεν φωνῇ μεγάλῃ Κύριε, μὴ στήσῃς αὐτοῖς ταύτην τὴν ἁμαρτίαν· καὶ τοῦτο εἰπὼν ἐκοιμήθη.

These doublets seem to be more than merely infelicitous repetitions, and really represent two traditions. According to one Stephen was lynched, according to the other he was executed—with some informality—by the Sanhedrin. The existence of this divergence is obscured by the insertion of the speech which implies that the Sanhedrin acted as judges.

This much seems probable, but some critics have gone further and analysed the speech of Stephen into two sources.[1] Many of these analyses are ingenious, and momentarily attractive, but none of them survive the test imposed by the question whether the text as it stands is improbable. The doublets in the narrative are real enough, but the supposed *strata* in the speech are imaginary and are not doublets. There seems more to be said for the theory that the whole speech—which bears so little

The speech of Stephen.

---

[1] The least unreasonable analysis is that of Feine. He postulates a Jewish-Christian source containing vi. 9-11, vii. 22-28, 35-43, 51-56, 59-60, viii. 1b, 2, and a Hellenistic source containing vi. 12-14, vii. 2-21, 29-34, 44-50, 57-58, viii. 1a, 3.

relation to the accusations brought against Stephen—is a free composition, either by the writer of Acts or by the author of the source [1] which regards the death of Stephen as due to the Sanhedrin, inserted into an earlier narrative which related that he was lynched. If any one will read Acts vi. 8-11, and vii. 54–viii. 1, omitting the intermediate verses, he will not detect any break in the narrative. This is of course no proof, but the suspicion will probably always remain that we have here a later edition of an early narrative, not its original form.

For the historian the important point is that, though no one of the complicated theories of Feine, Spitta, etc., is probable, they all rest on a few real facts which point to the general hypothesis that Acts vi. 8-11 with the conclusion of the narrative (especially if this be limited to vii. 54-58a) describe the martyrdom of Stephen as an act of lynching, prepared by a vigilance committee of Hellenistic Jews, while Acts vi. 12–vii. 53 taken with vii. 58b-60 describe a judicial execution by the Sanhedrin. Which is the more probably true? It is in general very unlikely that during the Roman dominion in Jerusalem the Sanhedrin could have carried out such an execution. Moreover, unless the whole tradition of Paul's connection with the martyrdom be unhistorical, Stephen's death cannot be placed at any date when the Romans were not in power; for Herod Agrippa had no authority in Jerusalem until 41 A.D.

Thus analytic criticism of Acts at this point really contributes something to the clearer statement of the historical problems. At the same time it does not seem that even the moderate suggestion made above has quite as much probability as the analysis of chapters i.-v. It is possible that the doublets in the narrative are accidental, and due to mere roughness of style; that Stephen really was tried before the Sanhedrin, which had no intention of inflicting an illegal sentence, but the crowd intervened and hurried Stephen to his death. The reason for

---

[1] The facts given in pp. 112 ff. as to Luke's use of the speeches in Mark support this alternative.

preferring the analytic view is that the existence of the doublets, in the accounts of the accusation and death of Stephen is rather strong evidence, and that the references to the witnesses and the garments seem intended to show that the death of Stephen really was by judicial process, but are historically inaccurate. It is true that according to the tractate *Sanhedrin* the witnesses had to begin the stoning and that the disposition of the 'garments' was also regulated : it was, however, the garments of the convict not of the witnesses.

It should be noted that the introduction of a trial which throws the opprobrium of judicial murder on the Jewish authorities, not on the people or on the Romans, is quite in keeping with the interest of the author of Acts, who is always anxious to show that Jesus, Peter, Stephen, and Paul were the victims of injustice at the hand of the Jewish rulers who condemned them when obviously innocent, while the Roman officials acquitted them, or acquiesced in the crime under protest.

Harnack, as usual, has disregarded these minor points, in order to grasp with more vigour the main contention of the writer of Acts, that the death of Stephen, and the persecution of the Hellenistic Christians which followed, were turning-points in the history of Christianity, because through them came the mission to the Gentiles; and therefore the evangelisations of Samaria and Antioch are connected with the persecuted Hellenists by the formula οἱ μὲν οὖν (in viii. 4 and xi. 19). But it is at least open to doubt whether Harnack is right in thinking that this formula in xi. 19 so far connects the story of Antioch with Stephen as to justify us in calling the story of Stephen the beginning of the Antiochian narrative. Nor does he adequately discuss the possibly composite character of the tradition of Stephen and the relation of this question to his theory. It seems at least possible that the stories of Stephen's death are part of the traditions of Jerusalem, and that the connection of Acts xi. 19 with Stephen is redactorial, though probably correct. It must, however, be noted that Acts vi. can scarcely come from the same documentary source as Acts i.-v. since with it begins the common use of μαθητής in the sense of Christian, of which there is no example in Acts i.-v.

As Harnack has seen, the Caesarean and Samaritan traditions are linked together by the names of Philip and Peter, and the characteristic recurrence of John as Peter's companion in the Samaritan section suggests a close relation with source *A* in Acts i.-v.

Personal or local traditions.
Was it around persons or around places that these traditions grew up ? No one can answer certainly, for history shows that traditions do both. The question then arises whether the Petrine portion of the Samaritan narrative, the only part of this section of Acts at all reminiscent of the Jerusalem Source *A*, does not represent a different story as to early Christianity in Samaria from that in the Philip section. The general schematisation by the editor is very apparent. He clearly wishes his reader to be convinced that though the evangelisation of a gradually increasing district was the work of the Hellenists, the original disciples— especially Peter—approved and co-operated. Access to the Pauline epistles probably will lead the historian to think that the spread of the Church was less peaceful. He may even accept the suggestion that the difference between Peter's hostility and Philip's friendliness towards Simon Magus is a hint of deeper differences, as to which the writer of Acts is silent consistently with his general policy of omitting almost all references to quarrels among Christians. The possibility cannot be ignored that there were two traditions as to the foundation of Caesarean Christianity, one attributing it to Philip, the other to Peter, and that the writer of Acts has combined them.

The conversion of Paul.
Besides this possibly composite account of the spread of Christianity as far as Antioch, the editor has prepared the way for the great theme of the second part of his book by telling the story of Paul's conversion. He does so three times in the course of Acts. Had he more than one source at his disposal ? There is no sufficient evidence, but there is something to be said for

THE INTERNAL EVIDENCE OF ACTS 153

the view that the account in Acts xxii. and xxvi. is nearer to Paul's own story, and that in Acts ix. there has been some editing in accordance with other versions, which made Paul more dependent on those who were Christians before him. The story of Ananias, as told in Acts ix., in Damascus, seems to be exactly the kind of story against which Paul protests in his epistles, urging that he was an apostle "neither of man nor through man." Thus the possibility—it does not amount to more—exists that Acts ix. partially represents the tradition of Jerusalem as to the conversion of Paul.

In the second part of Acts xi. and the following chapters there is clearly a fragment of Antiochian tradition. It covers xi. 19-30 and xii. 25–xiv. 28. It describes Paul and Barnabas as preaching in Antioch and undertaking a mission to Cyprus and Galatia. Harnack also reckons to this Antiochian source Acts xv. But why should this be so? Schwartz's view that Acts xv.-xvi. 5 represents the Jerusalem tradition of the same events as Acts xi. 19 ff. seems preferable. The reason is not any inconsistency or 'seam' in the narrative as it stands, but that no other theory seems equally well to solve the problem provided by the comparison of Acts xv. with Gal. ii. *Acts xi. 19-30 and xii. 25- xiv. 28.*

The main points of this famous puzzle are that in some ways Acts xv. seems to represent the same incidents as Gal. ii., but to give a very different account of them, and that though, according to Acts, this visit of Paul to Jerusalem was his third, in Galatians he calls God to witness that it was only his second. *Acts xv.*

The result of this difficulty has been to induce some writers to identify the visit mentioned in Gal. ii. with that in Acts xi. in connection with the famine relief,[1] and to suppose that Galatians contains no reference to the events described in Acts xv. because it was written before the meeting in Jerusalem took place. This satisfactorily answers the difficulties provided by Galatians, but it leaves the equally great ones of 1 Corinthians quite untouched. How could Paul treat of $εἰδωλόθυτα$ as he does in

[1] See pp. 277 ff. for the argument in favour of this view.

1 Corinthians, if an agreement on the subject had been reached by him and the Church of Jerusalem ?[1] If Acts xv. represents an Antiochian version of the incidents at Jerusalem no answer can be given; but the matter becomes altogether easier if it be supposed that Acts xv. is the tradition of Jerusalem. In this case it may well be a doublet of the account in Acts xi. which is clearly Antiochian, of the visit of Paul and Barnabas to relieve the famine in Judaea. It should be noted that there is no reason to suppose that either account is insincere. Unless written records are preserved the most extraordinary discrepancies arise in an incredibly short time even among the most careful and trustworthy persons. Any member of any faculty of any university could probably illustrate this fact from his own experience. It would be consistent with all that is known of redactorial methods to suppose that the editor of Acts found two accounts of the arrival at Antioch of messengers from Jerusalem, followed by a mission to Jerusalem of Antiochian representatives. According to the Antiochian account it was chiefly concerned with the obtaining of relief for the poor in Jerusalem; according to that of Jerusalem it was an attempt on the part of that Church to keep Antioch in the path of orthodoxy. The editor perceived the difference between them, thought that they referred to separate events, and separated them by the story of Paul and Barnabas' missionary expedition to Cyprus, Pamphylia, and Galatia.

Schwartz's corollary.

But Schwartz has seen that this conclusion carries with it a further consequence. The unavoidable corollary is that just as the meetings in chapters xi. and xv. are one and the same, so also the journeys which follow them are also identical. It then becomes worthy of renewed notice that neither account is complete. The story of the first journey stops, so far as any detailed account is concerned, in Lystra and Derbe, and is suddenly wound up by a few sentences which are surely

[1] The more the present writers have considered this point, the more does this objection impress them. See, however, pp. 272 ff. and 322 ff.

THE INTERNAL EVIDENCE OF ACTS 155

redactorial. The story of the so-called second journey begins with a passage which summarises the first part, but in Lystra begins again with a detailed narrative. Leave out the summary descriptions at the end of the first journey and the beginning of the second and there is a tolerably full and connected narrative. We cannot, of course, be quite certain as to the original text of the juncture; Schwartz suggests that Barnabas actually did return to Antioch from Lystra and Derbe though Paul did not do so. In this case we have in Acts the record of one long missionary expedition of Paul through Cyprus, Galatia, Asia, Macedonia, and Achaia. During the first part of it he was accompanied by Barnabas, but not during the second, for Barnabas went back to Antioch after preaching in Galatia, and did not go on into Asia. If this be so, it is natural to ask whether the division of this missionary expedition into two was not due to the fact that the writer of Acts had seen or heard of a tradition which described Barnabas and Paul's conjoint journey, and, being written by some one nearer to Barnabas than to Paul, said nothing about what happened to Paul after Barnabas left him.

This theory is attractive : but from the nature of the case can never be certainly proved. The writer of Acts was convinced that there were two journeys, and not one, and it is no more possible to undo his redactorial work than it would be in the gospel if we did not possess Mark. All that can be said is that just as Mark justifies the certain assignment of various parts of the gospel of Luke to different sources, so the existence of Galatians justifies the tentative suggestion that Acts xi. and xv. are parallel traditions of the same visit of Paul to Jerusalem, and the corollary that the journey described in Acts xiii. f. is the same as that summarised in the opening verses of Acts xvi.

The whole question revolves round Acts and Galatians ii. If we had not Galatians, which is to the criticism of Acts what Mark is to the criticism of Luke, the problem would be invisible. The account in Acts would lose most of its difficulties ; but it

156 THE COMPOSITION AND PURPOSE OF ACTS

is hard to reject[1] the classical view that Acts xv. corresponds to Galatians ii., and the central fact in the problem then becomes Paul's testimony that this was his second and not his third visit to Jerusalem. If so there is no reasonable solution except that which identifies Acts xi. with Acts xv., and explains the problem as the result of a loose use of sources.

Acts xii. One chapter remains to be treated. Chapter xii. gives the account of Peter's imprisonment and escape in the reign of Herod Agrippa I. This is one of the few passages in the early part of Acts of which the chronology is relatively certain. It must have happened in A.D. 44,[2] and before the famine in Jerusalem, which did not take place, according to Josephus, before 45 if not 46. Therefore chapter xii. ought to come before chapter xi. In other words, it is placed correctly with regard to the Jerusalem version of the visit of Paul to Jerusalem, but wrongly with regard to the Antiochian account. This is not unnatural, for it obviously belongs to the Jerusalem tradition.

It may, however, be legitimate to suggest a further complication in the Jerusalem tradition. Acts ix. 32 suddenly introduces Peter as journeying through the whole country, but there is no explanation as to how he came to be doing so. If chapter xii. 1-17 be inserted before Acts ix. 32, an admirable connection is given.

A curious and in some ways attractive consequence would follow from the acceptance of this rearrangement, which is in

---

[1] An attempt to reject it is made in K. Lake's *Earlier Epistles of St. Paul*, but on further consideration it seems that the arguments then given only emphasise the differences in detail and the different points of view in the two accounts. The general impression of identity remains, though if the analysis of sources in Acts be rejected, the position adopted in the *Earlier Epistles* seems inevitable. See also pp. 277 ff.

[2] It is plain that Peter left Jerusalem at the time of or just before the death of Herod Agrippa. Therefore the departure of Peter can be dated with great probability as the spring of 44 A.D. It is interesting to note that Eusebius, apparently in order to accommodate the facts to the belief that Peter was bishop of Rome for twenty-five years, puts the foundation of the Church of Antioch and the departure of Peter for Rome in the year 42 A.D., though he puts the death of Herod Agrippa correctly in 44 A.D.

itself by no means radical, representing only a change in the order of a source, to which several parallels could be adduced from the way in which Luke made use of Mark. The activity of Peter in Lydda, Joppa, and Caesarea could reasonably be supposed to occupy the greater part of a year. If Peter returned to Jerusalem at the end of this period he would have arrived at just about the same time as Paul and Barnabas came from Antioch on the mission described in chapter xi. In that case the discussion between Peter and the stricter sect of Christians in Jerusalem must have taken place at the same time as the discussion between the same group and Paul and Barnabas.

It is noticeable that in Acts xv. the speeches of both Peter and James refer to Peter's preaching to the Gentiles and his mission to them, and say nothing about Paul and Barnabas. If it were not for the context in which these speeches are placed one would say that they are much more appropriate to a discussion of the episode of Cornelius than to that of the Church in Antioch. A good many difficulties would be cleared up if the discussion at Jerusalem were supposed to be dealing with Peter and Cornelius as well as with Antioch and Paul.

If this reconstruction were accepted the chronological order of events would be : (1) the death of Herod and Peter's departure from Jerusalem ; (2) Peter's journey through Palestine to Caesarea ; (3) the famine in Palestine ; (4) Peter's return to Jerusalem and the Apostolic Council, related from the Antiochian point of view in Acts xi. and Galatians ii. and from the point of view of Jerusalem in Acts xv.

The second part of Acts is written in a style which is obviously different from that of the first, though the difference is not susceptible of statistical demonstration and does not exclude a remarkable unity in all parts of the book. It presents fewer problems in the identification of sources than the first part, but raises questions of the greatest importance for the authorship of the book.

158 THE COMPOSITION AND PURPOSE OF ACTS

The we-sections.

The most remarkable phenomenon in these chapters [1] is the alternation of style between the first person plural and the third person. The change is made as follows:

(1) Acts xvi. 1, first person.
(2) Acts xvi. 17, third person.
(3) Acts xx. 4, first person.
(4) Acts xxi. 27, third person.
(5) Acts xxvii. 1, first person.
(6) Acts xxviii. 17, third person.

Thus there are three sections written in the first person plural. The first begins in Troas, and ends with the arrest of Paul and Silas at Philippi. The second begins in Philippi—the place where the first "we section" ended, and ends with the interview in Jerusalem between Paul and James. The third and last begins when Paul leaves Palestine, and ends when Rome is reached.

Between these passages come long sections of narrative in which Paul is the chief subject and the first person is not used. In general it may be said that whereas there is some difference in style between Acts i.-xv. and the second part of the book, there is none between the "we" sections and the narrative in which they are embedded.

This presents a curiously difficult problem. On one point only is there a decided majority of favourable opinion. Few students doubt that the origin of the "we" sections is the actual diary of a companion of Paul. But to what extent this diary went, and the relation of the diarist to the compiler of Acts is disputed.

Four possibilities have received considerable assent, but none unanimous support.

(1) The traditional view is that the diarist is identical with the compiler of Acts and uses the first person to show that he was present during these parts of the events narrated.

---

[1] In the Western text of Acts xi. 20, there is another "we," but it is probably not genuine.

THE INTERNAL EVIDENCE OF ACTS

(2) The diarist is not the compiler of Acts but added to his own diary the intervening sections of narrative, thus producing a connected whole, which was later taken over by the compiler of Acts and formed the main source of Acts xvi.-xxviii.

(3) The diarist wrote nothing except the "we" sections; another writer added the intervening parts in Acts xvi.-xxviii., and the final editor added this composite work to Acts i.-xv.

(4) The diarist wrote nothing except the "we" sections, and the compiler added the intervening sections as well as Acts i.-xv. from other information.

No one of these theories can be lightly dismissed as absurd, and the difficulties of each are the strong points of the others.

The most clarifying and convenient procedure is to begin with a consideration of the possible meaning of the first person in the "we sections" and of its difficulty on any hypothesis.

The certainty with which eminent critics have put forward contradictory statements on this question seems due to their unconscious assumption of a previous point which they have very rarely discussed. That point is whether in their original form the two λόγοι sent to Theophilus contained a direct statement of authorship. Unfortunately that is exactly what we do not and cannot know. In the first place the title "the Gospel according to Luke" is surely not original, but was given to the first "treatise" after it had been separated from the second and incorporated into the fourfold canon of the Gospels. Its value as evidence is not that of an integral part of the original book, but of a summary of ecclesiastical tradition probably made in the second century.[1] Thus we do not know whether the original form of the first treatise was anonymous, as it is now, or contained a statement of authorship. In the second place who was Theophilus? No one knows. There is no early tradition, and Origen was inclined to think that Theophilus is merely an imaginary name for Christian readers in general.

If Theophilus was a real person, no doubt he knew who

[1] The value of this tradition is discussed on pp. 250 ff.

wrote the book sent to him, but if not the work may have been really as well as formally anonymous.

But in discussing the " we " sections this difficulty has been passed over. One group of writers has unconsciously assumed that of course the original readers knew who wrote the book—and therefore that the " we " sections were intelligible as a reference to the author. Another group has assumed equally unconsciously that the book was anonymous, and therefore that the " we " sections had no such reference. Each group started with its own assumption, but was unconscious of it, and treated it as a triumphant conclusion when it emerged again from the scientific consideration of the first person. Unfortunately an assumption cannot change its nature by being passed through never so many scientific processes.

If no such assumption be made—and only by an effort of will can we refrain from making it—the difficulty of the " we " sections appears equally great on either of the main hypotheses. In the first place the importance of being an eye-witness was well enough understood in the first century, and the use of the first person, of which there are many examples, is a natural method of expressing it. But the value of such direct testimony depends partly on who gives it. There are few or no parallels to the use of the first person by a writer who does not reveal his identity in the text of his work. On the other hand, if the use of the first person be not a claim to give first-hand evidence it remains equally a puzzle why the writer of the whole did not say who was the writer of the source to which he attached so much value. It is of course possible that he had found the diary, or a document about Paul including the diary, and used it as a source, preserving the passages in the first person to prove that he had here fulfilled the claim made in the preface to give the evidence of eye-witnesses. But there is no proof that this is the case. Therefore the frequent contention that the " we " sections prove the authorship of Acts by a companion of Paul is ungrounded. The truth rather is that they are a remarkably difficult pheno-

THE INTERNAL EVIDENCE OF ACTS 161

menon, and their interpretation depends on, and does not solve, the problem of the authorship of Acts.

They prove that certain parts of Acts were originally written by a companion of Paul, but they are explicable (with about equal difficulty) either on the hypothesis that he edited the whole of the Gospel and Acts, or that the editor of the whole made use of them, changing their style in places, but preserving the idiom as showing the value of these sections.

A plausible but fallacious argument[1] has sometimes been put forward to show that linguistic considerations prove identity of the editor with the writer of the 'we' sections. This was done first in 1866 by Klostermann in his *Vindiciae Lucanae*, with greater clearness, though with a characteristically correct reserve of judgment, by Sir John Hawkins in *Horae Synopticae*, and in a more spectacular manner by Harnack in his *Beiträge zur Einleitung in das Neue Testament*, especially Parts I., III., and IV., published between 1906 and 1911.

The linguistic argument.

Harnack's method, which has attracted attention in wider circles than those reached by the earlier books, was to examine word by word two of the 'we' passages, discussing those words or idioms which are characteristic of Luke's style. Then he makes a list of words that occur in the 'we' passages and elsewhere in Luke and Acts, but not in Matthew, Mark, or John.[2] Finally he prints the whole text of the 'we' passages, underlining the Lucan phrases and words. By all these methods the same fact is proved,—the great similarity of language in the 'we' passages and in the rest of Luke and Acts. This fact is not and never has been denied. But when Harnack makes deductions from the fact, his statements become less reliable. For he assumes that the relative abundance of Lucan words in a passage is evidence for or against the use of a source. In the 'we' passages the identity of language is, he believes, too great to allow

---

[1] The following section on the linguistic argument is by Dr. H. J. Cadbury.
[2] According to Harnack, *Luke the Physician*, p. 78, there are about 130 such words or phrases in 190 places in the 97 verses of the 'we' sections.

of the hypothesis that a source was used for these sections. The author of the whole historical work must be himself the author of those 'we' passages within it, must be, in short, a companion of Paul, presumably Luke the Physician. To the objection that many other parts of this work appear to have been based on sources, and yet have been revised by the editor so as to bear marks of his own distinctive style and vocabulary, Harnack makes a twofold answer: (*a*) Certain parts of the Gospel of Luke are dependent, it is true, on Mark and on another source (Q), yet where these sources are used, the author has only slightly transformed them, adding a few touches of his own, but retaining so much of the vocabulary of the original source that if no other Gospel were in existence we should know that Luke was dependent on a written source. (*b*) In Luke i., ii., and Acts i.-xii., xv., "the vocabulary and style are so absolutely Lucan that, in spite of all conjectures that have been made, the hypothesis of a Greek source is impossible, for there is nothing left for it."

Closely criticised, this argument appears fallacious, but in its method and principles rather than in the details. For it assumes that it is possible by the vocabulary and style of a passage in Luke or Acts to determine whether or not a Greek source has been used in its composition. But the style of these writings is throughout homogeneous, and the relative abundance of Lucan terms is not always due to the influence of sources. It cannot be denied that the 'we' sections abound in characteristic Lucan words and phrases. But if we are to put confidence in numerical comparisons we shall have to confess that Luke i., ii., for which Harnack claims equal originality and independence, uses such terms with less than half the frequency of the 'we' sections. In fact even the 'Q' passages of Luke, in spite of their faithfulness to their source, have nearly as many Lucan expressions as these chapters of the Infancy. And particularly where Luke is using Mark—for this is the surest ground for comparison—we are able to see how effectively the author covers over his sources, even when dealing with material which permitted less freedom than other parts of his history.

In these matters Harnack's statements are especially misleading. In connection with an analysis of two short passages taken by Luke from Mark he makes the following statements: " In spite of all the freedom with which the author of the third Gospel treats his source, the style, the syntax, and also the vocabulary of that source are still everywhere apparent." " The source is, as one sees, on the whole only slightly altered (some characteristic idioms and solecisms of Mark are nevertheless erased); moreover, its peculiar style here stands out clearly in comparison with those parts in which Luke could give himself freer rein, for it is evident that in chapter iii. ff. he has kept as closely as possible to the already existing type of Gospel narrative. Compare the καί beginning a new sentence ten times repeated (just as in the source, and quite in opposition to his own style)." " Here also the constant occurrence of καί at the beginning of sentences is for every careful reader of the Acts an evident proof that the author is following a source and not speaking in his own words. Otherwise the narrative is in detail (in style) so much altered and polished that the special character of the source is not immediately discernible " (*Luke the Physician*, pp. 87, 89 f., 93). But let us examine these statements. Harnack mentions the use of καί to begin a new sentence as due to Mark and gives some statistics in a footnote. But by actual count καί is also much more abundant than δέ in Luke i. ii., which by his hypothesis are not from a source. He says that the vocabulary of Mark is still apparent through the Lucan editing. Yet an actual count of the occurrence in Lucan writings of words impartially chosen as characteristic of Mark [1] shows that these occur as often or oftener in the parts of Luke and Acts not derived from Mark. And when Harnack says that in these Marcan passages Luke kept as closely as possible to the already existing type of Gospel

---

[1] See lists in Hawkins, *Horae Synopticae*, pp. 9 ff., and Swete, *St. Mark*, p. xliii.

narrative, imitated the phraseology of Mark, etc., he plainly admits that in "those parts in which St. Luke could give himself freer rein" he could show more abundantly features of his own style, even were he using a source. In other words the comparative abundance of Lucan terms in the 'we' sections is not final proof that no source was being used.

And sometimes at least even in copying Mark the Lucan characteristics are almost as abundant as in the 'we' passages. One illustration may here be sufficient. Harnack, in returning again to this argument in *The Date of the Acts*, pp. 15 ff., expresses himself as follows:

Let us take, by way of trial, the account of the shipwreck! If a source were present here it would be exceedingly improbable *a priori* that we should discover between it and the rest of the Acts of the Apostles or the Gospel of Luke any relationship either in language or in style that would be worthy of mention; for neither work is elsewhere concerned with sea voyages. And yet, how overwhelming even here is the multitude of coincidences! *Let us consider only the first three verses.*

Here follows a full commentary on Acts xxvii. 1-3, showing its Lucan characteristics, including eight of the kind noted above, that is, expressions found elsewhere in the Lucan writings but not in the other Gospels. Harnack then continues:

All these coincidences are found in the small compass of three verses. That this is due to accident, and that through accident the author of the Acts had come into the possession of an original document whose style and vocabulary so completely, and in every tiny detail, coincided with his own, is an impossible assumption. Hence, if one would escape from the admission of identity, there remains only the hypothesis that the author has entirely recast the document that had come into his hands. But what were the words of this document, and what could have led the editor to recast a record so absolutely simple in character? No! every one must recognize that we have here primary narrative, that there has been no working up nor revision.

There is, however, in spite of Harnack, in Luke's writings one other account of a sea voyage—the storm and threatened shipwreck of Jesus and his disciples on the Lake of Galilee in Luke viii. 22-24. Neither Harnack nor any one else will maintain that these are the independent composition of Luke. They are plainly a revision of Mark iv. 35-39, for they agree with it in thought, in position, and in several verbal details. The following is the text of the two passages. Words characteristic of Luke are underlined as in Harnack.

Mark.	Luke.
³⁵ Καὶ λέγει αὐτοῖς ἐν ἐκείνῃ τῇ ἡμέρᾳ ὀψίας γενομένης <u>Διέλθωμεν εἰς τὸ πέραν</u>. ³⁶ καὶ ἀφέντες τὸν ὄχλον παραλαμβάνουσιν αὐτὸν ὡς ἦν ἐν τῷ πλοίῳ, καὶ ἄλλα πλοῖα ἦσαν μετ' αὐτοῦ. ³⁷ καὶ γίνεται λαῖλαψ μεγάλη ἀνέμου, καὶ τὰ κύματα ἐπέβαλλεν εἰς τὸ πλοῖον ὥστε ἤδη γεμίζεσθαι τὸ πλοῖον. ³⁸ καὶ ἦν αὐτὸς ἐν τῇ πρύμνῃ ἐπὶ τὸ προσκεφάλαιον καθεύδων· καὶ ἐγείρουσιν αὐτὸν καὶ λέγουσιν αὐτῷ Διδάσκαλε, οὐ μέλει σοι ὅτι ἀπολλύμεθα; ³⁹ καὶ διεγερθεὶς ἐπετίμησεν τῷ ἀνέμῳ καὶ εἶπεν τῇ θαλάσσῃ Σιώπα, πεφίμωσο· καὶ ἐκόπασεν ὁ ἄνεμος, καὶ ἐγένετο γαλήνη μεγάλη.	²² <u>Ἐγένετο δὲ ἐν μιᾷ τῶν ἡμερῶν</u> καὶ αὐτὸς ἐνέβη εἰς πλοῖον καὶ οἱ μαθηταὶ αὐτοῦ, καὶ εἶπεν πρὸς αὐτούς <u>Διέλθωμεν εἰς τὸ πέραν</u> τῆς λίμνης. καὶ ἀνήχθησαν. ²³ <u>πλεόντων δὲ αὐτῶν ἀφύπνωσεν</u>· καὶ κατέβη λαῖλαψ ἀνέμου εἰς τὴν λίμνην, καὶ <u>συνεπληροῦντο καὶ ἐκινδύνευον</u>. ²⁴ <u>προσελθόντες δὲ διήγειραν</u> αὐτὸν λέγοντες Ἐπιστάτα, ἐπιστάτα, ἀπολλύμεθα. ὁ δὲ διεγερθεὶς ἐπετίμησεν τῷ ἀνέμῳ καὶ τῷ κλύδωνι τοῦ ὕδατος· καὶ ἐπαύσαντο. <u>καὶ ἐγένετο γαλήνη</u>.

Here again within the small compass of three verses are found many Lucan characteristics, including at least nine words or phrases peculiar to Luke among the evangelists.

To use Harnack's words, "the author has entirely recast the document that had come into his hands." If his original had not been preserved we should never have suspected from his language that this was the case, but should have asked with incredulity, "What were the words of this document, and what could have led the editor to recast a record so absolutely simple in character ?"

Conclusions. The general conclusion from any discussion of these linguistic questions is that they lead to nothing, if no assumption be made at the start.

The fact which emerges most clearly is that there are slight differences of style between various parts of Luke and Acts, and that the style of the 'we' sections is closer to the style of the redactorial changes in the sections known to be taken from Mark than the first part of Acts. This shows that the editor's style resembled that of the diarist more nearly than it did that of Mark or of the source used in Acts i.-xv. It does nothing more ; and the fact is not in itself very significant if the Aramaic element in Mark and Acts i.-xv. be taken into account. If it be held on other grounds that Acts probably was written by a companion of Paul the linguistic facts fit in admirably with this conclusion. But they fit no less well if it be thought that the authorship of Acts by a companion of Paul is impossible. Similarly, if it be believed that the writer of Acts was a physician the language of Acts offers no obstacles ; but neither does it forbid the view that he was nothing of the kind.

This negative conclusion ought not to be surprising, for, as is shown on pp. 112 ff., the indisputable evidence of Mark— the one still extant document which Luke used—discredits the suggestion that we can distinguish the sources of Luke by linguistic evidence. Though there are variations of vocabulary and idiom between various parts of the Lucan writings these often prove to be fallacious as tests when they can be controlled, and should not be trusted when they cannot.

The final decision whether the editor of Acts was the companion of Paul who wrote the 'we' sections depends on the argument as to the comparison of Acts with the Epistles.

If on these grounds it be held that the editor of the whole is identical with the writer of the 'we' sections the analysis of Acts may end here. It is true that such a conclusion does

THE INTERNAL EVIDENCE OF ACTS 167

not preclude the opinion that occasional sentences may be interpolations, but their consideration belongs to the commentary rather than to an introduction.

If, on the other hand, it be thought that the description of Paul in Acts is too different from the Paul revealed by the Epistles to come from the pen of one of his companions, the choice remains between the last three of the four alternatives already given. The writer of the 'we' sections may have himself supplied the intervening sections of narrative; or the combination of the 'we' sections with the intervening narrative may have been made by some other Greek writer, and the editor of Acts, who revised the whole, used it in this already composite form; or finally the combination may have been made by the editor himself.

The first of these possibilities will appeal to those who think that Acts xv. and the Apostolic decrees cannot have been accepted as true by a companion of Paul, but see no difficulty in the description of the events in Jerusalem in Acts xxii. But otherwise it has little advantage over the conservative view, for it is not necessary to think that a companion of Paul—or even Paul himself—knew everything about the early church in Jerusalem, and the extremest analytic view of the first part of Acts is quite consistent with the editing of the whole by Luke, the companion of Paul, if the references to Paul in Acts ix. and xv. be regarded as not too contradictory of Paul's own statements in the Epistles to be attributed to one of his companions.

The second possibility has similarly little to commend it in preference to the third, unless it be held that there are many relatively small interpolations in the text of the later chapters of Acts and several incidents in them which are not historical and readily distinguishable from the general body of the narrative. It is hard to see convincing evidence that this is the case, even though certain sections—such as the story of Scaeva—raise occasional doubts. Again, it seems better to discuss such points in the body of the commentary.

168 THE COMPOSITION AND PURPOSE OF ACTS

The growth of Acts.

Before passing on to consider the purpose of Acts, it may conduce to clearness if a summary be given of the stages which apparently have been passed through before Acts reached its present form, and of the difference made to the historian by the results of analytic criticism.

1. The automatic action of human memory, and the natural desire to preserve the records, led to the formation of local tradition in every place where a Christian church was founded. The problems needing further discussion in this stage are: (a) Were these traditions already in writing, and if so, in what language? (b) Did they already contain parallel traditions of the same events, thus creating doublets? The present writers think that they already existed in Aramaic writing and that they did contain doublets. But the question is obscure and incapable of complete solution.

2. The second stage was the collection of several of these local traditions into a connected narrative. That this was ultimately done is shown by Acts. The problems relating to it are whether this collection was first made in Aramaic or in Greek, and whether it was made first by the editor of Acts or by some predecessor whose work he used. That it was—so far as we know—never more than a partial collection is shown by the fact that the editor of Acts was only acquainted with the traditions of Jerusalem, Caesarea, and Antioch. He has nothing to say as to the tradition of the spread of Christianity in Damascus or in Tarsus.[1] It is worth considering that these are both traditions which must have been well known to Paul, and it is hard to think that they were unknown to any of his intimate companions, especially to a companion with an interest in the story of the beginnings of Christianity.

3. A new stage in the growth of formulated tradition was reached by the diarist who preserved an account of his travels in company with Paul. The essential difference between this

---

[1] It is possible that he knew, but preferred not to use these other traditions; but to the present writers this seems very improbable.

THE INTERNAL EVIDENCE OF ACTS

and the preceding stages is that it is concerned with individuals and with the missionary enterprise of an apostle, not with the local tradition of churches.

4. A further stage was the completion of the diary of the journeys with Paul by the intervening narrative of Paul's labours. Was this done by the diarist himself or by some one else ?

5. The whole of the preceding stages were revised by the editor of the two λόγοι sent to Theophilus. Once more, was this editor the same as the diarist ?

6. Somewhat later the two λόγοι were divided, and the first made into an εὐαγγέλιον, while the second was given (or retained ?) the title of πράξεις.

7. A final stage was reached when the whole of the Gospel and Acts was revised and vigorously amended textually. This stage will be dealt with in another place, but it is mentioned here because of the belief entertained by Blass and Zahn that it came before, not after, the preceding stage and was undertaken by the diarist himself.

That these stages were passed through before Acts reached its present form is certain. The problems involved are all internal to the various stages ; with their consideration we pass out of the domain of certainty into that of variously graduated probability. Assuming that the name of the diarist was Luke the choice of possibilities seems to extend from the view which attributes to him only stage 3, to that which attributes to him all except stage 1, and thinks that this stage was not in writing before his time. The present writers are more inclined to the former than to the latter extreme, but do not feel able to exclude a series of possibilities, down to the admission that the final editor may have been a companion of Paul at times, but if so he did not have a good understanding of the mind of Paul as shown in the Epistles.

The points on which the analytic arrangement of sources *Reconstruction of history.*

and a comparison with the Gospels and Acts give a different view of the course of events from that presented by the text of Acts as the editor arranged it, are, after all, not very many, and it is impossible sufficiently to emphasise the fact that the main reason for ever deserting the opinion of the editor is not subjective criticism of Acts, but the definite statements of Mark and Paul. It is their evidence, not his own suspicions, which forces the critic to seek in *Quellenkritik* some solution for the differences presented by three such early witnesses as Mark, Paul, and Luke. Led in this way to the analysis of the narrative, he is sometimes induced to go further, and to apply the same methods to solve the problems presented by the less perceptible, less important, yet surely not imaginary, discrepancies which are revealed by the text of Acts itself.

Beyond doubt, Luke and Acts give a connected and intelligible account of the events which intervened between the arrest of Jesus and the growth of Hellenistic Christianity. If we had not other documents, we should have no power and little reason to go behind it. The most that could be said is that the reference to Christians in Damascus shows that the spread of Christianity was somewhat wider and progressed somewhat faster than Acts would suggest. But the evidence of Mark shows that there was another tradition which represented the appearance of the risen Lord as taking place in Galilee, so that a full narrative of the events ought to include the flight of the disciples to Galilee, the appearance of the risen Lord, and their return to Jerusalem. It is true that certain alternatives have been suggested. The best known of these, and the most attractive, is offered by Johannes Weiss in his *Urchristentum*. He believes that the Marcan tradition is wrong. What really happened, according to him, is this: Jesus said,[1] in his conversation with his disciples just before entering the Garden of Gethsemane, "After I am risen, I will lead you into Galilee." This was misinterpreted, and reappears in a later and mistaken form as,

[1] Mark xiv. 28.

"After I am risen, I will go before you into Galilee; there ye shall see me."[1] Thus the Galilean tradition is an unhistorical attempt to provide a fulfilment for the words of Jesus. The true interpretation of the Greek implies that the disciples remained in Jerusalem waiting for the return of their master to lead them to Galilee: he never came, but he was seen, and the disciples received the Spirit instead of the Parousia which they expected. This is ingenious, but it is difficult to think that the Marcan tradition can really be explained in this way. It is bound up with Johannes Weiss's view that the whole story of the empty tomb is a relatively late tradition.[2]

A more subtle theory has been suggested, though never fully expounded, by F. C. Burkitt, to the effect that the lost conclusion probably contained a statement of how the disciples started for Galilee, but were turned back by a vision of the risen Lord while they were still near to Jerusalem. The objection to this theory would be that it is difficult to believe in the survival of, and indeed emphasis on, the tradition that Galilee was the place where the risen Lord was seen, if, as a matter of fact, he was really seen somewhere else.[3]

Thus the historian is driven to the conclusion that the account given by the editor of Luke and Acts is wrong, not primarily because of any subtle criticism, but from a preference for the earlier tradition of Mark. It is not the critic but the evangelist who raises the difficulty. But the recognition of this difficulty justifies a consideration of the suggestion of internal criticism that in Acts i. 1–v. 42 we are dealing with a narrative which has two Aramaic documents behind it. It is probable that Acts i. and ii. continue the Jerusalem tradition found in the last chapters of Luke, and that iii.-iv. 35 is another tradition of the same

---

[1] Mark xvi. 7.

[2] For the critical reasons in favour of the truth of the Marcan tradition that the women visited the tomb on the third day, see K. Lake, *The Resurrection of Jesus Christ*, pp. 166 ff.

[3] It is of course presumed that Matt. xxviii. 9 is a doublet of the words of the young man seen by the women at the tomb.

events. Acts iv. 36–v. 16 is a record of three incidents in the history of the Church in Jerusalem, any or all of which may be connected with either or neither of the preceding sources; but the story of the trial in v. 17-42 is probably another version of the event described in iv. 1-31. The historian is thus dealing with narratives which are more probably parallel versions of the same incidents than a consecutive account of separate ones.

The two accounts of the early Church in Jerusalem agree in representing the disciples: (1) as under the leadership of Peter; (2) as inspired—at least some of them and sometimes —by the Holy Spirit; (3) as opposed, but not seriously persecuted, by the Sanhedrin; and (4) as organised on a communistic basis. One of these accounts, but the obviously inferior one, gives a narrative which is linked directly with the Jerusalem tradition of the Gospel of Luke,—it represents the apostles as staying permanently in Jerusalem after the crucifixion. The other narrative seems to have no beginning, and it is impossible to notice this without thinking of the Galilean tradition—which has in the Gospel no completion. The historian is more than ever confirmed in the view that Mark gives the oldest account, but that for some reason, now untraceable, the Church forgot or ignored the 'Galilean episode' in which the disciples went back to (or towards?) Galilee, saw the risen Jesus and returned to Jerusalem. Whether the A source in Acts really represents a fragment of this tradition cannot be decided; but it is an attractive guess that the Galilean episode was related at the lost beginning of the A source, and that Luke felt that it was incompatible with the Jerusalem tradition of his choice. This much may even seem probable; but it is more hazardous to assume that the whole of this Galilean tradition was part of the lost conclusion of the Gospel of Mark.[1] Indeed this assumption seems to be positively improbable in view of the fact that source A seems to have been Aramaic, while Luke knew Mark in

[1] This view has the support of J. Weiss and F. C. Burkitt.

Greek.[1] Probably Mark and source *A* represent two extracts of the same originally Aramaic Galilean tradition. A tenable alternative is that, contrary to Torrey's view, Luke used Greek translations of all his Aramaic sources, as he did for Mark. In this case the translator whom Torrey has detected is not identical with the editor of Acts.

Similar help is given to the historian by the analysis of Acts vi.-xv. If Galatians were not extant it would be possible to hold that the course of events was that which the editor of Acts believed it to have been, that is to say the Church passed over to the evangelisation of the Gentiles by a series of events which followed each other. The first stage was the preaching of Philip in Samaria, if indeed the editor regarded that as preaching to the Gentiles. The second stage was the conversion of Cornelius to Christianity and of Peter to the recognition of the Gentiles. The third stage was the Gentile mission in Antioch. Few can doubt that the editor of Acts regarded these events as consecutive rather than synchronous. Moreover, the result of the Antiochian mission was, he thought, two distinct visits of Paul and Barnabas to Jerusalem, one to relieve the distress caused by famine, the other to discuss the legitimacy of the mission to the Gentiles.

The whole story is intelligible, and, at least at first sight, contains nothing to rouse suspicion, but the historian is faced at this point by two pieces of evidence which really raise legitimate doubt. In the first place, before the death of Stephen there were already Christians in Damascus, and in the second place the account given by Paul himself in the Epistle to the Galatians cannot be reconciled with that in Acts. At this point, therefore, the historian is justified in considering whether an appeal from the editor of Acts to the sources which he used is not a possible solution of the problem. It then becomes clear that the theory

[1] It is true that Torrey thinks that Mark is a translation, and that Luke knew both the Aramaic original and the translation, but there seems to be no sufficient evidence in favour of the latter part of this complex hypothesis.

of sources drawn from at least two centres of tradition and representing parallel accounts of the incidents common to both traditions brings Acts into harmony with Galatians, instead of leaving them irreconcilable as is the case when the editor is followed without criticism.

So far there is a reasonably strong case for the theory which divides Acts into parallel sources even while admitting that their exact delimitation is impossible. Anything further is hazardous, but it is just as hazardous to assume that the editor may be trusted as it is to rearrange his material. The point of most importance is obviously the relation between Acts xii. 17 and Acts ix. 32 ff. If a dislocation of sources such as can be paralleled from Luke's treatment of Mark be supposed, the return of Peter to Jerusalem from the conversion of Cornelius synchronises with the visit of Paul and Barnabas to Jerusalem, or is, at most, separated from it by a very short interval of time. This result is much less certain than the identification of the famine relief visit with the Apostolic Council of Acts xv. But if it be true it gives a very probable picture of events. The Church was spreading in every direction from Jerusalem. The two problems which became pressing were the relation of the Church to the Jewish law as applied to Gentile converts and the economic necessities of Jerusalem. The same people were concerned with both problems, and the criticism of sources suggests that their discussion came to a head in Jerusalem at the same time rather than, as the editor's use of the sources would suggest, at three separate moments. The effect of this discussion was to send Paul on his journey through Asia Minor and Greece. We are not told what happened to Peter, but other evidence assures us that it had the same effect upon him, for the Pauline Epistles give us glimpses of him in Antioch and Corinth, and tradition, which there is no reason to reject, tells us that he reached Rome.[1]

[1] The statements of Paul in Galatians suggest that Peter originally intended to preach only to Jews. But tradition seems to show that he did, in fact, make converts also among the Gentiles. Probably both he and Paul began by preaching in the synagogues, but found their chief success outside of them.

THE INTERNAL EVIDENCE OF ACTS 175

After Acts xv. the historian has but little to learn from analytic criticism. Various attempts have been made to dissect the second part of Acts into two sources ; but none has won any permanent place in the esteem of scholars. All that need be said is that 1 and 2 Corinthians [1] play here somewhat the same part as Mark and Galatians do in the consideration of Acts i.-xv. They warn the reader how imperfect and one-sided a record Acts is. It omits all the story of the dissensions in the Corinthian church, and nothing in Acts would account for the strong language which Paul uses in Corinthians about his misfortunes at Ephesus. The writer of Acts obviously omits and compresses : did he do so from ignorance or deliberately ? If he was ignorant, can he have been a companion of Paul for any long period ? If he did it deliberately, he surely was not writing with the primary object of telling the facts about the spread of the Gospel. He has suppressed the struggle between Paul and the extreme Greek party, just as he modified the story of the struggle between Paul and the Judaising party. Not to give a complete record, but to fulfil a didactic and possibly apologetic purpose was the object of the writer.

Whatever views may be held as to the analysis of Acts and the recovery of the sources used by the editor, it remains necessary to carry further the question raised by the last paragraph, What was the plan and purpose of the editor ? *The literary plan of Acts.*

So far as the plan of the editor, in the sense of merely literary composition, is concerned, it is obvious that he arranges his material in a natural and orderly manner, so as to describe the spread of the Church from Jerusalem to Rome, and divides

---

Missionaries may preach where they choose, but they make converts where they can.

[1] An attempt was made in K. Lake's *Earlier Epistles of St. Paul* to summarise the evidence of 1 and 2 Corinthians. This should be supplemented by a consideration of J. Weiss's commentary on 1 Corinthians. But it is perhaps worth mentioning that it was the sense of contrast of 1 Corinthians with Acts which led the writer of the *Earlier Epistles* to turn to Acts, before going on to the *Later Epistles*, which he has not, however, forgotten.

his narrative by short summaries of the progress made. Far the best statement of this is given by Professor C. H. Turner in the article on Chronology in Hastings' *Dictionary of the Bible*. He writes as follows : " The picture is cut up, as it were, into six panels, each labelled with a general summary of progress, and with so careful an artist, the divisions thus outlined are, in the absence of more precise *data*, the natural starting-point of investigation. (i.) *First period*, i. 1 : The Church in Jerusalem and the preaching of St. Peter : summary in vi. 7 : ' And the word of God was increasing, and the number of disciples in Jerusalem was being greatly multiplied, and a large number of the priests were becoming obedient to the faith.' (ii.) *Second period*, vi. 8 : Extension of the Church through Palestine ; the preaching of St. Stephen ; troubles with the Jews : summary in ix. 31 : ' The Church throughout all Galilee and Judaea and Samaria was having peace, being built up, and walking in the fear of the Lord and in the consolation of the Holy Spirit was being multiplied.' (iii.) *Third period*, ix. 32 : The extension of the Church to Antioch ; St. Peter's conversion of Cornelius ; further troubles with the Jews : summary in xii. 24 : ' And the word of the Lord was increasing and being multiplied.' (iv.) *Fourth period*, xii. 25 : Extension of the Church to Asia Minor ; preaching of St. Paul in ' Galatia ' ; troubles with the Jewish Christians : summary in xvi. 5 : ' The Churches then were being confirmed in the faith, and were abounding more in number daily.' (v.) *Fifth period*, xvi. 6 : Extension of the Church to Europe ; St. Paul's missionary work in the great centres, such as Corinth and Ephesus : summary in xix. 20 : ' So forcibly was the word of the Lord increasing and prevailing.' (vi.) *Sixth period*, xix. 21 : Extension of the Church to Rome ; St. Paul's captivities : summarised in xxviii. 31 : ' Proclaiming the kingdom of God and teaching the things concerning the Lord Jesus Christ with all boldness unhindered.'

" Of these six sections, the protagonist in the first three is St. Peter, in the last three St. Paul, and the two halves into which

THE INTERNAL EVIDENCE OF ACTS 177

the book thus naturally falls make almost equal divisions at the middle of the whole period covered."

There is only one point on which this statement may perhaps be supplemented or corrected. The general statement that Acts is arranged by the editor into a series of 'panels' is incontrovertible; but are there only six ? The doubt arises from the fact that at least two other passages may be taken as 'summaries' similar to those mentioned by Professor Turner—Acts ii. 47 and xi. 21. But this is a relatively minor question,[1] and the general correctness of the analysis is probable.

The purpose of the editor, as distinct from the plan of composition which he followed, is more important and more difficult. It can hardly be described by any simple formula. Few books are ever written with a single purpose. The preceding discussion shows that 'pure history'—the correct narration of all important events—cannot have been the aim of the editor. It was rather that object for which the Lucan writings have always been used—to give religious instruction. Therefore, by taking the Gospel and Acts as they stand, it is possible to form an accurate idea of the type of Christian teaching which he put forward and his contemporaries accepted. But before considering this side of the matter it is well to notice another, which, even if secondary, was probably far more important to the mind of the writer than it is obvious to ours. Are not the Lucan writings an apology for Christianity to the heathen as well as a manual of instruction for the Christian ? *The purpose of the Editor.*

It has often been recognised that, whatever else was the purpose of the writer of Acts, he was anxious to defend the *Acts as an apology for Christianity.*

---

[1] See also Prof. C. J. Cadoux, *Journal of Theological Studies*, 1918, pp. 333 ff., and Prof. B. W. Bacon in the *Harvard Theological Review*, April 1921. Both these writers go beyond Prof. Turner, and press the chronological aspect of the 'panels.' Their suggestions are full of interesting possibilities, but bear chiefly on the problem of Chronology, which will demand separate treatment in the Commentary. Reference may also be made to Moffatt's *Introduction to the New Testament*, pp. 284 ff. Moffatt thinks that the progress in the narrative implied by these 'panels' is geographical rather than chronological. More probably it is both : progress usually is.

Church against the suspicions of the official world. The general truth of this view rests securely on the internal evidence of the whole book, but it is difficult to formulate, because many facts well known to the writer are obscure to us. These are implied, but not explained, in the Preface, in which the writer addresses Theophilus as 'most excellent,' and endeavours to help him to 'know the certainty' of the information which he has received. The whole problem turns on these phrases. It may be resolved into three questions: (1) Who was Theophilus? (2) What is the meaning of the title 'most excellent'? (3) What kind of information is implied by the words περὶ ὧν κατηχήθης λόγων?

Theophilus. (1) There is absolutely no tradition of any historical value as to Theophilus. It has even been suggested that his name, 'Lover of God,' merely means 'the Christian Reader.' There is, however, no evidence of this custom in antiquity, and it is far more likely that Theophilus was a real, though forgotten, person. The notes appended to MSS. of the Gospels sometimes say that Theophilus was a disciple of Luke (H. von Soden, *Die Schriften des N.T.* i. p. 319), sometimes that he was a man of senatorial rank (συγκλητικὸν ὄντα καὶ ἄρχοντα ἴσως), because he is addressed as κράτιστος (*op. cit.* p. 324), but these statements are obviously only deduced from Luke, and are important as showing the absence of any independent tradition.

κράτιστος. (2) The title κράτιστος is usual in Greek to represent high official position. It is so found three times in Acts—of Felix in the letter sent to him by Lysias, and again in the speech of Tertullus, and of Festus in the speech of Paul.[1] It is also used by other writers in their dedicatory addresses, for instance, by Dionysius of Halicarnassus, who dedicates his *De orat. antiq.* to κράτιστε Ἀμμαῖε. On the other hand, the adjective is nowhere used by a Christian in the first two centuries of a brother Christian. It is, of course, scarcely probable that a Roman governor had the Greek name Theophilus, but the Greeks were notoriously apt to extend by courtesy the application of titles, and it remains

[1] Acts xxiii. 26, xxiv. 3, and xxvi. 25.

extremely probable that Theophilus was an official of some kind.

(3) The meaning of κατηχέω is in itself probably neutral. It is used in the Church to describe the instruction given to young converts, and the interpretation of Acts has been profoundly influenced by this custom. It is so used in Acts xviii. 25 of Apollos. But it is also twice used in Acts of the false information given about Paul by his enemies to the Jews in Jerusalem,[1] and a variant of the phrase 'to know the certainty' is also twice used of official investigation.[2]

Thus the evidence of Lucan usage does not support the usual explanation of commentators that Theophilus was a catechumen, thirsting for religious instruction, but rather suggests that he was a Roman official concerned with the public safety and legal procedure. He had heard stories damaging to Christians, perhaps especially to Pauline Christians, and the purpose of the writer was to disabuse him of these slanders by putting before him the exact facts.

The questions which would naturally occur to a magistrate's mind were two. Were the Christians practising a lawful religion ? Were they doing anything by word or deed which called for 'administrative' action ?

The earlier the date ascribed to Theophilus, the more probable it is that the question of the illicit character of the Church was in his mind, for in the Empire the distinction between a lawful and unlawful religion was rapidly being forgotten.[3] The theory

[1] Acts xxi. 21, 24.   [2] Acts xxi. 34, xxii. 30.
[3] See K. J. Neumann, *Der römische Staat und die allgemeine Kirche bis auf Diocletian*, i., 1890 ; P. Allard, *Histoire des persécutions pendant les deux premiers siècles*, tom. i. ; also his article on." La situation légale des chrétiens pendant les deux premiers siècles " (*Revue des questions historiques*, 1896, pp. 5 ff.) ; L. Guerin, " Étude sur le fondement juridique des persécutions dirigées contre les chrétiens pendant les deux premiers siècles de notre ère " (*Revue hist. de droit français et étranger*, 1895, pp. 713 ff.) ; J. E. Weis, *Christenverfolgungen*, 1899 ; Th. Mommsen, *Historische Zeitschrift*, 1890, S. 389 ff. ; *Römisches Strafrecht*, 1899 ; E. G. Hardy, *Christianity and the Roman Government*, 1894 ; W. M. Ramsay, *The Church in the Roman Empire before 170* (1893) ; A. Linsenmayer, *Die Bekämpfung des Christentums durch den römischen Staat*, 1905.

180 THE COMPOSITION AND PURPOSE OF ACTS

was that all religions were forbidden unless they had been definitely sanctioned; but, in the Provinces especially, the general principle was to accept any local cult, provided it contained nothing detrimental to good order. Still, to be able to prove that a religion was lawful was a point which any apologist would be likely to make.

How could a Christian do this? No religion could in practice expect to be tolerated unless it was that of a recognised 'race' of men, and no new religion could be licensed. This explains why all the Apologists, except Aristides, argue that Christianity is the true religion of Israel, and Aristides tries to cover the same point by arguing that the Christians are a 'new race,' and therefore—so it is implied—have a right to a new religion.

That Luke has anticipated the Apologists in this respect can be seen in the Gospel as well as in Acts.

The Gospel as an Apology.
The preface to the Gospel is so worded as to lead the reader to suspect that he is about to peruse an ordinary work by a literary man of the period, but suddenly he finds the author adopting the Hebraic style of a native of Palestine. It may be that at this point he is translating from a Semitic source, but in any case he introduces Theophilus in this manner to the first stage of his argument, the origin of the new faith in the Temple at Jerusalem. In contradiction to Matthew, who desires to emphasise that Jesus was born as Christ, in accordance with prophecy, at Bethlehem, the Third Gospel dwells on the connection both of the Forerunner and of Jesus with the Temple. The scene opens with the ministration of Zacharias in the Sanctuary; and the Temple, throughout the first two chapters, is always the background. The predictions of the future glories of the divine child clearly foreshadow the attributes of the risen Lord in Acts. Thus the promises made by Gabriel to Mary at the Annunciation are that the child shall be great and shall be called υἱὸς ὑψίστου, he shall sit upon the throne of David his father, and he shall be called υἱὸς θεοῦ. The Virgin is to conceive when the Holy Spirit comes upon her (πνεῦμα ἅγιον ἐπελεύ-

σεται ἐπὶ σέ). In the *Magnificat* we have an undoubted echo of Hannah's song on the birth of Samuel, who was destined to be the prophet deliverer of Israel, and in i. 54 the words ἀντελάβετο Ἰσραὴλ παιδὸς αὐτοῦ are a reminder of the passages in Isaiah which lead up to the revealing of the 'servant of Jehovah.' In the *Benedictus* a similar note is struck. The 'horn of salvation' is to arise from the House of David, καθὼς ἐλάλησεν διὰ στόματος τῶν ἁγίων ἀπ' αἰῶνος προφητῶν αὐτοῦ, and it is the sign of salvation from our enemies. In like manner the angels announce that a Saviour is born ὅς ἐστιν χριστὸς κύριος, and Simeon on seeing the child Jesus calls him τὸ σωτήριόν σου ὃ ἡτοίμασας.

The point throughout is that Jesus and his work are the proper culmination of the history of Israel, foretold by the prophets, and by those who represent the true leadership of the nation.

In the succeeding chapters of the Gospel and in Acts the keynote is the unity of the progress of the Gospel inaugurated by Jesus, continued by the Twelve, and carried to the ends of the world by Paul. The difficulty lay in bridging the gulf which separated the Pauline teaching and the primitive Christian message. Paul as presented in the Lucan literature is not the Paul self-revealed in his epistles, a man relying on his own spiritual experiences, and almost fiercely independent of those of others; but an earnest missionary, scrupulously deferential to the authority of those older than himself in the faith. We are more impressed by the 'correctness' of Paul's attitude than by his greater qualities. He is scrupulous in offering the Gospel in due order, seeking out the synagogue directly he arrives in a new city. His conduct to the Church of Jerusalem is represented as irreproachable, his attitude towards the Jews is beyond criticism, the concluding chapters are mostly devoted to forensic matter, that is, to speeches proving the legality of Paul's position. Nothing to all appearance could be a more unexpected sequel to the story of the preaching and death of Jesus and the signs following the Resurrection than the defence of Paul in Acts, yet it is germane to the argument of the author. He is anxious to show the unity between Israel and Jesus, Jesus and the Twelve, the Twelve and Paul in order to establish the legitimacy of Christianity as the religion of the Chosen People. Therefore he obviously schematises the stories of Jesus, of Peter, and of Paul so as to bring out the parallelism between them.

Just as in Acts Paul begins his ministrations everywhere in the synagogue, so in the section peculiar to Luke had Jesus done before him; and as at Lystra Paul was dragged ἔξω τῆς πόλεως to be stoned, so had it been with Christ at Nazareth.[1] The writer of the Gospel is naturally bound by his sources, and possibly by tradition, as to his manner of relating the story of Jesus; yet when he comes to the appointment of the Twelve he carefully disconnects it from the mission to Jews only, as in Matthew x., and gives the incident an additional importance by stating[2] that Jesus bestowed on them the name of 'apostles' (οὓς καὶ ἀποστόλους ὠνόμασεν). Just as Barnabas and Saul were chosen for the mission to Gentile lands after prayer, so were the Twelve selected after Jesus had been διανυκτερεύων ἐν τῇ προσευχῇ τοῦ θεοῦ. The introduction to the discourse in chapter vi. differs significantly from that to the Sermon on the Mount, in which Jesus, like another Moses, goes up into the mountain, followed by his disciples. In 'Luke' Jesus chose (ἐκλεξάμενος) the apostles on the mountain, and came down with them (καταβὰς μετ' αὐτῶν) to give his instruction with his disciples to the multitude. Here the design of 'Luke' is evident. He represents the Twelve as the official preachers of the Gospel, descending with the Master when he proclaims its moral principles. The same appears in the discourse itself. In Matthew it is the interpretation of the Law

---

[1] "Ὥστε κατακρημνίσαι αὐτόν. In the Mishna (Sanhedrin) the man to be stoned was cast down before he was stoned, with the idea that he might be killed by the fall.

[2] So also in Mark; but the text is here doubtful, and may be an accommodation to Luke.

by Jesus, whereas in 'Luke' it is a missionary address in which the Law is not mentioned or quoted. 'Luke' is careful to show that in his opinion the apostolate was a permanent and not a temporary office, as is implied by Matthew; for, whereas Matthew makes the selection of the Twelve precede the discourse about preaching in Palestine 'to the lost sheep of the house of Israel,' Luke connects it with the sermon which contains the essence of a world-wide propaganda.

Although the other evangelists mention the preaching of Jesus from town to town, they do not appear to do so with the set purpose, seen in the Third Gospel as compared with Acts, showing that the missionary work of the Apostles was in conformity with the precedent set by Jesus.

But, it might have been said, the Jews rejected Jesus and his followers. How, then, could Christianity be the true religion of Israel? The answer which the writer seems to suggest is the traditionally Christian one, that the Jews had always rejected the teachers whom God had raised up. Their treatment of Jesus was unjustifiable; Pilate and Herod did not condemn him, they only yielded to pressure. The righteous man in the Sanhedrin, Joseph of Arimathea, had opposed his execution[1] and given him honourable burial, but his colleagues had gone their wicked way, as their fathers had done. Similarly in Acts, Gamaliel, the most prominent Jewish teacher, befriends the Apostles, though the priests persecuted them as far as they dared. Stephen is condemned and stoned, and his defence is nothing but a long argument to show that this is exactly what the Jews might have been expected to do; it confirmed rather than refuted the claim of the Church to be the true Israel.

So also Paul is accused by the Jews, but supported by the Pharisees and by King Agrippa; and in Rome the prophets are quoted to show that nothing but the obstinate refusal to recognise their own religion could be expected from the nation.

The conclusion is obvious: the writer desires Theophilus to

[1] A point, be it noted, peculiar to Luke.

understand the claim of the Church to be the true Israel, and consequently that its worship was lawful in the Roman Empire.

Equally plain is the running stream of suggestion that the Church was harmless, had always been found so, and could not justly be punished. A comparison of the trial of Jesus in Mark with that in Luke shows how strongly Luke brings out the favourable judgment of Pilate. The same purpose is naturally less visible in the early chapters of Acts, but even there the general description of the Church seems calculated to disarm criticism. In the story of Paul it is very plain.

He was the subject of constant persecution but in no instance has it so much as a show of legality. On the contrary, all who are in authority, notably the Roman officials, are made to show him marked consideration. Until the Council of Jerusalem he and Barnabas are not molested save by the envy of the Jews, who stir up the people and drive them from city to city, and at Lystra Paul is stoned by the mob but is not seriously hurt.[1] The only Roman mentioned in this section is the proconsul, Sergius Paulus, who became a believer.

Paul's second journey (ch. xvi. ff.) is marked by persecution. At Philippi he is accused as a disturber of the peace and of introducing customs which it was unlawful for Romans to observe. He and Silas, however, complained that they were unjustly imprisoned and scourged as men who had not been condemned, and pleaded their Roman citizenship so that they were at their insistence publicly acquitted. It appears indeed to be the point of the whole story to show that they were absolutely guiltless of the charge of rioting or teaching unlawful practices.[2] At Thessalonica Jason, their host, was accused of harbouring men who were violating the law and proclaiming Jesus a

---

[1] Acts xiv. 19-20. Paul was supposed to be dead. He was stoned in a riot, but when the disciples stood round him he arose and went into the city. The incident recalls the escape of Jesus at Nazareth, Luke iv. 28-30.

[2] Acts xvi. 37 δείραντες ἡμᾶς δημοσίᾳ ἀκατακρίτους . . . καὶ νῦν λάθρᾳ ἡμᾶς ἐκβάλλουσιν. The contrast is between the public nature of the insult and the privacy of the would-be apology on the part of the magistracy.

rival emperor (βασιλέα). The politarchs dismiss the charge as absurd, take security of Jason and set them at liberty.[1] At Corinth Gallio declares that he can take no cognisance of purely Jewish disputes and refuses to hear the charges made against Paul. At Ephesus the Asiarchs protect Paul by sending their advice that he should not show himself in the theatre, and the town-clerk (γραμματεύς) pointedly acquits Gaius and Aristarchus, who were brought before him, of being temple robbers or blasphemers of the goddess Artemis.

The section xxi. 14–xxvi. 32 is a defence of the legality of Paul's position. In deference to the desire of the Jewish Christians he had consented to bear the expenses of certain brethren in discharge of vows they had taken. On being seen in the Temple he was attacked by the fanatical Jews and accused of bringing heathen Greeks into the Temple. This was a capital charge, but the Jews, and apparently the high priest, were determined to have Paul killed whether guilty or not, and a band of assassins was formed to slay him. Paul, who had declared himself to be a Roman citizen, was carefully protected from injury by Claudius Lysias and sent under a strong guard to Felix the procurator at Caesarea. As has been already stated, his defence to the Jews was that as a Pharisee he had always observed the Law. Before Felix he was charged by Tertullus with being a disturber of the peace throughout the Empire, a leader of the faction of the Nazarenes, and one who had tried to pollute the Temple at Jerusalem.[2] Paul's answer was virtually that the Jews had no proof, as they had not produced the Asiatic Jews, the only witnesses whose testimony would have been of service to them.[3] Felix is represented as knowing too much about the new religion (ἀκριβέστερον εἰδὼς τὰ περὶ τῆς

[1] Acts xvii. 5 ff.
[2] Acts xxiv. 5-6. Paul is accused generally as a disturber of the peace, as the head of the Nazarenes, and particularly of trying to pollute the Temple. Note Tertullus does not charge him, as did the Jews (xxi. 28), with having actually done so.
[3] Acts xxiv. 19

ὁδοῦ) to listen to this charge and to have kept Paul under arrest merely because he hoped to extract more money from him. Festus, his successor, acted with prudence and refused to be hurried into precipitate action on his arrival. He offered Paul a trial at Jerusalem, and accepted without hesitation his appeal to Caesar.[1] Herod Agrippa next appears on the scene. Being a Jew, he was more capable than a Roman of deciding the issue. His verdict was decisive: "This man doeth nothing worthy of death or bonds. . . ." He might have been released but for his appeal. Arrived at Rome, no more is said of the charges against Paul. He is simply allowed to live in a private house of his own, to receive his friends, to preach the kingdom of God, and to teach about Jesus. The meaning of the last two verses of Acts is that Paul was either acquitted or allowed to live in a house of his own to which his friends were given free access.[2]

Significance of the acquittal of Paul.

The termination of Acts is extremely significant. The climax is the freedom accorded to Paul. A very large proportion of Acts has been devoted to the discussion of the charge made against him that he was a seditious person who had tried to profane the Temple. The Jews had spared nothing to secure his condemnation. The High Priest Ananias had showed the utmost animus in the trial before the Sanhedrin. Yet Felix, venal and unjust as he was, desirous as he was to gratify the Jews, dared not pronounce sentence against Paul. Festus tried to induce Paul to go to Jerusalem to be tried, but was forced to allow the appeal to Caesar. Agrippa, a Jew, not blinded by prejudice, heard the Apostle and proclaimed him innocent without hesitation. At Rome, even the Jews disclaim all interest in the prosecution, and though nothing is said of his trial before Caesar, he is left free in his own hired house, at perfect liberty to see his friends and to preach and teach his message. Of what

[1] Acts xxv. 12.
[2] Acts xxviii. 16. On Paul's arrival at Rome he was allowed to live where he chose under guard, but in 30-31 the soldier who kept him is not mentioned.

THE INTERNAL EVIDENCE OF ACTS 187

happened to him later there is no record,[1] but the writer of Acts might well have added : "So you see nothing could be laid to Paul for his preaching Jesus. As a Jew and as a Roman he was legally guiltless." The religion which he preached was the ancient faith of Israel, rejected by the Jews, only by reason of their traditional lack of obedience to the guiding of God and of his prophets. It was therefore a lawful religion in the Empire. In its lawful pursuit neither Jesus nor Paul had ever been convicted of bad behaviour by a competent magistrate. In the capital of the Empire itself, Paul, while still under surveillance, had preached without let or hindrance from the authorities.

The didactic purpose of the editor of Acts is clearer than his apologetic object, and has often been described. *The didactic purpose of Acts.*

It can be treated in several ways, each with its appropriate advantages. Following the order of theological importance, it would be natural to take successively the teaching about God, about Christ, about the Spirit, and about the Church. But there is much to be said for taking rather the order in which the Gentile world would have faced the matter. The first question would have been as to the Church. What did it claim to be and what was its message ?

The answer, that the Christian Church was the ancient people of God, was at least as important for the instruction of converts as it was as a justification before Roman lawyers. It was indeed more likely to be accepted as a privilege than entertained as a defence. As has been said already, this point is emphasised by Luke more than by Matthew, and far more than by Mark. Indeed, the Lucan writings stand out as the earliest documents which represent the self-consciousness of the Church and the belief that its history was the final development of the divine promise that the true Israel should be God's own people. That development involved the provision for the changing of the *The Church.*

---

[1] Acts never tells what happened to any of such leading characters as Peter or Barnabas : they simply drop out of the narrative. James only is mentioned as being beheaded.

basis of the promise in the last days, so that the opportunity of enjoying its privileges should be extended to the Gentiles, and the congregation, or people of God, be no longer on a national basis. The Christians, therefore, adopted, in speaking of themselves, the title of *Ecclesia*, which to Hellenistic ears must have inevitably taken with it the claim that they were the chosen people, the true Israel. For ἐκκλησία is used in the Septuagint, except in Genesis, Exodus, Leviticus, and Numbers, to mean the People of the Lord assembled together for common action, and it is this use of the word in the Septuagint which is really important, rather than any considerations derived from Greek etymology.[1]

This contention necessitated a new series of arguments from prophecy, and Acts shows how part of the Christian theology was the elaboration of proof texts to demonstrate that the promise was not to the Jews only, but also to a congregation chosen out from the Gentiles. We have, in fact, the beginning of the arguments of the Christian apologists, and of such writers as the authors of Hebrews and Barnabas, who desire to show that the whole of the Old Testament foretells the Christian Church and belongs to it.

The true God. Inasmuch as the Church was the 'ancient people of God,' it followed naturally that the primary object of the earliest Christian mission to the Gentiles was in one respect entirely identical with that of the Jewish mission. Both the Church and the Synagogue believed in the God of the Jews, held that he was the only true God, and endeavoured to turn the heathen from the

[1] Etymologically ἐκκλησία means the assembly 'called out' from a Greek city by the herald, but as is usually the case with well-known and often-used words, this original sense, referring to the method of the assembly, was completely merged in the acquired sense of the persons composing the assembly. It translates *qahal*, but for those who, like the first Christians, took the Septuagint as their sacred book, the fact that it represented *qahal* rather than 'e dhah would be a point of small importance. The word would be familiar to all as the characteristic designation of Israel, the people of God, especially in Chronicles, Ezra, and Nehemiah. This remains true even though the origin of the word is probably the translation of Keneseth, the ordinary word for a synagogue. See F. J. A. Hort, *The Christian Ecclesia*, pp. 3-15 and vol. i. p. 304.

THE INTERNAL EVIDENCE OF ACTS 189

worship of idols to his service. So far as the Gospel and the early chapters of Acts are concerned there is of course little trace of this propaganda, for there was no controversy on this point between Jesus and the Jews or between them and his disciples. There are really only four places in which Acts gives a direct account of Christian preaching to the Gentiles, and in these the worship of the true God is put into the foreground. At Lystra Paul begins his speech, " We are men of like passions with you, and our message to you is to turn from these vanities to a living God." Similarly at Athens the message of Paul to the Greeks is that he announces to them the God ' who made the world and all that is in it.' It is not until the end of his speech that he mentions Jesus, and then not as ' the Lord,' but as a man whom God had ' appointed to judge the world.' [1] Much the same may be said, though with less certainty, of the speech of Paul at Miletus to the Ephesian elders where he summarises his teaching as ' testifying both to Jews and Greeks of repentance (or conversion) to God and faith in our Lord Jesus.' Once more, in explaining his preaching to Agrippa II., Paul describes his mission to the Gentiles as ' a call to repentance and conversion to God.' Moreover, apart from these special references, it must be remembered that to Gentile eyes the whole of the Gospel and of Acts would appear as one continuous plea for belief in the God of Israel, the claim of whose missionaries was justified by history, by prophecy, by miracles, and by the resurrection of his anointed servant, Jesus.

More controversial, and in some ways more important, than Jesus.

---

[1] It is noticeable that this is an example of an unmixed " Son of Man " Christology. It seems to us to belong to a less developed form of thought than that of the editor of Acts. This is one of the minor reasons in favour of the view that there is a documentary source behind the second part of Acts. It is well to remember in this connection that although there is abundant evidence that the speeches in the literature of this period are the least likely part of any book to have escaped revision, and may even be the free invention of editors, it is also true that the comparison of Luke with Matthew and Mark suggests that he found speeches in his sources, and contented himself with comparatively small revisions.

the preaching of the true God, which marked the connection of the Church with Judaism, was a change in the view held as to Jesus.

Two points stand out here as characteristic of the Lucan writings. Though Jesus is the Son of God, Messiah, the Davidic King, and the Son of man, these titles and their implications come from the sources used in the Gospel or in Acts. They are accepted by the writer and are not peculiar to him. But in no writing certainly earlier than Luke is the statement to be found that Jesus was the Son of God because he was born of the Virgin Mary by the operation of the Holy Spirit.[1] In Mark the divine sonship of Jesus begins at the Baptism.[2] It is true that the Lucan view is also held in Matthew, but it is less emphasised; and it is by no means certain that Luke is later than, still less dependent on, Matthew. Thus Luke is clearly differentiated from Mark on the one hand and from John on the other by his doctrine of the Divine generation of the Son by birth from the Holy Spirit and Virgin Mary,[3] not by the descent of the Spirit at the Baptism, nor by eternal pre-existence as in Johannine Christianity.[4]

Equally important and equally characteristic of Luke is the

---

[1] Luke i. 35. Cf. Vol. I. pp. 398 and 400.

[2] The words in Mark i. 9 ff. can originally have meant nothing but that Jesus became at the Baptism the Son of God by the impartation to him of the Holy Spirit. Only when the nativity stories were prefixed, could it be taken to mean that Jesus was then announced to be what he had been in reality from the beginning.

[3] See further, p. 200.

[4] It is impossible to discuss here the difficulties of a precise formulation of the Johannine doctrine, or the history of Christian doctrine on the subject before Origen. But it is permissible to point out that a promising line of enquiry begins by asking whether John i. 14 used the phrase μονογενής of the incarnate or the pre-incarnate Logos. Hort's famous dissertation is the beginning of wisdom for students approaching this subject, but it may be added that even if the variant in John i. 13 (ὃς ἐγεννήθη κ.τ.λ. instead of οἳ ἐγεννήθησαν) be not genuine, it is very early, and thus reflects the belief that the Logos who had existed with the Father from the beginning was begotten in time, and so became μονογενής. John holds to the pre-existence of the Logos, but this is not the same as the doctrine of the eternal generation. Nor is it germane to the subject that the Fathers of the later centuries thought one way or the other.

sense that Jesus was the living head of the Christian Church. This marks the divergence from Judaism, and the self-consciousness of Christians that even though they are the Congregation of the Lord they are not the Synagogue of the Jews. This is a real change from anything which can have existed in the original Jewish community, and is marked by the adoption of the title Lord for Jesus. It means that to the writer Jesus was not so much the national king of the Jews or the supernatural judge of the living and the dead (though he was these also) as the supernatural leader of the Church.

Is it fair to go further and say that to the editor of Acts Jesus was the centre of worship or even an object of it ? Here again much depends on the discrimination of sources. In the early chapters of Acts the centre of worship is God—the God of the Jews. Jesus is his holy servant through whose name miracles are wrought; prayer is directed to God, not to Jesus.[1] It is true that the dying words of Stephen are an appeal to Jesus to receive his spirit, but it must be remembered that at that moment he was seeing the vision of the risen Lord at the right hand of God; the words are a petition for help, not an act of divine worship. "He saw his Master in the skies, and called on him to save." On the other hand, the appellation of Jesus as Lord, which is certainly characteristic of the editor of Acts, was a long step in the direction of deification and consequent worship.[2]

What in any case stands out clearly is that just as the relation to the true God marked the 'ancientness' of the Church, its relation to the Saviour marked its 'newness.' The Church is

[1] Cf. iv. 24 ff.
[2] J. Weiss and others seem somewhat to exaggerate the evidence for the worship of Jesus by the first Christians. To regard him as a supernatural protector and helper—the Saviour—and as one whose name was potent to influence God and to conquer devils is one thing, but to worship him with the same worship that is given to God is a different matter, against which all Jewish tradition would have revolted. The question may be raised in this connection of the meaning of Revelation xxii. 6-9. Is it possible to avoid the identification with Jesus of the angel, who announces that he will come quickly, but repudiates worship ?

the ancient people of God, but it is also a new thing in the history of the world. Of course the writer would have said that this was the fulfilment of prophecy and was part of the divine plan. In this respect Acts is the logical antecedent of Aristides with his startling claim that Christians are a new race. On the negative side there is a noteworthy absence of any metaphysical speculation as to the original relation between God and the Lord. Nor indeed would this be otherwise. The Lord was the Son of God 'begotten'—not 'of his Father before the world,'—but 'of the Holy Ghost and the Virgin Mary.'

The Holy Spirit.
A third point which characterises the thought of the editor is the belief that Christians were inspired by the Spirit owing to their membership in the *Ecclesia* and its connection with the Lord Jesus. The connection of the *Ecclesia* with the Lord Jesus is implied throughout Acts, as it is in all other early Christian literature; the apostles are specifically his missionaries, and to his service Paul is converted. But it is not less plain that the members of the Church were regarded as gifted with the Holy Spirit, even though certain points are obscure in the view which is presented of the working of the Spirit.[1] It seems plain that the Spirit is the 'Spirit of the Lord' of the Old Testament, but it is also sent from God by Jesus (Acts ii. 33), and in one place it is apparently described as the Spirit of Jesus (Acts xvi. 7). This reminds us of the manner in which in Romans viii. the words 'Christ,' 'the Spirit of Christ,' 'the Spirit of God,' 'the Spirit,' are interchanged, with no apparent difference of meaning; but in Acts the connection of the Spirit with the Lord has not quite reached the stage of identification represented by such passages, or still more by the direct statement, "The Lord is the Spirit" in 2 Cor. iii. 17. Moreover, the apparent exchange of usage between 'Spirit' and 'angel of the Lord' in the story of Philip (Acts viii. 26, 29, 39) suggests the confusion between angel and Spirit which is noticeable in Hermas and Tertullian, and seems to have its origin in a remote chapter

[1] Cf. Vol. I. pp. 325 ff.

THE INTERNAL EVIDENCE OF ACTS 193

of Jewish theology. There is, however, nothing which really enables us to answer the question whether the Spirit was completely hypostatised or was regarded as an impersonal element sent by or from God. On the one hand, the Spirit ' speaks,' which is a personal act; but on the other hand it is ' poured out,' which points rather to the view that it was an element, or, to use the customary and convenient phrase adopted by the Germans, a *Fluidum*. Constant combination of these views, inconsistent with each other though they seem to us, is as noticeable in Acts as it is in almost all early literature. It is as common to say that a man was filled with the Spirit and therefore spoke, as to say that the Spirit spoke through the man.

Psychologically this difference of expression and the apparent confusion of views which it implies is due to an underlying difference of experience. The prophetic speaker feels that he speaks because the Spirit first spoke to him; the message which he delivers is not his own, but that of the Spirit which constrains him; the Spirit is greater than he is, and if there is any question of absorption, it is the ' Spirit ' and not ' himself ' which predominates and survives. But from the people this feeling of the prophet is hidden : to them it is clear that the prophet speaks, and the Spirit is looked on as an element which affects him in a manner analogous to the working of wine. It would be out of place to discuss here the degree of truth reached by these theories; but it is important to notice that the double line of thought which is so clear in Acts is not merely due to the survival of various forms of primitive theology, though this no doubt affected it, but also to the fact that we have the description of the phenomena of inspiration from two angles of vision—that of the prophet, who regarded them from the point of view of perception from within, and that of the people, who regarded them from the point of view of observation from without. Ancient and mediaeval theology erected a doctrinal edifice by means of the application of logic and metaphysics to the data provided by these two descriptions of the phenomena of inspiration, but the productive work of the future will consist chiefly in the attempt to go behind these descriptions to discover the actual facts. In other words, we are brought here to the territory which has been marked out as his own by the student of psychology and to that particular part of it which has become famous from the application to its dark recesses of the theory of subliminal consciousness.

The general conception in Acts is that Christians normally receive the Spirit, but not that all their actions are inspired by it. It is, as it were, only sometimes that the Spirit takes possession of them, and they speak 'in the spirit,' either with or without *glossolalia*, or perform miracles of healing or of punishment by its means. The Christian is not so much a man who is always and entirely possessed by the Spirit, as one who is capable of obsession, or, one might almost say, liable to obsession, at critical moments. It is, however, not wholly plain in what way the editor conceived the means whereby the Spirit was imparted to Christians. It was certainly given to the apostles, and only the apostles could impart it to others; but was it by baptism or by the laying on of the hands of the apostles or by both?[1]

The Church as the Kingdom of God.

The benefits derived from membership in the Church are not elaborately stated, but they can be discerned with reasonable clearness. The editor of Acts and possibly the source of the later chapters agreed with Matthew in regarding the Church of the Lord as identical with the 'Kingdom of God' of which Jesus had spoken. That he did so is clear by the passages in which the Kingdom of God is spoken of in Acts[2] even though in the gospel other passages taken from Mark or Q represent an earlier use. In none of the passages in Acts is it impossible that the Kingdom means the Church, and in most of them this is the most obvious meaning. Nevertheless the phrase Kingdom of

---

[1] See Vol. I. pp. 337 ff. for a discussion of the relation of the editor to his sources in connection with baptism.

[2] Acts i. 3, 6, viii. 12, xiv. 22, xix. 8, xx. 25, xxviii. 23, 31. See also Vol. I. pp. 324 ff.

THE INTERNAL EVIDENCE OF ACTS 195

God is relatively uncommon in Acts,[1] and its use ought not to be unduly emphasised.

A further point closely connected with the Church, and emphasised in Acts, but either not found or quite subordinate in Matthew or Mark, is the forgiveness of sins. In the speech of Peter in Acts ii. the Messianic prophecies are explained as fulfilled by the gift of the Spirit to the Church and the forgiveness of sins. In the speech of Peter to Cornelius in Acts x. the conclusion of the whole is the offer in v. 43, supported by prophecy, of forgiveness of sins to all who believe in Jesus. In the speech of Paul to the Jews at Pisidian Antioch in Acts xiii. the point to which everything leads is v. 38, " through him is forgiveness of sins announced to you, and from all things from which by the law of Moses you could not be justified, by him every believer is justified." In his speech before Agrippa in Acts xxvi. he claims that his mission to the Gentiles has for its object that "they should receive remission of sins and a part among those sanctified by faith" in Jesus. Finally, in his last speech to the Jews in Rome in Acts xxviii. he seems to treat the Kingdom of God of which he testified (v. 23) as identical with the salvation (or message of salvation, $\sigma\omega\tau\eta\rho\iota\sigma\nu$) of God ($v$. 28).

The point of view of these passages seems to be different from the purely Jewish view of repentance as the adequate basis for salvation, which is replaced by the miraculous action of the Lord. It is, in fact, not merely forgiveness in the sense in which Ezekiel, for instance, connected it with the repentance of 'turning' of the wicked, but a complete change of nature.

It is easy to see that this development may be entirely due to Hellenistic influences akin to the sacramental view of grace which dominated Catholic Christianity and the other mystery or sacramental cults of the first four centuries. But it is also found in some Jewish sources of the Diaspora, notably the *Oracula Sibyllina*, where the work of bestowing

[1] Acts i. 3, viii. 12, xiv. 22, xix. 8, xxviii. 23, 31.

miraculous freedom from sin is one of the functions of the Messiah.[1]

The Resurrection. Finally, it would seem that a resurrection to immortality is one of the benefits offered by the Church, though it is curious how small a part is played in Acts by this doctrine. In the earlier chapters it is mentioned in Acts iv. 2, but only because the Sadducees objected to the preaching that Jesus had risen, as justifying a belief which they rejected. Obviously there was no more controversy between the first Christians and the Jews in general—as distinct from the Sadducees—as to a belief in a general resurrection [2] than there was as to the nature of God. But just as the nature of God became important in Christian preaching to the Gentiles, so also did the general resurrection, and it is consequently mentioned five times, in Acts xvii. 18 and 32, in Paul's speech at Athens, and in Acts xxiii. 6, xxiv. 15 and 21, in Paul's defence before the Sanhedrin and before Felix, where he contends that in preaching a resurrection he was justified by the best Jewish tradition of the Pharisees. Clearly a general resurrection was part of the Christian teaching which the editor of Acts accepted, but it appealed to him as part of the Jewish tradition. The resurrection of Jesus was the evidence that Jesus was the Messiah, rather than proof of the general resurrection.[3]

Comparison of Acts with other books. It is desirable, in conclusion, to attempt roughly the task of fixing the general position of this system of theology as compared with that of the other main documents of New Testament theology. It is clear that the point which really divides the Lucan theology from that of Mark or of Matthew is the conception of the Church as a community separate from Judaism,

---

[1] Cf. H. Windisch, *Taufe und Sünde im ältesten Christentum*, pp. 34-45.

[2] Of all men or of Jews and Christians only ?

[3] In that respect Paul's epistles are the complement of Acts. He bases his argument in favour of a resurrection on Jewish eschatological belief, with the addition—where he speaks to the Gentiles—of the clinching argument that Jesus had actually risen. Norden missed this point in *Agnostos Theos*, where he treats the Resurrection as synonymous with $ἀθανασία$. Cf. F. C. Burkitt, *J.T.S.*, 1914, pp. 455 f.

THE INTERNAL EVIDENCE OF ACTS 197

but at the same time the true representative of the ancient 'people of God.' That is why Luke, unlike Matthew and Mark, was obliged to produce a second book, and not merely confine himself to recounting the life and the teaching of Jesus.

Mark seems to have had the single object of persuading his readers that Jesus was the Messiah, in spite of the fact that Jesus himself had not proclaimed this openly. In order to establish his case he tells the story of the wonderful deeds of Jesus; as a second line of evidence he quotes the testimony given on two occasions by the voice of God, first at the Baptism to Jesus himself, and the second time, in identical words, to three disciples on the Mount of Transfiguration; and as a final corroboration of these two lines of proof he adds the culminating witness of God in the resurrection. It does not appear to be any part of his plan to suggest that the teaching of Jesus was a new law, different from the law of Moses, or that his disciples were a new community, different from the community of the Jews. Mark.

Matthew accepts the position of Mark, but wishes to go further and expound his view that the teaching of Jesus had the force of a new law. Therefore, while making use of the material already collected by Mark he adds to it from other sources all that he could find bearing upon the teaching of Jesus, and edits this so as to prove his point. His interest in Christianity is not that the disciples form a new community, but that they have been entrusted with a new law which supplements and takes the place of the law of Moses. Matthew.

Luke, like Matthew, accepts the position of Mark and wishes to supplement it; but his supplement is that the Christians are a divinely instituted Church, and therefore, although it is as necessary to his plan as it is to that of Matthew to repeat and expand the Marcan document, it is also necessary for him to give the evidence justifying his claims not merely for the Christ, but also for the Church of the Christians. It would not, however, be fair to say that Luke in this respect necessarily represents Luke.

a position chronologically more advanced than Matthew; the truth is rather that he and Matthew stand for two different lines of development, probably in different places. Both of them are clearly later than Mark, but we cannot say that either is necessarily the later of the two, for neither seems derived from the other.

Paul. More striking still is the fact that the theology of Acts and the theology of Paul seem in the same way to represent separate lines of development. Even the most radical critics have been so much under the influence of the tradition that Luke was a pupil of Paul that they have been anxious, sometimes perhaps unconsciously, to find traces of Paulinism in Acts. But an unprejudiced inquiry rather goes to show that Acts and Paul are singularly independent of each other, for sometimes one and sometimes the other seems to be the more advanced, and there is no satisfactory evidence that either borrows from the other.

Three sets of facts are especially cogent in this connection. As we study the use of the word 'Christ' in Acts and in the Pauline epistles, Paul represents a greater divergence from what must have been the original usage of the word than Acts. In the Pauline epistles 'Christ' is almost always used as a name, but in Acts, except in certain formulae of belief, 'Christ' is nearly always used as a title, and not as a name. There can be no doubt that the Acts stands in this respect nearer to primitive custom than Paul.

In the same way in the Pauline epistles the soteriological explanation of the death of the Christ represents a more advanced type of thought than anything which is found in Acts. In most of the speeches in Acts, in which the crucifixion is alluded to, there is little or no suggestion of any soteriological doctrine, and it is regarded primarily as the wicked act of the Jews. Here again Luke seems to be less advanced than Paul, though, unless one is prepared to maintain that they both belonged from the beginning to the same circle, 'less advanced' is not necessarily the same as 'earlier.'

THE INTERNAL EVIDENCE OF ACTS 199

Against these two points, which go to show that the Pauline theology is in some respects more advanced than the Lucan, must be set the fact that the interpretation of the figure of the Servant of the Lord in Isaiah as a reference to the Messiah is markedly characteristic of Luke and is not found in Paul, although one would have supposed that, had he known it, Paul would certainly have made use of it to support his soteriological arguments. It seems, therefore, to be clear that, just as Matthew and Luke represent two lines of development in Christian thought—though closely related—rather than two points on the same line of development, so also do Paul and Acts.

But the most striking comparison with Acts is not offered by any book in the new Testament, but rather by the Apostles' Creed. If the foregoing analysis of Acts and Luke were summarised the objects of belief could be stated as follows :—

(1) God, as
    (a) the Creator of the World, and
    (b) the Father of the Lord and of his People.
(2) Jesus, the Christ, as
    (a) the Son of God, born of the Holy Spirit and the Virgin Mary ;
    (b) the Lord,
        who suffered under Pontius Pilate and Herod,[1] died, was buried, rose again on the third day, ascended into Heaven, sits at God's right hand, and is coming to judge the world.
(3) The Holy Spirit.
(4) The Church.
(5) Baptism, and the Apostolic Laying on of hands.
(6) The Forgiveness of Sins.
(7) The Resurrection of the Dead.

It is scarcely necessary to print the Apostles' Creed to draw attention to its extraordinary similarity to this summary. The

[1] Once more the comparison with Aristides is suggestive.

resemblance is illustrated by the remarks of K. Holl to the Berlin Academy in January 1919.¹ In this he deals with the interpretation of the second article of the Apostles' Creed in a manner which was immediately accepted by Harnack and others as convincing though new. He points out that the second article of the Creed begins with a double description of Jesus Christ as (1) τὸν υἱὸν αὐτοῦ τὸν μονογενῆ, (2) τὸν κύριον ἡμῶν, and that this double description is then explained by two paragraphs each enclosed, as it were, by the repetition of the article, τὸν γεννηθέντα ἐκ πνεύματος ἁγίου καὶ Μαρίας τῆς παρθένου, τὸν ἐπὶ Ποντίου Πιλάτου σταυρωθέντα καὶ ταφέντα. As Holl points out, there is no other document than Luke which treats the divine sonship of Jesus as beginning with his birth of the Holy Spirit and the Virgin Mary. Luke certainly does so, and an unprejudiced reading of the Apostles' Creed gives the same explanation. There is also no other document in the New Testament which treats the Ascension as an event separate from the Resurrection. The combination is very striking, and shows that the Apostles' Creed is more closely associated with Lucan documents than with any others. The fact has scarcely received sufficient attention from the investigators of Christian doctrine, partly because, at least since the fourth century, the Synoptic Gospels have always been interpreted in the light of the Fourth Gospel, and the Apostles' Creed in the light of the Council of Nicea. The problem which is opened up for the Church historian is to distinguish, so far as possible, the traces of that type of Christianity which is represented by the Synoptic Gospels, Acts, and the Apostles' Creed, from that other great line of thought, ultimately triumphant, which is represented by the later epistles of St. Paul, by the Fourth Gospel, and by the Alexandrian School of theology, and found final expression in the Nicene Creed.

The provenance of Acts.

Where was Acts compiled ? The oldest tradition, which

¹ *Sitzungsberichte der preussischen Akademie der Wissenschaften*, 1919, pp. 2 ff.

cannot be traced back beyond the third century,[1] connects Luke with Antioch. This may be a true tradition of the birthplace of Luke, the companion of Paul, or an inference from the emphasis laid on Antioch in the Acts, or a real tradition as to the place where the Third Gospel and Acts were first used. There can be no certainty on the point, but even assuming that the tradition is merely an inference, it is one which the modern investigator is tempted to repeat. Antioch is certainly a Church which was well known to the editor; if the foregoing analysis of sources be in any degree correct, he was in possession of good Antiochian traditions, and—a very significant fact—knows nothing of the details of Paul's missionary work until he came to join Barnabas in Antioch. The Western text of Acts in Acts xi. 28 which introduces a 'we' clause [2] is probably not original. Still less acceptable is the variant in Acts xiii. 1, which introduces into the list of the prophets at Antioch "Lucius of Cyrene, who still survives." But both passages probably represent the belief that Luke was the 'I' implied by the we-clauses, that he was the editor of the book, and that he came from Antioch, so that the we-clauses ought to begin in that city, not in Troas. It is probably far the oldest testimony which we possess as to early opinion about the place to which the writer of Acts belonged; it is based on an intelligent interpretation of the facts, but it is not conclusive.

To have survived at all, the Gospel and Acts must have belonged to some large and important Church. The places which challenge Antioch for consideration are Jerusalem, Ephesus, and Rome.

There is least to be said in favour of Jerusalem. Nothing Jerusalem. in Acts suggests that the writer was a member of the Church in that city, except that he used documents which probably came from it, and the fact that Acts is a Greek, not an Aramaic, book

---

[1] It is first found in Eusebius, but may be taken from Julius Africanus. See pp. 232 and 247.

[2] συνεστραμμένων δὲ ἡμῶν ἔφη εἶς ἐξ αὐτῶν ὀνόματι "Αγαβος κτλ.

Ephesus. almost suffices to exclude Jerusalem. Ephesus seems similarly excluded by two facts. In the first place, Acts is noticeably lacking in full or accurate information as to Paul's career in Ephesus. The Epistles to the Corinthians show that much happened in Corinth and Ephesus, of which Acts says not one word. In the second place, the Johannine, not the Lucan, tradition and theology are typically Ephesian. These two points are, however, not conclusive: it will probably prove that the form of Synoptic tradition [1] which is behind the Fourth Gospel is precisely that of Luke, and if so, the case for Ephesus as the original home of Acts would have to be reconsidered.

Rome. Rome is supported by two facts, of which one at least is certain. Acts ends with the 'diarist' in Rome. There is therefore a slight—very slight—probability that the diary was found and used there.[2] So far as it goes, this is certain. The other point is more doubtful, though very important. It has been pointed out above that Luke and Acts would serve, as no other documents would, as *pièces justificatives* for the Apostles' Creed. If it were certain that this creed was really Roman in origin, it would be strong evidence in favour of Rome as the place of origin for the Lucan writings. But is it certain? The early history of the Apostles' Creed has not yet been fully written. It was doubtless used in Rome at a very early time in almost exactly the form in which we know it.[3] But there are traces of earlier forms elsewhere, for instance, the fivefold creed in the *Epistola Apostolorum*,[4] and the only slightly divergent form in the Der-Balyzeh papyrus,[5] of which the latter comes from Egypt and the former probably from Ephesus. Lietzmann is, no doubt,

---

[1] See especially on this point Holtzmann, "Die schriftstellerische Verhältnis des Johannes zu dem Synoptik," *Z.W.Th.*, 1869, pp. 62 ff., and Harnack, *Lukas der Arzt*, pp. 157 ff.

[2] This is Jerome's view (see pp. 236 ff.). But it is merely his guess, he does not refer to tradition.

[3] For this Marcellus of Ancyra and Rufinus are the chief witnesses, and Hippolytus may perhaps be added.

[4] C. Schmidt, "Gespräche Jesu," *T.U.* xliii. p. 32.

[5] *Revue bénédictine*, xxvi. p. 34 ff. Cf. Th. Schermann in *T.U.* xxxvi. 1 b, and H. Lietzmann in the Berlin *Sitzungsberichte* for March 27, 1919.

right in thinking that these simple creeds are more primitive than the fuller forms. There are also intermediate variations; for instance, the baptismal service of the Verona fragments contain the following baptismal service, unhappily imperfect at the beginning: "... manum habens in caput inpositam baptizet semel. Et postea dicat: 'Credis in Christum Iesum, filium Dei, qui natus est de spiritu sancto ex Maria uirgine et crucifixus sub Pontio Pilato et mortuus est et sepultus et resurrexit die tertia uiuus a mortuis et ascendit in caelis et sedit ad dexteram patris uenturus iudicare uiuos et mortuos?' Et cum ille dixerit: 'Credo,' iterum baptizetur. Et iterum dicat: 'Credis in spiritu sancto et sanctam ecclesiam et carnis resurrectionem?' Dicat ergo, qui baptizatur: 'Credo.' Et sic tertia uice baptizetur." If, as E. Schwartz and R. H. Connolly have rendered all but certain, this text comes from the lost *Traditio apostolica* of Hippolytus,[1] we have here a Roman creed of the beginning of the third century. But we still do not know whether it originated in Rome, and it is therefore valueless as evidence for the origin of Acts. The problem may be stated thus: we have in Luke and Acts the justification, in the form of a history, of a definite type of Christian doctrine, formulated in the Apostles' Creed. That creed is a development of simpler forms, possibly at first merely the baptismal formula, possibly some such simple fivefold statement as is found in the *Epistola Apostolorum* or in the papyrus of Der-Balyzeh. It developed mainly by the growth of the statements about the life of Jesus, and these statements are all of them justifiable out of Luke and Acts, but not out of any other single book in the New Testament. It is therefore not unlikely that the development took place in some Church which was especially Lucan. Find this Church, and you have reason to say that the development of the creed is likely to have taken place there; or identify the place where the creed developed,

[1] Ed. Schwartz, in *Über die pseudo-apostolischen Kirchenordnungen*, Strassburg, 1910, was the first to make this suggestion, which was independently reached by Dom R. H. Connolly in his magistral "The So-called Egyptian Church Order," in *Texts and Studies*, viii. 4, in 1916.

and you have a right to say that Luke and Acts are likely to have been cherished by the Church in that place. Unfortunately neither end of the problem has yet been solved. It is legitimate to think that, here at least, Rome holds the keys; but who can prove it?

II
THE IDENTITY OF THE EDITOR OF LUKE AND ACTS

INTRODUCTION

THE tradition of early Christian writers ascribes the Third Gospel and Acts to Luke the Physician, the companion of Paul. Whether this be correct or not has been widely discussed.

On one point there is practical agreement—the author of the two works is the same. This seems to be proved by the common address to Theophilus, by the description in Acts i. of a book corresponding to the Third Gospel, and by the identity of the two books in style and language, even in subtle details and mannerisms.

The two points which at first sight seem decisively in favour of the tradition prove susceptible of interpretation in such divergent manners that they are not likely to provide convincing proofs for or against Lucan authorship. The 'we' in certain sections of Acts may be interpreted either as due to the use of an autobiographical source embodied in the text, or to personal reminiscences of the author. The first alternative would exclude, as the second would prove, Lucan authorship. But neither interpretation of the 'we' passages is so easy as to be certain. Each involves literary awkwardness, for the unexplained and abrupt appearances and disappearances of the 'we' are difficult, whether due to the author's own presence on certain occasions, or to a source which has been otherwise adapted in style to the rest of the book. When all possible parallels to either method of procedure have been collected, it will still be doubtful which interpretation is in this case the less unlikely.

The other ambiguous factor in the problem is the relation of the author to Paul. On the one hand, he reveals an intimate knowledge of Paul's movements, whether derived from his own experience, or from his sources, and a general similarity of religious view; on the other hand, he frequently varies from the statements in the Pauline Epistles both in matters of minor detail and in general attitude. If his knowledge be emphasised, authorship by a companion of Paul will seem a possibility or even a probability; if stress be laid on his ignorance, such authorship will appear unlikely. But on neither side is the evidence overwhelmingly convincing. It is as hazardous to define what a companion of Paul could not have written as to determine what one who was not his companion could not have known.

In the following sections will be discussed :
(1) The Tradition.
(2) The case for the Tradition from internal evidence.
(3) The case against the Tradition from internal evidence.
(4) Subsidiary points.

I

THE TRADITION

By Henry J. Cadbury

1. The Earliest Testimonia

The tradition of Christian writers since the second century has been that the Third Gospel and the Acts were written by Luke the Physician who is mentioned by Paul in Colossians, Philemon, and 2 Timothy.

The external evidence which constitutes this tradition is given in the following catena of testimonia, which includes the principal references in early patristic literature to the tradition of Luke's authorship of the gospel and Acts. They are typical, though not exhaustive.

The text of the difficult and obscure Canon of Muratori is given in unemended form according to the readings of the single Milan MS. in which it is preserved. For the other selections a modern critical text has been used so far as possible, usually that of the two standard editions, *Corpus Scriptorum Ecclesiasticorum Latinorum* (Vienna) and *Die griechischen christlichen Schriftsteller der ersten drei Jahrhunderte* (Berlin).

The translations have been made directly from the text employed, but have been compared and corrected by comparison with other versions in modern languages. But in quotations from scripture the English of the Revised Version has been generally used where the same original text occurs in, or appears to underlie, the patristic text.

The Canon of Muratori.

Lines 1-8 : [1]

quibus tamen interfuit et ita posuit.
tertio euangelii librum secando lucan
lucas iste medicus post acensum $\overline{\chi\rho\iota}$.
cum eo paulus quasi ut iuris studiosum
secundum adsumsisset numeni suo
ex opinione concriset $\overline{dnm}$ tamen nec ipse
quidit in carne et idem pro asequi potuit.
ita et ad natiuitate iohannis incipet dicere.

Lines 34-39 :

Acta autem omnium apostolorum
sub unu libro scribta sunt lucas obtime theofi
le conprindit quia sub praesentia eius singula
gerebantur sicuti et semote passionem petri
euidenter declarat sed profectionem pauli au vr
bes ad spaniam proficescentis.

[1] This text is that given by E. S. Buchanan in the *Journal of Theological Studies*, 1907, pp. 540 ff. So many corrections are necessary that it is easier to print as a whole the emended text, translated above, than to indicate changes in separate notes.

Lines 1-8:
    quibus tamen interfuit et ita posuit. tertium euangelii librum secundum lucam, lucas iste medicus post ascensum christi, cum eum paulus itineris sui socium secum adsumsisset, nomine suo ex opinione conscripsit. dominum tamen nec ipse uidit in carne, et ideo prout adsequi potuit. ita posuit et ad natiuitatem iohannis incipit dicere.

Lines 34-39:
    Acta autem omnium apostolorum sub uno libro scripta sunt. lucas optimo theofilo comprendit quae sub praesentia eius singula gerebantur; sicuti et semote passione petri euidenter declarat sed et profectione pauli ab urbe ad spaniam proficiscentis.

It is obvious that many of these emendations are extremely doubtful, and many others have been suggested by editors of the fragment.

The Canon of Muratori.

Lines 1-8:

. . . at which, however, he was present and so he set them down.

The third book of the Gospel, according to Luke, Luke that physician, who after the ascension of Christ, when Paul had taken him with him as companion of his journey, composed in his own name on the basis of report. However, he did not himself see the Lord in the flesh and therefore as he could " trace the course of events " he set them down. So also he began his story with the birth of John.

Lines 34-39:

But the Acts of all the apostles were written in one volume. Luke compiled for " most excellent Theophilus " what things were done in detail in his presence, as he plainly shows by omitting both the death of Peter and also the departure of Paul from the city, when he departed for Spain.

Irenaeus.

Adv. haer. iii. 1 (Ed. Harvey, ii. p. 6):

Et Lucas autem sectator Pauli, quod ab illo praedicabatur Evangelium, in libro condidit.[1]

Adv. haer. iii. 14 (Ed. Harvey, ii. pp. 74 ff.):

Quoniam autem is Lucas inseparabilis fuit a Paulo, et cooperarius ejus in Evangelio, ipse facit manifestum, non glorians, sed ab ipsa productus veritate. Separatis enim, inquit, a Paulo, et Barnaba et Johanne, qui vocabatur Marcus, et cum navigassent Cyprum, nos venimus in Troadem : et cum vidisset Paulus per somnium virum Macedonem dicentem : Veniens in Macedoniam opitulare nobis, Paule ; statim, ait, quaesivimus proficisci in Macedoniam, intelligentes quoniam provocavit nos Dominus evangelisare eis. Navigantes igitur a Troade, direximus navigium in Samothracen : et deinceps reliquum omnem ipsorum usque ad Philippos adventum diligenter significat, et quemadmodum primum sermonem locuti sunt : Sedentes enim, inquit, locuti sumus mulieribus quae convenerant ; et quinam crediderunt, et quam multi. Et iterum ait : Nos autem navigavimus post dies azymorum a Philippis, et venimus Troadem, ubi et commorati sumus diebus septem. Et reliqua omnia ex ordine cum Paulo refert, omni diligentia demonstrans et loca et civitates et quantitatem dierum, quoadusque Hierosolymam ascenderent : et quae illic contigerint Paulo, quemadmodum vinctus Romam missus est ; et nomen centurionis qui suscepit eum, et parasema navium, et quemadmodum naufragium fecerunt, et in qua liberati

---

[1] This statement is repeated in *Adv. haer.* iii. 10: "Lucas autem sectator et discipulus apostolorum."

Irenaeus.

Adv. haer. iii. 1:

And Luke the follower of Paul recorded in a book the gospel that was preached by him.

Adv. haer. iii. 14. 1:

But [1] that this Luke was inseparable from Paul and was his fellow-worker in the gospel he himself makes clear, not boasting of it, but compelled to do so by truth itself. For after Barnabas and John who was called Mark had parted from Paul and when they had sailed to Cyprus, he says, " We came to Troas "; and when Paul had seen in a dream a man of Macedonia, saying, " Come into Macedonia and help us, Paul," " straightway," he says, " we sought to go forth into Macedonia, concluding that the Lord had called us to preach the gospel unto them. Setting sail therefore from Troas we steered our course to Samothrace "; and thereafter he carefully relates all the rest of their journey as far as Philippi and how they made their first address; " For," says he, " we sat down and spake unto the women that were come together "; and he tells who believed and how many. And again he says, " And we sailed away from Philippi after the days of unleavened bread and came to Troas, where also we tarried seven days." And he relates everything else while with Paul in order, carefully indicating both the places and cities and number of days until they went up to Jerusalem; and what things befell Paul there, how he was sent bound to Rome, and the name of the centurion that took him, and the sign of the ships, and how they were shipwrecked, and in what island they

---

[1] The purpose of this passage is to meet the argument of those who claim that Paul alone knew the truth. Irenaeus argues that, if that were the case, Luke would have known and recorded Paul's secrets, since he was inseparable from Paul and as it is he has recorded much that is not in other gospels. The heretics who claim to follow Paul have no right to claim more or less than Luke records. Certainly they are not justified in accepting part of Luke's gospel and rejecting the rest.

sunt insula; et quemadmodum humanitatem ibi perceperunt, Paulo curante principem ipsius insulae; et quemadmodum inde Puteolos navigaverunt, et inde Romam pervenerunt, et quanto tempore Romae commorati sunt. Omnibus his cum adesset Lucas, diligenter conscripsit ea, uti neque mendax, neque elatus deprehendi possit, eo quod omnia haec constarent, et seniorem eum esse omnibus qui nunc aliud docent, neque ignorare veritatem. Quoniam non solum prosecutor, sed et cooperarius fuerit Apostolorum, maxime autem Pauli, et ipse autem Paulus manifestavit in epistolis, dicens: Demas me dereliquit, et abiit in Thessalonicam, Crescens in Galatiam, Titus in Dalmatiam: Lucas est mecum solus. Unde ostendit quod semper junctus ei et inseparabilis fuerit ab eo. Et iterum in ea epistola quae est ad Colossenses, ait: Salutat vos Lucas medicus dilectus. Si autem Lucas quidem, qui semper cum Paulo praedicavit, et dilectus ab eo est dictus, et cum eo evangelisavit, et creditus est referre nobis Evangelium, nihil aliud ab eo didicit, sicut ex verbis ejus ostensum est, quemadmodum hi qui nunquam Paulo adjuncti fuerunt, gloriantur abscondita et inenarrabilia didicisse sacramenta?

2. Quoniam autem Paulus simpliciter quae sciebat, haec et docuit, non solum eos qui cum eo erant, verum omnes audientes se, ipse facit manifestum. In Mileto enim convocatis episcopis et presbyteris, qui erant ab Epheso et a reliquis proximis civitatibus, quoniam ipse festinaret Hierosolymis Pentecosten agere, multa testificans eis, et dicens quae oporteret ei Hierosolymis evenire, adjecit: Scio quoniam jam non videbitis faciem meam: testificor igitur vobis hac die, quoniam mundus sum a sanguine omnium. Non enim subtraxi uti non annuntiarem vobis omnem sententiam Dei. Attendite igitur et vobis, et omni gregi, in

were set free, and how they received kindness there, when Paul healed the chief man of that island, and how they sailed thence to Puteoli, and thence they came to Rome, and for what length of time they remained in Rome. Since Luke had been present at all these events, he carefully wrote them down, so that he can be convicted of neither lying nor boasting, because all these things prove both that he was earlier than all those who now teach otherwise, and that he was not ignorant of the truth. That he was not only a follower, but also a fellow-worker of the apostles, especially of Paul, Paul himself made clear in his letters, saying, " Demas forsook me and went away to Thessalonica, Crescens to Galatia, Titus to Dalmatia ; only Luke is with me." By this he shows that he was always joined to him, and was inseparable from him. And again in that letter which is to the Colossians he says, " Luke, the beloved physician, saluteth you." Now if this Luke, who always preached with Paul and was called by him " beloved," and preached the gospel with him, and was entrusted with handing on the gospel to us,[1] learned from him nothing else, as has been shown from his words,—how do they, who were never associated with Paul, boast that they have learned hidden and unspeakable mysteries ? [2]

2. But that Paul taught plainly what he knew not only to those who were with him but also to all who heard him, he himself makes clear. For when the bishops and elders who were from Ephesus and from other nearby cities had been called together in Miletus, since he himself was hastening to keep Pentecost at Jerusalem, he testified to them of many things and told what must befall him in Jerusalem, adding, " I know that ye shall see my face no more ; therefore I testify unto you this day that I am pure from the blood of all men. For I shrank not from declaring unto you the whole counsel of God. Take heed, therefore, both unto yourselves and unto

---

[1] Or " is believed to have recorded the gospel for us."
[2] Assuming that here, as often, *sacramenta* is for μυστήρια.

quo vos Spiritus sanctus praeposuit episcopos, regere ecclesiam Domini, quam sibi constituit per sanguinem suum. Deinde significans futuros malos doctores, dixit : Ego scio quoniam advenient post discessum meum lupi graves ad vos, non parcentes gregi. Et ex vobisipsis exsurgent viri loquentes perversa, uti convertant discipulos post se. Non subtraxi, inquit, uti non annuntiarem omnem sententiam Dei vobis. Sic Apostoli simpliciter, et nemini invidentes, quae didicerant ipsi a Domino, haec omnibus tradebant. Sic igitur et Lucas nemini invidens, ea quae ab eis didicerat, tradidit nobis, sicut ipse testificatur dicens : Quemadmodum tradiderunt nobis qui ab initio contemplatores et ministri fuerunt Verbi.

3. Si autem quis refutet Lucam, quasi non cognoverit veritatem, manifestus erit projiciens Evangelium, cujus dignatur esse discipulus. Plurima enim et magis necessaria Evangelii per hunc cognovimus, sicut Johannis generationem, et de Zacharia historiam, et adventum angeli ad Mariam, et exclamationem Elizabeth, et angelorum ad pastores descensum, et ea quae ab illis dicta sunt, et Annae et Simeonis de Christo testimonium, et quod duodecim annorum in Hierusalem relictus sit et baptismum Johannis et quot annorum Dominus baptisatus sit, et quia in quintodecimo anno Tiberii Caesaris. Et in magisterio illud quod ad divites dictum est : Vae vobis divites, quoniam percipitis consolationem vestram. Et, vae vobis qui satiati estis, quoniam esurietis : et qui ridetis nunc, quia plorabitis. Et, vae vobis cum benedixerint vos homines omnes. Secundum haec enim faciebant et pseudoprophetis patres vestri. Et omnia

all the flock, in which the Holy Spirit hath made you bishops to rule the church of the Lord, which he hath established for himself through his own blood." Then pointing out that there will be evil teachers he said, "I know that after my departure grievous wolves shall enter in among you, not sparing the flock; and from among your own selves shall men arise, speaking perverse things, to draw away the disciples after them." "I shrank not," he says, "from declaring unto you the whole counsel of God." So the apostles, plainly and grudging no man,[1] delivered to all those things which they themselves had learned from the Lord. So therefore Luke also grudging no man delivered to us those things which he had learned from them, as he himself testifies, saying, "Even as they delivered unto us, who from the beginning were eye-witnesses and ministers of the word."

3. But if any should reject Luke, on the ground that he did not know the truth, he plainly throws over the gospel of which he claims to be a disciple. For through him we have learned very many quite important parts of the gospel, as the birth of John and the story about Zacharias, and the coming of the angel to Mary, and the cry of Elisabeth,[2] and the coming down of the angels to the shepherds, and the things that were spoken by them, and the testimony of Anna and Simeon concerning the Christ, and how when twelve years old he was left behind in Jerusalem, and the baptism of John and at what age the Lord was baptized, and that it was in the fifteenth year of Tiberius Caesar. And in his instruction, that which was said to the rich, "Woe unto you, ye rich, for ye receive your consolation," and "Woe unto you that are filled, for ye shall hunger; and who laugh now, since ye shall mourn," and, "Woe unto you when all men shall speak well of you, for in this manner did your fathers also to the false prophets." And

---

[1] That is, there was no secret teaching.
[2] Possibly the Magnificat, which in iv. 7. 1 is assigned by Irenaeus to Elisabeth; but the loud cry of Luke i. 42-45 may be intended here.

hujusmodi per solum Lucam cognovimus, et plurimos actus Domini per hunc didicimus, quibus et omnes utuntur : ut et multitudinem piscium, quam concluserunt hi qui cum Petro erant, jubente Domino ut mitterent retia : et illa quae per octodecim annos passa, curata fuerat mulier die sabbatorum : et de hydropico, quem curavit Dominus die sabbatorum, et quemadmodum disputavit quod curavit in hac die : et quemadmodum docuit discipulos primos discubitus non appetere : et quoniam pauperes et debiles vocare oportet, qui non habent retribuere : et qui pulsavit nocte sumere panes, et propter instantiam importunitatis sumit : et quoniam apud Pharisaeum recumbente eo, peccatrix mulier osculabatur pedes ejus et unguento ungebat, et quaecunque propter eam dixit ad Simonem Dominus de duobus debitoribus : et de parabola divitis illius qui reclusit quae ei nata fuerant, cui et dictum est, In hac nocte expostulabunt animam tuam a te : Quae autem praeparasti, cujus erunt ? similiter autem et divitis qui vestiebatur purpura, et jocundabatur nitide, et egenum Lazarum : et eam quam ad discentes suos dixit responsionem, quando dixerunt ei : Adjice nobis fidem : et eam quae ad Zacchaeum publicanum facta est confabulationem : et de Pharisaeo et publicano, qui simul adorabant in templo : et de decem leprosis, quos simul emundavit in via : et quoniam de vicis et plateis claudos et luscos [1] jussit colligi ad nuptias ; et parabolam judicis qui Deum non timebat, quem instantia viduae fecit ut vindicaret eam : et de arbore

---

[1] The Arundel MS. reads *caecos*, which is possibly a correct gloss, for it is doubtful whether *luscos* meant more than this to the translator of Irenaeus. But it may represent an original μονοφθάλμους in the Greek of Irenaeus, due to confusion between Luke xiv. 13 and Mark ix. 47 or Matt. xviii. 9.

THE TRADITION 219

everything of this kind we know through Luke alone, and very many of the Lord's deeds we have learned through him, which all use,[1] as the multitude of fishes, which Peter and they that were with him inclosed, when the Lord commanded to let down the nets; and what the woman had suffered for eighteen years and then was cured on the sabbath day, and about the man with the dropsy whom the Lord cured on the sabbath day, and how he reasoned because he cured on that day, and how he taught his disciples not to seek the chief seats at feasts; and that we should invite the poor and the sick who cannot recompense; and of him who knocked at night to get bread and on account of the perseverance of his importunity got it; and how while he lay at meat in a Pharisee's house, a woman that was a sinner kissed his feet and anointed them with ointment, and what the Lord said to Simon on account of her about two debtors; and about the parable of that rich man who stored his produce,[2] to whom also it was said, " This night shall thy soul be required of thee; and the things which thou hast prepared, whose shall they be ? " Likewise also of the rich man who was clothed in purple and fared sumptuously, and the beggar Lazarus; and that reply which he made to his disciples when they said to him, " Increase our faith "; and that conversation which he had with Zacchaeus the publican; and about the Pharisee and the publican who prayed at the same time in the temple; and about the ten lepers whom he cleansed at the same time on the way; and that he commanded the lame and those with one eye to be gathered to the marriage from the lanes and streets; and the parable of the judge who feared not God, but the perseverance of a widow led him to do her justice,

[1] Many editors put these words in brackets and understand all of the evangelists—as if Irenaeus were here noting that there is beside Luke's peculiar matter other matter which he shares with the other evangelists. Probably the reference is to Luke's peculiar matter throughout and the all is meant to show, as below, that the heretics use Luke.

[2] Translating τὰ γενήματα (not γεννήματα, see Moulton and Milligan, *Vocabulary of the Greek Testament*, pp. 123 f.), which lies behind the Latin.

fici quae erat in vinea, quae non faciebat fructum. Et alia multa sunt quae inveniri possunt a solo Luca dicta esse, quibus et Marcion et Valentinus utuntur. Et super haec omnia post resurrectionem in via ad discipulos suos quae locutus est, et quemadmodum cognoverunt eum in fractione panis.

4. Necesse est igitur et reliqua quae ab eo dicta sunt, recipere eos, aut et his renuntiare. Non enim conceditur eis ab his qui sensum habent, quaedam quidem recipere ex his quae a Luca dicta sunt, quasi sint veritatis ; quaedam vero refutare, quasi non cognovisset veritatem. Et si quidem refutaverint hi qui a Marcione sunt, non habebunt Evangelium : hoc enim quod est secundum Lucam quemadmodum praediximus, decurtantes, gloriantur se habere Evangelium ; hi vero qui a Valentino sunt, cessabunt a plurimo vaniloquio suo : ex hoc enim multas occasiones subtililoquii sui acceperunt, interpretari audentes male, quae ab hoc bene sunt dicta : si autem et reliqua suscipere cogentur, intendentes perfecto Evangelio, et Apostolorum doctrinae, oportet eos poenitentiam agere, ut salvari a periculo possint. (See also *Adv. haer.* iii. 15. 1.)

Clement of Alexandria.

Strom. v. 12 (G.C.S. xv. p. 381) :

λείπεται δὴ θείᾳ χάριτι καὶ μόνῳ τῷ παρ' αὐτοῦ λόγῳ τὸ ἄγνωστον νοεῖν, καθὸ καὶ ὁ Λουκᾶς ἐν ταῖς Πράξεσι τῶν ἀποστόλων ἀπομνημονεύει τὸν Παῦλον λέγοντα· ἄνδρες Ἀθηναῖοι, κατὰ πάντα ὡς δεισιδαιμονεστέρους ὑμᾶς θεωρῶ κτλ.

Adumbr. in 1 *Petr.* (G.C.S. xvii. p. 206):

Marcus, Petri sectator, praedicante Petro evangelium palam Romae coram quibusdam Caesareanis equitibus et multa Christi testimonia proferente, petitus ab eis, ut possent quae dicebantur

THE TRADITION 221

and about the fig tree which was in a vineyard which bore no fruit. And there are many other things that can be found to have been told by Luke alone, which both Marcion and Valentinus use. And beside all these what he said to his disciples on the way after the resurrection and how they knew him in the breaking of bread.

4. It is necessary, therefore, that they should accept also the other things that were said by Luke or that they should give up these as well. For it is not permitted to them by those who have sense, to accept as being true some of the things that were said by Luke, but to reject certain others, as if he had not known the truth. And if those who are of Marcion's party reject them, they will not have the gospel (for mutilating, as we have said before, this gospel which is according to Luke, they boast that they have the gospel); while those who are of the party of Valentinus will cease from their copious nonsense; for from this gospel they draw many of their occasions for quibbling, presuming to interpret badly what he had said well. But if they are compelled also to accept the whole, paying heed to the entire[1] gospel and to the teaching of the apostles, they must repent, in order to be saved from danger.

Clement of Alexandria.

Strom. v. 12:

It follows then that it is by God's grace and only by the Logos that comes from him that we perceive the unknown, as also Luke in the Acts of the Apostles records that Paul said, " Ye men of Athens, in all things I perceive that ye are very religious, etc."

Adumbr. in 1 *Petr.:*

While Peter was preaching openly at Rome in the presence of certain knights of Caesar and putting forward much

[1] As compared to the mutilated Luke of Marcion.

memoriae commendare, scripsit ex his quae a Petro dicta sunt evangelium quod secundum Marcum vocitatur ; sicut Lucas quoque Actus apostolorum stilo exsecutus agnoscitur et Pauli ad Hebraeos interpretatus epistolam.

Tertullian.

Adv. Marc. iv. 2 (C.S.E. xlvii. 426 ff.) :

Habes hanc ad Antitheses expeditam a nobis responsionem. Transeo nunc ad evangelii, sane non Iudaici sed Pontici, interim adulterati, demonstrationem, praestructuram ordinem, quem adgredimur. Constituimus inprimis evangelicum instrumentum apostolos auctores habere, quibus hoc munus evangelii promulgandi ab ipso domino sit impositum. Si et apostolicos, non tamen solos, sed cum apostolis [et postapostolicos], quoniam praedicatio discipulorum suspecta fieri posset de gloriae studio, si non adsistat illi auctoritas magistrorum, immo Christi, quae magistros apostolos fecit. Denique nobis fidem ex apostolis Ioannes et Matthaeus insinuant, ex apostolicis Lucas et Marcus instaurant, isdem regulis exorsi, quantum ad unicum deum attinet creatorem et Christum eius, natum ex virgine, subplementum legis et prophetarum. Viderit enim si narrationum dispositio variavit, dummodo de capite fidei conveniat, de quo cum Marcione non convenit. Contra Marcion evangelio, scilicet suo, nullum adscribit auctorem, quasi non licuerit illi titulum quoque adfingere, cui nefas non fuit ipsum corpus evertere. Et possem hic iam gradum figere, non agnoscendum contendens opus, quod non erigat frontem, quod nullam constantiam praeferat, nullam fidem repromittat de plenitudine tituli et professione debita

THE TRADITION

evidence to Christ, Mark, the follower of Peter, wrote at their request the Gospel which is called " according to Mark," out of those things which were said by Peter, in order that they might be able to commit to memory what was told, just as Luke also is recognised to have described with his pen the Acts of the Apostles and to have translated Paul's letter to the Hebrews.

Tertullian.

Adv. Marc. iv. 2 :

Here then is the answer which we give to the Antitheses. I now pass to the exposition of his gospel, which is not of Judaea but of Pontus and corrupted into the bargain; this will provide the scaffolding for the argument we are undertaking. In the first place we assert that the gospel documents have apostles for their authors, for to them did the Lord himself commit the office of making known the gospel. And even if they were merely followers of the apostles, they did not work alone, but with the apostles, for as disciples their preaching might have been suspected of vain glory, had it not been supported by the authority of their masters, yea and of Christ; for it was his which made their masters apostles. In fine our faith is based on John and Matthew, it is built up on Luke and Mark, followers of the apostles. They start from the same principles, namely that God the Creator is one, and that his Christ born of a Virgin is the fulfilling of the Law and the prophets. It matters little if the arrangement of the accounts is different, provided it agrees with the fundamentals of our faith, and here disagrees with Marcion. He, unlike us, ascribes his gospel to no author at all, as though he felt himself prohibited from setting a superscription over the body which he had not scrupled to destroy. And here I might make a stand and maintain that a book is not worthy of recognition which does not hold up its head and come boldly forward, and give no reason for our confidence by supplying us with a title and the declaration

224 IDENTITY OF EDITOR OF LUKE AND ACTS

auctoris. Sed per omnia congredi malumus, nec dissimulamus quod ex nostro intellegi potest. Nam ex his commentatoribus, quos habemus, Lucam videtur Marcion elegisse quem caederet. Porro Lucas non apostolus, sed apostolicus, non magister, sed discipulus, utique magistro minor, certe tanto posterior quanto posterioris apostoli sectator, Pauli sine dubio, ut et etsi sub ipsius Pauli nomine evangelium Marcion intulisset, non sufficeret ad fidem singularitas instrumenti destituta patrocinio antecessorum. Exigeretur enim id quoque evangelium, quod Paulus invenit, cui fidem dedidit, cui mox suum congruere gestiit, siquidem propterea Hierosolymam ascendit ad cognoscendos apostolos et consultandos, ne forte in vacuum cucurrisset, id est ne non secundum illos credidisset et non secundum illos evangelizaret. Denique ut cum auctoribus contulit et convenit de regula fidei, dextras miscuerunt, et exinde officia praedicandi distinxerunt, ut illi in Iudaeos, Paulus in Iudaeos et in nationes. Igitur si ipse inluminator Lucae auctoritatem antecessorum et fidei et praedicationi suae optavit, quanto magis eam evangelio Lucae expostulem, quae evangelio magistri eius fuit necessaria? (See also *De ieiunio*, 10 (C.S.E. xx. 1, 286), where the book of Acts is referred to as *Commentarius Lucae*.)

Origen.

Apud Eus. *H.E.* vi. 25 (G.C.S. ix. 576):

ὡς ἐν παραδόσει μαθὼν περὶ τῶν τεσσάρων εὐαγγελίων, ἃ καὶ μόνα ἀναντίρρητά ἐστιν ἐν τῇ ὑπὸ τὸν οὐρανὸν ἐκκλησίᾳ τοῦ θεοῦ, ὅτι πρῶτον μὲν γέγραπται τὸ κατὰ τόν ποτε τελώνην, ὕστερον δὲ ἀπόστολον Ἰησοῦ Χριστοῦ Ματθαῖον, ἐκδεδωκότα αὐτὸ τοῖς ἀπὸ Ἰουδαϊσμοῦ πιστεύσασιν, γράμμασιν Ἑβραϊκοῖς

of its authors which is our due. But we prefer to join issue on every point and do not conceal what can be understood from our text. For from the gospel writers whom we have Marcion is seen to have selected Luke for mutilation. Luke, not an apostle, but a follower of the apostles, not a master but a disciple, at any rate inferior to a master and so far later than the others as he was the follower of a later apostle, of course of Paul. So that even if Marcion had introduced his gospel under Paul's own name, a canon containing only one gospel, one document alone unsupported by his predecessors, would not be sufficient proof. For what would still be required is the gospel which Paul found and gave adherence to, and was anxious that his own should agree with it; since on this account he went up to Jerusalem to become acquainted with the Apostles and to consult them lest haply he had run in vain, meaning lest he might have not believed as they did or preached the gospel as they did. Accordingly after he had conferred with the original leaders and had come to an agreement as to the rule of faith, they joined hands, and henceforward distinguished between their spheres of evangelisation, that they should go to the Jews, and Paul to the Jews and Gentiles. Therefore if the man who brought the light to Luke himself desired the authority of those who were before him alike for his faith and his message, how much more right have I to demand for the gospel of Luke the support which was necessary for the gospel of his master.

Origen.

Apud Eus. *H.E.* vi. 25 :

. . . as having learned by tradition concerning the four Gospels, which alone are undisputed in the church of God throughout the world, that the Gospel according to Matthew, who was once a publican, but afterwards an apostle of Jesus Christ, was written first. He published it for those who had become converts from Judaism, and composed it

συντεταγμένον· δεύτερον δὲ τὸ κατὰ Μάρκον, ὡς Πέτρος ὑφηγήσατο αὐτῷ, ποιήσαντα, ὃν καὶ υἱὸν ἐν τῇ καθολικῇ ἐπιστολῇ διὰ τούτων ὡμολόγησεν φάσκων " ἀσπάζεται ὑμᾶς ἡ ἐν Βαβυλῶνι συνεκλεκτὴ καὶ Μάρκος ὁ υἱός μου"· καὶ τρίτον τὸ κατὰ Λουκᾶν[1], τὸ ὑπὸ Παύλου ἐπαινούμενον εὐαγγέλιον τοῖς ἀπὸ τῶν ἐθνῶν πεποιηκότα· ἐπὶ πᾶσιν τὸ κατὰ Ἰωάννην.

Hom. in Luc., Jerome's translation (Migne, *P.L.* xxvi. 231 ff.):

Sicut olim in populo Judaeorum multi prophetiam pollicebantur, et quidam erant pseudoprophetae, e quibus unus fuit Ananias filius Agot: alii vero prophetae et erat gratia in populo discernendorum spirituum, per quem alii inter prophetas recipiebantur, nonnulli quasi ab exercitatissimis trapezitis reprobabantur: ita et nunc in novo testamento multi conati sunt scribere evangelia, sed non omnes recepti. Et ut sciatis, non solum quatuor evangelia, sed plurima esse conscripta, e quibus haec, quae habemus, electa sunt, et tradita ecclesiis, ex ipso prooemio Lucae, quod ita contexitur, cognoscamus: Quoniam quidem multi conati sunt ordinare narrationem. Hoc quod ait, conati sunt, latentem habet accusationem eorum, qui absque gratia spiritus sancti ad scribenda Evangelia prosilierunt. Matthaeus quippe, et Marcus, et Joannes, et Lucas non sunt conati scribere; sed Spiritu sancto pleni scripserunt Evangelia. Multi igitur conati sunt ordinare narrationem de his rebus, quae manifestissime cognitae sunt in nobis. Ecclesia quatuor habet Evangelia, haereses plurima: e quibus quoddam scribitur secundum Aegyptios, aliud juxta duodecim apostolos. Ausus fuit et Basilides scribere Evangelium, et suo illud nomine titulare. Multi conati sunt scribere: sed et multi

---

[1] See also Eus. *H.E.* vi. 25. 14, where Eusebius quotes Origen as referring in his homilies on Hebrews to the Lucan authorship of Acts.

in Hebrew; second came that according to Mark, who wrote it as Peter directed him. And in his general epistle Peter acknowledges him as a son in these words, declaring, "She that is in Babylon, elect together with you, saluteth you; and so doth Mark my son;" and third came that according to Luke, who had made for converts from the Gentiles the gospel praised by Paul; last of all came that according to John.

Hom. in Luc. :

Just as formerly among the people of the Jews when many professed themselves prophets, some were false prophets, one of whom was Hananiah the son of Azzur,[1] but others were true prophets, and there was the gift of the discerning of spirits in the people, whereby some were accepted as among the prophets, others were rejected as though by skilled money-changers; so also now under the new covenant many have tried to write Gospels, but not all have been accepted. And that you may know that not only four Gospels but many have been written, from among which those which we have have been selected and delivered to the Churches, let us learn directly from the preface of Luke which is constructed thus;— " Forasmuch as many have taken in hand to draw up a narrative." The expression " have taken in hand " contains a hidden accusation of those who leapt forward without the grace of the Holy Spirit to write Gospels. Now Matthew and Mark and John and Luke did not " take in hand " to write, but filled with the Holy Spirit wrote Gospels. " Many " therefore " have taken in hand to draw up a narrative concerning those things which have been clearly known among us." The Church has four Gospels, the heretical sects many. Of these one is described as " according to the Egyptians," another " according to the twelve apostles." Basilides also dared to write a Gospel and to put his own name in the title. " Many have taken in hand " to write, rather, " many have taken in hand " to draw

[1] Lat. *Azot*, Gk. (LXX.) 'Αζώρ, Jer. xxviii. 1.

conati sunt ordinare. Quatuor tantum Evangelia sunt probata, e quibus sub persona Domini et Salvatoris nostri proferenda sunt dogmata. Scio quoddam Evangelium, quod appellatur secundum Thomam, et juxta Mathiam, et alia plura legimus, ne quid ignorare videremur, propter eos qui se putant aliquid scire, si ista cognoverint. Sed in his omnibus nihil aliud probamus, nisi quod Ecclesia, id est quatuor tantum Evangelia recipienda.

Haec idcirco, quia in principio lectum est : Multi conati sunt ordinare narrationem de his rebus quae confirmatae sunt in nobis. Illi tentaverunt atque conati sunt de his rebus scribere, quae in nobis manifestissime sunt compertae. Effectum suum Lucas indicat ex sermone, quo ait : In nobis manifestissime sunt ostensae, id est, πεπληροφορημένων quod uno verbo Latinus sermo non explicat. Certa enim fide et ratione cognoverat, neque in aliquo fluctuabat, utrum ita esset, an aliter. Hoc autem illis evenit, qui fidelissime crediderunt, et id quod Propheta obsecrat, consecuti sunt, et dicunt : Confirma me in sermonibus tuis ; unde et Apostolus de his qui erant firmi, atque robusti, ait : Ut sitis radicati et fundati in fide. Si quis enim radicatus in fide est atque fundatus, licet tempestas fuerit exorta, licet venti flaverint, licet se imber effuderit, non convelletur, nec corruet, quia super petram aedificium solida mole fundatum est. Nec putemus oculis istis carnalibus firmitatem fidei dari, quam mens et ratio tribuit. Infideles quique credant signis atque portentis, quae humana acies contuetur. Fidelis vero magis prudens atque robustus rationem sequatur et verbum, et sic dijudicet quid verum, quidve falsum sit.

"Sicut tradiderunt nobis, qui ab initio ipsi viderunt, et ministri fuerunt sermonis."

THE TRADITION

up. Only four gospels are approved from which doctrines are to be set forth with the authority [1] of our Lord and Saviour. I know a certain Gospel which is called " according to Thomas," and one " according to Matthias," and several others we have read,—that we may not seem to be ignorant, for the sake of those who think they know something if they know those Gospels. But among all these we approve of none except what the Church does, that is, only four accepted Gospels.

These four because in the beginning it reads : " Many have taken in hand to draw up a narrative concerning those things which have been confirmed among us." They have essayed and taken in hand to write about those things which have been clearly ascertained among us. The result in his own case Luke indicates by his language, in which he says, " Among us have been clearly shown," that is $\pi\epsilon\pi\lambda\eta\rho o\phi o\rho\eta\mu\acute{\epsilon}\nu\omega\nu$, which the Latin language does not express in a single word. For he had learned with sure faith and reason, nor did he hesitate in any matter as to whether it was this way or the other. But this was the outcome in those who faithfully believed, and they obtained that for which the prophet prays, and they say, " Confirm thou me in thy words." Wherefore the apostle also says of those who were fixed and firm, " That ye may be rooted and grounded in faith." For if any one is rooted and grounded in faith, though the storm arise, though the winds blow, though the rain pour down, he will not be torn loose, he will not fall, because the building is founded with solid strength upon a rock. And let us not suppose that those physical eyes give the firmness in faith which mind and reason supply. Faithless are such as believe in the signs and portents which human sight beholds. But let the faithful man of more judgment and strength follow reason and the word, and so let him distinguish what is true and what is false.

" Even as they delivered to us who from the beginning were eyewitnesses and ministers of the word." In Exodus it

---

[1] *Sub persona* seems to be best so rendered.

In Exodo scriptum est : Populus videbat vocem Dei. Et certe vox auditur prius quam videtur ; sed propterea scriptum est, ut ostenderetur nobis aliis oculis videre vocem Dei, quibus illam aspiciunt qui merentur. Porro in Evangelio non vox cernitur, sed sermo, qui voce praestantior est. Unde nunc dicitur : Sicut ab initio tradiderunt nobis, qui a principio ipsi viderunt, et ministri fuerunt sermonis. Igitur apostoli ipsi viderunt sermonem : non quia aspexerant corpus Domini Salvatoris, sed quia verbum viderunt. Si enim juxta corpus vidissent Jesum, hoc est, Dei vidissent sermonem, ergo et Pilatus qui condemnavit, sermonem Dei vidit, et Judas proditor, et omnes qui clamaverunt : Crucifige, crucifige eum, tolle de terra talem, Dei viderunt sermonem. Sed absit ut quisquam incredulus sermonem Dei viderit. Videre sermonem Dei, tale est quale Salvator ait : Qui videt me, videt et Patrem qui misit me. Sicut tradiderunt nobis qui a principio ipsi viderunt, et ministri fuerunt sermonis. Clam Lucae sermonibus edocemur, quod cujusdam doctrinae finis sit ipsa doctrina, alterius vero doctrinae finis in opere computetur. Verbi gratia : Scientia geometriae finem habet ipsam tantum scientiam atque doctrinam. Alia vero scientia est, cujus finis opus exigit : velut in medicina oportet me rationem et dogmata scire medicinae, non ut tantummodo noverim quid debeam facere, sed ut faciam, id est, ut secem vulnera, victum moderatum castigatumque disponam, aestus febrium in pulsum venarum sentiam, ut curationibus cyclicis humorum abundantiam siccem, temperem atque restringam. Quae si quis tantum scierit et non opere fuerit subsecutus, cassa erit ejus scientia. Simile quid scientiae medicinae et operi, etiam in notitia minis-

is written, "The people saw the voice of God." Well, surely a voice is heard rather than seen; but for this reason it is written, to show us how to see the voice of God with those other eyes with which they have sight to whom he grants it. Nay more, in the Gospel it is not the voice that is seen but the word, which is more excellent than the voice. Wherefore it is now said, "Even as they delivered to us who from the beginning were eyewitnesses and ministers of the word." So the apostles themselves were eyewitnesses of the word, not because they had looked at the body of the Lord and Saviour, but because they saw the word. For if they had seen Jesus, that is, had seen the word of God, in bodily wise, then Pilate who condemned him saw the word of God, and Judas the betrayer, and all who cried "Crucify him, crucify him," "away with such a fellow from the earth,"[1] saw the word of God. But God forbid that any unbeliever saw the word of God. To see the word of God is such a thing as the Saviour says, "He that seeth me, seeth also the Father that sent me." "Even as they delivered to us who from the beginning were eyewitnesses and ministers of the word." We are secretly taught by Luke's words that of one teaching the end is the teaching itself, but of another teaching the ultimate value is in practice. For example, the science of geometry has as its end only the science itself and the teaching. But there is another kind of science whose purpose requires practice, just as in medicine I must know the reason and the rules of medicine, that I should not merely know what I ought to do, but that I should do it, that is that I should operate on wounds, that I should arrange for a moderate and strict diet, that I should feel the heat of fevers in the pulse of veins, that I should by routine treatments remove, temper, and curtail excess of humours. For if one only knows these things, and does not follow them out in practice, his knowledge is futile. Something like the knowledge of medicine and the practice of it is also in the knowledge and the ministry of the word: "Even

---

[1] Including *talem* in the quotation and supposing it to represent Acts xxii. 22.

terioque sermonis est : Sicut tradiderunt nobis qui a principio ipsi viderunt, et ministri fuerunt sermonis. Ut ex eo quod dixit, ipsi viderunt, doctrinam et scientiam significari, et ex eo quod dixit, ministri fuerunt sermonis, demonstrari opera cognoscamus. Assecuto a principio : Visum est et mihi assecuto ab initio : inculcat ac replicat, quoniam ea quae scripturus est, non rumore cognoverit, sed ab initio ipse fuerit consecutus. Unde et ab Apostolo merito collaudatur, dicente : Cujus laus in Evangelio est per omnes Ecclesias. Hoc enim de nullo alio dicitur, et nisi de Luca dictum traditur.

Visum est et mihi assecuto a principio omnia diligenter ex ordine tibi scribere, optime Theophile. Putat aliquis, quod ad Theophilum quempiam Evangelium scripserit : omnes qui nos auditis loquentes, si tales fueritis ut diligamini a Deo et vos Theophili estis, et ad vos Evangelium scribitur. Si quis Theophilus est, iste optimus et fortissimus est (hoc quippe significantius Graeco sermone dicitur κράτιστος).[1] Nemo Theophilus infirmus est.

Eusebius.

Historia ecclesiastica, iii. 4 (G.C.S. ix. 192 ff.) :

Λουκᾶς δὲ τὸ μὲν γένος ὢν τῶν ἀπ' Ἀντιοχείας, τὴν ἐπιστήμην δὲ ἰατρός, τὰ πλεῖστα συγγεγονὼς τῷ Παύλῳ, καὶ τοῖς λοιποῖς δὲ οὐ παρέργως τῶν ἀποστόλων ὡμιληκώς, ἧς ἀπὸ τούτων προσεκτήσατο ψυχῶν θεραπευτικῆς ἐν δυσὶν ἡμῖν ὑποδείγματα θεοπνεύστοις κατέλιπεν βιβλίοις, τῷ τε εὐαγγελίῳ, ὃ καὶ χαράξαι μαρτύρεται καθ' ἃ παρέδοσαν αὐτῷ οἱ ἀπ' ἀρχῆς αὐτόπται καὶ ὑπηρέται γενόμενοι τοῦ λόγου, οἷς καί φησιν ἔτ' ἄνωθεν ἅπασι παρηκολουθηκέναι, καὶ ταῖς τῶν ἀποστόλων

[1] This parenthesis is of course added by Rufinus, and it is probable that the double phrase " optimus et fortissimus " is also due to his difficulty in rendering κράτιστος.

as they delivered to us who from the beginning were eyewitnesses and ministers of the word." So that we learn that by the expression " were eyewitnesses," is meant the teaching and knowledge, and by the expression " were ministers of the word," their practice is indicated.

" Having traced from the beginning " ; " it seemed good to me also having traced the course from the first." He emphasises and repeats, since he has not learned by vague report the things that he is about to write, but from the first has followed them himself. Wherefore also he is justly praised by the apostle who says, " Whose praise in the Gospel is in all the Churches." For this is said about no one else, nor accepted as said, except about Luke.

" It seemed good to me also, having traced the course of all things accurately from the first, to write unto thee in order, most excellent Theophilus." One imagines that he wrote the Gospel to a definite Theophilus. You all, who hear us speaking, if you are such as to be loved by God,[1] you too are Theophiluses, and to you the Gospel is written. If any one is a Theophilus he is best and strongest (this indeed is more clearly expressed in the Greek word κράτιστος). No Theophilus is weak.

Eusebius.

Historia ecclesiastica, iii. 4 :

Luke, being by birth one of the people of Antioch, by profession a physician, having been with Paul a good deal, and having associated intimately with the rest of the apostles, has left us examples of the art of curing souls that he obtained from them in two divinely inspired books,—the Gospel, which he testifies that he wrote out even as they delivered to him who from the beginning were eyewitnesses and ministers of the word, all of whom [2] he says he had followed even

---

[1] In reference to the etymology of Theophilus—" loved by God."

[2] Possibly, " all of which facts," but Eusebius appears to give the ambiguous πᾶσιν in Luke i. 3 the personal force.

Πράξεσιν, ἃς οὐκέτι δι' ἀκοῆς ὀφθαλμοῖς δὲ παραλαβὼν συνετάξατο. φασὶν δ' ὡς ἄρα τοῦ κατ' αὐτὸν εὐαγγελίου μνημονεύειν ὁ Παῦλος εἴωθεν, ὁπηνίκα ὡς περὶ ἰδίου τινὸς εὐαγγελίου γράφων ἔλεγεν κατὰ τὸ εὐαγγέλιόν μου. τῶν δὲ λοιπῶν ἀκολούθων τοῦ Παύλου Κρήσκης μὲν ἐπὶ τὰς Γαλλίας στειλάμενος ὑπ' αὐτοῦ μαρτυρεῖται, Λίνος δέ, οὗ μέμνηται συνόντος ἐπὶ Ῥώμης αὐτῷ κατὰ τὴν δευτέραν πρὸς Τιμόθεον ἐπιστολήν, πρῶτος μετὰ Πέτρον τῆς Ῥωμαίων ἐκκλησίας τὴν ἐπισκοπὴν ἤδη πρότερον κληρωθεὶς δεδήλωται· ἀλλὰ καὶ ὁ Κλήμης, τῆς Ῥωμαίων καὶ αὐτὸς ἐκκλησίας τρίτος ἐπίσκοπος καταστάς, Παύλου συνεργὸς καὶ συναθλητὴς γεγονέναι πρὸς αὐτοῦ μαρτυρεῖται.

Historia Ecclesiastica, iii. 24. 15 (G.C.S. ix. 250) :

ὁ δὲ Λουκᾶς ἀρχόμενος καὶ αὐτὸς τοῦ κατ' αὐτὸν συγγράμματος τὴν αἰτίαν προύθηκεν δι' ἣν πεποίηται τὴν σύνταξιν, δηλῶν ὡς ἄρα πολλῶν καὶ ἄλλων προπετέστερον ἐπιτετηδευκότων διήγησιν ποιήσασθαι ὧν αὐτὸς πεπληροφόρητο λόγων, ἀναγκαίως ἀπαλλάττων ἡμᾶς τῆς περὶ τοὺς ἄλλους ἀμφηρίστου ὑπολήψεως, τὸν ἀσφαλῆ λόγον ὧν αὐτὸς ἱκανῶς τὴν ἀλήθειαν κατειλήφει ἐκ τῆς ἅμα Παύλῳ συνουσίας τε καὶ διατριβῆς καὶ τῆς τῶν λοιπῶν ἀποστόλων ὁμιλίας ὠφελημένος, διὰ τοῦ ἰδίου παρέδωκεν εὐαγγελίου.

Jerome.

Comment. in Esaiam (Migne, *P.L.* xxiv. 98) :

Evangelistam Lucam tradunt veteres Ecclesiae tractatores medicinae artis fuisse scientissimum, et magis Graecas litteras scisse quam Hebraeas.[1] Unde et sermo ejus tam in Evangelio, quam in Actibus Apostolorum, id est, in utroque volumine

---

[1] Cf. Jerome, *ibid.* p. 331 (on Is. xxviii. 13) and *Quaest. hebr. in Gen.* (Migne, *P.L.* xxiii. 1053).

from the beginning, and the Acts of the Apostles, which he composed, receiving his information with his own eyes, no longer by hearsay. And they say that it was actually the Gospel according to him that Paul used to mention whenever, as though writing about some Gospel of his own, he used the expression " according to my Gospel." But of the other followers of Paul Crescens is recorded by him to have gone to the Gallic provinces,[1] and Linus, whom he mentions as with him at Rome, according to the second letter to Timothy, we have shown above to have been the first after Peter to inherit the bishopric of the church of the Romans. Moreover Clement also (he too was appointed as the Roman church's third bishop) is recorded by Paul to have been his fellow-worker and fellow-contestant.

Historia Ecclesiastica, iii. 24, 15 :

And Luke himself also in beginning the work that bears his name set forth the reason why he made the composition, showing that while many others had somewhat too rashly engaged in making an account of the things of which he himself was fully assured, thus expressly freeing us from doubtful suspicion about the others, he had delivered to us through his own gospel a sure and certain record of what he was convinced to be true, aided by his continued and intimate fellowship with Paul and by his intercourse with the rest of the apostles.

Jerome.

Comment. on Isaiah, iii. 6 :

The ancient writers of the church say that the evangelist Luke was very learned in the art of medicine, and that he knew Greek better than Hebrew. And therefore, too, his language in the Gospel, as well as in the Acts of the Apostles,

[1] The reference is to 2 Tim. iv. 10. Where some of the best manuscripts read Γαλλίαν, though some read Γαλατίαν. Similarly the Syriac version of Eusebius reads 'Galatia.'

comptior est, et saecularem redolet eloquentiam, magisque testimoniis Graecis utitur quam Hebraeis.

Epistula, xx., *ad Damasum* (C.S.E. liv. 108):

De verbo vero " osianna," quia in Graecum non poterant transferre sermonem, sicut et in " alleluia," et in " amen," et in plerisque factum videmus, ipsum Hebraeum posuerunt, dicentes, " osianna." Lucas igitur, qui inter omnes evangelistas Graeci sermonis eruditissimus fuit, quippe ut medicus et qui in Graecis Evangelium scripserit, quia se vidit proprietatem sermonis transferre non posse, melius arbitratus est tacere, quam id ponere, quod legenti faceret quaestionem.

Epistula, liii., *ad Paulinum* (C.S.E. liv. 463):

Actus Apostolorum nudam quidem sonare videntur historiam, et nascentis ecclesiae infantiam texere : sed si noverimus scriptorem eorum Lucam esse medicum, cujus laus est in Evangelio, animadvertimus pariter omnia verba illius languentis animae esse medicamina.

De viris illustribus (Richardson, *Texte und Untersuchungen*, xiv. 1. 11 f.) :

Lucas medicus Antiochensis, ut eius scripta indicant, Graeci sermonis non ignarus fuit, sectator apostoli Pauli, et omnis eius peregrinationis comes, scripsit Evangelium, de quo idem Paulus : Misimus, inquit, cum illo fratrem, cuius laus est in evangelio per omnes ecclesias, et ad Colossenses : Salutat vos Lucas medicus carissimus, et ad Timotheum : Lucas est mecum solus. Aliud quoque edidit volumen egregium, quod titulo Apostolicorum πράξεων praenotatur, cuius historia usque ad biennium Romae commorantis Pauli pervenit, id est, usque ad quartum Neronis annum. Ex quo intelligimus, in eadem urbe

that is, in both volumes is more elegant, and smacks of secular eloquence, and he uses Greek quotations rather than Hebrew.

Epistle xx. 4 :

With regard to the word, hosanna, because they could not translate it into the Greek language, just as we see was done also in the case of hallelujah, and of amen and in most other words, they put down the Hebrew itself, saying, hosanna. Luke therefore, who was the most learned in the Greek language among all the evangelists, since he was a doctor and wrote his gospel among the Greeks, because he saw that he could not translate the proper meaning of the word, thought it better to omit it, than to put down what would raise a question in the reader's mind.

Epistle liii. 9 :

The Acts of the Apostles, it is true, seems to present bare history, and to weave the story of the new-born church's infancy ; but if we realise that the author of this book is Luke the physician "whose praise is in the Gospel" we observe that all his words alike are medicine for the sick soul.

De viris illustribus, vii. :

Luke the physician, an Antiochian, as his writings show, was not ignorant of the Greek language. The follower of the apostle Paul and comrade of all his travels, he wrote the Gospel, of which the same Paul says, "We have sent together with him the brother whose praise is in the gospel through all the churches ; " and to the Colossians, "Luke the beloved physician greeteth you," and to Timothy, "Only Luke is with me." He also published another excellent volume, which is designated by the title 'apostolic πράξεις,' the narrative of which extends up to the two-year period of Paul's stay in Rome, that is, to the fourth year of Nero. From this also we learn that the book was written in the same city. There-

librum esse conpositum. Igitur περιόδους Pauli et Theclae et totam baptizati leonis fabulam inter apocryphas scripturas conputemus. Quale enim est, ut individuus comes apostoli, inter ceteras eius res hoc solum ignoraverit? Sed et Tertullianus, vicinus illorum temporum, refert presbyterum quemdam in Asia σπουδαστὴν apostoli Pauli, convictum apud Johannem quod auctor esset libri, et confessum se hoc Pauli amore fecisse, loco excidisse. Quidam suspicantur, quotiescumque Paulus in epistulis suis dicat, iuxta evangelium meum, de Lucae significare volumine et Lucam non solum ab apostolo Paulo didicisse evangelium, qui cum Domino in carne non fuerat, sed et a ceteris apostolis. Quod ipse quoque in principio voluminis sui declarat dicens: Sicut tradiderunt nobis, qui a principio ipsi viderunt et ministri fuerunt sermonis. Igitur Evangelium, sicut audierat, scripsit; Acta vero apostolorum, sicut viderat ipse, conposuit. Sepultus est Constantinopolim, ad quam urbem, vicesimo Constantii anno, ossa eius cum reliquiis Andreae apostoli translata sunt.

Praefatio in Commentarios in Matthaeum (Migne, *P.L.* xxvi. 18):

Tertius Lucas medicus, natione Syrus Antiochensis, cuius laus in Evangelio, qui et ipse discipulus apostoli Pauli, in Achaiae Boeotiaeque partibus volumen condidit, quaedam altius repetens, et ut ipse in prooemio confitetur, audita magis, quam visa describens.

fore we reckon the περίοδοι[1] of Paul and Thecla, and the whole tale of the baptized lion, among the apocryphal writings. For how strange it would be if the inseparable companion of the apostle should be ignorant of this alone among all his affairs. Moreover Tertullian, who lived near those times, reports that a certain elder in Asia, a σπουδαστής[2] of the apostle Paul, was convicted in the presence of John of being the author of the book, and, having confessed that he had made it out of affection for Paul, lost his rank. Some men suspect that whenever Paul says in his letters "according to my gospel" he means the volume of Luke, and that Luke had learned the gospel not only from the apostle Paul, who had not been with the Lord in the flesh, but also from the rest of the apostles. And this he also declares himself in the beginning of his volume saying, "Even as they delivered to us who from the beginning were eyewitnesses and ministers of the word." The Gospel, therefore, he wrote as he had heard; but the Acts of the Apostles he composed as he had seen. His tomb is at Constantinople, to which city his bones, together with the remains of the apostle Andrew, were transferred in the twentieth year of Constantius.

Preface to the Commentary on Matthew:

The third,[3] Luke the physician, by birth a Syrian of Antioch, " whose praise is in the gospel," and himself a disciple of the apostle Paul, composed his book in the districts of Achaia and Boeotia,[4] investigating some things from an earlier time, and, as he himself confesses in his preface, describing what he had heard rather than what he had seen.

---

[1] Journeyings.   [2] An admirer.   [3] *I.e.* of the Evangelists.
[4] Some MSS. read Bithynia (see Monarchian prologue), but elsewhere Jerome suggests that Luke died in Thebes. An earlier reference to Luke's activity in Achaia is in Greg. Naz. *Or.* xxxiii. 11.

Adamantius.

Dialogus De recta in deum fide, v. (G.C.S. iv. 8 ff.):

ΜΕΓΕΘΙΟΣ. . . . εἰπὲ δὲ πρῶτον τὰ ὀνόματα τῶν γραψάντων τὰ εὐαγγέλια.

ΑΔΑΜΑΝΤΙΟΣ. Οἱ μαθηταὶ τοῦ Χριστοῦ γεγραφήκασιν, Ἰωάννης καὶ Ματθαῖος, Μᾶρκος καὶ Λουκᾶς.

ΜΕΓ. Μᾶρκον καὶ Λουκᾶν οὐκ ἔσχε μαθητὰς ὁ Χριστός· ἐντεῦθεν ἐλέγχεσθε φάλσα ποιοῦντες. διὰ τί γὰρ οἱ μαθηταί, ὧν γέγραπται τὰ ὀνόματα ἐν τῷ εὐαγγελίῳ, οὐκ ἔγραψαν, ἀλλ' οἱ μὴ ὄντες μαθηταί; τίς οὖν ἐστὶ Λουκᾶς ἢ Μᾶρκος; ἠλέγχθητε ἐπὶ τούτῳ ὀνόματα ⟨οὐ⟩ γεγραμμένα ἐν τῇ γραφῇ προφέροντες.

ΕΥΤΡΟΠΙΟΣ. Ἔχων μαθητὰς ὁ Χριστὸς οὐ μᾶλλον τούτοις ἐνεχείριζεν ἢ τοῖς μὴ οὖσι μαθηταῖς; φαίνεταί μοι τοῦτ' οὐ καλῶς ἔχειν· ἔδει γὰρ τοὺς μαθητὰς αὐτοὺς ἐμπιστευθῆναι μᾶλλον.

ΑΔ. Μαθηταί εἰσι καὶ οὗτοι τοῦ Χριστοῦ.

ΜΕΓ. Ποίησον ἀναγνωσθῆναι τὸ εὐαγγέλιον καὶ εὑρήσεις ὅτι οὐ γέγραπται τὰ ὀνόματα ταῦτα.

ΕΥΤΡ. Ἀναγνωσθήτω.

ΑΔ. Τῶν δώδεκα ἀποστόλων ἀνεγνώσθη τὰ ὀνόματα, οὐχὶ καὶ τῶν οβ'.

ΕΥΤΡ. Πόσους ἔσχεν ὁ Χριστὸς ἀποστόλους;

ΑΔ. Πρώτους ἀπέστειλε ιβ' καὶ μετὰ ταῦτα οβ' εὐαγγελίσασθαι. Μᾶρκος οὖν καὶ Λουκᾶς, ἐκ τῶν οβ' ὄντες, Παύλῳ τῷ ἀποστόλῳ συνευηγγελίσαντο.

ΜΕΓ. Ἀδύνατον ὅτι ποτ' εἶδον οὗτοι Παῦλον.

ΑΔ. Δείκνυμι αὐτὸν τὸν ἀπόστολον μαρτυροῦντα Μάρκῳ καὶ Λουκᾷ.

ΜΕΓ. Τῷ σῷ φάλσῳ οὐ πιστεύω ἀποστολικῷ.

ΑΔ. Προένεγκε τὸ ἀποστολικόν σου, εἰ καὶ τὰ μάλιστα

Adamantius.

Dialogue on the True Faith :

Megethius. . . . Tell me first the names of those who wrote the Gospels.

Adamantius. The disciples of Christ wrote them, John and Matthew, Mark and Luke.

Meg. Christ had no disciples Mark and Luke; so you are convicted of forgery. For why did the disciples whose names are written in the gospel not write them, rather than those who were not disciples ? Who then is Luke, or Mark ? This convicts you of bringing forward names not written in Scripture.

Eutropius. Was not Christ, since he had disciples, more likely to entrust the task to them than to those who were not disciples ? This does not seem to me to be right, for the disciples themselves ought to be trusted more.

Ad. These too are disciples of Christ.

Meg. Have the Gospel read and thou wilt find that these names are not written in it.

Eutr. Let it be read.

Ad. The names of the twelve apostles have been read, but not of the seventy-two.[1]

Eutr. How many apostles had Christ ?

Ad. First he sent out twelve and after that seventy-two to preach the gospel. So Mark and Luke, being from the number of the seventy-two, preached the gospel together with Paul the apostle.

Meg. It is impossible that these men ever saw Paul.

Ad. I can show the apostle himself testifying to Mark and Luke.

Meg. I do not believe in thy forged apostolicon.[2]

Ad. Bring thy own apostolicon, even though it is mutilated

---

[1] Some MSS. of Luke x. 1 read 72 instead of 70.

[2] *Apostolicon,* that is, the group of letters of Paul accepted into a canon of scripture.

περικεκομμένον ἐστί, καὶ δείκνυμι ὅτι Μᾶρκος καὶ Λουκᾶς συνήργησαν Παύλῳ.
ΜΕΓ. Δεῖξον.

ΑΔ. Ἀναγινώσκω ἐν τοῖς τελευταίοις τῆς πρὸς Κολοσσαεῖς Παύλου· Ἀσπάζεται ὑμᾶς, φησίν, Ἀρίσταρχος, ὁ συναιχμάλωτός μου, καὶ Μᾶρκος, ὁ ἀνεψιὸς Βαρνάβα, περὶ οὗ ἐλάβετε ἐντολὰς ἵνα ἔλθῃ πρὸς ὑμᾶς· δέξασθε οὖν αὐτόν· καὶ Ἰησοῦς ὁ λεγόμενος Ἰοῦστος, οἱ ὄντες ἐκ περιτομῆς. οὗτοι μόνοι μού εἰσι συνεργοὶ εἰς τὴν βασιλείαν τοῦ θεοῦ, οἵτινες ἐγενήθησάν μοι παρηγορία, καὶ τὰ ἑξῆς. ἀσπάζεται ὑμᾶς Λουκᾶς καὶ Δημᾶς. παρέσχον τὰς ἀποδείξεις τῆς ἐπιστολῆς. ὁρᾷς ὅτι καὶ αὐτὸς ὁ ἀπόστολος μαρτυρεῖ αὐτοῖς.

ΕΥΤΡ. Δήλη ἡ περὶ τούτων ἀπόδειξις.

Priscillian.[1]

Argumentum in Lucam :

Incipit argumentum euangelii secundum Lucam. Lucas Syrus natione Antiochensis, arte medicus, discipulus apostolorum, postea Paulum secutus usque ad confessionem eius, seruiens deo sine crimine. Nam neque uxorem umquam habens neque filios lxxiiii annorum obiit in Bithynia plenus spiritu sancto. Qui cum iam descripta essent euangelia per Mattheum quidem in Iudaea, per Marcum autem in Italia, sancto instigante spiritu in Achaiae partibus hoc scripsit euangelium, significans etiam ipse in principio ante alia esse descripta. Cui extra ea quae ordo euangelicae dispositionis exposcit, ea maxime necessitas fuit laboris, ut primum Graecis

[1] The origin of these Prologues is not certain, but the most popular theory, advocated especially by Dom Chapman, attributes them to Priscillian. Zahn, however, now (*Kommentar zum N.T.* iii. 738 ff.; cf. 13 ff.) prefers G. Morin's guess of the Priscillianist Instantius. But—what is more important—reversing the usual theories of their relation, he believes that the shorter Latin version is earlier than the Monarchian, and that the Greek version is the original of the short Latin one. This would carry the principal elements of the tradition about Luke (as distinct from the Priscillianist theology) back to at least 330-350 A.D. It is fortunately not necessary for the present

THE TRADITION 243

very extensively, and I can show that Mark and Luke worked together with Paul.

Meg. Show me.

Ad. I am reading in the closing part of Paul's letter to the Colossians; "Aristarchus my fellow-prisoner," he says, "saluteth you, and Mark the cousin of Barnabas (touching whom ye received commandments that he should come to you; therefore receive him), and Jesus that is called Justus, who are of the circumcision: these only are my fellow-workers unto the Kingdom of God, men that have been a comfort unto me," and so forth. "Luke and Demas salute you." I have supplied the proofs of the epistle. Thou seest that the apostle himself testifies to them.

Eutr. The proof in their case is clear.

Priscillian.

'*Monarchian*' *Prologue* to Luke.

Luke, a Syrian of Antioch by nation, by profession a physician, a disciple of the Apostles, later followed Paul until his confession, serving God without blame. For he never had wife or children, and died at the age of seventy-four in Bithynia, full of the Holy Ghost. When Gospels had already been written, by Matthew in Judaea and by Mark in Italy, at the instigation of the Holy Spirit he wrote this Gospel in the parts of Achaia, and he also signified in the commencement that others had previously been written. Apart from the demand made by the order of the disposition of the Gospels [which made his Gospel necessary] the principal object of his toil was that he should labour that the Greek faithful might, by the manifestation of

---

purpose to discuss the exact meaning of the Prologue to Luke, which is hard to understand and even harder to translate. After rejecting several attempts of their own the editors and Dr. Cadbury have thought it best to reproduce Dom Chapman's text and rendering, but those interested in the translation or interpretation should read Corssen, *Texte und Untersuchungen*, xv. 1., and Dom Chapman's discussion in his *Early History of the Vulgate Gospels*.

fidelibus omni perfectione venturi in carnem dei manifestata, ne Iudaicis fabulis intenti in solo legis desiderio tenerentur vel ne hereticis fabulis et stultis sollicitationibus seducti excederent a veritate, elaboraret; dehinc ut in principio euangelii Iohannis natiuitate praesumpta, cui euangelium scriberet et in quo electus scriberet, indicaret, contestificans in se completa esse quae essent ab aliis inchoata. Cui ideo post baptismum filii Dei a perfectione generationis in Christo impletae et repetendae a principio nativitatis humanae potestas permissa est, ut requirentibus demonstraret, in quo adprehendens erat, per Nathan filium introitu recurrentis in deum generationis admisso indispartibilis deus ut, praedicans in hominibus Christum suum perfecti opus hominis redire in se per filium faceret, qui per Dauid patrem venientibus iter praebebat in Christo. Cui Lucae non inmerito etiam scribendorum apostolicorum actuum potestas in ministerio datur, ut deo in deum pleno ac filio proditionis extincto oratione ab apostolis facta sorte domini electionis numerus compleretur, sicque Paulus consummationem apostolicis actibus daret, quem diu contra stimulos recalcitrantem dominus elegisset. Quod legentibus ac requirentibus deum etsi per singula expediri a nobis utile fuerat, scientes tamen, quod operantem agricolam oporteat de fructibus suis edere, vitamus publicam curiositatem, ne non tam demonstrare volentibus deum videremur quam fastidientibus prodidisse. Explicit argumentum evangelii secundum Lucam.

THE TRADITION

all the perfection of God coming in the flesh, be prevented from giving themselves to the study of Jewish fables, and from being held by the desire of the law only, and that they might not be seduced by heretical fables and foolish questions, and so depart from the truth. And further, that in the beginning of his Gospel, having first given the birth of John, he might point out for whom [viz., for Theophilus] he wrote his Gospel, and the purpose of his election to write it, attesting that what was begun by the others was finished in him. To him power was granted after the baptism of the Son of God [Luke iii.] to reckon back the human birth from its beginning, starting from the perfection of the generation fulfilled in Christ, in order that he might show forth to seekers (in that he had himself apprehended), by admitting into the list the entrance of a genealogy running back to God through the son Nathan, how the indivisible God, proclaiming His Christ among men, has made the work of the perfect man return to Himself by the son of David—He who by David the father offered in Christ a way to those who came to Him. To this Luke ministerial power was deservedly given of also writing the Acts of the Apostles, that God being full in God, and the son of perdition being dead, after prayer had been made by the Apostles, the number of election (twelve apostles) might be made complete by the lot of the Lord, and that thus Paul might supply the consummation of the Acts of the Apostles,[1] whom the Lord chose after he had long kicked against the pricks. And though it had been useful for us to explain this in detail for readers and seekers after God, yet knowing that the working husbandman ought to eat the fruits of his own labour, we avoid the curiosity of the public, lest we should appear less to be re-revealing God to the desirous, than to have betrayed Him to scorners."

---

[1] Or, reading *Paulum*, "that he might give Paul as the consummation (the thirteenth Apostle) to the Acts of the Apostles." That this is the true reading is attested by the Prologue to Acts. See Chapman, ch. xiv. p. 255.

II. LUKE IN LATER TRADITION

Many accounts of Luke, later than the *testimonia* given above, occur in church histories, commentaries, church calendars, lists of apostles, saints, or martyrs, and in New Testament manuscripts. One of the earlier is given in "The Doctrine of the Apostles," from *Ancient Syriac Documents*, edited by W. Cureton (1864), pp. 34 ff. "Byzantium, and all the country of Thrace, and its environs, even to the great river, the border which separates between the Barbarians, received the Apostles' Hand of Priesthood from Luke the Apostle, who built a Church there, and ministered there in his office of Ruler and Guide there.... But Luke the Evangelist had this diligence, and wrote the Triumphs of the Acts of the Apostles, and the Ordinances and Laws of the ministry of their Priesthood, and whither each one of them went. By his diligence, therefore, Luke wrote these things, and more than these, and he placed them in the hand of Priscus and Acquilas, his disciples; and they accompanied him even up to the day of his death: like as Timothy and Erastus, of Lystra and Menaus, the first disciples of the Apostles, accompanied Paul until he went up to the city of Rome, because he had withstood the orator Tertullus. And Nero the Emperor slew him with the sword, and Simon Cephas, in the city of Rome." This heterogeneous material is conveniently summarised in R. A. Lipsius, *Die apokryphen Apostelgeschichten und Apostellegenden*, II. ii. (1884), pp. 354-371, and T. Schermann, "Propheten- und Apostellegenden," in *Texte und Untersuchungen*, xxxi. 3 (1907), pp. 288-289. The numerous Greek texts are published by T. Schermann in the Teubner text series under the title *Prophetarum vitae fabulosae*, etc., 1907. For some of the material in New Testament manuscripts see von Soden, *Die Schriften des N.T.* I. i. (1902), pp. 305-333.[1]

---

[1] Much bibliographical material on the traditions about Luke, together with brief quotations, will be found in Zahn, *Einleitung in das N.T.*³, § 58 *notes*, and in

In this literature the statements of the earlier writers are repeated with additions. Some of the commonest are as follows :

Luke, the physician, the companion of Paul and author of the two λόγοι to Theophilus, is identified with the unnamed companion of Cleopas on the walk to Emmaus in Luke xxiv.

Moreover, the suggestion made in the passage of Adamantius given above that he was one of the seventy of Luke x., and the statement of Jerome following a suggestion of Origen that he was the anonymous brother of 2 Corinthians viii. 18, whose praise is in the gospel, recur as unqualified assertions. The view that Luke is the Lucius of Romans xvi. 21 is mentioned but not asserted by Origen.[1]

That Luke was from Antioch is plainly stated by Eusebius, *H.E.* III. iv. 7 Λουκᾶς δὲ τὸ μὲν γένος ὢν τῶν ἀπ' Ἀντιοχείας, τὴν ἐπιστήμην δὲ ἰατρός κτλ. (For the manner of expression compare 4 Macc. v. 4 Ἐλεάζαρος, τὸ γένος ἱερεύς, τὴν ἐπιστήμην νομικός.) Earlier in this chapter Eusebius has referred to the letter of Julius Africanus to Aristides about the genealogies in Matthew and Luke, and it is possible that the statement here about the latter is derived from that source also, for in sections of that letter not quoted by Eusebius but preserved in MSS. purporting to quote it through a catena of Nicetas (Spitta, *Brief des Africanus an Aristides*, p. 111), we read : ὁ δὲ Λουκᾶς τὸ μὲν γένος ἀπὸ

---

his *Kommentar zum N.T.* vol. iii. pp. 1-19, 738-745. The acts of Luke will be found in the Bollandist *Acta Sanctorum*, vol. lvi. (1868), pp. 282-313.

[1] Zahn, *Introduction to the N.T.* iii. 5, n. 4. Deissmann has recently accepted this identification in *Festgabe A. von Harnack dargebracht*, Tübingen, 1921, pp. 117 ff. There seems to be no early example of identification of Luke with the Lucius of Cyrene of Acts xiii. 1, unless the clause *qui manet usque adhuc* added to his name in the Codex Sangallensis of the *Prophetiae ex omnibus libris collectae* be thought to assume such an identification of Lucius with the author. On this treatise see A. Amelli, *Miscellanea Cassinese*, 1897, part 6; *Geschichtliche Studien Albert Hauck zum 70 Gebeurtstag*, 1916, pp. 52 ff., and Th. Zahn, *Forschungen*, ix. p. 21.

τῆς βοωμένης Ἀντιοχείας ἦν κτλ.[1] The statement reappears in Jerome (see the three passages given elsewhere) and in the Priscillianist Latin prologue to Luke (see p. 242, and cf. the Latin prologue to Acts). Modern scholars have attempted to confirm the tradition in various ways. (*a*) Thus Zahn (*Introduction to the New Testament*, § 59, *n*. 5, and elsewhere) notes the early tradition about a Theophilus of Antioch, later identified with Luke's Theophilus and even with the bishop of Antioch of the same name of about 180 A.D. (*b*) Bacon (*Expositor*, Oct. 1920, p. 291) notes that Basilides and Cerdo both came from Antioch and, like Cerdo's famous pupil Marcion, both used only Luke's gospel. It should be remembered, however, that with the possible exception of Ephrem Syrus none of the various Fathers who suggest a place of writing for Luke's gospel name Antioch. (*c*) Harnack (*Luke the Physician*, Eng. trans., pp. 20-24) very forcibly argues from internal evidence in Acts the author's interest in Antioch.

But here as in other similar traditions the real question is whether there was any independent knowledge on the subject still current in the Church or whether the assertion of Luke's Antiochian origin is a conjecture from the text. For the so-called 'Western text' of Acts xi. 28, as found not only in Codex Bezae but also in Augustine and several other Latin authorities, introduces a 'we' in an incident at Antioch. This reading is certainly as early as the tradition of Luke's Antiochian provenance —some would say it is the original text of Acts—and it is more likely to be the cause than the effect of that tradition. Readers of such a text could naturally infer from this, the first occurrence of the 'we,' that the writer must himself have been an Antiochian, just as readers of the other text have assumed from the first

---

[1] It seems more likely, however, as Reichardt (*Texte und Untersuchungen*, xxxiv. 3 (1909), pp. 48-50) has more recently argued, and as even Zahn now agrees, that this passage in the catena of Nicetas on Luke, although it occurs between quotations from Africanus, is really the work of Eusebius and is taken bodily along with the quotations from Africanus from the lost *Quaestiones Evangelicae* of Eusebius.

occurrence of the 'we' in their text at xvi. 10, and its disappearance and reappearance at Philippi, that the writer was 'a man of Macedonia.' Granted that the 'we' indicated the presence of the ultimate author, the fertile and clever inference of scholars in an age when all possible information and conjecture about the four evangelists was carefully compiled and compared could be trusted to determine both the name and home of the diarist. With the Western text Antioch was quite as easily settled on for the latter as Luke the physician was for the former.

The scene of his literary labours is given by Jerome as in the parts of Achaia and Boeotia.[1] Gregory of Nazianzus confines his activity to Achaia. According to Epiphanius Luke preached in Dalmatia, Gallia, Italy, and Macedonia. Dalmatia and Gallia are evidently due to their close association with the name of Luke, in 2 Timothy iv. 10 f. The other place names [2] are apparently inferences from the 'we'-passages (including the 'we'-passage at Antioch in the Western text of Acts xi. 28).

In the earlier forms of tradition no mention is made of Luke's martyrdom, and later it is explicitly denied. But it is inevitable that he should be ranked by some as a martyr. The translation of his relics to Constantinople in 357 A.D., along with those of Andrew, appears to have suggested both the fact of his martyrdom, and the method (crucified on an olive tree). The translation is mentioned and dated by Jerome. The day of Luke's death appears with some exceptions as October 18, as in the most modern church calendars. His age is usually given as between

[1] Some Peshitta MSS. give Alexandria, the traditional scene of Mark's work; but this is perhaps due to confusion such as is frequent between the evangelists. One Peshitta MS. assigns Luke's gospel to Ephesus (instead of John's). Similarly, Ephraem Syrus assigns John's gospel to Antioch (instead of Luke's). Note further how in some of the pseudo-Epiphanius lists Luke's gospel is written at the instigation of Peter (instead of Mark's) and his death is placed at Ephesus (instead of John's).

[2] Neither Boeotia nor Thebes (where Luke's martyrdom is usually placed) is mentioned in the N.T. But Boeotia has as variants the Biblical names Bithynia and Bethania, and it is hard to determine the original. 2 Cor. xi. 10 may be suspected as the source of the phrase " in the parts of Achaia."

seventy and ninety—often as eighty-four, the years assigned to the widow Anna in Luke ii. 37.[1] Thebes is often given as the place of his death. Arabic and Coptic sources, however, locate his martyrdom at Rome under Nero and give a full and independent account of the marvellous circumstances attending it.[2]

The tradition that Luke was a painter and the first to make a picture of the Virgin is widespread in the later Greek Church, but its origin and antiquity are not known. Except for a claim of Nicephorus Callistus that he is quoting from Theodorus Lector, this tradition has not been definitely traced earlier than the tenth century.

III. THE VALUE OF THE TRADITION

The foregoing passages indicate how early and undisputed is the attribution of the two books to Luke, the companion of Paul. Such evidence is usually explained as due to an accurate memory of the actual facts of authorship handed down from generation to generation. Its value is enhanced by its early date and unanimity, and according to ordinary standards, Luke and Acts have an almost unexcelled attestation among those books of the New Testament which do not plainly declare their real or professed authorship. It is often called external tradition. But external tradition ought to mean the preservation of facts concerning a book, which could not have been guessed at by a study of its contents and are thus 'external.' The question is whether much of the tradition concerning the New Testament is really external in this sense,[3] or ought to be

---

[1] It is also usually said that he had neither wife nor children, which may also be connected with the same passage. But Zahn, *Kommentar*, iii. 16, thinks these statements genuine tradition since they are not derived from any New Testament suggestion.

[2] Syriac sources for the same legend have also been found. An English translation of a document of this type will be found in E. A. W. Budge, *The Contendings of the Apostles*, vol. ii. (1901), 137-145.

[3] A deep, though often unconscious, difference of attitude on this point

THE TRADITION

regarded as the earliest inference from the contents of the documents.

To estimate its value, it is necessary to consider the general character of the allusions in the literature of the early Church to the origin of the canonical books.

There is much obscurity about the growth of the New Testament canon. The books of the New Testament and other cognate literature were written separately, often anonymously, between A.D. 50 and 150. By the end of the fourth century the number of canonical books was definitely fixed and they were declared to be the inspired writings of apostles or their companions. It is their treatment during the intervening period that requires attention.

To a considerable extent the development is that of the attitude of the readers of the New Testament, for the canonisation of books merely registers the feeling entertained towards them; and one may say that a theory of canonicity existed in the Church almost from the first. Briefly stated, the requirements for the acceptance of a book as authoritative were popularity, orthodoxy, and apostolicity. It is obvious that the popularity of any book was a matter of fact—it either was or was not generally known and read in churches. It is equally obvious that orthodoxy was a matter of personal and collective opinion. The book itself sometimes stated its authorship, and thus established or refuted a claim to canonicity.[1] But in the case of an anonymous book its authorship could be inferred by conjecture from its contents or by comparison with other books, and repetition soon added authority to conjecture. Nevertheless, such inference, however justifiable, is based on judgment, not on knowledge,

Requisites for canonicity.

---

has usually characteristically divided English from continental scholars. The English attitude has been to accept without sufficient inquiry the earliest evidence as necessarily external, the continental to be unduly suspicious of it, and to treat it almost as if it were necessarily untrue. Harnack represents a reaction against this attitude.

[1] 2 Peter and Hermas, for instance, were respectively accepted and rejected on this ground.

and is identical with what is commonly known as 'internal evidence.'

Even when actual apostolic authorship seemed impossible, there would be a tendency in the case of books otherwise acceptable or actually accepted in the canon to assign them apostolic authority. Numerous instances can be collected where apostolic connection was inferred from the contents. Hebrews was evidently not written in Paul's own style, but the thought was regarded as Paul's and so the book was assigned indirectly to him through Luke or some other amanuensis or translator.[1]

Tertullian. Tertullian plainly represents the feeling of the orthodox Church concerning the necessity of knowing the authorship of the Gospels when he argues that, unlike Marcion's gospel, they are not anonymous, for "a work ought not to be recognised which holds not its head erect, which shows no boldness, which does not assure of its trustworthiness by fullness of title and the fitting declaration of its author." "We lay it down as our first position that the evangelical instrument has apostles for its authors, to whom was assigned by the Lord himself this office of publishing the gospel. Even if they were apostolic" (*apostolici*, that is, belonging to the next generation, as we speak of the 'Apostolic fathers'), "they do not stand alone but are with apostles and after apostles." [2]

"That which Mark published may be affirmed to be Peter's, whose interpreter Mark was. For even Luke's form of the gospel men usually ascribe to Paul. And it may well seem that the works which disciples publish belong to their masters." [3]

... "But Luke is not an apostle, but an apostolic man: not a master, but a disciple, and so inferior to a master—at least as

---

[1] Clem. Alex. *apud* Eus. *H.E.* vi. 14; Origen, *ibid.* vi. 25; Eusebius, *ibid.* iii. 38; Jerome, *De vir. ill.* 5.

[2] *Adv. Marc.* iv. 2. Tertullian alludes to the African order of the Gospels, John, Matthew, Luke, Mark, which he seems in this treatise to regard as representing chronological order.

[3] *Adv. Marc.* iv. 5.

THE TRADITION

far behind him as the apostle whom he follows (and that no doubt was Paul) was behind the others : so that, had Marcion even published his Gospel in the name of Paul himself, the single authority of the document, destitute of all support from preceding authorities, would not be a sufficient basis for our faith. There would still be wanted that Gospel which Paul found in existence, to which he yielded his belief, and with which he so earnestly wished his own to agree, that he actually on that account went up to Jerusalem to know and consult the apostles, ' lest he should run, or had been running in vain ' ; in other words, that the faith which he had learned, and the gospel which he was preaching, might be in accordance with theirs. Then, at last, having conferred with the authors, and having agreed with them touching the rule of faith, they joined their hands in fellowship, and divided their labours thenceforth in the office of preaching the gospel, so that they were to go to the Jews, and Paul to the Jews and Gentiles. Inasmuch, therefore, as the enlightener of Luke himself desired the authority of his predecessors for both his own faith and preaching, how much more may not I require for Luke's gospel that which was necessary for the gospel of his master." [1]

It is clear from this that Tertullian possessed a tradition which was not an inference so far as he was concerned, but that the argument which weighed with him was apostolic propriety rather than anything which we should regard as facts. It is, moreover, noticeable how much emphasis he lays on the impropriety of an anonymous gospel : Marcion did not share this view and presented the gospel without giving the name of the writer. Did he know it ? It is strange how many inquiries in early Christian tradition take us back to the period of the Marcionite controversy, but no further.

That that tradition was not really fixed but grew can be seen clearly in the connection of Peter with Mark's Gospel. Papias and Irenaeus in the second century speak of it as written by Mark,

[1] *Adv. Marc.* iv. 2.

apparently on the basis of Peter's preaching after Peter's death.[1] Clement goes further and dates it before Peter's death, though he says that Peter "neither directly forbade nor encouraged it";[2] but Eusebius says that the Gospel "received the sanction of Peter's authority for reading in the churches,"[3] while even earlier Origen, followed later on by Jerome, had already gone still further, and implied that Peter dictated it to Mark.[4]

Similarly, in the case of Luke and Acts, though actual apostolic authorship is excluded by the preface (Luke i. 2), the early Church interpreted the reference to "eyewitnesses and ministers of the word" as showing that Luke was "not merely a follower but also a fellow-worker of the disciples, especially of Paul."[5] His intimate Pauline connection was proved by explaining the 'we' passages as a mark of the author's own presence,[6] and by identifying his book with the gospel preached by Paul,[7] and the writer himself with the unnamed "brother whose praise in the gospel is in all the churches."[8]

Furthermore, a survey of the earliest literature shows that in the second century there were already growing many artificial theories about the origin, number, relation, and authority of New Testament books. These persisted through the following century, and became the commonplaces of the Fathers. In

[1] Eus. *H.E.* iii. 39; Iren. iii. 1. The text of Irenaeus is μετὰ δὲ τὴν τούτων ἔξοδον. It is just possible to interpret this as meaning "after Peter and Paul had left Rome"—the time referred to in the previous sentence. But ἔξοδος is an almost technical term for death. It is therefore hard to accept this view which is stated best by Dom Chapman in the *J.T.S.*, 1905, 563 f.

[2] Eus. *H.E.* vi. 14.

[3] *Ibid.* ii. 15; cf. Jerome, *De vir. ill.* 8.

[4] Origen, *apud* Eus. *H.E.* vi. 25; Jerome, *Ad Hedib.* ii. "Petro narrante et illo scribente."

[5] Iren. iii. 14; Eus. iii. 4 and 24.

[6] Iren. iii. 14.

[7] Rom. ii. 16, xvi. 25; 2 Tim. ii. 8; cf. also Gal. i. 11; 1 Cor. xv. 1, *et al.*; Iren. iii. 1; Tertull. *Adv. Marc.* iv. 58; Eusebius, *H.E.* iii. 4; Jerome, *De vir. ill.* 7, *Ep. II., ad Paulinum.*

[8] 2 Cor. viii. 18; Origen, *apud* Eus. *H.E.* vi. 25. 6; Jerome, *loc. cit.* See also the Collect for St. Luke's Day. In all these cases Paul's 'gospel' has been understood to mean a written gospel, an interpretation which is altogether unlikely.

THE TRADITION   255

the construction of such theories exactly the same use of general propriety and what we should call ' internal evidence ' was made as is employed by Tertullian in proving the Pauline authority of the Third Gospel and Acts.

It is unnecessary to deal with the whole mass of this evidence : Canon of it is all of the same nature, and represents a single catena of Muratori. statement. There is no serious difference between the Canon of Muratori, Irenaeus, Clement, Tertullian, or Origen. They all say the same things, and none has any reason for his statements beyond what is common to all. Under these circumstances, then, the value of the whole can be tested by an examination of the Canon of Muratori, the earliest witness to the Lucan tradition. Is its evidence certainly based on knowledge, or may it be due to inference ?

It was published in 1740 by Muratori from an eighth (?) century Latin MS. and appears to come from Rome, about the year 170.[1] Though it is broken at the beginning and end and often is almost unintelligible either from faulty grammar and spelling or from conciseness of phraseology, its general character is plain. It is not only a list of accepted and rejected books, but also a condensed and laconic essay on the origin, contents, relation, and number of books, or, as we should say, a "New Testament Introduction."

The first point to be noticed is that the precise number of books of Scripture was at this time a matter of serious interest. Thus the Old Testament had to consist of exactly twenty-two

[1] This date is derived from lines 73 ff., which say that the *Shepherd of Hermas* was written " very recently in our own times while Pius his brother the bishop was sitting on the chair of the church of the city of Rome." Pius appears to belong about A.D. 139–154. " Very recently " is of course a relative and indefinite term as Irenaeus reminds us when he speaks (about A.D. 185) of the end of Domitian's reign (A.D. 96) as being " not long ago, but almost in our own generation " (v. 30. 3). But any natural interpretation of the Canon of Muratori certainly implies a date within the second century. Few scholars have suggested a later origin. The arguments here drawn from it are largely independent of its early date, though they tend to confirm it, for illustrations of the same characteristics can be quoted from the successive Fathers of the Church back into the second century.

books in order to correspond with the letters of the Hebrew alphabet. In the same way Irenaeus advances ingenious arguments to show that there can only be four Gospels.[1]

With a similar object the Canon of Muratori comments on the number of Paul's letters; Paul, " the blessed apostle himself, following the order of his predecessor John, writes by name only to seven churches "—" for John in his apocalypse though he writes to seven churches nevertheless speaks to all," for " the church which is scattered throughout the whole world is nevertheless recognised to be one." This is the secret of the number. Seven is symbolic of unity and universality.[2] The Canon of Muratori

[1] " It is not possible that the Gospels can be either more or fewer in number than they are. For, since there are four zones of the world in which we live, and four catholic spirits (*i.e.* four principal winds), while the church is scattered throughout all the world, and the pillar and ground of the church is the gospel and the spirit of life; it is fitting that she should have four pillars . . . the gospel under four aspects, but bound together by one spirit " (Iren. *Adv. Haer.* iii. 11. 11).

Irenaeus's explanation of the four faces of the living creatures of Ezekiel as applied to the evangelists illustrates another artificial treatment of the quadriga of the gospels. It is repeated and varied in later Fathers, and played an important part in Christian art. See Th. Zahn, *Forschungen zu Kanongeschichte,* vol. ii. pp. 257 ff.

[2] This view is not confined to this author. Cf. Victorinus Petavius *in Apoc.* i. 20 : " Those seven stars are the seven churches, which he names in his addresses by name, and calls them to whom he wrote epistles. Not that they are themselves the only, or even the principal churches ; but what he says to one, he says to all. For they are in no respect different, that on that ground any one should prefer them to the larger number of similar small ones. In the whole world Paul taught that all the churches are arranged by sevens, that they are called seven, and that the catholic church is one. And first of all, indeed, that he himself also might maintain the type of seven churches he did not exceed that number. But he wrote to the Romans, to the Corinthians, to the Galatians, to the Ephesians, to the Thessalonians, to the Philippians, to the Colossians ; afterwards he wrote to individual persons, so as not to exceed the number of seven churches. And abridging in a short space his announcement, he thus says to Timothy : ' That thou mayest know how thou oughtest to behave thyself in the church of the living God.' We read also that this typical number is announced by the Holy Spirit by the mouth of Isaiah : ' Of seven women which took hold of one man.' The one man is Christ, not born of seed ; but the seven women are seven churches, receiving his bread and clothed with his apparel, who ask that their reproach should be taken away, only that his name should be called upon them. The bread is the Holy Spirit, which nourishes to eternal life, promised to them, that is, by faith. And his garments wherewith they desire to be clothed are

gets its number by counting only churches, and the additional letters need explanation. "To the Corinthians and Thessalonians he writes a second time for correction," "To Titus he writes one letter and to Timothy two out of love and affection. Yet they are sanctified in the honour of the catholic church for the ordaining of ecclesiastical discipline."

It is also noticeable that the differences of the four Gospels were observed from the first and demanded explanation. Their different beginnings or *principia* were compared and allegorically explained,[1] and various lines of primitive thought in gospel harmonisation appear somewhat cryptically and briefly presented in the Canon of Muratori.

In the fragment as we have it the starting-point of Luke is the only one mentioned. "He began to narrate from the birth of John," but later he says, "and therefore though the several

---

the glory of immortality, of which Paul the apostle says: 'For this corruptible must put on incorruption, and this mortal must put on immortality.'" So also Cyprian, inverting the order of John and Paul, refers twice to their common use of seven: in the *De exhort. martyr.* 11 he says: "And the apostle Paul, who remembered this regular and fixed number, writes to seven churches. And in the Apocalypse the Lord writes his divine commands and heavenly precepts to seven churches"; and in the *Testim. adv. Jud.* i. 20 he says: "Likewise in the first book of Kings (1 Sam. ii. 5): 'The barren has born seven and she who had very many sons is weakened.' Now the seven sons are seven churches. Wherefore also Paul wrote to seven churches, and the Apocalypse puts seven churches, that the sevenfold number might be preserved, etc." Jerome says: "Paul the apostle writes to seven churches (for the eighth (letter) to the Hebrews is put outside the number by most); he gives instructions to Timothy and Titus, and intreats Philemon in behalf of a fugitive slave" (*Epist. II. ad Paulinum*). On the unity of the scattered Church similar thoughts are expressed by Irenaeus: "For the church preaches the truth everywhere, and she is the seven-branched candlestick which bears the light of Christ" (*Adv. Haer.* v. 20. 2).

Later collections of letters number seven, as the letters of Ignatius. Eusebius mentions seven letters of Dionysius of Corinth to special churches, but calls them catholic or universal letters (*H.E.* iv. 23). So our own seven catholic epistles perhaps should be connected both in name and in number with the symbolic principle implicit in the Canon of Muratori.

It is worth noting that the later canon of Paul had fourteen (2 × 7) letters which could still be used symbolically. Cf. Origen, *Hom. on Josh.* 7.

[1] E. A. Abbott, *The Four-fold Gospel, Introduction*, p. 82 ff., explains Papias' famous criticism of Mark as being "not in order" as an allusion to the starting-point of Mark.

books of the gospel are shown to have different beginnings, nevertheless it makes no difference to the faith of the believers, since by the one and principal spirit are declared in all of them all things concerning his birth, death, resurrection, intercourse with his disciples, and his twofold coming, the first in humility, despised, which has been, the second in royal power, illustrious, which is to be." The fragment seems to refer, in the first lines now extant, to the presence or absence of Mark or Peter at events recorded in the Second Gospel,[1] and it goes on to say that Luke wrote *ex opinione* (perhaps, 'from hearsay'), but had not seen the Lord in the flesh and so he wrote as best he could "trace the course of events"—(*asequi* (*sic*)). But in Acts—" he wrote in detail the things that had occurred in his presence, as his omission of the passion of Peter and of the departure of Paul, when he departed from the city (Rome) to Spain shows clearly."[2]

"John, however, expressly mentions in his epistle the several relations he had to evangelic material, saying of himself, 'What we have seen with our eyes and have heard with our ears and our hands have handled, that we write to you.' For thus he professes to have been successively not merely a seer and hearer, but also a writer of all the wonderful deeds of the Lord."

The fragment says that Luke and John wrote "in their own name" (lines 5, 15). This means that though they were the authors, they were not the only authority for their works. In the case of Luke, presumably Paul or the sources of his preface are meant to be understood as his authorities. With regard to John, the double authorisation of his gospel, divine and human, is distinctly noted—divine revelation and the approval of his

---

[1] ". . . quibus tamen interfuit et ita posuit."

[2] This seems to be the general meaning of the sentence, though it would be difficult to restore with certainty its spelling and construction. The distinction between Luke and Acts is concisely expressed by Eusebius and Jerome. The former says of Acts (*H.E.* iii. 4): "He composed it, no longer from hearsay, but perceiving with his eyes." The latter (*De vir. ill.* 7): "So he wrote the gospel as he had heard, but he composed the Acts of the Apostles as he himself had seen."

fellow-disciples and bishops. "John, one of the disciples,[1] when his fellow-disciples and bishops urged him (to write a gospel) said: 'Fast with me to-day for three days, and whatever is revealed to each let us tell one another.' The same night it was revealed to Andrew, one of the Apostles, that John should write everything in his own name, while all revised and certified it (*recognoscentibus*)."

This story, no doubt based on the mysterious 'we' in John xxi. 24, recurs in Jerome,[2] thus : " He was urged by nearly all the bishops of Asia at that time and by delegations of many churches to write, etc. . . . And ecclesiastical history relates that when he was urged by the brethren to write he replied that he would do so if all should declare a fast and pray God in common. When this was done, filled with revelation, he burst forth with that prologue, etc." Clement of Alexandria[3] says he wrote it at the instigation of his acquaintances ($\pi\rho o\tau\rho a\pi\acute{\epsilon}\nu\tau a$ $\dot{\upsilon}\pi\grave{o}$ $\tau\hat{\omega}\nu$ $\gamma\nu\omega\rho\acute{\iota}\mu\omega\nu$; Rufinus *deprecatum a discipulis*). Irenaeus seems to identify the witnesses of John xxi. 24 with " all the elders who met John the disciple of the Lord in Asia." [4]

Similar stories of composition by request occur about Mark in Clement (*apud* Eus. *H.E.* vi. 14) and Eusebius (*ibid.* ii. 15). In the latter it is said that Peter learned of what Mark had done by a revelation of the Spirit. Of course all the Gospels are naturally assumed to be inspired.

The bearing of these characteristics of the Canon of Muratori and other early Christian literature on the tradition of Lucan authorship is evident. They show that speculation on the origin of the New Testament books was already abundant in the second century. Whether authentic external evidence was

Conclusions.

---

[1] This use of 'disciple' is striking, as Andrew is called an apostle just below. So Irenaeus (iii. 11. 7, *et al.*; cf. also *Epideixis*, xliii.) calls John 'disciple.' But the term does not aim to exclude him from the apostles, but is due rather to the use of 'disciple' in John xxi. 24, and other passages which refer to the " disciple whom Jesus loved," and include him in the number of the twelve.

[2] *Comm. in Matt. Praef.*

[3] Eus. *H.E.* vi. 14.

[4] *Ibid.* iii. 23; Iren. ii. 22.

available or not, the inner characteristics of the books gave rise to more or less fanciful theories about the occasion, date, purpose, authority, and even the authorship of individual books, and about the relation of the several books to each other. These theories became gradually the uniform tradition of the Church. The earlier the date of the Canon of Muratori the less assuring appears to be its witness to the tradition of Lucan authorship. For it shows that from the beginning the assertion of Lucan authorship was inextricably bound up with reasoning which is obviously derived from fiction, allegory, and conjecture devised to explain obscure phenomena in the books of the New Testament and to satisfy curiosity in regard to gaps in knowledge where no real information was available. Nor does the consistency of this tradition, as it continues through the times of Origen, Eusebius, and Jerome, give it any special value, for the more fanciful theories are similarly repeated in later writers.

Whether any actual knowledge about the author of the Third Gospel and Acts was handed down from early times or not, the first statements made about it can be largely explained as inferences from the text. Thus the statement that the author had not seen Jesus, but knew men who had seen him, clearly states nothing which cannot be inferred from Luke's preface. The omission from Acts of Peter's martyrdom and Paul's departure to Spain are obvious to any reader; but they seemed to need explanation to Romans of the second century, and the explanation is suggested by the 'we' passages. In them and indeed in the whole book the author " wrote what was done in his presence," omitting other contemporary events. Under any explanation the 'we' passages are a most striking phenomenon and demand explanation.[1] Any modern scholar who believes that they are most naturally explained as showing that the author of both books was a companion of Paul, must admit that the same explanation might suggest itself in the second century. And

---

[1] It is instructive to notice how much attention and conjecture was called forth by the single 'we' passage in John xxi. 24. See above, pp. 258 f.

THE TRADITION

then at once the question presses for solution, What companion ? Why the early church answered 'Luke' we can only guess. That it knew is of course not impossible ; but our study has led us to believe that whether it knew or not it would be sure in time to answer such a question. The New Testament books themselves would be scanned for a reply with a critical zeal and imagination scarcely surpassed in modern times. The 'we' continues to Paul's two years in prison at Rome. From prison Paul writes several letters and mentions several companions —Epaphras, Mark, Aristarchus, Demas, Luke (Philemon 23, 24), Jesus Justus (Col. iv. 11). Perhaps Luke's selection was due to a process of elimination, for Aristarchus is excluded by Acts xxvii. 2, " Aristarchus being with us." He as well as Jesus Justus and Mark are called, in Col. iv. 10, 11, " of the circumcision." Epaphras is a Colossian (Col. iv. 12). According to 2 Tim. iv. 9-12, neither Demas nor Mark is with him, nor, of other frequent companions, either Crescens, Titus, or Timothy himself. Possibly, therefore, opinion was influenced by the statement of 2 Tim. iv. 11, " Only Luke is with me." [1]

It is not necessary to determine exactly what passages were used, nor what inferences and conjectures were drawn from them in order to assign the Third Gospel and Acts to Luke. Sometime before A.D. 180 the assignment was made, and before that

[1] To the author of the fragment, believing as he did both in the genuineness of the pastoral epistles and in the tradition of Paul's journey to Spain, practically no other date was possible for this passage than the two years in Rome. Furthermore, the author of Acts must have been present those two years since " he mentions only what was done in his presence." Eusebius, applying the same method of inference to this same passage and to the statement in a subsequent verse, " At my first defence no one took my part, but all forsook me," draws the following somewhat opposite conclusions : Paul was twice imprisoned and tried at Rome, but preached in the interval, since he says God rescued him at the first trial that he might preach to the Gentiles. " At this second defence only Luke was with him, at his first not even he. Wherefore, probably Luke composed the Acts of the Apostles about that time, telling the story as far as he was in Paul's company. This we have said is evidence that Paul's martyrdom was not accomplished during his sojourn at Rome which Luke records." See the whole passage in *H.E.* ii. 22.

date we have no records dealing with the authorship of the books.[1] Evidences of their use may exist thirty years before, perhaps still earlier, but evidence of use is not evidence as to authorship. The origin of the assignment of the gospel and Acts to Luke is therefore uncertain. But even in the earliest Christian records the treatment of authorship and kindred topics is evidently based primarily on various words and phrases of Scripture selected, combined, interpreted, allegorised, elaborated and repeated until the very interpretation of them became a fixed tradition. And it is not unfair to suppose that the methods of the writers of Alexandria, Asia, Rome, and Gaul at the end of the second century were also the methods of their predecessors, from whom the tradition of Lucan authorship was derived. It is therefore possible that this tradition is merely the earliest conjecture without any independent value.

Whether the conjecture was correct is quite a different question. Much of the earliest criticism seems to us fanciful and crude and altogether lacking in scientific and historical method, or in any sense of literary or psychological probabilities. Two tendencies especially biased their theories of authorship—the desire to identify the author with some definite name, and the desire to give him apostolic authority. And it was these tendencies also that made conjecture inevitable. Origen's confession that no one knew the authorship of the epistle to the Hebrews[2] is a surprising example of the modernity of his criticism. Even when much shrewdness is displayed by the Fathers in dealing with internal evidence the argument is often more clever than convincing. It is striking how obvious evidence is passed

[1] It may perhaps be inferred from the silence of Eusebius that Papias did not discuss the authorship of Luke or Acts or John. It is difficult to say how early should be dated the evidence for Lucan authorship implied in the title "According to Luke" found in the earliest MSS. It certainly records the general opinion of the fourth century. The transliteration *cata Lucan* in the Old Latin MS. *e* hardly proves, as some have said, that the Greek original of the translator read so.

[2] "But as to who wrote the letter, God alone knows the truth" (Eus. *H.E.* vi. 25).

THE TRADITION

over in silence; it is the obscure and the unknown that arouse the curiosity and call forth the ingenuity of early patristic scholarship. Their answers prove the existence of very little really *external* tradition, even only a few generations after the New Testament books were written. As the quotations given above prove, the solution is generally found by symbols, allegories, numbers, and the forcing of words and texts. Certainly in modern times we shall read with interest all these suggestions, but in trying to discover how the canonical Gospels really came to number four, or the churches of Paul's letters seven, under what circumstances the Fourth Gospel was written, and how the gospels were to be harmonised in their various differences, we shall give little weight to the tradition of the Fathers. It is neither possible nor right to prevent this fact from influencing our judgment on the ascription of authorship in early tradition. If these writers had merely stated that, for instance, Luke wrote Acts we should have reason to say that presumably this was what their predecessors had said, and when their evidence is thus summarised and repeated, it is not strange that many students accept it at once, and regard any hesitation to do so as hypercritical. It is only when we read the tradition as a whole that the reason for scepticism is apparent. No one who has done this can deny that the witnesses are remarkable for an inability to distinguish fancy from fact, and betray their ignorance by their statements rather than by their silence.

It must be admitted as possible that the whole tradition of Apostolic authorship may in such cases represent the tendency to assign to Apostolic persons documents possessing the necessary qualifications for inclusion in the canon on the ground of their contents, rather than the fact that in the second century men remembered who the author really was. If so, much which is called ' external tradition ' may be neither external nor tradition, but the earliest statement of the internal evidence interpreted in the light of a canonicity which had been already conceded.

Thus we may consider it safer to draw our conclusions as to

the authorship of Luke-Acts directly from the books as we have them. If the internal evidence unmistakably proves or disproves Lucan authorship, its testimony is worth more than tradition; if it is inconclusive, the tradition may be right, but is not adequate proof, and we must be content, as in the case of many other of the greatest books, to be ignorant of the author.

II

THE CASE FOR THE TRADITION

THE PAUL OF ACTS AND THE PAUL OF THE EPISTLES

By C. W. EMMET

It is perhaps not quite so superfluous as might at first appear to emphasise the fact that we can no longer approach such a subject as this on the old basis of a belief in verbal inspiration. For neither those whose main interest is the defence of the accuracy of the New Testament writings, nor those whose ideal is that of the impartial historian, always realise what is implied in the changed point of view. Both still show at times the subconscious influence of presuppositions which in theory have been long abandoned, and look for an unreasonable amount of agreement in the New Testament writings. The result is that the one class sometimes forces this agreement by the use of the methods associated with the 'Harmonisers' of an earlier period, while the other is tempted to draw from the discrepancies which it finds damning conclusions which it would hardly draw in the case of writings outside the Canon.

We have no right to expect a complete agreement between the Acts and Paul; the real questions we have to ask are whether the differences between the two are so great that one or the other—presumably Acts—must be regarded as a late and unreliable witness, and whether the general presentation of the facts in Acts is such as we might ascribe to a companion of Paul.

It will be convenient to group the material under the following heads :

I. Accounts in which Acts and the Pauline Epistles seem to overlap.

II. Indirect coincidences or discrepancies.

III. The general presentation in Acts of Paul as compared with the impression given in his own writings.

I. ACCOUNTS IN WHICH ACTS AND THE PAULINE EPISTLES OVERLAP

1. The life of Paul before his conversion.

Our two authorities agree as to the strict Pharisaism and fanatical enthusiasm of Paul's early days,[1] but we may note that Acts is our only authority for his connection with Tarsus. Further, there is agreement as to his attitude towards Christianity ;[2] but a question arises as to his early activity as a persecutor in Jerusalem.

The evidence for this is derived wholly from Acts, and it has been urged that it is inconsistent with the statements in the Epistles. In Gal. i. 13 ff. Paul says that he had been persecuting the Church of God, that after his conversion he 'returned' to Damascus, and that he remained 'unknown by face' to the churches of Judaea. Only they heard that " he who once persecuted us is now preaching the faith of which he once made havoc." The most natural interpretation of this passage would be that Paul had persecuted Christians in Damascus, that he went back to Damascus after his conversion, and never went near Jerusalem until the time, three years later, when he went up to see Peter. The ' us,' in the phrase " he who persecuted us," is on this view taken to refer to the brethren in Damascus, as a prominent persecuting official cannot well be unknown by sight to his victims.

---

[1] Acts xxii. 3, xxiii. 6, xxvi. 5 ; Gal. i. 14 ; 2 Cor. xi. 22 ; Phil. iii. 5.

[2] Acts vii. 58, ix. 2 ff., etc. ; Gal. i. 13 ; 1 Cor. xv. 9 ; Phil. iii. 6 ; 1 Tim. i. 13. It is worth noting that πορθεῖν occurs in N.T. only in this connection, *i.e.* in Acts ix. 21 ; Gal. i. 13, 23.

THE CASE FOR THE TRADITION 267

It is therefore held that the connection between Paul and Stephen in Acts is imaginary, and that the 'letters to Damascus' are an artificial link forged in order to bring him to Damascus for his conversion. It has also been argued that Paul's Judaism was not the contemporary Rabbinic Judaism of Jerusalem, and therefore suspicion falls on the statement of Acts that he was brought up at the feet of Gamaliel.[1]

The answer to these objections is :

(1) There is nothing intrinsically improbable in the account given in Acts ;[2] the conversion becomes in fact harder to explain, if we abandon the connection of Paul with Stephen.

(2) Even if the view that Paul was a Hellenist be accepted, it does not exclude a period of training at Jerusalem ; young men are not always chameleons, and Gamaliel himself is credited with liberal tendencies.

(3) It is possible that the ' churches of Judaea,' in Gal. i. 22, is to be taken as excluding rather than including Jerusalem, since Paul has just mentioned a visit to Jerusalem. It has, however, to be admitted that this is not the most obvious meaning of the words. Paul seems to be saying merely that, though he did go up to Jerusalem, he made no public appearance there or elsewhere in Judaea.

(4) In Rom. xv. 19 Paul says he preached the gospel " from Jerusalem . . . to Illyricum." If this be taken to include Jerusalem it may refer to the preaching described in Acts ix. 28 f.

(5) 'Persecuted us' in Gal. i. 23 has clearly more force if it refers to the persecution of Christians in Jerusalem rather than Damascus, and ' unknown by face ' may mean that after his conversion the Judaean Christians never caught a glimpse of Paul—not that they would not have recognised him had they seen him. The *prima facie* impression of Galatians is unfavourable to the account of Acts, but it does not seem

---

[1] Montefiore, *Judaism and Paul*, p. 90 ; see also Bousset, *Kyrios Christos*, p. 92 ; Loisy, *Les Mystères païens*, p. 317.

[2] See Harnack, *Mission und Ausbreitung*, pp. 40, 237 ff., for the activities of Jewish ' apostles,' and the light thrown on the mission of Paul to Damascus.

altogether to exclude it, if we postulate a certain exaggeration and looseness of expression on Paul's part.

2. The conversion.

Paul regards his conversion as the turning-point in his life and connects it with Damascus (Gal. i. 15-17), but he emphasises the fact that no human intermediary had a share in it. According to Acts, however, he was instructed and baptized by Ananias.[1]

The divergence of these statements is obvious, but there is a fair case in favour of the substantial truth of Acts. It is extremely probable that in Galatians Paul somewhat exaggerates his independence of all human instruction. He writes as a πνευματικός [2] who relies on his own inspiration and is independent of teaching from 'flesh and blood.' What he is really concerned to show is, that his gospel, with its special mission to the heathen world, is his own. This is scarcely contradicted even by the words put into the mouth of Ananias, and elsewhere Paul admits that he had received some information about the life of Jesus (cf. the παρέλαβον of 1 Cor. xv. 3 and perhaps of 1 Cor. xi. 23); moreover, his language about baptism certainly suggests that he had himself been baptized.

Further difficulties arise with regard to Paul's movements after the conversion, as narrated in Acts and Gal. i. Galatians mentions a visit to Arabia following immediately on the conversion, of which Luke says nothing. He does, however, mention a period of preaching at Damascus omitted by Paul. Paul tells us he returned thither (Gal. i. 17), and there is no inherent improbability in supposing that he at once began to preach. According to Acts ix. 23, his stay at Damascus was cut short by a plot of the Jews against his life. An allusion to this may reasonably be found in the reference to the attempt of Aretas (2 Cor. xi. 32), though this differs in an important point from the account in Acts ix. This must be placed either here or in the visit to Syria implied in Gal. i. 21; but it is more natural

[1] Acts ix. and xxii., but not Acts xxvi.
[2] See Reitzenstein, *Die hellenistischen Mysterienreligionen*, pp. 48, 198 ff.; Watkins, *Der Kampf des Paulus um Galatien*, pp. 47, 70 (Eng. trans. *St. Paul's Fight for Galatia*, pp. 104, 158).

THE CASE FOR THE TRADITION 269

to refer the latter to Antioch rather than to Damascus, and the coincidences of the language of 2 Cor. xi. with Acts are too close to justify the rejection of the traditional interpretation without good reason. It has indeed been argued from the evidence of coins that Aretas could not have had control over Damascus before A.D. 37, and that therefore the incident cannot on any dating be connected with the conversion. This conclusion, however, does not hold good. For the term 'Ethnarch' does not imply that Damascus formed part of the *dominions* of Aretas, but simply that he had a representative there (a 'consul' in the modern sense). It has been suggested that Paul may have roused the hostility of Aretas by his preaching in Arabia, while even if we regard it as improbable that the visit to Arabia was undertaken for this purpose, there is no difficulty in ascribing the action of Aretas to a desire to win the favour of the Jews of Damascus.

A far more complicated problem turns mainly on the relation between Acts and Gal. i. and ii.

3. Visits to Jerusalem.

Both these authorities narrate a visit placed soon after the conversion; the accounts may be placed in parallel columns:

(a) The first visit.

Acts ix. 26-29.	Gal. i. 18-24.
And when he was come to Jerusalem, he assayed to join himself to the disciples: and they were all afraid of him, not believing that he was a disciple. But Barnabas took him, and brought him to the apostles, and declared unto them how he had seen the Lord in the way, and that he had spoken to him, and how at Damascus he had preached boldly in the name of Jesus. And he was with them going in and out at Jerusalem preaching boldly in the name of the Lord: and he spake and disputed against the Greek-speaking Jews; but they went about to kill him.	After three years I went up to Jerusalem to become acquainted with Cephas, and tarried with him fifteen days. But other of the apostles saw I none, save James the Lord's brother. Now touching the things which I write unto you, before God, I lie not. Then I came into the districts of Syria and Cilicia. And I was unknown by face unto the churches of Judaea which were in Christ: but they only heard say, He that persecuted us once now preacheth the faith of which he made havoc; and they glorified God in me.

There are obvious differences between these two accounts, Luke giving the impression that this visit took place sooner, lasted longer, and was of a more public character than is suggested in Galatians. The notes of time in Acts are: " he was certain days with the disciples which were at Damascus " (ix. 19), and " when many days were fulfilled " (ὡς δὲ ἐπληροῦντο ἡμέραι ἱκαναί, ix. 23). In view of Luke's vague use of ἱκανός, these are not necessarily inconsistent with Paul's ' after three years,' which may mean only one year and two fractions, the inference being that Luke had no definite data for the chronology of this period. It is, however, argued that the character of Paul's reception at Jerusalem implies that the conversion was so recent that news of it had not yet reached that city. A possible explanation is that Paul had disappeared for some time to Arabia before his conversion had become generally known in Damascus. It was only when he returned and preached that the fact became public, and therefore no report of it may have reached Jerusalem before his visit.

With regard to the events of the visit, since Luke does not call James (the brother of the Lord) an ' apostle,' the plural of ix. 27 ("brought him to the apostles ") is inconsistent with Gal. i. 19, " other of the apostles " (*i.e.* than Cephas) " saw I none, save James," while Paul's account, even if it be supposed to leave room for preaching during a short period ('fifteen days '), gives an entirely different impression from that left by Acts ix. 27 ff. The phrase " unknown by face to the churches of Judaea," even if it be understood as not including Jerusalem, must exclude the public ministry implied in Acts, and certainly contradicts Acts xxvi. 20 (" declared both to them of Damascus first, and at Jerusalem, and throughout all the country of Judaea, and also to the Gentiles, that they should repent "), since it is difficult to find room for any preaching in Judaea at an altogether later period. These discrepancies, however, need not imply that the whole account of the visit as given in Acts ix. is an invention; they rather suggest that Luke had no

THE CASE FOR THE TRADITION 271

detailed knowledge of the events of this period and filled in the picture in general terms. Gal. i. 20 seems to hint that erroneous accounts of that visit were already current.

As to Paul's subsequent movements, he himself says that he went to Syria and Cilicia (Gal. i. 21), while Luke takes him to Tarsus (Acts ix. 30) and then to Antioch (xi. 26), thus reversing the order. It is possible that Syria is mentioned first by Paul as being the more important, as Cilicia was constantly little better than an appendage of Syria.

The crux of the problem is the second visit to Jerusalem. The common assumption that Gal. ii. and Acts xv. are accounts of the same events give rise to a double difficulty : *(b) The second visit to Jerusalem.*

(1) Paul's omission of any reference to the events of Acts xi.

(2) The considerable divergence between the two accounts of the negotiations at Jerusalem. On the natural ground that Paul's account is first-hand, conclusions are drawn in both cases unfavourable to Acts. On the one hand, it is maintained that the visit of Acts xi. never took place, or is a duplicate of Acts xv. ; on the other hand, Acts xv. is pronounced unhistorical, as a literary attempt to amplify the private negotiations alluded to in Galatians. Naturally these views make it difficult to regard Acts as a reliable historical document. The Council clearly occupies a central place in Luke's scheme, and is intended to mark a critical point in the history of the Church ;[1] the narrative refers to well-known public and official events. If Acts is not here in substance accurate, the author must deliberately have invented facts, or relied on traditions obscured by time and unsupported, at any rate at this point, by first-hand authorities.

The difficulties which arise if Acts xv. and Gal. ii. refer to the same events call for detailed consideration. (*a*) In the first place, if the visit of Acts xi. is historical why is it omitted by *The omission of the second visit of Acts xi.*

---

[1] Cf. J. Weiss, *Über die Absicht u. lit. Char. der Apg.*, p. 25 : " Die Erzählung vom Apostel-Conzil bildet nicht nur äusserlich ziemlich genau die Mitte des Buches, sondern stellt sich auch sachlich als Mittelstück und eine Art Wasserscheide dar."

Paul ? To argue that Paul may have passed it over in his survey, because he does not claim to be giving an exhaustive list of his visits to Jerusalem, fails to meet the difficulties; for the implication of Galatians is not merely that Paul had not received his gospel from men, in other words, been a pupil of the Apostles or of the Jerusalem Church (both come into consideration), but that *he had had no opportunity of doing so*; the nature of his movements after the conversion made it impossible. For this reason we have the successive notes of time: 'immediately' (i. 16), 'then after three years' (v. 18), 'then' (v. 21), 'then after the space of fourteen years' (ii. 1). It is therefore very difficult to believe that between these two 'thens,' and during the very interval covered by vv. 21-24, Paul had paid an official visit to Jerusalem as a delegate from Antioch. Whether he saw the apostles in the course of it, or whether the business was purely restricted to the question of relief, is not for the moment important. The point is that here was in fact an opportunity for intercourse with the Jerusalem Church. If the opportunity was not actually used and the visit had no further bearing on the questions at issue, it would have been all the easier for Paul to dispose of it in a sentence or parenthesis (and Paul is not afraid of parentheses!), instead of giving an obvious handle to his opponents to accuse him of disingenuousness at the very moment when he was appealing to God in token of his accuracy.

This point, indeed, is admitted by most critics. Those who can find no mention of 'the Famine visit' in Galatians often feel themselves compelled to get rid of it altogether by rejecting it as unhistorical [1] or by regarding it as a doublet of Acts xv. from a different source (so *e.g.* Pfleiderer and McGiffert).

With respect to all such solutions, it should be clearly understood that there is nothing suspicious in the story of Acts xi.

[1] See Moffatt, *Intr. to the Lit. of the N.T.*, for a list of critics who take this view. Wendt regards the whole story of the famine and its sequel as a mistake arising from a literal interpretation of a prophecy of a famine which was intended figuratively, referring to a " famine of the word of the Lord " (cf. Amos viii. 11).

THE CASE FOR THE TRADITION 273

as it stands; the objections arise solely from the supposed difficulty of finding room for it in Galatians.

(b) Secondly, even if Acts xv. stood in Luke's account as the second visit of Paul to Jerusalem after his conversion, instead of the third, there would still be grave objections to identifying it with the visit in Gal. ii. Why does not Paul so much as refer in Galatians to the decree of the Council—not merely the restrictive clauses, but even the main decision to the effect that Gentile Christians need not be circumcised? We are told of the recognition by the 'pillars' of the mission to the Gentiles, but this falls far short of what we should expect. For, according to Acts, what the Council gave to Paul was an authoritative decision that Gentile Christians were exempt from circumcision and from the keeping of, at any rate, the great mass of the Jewish Law. Paul was bound to bring this forward in his controversy with the Judaisers who had appealed to the authority of Jerusalem. No doubt he might have gone on to support it by arguments derived from the Old Testament and by other considerations, but this must of necessity have been his starting-point. To say that it was so familiar to the Galatians that it could be taken for granted is not *ad rem*. For if the decree existed when Paul wrote, both they and the Judaisers were ignoring it, and the first thing was to remind them of it in the clearest and most emphatic manner possible.[1]

Acts xv. and Gal. ii.

A word must be said as to the omission of any reference to the restrictive clauses of the decree. Are they compatible with St. Paul's statement that the only restriction was "that

---

[1] The difficulty is not greatly eased by the view of Wendt that the decrees were really only local, addressed solely to Syria and Cilicia, their scope being wrongly extended by Luke in Acts xvi. 4, xxi. 25. It is argued in support that the Jewish-Gentile difficulty was probably most acute in the countries nearer to the centre. But even if this be true with regard to the purpose of the decrees, they were clearly relevant to the Galatian controversy, and St. Paul had every reason to assume that a liberal solution adopted for Syria and Cilicia would not be refused for Galatia. He had only to say, "In churches where this question has arisen the Jerusalem Church has removed the burden, so that the question is practically settled for you too."

we should remember the poor "? On the ordinary view that they are ceremonial restrictions their omission does not seem to be honest, and certainly adds to the difficulty of the identification. On the other hand, if the 'Western' or B text be adopted they are not ceremonial restrictions.

The Western text describes the restriction as abstinence from εἰδωλοθύτων αἵματος and πορνείας, omitting πνικτοῦ. Two interpretations of this text are possible : (1) the three offences indicated are idolatry, murder, and fornication ; (2) they are three characteristic forms of heathen sacrificial practice. In neither case are they ceremonial restrictions in the same way as a food law.[1]

Still, even if this text be accepted, the omission of all mention of the Decree by Paul remains very hard to explain. It was obviously in Paul's interest to quote the whole Decree, since, on this view, it marked the most complete victory for his principles.

There is a similar difficulty in regard to 1 Corinthians which was certainly written after the Council. But in discussing the question of eating things offered to idols the Apostle had no need to introduce the main decision of the Council. There was no controversy as to circumcision at Corinth. With regard to the restrictive clauses, the regulation about εἰδωλόθυτα is not really relevant, since the point at issue was the relation between Gentile Christians and their heathen neighbours, not the relation between Gentiles and Jews within the Church. This part of the decree was in fact only local and temporary, and did not apply to a predominantly Gentile Church such as Corinth, being intended to regulate social intercourse between Jewish and Gentile Christians.[2] It is true we have rejected this argument as explaining why the decision abolishing the requirement of circumcision is ignored in Galatians, but the case here is quite different. The exemption of Gentile converts from the burden of the Law was

---

[1] See pp. 324 ff., and in the commentary on this passage.
[2] So Wendt, p. 236 ; Sanday, *The Apostolic Decree.*

THE CASE FOR THE TRADITION 275

a fundamental principle which if adopted for mixed Churches in the neighbourhood of Jerusalem applied *a fortiori* to all other Churches; *the conditions*, if they did in fact constitute a food-law, took the form of restrictions which might well be only local and temporary in their operation. As a fact of history this is what happened; the main decree was applied universally in the Christian world; the restrictions dropped into oblivion, and little is heard of them subsequently. If we accept the ' Western ' text, the difficulty is even less, for the question of εἰδωλόθυτα at Corinth was not one of morality or of deliberate participation in idolatrous worship.

(c) What St. Paul actually does say in Gal. ii. is quite inconsistent with Acts xv.:

> Then after the space of fourteen years I went up again to Jerusalem with Barnabas, taking Titus also with me. And I went up by revelation; and I laid before them the gospel which I preach among the Gentiles, but privately before them who were of repute, lest by any means I should be running, or had run, in vain. But not even Titus who was with me, being a Greek, was compelled to be circumcised: and that because of the false brethren privily brought in, who came in privily to spy out our liberty which we have in Christ Jesus, that they might bring us into bondage; to whom we gave place in the way of subjection, no, not for an hour;[1] that the truth of the gospel might continue with you. But from those who were reputed to be somewhat (whatsoever they were, it maketh no matter to me; God accepteth not man's person)—they, I say, who were of repute imparted nothing to me: but contrariwise, when they saw that I had been intrusted with the gospel of the uncircumcision, even as Peter with *the gospel* of the circumcision (for he that wrought for Peter unto the apostleship of the circumcision wrought for me also unto the Gentiles): and when they perceived the grace that was given unto me, James and Cephas and John, they who were reputed to be pillars, gave to me and Barnabas the right hands of fellowship, that we should go unto the Gentiles and they unto the circumcision; only they would that we should remember the poor; which very thing I was also zealous to do.

---

[1] The text is doubtful, but it is in any case ambiguous; see Zahn's *Kommentar zum Neue Testament*, ix. 1905; and Lake, *Earlier Epistles of St. Paul*, pp. 275 ff.

Public or private discussion?

Here we have a private discussion between Paul and Barnabas on the one hand, and James, Cephas, and John on the other, leading to a recognition of the fact that Paul has been entrusted with the duty of preaching to the Gentiles, with a consequent division of the spheres of labour; the terms on which Gentiles were to be admitted may have been understood, but it is not stated that they were explicitly settled. Acts xv., on the other hand, describes a formal and public discussion, in which Peter takes the lead and by speaking of his own admission of Gentiles in the past, brings about a decision, embodied in writing, with regard to circumcision and the Law. No doubt this public debate may have been, and indeed probably was, preceded by private conferences, and it is perfectly natural that Luke should say nothing of them. But it is an altogether different thing when Paul speaks of the private conference as though it were the only thing which happened, and ignores the formal and public decision altogether. Paul's language, indeed, excludes any such public discussion; 'but privately' cannot mean "privately in the first place and then publicly before the Church," and it would seem impossible to accept the view of Lightfoot and others that while Luke writes from the official and public point of view, Paul confines himself to the history of the private negotiations.[1] If we suppose a missionary sent home to discuss an important point of Church policy, and invited to address Convocation on the subject, with the result that that body came to a formal decision in his favour, it would be inconceivable that he should write back, "I went to London, and discussed the matter, but privately, with three or four leading bishops," simply because he had had a private conference at Lambeth before the public debate, passing over the latter in complete silence.

Suggested solutions.

It is indeed suggested,[2] partly on the ground of supposed traces of differences of sources, that the real decision in Acts xv.

---

[1] Cf. C. W. Emmet, "The Epistle to the Galatians" in *The Reader's Commentary*.
[2] Watkins, *op. cit.* p. 94 (Eng. trans. p. 222).

is taken by the Apostles, while the rank and file play no part. No doubt these may have been little more than listeners, but Luke's story must be very drastically edited and cut down before it can represent merely a private conference between half a dozen leading men; and even then this hypothesis does not solve the problem why the terms of the decision are not more definitely reproduced in Galatians.

Once more the reality of these difficulties is very generally recognised, only to be solved, as before, at the expense of Acts. Acts xv. is either rejected as unhistorical, or else it is regarded as the antedating of a decree which only came into existence at a later period in the history of the Church and after the writing of Galatians and 1 Corinthians.[1] A somewhat favourite form of this theory is that supported by J. Weiss, who argues that the original account of the Council made no mention of Paul and Barnabas, their presence being due entirely to a secondary source. Support for this view is found in Acts xxi. 25, where Luke represents James as informing Paul of the restrictive decrees of the Council, as though he had never heard of them. The verse, however, may either be a gloss (its removal improves the connection between verses 24 and 26), or else, more probably, it is a not very necessary note on the part of Luke, put into the mouth of James but really intended for the benefit of the reader, not representing information given to Paul.[2] It is a *tour de force* of criticism to exclude the Apostle of the Gentiles from any share in the decision which was the charter of their liberty.

It remains then to consider whether there is any alternative to the hypothesis that Gal. ii. and Acts xv. refer to the same events. Why should not the second visit mentioned by Paul be the same as the second recorded in Acts, *i.e.* the 'Famine

Identification of visits of Acts xi. and Gal. ii.

---

[1] For details see Moffatt, *op. cit.* pp. 307 f.

[2] A modern writer would have simply added a footnote, "See above for the arrangement already made with respect to Gentiles." But footnotes not being known the remark has to be put into the mouth of James, somewhat to the confusion of the critic. It might be well worth while to trace in ancient literature the results of the non-use of this great stand-by of the modern writer, and the methods by which the gap was filled.

visit' of Acts xi. ? This visit was undertaken by Barnabas and Paul in order to bring contributions from the Christians of Antioch for the relief of the Jewish Church. Barnabas had been sent to Antioch as a representative of the Mother Church to superintend the growth of the new community, with special reference to the preaching to Gentiles, and Paul had been already preaching and teaching actively for some time in the Gentile world (Acts xi. 26; Gal. i. 22 f.). Hence, even if we had been told nothing about it, we should have been bound to assume that Barnabas made some sort of report to those by whom he had been sent, and that the Gentile question came under discussion. The idea that this question could not have been raised at so early a period is contradicted by the notices in Acts xi. of the missionary activity of the Antiochean church [1] as well as by all *a priori* probabilities.

It becomes increasingly clear that it is a mistake to regard Paul as the founder of Hellenistic or even of Hellenic Christianity. There were Christians in Damascus before the conversion of Paul; the Greek Christianity at Antioch had its origin apart from his efforts; even the Church at Rome—certainly consisting of Greek as well as Jewish Christians—was in existence before Paul came to Italy.[2] The problem of the recognition of these communities and their missionary activity must have soon attracted notice. The kind of discussion implied in Gal. ii. is precisely what we should expect at this stage. It is private and informal, dealing with the general principle of a mission to the Gentile world. If details as to the conditions on which the new converts were to be accepted were raised at all, they

---

[1] In Acts xi. 20, Ἕλληνας ('Greeks,' *i.e.* Gentiles), not Ἑλληνιστάς (Greek-speaking Jews), is probably the right reading; see commentary.

[2] Bousset has a remarkable paragraph on this point in his *Kyrios Christos*, p. 92. "Between Paul and the Palestinian primitive church stand the Hellenistic churches in Antioch, Damascus, Tarsus. . . . In any case the development of the Apostle's life took place in the foundation of the Hellenistic churches." See also Heitmüller's article "Zum Problem Paulus und Jesus," in the *Zeitschrift f. neutestamentl. Wiss.* xiii. (1912), pp. 320 ff., and Loisy, *Les Mystères païens*, pp. 318 ff.

THE CASE FOR THE TRADITION 279

clearly remained unsettled. There is therefore ample room for the public and formal Council of Acts xv., where outstanding questions were debated and more or less settled, and we need not be seriously disturbed by the suggestion that we are making history repeat itself.

There are one or two minor points which go to confirm this view. (a) 'Went up by revelation' in Gal. ii. 1 corresponds excellently to the prophecy of Agabus in Acts xi. (b) There is no difficulty in placing the dispute at Antioch (Gal. ii. 11 ff.) in its proper place before the Council, perhaps during the events of Acts xv. 1 ff. On the ordinary view we have either to place this episode after the Council or else to suppose that St. Paul introduces it entirely out of its proper order; each of these alternatives is attended by serious objections.[1] (c) In Gal. ii. 10 we read that the apostles laid down the condition "only they would that we should remember the poor, which very thing I was also zealous to do." The aorist $\dot{\epsilon}\sigma\pi o\acute{v}\delta a\sigma a$ fits in well with the fact that Paul had actually just brought alms to Jerusalem: it is almost a pluperfect.[2] On the other hand, if we transfer the whole scene to a later date and see in the remark an anticipation of the great collection for the Saints, the tense is quite wrong. We should expect either $\ddot{\eta}\mu\epsilon\lambda\lambda ον$ $\pi οι\epsilon\hat{\iota}ν$ 'was about to do,' from the point of view of the interview, or else 'am eager to do' from the point of view of the period at which the Epistle was written, since, on the ordinary dating, Galatians belongs to the group in which this collection plays a prominent part.

It is, however, objected that there were no apostles in Jerusalem at the time of the Famine; presbyters alone are mentioned in Acts xi. 30, and it is suggested that all the Twelve had left Jerusalem on account of Herod's persecution. The fact, however,

<small>Apostles in Jerusalem.</small>

---

[1] See p. 326.
[2] "The pluperfect was never very robust in Greek. . . . The conception of relative time never troubled the Greeks; and the aorist which simply states that the event happened is generally quite enough to describe what we should like to define more exactly as preceding the time of the main verb" (Moulton, *Grammar of N.T. Greek*, i. p. 148).

that the alms were handed over to the presbyters does not necessarily imply that there were no apostles to receive them, but merely carries out the principle of Acts vi. that it was not their business 'to serve tables.' Further, if we regard the narrative of Acts as arranged in strict chronological order, Paul and Barnabas reached Jerusalem *before* the outbreak of Herod's persecution, in which case there is no reason to assume the absence of the Apostles. The probability, however, is that this order is not closely observed. Luke is passing backwards and forwards from Jerusalem to Antioch. Having brought the story of Antioch up to the famine (*circa* A.D. 46), he resumes the thread of events at Jerusalem with chapter xii., leading up to the death of Herod in A.D. 44. But Acts xii. does not suggest that all the apostles or even Peter [1] fled from Jerusalem to escape persecution. And even if we do assume that he and others left the city there is no reason whatever why they should not have returned by A.D. 46–47, since the persecution ceased with the death of Herod.

Chronology. A more serious difficulty arises in connection with the chronology. In Gal. i. 18 we read, "Then after three years ($\mu\epsilon\tau\grave{\alpha}$ $\tau\rho\acute{\iota}\alpha$ $\emph{ἔ}\tau\eta$) I went up to Jerusalem"; and in ii. 1. "Then after the space of fourteen years ($\delta\iota\grave{\alpha}$ $\delta\epsilon\kappa\alpha\tau\epsilon\sigma\sigma\acute{\alpha}\rho\omega\nu$ $\grave{\epsilon}\tau\hat{\omega}\nu$) I went up again to Jerusalem." The question is whether the 'fourteen years' are to be reckoned from the conversion, or from the former visit. The two expressions are clearly parallel; in the first the 'after three years' seems to be reckoned from the conversion, and not from the return from Arabia to Damascus, which is the last-mentioned movement. It is therefore quite possible that the 'after fourteen years' is to be calculated on the same principle; and that Paul throughout is dating his movements from his conversion, which he takes as his starting-point. In this case we only require 'fourteen years' from the

---

[1] The theory that Peter left Jerusalem depends entirely on the interpretation of ἕτερος τόπος in Acts xii. 17, as meaning 'another city.' It may mean 'another house,' cf. Acts iv. 31.

THE CASE FOR THE TRADITION 281

conversion to the famine visit, and the chronological difficulty disappears. We have, however, to reckon with the possibility that the 'fourteen years' are to be reckoned from the 'three years.' Even so, it is still open to us to date Gal. ii. at the time of the famine. We must remember that according to the old method of reckoning time, fractions of a day or year were often spoken of as wholes; *e.g.* 'after three days' might mean from late on Friday afternoon till early on Sunday morning.[1] Accordingly, we have no right to add the three years and the fourteen together, and to speak of an interval of *seventeen* years, as is usually done. The true state of the case may be best represented as follows:

'After three years' $= x + 1 + y$;
'After fourteen years' $= (1 - y) + 12 + z$;

where x, y, z are unknown numbers of months. The total period is therefore fourteen years + $(x + z)$ months, where x and z may be quite small. To put it in another way, December 1909 to March 1911 might be the first period, and March 1911 to January 1924 the second, the whole period from December 1909 to January 1924 being just over fourteen years. Since the famine visit probably took place in A.D. 47, the resultant date for Paul's conversion is about A.D. 32, which is by no means impossible.[2]

Assuming, then, the identity of the visits of Acts xi. and Gal. ii. we remove the difficulty which arises on account of the supposed omission of the former by Paul. We have still, however, to explain why he does not continue his story up to the time of the Council, and clinch his argument by quoting its decision. The obvious answer is that the Council had not yet taken place; in other words, Galatians was written at the close of the first

Date of Galatians.

---

[1] Cf. Ramsay, Hastings's *Dict. of the Bible*, v. p. 474.

[2] A different solution may be found in the suggestion, based on quite other grounds, of a primitive corruption in the text of Gal. ii. 1, whereby, by the addition of a single iota, 'fourteen' has been substituted for 'four.' See Lake, "The Date of Herod's Marriage with Herodias" (*Expositor*, November 1912).

Missionary Journey, and not, as is usually assumed, during the course of the third. A full discussion of this view obviously belongs primarily to a commentary on that Epistle,[1] but at the same time it has a direct bearing on Acts, since, as has been pointed out, the omission in Galatians of any real reference to the decrees of the Council makes it almost impossible to accept Luke's account, except on the assumption that it lay still in the future. It must here be taken for granted that the Epistle was in fact addressed to the Churches of South Galatia, evangelised on the First Journey;[2] on the rival view the hypothesis of the early date becomes of course impossible. On his return from this journey Paul remained at Antioch 'no little time' (Acts xiv. 28); and we have no right to assume that events summarised in a few verses all happened in a few days. During this period Judaisers from Jerusalem came to Antioch; and there is nothing improbable in supposing that they also extended their propaganda to the Churches just founded by Paul, in which the strong Jewish element described in Acts xiii., xiv. guaranteed a favourable soil. St. Paul, while occupied in the controversy at Antioch, hears of the defection of the Galatian Churches which has been brought about with an unexpected ease and celerity (Gal. i. 6). He cannot visit the scene himself (iv. 20), perhaps because he knows he must go to Jerusalem, or is even already on the way there. Accordingly he writes this urgent appeal in order to stop the mischief at once; and on the first opportunity he follows it up by a personal visit, in which he explains the decisions of the Council (Acts xvi. 1-6). On this reconstruction of the course of events Acts and Galatians dovetail into one another quite naturally without any forcing of language or adroit manipulation.

[1] See Emmet, *Commentary on Galatians*, quoted above, and Lake, *The Earlier Epistles of St. Paul*, pp. 297 ff. A similar conclusion as to the date of Galatians has now been reached by Ramsay, though on somewhat different lines; see *The Teaching of Paul*, pp. 372 ff. Cf. also Douglass Round, *The Date of Galatians*.

[2] See note on xvi. 6.

THE CASE FOR THE TRADITION 283

The possible objections are slight. It is urged that τὸ πρότερον in Gal. iv. 13, implies that Paul had visited Galatia twice at the time of his writing, whereas the theory advanced implies that the Epistle was sent after his first visit and before the second. But, even assuming that τὸ πρότερον in Gal. iv. 13 means 'the first time' and not merely 'formerly,' the reference may quite well be to the double journey mentioned in Acts. Each town, except Derbe, was visited twice, and on the return visit Paul stayed long enough to instruct his converts and appoint Elders.

It is also argued that Romans, Galatians, and the two epistles to the Corinthians are so closely connected that they must all belong to the same period, that is to the time of Paul's Corinthian-Ephesian mission. But the close connection in language, subject, and style between Galatians and Romans, and to a lesser degree 1 and 2 Corinthians, does not compel us to suppose them all to have been written at the same period. Galatians is clearly the hasty sketch, thrown out on the spur of the moment, under the pressure of an urgent crisis, while Romans represents the carefully matured, almost philosophical development of the same theme, written at a time when the most pressing danger had passed away.[1] Nor need we be greatly troubled by suggestions that Paul's theology could not have reached the stage of development shown in Galatians at so early a period. He had been a convert and a preacher for many years, and by the time

^{Romans and Galatians.}

---

[1] To argue from similarity of style to identity of date is one of those critical rules of thumb which, except where it is confirmed by other indications, only simplifies at the cost of misleading. There are literary parallels in plenty, where a writer produces works marked by the same style, separated by others in which a quite different style is found. We may instance Tennyson and *The Idylls of the King*. "Morte d'Arthur" was written in 1842, "Balin" thirty years later, the rest being produced at varying intervals. The fact that the student of Tennyson may be able to detect differences between the earlier and later parts, does not affect the general homogeneity of language and style in works published at very different times and separated from one another by poems in which quite other styles were adopted.

With regard to the admitted priority of Galatians see Turner, *H.D.B.* i. p. 423; Sanday and Headlam, *Romans*, p xxxviii.

of the Council he must certainly have thought out the general lines on which he was to defend the inclusion of Gentiles. The question is not referred to in the subsequent epistles to Thessalonica, simply because it had not arisen in that Church; a missionary and less argumentative type of letter is all that is needed.

A minor objection has been found in the language of Acts xv. 3,[1] "They [sc. Paul and Barnabas] . . . passed through both Phoenicia and Samaria, declaring the conversion of the Gentiles; and they caused great joy unto all the brethren." It is argued that this excludes the supposition that there was at this very time a grave danger of defection in the Galatian Church. But all that is implied in the words is that the Apostles told the story of their successes, and that the news was welcomed. The fact of the conversion of the Gentiles still remained, even if at the moment there was cause for anxiety. Luke, it is true, omits to mention the troubles with the Galatians—a far less significant fact than his silence about those at Corinth—but this makes no difference to the argument as to whether the Galatian difficulty arose early or late.

Luke's silence.

With regard to Luke's silence itself we must remember that he wrote at a time when these temporary disagreements had been settled. They loom large to us because we happen to have letters written at a time when they were acute. But to the historian, writing after a lapse of years, they may well have appeared comparatively unimportant. The fact that he mentions the differences of opinion which led to the Council, and such things as the deceit of Ananias and Sapphira, and the quarrel between Paul and Barnabas, may be enough to absolve him from the charge of deliberately glossing over the troubles of the early Church. There was, however, no reason why he should mention them all, nor did he write with the view of enabling future generations to illustrate the letters of his friend.

[1] See Maurice Jones, *The New Testament in the Twentieth Century*, pp. 249 ff.

THE CASE FOR THE TRADITION 285

It may be said again that if the Council were already in prospect when Paul wrote the Epistle, we should still expect him to refer to it; and thus the old difficulty recurs in a new though less serious form. The answer, however, is not hard to find. Paul's position at the time of the Council must have been that if the decision was fairly favourable to him he would accept it, but not otherwise; we cannot conceive of the writer of Galatians as ready to acquiesce if the Apostles had taken the side of the Judaisers.[1] Hence while the Epistle seems to be a sketch of the arguments he was using in the controversy, he could not tie his hands by telling his converts to wait patiently for the result of a conference which he might find himself obliged to throw over. It is further quite possible to escape the difficulty altogether by supposing that the Epistle was written before the decision to go to Jerusalem was arrived at.

A last objection is found in the circumcision of Timothy, which, it is urged, is inconceivable after the writing of Galatians. This, however, can hardly hold good in view of the special circumstances attending the case; see further p. 293 below.

To sum up; it has been necessary to treat with some fulness the difficulties connected with the relation of Acts and Galatians, since their solution is crucial to the position of the former as a historical document. It has been suggested that these difficulties disappear almost entirely if the three points for which we have argued can be made good : (1) That Acts xi. and Gal. ii. refer to the same events; (2) that Galatians was written to the Churches of South Galatia; (3) that it was written before the Council of Acts xv. It may be maintained with some confidence that the objections are in no case serious; the positive arguments are derived from the *prima facie* evidence of both

[1] " Lest by any means I should be running, or had run, in vain," cannot be understood as implying that Paul was ready to confess that he had been wrong if the decision went against him. What the words mean is that such a decision might involve the practical failure of his work and the ruin of Gentile Christianity.

286 IDENTITY OF EDITOR OF LUKE AND ACTS

books, if only we approach that evidence without presuppositions which have held the field too long unchallenged.

II. INDIRECT COINCIDENCES AND DISCREPANCIES

The coincidences between Acts and the Pauline Epistles are as follows : (1) Jerusalem, not Galilee, as we should have expected from Mark and Matthew, became the centre of the primitive church. (2) Believers are called ' disciples,' ' saints,' ' brethren,' but Luke, though he knows the name, agrees with Paul in not calling them Christians. (3) The Twelve are the rulers of the community; and Luke and Paul both specifically mention Peter and John by name. (4) Side by side with them are other apostles, Barnabas (Acts xiv. 14) being mentioned. (5) James and the other brethren of the Lord take a prominent place. (6) Baptism is connected with the forgiveness of sins, and is administered by the Apostles and others in the name of Jesus (Acts viii. 16, xix. 5 ; 1 Cor. i. 14 ff.). (7) Thanksgiving ($εὐχαριστία$) and the Breaking of Bread are closely connected (Acts xx. 7, xxvii. 35 ; 1 Cor. x. 16, xi. 23, xiv. 16). (8) The death and resurrection of Jesus hold the central place, though we must admit that Luke does not interpret them in the characteristically Pauline way. (9) The expectation of the Parousia is prominent both in the early chapters of Acts and in the earlier Pauline Epistles. Some of these coincidences may seem obvious and commonplace but they are significant collectively.

References to the Pauline Churches. (a) Galatia.

On the North Galatian theory we of course learn nothing from Acts beyond the mere fact of the founding of the Church, but on the South Galatian theory we find several coincidences between Galatians and Acts xiv., e.g. in the mention of Barnabas as well known (Gal. ii. 1), miracles (iii. 5), persecutions (iii. 4, v. 11, vi. 12 ; cf. 2 Tim. iii. 11),[1] and possibly the reception

---

[1] Even if the Pastorals are not Pauline, this may well be one of the Pauline notes embodied in them.

THE CASE FOR THE TRADITION 287

of Paul as "an angel of God," iv. 14 ff.; cf. Acts xiv. 11, where Paul is Hermes, the messenger, or *angelos*, of the gods.[1]

(b) Thessalonica.

Acts and the Epistles to the Thessalonians confirm one another in the following points: the presence of a large Gentile element in the Church (Acts xvii. 4; 1 Thess. i. 9, ii. 14), the hostility of the Jews (Acts xvii. 5; 1 Thess. ii. 14), the close association of Silas and Timothy, and the stress laid by Paul on 'the kingdom' (Acts xvii. 7; 1 Thess. ii. 12; 2 Thess. i. 5), with the consequent special interest in the Parousia.

There is sometimes supposed to be a contradiction between Acts and these Epistles with regard to the length of Paul's stay in Thessalonica. The Epistles seem to imply that this lasted for some time while Acts only mentions three Sabbaths (xvii. 2). The latter, however, may refer only to the period of preaching to the Jews, and it may be reasonably argued that Luke's narrative as a whole suggests a longer stay.

A somewhat complicated, though not really important, question arises with regard to the movements of Timothy and Silas. According to Acts xvii. 14, they are left in Beroea and rejoin Paul at Corinth (xviii. 5). But 1 Thess. iii. 1 ff.[2] seems to imply that they were at one time with Paul at Athens, and that Timothy was sent from there to Thessalonica. It is possible to combine the two accounts by supposing that Timothy and Silas did in fact rejoin Paul at Athens, and that Timothy was sent away again to Thessalonica, and Silas on some other mission, perhaps to Philippi, both meeting Paul again at Corinth. If this be the explanation, we admit that Luke was either not accurately informed of the movements of Paul's companions, or else expressed himself badly. This point is of so little importance to the historian that he may well be

---

[1] This need not imply that Paul would have acknowledged Hermes as an angel of God.

[2] "Wherefore when we could no longer forbear we thought it good to be left behind at Athens alone; and sent Timothy our brother . . . to establish you. . . . But when Timothy came even now unto us from you . . ."

forgiven if he did not consider meticulous accuracy to be required.¹

(c) Corinth. Paul's work at Corinth coincided with a period of weakness and depression (1 Cor. ii. 3, "And I came to you,"), which is readily explained by his experiences in Europe and his failure at Athens as narrated in Acts; he needed a special vision to encourage him (Acts xviii. 9 ff., 'fear not'). Special references are made to his practice of continuing to work at his trade (xviii. 3; 1 Cor. ix. 15 ff.; for other references see Acts xx. 34; 1 Thess. ii. 9; 2 Thess. iii. 7). Crispus is a prominent convert (Acts xviii. 8; 1 Cor. i. 14); Aquila and Priscilla are known at Corinth (xviii. 3; 1 Cor. xvi. 19), and have moved to Ephesus Acts xviii. 18 ff.).² The presence of Apollos in Corinth (1 Cor. i. 12, etc.), though only for a short time, since xvi. 12 mentions him at Ephesus, is attested by Acts xviii. 27, and Luke's mention of his visit to Achaia may indicate that he was aware that it had had important consequences. Apollos was evidently in a sense responsible for the divisions referred to in 1 Corinthians, and Luke may be hinting at these in this passage, though he makes no further reference to them.³ A final visit to Corinth by way of Macedonia is attested both by Acts xx. 1, and 2 Cor. ii. 12,⁴ while Acts xx. 3 ff. explains why Paul returned the same way and did not carry out his intention of going direct from Corinth to Jerusalem (2 Cor. i. 16).

The reference in 1 Cor. xv. 32 is hardly to the affair of

---

¹ E. von Dobschütz holds that Timothy and Silas were stopped from coming to Athens by a message from Paul sending them elsewhere, and that they did not actually rejoin him till he was at Corinth; but 1 Thess. iii. implies that Paul had not previously been alone.

² The Sosthenes of 1 Cor. i. 1, is probably not identical with the Sosthenes of Acts xviii. 17, who is a Jew, and hostile to Paul, unless it be supposed that he afterwards became a convert and migrated to Ephesus. "The name Sosthenes was not rare among the Greeks" (Wendt).

³ In the same way we hear nothing in Acts of the trouble dealt with in 2 Corinthians and of the implied journeys and missions between Ephesus and Corinth.

⁴ 1 Cor. xvi. 5 may refer to an earlier visit or to a plan which was not carried out; see 2 Cor. i. 15 ff.

Demetrius, in Acts xix., since Paul did not figure directly in it. It may refer to some danger or imprisonment about which Acts is silent; cf. 2 Cor. i. 8, xi. 23. For the relation of 1 Corinthians to the Council, see above, pp. 274 f.

Romans and Acts agree in implying that at the time the Epistle was written Paul wished to visit Rome, but had been unable to do so (Acts xix. 21; Rom. i. 13, xv. 23); the passage in Acts emphasises precisely the point he mentions himself, that he must first visit Jerusalem.[1] A somewhat perplexing difficulty arises from the language of Acts xxviii. 21 ff.,[2] where the Jews in Rome are represented as knowing nothing of Paul or even of Christianity except that "it is everywhere spoken against." It is argued that this is inconsistent with the epistle, which implies the existence of a Christian Church in Rome, comprising a Jewish as well as a Greek element, and interested in the relation between Christianity and the Law: in view of this, it is hard to believe that there had been no collisions between Jews and Christians in Rome,[3] or that the former could have been entirely ignorant of the new religion. The explanation of Luke's language may be that the Jews in Rome were in fact less hostile than elsewhere, while for reasons of their own they disavowed acquaintance with Christianity. At any rate, the statement is not one which a writer—least of all a late writer with Romans before him—would be likely to invent, though he may, of course have misunderstood the position of the Roman Jews. Acts ii. 10 and xxviii. 15 show that Luke did in fact recognise the existence of Christianity in Rome before Paul's visit.

(d) Rome.

There are somewhat remarkable coincidences in the names

Minor points of contact.

[1] "If we closely compare Acts xix. 21 with Rom. xv. 23-25, we are astonished at the completeness of coincidence in the two passages" (Harnack, *Neue Untersuchungen zur Apg.* p. 49, n. 1 (Eng. trans., *Date of the Acts and the Synoptic Gospels*, p. 69, n. 2)).

[2] See on this passage Harnack, *Lukas der Arzt*, p. 92, n. 3 (Eng. trans., *Luke the Physician*, pp. 130 ff. n.).

[3] The words of Suetonius (*Claud.* 25), "Iudaeos impulsore Chresto assidue tumultuantes Roma expulit," certainly suggest such collisions.

of minor characters in the Acts and the Pauline Epistles. Apollos, Aquila and Priscilla, and Timothy have already been referred to. There is no reason to doubt the identity of the Silas of Acts with the Silvanus [1] of 1 Thess. i. 1 ; 2 Thess. i. 1 ; 2 Cor. i. 19. In the list in Acts xx. 4 f., Sopater is probably the Sosipater of Rom. xvi. 21 ; Aristarchus (cf. xix. 29, xxvii. 2) is mentioned in Col. iv. 10, Philem. 24 ; Tychicus occurs in Col. iv. 7, Eph. vi. 21, 2 Tim. iv. 12, Titus iii. 12 ; Trophimus (cf. xxi. 29) in 2 Tim. iv. 20, while Gaius of Derbe might be identical with the Gaius of Rom. xvi. 23, though the name is common.[2] On the other hand, the Secundus of Acts xx. is not elsewhere mentioned, a fact which suggests that the list is not made up of names taken at random from the Pauline Epistles. A similar conclusion may be drawn from the omission in Acts of the names of Titus and Luke.

The references in Acts and in the Epistles to the collection for the Saints afford an example of undesigned coincidence, in the language of psychical research ' a cross-correspondence,' being quite incidental and yet supplementing one another in a very remarkable manner. Luke says nothing about the bringing of alms as the main reason of Paul's last journey to Jerusalem until xxiv. 17, where it appears clearly.[3] On the other hand, in the Epistles of this period there are frequent references showing the importance Paul attached to the collection and the trouble he took in securing contributions from all his Churches (Rom. xv. 25 ff. ; 1 Cor. xvi. 1 ; 2 Cor. viii. ix.). The charge and promise of Gal. ii. 10 explain why Paul felt himself

---

[1] The view of Weizsäcker is that a Jerusalem Silas has been substituted for the Pauline Silvanus as a companion of Paul in order to emphasise his close connection with the Jerusalem Church. But if they were really different persons, the natural thing would have been for the writer of Acts to complete the identification by using the name Silvanus instead of the ambiguous Silas.

[2] But not with the Gaius of Acts xix. 29, who is a Macedonian, or the Corinthian of 1 Cor. i. 14 ; the Gaius of Rom. xvi. 23 is generally identified with the latter. The point depends on the *provenance* of Romans xvi.

[3] Wendt suggests that the διακονία of xx. 24 may have originally (*i.e.* in the supposed source) referred to this.

THE CASE FOR THE TRADITION 291

especially bound to this work, a point which Acts does not mention. In the light of these references, it becomes clear that the companions of Paul (Acts xx. 4) whose presence is not explained, are, in fact, the delegates chosen by the Churches (1 Cor. xvi. 3; 2 Cor. viii. 18 ff.). There is no serious difficulty in the fact that Paul in Acts xxiv. 17 speaks of the collection as a gift to the Jewish nation; it was intended specifically for *Jewish* Christians, and the Church was regarded as the true representative of the nation.

III. THE GENERAL PRESENTATION OF PAUL IN ACTS

Is the description in Acts of Paul's conduct inconsistent with the Epistles?[1] Before entering into detail the right point of view must be sought. If we confine our attention to Galatians, an Epistle written in the heat of controversy, we obtain a very one-sided impression of Paul's attitude. Both Corinthians and Romans contain indications of a more moderate standpoint, particularly when it comes to practical matters (see especially 1 Cor. ix. 20), while even Galatians itself shows that Paul's own conduct was open to the charge of inconsistency. The fact was that he never forgot that he was a Jew, nor did he throw off altogether the effects of his early training. The wider the breach between his nation and Christianity, the more burning was his patriotic love, and the stronger the stress laid on the real privileges of the Jew (Rom. ix., x.). His behaviour did not arise from a desire for accommodation so much as from a certain illogicality inherent in his position. He never drew the conclusion that the Jewish Christian should cease to be a Jew or

Paul and the Law.

---

[1] For a very full treatment of the question see Harnack, *Neue Untersuchungen zur AG*, etc. (Eng. trans., *Date of the Acts*, etc.), chap. ii.; Pfleiderer, *Paulinism*, ii. pp. 242 ff., both of whom defend the general presentation as given in Acts. For a statement of the case on the other side, see Jülicher, *Neue Linien i. d. Kritik d. evangel. Überlief.* pp. 59 f. (quoted by Harnack, pp. 25 f. (Eng. trans. p. 36)).

hold himself exempt from the Law.¹ This conclusion was drawn by a later generation and was no doubt implied in Paul's own teaching, especially in Galatians, but in a time of transition few men are entirely consistent or prepared to work out their principles to their logical issue when they run counter to long-established modes of thought. What Paul opposed in the Law was mainly its exclusiveness. The essential things for which he contended were the liberty of the Gentiles and the duty of the Jewish Christians to accept them as brethren. Here Acts suggests no tendency to compromise. It remains to examine the details of the objection.

It is suggested that the view of Acts according to which Paul made it his practice to appeal first to Jews on his missionary journeys, and to preach in the synagogues as long as he was allowed to do so, is inconsistent with the arrangement made in Gal. ii. that he should go to the Gentiles and Peter to the Jews. But in any case, as the evidence of the Epistles shows, the separation of spheres spoken of here cannot be taken as more than a vague working agreement. It cannot have implied that Peter was never to preach to Gentiles or Paul to Jews. We find the former in the Gentile Churches of Antioch and, probably, Corinth. For though there must always be some doubt on the point, the mention in 1 Corinthians of a party of Cephas raises a presumption that Peter had been in Corinth, though it does not of course follow that he at once preached to the heathen. Similarly at Antioch Peter clearly mixed at first with all the Christians, though he afterwards had scruples (cf. Gal. ii. 11 f.). Once more this does not necessarily mean that he immediately preached to unconverted heathen, but the influence of Gentile Christians

---

¹ See to the contrary Gal. v. 3 ; 1 Cor. vii. 18. An interesting parallel may be found in the position of Luther. He began with a moderate position, and it was only force of circumstances which compelled him to go further. "Only gradually did he reach the position that a man can be saved apart from the Pope; and he ended by saying that a man cannot be saved unless he opposes the Pope" (A. Plummer, *The Continental Reformation*, p. 102). Paul was less logical.

THE CASE FOR THE TRADITION   293

would inevitably bring him into contact with their unconverted friends. Paul, on his side, includes Jews in his letters, and is obviously concerned with them; the arrangement was clearly understood as admitting of some overlapping. It was in fact inevitable that Paul should begin by preaching in the synagogues when he reached a fresh city, since it was there that he would find the 'God-fearers' who formed the nucleus of each new Church.

The acceptance of the Conciliar decrees has been implicitly dealt with already (see above, pp. 273 ff.). If the Western text be adopted, there is, of course, no difficulty. But with the ordinary reading the restrictive clauses are not to be interpreted as though they laid down a minimum of law necessary to salvation; this, indeed, Paul could never have acknowledged. They are rather the practical recognition of certain usages, very possibly usages which already existed, intended to facilitate intercourse between the two sections of the Church; to them the Paul of the Galatian Epistle might readily agree.

The circumcision of Timothy (Acts xvi. 3) laid Paul open to a charge of inconsistency. This is naturally bound up with the vexed question whether Titus [1] was circumcised or not. However, in neither case had he yielded to the prejudices of the Judaisers in the Church. In view of what has been said above with regard to the peculiar, if we will the inconsistent, position Paul was bound to adopt at a time of transition, it is impossible to maintain that he could never have circumcised a half Jew, whether before or after the writing of Galatians.

With regard to Paul's vow at Corinth (Acts xviii. 18), there is some doubt as to its nature, and also whether it was, in fact, taken by Paul or Aquila. Assuming the former, whatever the reason of the fact and of its mention by Luke, it must be considered in connection with Paul's similar action at Jerusalem. It is here that the objections as to the behaviour attributed to

Paul at Jerusalem.

---

[1] The text of Gal. ii. 3 ff. is very doubtful.

Paul in Acts are at their strongest,[1] and it may at once be admitted that there is much obscurity in the narrative of Acts xxi. 17 ff. But, as we have seen, it is clear from the Epistles that Paul lived as a Jew among Jews, and never urged them to abandon their nationality. Hence Luke's object was not so much to show that Paul was a strict Jew, but that he was still so far in sympathy with Judaism as to be able to take his part in a religious rite which did not compromise his principles. The false report of *v.* 21 which is thus to be refuted concerns his attitude towards Jews, not Gentile Christians. Paul's action does not necessarily imply that he himself had taken a vow, still less that he recognised the ceremonial law as a means of securing salvation; it is precisely the rôle that could be played by any liberal sympathiser with Judaism like Agrippa.[2] The action was performed at a period when Paul was anxious to avoid any formal breach with the Mother Church of Jerusalem, and if possible to win his nation (cf. Romans). Further, as both Pfleiderer and Harnack[3] point out, Luke's silence as to any further help or support of Paul on the part of the Jewish Christians is strongly against the view that the whole incident is an invention due to a 'tendency' to over-emphasise the friendly relations between the two. The difficulty is psychological rather than historical.

With respect to Paul's attendance at feasts, if this seems to be inconsistent with Gal. iv. 10, so is 1 Cor. xvi. 2 (cf. Rom. xiv. 5 ff.). Paul's object in visiting Jerusalem at the festal seasons may have been to meet friends from all quarters of the world,[4] though he had also the idea of proving publicly that he had not broken entirely with Judaism.

[1] Cf. pp. 320 f.
[2] See Josephus, *Ant.* XIX. 6. 1, where Agrippa "ordered that many of the Nazirites should have their heads shorn," *i.e.* paid for their sacrifices. Was Paul's action, as Harnack suggests, a way of expending part of the contribution he had brought?
[3] *Paulinism*, ii. p. 245; *Date of the Acts*, pp. 51, 81.
[4] The fact that a man may desire to spend Easter in Rome does not imply a complete sympathy with the teaching and practice of Roman Catholicism.

THE CASE FOR THE TRADITION 295

It has often been assumed that if Acts is by a companion of Paul, not only must his teaching as represented therein be clearly and exclusively 'Pauline,' but the teaching of Acts as a whole must fit in with the same scheme. The fallacy is obvious; Luke may have admired the Apostle without really understanding him or accepting his full system, and there is certainly no reason to expect the whole of Acts, or the Third Gospel, to be impregnated with more than a mild solution of Paulinism. The controversial Epistles do not represent Paul's normal missionary preaching; of this the Epistles to the Thessalonians are a far better type. And with regard to the representation in Acts of the teaching of Paul himself it must be borne in mind that a companion of Paul might well have composed speeches for his hero, though indeed many have seen traces of Pauline thought in these. In the speech in the synagogue at Pisidian Antioch the first part is obviously a repetition of the sort of arguments put into the mouth of Stephen in Acts vii. Yet in the second part there are clear affinities with Galatians and Romans.[1]

Paul's teaching in Acts.

The speech at Athens is more important, especially in regard to the theory of Norden propounded in his *Agnostos Theos*, that it is based on a conventional type of preaching. But this is discussed elsewhere.[2] The speech, moreover, has a parallel in Rom. ii. when Paul appeals to the natural religious consciousness of the Gentile world.

With regard to the later speeches the main difficulty is connected with the line of defence adopted by Paul in Acts xxiii. 6, xxiv. 21, xxvi. 5 ff., where he tries to enlist the sympathy of

Paul and the Pharisees.

---

[1] Cf., for instance, the allusions to the Promise in Acts xiii. 23, 32, with Galatians, the phrase "the fullness of time" in Acts xiii. 27, 33, with Gal. iv. 4, and the 'tree' (used of the Cross) in xiii. 29 with Gal. iii. 13. The words in xiii. 38, "By him every one that believeth is justified from all things, from which ye could not be justified by the law of Moses," can be interpreted as meaning that the gospel is complementary to the Law. But this is not certain, and even if this be the meaning, it might be a contemporary's misconception of Paul's difficult and subtle doctrine.

[2] See pp. 330 ff. and commentary *ad loc.*

the Pharisees by suggesting that the only question at issue is the Resurrection of the dead. It is argued that this is disingenuous and unworthy of Paul, and that we cannot conceive him thus minimising his divergence from the Pharisees. But such a touch, if not authentic, must come from a period and author interested in suggesting a *rapprochement* between Christianity and Pharisaism. There are, however, in later times, few, if any traces of such tendency; on the contrary, each decade shows an increasing desire on both sides to emphasise the gulf between the Christian and the Jew. It is therefore probable that this line of defence was that actually adopted by Paul. We know from Romans that this was just the period when he was especially eager and hopeful with regard to the conversion of his nation. It was quite natural that he should over-emphasise the position that Christianity was after all only the logical and historical development of Judaism, and argue that all turned on the resurrection, a belief which he shared with some of his opponents.[1] Just as the Church is the true Israel, so is he himself the true Pharisee.[2] And if there was any disingenuousness in the argument the difficulty is moral, not historical.

The character of St. Paul. Jülicher [3] finds in the Paul of Acts " a colourless rhetorical representative of average Christianity "; his portraiture is " woefully deficient and poor, just because it preserves absolutely nothing of the peculiar characteristics of the man "; the writer has not been able to " introduce into his portrait even one of the grand and noble characteristics of the Apostle," the conclusion of course being that Acts cannot be regarded as a historical work by a companion of Paul. It is evident that we are here on ground where subjective considerations play a very large

---

[1] In the same way a Christian Scientist might, and in fact often does, try to conciliate Church opinion by arguing that he is only insisting on the reality of prayer and the supremacy of spirit over matter.

[2] It is possible that this is suggested in the phrase of Gal. i. 15: " Separated me from my mother's womb."

[3] As quoted by Harnack (see above, p. 291): for Harnack's brief reply on this point, see *op. cit.* p. 89.

THE CASE FOR THE TRADITION

part. It will probably be agreed that Luke's forte is not character-drawing; he is interested rather in facts. But, none the less, the portrait of Paul is correct so far as it goes. We have tried to show that there is nothing in Acts which is really unworthy of the Paul of the Epistles; nor can the hero of the shipwreck narrative be described as a purely conventional or colourless figure. In the farewell at Ephesus we have a good example of the Apostle's love of his Churches, a characteristic which is very prominent in the Epistles, while the Barnabas episode (Acts xv. 37 ff.) illustrates his stern insistence on his own point of view. And throughout the story there runs that combination of the mystical and practical elements in Paul which is generally recognised as his peculiar characteristic. We have no right to demand more than this from a companion of the Apostle.

To sum up: we have devoted considerable space to the details of the relationship between Acts and the Pauline Epistles since apart from them it is easy to paint an impressive picture in general terms, either of agreement or contrast; the real test can only be found in the details. One result at least stands out; Acts is independent of the Epistles.[1] It neither uses them nor corrects them in such a way as to suggest that they are before the writer. On the other hand, there is a sufficiently remarkable general agreement in the picture of early Christianity, in the doings of Paul and his companions, and in the conception of his work and teaching. It is true that there are also apparent contradictions, but these are mainly on minor points; if the cautions suggested above (p. 265) be borne in mind they do not affect the general credibility of Acts, or destroy the possibility of its coming from a companion of the Apostle. The most critical point is the story of Acts xv., and even here, as we have tried to show, there is a fair and reasonable solution of the difficulty, a solution not forced by any apologetic necessity, but suggested by Galatians itself.

Summary.

[1] *En. Bib., s.v.* Acts, col. 42. Moffatt, *Intr. Lit. N.T.* p. 300, argues that there is no special resemblance in vocabulary between the two.

III

THE CASE AGAINST THE TRADITION

By H. Windisch

The evolution of the problem and its present status.

THE tradition that Luke, the pupil of Paul, wrote the third Gospel and the Acts of the Apostles was thoroughly first disputed by the Tübingen School, who fortified their position with a mass of evidence and incisive criticism.[1]

Preparatory work had been done by M. Schneckenburger in his *Über den Zweck der Apostelgeschichte* (1841). For although he held fast to the trustworthiness and traditional authorship of Acts, he nevertheless attempted to prove that it is an historical work with the special purpose of defending Paul against his Judaistic opponents. He argued that only this special purpose will account for the peculiar selection of incidents, for the theological colouring which appears in the attribution to Peter of distinctly Pauline characteristics, and to Paul of Judaistic tendencies, and in general for the assimilation of the two chief Apostles to each other and for the frequency, in the last chapters, of Paul's speeches in his own defence.[2]

---

[1] Chief works: F. Ch. Baur, *Paulus, der Apostel Jesu Christi*, 1845, English translation by Menzies, 1873, 1875; Ed. Zeller, *Die Apostelgeschichte nach ihrem Inhalt und Ursprung untersucht*, 1854; cf. ii. p. 72 ff., English translation by J. Dare, 1875, together with a translation of F. Overbeck's valuable essay (1870) in De Wette's *Handbuch*, in Williams and Norgate's Theological Translation Fund Library; Schwegler, *Geschichte des nach-apostolischen Zeitalters*, 1846.

[2] In his *Paulus* (1845), p. 5 ff., Baur refers directly to Schneckenburger. He acknowledges the reasonableness of Schneckenburger's fundamental methods of approach, but would carry them on further, alleging that Luke's authorship is inconsistent with his results. Cf. also Schwegler, *Nachapost. Zeitalter*, ii.

THE CASE AGAINST THE TRADITION 299

Following out these ideas consistently, Baur and his school subjected the Acts of the Apostles to their investigations, which included all early Christian literature, and tested it everywhere for such special purposes (*Tendenzen*). What D. F. Strauss had done for the Gospels with his destructive criticism of their narratives, Baur and Zeller accomplished for Acts. But they did not limit themselves, as Strauss had done, to the narratives, but strove especially to make clear the untrustworthiness of the speeches. The element of greatness in the Tübingen criticism is to be found in the unity of the fundamental ideas by which it is dominated. We have to deal not with a rationalistic criticism of details, but with a brilliantly chosen point of view from which to examine and interpret the whole of the apostolic and post-apostolic age. In accordance with the Hegelian watchword that all which happens is determined by the sequence, *Thesis, antithesis, synthesis*, the Tübingen School constructed two periods; the first was one of embittered conflict between Paul and the Judaisers, who were at one with the original Apostles ; and the second was a period of conciliation, which gradually made itself effective and marked the transition from primitive Christianity to Catholicism. Acts was classed under the documents of a conciliatory character. The Tübingen School argued that by a falsification of all the transmitted data, it painted a picture of complete harmony in thought and deed. From the beginning the original Apostles plan missions to the Gentiles ; Peter performs the first baptism of a Gentile, and justifies it with success before the original congregation ; in common with James he brings about the complete recognition of Paul's missionary work among the Gentiles, except that a measure of ritualistic observance is imposed upon the Gentiles, to which Paul obediently submits. On the other hand, Paul appears as a true Jewish

The School of Tübingen.

---

p. 75. Still greater agreement with Baur is to be seen in K. Schrader, *Der Apostel Paulus*, vol. v., 1836, and Aug. Gfrörer, *Geschichte des Urchristentums*, ii., "Die heilige Sage," 1838, (1) pp. 383-452; (2) pp. 244-47. Both scholars have disputed the trustworthiness of the Acts and the authorship of Luke, but they have had no influence upon the evolution of the criticism.

Christian, unshakably faithful to the hopes and customs of his people; as the reward of this conservatism he is recognised by all as the co-equal of the other Apostles. For this assertion evidence is to be found in the fact that in Acts miracles of the same value are ascribed to him as to Peter. If this is a fair picture of the special purposes (*Tendenzen*) to be found in Acts, then a comparison of this delineation with the four Pauline Epistles accepted as genuine by the Tübingen School (Rom., 1 Cor., 2 Cor., Gal.) shows clearly that throughout the whole document the facts have been tampered with. The historical Paul was an irreconcilable anti-Judaist. The original Apostles had to take him exactly as he was without dictating anything to him whatsoever; the mission to the Gentiles was rejected by the primitive congregation and assigned to Paul alone; all his life long Paul had to suffer under the attacks of the Judaisers. The obvious conclusion was that it is not possible to consider Luke the author of Acts; only a later comer could have produced such a document. No pupil of Paul could have falsified his own memories of Paul and his doctrines, corrected the import of his letters, invented miracles for his glorification, and on the other hand denied his autonomy, liberty, and independence.

Antagonism to Tübingen theory. The dispute which grew out of the position taken by the Tübingen School was long carried on. The opponents of the Tübingen School held their criticism of Acts to be exaggerated, endeavoured to harmonise the narrative of Acts with the testimony of the Pauline Epistles, and attributed to the sources which Luke used or to the inaccuracy of his memory anything which might be found incredible. The assumption that there were distortions of fact for special purposes was most vigorously rejected.

Present attitude. The notion that Biblical criticism has constantly to be on guard against the influence of special purposes in the documents which it investigates (*Tendenzkritik*) has been given up more and more in the course of years even among the friends of courageous criticism. We no longer talk about the policy of union, or about the deliberate assimilation of the pictures of the two apostles. Nevertheless, Luke's authorship of Acts is denied. The chief positions maintained to-day are : (1) The separation of the 'we' source, which was the work of a companion of Paul, probably Luke, from the other material which the actual author of Acts has combined with it. (2) The demonstration that the author of Acts was unfamiliar with the general trend of primitive Christianity ; that, for example, he does not understand the gift of tongues—hence his presentation of the miracle of Pentecost—and represents, contrary to the historical facts, the original Apostles as initiating the missions to the Gentiles. (3) The demonstration that the author of Acts is ignorant of the peculiar character of Paul, obliterates his anti-Judaism, leaves unnoticed or reproduces in a completely distorted form the experiences that were decisive for him, especially his conflicts, and does all this not so much because he has some special purpose in mind as because he is naïvely of the opinion that complete harmony prevailed between Paul and the original Apostles.[1]

A new phase in the conflict about the author of Acts was recently introduced by A. von Harnack.[2] He believes that, once the critical point of view of the Tübingen School has been given up, the retention of their denial of the authorship to Luke is inconsistent and can only be founded on prejudice or an inability to think psychologically. Harnack is far from defending

Harnack's defence of Lucan authorship.

[1] Cf. A. Jülicher, *Einleitung in das Neue Testament,* 1906, p. 391 ff.; P. W. Schmiedel, "Acts of the Apostles" in *Encycl. Bibl.* pp. 37-57 ; P. W. Schmidt, *Die Apostelgeschichte bei De Wette, Overbeck und bei Adolf Harnack,* 1910 ; P. Wendland, "Die Literaturformen des Neuen Testaments" (Lietzmann's *Handb. zum N.T.* i. (2) p. 314 ff.) ; H. H. Wendt, "Die Apostelgeschichte" (Meyer's *Commentar,* iii. 9th ed.), 1913 ; W. Brückner, *Prot. Monatshefte,* 1911, pp. 139 ff., 179 ff., 219 ff., 270 ff., etc.; G. Hoennicke, *Die Apostelgeschichte,* 1913, p. 18 ff.

[2] *Lukas der Arzt,* 1906 ; *Die Apostelgeschichte,* 1908 ; *Neue Untersuchungen zur Apostelgeschichte und zur Abfassungszeit der synoptischen Evangelien,* 1911. Cf. concerning these, Schürer, *Theol. Literaturzeit.* 1906, p. 405 ff.; C. Clemen, *Theol. Rundschau,* 1907, p. 97 ff.; *Hibbert Journal,* viii. pp. 780-799; W. Bousset, *Theol. Rundschau,* 1908, p. 185 ff.; A. Jülicher, "Die jüdischen Schranken des Harnackschen Paulus," *Prot. Monatshefte,* 1913, pp. 1-20; M. Jones, *The N.T. in the 20th Century,* 1914, p. 227 ff.

the credibility of the whole book when he defends its authenticity. He thinks that Luke was a credulous practitioner of medicine who was delighted to propagate the stories of miracles which were told him. But the representation of Paul seems to him on the whole to be correct. His chief arguments are the following: (1) The so-called 'we' source comes from the author of the whole Lucan historical work, as is shown by the linguistic and stylistic unity.[1] (2) The Jewish-Christian character of the narratives and speeches, the importance attached to the original apostles, etc., are to be explained by the fact that Luke, the converted Gentile, held the Old Testament and the revealed Jewish religion in high respect.[2] (3) The Jewish-Christian garb in which Paul appears in word and deed corresponds on the whole to the historical truth. Critics are inclined to exaggerate the freedom and the anti-Judaism of Paul. On the basis of the Epistles it can be demonstrated that Paul as far as he personally was concerned and in his hopes continued to be a genuine Jewish-Christian.[3] To the contention that the Paul of Acts is not really the true Paul, it can be answered that Luke, though a friend of Paul, was no 'Paulinist,'[4] and was hardly able to conceive sympathetically and to the full the true nature of the great apostle.

Harnack set Biblical criticism new tasks to accomplish. Every new investigator of the problem of the authorship must learn from him, and must meet his arguments.

Dutch reversal of Tübingen hypothesis. While the authenticity and integrity of the most important of the epistles of Paul are taken for granted by the scholars who are under the influence of the Tübingen School, and are used by them as a basis for discussing the credibility and authenticity of Acts, there have been scholars, notably among the Dutch, who have exactly reversed the presuppositions of the problem. They deny the authenticity of all the epistles and maintain that the representation of Paul as found in Acts is

---

[1] Cf. *Lukas der Arzt*, p. 28 ff.; *Neue Untersuchungen*, p. 1 ff.
[2] Cf. *Lukas der Arzt*, p. 91.
[3] Cf. *Neue Untersuch.* pp. 21-62.   [4] Cf. *Lukas der Arzt*, p. 99 ff.

nearer the actual historical truth than the one in the Epistles.[1] The reasons for this opinion are very various; the following are probably the essential ones: (1) The Paul of the Epistles is so superior in his christology to the synoptic tradition and so radical in his antinomism that he cannot possibly have been a younger contemporary of the Apostles. Decades were necessary before the evolution of the original Jewish-Christian Gospel had reached the point where Judaism could be done away with. The historical Paul cannot at best have advocated more advanced ideas than the doctrines and principles of the Paul of Acts. But these very doctrines and principles cannot be harmonised with those of the Epistles except in so far as they already represent a post-Pauline standpoint.

In the place of the Hegel-Baur watchwords—thesis, antithesis, synthesis—the Dutch radicals have put the principle of Slow Evolution from Conservatism to Radicalism. The same phenomena which the Tübingen School interpreted as indicative of a desire for union and conciliation, are held by the Radicals to be intermediate stages of the evolutionary process.

(2) They hold that the form no less than the content forbids the belief that the Epistles are authentic Pauline productions. They are not unified, but patched and interpolated, as general quite incomprehensible and impossible as letters. How could the Christians of Galatia have understood the dialectics of the Epistle bearing their name? When would anybody ever have sent as a letter such a dogmatic disquisition as the Epistle to the Romans? Every effort to discover the conditions out of which the Epistles might have arisen, the circumstances of the persons to whom they are addressed, the relation of the writer to them, has been quite fruitless.

Pauline authorship of Epistles denied.

[1] Main works: Bauer, *Kritik der paulinischen Briefe*, 1852; Loman, *Quaestiones Paulinae Theol. Tijdschr.*, 1882 ff.; A. Pierson and S. A. Naber, *Verisimilia*, 1886; van Manen, *Paulus*, i. 1890, ii. 1891, iii. 1896; R. Steck, *Der Galaterbrief nach seiner Echtheit untersucht*, 1888. Cf. the paragraphs by van Manen, in "Paul," *Encycl. Bibl.* pp. 3620-3638; G. A. van den Bergh van Eysinga, *Die holländische radikale Kritik des neuen Testaments*, 1912. The same author's *Radical Views about the New Testament*, 1912.

The entrance of the school of radical criticism into the discussion of the credibility and authenticity of Acts lends a new aspect to the whole situation, which, while it complicated the problem, increases its interest. To be sure, the Radicals do not dream of ascribing Acts to Luke, but they compel us to reconsider ever anew the question of the relation of the 'Pauline' Paul and the 'Lucan' Paul.

The assumptions on which our decision must rest.

Considerations of space render it impossible to treat in detail all the critical questions of importance for the problem of authorship, but as any opinion about the author depends entirely on the other problems of literary criticism connected with Acts, a brief consideration of the following propositions is essential:

(1) The 'we' sections.

(1) First comes *confidence in the reliability of the 'we'* in the so-called 'we' sections (xvi. 10-17, xx. 4-16, xxi. 1-18, xxvii. 1-xxviii. 16).[1] The effort has been made indeed to explain the 'we' as a literary fiction on the part of the author,[2] but the simplicity and the comprehensibility of the 'we' narratives in contradistinction to all the others is, in my opinion, a sufficient proof of their genuineness.

The question of the extent of the 'we' narrative must be left undecided. There are three possible assumptions: (*a*) While only the above-mentioned sections are to be ascribed with confidence to the 'we' narrative, they are to be conceived of as fragments of an originally more extended itinerary.[3] (*b*) To the 'we' narrative belong still more extensive parts of the other reports about Paul, perhaps also parts of the narratives the scene

---

[1] The 'we' in the β-text xi. 28 I do not believe to be genuine. Cf. Harnack, *Sitzungsberichte der Berliner Akademie*, 1899, pp. 316-327, though many scholars are of a different opinion. Cf., for example, Zahn, *Einl. in das N.T.* ii. p. 338; *Die Apostelg.* p. 377 ff.

[2] Thus B. Bauer, *Die Apostelg.*, 1850, R. Reitzenstein, *Hellenistische Wundererzählungen*, p. 54, and in Ilberg's *Neue Jahrbücher f. d. klass. Altertum*, 1913, i. p. 417 f.) has recently expressed critical doubts and gives analogous cases of fictitious 'I' and 'we,' but he is unwilling to deny that the 'we' in Acts has reference to actual personal experiences.

[3] Cf. Jülicher, *Einl. in d. N.T.* p. 405 ff.

THE CASE AGAINST THE TRADITION   305

of whose action is in Antioch and Jerusalem.[1] (c) By the 'we' is to be understood the author of the whole book, who therefore must have made use of his diary or was narrating from memory his own personal experiences.[2] Since it is generally assumed that the 'I' who is concealed behind the 'we' sections, is Luke, the acknowledgment of the validity of the third point of view would solve our problem in advance in agreement with the traditional belief. The decision of this question must be reserved.

(2) With apparent leaning toward the traditional view, attention must be called to the pervasive lexical, stylistic, and redactional *unity* of Acts as it has been demonstrated by the representatives of the most varied points of view, and, what is especially important, with the inclusion of the 'we' sections.[3] This assumption is far from settling the main problem in advance in favour of the tradition. The actual state of affairs permits here again two possibilities: the first, that the eye-witness who is speaking in the 'we' sections did actually write the whole book; and the second, that the 'we' sections represent one of the sources which an author, not the 'I' of the narrative, combined with other sources, and in the process created a literary unity out of the whole by revising all the sources to conform to his own style and language. Our decision and the reasons for it must again be withheld. *(2) Unity of Acts.*

(3) Closely involved with the question of the (relative) unity of Acts is the question of its *homogeneity with the Third Gospel*, which has been disputed frequently without adequate *(3) Acts and the Third Gospel.*

---

[1] Spitta, *Die Apostelgeschichte*, 1891 (Source A); J. Weiss, *Über Absicht und lit. Charakter der Apg.* pp. 34-51; H. Wendt, *Die Apg.* pp. 15-40; Ed. Norden, *Agnostos Theos*, p. 313 ff.

[2] This is the traditional conservative opinion recently defended by Harnack (cf. above). Cf. also Moffatt, *Introduction to the Literature of the N.T.* 2nd ed. pp. 294-296.

[3] Cf. Ed. Zeller, *Die Apostelgeschichte*, pp. 387-413; van Manen, *Paulus*, i. 1-17; Th. Zahn, *Einleitung in das N.T.* 3rd ed. ii. pp. 415-425, 442-446, 498 ff.; Ad. Harnack, *Lukas der Arzt*, p. 29 ff.; Moffatt, *Introduction*, p. 297 ff.; Sir John Hawkins, *Horae Synopticae*, 2nd ed. pp. 182-189—the first edition of this work appeared in 1899.

reason.¹ But lexical, stylistic, and material points of contact between the two prove that both documents derive from the same author, so that Acts i. 1 is not a fiction.² In this case again we do not anticipate the decision of the question whether Luke was this author or whether it was some unknown person who only used a writing of Luke's.

(4) Legends and speeches in Acts.

(4) Acts, which in this also is similar to the Third Gospel, contains both accounts of events developed in legendary form or even legendary inventions, and freely composed speeches. Harnack especially has correctly pointed out that Luke himself was quite capable of taking over legends and of putting speeches of his own composition into the mouths of others, even of Paul. And the same scholar has laid especial emphasis on the fact that the miracles in the report of Paul's doings are much less marvellous and much less numerous than those of the first part of Acts.³ The question therefore reduces itself to this : Do the miracles and other distortions of history which we perceive in Acts, and the liberties which the author has allowed himself in the composition of the speeches, exceed the limit which we should naturally expect a man like Luke to observe ?

(5) Pauline Epistles authentic.

(5) A further important assumption is the *authenticity* of the Pauline Epistles, with the exception of the Pastoral Epistles and perhaps also of the Epistle to the Ephesians. For the criticism of Acts the decision about the portrayal of Paul is of crucial importance. The following discussion is based only on the undoubtedly genuine Epistles. We can still put the question in the same form as the Tübingen School : Does the Paul of Acts harmonise with the Paul of the authentic Epistles, and are the

---

¹ Cf. J. H. Scholten, *Is de derde evangelist de schrijver van het boek der Handelingen ?* 1873. Also A. Gercke, Hermes, 1894, p. 373 ff. has expressed doubts whether the author of the Lucan Gospel wrote Acts as well, especially the first part. Further discussion in C. Clemen, *Paulus*, i. p. 165.

² Cf. Ed. Zeller, *op. cit.* pp. 414-452 ; H. J. Holtzmann, *Lehrbuch der Einl. in das N.T.* 3rd ed. p. 391 ff. ; Th. Zahn, *Einleitung*, ii. p. 387 ff.

³ *Die Apostelg.* p. 111 ff.

differences of such a sort that the delineation of Paul as found in Acts is only comprehensible on the assumption that it is the work of one who had not personally known Paul ? We differ from the old Tübingen scholars only in not limiting the number of the authentic Epistles to four,[1] and in not demanding from a pupil of Paul in every respect a fully spiritual understanding and completely accurate presentation of Paul's activity and teachings.

It is here that there is a real difference between our method of procedure and that of the radical critics of Holland. The arguments against them are principally the following : (1) The doctrine concerning Christ as it appears in the Epistles of Paul is quite comprehensible in the apostolic age, if we take into consideration the fact that where it is concerned the union of an already completely developed Christology with the figure of Jesus as the Messiah is an essential presumption.[2] The antinomianism of the Epistles is explained by the special circumstances accompanying the conversion of Paul, the former Pharisee and enemy of Christ, and by the demands of a broadly inclusive plan for the conversion of the heathen ; perhaps also by assuming that Paul's pre-Christian religion was not mere rabbinic Judaism, but a religion less satisfying and more pessimistic (as, for instance, the religion of the Ezra-apocalypse).[3] And furthermore the antinomianism found in the Pauline Epistles is still very moderate compared with its later forms in Barnabas, the Gnosis, and in Marcion, since it still clings to the belief that the Old Testament is the enduring word of God's revelation and that the Jewish folk is still God's chosen people, or shall again become so. (2) However great is the difficulty which the Epistles offer us,

---

[1] By limiting themselves to the four Epistles the Tübingen School gave up a very important piece of evidence, and one which is still important—the great anti-Jewish or anti-Judaistic polemic of Paul in Phil. iii.

[2] Cf. M. Brückner, *Die Entstehung der paulinischen Christologie*, 1903 ; H. Windisch, " Die göttliche Weisheit der Juden und die paulinische Christologie " (*Neutestamentliche Studien für Heinrici*), 1914, pp. 220-234.

[3] Cf. C. Montefiore, *St. Paul and Judaism*, 1914.

they are nevertheless much more incomprehensible from a psychological point of view, if we take them to be pseudepigrapha or compilations. The radical criticism of Holland transfers the riddle from the first to the second century, but this transference is attended with the disadvantage that what is enigmatic in the first century becomes incomprehensible in the second.

Our refusal to accept the results of this radical criticism, therefore, receives the support of excellent witnesses whose testimony is of decisive importance in the discussion of the authorship of Acts by a pupil of Paul.

(6) Epistles not used in Acts.

(6) It is equally important to make clear that the Epistles of Paul cannot have been used by the author of Acts. The Tübingen School, consistently with their critical principle that Acts was written in defence of a special thesis, assume not only the use of the Pauline Epistles but the distortion of the historical data and the doctrine contained in them. When we have broken away from this principle we can assent to neither proposition. In fact very few of the similarities which some scholars still point out from time to time and wish to explain on the basis of the use of the Epistles,[1] are at all impressive, and they cannot be used to support the hypothesis of such use, since Acts is on the whole independent of the Epistles, and its narrative is only intelligible if its author did not know them.[2]

(7) Date of composition.

(7) The determination of the date, which we must note as the last of our assumptions, is closely connected with our assumption that the Pauline Epistles were not used by the author of Acts. *Acts must have been written at a time when, as yet, no collections of Paul's letters had been spread abroad,* and so could

[1] Cf. O. Pfleiderer, *Urchristentum*, 2nd ed. i. p. 532; H. J. Holtzmann, *Handkomm. zum N.T.* i. 2, *Die Apg.* 3rd ed., 1901, p. 10; H. Schulze, *Theol. Stud. und Kritiken*, 1900, pp. 119 ff.; W. Soltau, *Zeitschr. für neut. Wiss.*, 1903, p. 133; van Manen, *Paulus*, i. pp. 58-74; W. Brückner, *Prot. Monatsh.*, 1911, p. 284; Ramsay, *St. Paul the Traveller*, p. 385.

[2] Cf. against the theory of utilisation Sabatier, *L'Auteur du livre des Actes des Apôtres a-t-il connu et utilisé dans son récit les épîtres de St Paul?* 1889; R. Steck, *Theolog. Zeitschr. aus der Schweiz*, 1890, p. 153 ff.; Th. Zahn, *Einl.* ii. pp. 414-418, 429; Wendt, *Die Apg.* pp. 40-42.

not have been at the disposal of the author as an easily accessible source of information and one to be consulted as a matter of course. Nor could he have taken for granted that they would be in the hands of his readers. So that the preparation of an historical commentary to these letters cannot be taken as a motive for the composition of Acts. Now the first testimony to an acquaintance with one of Paul's Epistles outside the place for which it was originally intended is the first letter of Clement— where a knowledge at least of 1 Cor. and Rom. is manifest. A second witness is probably Ignatius, a third, Polycarp, etc.[1] We may conclude therefrom that the dissemination of some of Paul's letters was beginning to be general from about 90 to 120 A.D., and it does not seem advisable to set the date of the composition of Acts later than about the close of the first century; the 90's or the 80's would have much to recommend them in this respect. This *terminus ad quem* is commendable on other grounds likewise. General persecutions of the Christians, furthered by the Roman government, seem to lie outside the author's field of vision [2] or he would hardly else have emphasised so industriously the moderation of the Roman officials. The *gnostic* danger was, to be sure, already threatening (cf. xx. 29 f.), but as yet the author did not consider a detailed refutation necessary. Finally, the hope of a 'parousia' appears in Acts in a very weakened form. These three considerations recommend the period of the *80's or 90's of the first century*, although they do not exclude the assignment of Acts to the first decade of the second century.

At the same time they fix the correct *terminus a quo*. I feel compelled to reject the assumption which has recently become

[1] Cf. *The N.T. in the Apostolic Fathers*, 1905. The date of composition of 2 Peter (cf. iii. 15 f.) is uncertain, so that his testimony cannot be used here.

[2] The αὐτοὺς ἠνάγκαζον βλασφημεῖν which, in xxvi. 11, is put in the mouth of Paul, the Jewish persecutor of the Christians, cannot possibly be an imitation of the *maledicere Christo* demanded by Pliny (*Epist.* x. 96). Cf. Hausrath, *Jesus und die neut. Schriftsteller*, 1909, ii. p. 194.

very popular and which is recommended even by Harnack,[1] that the author of Acts—on this supposition naturally Luke—continued the narrative down to the date of composition, that is to say, he wrote it in Rome *during Paul's imprisonment* and completed it at the end of the first two years of his stay in that city. To be sure, this assumption is very enticing in that it is apparently the only one which really explains the enigmatic conclusion of Acts, which, from our point of view, is really no conclusion at all.[2]

But the hypothesis is rendered untenable by the consideration that the Third Gospel must, beyond dispute, have been written after the destruction of Jerusalem, and by the further consideration that Acts as a whole, with all its defectiveness and legendary character and other literary mannerisms, is a product of post-apostolic times. It seems strange at first, it must be confessed, that no reference is made [3] in Acts to the destruction of Jerusalem and the attendant humiliation of the Jews,[4] but the judgment which actually took place in the year 70 is adequately characterised in the Gospels and the disaster of the year 70 by no means resulted in breaking the pride and self-confidence of the Jews, least of all in the Diaspora. Attention need only be called to the defence of Josephus *Contra Apionem*, written

---

[1] Cf. *Apostelg.* p. 217 ff.; *Neue Untersuchungen*, p. 65 ff.; Belser, *Einl. in das N.T.* 2nd ed. p. 125 ff. For further representatives of this opinion, cf. Schäfer-Meinertz, *Einl. in das N.T.* 2nd ed., 1913, p. 385.

[2] The hypothesis seems particularly attractive in the form which D. Plooij has recently given it. He assumes that Theophilus was not by any means a catechumen, but stood in close relations with the council with which Nero had to discuss Paul's lawsuit, and that Luke wrote his Gospel and Acts to serve in Paul's defence, and that he handed both books over to Theophilus and the stratopedarch mentioned in the Bezan text of xxviii. 16, that is, to Burrhus, so that they might convince themselves of the political innocuousness of Paul and the teachings he brought forward. *Expositor*, ser. 8, viii. pp. 511-523, xiii. pp. 108-124; cf. M. Jones, *Exp.* ser. 8, ix. pp. 217-234. A similar effort was made earlier by Aberle, *Tüb. theol. Quartalsch.*, 1855, 1863. Cf. also Hilgenfeld, *Ztsch. für wiss. Theol.*, 1864, pp. 441-448; J. Weiss, *Urchr.* p. 106 f.; de Zwaan, *Handelingen der Apost.*, 1920, p. 7 f.

[3] Harnack calls attention to this, *loc. cit.*

[4] Cf. H. Windisch, "Der Untergang Jerusalems anno 70 im Urteil der Christen und Juden," *Theol. Tijdschr.*, 1914, pp. 519-550.

THE CASE AGAINST THE TRADITION 311

after A.D. 93. It is hardly to be supposed that the Jews in Asia Minor, Macedonia, and Achaia were more active against the Christians in the 80's and 90's than in Paul's time. A particularly good proof for Asia Minor is to be found in Rev. ii. 9, iii. 9. This attractive explanation for the conclusion of Acts must therefore be abandoned. The hypothesis which Ramsay, Zahn, and others favour, that Luke intended to write a third volume, though possible, seems to me to be precarious.[1]

More plausible are the suggestions that the author felt that he had done enough when he had brought the account of Paul's testimony to Christ down to the visit to Rome (cf. xix. 21, xxiii. 11, xxviii. 14), and that he kept silence about the unfortunate outcome of the trial, in order not to cloud the favourable picture of the Roman government which he paints elsewhere.[2] Even better seems the assumption that the Lucan source brought the record only as far as Rome, and that the author could not procure any very reliable information about the later events.[3] Whoever is unwilling to accept the validity of the latter explanation, has no choice but to put the close of Acts among the many things in the New Testament which, with all our knowledge, we are unable to explain. Under all circumstances the year 80 is to be maintained as the *terminus a quo*.[4]

In going no further than to set the years 80 and 110 A.D. as the extreme limits for the date of composition, no use is made of the possibility, which is, nevertheless, well worth taking into

Did Acts use Josephus?

---

[1] Cf. Zahn, "Das dritte Buch des Lukas" (*Neue kirchl. Zeitsch.*, 1917, pp. 373-395).
[2] Cf. J. Weiss, *Über die Absicht und den literarischen Charakter der Apostelg.*, 1897, pp. 52-54; van Manen, *Paulus*, i. pp. 9, 13; v. d. Bergh v. Eysinga, *Nieuw Theol. Tijdschr.* 1919, p. 366 f.; Ed. Schwartz, *Nachricht. d. Göttingen Gesellsch. d. Wiss.*, phil.-histor. Kl., 1907, p. 298 f.
[3] Cf. Bousset, *Theol. Rundschau*, 1908, p. 202; J.Weiss, *Das Urchristentum*, i. p. 106 f.
[4] Th. Zahn likewise combats the too early dating. Cf. *Einl. in d. N.T.* i. pp. 439-441; *Das Evangelium d. Lukas*, pp. 32-37. He was the first to call attention to the addendum to Acts xiii. 1, offered by *Cod. Sangall.* 133: *Lucius Cyrensis qui manet usque adhuc.* The text is probably not genuine. If it were genuine, it would in fact be positive evidence of the later composition of Acts.

consideration, that the author of the Lucan history made use of the writings of Josephus. There are beyond all doubt several passages in the writings of Josephus which are much clarified by passages in Luke's writings, in respect both to subject-matter and to expression. From this point of view the diligent book by M. Krenkel, *Josephus und Lucas*, 1894, is of permanent value. It is more difficult to decide definitely the question whether or not Luke had access to Josephus' writings. One is most tempted to give an assenting answer in the case of the speech of Gamaliel. This speech is surely a composition of the author, and the peculiar arrangement Theudas-Judas (v. 36 f.) is best explained as a rather inaccurate reminiscence of Josephus, *Antiq.* xx. 5. 1 f. Further confirmation is to be had in certain coincidences in expression, and in the fact that in the context in Josephus the same famine is mentioned which is also reported in Acts xi. 27-30.

If literary contact is assumed here, there will be many other parallel passages in the two authors about which we shall have to hold that the influence has been in the same direction, and the inevitable result of such a decision will be a new *terminus a quo* for the genesis of Luke's writings, namely the year 93 A.D. We should have won thereby a sure date on which to base our opposition to the traditional point of view. But since I cannot persuade myself that Luke's dependence on Josephus is a proved fact, I prefer to make no use of this hypothesis, in spite of the fact that it would materially simplify the work of criticism and make surer the results.[1]

[1] Compare in reference to the problem, H. Wendt, *Die Apostelgeschichte*, pp. 42-45; P. W. Schmiedel, "Acts of the Apostles," in *Encycl. Biblica*, i. p. 37 ff.; Hausrath, *Jesus und die neut. Schriftsteller*, ii. pp. 167 ff. ; van Manen, *Paulus*, i. pp. 133-139 ; Moffatt, *Introduction*, 2nd ed. pp. 29-31; K. Lake, *Dict. of the Apost. Age*, i. 20 f.; v. d. Bergh v. Eysinga, *Nieuw Theol. Tijdschr.*, 1917, pp. 141 ff. My reserve finds its justification in the circumstance that in the above-mentioned important parallels, as in the case of many others, there are noteworthy differences besides the points of similarity, which after all permit the possibility that Luke is independent of Josephus. Cf. Zahn, *Einl.* ii. pp. 400-403, 423-425, *Die Apg. d. Lucas*, i. p. 214 ff. Stählin confesses to similar doubts in Christ's *Geschichte der griech. Lit.* 5th ed., 1913, ii. 2. pp. 967-71.

THE CASE AGAINST THE TRADITION   313

I find it equally impossible to agree to Ed. Norden's[1] hypothesis, that the author, or final editor of Acts, borrowed an idea for the speech on Mars Hill out of the lost book of Apollonius, περὶ θυσιῶν. If this theory were accepted, the date of composition cannot be put earlier than the end of the first century, but Harnack's investigations have shown clearly that the effort to prove that a note in Philostratus's *Vita Apollonii* (vi. 3) had its source in the above-mentioned writing of Apollonius, is a *failure*.[2] I have no greater inclination to adopt the variant hypothesis of P. Corssen,[3] that the piece was taken from Damis's novel *Philostratus*, and that this novel is the model for Acts. I think it extremely probable that the author of Acts had literary models for the speech on Mars Hill, but I prefer, in this connection, not to give assent to any special hypothesis which creates a prejudice for or against a particular date of composition.

^{Alleged debt to Apollonius.}

All these propositions leave an open question the possibility that the tradition (concerning Luke as author of Acts) is correct, but do not bar the way to critical enquiry.

If we attempt a critical solution of the much-debated problem, we cannot assume that the result we favour is the most natural and the only conceivable one. The traditional opinion has the right to be taken seriously and demands that we weigh conscientiously the reasons for and against it.[4] And to the following extent the assumptions just made favour the retention of the traditional view.

^{The advantages of the traditional opinion.}

---

[1] *Agnostos Theos*, 1913. Cf. in reference to this, R. Reitzenstein in Ilberg's *Neue Jahrbücher*, 1913, i. pp. 146-155, 393-422 ; W. Jäger in the *Göttinger Gel. Anz.*, 1913, p. 569 ff. ; Burkitt, *J. Th. S.* xv., 1914, pp. 455-464.
[2] "Ist die Rede des Paulus in Athen ein ursprüngl. Bestandteil der Apg.?" (*Texte und Untersuch.* xxxix. 1, pp. 1-46). In reference to this R. Reitzenstein, *op. cit.* pp. 393-422 ; W. Jäger, *op. cit.* pp. 601-610. Cf. also Th. Birt, *Rhein. Museum für Phil.*, 1914, pp. 342-392.
[3] "Der Altar des unbekannten Gottes," *Ztsch. f. neut. Wiss.*, 1913, pp. 309-323. Cf. Hempel, *Apollonius v. Tyana*, 1920, p. 3 ff., 81 f.
[4] Cf. Harnack, *Lukas der Arzt*, pp. 9-18 ; K. Lake, *l.c.* 17.

314 IDENTITY OF EDITOR OF LUKE AND ACTS

(1) Argument from 'we' sections.

(1) If the 'we' is genuine, and if Acts and the Third Gospel form a unit, what is more natural than that we should explain the 'I' of the 'we' narrative, which surely refers to a companion of Paul, as the *autor ad Theophilum*, thus confirming a tradition which goes at least as far back as the second century?[1] Is it to be assumed that the books dedicated to Theophilus circulated at one time anonymously or under some other name? And more particularly, who are we to suppose had falsely attached Luke's name to the Third Gospel? If some unknown person had actually taken up the 'we' narrative and worked it over, the retention of the 'we' would be either incomprehensible negligence or a rather dangerous attempt to claim the credit himself as an eye-witness and so deceive the reader. When a 'we' without further explanation appears and vanishes again in a document dedicated personally to Theophilus, the natural interpretation is that the author is modestly pointing out the experiences and deeds of Paul in which he personally had a share.

(2) Non-use of Pauline Epistles.

(2) If Paul's letters were not used (cf. p. 308) this fact speaks for Luke. A later comer, who, since he was not an eye-witness, would certainly have sought diligently for sources of information, and who would have made especial use of his sources when he was, as the critical scholars assume, freely composing his reports and speeches, would probably have discovered the Epistles and would have made every effort to profit by them to the greatest possible extent. Luke was not looking for written sources, because he felt he had all the material he needed in his own recollections and the verbal accounts of other eye-witnesses.

(3) Luke could be alive at A.D. 80.

(3) It seems more advisable to put the date of composition of the 'Lucan histories' in the first century, and if the year 80 can still be reasonably set as a *terminus a quo*, we can further assume with great probability that Luke was still alive at this

---

[1] Irenaeus, *Adv. Haer.* iii. 14 ; 15, 1, ed. Harvey; *Canon Muratori*, l. 34 ff. Concerning Marcion cf. Zahn, *Einl. in das N.T.* 3rd ed. ii. p. 178 f. and *Das Evang. des Lukas*, 1913, p. 1 ff. About earlier traces see Moffatt, *Introduction*, pp. 313 f.

THE CASE AGAINST THE TRADITION 315

time.[1] If the works were written during his lifetime, then Luke himself must be the author.

(4) It appears further that everything we know about the personality of Luke confirms the tradition.

(4) Personality of Luke favours tradition.

(a) Luke was a personal pupil of Paul. Paul, however, mentions him only in his later letters (Col. iv. 14; Philemon 24; 2 Tim. iv. 11). As a matter of fact the author of Acts is especially interested in Paul and has the most accurate information about him. The main idea of Acts, the right of a missionary activity among the Gentiles unhampered by law, is an achievement for which the Church has chiefly Paul to thank. This idea is illustrated almost exclusively by examples taken from Paul's activity. According to the testimony of the 'we' narrative, Luke accompanied Paul on his first European journey from Troas to Philippi and again on the journey, undertaken to collect money, from Philippi to Jerusalem, and finally on the journey from Jerusalem to Rome. The fact that Paul does not mention Luke until the letters written during his captivity, is in excellent agreement with this. When he was writing the earlier epistles Luke was not present.

(b) Luke was a physician (Col. iv. 14). It is said that a careful examination of the Lucan history, including the Third Gospel as well, has made clear that the author was familiar with medical terminology, was interested in medical phenomena, and had perhaps even read medical works.[2] Luke is the only physician whom we meet in the primitive Christian community.[3] We cannot demand unconditionally that the medical calling of an author should appear in an evangelic and apostolic history.

---

[1] An old tradition has it that Luke died at the age of 84. Cf. Zahn, *Ev. des Lukas*, pp. 13 ff., 740 ff.

[2] Cf. Hobart, *The Medical Language of St. Luke*, 1882; Campbell, *Critical Studies in St. Luke's Gospel*, etc., 1891; Th. Zahn, *Einl. in das N.T.* 3rd ed. ii. 433 f., 442 f.; Harnack, *Lukas der Arzt*, pp. 9 ff., 122 ff.; Moffatt, *Introduction to the Lit. of the N.T.* 2nd ed. p. 298 f.

[3] Not until the second century do Christians with a medical training meet us again. Cf. Harnack, "Medicinisches aus der ältesten Kirchengeschichte" (*Texte und Untersuchungen*, viii. 4, p. 40 ff.).

316 IDENTITY OF EDITOR OF LUKE AND ACTS

If, however, we do find traces of such a professional education, we appear to have an unexpectedly brilliant confirmation of the tradition. It is further worth calling attention to the fact that the author of the prologue to the Gospel (Luke i. 1-4) and the author of Acts each has at his disposal no small skill in expression and general literary training. People of 'culture' were rare in the first century in the Christian community (cf. 1 Cor. i. 26 ff.). We should gladly seize upon the tradition which gives us the name of a physician.

(c) Luke was, according to Eusebius, a native of Antioch (*Hist. eccl.* iii. 4. 6).[1] Even though we deny the authenticity of the first 'we' passage of the 'Western' text (xi. 28) which leads us to Antioch (see above, p. 304), there are still sufficient indications that the author of Acts stood in especially close relations with Antioch (cf. vi. 5, xi. 19 ff., xiii. 1 ff., xv. 2, 23, 35, xviii. 23). This would be most easily explained if we could believe a native of Antioch to be the author.

(d) Luke was personally acquainted with Mark (Col. iv. 10, 14 ; Philemon 24 ; 2 Tim. iv. 11). In excellent agreement with this is the fact that the author makes use of the Gospel of this Mark and that the author of Acts is also well informed about him (xii. 25, xiii. 13, xv. 37 f.) and narrates an event which happened in the house of Mark's mother, in the course of which he even mentions the name of the maid-servant (xii. 12 ff.).

All these comparisons and considerations are strong arguments in favour of the correctness of the tradition. If we are to put them aside, we must have counter-arguments of exceptional weight.

Decisive objections to the traditional view.

The critical examination to which the Tübingen School had subjected the Acts of the Apostles had been carried on with more than usually close and accurate reasoning. But since, on the one hand, the view on which they based their whole argument has become untenable, and on the other hand, all the

[1] Cf. Zahn, *Das Evang. des Lukas*, pp. 10 ff. 738 ff.

THE CASE AGAINST THE TRADITION

circumstances and reasons which speak in favour of the tradition have been studied until they seem stronger than ever, it seems scientifically impossible to cast serious doubt upon the tradition.

Let us see, however, whether or not this prospect is deceptive. The chief argument of the Tübingen School was as follows: The Lucan Paul is not consistent with the Paul of the authentic epistles. Nor is the Lucan Peter consistent with the Peter of the Epistle to the Galatians. In other words, they deemed it impossible that Luke would be responsible for such an unhistorical attribution to Paul of Judaistic leanings and for such a similar remodelling of Peter's character to resemble more closely Paul's as we find in Acts.

When we proceed to test the correctness of this thesis, we must first of all fix definitely the method we are to employ in respect to two points which were not as yet clearly perceived and taken into account by the Tübingen School.

(1) When they noticed differences between the presentation of various events in Acts and Paul's own account, the Tübingen School declared immediately and without further consideration that the 'Lucan' account was false. They did so with some plausibility, for the genuine epistles of Paul are in comparison with Acts historical documents of the first rank. To-day, more correct emphasis is laid on the consideration that Paul himself in these very letters, especially in the Epistle to the Galatians, is a party-man, engaged in combat; and, as a partisan, naturally one-sided.[1] There is therefore a possibility that the account may be correct as it appears in Acts, even if it conflicts with Paul's, or even if he is silent on the subject. (1) Acts and Pauline letters conflict.

(2) Whether Acts is historical and whether it is to be attributed to Luke are two different questions (cf. p. 306). Even when a report about Paul or Peter appears unhistorical, it does not follow that Luke would have been able to recognise it as such, and would therefore have been incapable of accepting it as true. (2) Question of historical probability.

[1] Watkins, *Der Kampf des Paulus um Galatien*, 1911.

318 IDENTITY OF EDITOR OF LUKE AND ACTS

The question can rather be put in this form: Does the account diverge from the actual historical events so markedly that only a writer who had not known Paul personally could have accepted it as true, or could have invented it?

Some Tübingen arguments answered:

In view of these and of other considerations, some of the conflicting points in the various documents, upon which the Tübingen School founded their arguments, can be eliminated.

(1) Regarding Paul's conversion.

(1) Paul emphasises in Galatians the fact that no human intervention had had a share in his conversion, whereas Acts relates that a man by the name of Ananias had received the temporarily blinded Saul, and had been enabled by a vision to explain his recent experience and to predict his future work (ix. 10 ff., xxii. 12 ff.). Many scholars of the Tübingen School declared Ananias to be a pure invention.[1] But he could have hardly been erroneously introduced in this connection; and, even if the presentation of him is legendary, or has been given a conventional literary form by the narrator, we may admit that, while Acts may have attributed too much importance to him in the conversion of Paul, Paul, on the other hand, was probably wrong in entirely disavowing him. In the ardour of his self-defence and to maintain so fundamentally important a point as his independence he may have forgotten, or underestimated, the possibly limited influence and assistance of another, though without it his conversion and call to be the apostle to the Gentiles might never have taken place. There is no reason, therefore, why the account in Acts may not be attributed to Luke.

(2) Paul's first visit to Jerusalem.

(2) There is a considerable discrepancy between the accounts of Paul's first visit to Jerusalem after his conversion as they appear in Acts and in the Epistle to the Galatians. The very date is suspicious: 'some days' after the conversion (Acts ix. 23) in contrast to the three years of Galatians i. 18. Acts goes on to say that when, after some initial difficulties, Paul was finally brought to the 'Apostles' by Barnabas, he began to preach

[1] Cf. Overbeck in De Wette, *Erklär. der Apg.* 4th ed. (1870), p. 136.

THE CASE AGAINST THE TRADITION 319

publicly to the Jews and even to dispute with the Greek-speaking Jews (ix. 26 ff.). Paul, on the contrary, assures us solemnly that he tarried incognito only fifteen days in Jerusalem, that he talked only with Cephas and James, and so remained unknown by face to the Christian congregations of Judaea (Gal. i. 18 ff.).[1] In some points (the matter of Barnabas and the attendant circumstances) Acts may be a correct supplement to the Epistle to the Galatians : about the others the author is evidently poorly or wrongly informed. It is probable that the circumstances of a later visit to Jerusalem are incorrectly assigned to the first. It is strange that 'Luke' was ignorant of these matters; nevertheless, it is not impossible that he might have given an incorrect version of the matter.

(3) In the accounts in Acts Paul is obviously described as following the principle of first searching out the Jews in a strange city, and of transferring his efforts to the Gentiles only when the Jews rejected his word or gave other evidences of hostility (xiii. 46, xviii. 6, xxviii. 25-28). We should be inclined to conclude from this that Paul (Gal. i. 16, ii. 7 ff. to the contrary notwithstanding) regarded himself first of all as a missionary to the Jews, and that only when his efforts among them had failed did he feel forced to turn to the Gentiles. While the Tübingen School declared that this was invented for a particular purpose and therefore not to be attributed to Luke,[2] one is now compelled rather to acknowledge that Paul could have hardly found a wiser method of conducting his campaign than to seek out the synagogue first, in order to be sure of an audience and to gain proselytes from among the Gentiles. That Luke makes this Paul's invariable custom, and regularly makes him follow up failure with the Jews by turning to the Gentiles, is probably unhistorical. It seems, indeed, strange that a converted Gentile, like Luke, should have

(3) Paul's attitude to the Jews.

---

[1] Cf. Overbeck in De Wette, p. 145 ff.
[2] Cf., for example, Overbeck in De Wette, *op. cit.* p. 207 ff. H. J. Holtzmann, "Die Apostelgeschichte" (*Handkomm.* i. 2), p. 14 f.

made Paul's desire to convert the Gentiles depend on repeated failures to convert the Jews; but it may be explained as the counter-effect of a definite theological idea: the author wished to defend Paul's behaviour toward the Jews and the Old Testament, and to show that Paul separated from the Jewish Church only under the pressure of necessity.

(4) Circumcision of Timothy and Titus.

(4) There is a much debated point in connection with the question of circumcision. According to Acts xvi. 1-3, Paul out of consideration for the Jews circumcised Timothy, whose mother was a Jewess. According to Gal. ii. 3 he had a short time before, at the Council of Jerusalem, successfully opposed the demand that the Gentile Titus, who likewise was his travelling companion, should be circumcised.[1] If the report about Timothy is held to be false, then the question of the authorship of Acts is decided. Luke could not fail to know whether his travelling companion Timothy had been circumcised or not. In fact the substance of the report and the reason given for it are curious. According to 2 Tim. i. 5, Timothy had a pious Jewish mother and grandmother. It is hard to believe that Paul would have undertaken and accomplished what these two women did not feel necessary, and that out of consideration for the Jews! And yet it is not safe to reject the report summarily. It may have been unskilfully written, or there may have been circumstances in the case which made the circumcision seem to Paul really advisable.

(5) Paul's compliance with James and the Elders.

(5) The most palpable error seems even now to be the allegation that Paul on his last visit to Jerusalem was willing to enter into the bargain, which James and the elders proposed, and, in order to give a spectacular example of his fidelity to the Law, consented to join the four men who wished to fulfil their vow with due legal ceremony. Such behaviour, it may be

---

[1] This seems the most natural meaning of Gal. ii. 3, or, if the text and exegesis be adopted which imply that Titus was circumcised—but not under compulsion—it at least suggests that Paul would not immediately afterwards have considered circumcision as the proper treatment of a semi-Jewish convert like Timothy.

thought, would be hypocrisy in a man who outside of Jerusalem strongly opposed the compulsory observance of the Law, and preached everywhere that it had been done away in Christ. Again, the report of Acts seems incredible, and hardly conceivable as coming from 'Luke.' But the following considerations forbid its summary rejection. (1) It is not impossible that Paul, following the principle enunciated in 1 Cor. ix. 20 (cf. also x. 23, viii. 1 ff.; Rom. xiv.), made a point of observing the ceremonial Law when he lived among the Jews and, especially, when he was at a festival in Jerusalem.[1] (2) Paul may have felt that circumstances, of which we are unaware, justified his concession to Jewish legal scruples on this occasion. (3) Luke may even have related the incident with the special purpose of showing how grievously the Jews had sinned against one so scrupulous to obey the Law as Paul.

So much can be conceded; though it is impossible to feel perfectly at ease as to the last three points. The very frequency of the reports, which seem strange if they be held to be from Luke's pen, militates against a ready acceptance of the efforts to explain away the inconsistencies psychologically. But if to those already considered other important pieces of evidence can be added, which cannot be brought into consonance with what is known about the facts of Luke's existence, then the final results of the criticism of the old Tübingen School must be accepted, even though the arguments on which they were based are faulty from the standpoint of modern exegesis and psychology.

For the critical investigator the decisive point must always be the 'Lucan' presentation of the Council of Jerusalem.[2]

The Council at Jerusalem.

We must first block the clever and convenient exit which is

[1] Cf. O. Pfleiderer, *Das Urchristentum*, 2nd ed. i. p. 523; J. Wellhausen, *Abh. d. Gött. Ges. d. Wiss.* N.F. xv. 2, p. 45.

[2] Cf. résumé and literature in H. Holtzmann, "Die Apostelgeschichte," *Handkomm.* i. 2, pp. 100-103; K. Schmidt, Art. "Apostelconvent" in Hauck's *Realencykl. f. protest. Theol. u. Kirche*, i. pp. 703-711; P. W. Schmiedel, Art. "Council of Jerusalem" in *Encycl. Bibl.* i. col. 916 ff.; W. Brückner, *Prot. Monatshefte*, 1911, p. 278 ff.; J. Weiss, *Urchristentum*, p. 192 ff.

offered by the refusal to admit the comparison of Gal. ii. with Acts xv. on the ground that Paul's story refers to the second visit to Jerusalem which Luke mentions in xi. 30, xii. 25.¹ But there is a real difficulty here. If the negotiations to which Paul refers did not take place till the third visit, why is he silent about the second ? However, this question stands by itself. Either Paul passed over this journey in silence, because it was unimportant,² or the journey never took place at all. Barnabas went without Paul, and Luke erred, or—what is more probable—the one journey has been doubled by an erroneous interpolation of chapters xiii. and xiv., so that Gal. ii. = Acts xv. = Acts xi. 30.³ However that may be, Acts xi. 30 cannot be legitimately identified with Paul's report of what was done at Jerusalem to the exclusion of Acts xv. In the first place, it creates unnecessary difficulties. Why, for example, does Luke say nothing about those agreements which were so decisive for the question of the mission to the Gentiles ? And if Gal. ii. = Acts xi. how came it that fresh negotiations had to be entered upon at the formal meeting of Acts xv. ? Again, the reports (Gal. ii. ; Acts xv.) show so much similarity in their main points — cause, subject of contention, parties to the negotiation, principles of the leaders—that they must be two different accounts of the same event. Thus, though it is possible that Acts xi. 30 really refers to the same visit as Acts xv., we must rely on Acts xv. as the Lucan account of the events described in Gal. ii.

<small>Conflicting statements in Acts and Galatians.</small> Turning to the comparison of Acts xv. and Gal. ii., certain of the smaller differences can be easily eliminated. When

¹ Ramsay, *St. Paul the Traveller*, p. 55 ff. ; C. H. Turner, Art. " Chronology " in Hastings' *Dictionary of the Bible*, i. p. 415 ff. ; Douglass Round, *The Date of St. Paul's Epistle to the Galatians*, 1906 ; K. Lake, *The Earlier Epistles of St. Paul*, p. 279 ff. ; C. W. Emmet, *St. Paul's Epistle to the Galatians*, 1912, p. xvi. ff.

² Thus, for example, Watkins, *Der Kampf des Paulus um Galatien*, p. 73, 103 ff.

³ Thus Ed. Schwartz and J. Wellhausen, *Nachr. d. Gött. Ges. d. Wiss.*, phil.-hist. Kl., 1907, p. 269 ff. and p. 7 f. Acts xiii. f. is an independent account which the author interpolated on his own responsibility. The Apostolic Decree mentions only congregations in Syria and Cilicia. Cf. also A. Mentz in the *Zeitschr. f. neut. Wiss.* xviii. p. 177 ff.

THE CASE AGAINST THE TRADITION 323

Paul, according to Gal. ii. 2, went from Antioch to Jerusalem because of a 'revelation,' but according to Acts xv. 2 as an ambassador of the Church of Antioch; when in Acts xv. 6 a public transaction is described while in Gal. ii. 2 the private nature of the negotiations is emphasised, the one version can be taken as supplementary to the other. But there are three conflicting statements in the account in Acts xv. which remain, and no skill can explain these away.

(1) The speech of Peter, xv. 7-11. In this passage Peter speaks of himself as the first to be called to be a missionary to the Gentiles. This title is contrary to the facts as told by Paul in the Epistle to the Galatians (ii. 6), when he says expressly that Peter, James, and John had no influence on his policy ($\pi\rho o\sigma a\nu\acute{e}\theta\epsilon\nu\tau o$), but, on the contrary, they were convinced by him that the Gentiles ought to be evangelised. Could a man who had known Paul have allowed Peter to claim that God had long before made him the apostle of the Gentiles?[1] And further, no one even partially conversant with the facts could have made Peter condemn the Law as an intolerable yoke, and use the sort of language that we find later in the furiously anti-legalistic polemic of the Epistle of Barnabas (cf. Barn. iv. 6, etc.). *(1) Peter's mission to the Gentiles.*

(2) The speech of James in Acts xv. 14-21 makes use of Amos ix. 11, 12 in such a way as to prove that it must have been composed by the author of Acts. James says that God " will raise up the fallen tabernacle of David that the rest of men may seek the Lord," whereas in the Hebrew the last clause is " that they possess the remnant of Edom," which would be quite fruitless in this context. The quotation from Amos is a free rendering of the LXX. It is improbable that any one who knew from Paul's account what position James took (cf. Gal. ii. 11 f.), *(2) Speech of James.*

---

[1] Acts xv. 7, Peter is made to allude to the conversion of Cornelius, which can hardly be regarded as other than a legend. In Galatians, Peter was clearly, up to the time of his meeting with Paul, confining his work to Jews, and he and his companions, James and John, were convinced by what they had seen and heard that Paul was justified in going to the Gentiles.

(3) In dealing with the Apostolic Decree, xv. 20, 28 f., xxi. 25,[1] it is first necessary to establish the original text. Harnack rightly saw that the text (the ritualistic form: abstinence from the flesh of sacrifices, from blood, from the flesh of strangled creatures and from corruption in the broader Jewish sense of the word) is inconsistent with the assumption that Luke is the author. He has therefore been lately pleading the cause of the 'Western' text as a moral catechism, prohibiting idolatry, murder, and fornication, and adding the Golden Rule.[2] Th. Zahn also thinks he can maintain the genuineness of Acts and still retain the text.[3] Yet I am persuaded by the following reasons that the common text alone can be the original. (1) The Golden Rule is certainly an interpolation. (2) Πνικτοῦ is probably original, since its elimination is more comprehensible than its addition.[4] Then ἀπέχεσθαι has reference naturally to food and not to murder, an exegesis which would present linguistic difficulties.[5] (3) The whole situation demands that certain legal requirements, representing the minimum amount of conformity to the Mosaic Law, should be prescribed absolutely for Gentile converts (cf. xv. 28). It is purposed to do away with the most objectionable of the unclean practices of the Gentiles, so that a mutual intercourse between Jewish and Gentile Christians may be possible, without the ever-recurring feeling of pollution on the part of the Jews. (4) If the Apostolic Decree were intended to be put forth as a sort of moral catechism, it would be noticeably incomplete. What mention is made of theft, avarice, litigiousness, lying, —prominent vices among the Gentiles—which are combated

[1] Cf. Baur, *Paulus*, p. 131 ff.; Ed. Zeller, *Die Apostelg.* p. 241 ff.; Overbeck in De Wette, p. 229 ff.; P. W. Schmidt, *Die Apostelg. bei De Wette-Overbeck und bei A. Harnack*, pp. 20-27.
[2] *Die Apostelgeschichte*, p. 188 ff. A detailed defence of the 'Western' text in G. Resch, *Das Aposteldecret* (Texte und Untersuch. 28. 3, 1905).
[3] *Einl. in das Neue Testament*, ii. pp. 358 f., 438 f.
[4] Cf. Schürer, *Theol. lit. Ztg.*, 1908, col. 175; Bousset, *Theol. Rundschau*, 1908, p. 193 f.   [5] Cf. F. Blass, *Theol. Stud. u. Krit.*, 1900, p. 18.

THE CASE AGAINST THE TRADITION 325

everywhere else (cf. 1 Thess. iv. 6 ; Gal. v. 20 ; 1 Cor. v. 11 ; 2 Cor. xii. 20 ; Eph. iv. 28 and *passim*) ?

The reading which makes the Decree a food law must, there- A food law. fore, be held to be the genuine one.[1] The following conclusions are to be drawn from this :

(1) Paul declares (Gal. ii. 6 ff.) in no ambiguous terms that (1) If so no obligations touching the Law were imposed upon him for his Paul nor work of converting the Gentiles (cf. ii. 6). If the 'Lucan' report his opponents. were correct, he would necessarily have mentioned the Decree,[2] which contains precepts taken from the Law (cf. Lev. xvii. 11, 'the life of the flesh is in the blood '), and has as its purpose to make possible the reception of Gentiles into Christian congregations which up till then had consisted of Jews. But the main subject of discussion of the Epistle to the Galatians is whether for any reason whatsoever Gentiles should be compelled to accept the obligations of the Law. Even if the originators of the Decree did not consider the fulfilment of the four commands as directly necessary for salvation, nevertheless the stricter Judaists would assuredly have tried to insist that it was so; and Paul, foreseeing this, could therefore not have failed to discuss the Decree and its correct interpretation. And even if the Decree, corresponding to the address of the letter, was adopted at first only for Antioch, Syria, and Cilicia, nevertheless it is the natural assumption—at any rate it is the assumption of ' Luke '— that it should also apply to all future Christian congregations ; in fact, ' Luke ' himself states (Acts xvi. 4) that Paul published the Decree in the South Galatian communities. In this case, Paul must have bound those whom he had already converted to observe the Decree ; or, if the North Galatian theory be

[1] Cf. H. Oort, "Het besluit der Apostelsynode" (*Theol. Tijdschr.* 40, p. 97 ff.); Sanday, *Expos.* viii. 6, pp. 289-305; K. Lake, *The Earlier Epistles of St. Paul,* 1911, pp. 48-60; H. H. Wendt, *Die Apostelg.* pp. 232-237; P. Wendland, *Die urchr. Literaturformen,* p. 320; H. Diehl, *Ztschr. f. neut. Wiss.*, 1909, pp. 277-296 ; J. Wellhausen, "Kritische Analyse der Apostelg." (*Abh. d. Gött. Ges. d. Wiss.* N.F. xv. 2, 1914, p. 28).

[2] The validity of this conclusion has been incorrectly denied, for example, Watkins, *Der Kampf des Paulus um Galatien,* p. 80.

adopted, he may have done the same thing to people who had not yet heard the Gospel from him. Anyhow he could not have failed to mention the Decree, if for no other purpose than that its publication should be correctly interpreted, and not be used against him by his opponents. If he fails to mention it, it is because neither he, nor the Galatians, nor the Judaists knew anything about an Apostolic Decree.

(2) Conflicts with the dispute of Antioch.

(2) The report of the conflict between Peter and Paul in Antioch (Gal. ii. 11 ff.) likewise discredits the 'Lucan' account of the issue of an Apostolic Decree. It must be assumed that in point of time this conflict followed the Apostolic Conference described in Galatians. Paul narrates his story from Gal. i. 13 and onwards in historical sequence; and the point of the narrative would be lost if Paul had had his controversy with Peter before a discussion of principles had taken place. Had the Apostolic Decree been issued in advance, then the conflict could hardly have arisen. The least the Gentiles could obtain by observing the Decree was the privilege of breaking bread with the Jews. If the conflict between Peter and Paul had arisen in spite of the Decree, Paul had no alternative but to produce it in support of his position, both at Antioch and in his subsequent Epistle to the Galatians. It would have been a crushing retort to the Judaisers. In fact the conflict itself and the silence of Paul prove that the Decree did not exist at the time, and therefore also that it was not adopted at the Apostolic Council.

(3) Paul and "idol meats."

(3) As is well known, Paul discusses one of the points mentioned in the Decree, the position toward the $\epsilon i \delta \omega \lambda \acute{o} \theta \upsilon \tau a$ in 1 Cor. viii.-x. His involved, and not entirely consistent language proves that neither he nor the Corinthians knew about any custom confirmed by a decree. If 'Luke' were correct, Paul would certainly have imposed the Decree from the very beginning upon his Corinthian congregation; and no confusion could ever have arisen. If, however, for some incomprehensible reason, Paul had failed to communicate the Decree in the beginning, then it was high time to repair his negligence and so avoid

THE CASE AGAINST THE TRADITION   327

further disunion. If therefore Paul is not to appear both neglectful of his duty and foolish, we have a proof of the fictitious character of the Lucan narrative in Acts xv.

The unhistorical character of the Lucan narrative in chapter xv. having been thus clearly shown, the possibility must be considered whether such an error can be attributed to the historical Luke. This, too, is impossible. Luke must have known what was required of Gentile Christians in Antioch, Asia Minor, Macedonia, and Greece. He must have known that the Pauline congregations at Derbe and Lystra as well as at Philippi and Corinth were not acquainted with the Decree. To a companion of Paul it must have been on the face of it too palpable an invention to include it in his narrative. Even if 'Luke' was not at Paul's side during the Galatian conflict, he must have had opportunities for obtaining information about the matters under discussion, and Paul's attitude toward them. If the Decree was discussed on the occasion of Paul's last visit to Jerusalem, as appears by its being cited in Acts xxi. 25, Luke must certainly have learned when and under what circumstances it was issued, since he was with Paul at this time and later had ample opportunity of learning from Paul how the matter stood.[1]

If Acts xv. is unhistorical can it be by Luke ?

We may call attention to another special point of view. According to xvi. 11 ff., it is certain that the writer of the 'we' sections, let us say 'Luke,' was present at the founding of the congregation in Philippi, and perhaps even had a hand in winning over its first members. According to xx. 4 it is probable that he visited them again some years later, if only for a short time in passing; and it is even possible that he was constantly in Philippi or in the neighbourhood during the period between Acts xvi. and Acts xx. May we not assume from Paul's warning against the 'concision' (Phil. iii. 2), that the congregation at Philippi never received from Paul a decree so Jewish in tone as that in Acts xv. ? How could the 'Luke' who knew the congregation at Philippi so well, have believed that the Paul,

[1] A. Gercke, *Hermes*, 1894, p. 376.

who founded the Philippian Church had accepted in Jerusalem a decree imposing so much legalism on Gentile Christians, and had delivered it to the congregations in Antioch and Asia Minor ? Is it possible that the Philippians could have been ignorant that the apostle had accepted a decree entirely incompatible with the teachings they had previously received from Paul ?

How then can we account for the rise of the report in Acts xv ? The author of Acts may have had before him an account of negotiations in Jerusalem which were concluded by an agreement between Paul, Peter, and James, and also the text of a decree which was issued, some time later, by the authorities of Jerusalem without the participation of Paul (cf. xxi. 25). Since the author did not know precisely when the publication of the Decree took place, he combined it with the account of the conference between Paul, Peter, and James. Thus he portrays a state of affairs in accordance with which the Apostles to the Jews and the Apostle to the Gentiles meet to take common council and are so far agreed as to put the results of their conference into documentary form, which then in the guise of an official letter is communicated to the congregations. Only a later comer, ignorant of Paul's attitude towards the Law, who had no certain information regarding the publication of the Decree could have undertaken such a combination as we have before us in Acts xv.

The preceding investigations have shown us that the author of Acts has given us unreliable accounts of important events, which he further elaborates as seems good to him. This leads to the question of his sources and especially to the problem of the 'we' source.

This is a decisive criterion for the correct point of view toward Acts. In accordance with the assumptions which we made and with the conclusions which we drew from them (p. 314 f.) our criticism seems to be undermined by the 'we' sections,[1] however many and however cogent the other reasons may be which it can advance.

In answer to these objections, those who reject the 'tradition'

[1] First in Acts xvi.

THE CASE AGAINST THE TRADITION 329

may submit the following considerations. It is a rather astonishing characteristic of the 'we' sections that the 'we' begins suddenly to appear in Acts xvi. and vanishes just as suddenly, and equally without any explanation by the author. According to xvi. 1 ff., Paul had only Silas with him, on his journey from Antioch to Lystra. In Lystra he found Timothy. If the first person plural which appears suddenly in xvi. 10, implies neither Silas nor Timothy, it is strange that the author gives us no information how he came into Paul's company. It is very hazardous to assume as an explanation that it was unnecessary to inform Theophilus; nor is it certain that the book is intended for him alone. Even if this assumption were correct, it would be astonishing that the author should make no effort to explain the presence of this 'we' section in its new context. It is much easier to explain the facts as we have them, if we assume that the author of Acts on this occasion took over Luke's diary and copied a passage out of it; and perhaps for literary reasons or, possibly, through mere carelessness, failed to mention the name of the travelling companion who appeared here for the first time.

The 'we' leads us only to the beginnings of the work in Philippi. After the healing of the prophetess 'Luke' vanishes; and, even when Paul and Silas are welcomed by the brethren after their imprisonment, he does not reappear. If Luke himself were the narrator, he would most certainly have told us, if only briefly, what became of him. The truth is that the author used only a fragment of the diary, and after a fashion general in antiquity, omitted any mention of his change of sources.

The same is true of the second and third 'we' sections, xx. 5-16, xxi. 1-18. Here also Theophilus could reasonably expect his friend Luke to tell him how he again came among the companions of Paul, and what had happened to him in the meantime, possibly in Macedonia. Luke would certainly have indicated for the benefit of those who knew him, as well as for those who did not, why he vanishes again at the time of the

Second and third in Acts xx. and xxi.

negotiations with James, if he did not wish to give the appearance of abandoning his teacher at the most difficult moment. But everything is clear, if we assume that we have to reckon with the literary peculiarities of a later comer who used a diary which lay before him ; and, as seemed best to him, worked it over or left it out of consideration, without giving any account of his procedure.

Fourth in Acts xxvii. f.

Finally, at the beginning of the fourth and last ' we ' section (xxvii. 1-xxviii. 16),[1] Luke would most certainly have specified how it came about that he now suddenly appeared in Caesarea and had the privilege of accompanying Paul on the ship. It is much easier to understand how an adapter of Luke's diary did not feel an explanation to be necessary here.

The matters narrated within the ' we ' sections are in general credible, especially when we take into consideration that the ' Luke the physician,' as a Christian and as an admirer of Paul, was a believer in miracles, and so could have had miraculous experiences. Our judgment about the history of the ' we ' sections is confirmed by the observation that much of what is found in chapters xvi.-xxviii. outside the ' we ' sections cannot have been narrated by an eye-witness. The story of the imprisonment of Paul and Silas at Philippi (xvi. 19 ff.) is not consistent, nor is it credible in some details, and must therefore have been adapted by the author or appended to the fragment of Luke's diary from some other source. The account of the journeys of Paul and Silas (xvii. 14 ff., xviii. 5) is incorrect, as appears from 1 Thess. ii. 14, iii. 1 ff. ; and it is difficult to suppose that ' Luke ' here had been wrongly informed.

Greek wisdom in Acts xvii.

Since the researches of Ed. Norden the speech at Athens has claimed especial interest. The speech must be considered a free composition even if the hypothesis is not adequately proved that the author of Acts worked on the model of a writing of Apollonius himself or of Damis. Some of the ideas are not Pauline, as for example the apology for heathen idol-

---

[1] Perhaps with interpolations by the author; cf. xxvii. 9-11, 21-26.

worship, xvii. 30,[1] and the pantheistic quotation in xvii. 28. The whole method of entering into competition with Greek wisdom is quite unlike Paul, who plainly declares that he refused to satisfy the demand of the Greeks at Corinth to preach 'wisdom.' Indeed he affirms that he had 'determined to know nothing' but 'Christ crucified'; and, if we assume that he abandoned the attempt to adapt himself to Greek methods of teaching, because he had so singularly failed at Athens, we should have to admit that the apostle was guilty of equivocation. Now it is not impossible that Luke had not read 1 Corinthians, and therefore could attribute such a speech to Paul; but he must have known that Paul determined to avoid teaching Greek 'wisdom.' It is surely more probable that the author of the speech had not known Paul.

It is difficult to determine whether the account of Paul's farewell at Miletus belongs to the 'we' source or not. In spite of the Pauline sound of the speech (xx. 18 ff.) it seems improbable. The prophecy of future teachers of false doctrine (v. 29) is out of place, since as a matter of fact such wolves had long been disturbing the quiet of Paul's congregations, though 'Luke' is consistently silent about this.[2] The words of Jesus also in Acts xx. 35 are perplexing. Why was not so fine a saying inserted in the Gospel? Surely it would have been, if 'Luke the physician' were the *auctor ad Theophilum*. But it is conceivable that an author, who had never met Paul, might, after he had finished the Gospel, have come across this saying in a 'source' whilst at work on Acts.

In the parts of Acts dealing with Jerusalem there may have been other fragments of Luke's diary used than those marked by the occurrence of the 'we.' But we have to reckon again with embellishments and elaborations. Yet here, too, it can be shown that the adapter and completer cannot possibly have known Paul.

Farewell speech at Miletus.

---

[1] See Rom. i. 18 ff. for the expression of the contrary view.
[2] Cf. O. Pfleiderer, *Das Urchristentum*, i. p. 519.

332 IDENTITY OF EDITOR OF LUKE AND ACTS

The collection for the Church at Jerusalem.

This appears first from the account of the motive for Paul's last journey to Jerusalem. According to 1 Cor. xvi. 1-4, 2 Cor. viii.-ix., Rom. xv. 25-28, the chief reason and the chief desire of Paul was the delivery of the moneys collected. The historical 'Luke' must often have heard from Paul himself how significant it was to him, and must have seen the delivery with full consciousness of its import. When Acts mentions this chief factor only as an afterthought and incidentally (xxiv. 17), the hearsay character of the evidence is manifest. Though the witness knows what happened he is no longer able to appreciate it.

Paul's conversion in his speeches.

It is extremely important to discuss the account of Paul's conversion in his speeches in his own defence. The author has made Paul tell the story on two separate occasions (xxii. 3-21 and xxvi. 9-20. Cf. ix. 1-21). Even though a nucleus of historical truth were guaranteed by the utterances of Paul (1 Cor. ix. 1, xv. 8), the whole story is probably legendary. Now it is quite possible that a pupil of Paul should have embodied the story of his teacher's conversion in a legendary form; the only question is, how it happened. Two things especially urge us to caution. In the first place, one of the decisive factors in Paul's conversion is an occurrence which Paul alone mentions, but which is, in his estimation, the most important: " I have seen the Lord " (1 Cor. ix. 1, xv. 8). But this vision of the Lord is completely ignored in the description in Acts, and even its possibility is excluded. Paul saw only light, he only heard the Lord. And this corresponds to the style of such visions (cf. Mark ix. 2-7). 'Luke' would have most certainly mentioned the 'seeing of the Lord,' upon which Paul founded his apostleship.[1] In the second place, Acts gives a threefold version of the manner in which Paul was called to be an Apostle to the Gentiles. According to ix. 15, the call came through Ananias; according to xxii. 17-21, the Lord himself sent Paul to the Gentiles, in a special vision granted later

[1] Cf. Wellhausen, *Abh. d. Gött. Ges. d. Wiss.* N.F. xv. 2, p. 17.

in Jerusalem;[1] and according to xxvi. 16-18, the summons was given by the Lord at the time of the vision in Damascus. The three accounts show that the author had no certain information or found different accounts already existing, and rewrote them as he saw fit. Luke would undoubtedly have known what Paul was accustomed to tell about his call to be an Apostle to the Gentiles and can scarcely have written such varying accounts.

More decisive are the doubts caused by Paul's manner of defence before the Council (xxiii. 1-9). Little importance need be attached to the fact that Paul, according to the account in Acts, first reviles the High Priest (*v.* 3) and then excuses himself by a statement which, moreover, it is hard to believe true (*v.* 5). The essential consideration is that Paul announces himself before the Council to be a Pharisee, and with this confession immediately wins over to his side several members of that party. The whole picture can hardly be considered historical; for it implies hypocrisy on the part of Paul. The whole of the second epistle to the Corinthians contradicts Acts (cf. iii. 3-iv. 6; v. 17; xi. 22 ff.). If Paul could have behaved as Acts represents him here, and then write the sharp invective (Phil. iii. 2) against Pharisaism, he would have been a hypocrite. For he tells the Philippians that though he had been a zealous Pharisee he had given up all his privileges of birth and race for the sake of Christ (Phil. iii. 2), and he denounces the Jewish religion. An effort to harmonise these two passages is an insult to Paul! That Paul, since his conversion, had broken with Pharisaism could never have been forgotten by a personal friend and pupil, nor could such a one have failed to record it. Only a later comer, who knew Paul only by tradition, and not as yet through his letters, could have represented Paul's theology as that of a Pharisee believing in Jesus as the Messiah. A personal friend could not possibly have represented Paul as denying his convictions in order to save his life.

Paul's defence before the Jews.

---

[1] The scene is probably invented by analogy with Isaiah vi.

334 IDENTITY OF EDITOR OF LUKE AND ACTS

Paul and Felix.

Not dissimilar are the statements which the author attributes to Paul in his defence before Felix, but they do not leave quite so black a stain on his character. Paul is represented as defining his position thus (Acts xxiv. 14 ff.): "Believing all things which are according to the law, and which are written in the prophets, having hope towards God which these also themselves look for, that there shall be a Resurrection both of the just and unjust." Here the real point at issue is carefully suppressed; for Paul had declared the Law a thing of the past (Gal. iii. 15-25; Rom. vii., x. 4), and according to his conviction, the whole belief in the Resurrection was based on the Resurrection of Jesus Christ, which the Jews denied (1 Cor. xv.). In this case, Luke, a converted Gentile, would have been quite clear about Paul's ideas of the Law and the Resurrection. The hand of the stranger betrays itself again when Paul is portrayed as a Jewish Christian, faithful to the Law and clinging to his Pharisaism.

Paul and the Jews at Rome.

In the description of Paul's negotiations with the Jews in Rome, at which, according to the traditional view, Luke was himself present, one has a right to expect a thoroughly clear and unexceptional account. But the following points show that it was compiled by a writer who, though he had traditional material at his disposal, did not know much that was important, or else did not give heed to it because he was seeking an effective conclusion which should make perfectly clear one of the main ideas of his book.

(1) Conflict with Romans.

(1) Paul, before he started for Jerusalem, hoping that he would be free to come from thence to Rome, had sent a most important letter to the Roman congregation. It was probably his intention to convey some knowledge of himself in advance, and irrespective of the division into Jewish and Gentile Christians, and of the threatened danger from the Judaisers, to come to an understanding with the congregation about the chief points of his teaching,—its freedom from the constraint of the Law, its opposition to the Jewish religion but not to the Jewish

THE CASE AGAINST THE TRADITION 335

people. It must have been of predominant interest to an actual companion of Paul to learn and to recount afterwards how Paul was received by the Christian congregation in Rome. The author of Acts has preserved only a brief note on the subject (xxviii. 15): the 'brethren' in Rome came to meet 'us.' About the chief point of interest, about the real reception in Rome, the attitude of the Roman congregation toward Paul the preacher and theologian, he is silent. 'Luke' would certainly have given us something analogous to the narrative in Acts xxi. 17 ff.

(2) Instead of relating Paul's reception by the Christians, 'Luke' gives us an account of the meeting with the Jews. This is not strange in itself, for much might depend upon the attitude of the Jews. But Paul's words (Acts xxviii. 17-20) disappoint us. They are an excerpt of the preceding narrative, which itself has been written up by the author. The suspicious statement already mentioned, that Paul was a prisoner because of the hope of Israel (xxvi. 6 f.) appears again (xxviii. 20). And the second half of the answer of the Jews is incredible (xxviii. 22). They profess that the Christian faith was known to them only by unfavourable reports, and therefore they welcomed the opportunity of obtaining information about it. This statement ignores the fact that a Christian congregation had long since been in existence in Rome, so that the Jews of that city had had ample opportunity to familiarise themselves with Christianity.[1] From Suetonius (*Claudius*, xxv.) we may conclude that discussions about the 'Christus' had taken place, and had been the cause of the separation of the church from the synagogue. Luke has himself to admit, an undisputed

(2) Answer to the Jews cannot be composition of Paul's companion.

---

[1] There is an additional argument for the early presence of Christianity in Rome. Aquila and Priscilla (Acts xviii. 2) came to Corinth in consequence of Claudius' edict. Now it is nowhere said that they were subsequently converted or baptized, so presumably they were Christians. This would confirm Suetonius' statement that the Jews had been expelled from Rome on account of a riot *impulsore Chresto*. If this is the case, Acts xxviii. 22 implicitly contradicts xviii. 2, probably because the author did not notice that his sources were at variance.

'we' section, that there were brethren (*i.e.* Christians) who welcomed Paul on his way to Rome (Acts xxviii. 15). Paul, through his Epistle, had already provided the Roman Jews with an opportunity of learning what he thought about the matter; for his letter to the Romans is in parts (cf. ii. 1 ff.), if only for rhetorical purposes, addressed to the Jews. It is probable that, when Paul actually arrived in Rome, he reaped the benefit of his letter both among the Christians and the Jews, and the Epistles must have formed at any rate the basis of any discussion between Paul and the Roman Jews. But the report of Paul's conversation with the Jews is so conventional and betrays such ignorance of what he had written to the Romans and of the situation implied by the Epistle, that though we may concede that, from the author's point of view the conclusion of Acts is grandly conceived, we can never believe that it is the reminiscence of an eye-witness about the most important days in the history of the most successful and greatest Apostle of Jesus Christ.

Why Lucan authorship is impossible.

Thus the evidence has accumulated that the elaboration of the reports of an eye-witness (*sc.* the author of the 'we' sections) cannot possibly originate in the pupil of Paul, but must be ascribed to some post-apostolic author. We were justified in making rather greater demands on these parts of the narrative than on the others, since the eye-witness, whom tradition has caused to be currently accepted as the author, was a companion of Paul from Troas to Philippi, and again from Macedonia to Rome, and so had opportunity to inform himself from the best sources, viz., from Paul himself, about the events which he did not personally witness. The verdict 'unhistorical' is here nearly equivalent to the verdict 'not Lucan.'

Fatal discrepancies.

The case is not much different with the stories about Paul which are narrated in Acts before the commencement of the 'we' sections and the account of the Council of Jerusalem. Here again suspicious deviations from historical truth confirm our judgment. The conversion of Paul in chapter ix. has already been discussed. The presentation of the South Galatian

THE CASE AGAINST THE TRADITION 337

mission (c. xiii. f.) is suspicious. The speech of Paul at Pisidian Antioch (Acts xiii. 15-41) is very un-Pauline, and obviously the product of the author, for the following reasons. (1) It borrows from the Gospel of Luke (compare xiii. 25 with Luke iii. 16, xiii. 28 with Luke xxiii. 13 ff.). (2) It implies that the Lord appeared after the Resurrection only to those who had gone up with him from Galilee to Jerusalem (cf. ii. 32), thereby excluding Paul and implying that, contrary to his own repeated assertions, he was only a second-hand witness that Jesus had risen.[1] (3) It is dependent on the Pentecostal speech of Peter for its proof of the resurrection (xiii. 34-37 ; compare ii. 25-32, 38). When the author later introduces a sentence recalling Paul's doctrine of justification (xiii. 38 f.), which is the only one of its kind in Acts, it is obviously an endeavour to put into his mouth a phrase with a genuinely Pauline ring about it. But even this seems to be a misunderstanding of Paul's teaching. Faith seems to be a supplement of strict observance of the Law. For these reasons the composition of the speech cannot be by a companion of Paul.

According to Acts xv. 23, the apostolic letter was sent to the Syrian Antioch, and to the Churches of Syria and Cilicia. But according to Acts South Galatia had already been converted, and Galatians shows (on the South Galatian theory) that the Judaistic controversy raged there. Would all mention of Galatia have been omitted by the apostles in their letter ? Is it not more likely that the editor of Acts has combined his sources in a wrong chronological order ? But is such a mistake conceivable if the author of Acts was 'Luke' the companion of Paul and possibly a native of Syrian Antioch ?

In the chapters dealing with Paul, the adapter, who stands at a distance from the Apostolic age, betrays himself, as we have seen, by his treatment of his sources. He mingles reliable testimony of eye-witnesses with material obviously legendary, and with theological dissertations designed to present his own

The author a skilled adapter.

---

[1] Cf. the apocryphal 3 Cor. 3.

point of view. The author of Acts was a professional writer, a collector, adapter, and supplementer of sources. Even the second part of his book, which is distinguished by more exact information and greater historical fidelity, reveals the points of view which determine his selection, and these and the unaccountable lacunae in the narrative prove that it cannot be the work of an eye-witness.

Selection of incidents.

The author gives incidents taken from the missionary journeys of Paul and from the history of the congregations founded by him. But what incidents does he select? What is he interested in? He presents samples of Paul's missionary sermons and anecdotes which characterise the founding of a congregation, the cessation of Paul's activity, or his reasons for removing elsewhere. He presents the purely external characteristics of Paul's activity, his first, and, in general, his superficial successes. About the subsequent administrative and pastoral work, which, nevertheless, to judge by the very abundant testimony of the Epistles, produced much that was great and significant, we rarely learn anything really tangible (xix. 8-20, xx. 17-38). The author gives no examples illustrative of the fruitful points of view which Paul's Epistles abound in, of the manifold experiences and conflicts which the young Pauline congregations must have had after the period of their first enthusiasm. He is not interested in such things. But the hints which Paul himself gives us (2 Cor. xi. 23 ff.) show clearly how insufficient is the narrative of Acts.

Two chief reasons may be advanced to explain the peculiarity that so little is reported in Acts of all Paul's many activities which the Epistles describe. Both provide arguments against the traditional view of the authorship of Acts.

Ignorance of facts displayed.

In the first place, we may explain the silence as ignorance on the part of the author. But Luke, who was with Paul before and after the composition of the Epistles to the Thessalonians, Corinthians, Galatians, and Romans, must have known something about the circumstances which resulted in

THE CASE AGAINST THE TRADITION 339

the writing of these letters. We can account for such ignorance as meets us in Acts only by assuming that the author was a later comer, who had to collect traditions about Paul from others, but was unacquainted with the Epistles or incapable of estimating their importance.

Besides the author's ignorance, we have to take into consideration his intentional suppression or rejection of reports which gave an historically correct, but not altogether agreeable, picture of the Apostolic age. This is especially pertinent in regard to the conflicts which Paul had constantly to wage against Judaistic tendencies (*e.g.* with Peter and Barnabas in Antioch) or Judaistic agitations ; (cf. Gal. ; 1 Cor. i.-iv. ; 2 Cor. x.-xiii. ; Rom. xv. 30-32 ; Phil. iii. 2 ff.). To judge by what Acts tells us in chapter xv., and does not tell us in xvi.-xxviii., the controversy in Jerusalem before Paul's first great journey was concluded once for all by an excellent compromise. Paul has nothing more to say about disturbers of the peace and teachers of false doctrine until his prophecy about them at his leave-taking from the representatives of the congregation at Ephesus (xx. 29 f.). The author's conception of the struggles of the apostolic age is therefore a definite one, but thoroughly wrong. The compromise is no less fictitious than the end of the conflict. Paul's Epistles teach us that nothing occurred —least of all in Jerusalem—to assure permanent understanding and concord, that not even the simplest questions were settled between Peter, Barnabas, and Paul, that agitations emanating from Jerusalem threatened to discredit Paul's whole work and person in Asia Minor and Greece. The historical Paul had no need to prophesy the coming of false teachers. He had already had personal experience with their wolfish nature and had made war upon them with all the energy at his disposal. Luke, the converted Gentile, must have known the actual state of affairs and appreciated its importance. Only a post-apostolic writer could have falsified history so unhappily with his inventions and suppressions, because he had not himself experienced the conflicts and did not understand their importance, or because he was not acquainted with the Epistles or did not know much about them, and, in order to idealise his story, refused to attribute much importance to them.

Non-Pauline traditions in Acts.

There remain the non-Pauline traditions in Acts i.-xii. Obstacles which hinder the acceptance of the traditional view of the authorship are not here so easy to find. 'Luke,' who was himself a believer in miracles, had in these cases less reliable sources, and was more prone to accept legendary material. A companion of Paul might easily be guilty of the obviously improbable anachronism about Theudas in the speech of Gamaliel, nor is there any reason why he should not, if he wrote after A.D. 70, have incorporated into his narrative the mythical elaboration of the legend of the ascension (Acts i. 2 ff.). We can only reject 'Luke's' authorship in these cases if we come upon reports which are obviously in contradiction to what a pupil of Paul, the Apostle to the Gentiles, must have known. But in the first part of Acts there are two narratives which cannot be reconciled with the traditional view, namely, the story of Pentecost and that of Cornelius.

The "tongues" at Pentecost.

A companion of Paul must have known what the gift of tongues meant; for it must have frequently fallen within his experience, and speaking with tongues is referred to with apparent understanding of its real meaning in x. 46 and xix. 6; behind the account of the Pentecostal gift the real state of affairs can be dimly perceived. But the occurrence described as the outpouring of the Spirit at Pentecost is a linguistic marvel presenting a miracle greater than any which the early Christian history records, not an outbreak of, as the text stands, 'speaking with tongues.'[1]

What must we suppose to be the background of ideas out of which such a picture arose? Probably ignorance of the true

---

[1] Cf. Mosiman, *Das Zungenreden geschichtl. und psychol. untersucht*, 1911. P. W. Schmiedel, *Pfingsterzählung u. Pfingstereignis* (Prot. Monatsh. xxiv. p. 73 ff.).

nature of the gift of tongues. Any one who was familiar with this must have considered it sufficiently wonderful; and only one who had come in contact with it rarely, if at all, would think of making the gift a basis for the fabrication of a story of a more impressive miracle.

Again, the legend shows a desire to glorify the original apostles beyond the measure of historical truth. The legend of the descent of the Spirit at Pentecost presupposes that in accordance with Acts i. 8, the disciples were from the first intended to go forth on a world-embracing mission. The fact is that it was only when circumstances drove them to it, that they set foot outside Judaea. The author obviously understood that the apostles from the very beginning contemplated the conversion of the Gentiles as well as the Jews. Thus Peter and the other original apostles are 'Paulinised,' and in like manner judaising tendencies are attributed to Paul.[1] Such a perversion of the actual historical facts can certainly have been accomplished only by one who was as unfamiliar with the history of the primitive congregations as he was with the conflicts which Paul had to wage. It is inconceivable that Luke should have constructed a legend like that of Pentecost, and equally inconceivable that he should have incorporated it into his history.

These same suspicions are still more justified in reference to the story of Cornelius (x. 1–xi. 18; cf. xv. 7-9). It is not the legendary character in itself, the frequency of visions and angelic appearances which is inconsistent with Luke's authorship, but the whole significance which the author attributes to the event.

Conversion of Cornelius.

In the first place, by a revelation that could not be misunderstood, Peter would have been enlightened about the absence of distinction between clean and unclean food. This is flatly contradicted by his hesitation in Antioch (Gal. ii. 11-13).

In the second place, this vision, if it were consistently

---

[1] Jülicher, *Einl. in das Neue Testament*, p. 398-402.

thought out or interpreted symbolically and taken in combination with that of Cornelius and the pouring out of the gift of the Holy Ghost in which the Gentiles shared and which impelled Peter to baptize them, would have given Peter not only the right to convert the Gentiles, but would have made it his duty. Peter would have to be considered as the first chosen instrument for the conversion of the Gentiles, as the pioneer by the grace of God, who opened the way through all of the old prejudices to the great work.

Thirdly, the reference to the baptism of Cornelius (xv. 7-9), which is certainly the work of the author of Acts, shows us clearly why the author introduced the story into his scheme. He considered it important to show that it was not Paul, but Peter, who was the first to receive the call to convert the Gentiles; and that it was not Paul, but Peter, who was the first pioneer in the work. It is difficult to attribute such a depreciation of Paul's position to a personal pupil.[1]

Thus the first part of Acts strengthens the arguments which make Luke's authorship incredible. For the whole work we may maintain the thesis that the author had never come into personal contact with Paul, and for this reason alone was able to present the history of the Apostolic age calmly and consistently, and to date back to the earliest times the compromise between Jerusalem and the Diaspora, which was not attained until post-apostolic times.

There remains for us only the further task of presenting briefly our opinion of the origin of Acts.

The author used Luke's diary. The author was not Luke; but he used as a source a diary of Luke's, and this circumstance is sufficient to explain his interest in Paul. He probably collected further traditions about Paul and likewise sought for informants about the acts of the original apostles. He probably learned many things in Antioch and Caesarea. But he must have been able to discover much less about the original apostles than about Paul. He himself, or

[1] Cf. Bousset, *Theolog. Rundschau*, 1908, p. 190 f.

THE CASE AGAINST THE TRADITION 343

his informants, were interested in the early history only in so far as it made clear the harmony between the original apostles, the first preachers, and Paul, and prepared the way for his work. The author was already so far removed from the conflicts and successes of Paul that he no longer thought it derogatory to his hero to credit the original apostles with having been the first labourers in the work of converting the Gentiles. Nor did he feel that he was perverting history when he reduced the long story of the conflicts between Paul and the Judaisers to a formal agreement made after a single discussion at a council of apostles and elders at Jerusalem.

That the author employed the first person plural in some places without giving any explanation seems strange to us (cf. pp. 304 f., and 329), but can be accounted for by the literary methods of antiquity, which was less careful of such details than our age demands, and by analogy with Ezra vii. 27–viii. 34 ; Neh. i. 1–vii. 5, xii. 31, xiii. 6-31. The dedication to Theophilus is not to be understood as though the work were adapted entirely to the personal circumstances of Theophilus. It was from the very beginning destined for the public, for the Christian Church, and probably also for non-Christian readers, hence the apologetic tendency. The method corresponds to the habits of antiquity, which were different from those of the twentieth century. What we condemn as deception to-day is in antiquity to be ascribed to a certain ingenuousness. The same naïveté which impels the author of Acts to leave the 'we' of another's diary which he incorporates into his history appears elsewhere, when he attributes speeches which he himself invented or elaborated to Peter, Gamaliel, Stephen, or Paul. Particularly crass examples are to be found in i. 18 f. and v. 36. We must assume that the name of the author was lost when the whole work was published. Tradition, which felt the need of a name from Apostolic times for such an important work, found in the 'we' sections the way pointed to a companion of Paul. Perhaps it was still known that Luke had written a diary, or else the fact was correctly

Use of the first person.

surmised from recollections still current in Jerusalem or in Rome concerning the travelling companions with whom Paul appeared in Macedonia or on the journey he undertook to raise moneys.

Third Gospel not Lucan.

When we have disproved the truth of the tradition concerning the authorship of Acts, we have of course done the same for the Third Gospel. It has often been emphatically stated that the Gospel itself gives criticism no hold. As a matter of fact, the result of a critical examination points the way to a consideration, important though seldom noted. It would be very strange—one can of course not say more—if the fullest of the synoptic Gospels had been written by a pupil of Paul, while the Pauline Epistles rather ignore the synoptic tradition. What is strange in this identification, which criticism has now dissolved, has usually been concealed by talk of the Paulinism of Luke.[1] This Paulinism is a fiction. The comforting announcement of forgiveness and grace, as we read it in Luke (xviii. 9-17, xv., xxiii. 41-43) is far from being Paulinism. If we decide on the shorter text in Luke's account of the Lord's Supper, then Luke appears as the Gospel farthest removed from Paulinism, since no account is taken in any way of the death of Christ as a means of salvation. The real author of the 'Lucan history' was acquainted with some phrases of Pauline theology (cf. Acts xiii. 38 ff.; xv. 11), but was far from enriching the primitive Gospel with Pauline dogmas and formulas.

Linguistic characteristics similar throughout Acts.

The extensive linguistic similarities between the 'we' sections and the rest of Acts do not stand in the way of this conclusion. In the first place, the so-called 'lower criticism' is never able to solve such complicated problems or even maintain itself against 'higher criticism.'[2] Further, it is possible to

---

[1] Cf. Schwegler, *Nachapost. Zeitalter*, ii. p. 41 ff.; Hilgenfeld, *Einl. in das N.T.*, pp. 571-574; H. J. Holtzmann, *Lehrb. der Einl. in das N.T.*, 3rd ed., p. 388 ff.; Jülicher, *Einl. in das N.T.*, p. 291 f.; Van de Sande-Bakhuijzen, *Het dogmatisch karakter van Lc*, 1888; Meyboom, *Theolog. Tijdschr.*, 1889, pp. 366-406; Rud. Steck, *Der Galaterbr.*, 1888, pp. 191-211.

[2] P. Wendland, *Literaturformen*, p. 335; R. Reitzenstein in Ilberg's *Neue Jahrbücher für das klass. Altertum*, 1913, i. pp. 410-422. (Noteworthy criticism of Harnack's method.)

point out linguistic differences between the 'we' sections and the rest of the document.¹ We must assume, therefore, that the author of Acts extensively revised his sources, even the 'we' source; the Third Gospel is one excellent illustration of this method,² the *Antiquities* of Josephus is another. Perhaps, too, the historic Luke and the author of Acts may have been members of the same language group.³

It is further possible that the 'we' sections were originally an independent document, the original πράξεις of Luke; that therefore the Gospel is genuine and Acts only an unhistorical revision and elaboration of this πράξεις of Luke.⁴ There is a good deal in favour of this hypothesis, among other things, the circumstance that the introduction to Acts (including the dedication) has manifestly been revised. But the attempt to separate the two elements by assigning to the original πράξεις all that seems credible to the modern critic, and to the reviser all that seems unthinkable in the mouth of a pupil of Paul, depends altogether too much upon the subjective and arbitrary decisions on individual points. It is probably impossible to avoid the assumption that the last editor of Acts must have revised the Gospel again as well. It seems to me, therefore, more simple to conclude that the reviser of the 'Lucan history,' the one who is responsible for the composition and style of both documents and who cannot have been a pupil of Paul, is identical with the *auctor ad Theophilum*.

The date assigned to the composition of Acts is not really opposed to the conclusion that Luke is not the author. Whether he actually lived to be eighty-four years old or not need not here be discussed. In any event, if Luke is the author

---

¹ Cf. W. Brückner, *Protest. Monatshefte*, 1911, p. 147 ff. Overbeck-De Wette, *Erkl. der Apg.* p. xxxix ff.
² Cf. Wendt, *Die Apg.* p. 22 ff.
³ Cf. P. W. Schmidt, *Die Apg. bei De Wette-Overbeck*, p. 46 ff.; E. Schürer, *Theolog. Lit.-ztg.*, 1906, col. 405.
⁴ Thus, with variations, F. Spitta, *Die Apg.*, 1891 (Source A.); A. Gercke, "Der δεύτερος λόγος des Lukas," *Hermes*, 1894, p. 373 ff. Ed. Norden, *Agnostos Theos*, p. 314 ff.; W. Soltau, *Protest. Monatsch.*, 1903, p. 296 ff.

of Acts, he must have written his histories at a considerable age. But we find no traces of senility in the skill displayed in the arrangement and composition of the book. If, however, Acts is as late as the beginning of the second century, Luke's authorship is of course impossible.[1]

Answer to argument that Luke would not need Paul's letters.

The assumption that the Pauline Epistles were not utilised in the composition of Acts is consistent with our result. When conservative criticism declares that a man like Luke would not have needed to consult the Epistles, since his own experiences and the verbal reports of many eye-witnesses offered him sufficient material for the story of Paul's missionary work, while a later comer could not do without the Epistles, and would surely have known of their existence, we may answer that Luke, to be sure, did not need to have recourse to the Epistles, but he had no right to suppress in his story all the things that we fortunately know from the letters, and that he could not diverge so much from the historical facts which Paul himself gives us in his Epistles. What we know from the letters, 'Luke' must certainly have known as an eye-witness and an acquaintance of eye-witnesses; and with his knowledge he would surely have considered it worth using it to make his narrative fuller and more correct than he did. But one cannot correctly maintain that Luke had no reason to consult the Epistles. He must have known that Paul had written letters—he was himself present when Paul wrote the Epistles to the Colossians and to Philemon—he therefore certainly knew that Paul's letters contained much information relative to the history of his missionary work. If a friend of Paul's composed Acts with the same care that, according to the prologue (Lk. i. 1-4), he expended on the Gospel, then he certainly would have consulted the letters in so far as they were accessible to him. It is much easier to believe that a later comer, who utilised predominantly documentary sources, did not have

---

[1] If we are no longer confined to the eighties, the hypothesis that 'Luke' utilised Josephus becomes, not sure, but more probable; and the assumption that he utilised a document by or about Apollonius of Tyana gains the *conditio sine qua non*.

THE CASE AGAINST THE TRADITION 347

recourse to the letters. Perhaps he was not acquainted with the most important Epistles, such as those to the Corinthians, Galatians, and Romans, or they were not at hand when he wrote his book. Such of Paul's Epistles as were accessible to him offered him no material that he could use. Thus we can explain also why the spirit of the Epistles of Paul remained alien to him and why he did not mention the fact that Paul had written any letters.

The preceding considerations eliminate those points which seem to controvert the critical view and support the traditional one. We have only a little to add. No one has as yet proved that the 'Lucan histories' must have been written by a physician (cf. p. 315 f.). When criticism forbids the view that Luke the physician composed the documents, it is not refuted by the indication of interest in medicine and of technical terms. These are even more compatible with the assumption that the author probably was not a physician at all, since they may also be explained by the assumption that the author possessed a certain amount of medical knowledge—the majority of the authors of antiquity must have belonged to the medical profession according to the demonstrations of Hobart, Harnack, and Zahn—to say nothing of the fact that, as a last solution, it would be possible to assume that both Luke and the author of Acts were physicians.[1]

Luke the physician.

If the more important arguments in favour of the traditional view turn out to be fallacious, the less important ones become less cogent than ever. The frequent references to Antioch (p. 316) can be adequately explained by the importance of the city, and perhaps by the utilisation of traditions originating from it.[2] It is not necessary to assume that the tradition that Luke was

---

[1] Cf. C. Clemen, *Theolog. Rundschau*, 1907, pp. 99-103; P. W. Schmidt, *Die Apg.* pp. 6-18; Wendland, *Literaturformen*, p. 335; H. J. Cadbury, *Style and Literary Method of Luke*, p. 39 ff., and see below p. 349 ff.

[2] It is just as legitimate to speak of Antiochian traditions as it is to speak of Jerusalem traditions. Cf. Harnack, *Die Apg.* p. 134 ff. The origin of the tradition has no bearing on the origin of the author.

born in Antioch is correct. Its first appearance in Eusebius is suspicious.¹

Author of Lucan books and Mark. The relations between Luke and Mark are quickly disposed of. The author of the 'Lucan histories' knew and utilised Mark's Gospel just as did the author of 'Matthew,' and he obtained information from Jerusalem or elsewhere about the household of Mark's mother. In view of the other facts, it is not permissible to draw any definite conclusions from these two data.

Conclusion. This much of the Tübingen criticism remains firmly established: Acts cannot have been written by Luke, the contemporary of the apostles and the companion of Paul, because above all the author had no longer a correct idea of the events before and during Paul's missionary activity, of what Paul accomplished, or of the fundamental ideas of Pauline theology. The other part of their theory is untenable, that a special purpose, of furthering the plans of a definite party, controlled the pen of the author, and led him to revise what he knew to be a reliable tradition. We may find traces of a special purpose in the circumstance that the author has suppressed all sorts of unpleasant matter—only it is now no longer possible to prove what he knew but kept silent about. He was, for the rest, more unconsciously than consciously controlled by the conviction that in the Apostolic age all was harmonious, and that the work of converting the Gentiles was from the very beginning a part of the plan of the original apostles. Such a view may well have been held in good faith by a man living in post-apostolic times (A.D. 80–110). The historic Luke would have uttered it knowing its untruth. Thus the critical attitude, without making the special attempt, has in the end an apologetic result. It re-establishes the honesty of Paul and of the author of Acts.

¹ Cf. also the enticing idea of Ramsay (*St. Paul*, p. 200 ff.), that Luke was a Macedonian and was himself the man who appeared to Paul in the dream, Acts xvi. 9. Since the 'we' first appears in connection with this vision, and since the narrator employing the first person actually has relations with Philippi (cf. Acts xvi., xx. 5 f.), it is possible to entertain this idea. But the hypothesis is far from sure. Cf. Wendt, *Die Apg.* p. 244.

IV

SUBSIDIARY POINTS

By H. J. CADBURY and the EDITORS

IT remains to discuss three points which are subsidiary in importance chiefly because they lead to no clear result. (1) The possibility that the presence of medical language in Acts confirms the tradition that the writer was a physician. (2) The possibility that Acts shows a knowledge of Josephus. (3) The general question of the chronological limits within which the writing of the Gospel and Acts must be placed.

The tradition of the Church identifies the writer of Acts with the 'Luke the physician' mentioned in Col. iv. 14. Starting with the assumption that this is true, early commentators illustrated it by drawing attention to medical phrases in Acts. Wettstein collected most of these illustrations into his commentary. But a new turn was given to the matter in 1882 by W. K. Hobart in a treatise entitled *The Medical Language of St. Luke*. This book collected parallels to Luke and Acts from medical writers. Many of these had been noted before, but always as illustration of the fact that Luke was a physician—regarded as a known truth —not to prove that he must have been so. The special feature of Hobart was that he converted illustration into argument. He went too far, and his argument was for some time discredited; but it was revived by Harnack in 1906 in his *Beiträge* with such skill that his readers were in many cases swept off their feet. Finally, in 1920, the subject was again taken up by Henry Cadbury,

Medical language.

who in his *Style and Literary Method of Luke*[1] submitted Harnack's arguments to fresh criticism, and reached the result that they fail to establish the conclusions put forward.

Referring to Hobart, Harnack says that "those who have studied it carefully will find it impossible to escape the conclusion that the question is not one of merely accidental colouring, but that this great historical work was composed by a writer who either was a physician or was quite intimately acquainted with medical language and science" (p. 14). He accordingly collects in an appendix to his book the most telling examples. His arguments may be summarised in his own language as follows :

(1) "In those passages where the author speaks as an eye-witness medical traits are especially and prominently apparent."

(2) "Nearly all of the alterations and additions which the third evangelist has made in the Marcan text are most simply and surely explained from the professional interest of a physician."

(3) In "the stories of diseases and subjects of allied character peculiar to St. Luke . . . traits appear which declare the interest or the sharp eyes or the language of the physician."

(4) "The representation of our Lord given in the third Gospel is dominated by the conception of Him as a wondrous Healer and Saviour of the sick."

(5) "The language of St. Luke elsewhere is coloured by medical phraseology."

The fallacy of Harnack's evidence could be shown completely only by a refutation as lengthy as his own proof. Many of his proofs are highly subjective, based on assumptions as to what a physician in antiquity would or would not have been likely to say. Others, especially (4), are drawn from the prominence of medical subjects and details in the narrative, an emphasis which, as Harnack himself agrees, might be due to the subject-matter, or to an entirely unprofessional interest of the writer. The real weight of his arguments rests upon the alleged technical medical

[1] *Harvard Theological Studies*, vi.

SUBSIDIARY POINTS 351

character of Greek words and phrases occurring in these writings. Here we must content ourselves by reviewing in order these verbal arguments only.[1]

(1) In the 'we' passages Harnack notes the following (pp. 176-181): Acts xxviii. 1-7 θέρμη, καθάπτειν = 'infect,' θηρίον = ἔχιδνα, πιμπρᾶσθαι, καταπίπτειν, μηδὲν ἄτοπον. Acts xvi. 16 ff. πύθων. Acts xx. 9 καταφερόμενος ὕπνῳ βαθεῖ and κατενεχθεὶς ἀπὸ τοῦ ὕπνου. Acts xxvii. 3, 17 ἐπιμέλεια (cf. ἐπιμελεῖσθαι, ἐπιμελῶς, Luke x. 34, 35, xv. 8), βοήθεια, ὑποζωννύναι. But θέρμη, of which Harnack says " this word, rare, I believe, in ordinary use, and only found here in the New Testament, is among physicians the general term for θερμότης," occurs apparently more frequently in Hellenistic Greek than θερμότης, while the latter, as a matter of fact, is not at all infrequent in medical writings. The meaning which Harnack assigns to καθάπτειν is very doubtful; in the sense 'to fasten on,' as it is usually here translated, it is a very common word in all kinds of writing. Θηρίον is also used of reptiles, especially poisonous ones, by lay writers, as Plutarch and Lucian.[2] Πιμπρᾶσθαι and καταπίπτειν in the sense applied by Acts occur in Greek writers from the time of Homer.[3] Ἄτοπος is especially frequent in litotes in all grades of Greek literature from Thucydides to the papyri. Πύθων does not appear to occur in medical writings (Hobart does not mention it); it is Plutarch who tells us that it meant 'ventriloquist.'[4] And even though " Passow gives only medical authorities for καταφέρεσθαι and καταφορά in the sense of sleep" (Harnack, p. 180), yet Wettstein's examples from Aristotle, Josephus, Diodorus, Plutarch, Lucian, and other non-medical writers show that the expressions in Acts xx. 9 are not technical terms. Of course ἐπιμέλεια and its cognates are not rare, and even in the special sense of medical attention which Harnack assumes for Acts xxvii. 3 they occur in ordinary writers. What-

[1] See *Style and Literary Method of Luke* for a fuller discussion of the details.
[2] It is the common word for 'snake' in modern Greek.
[3] For examples from the Greek Bible see Num. v. 21-27; 4 Macc. iv. 11.
[4] *De defectu oracul.* ix. (414 E).

ever may be the meaning of the words βοήθεια and ὑποζωννύναι as applied to the manœuvres of the sailors in the storm, it must be confessed that their use is as likely due to nautical as to medical terminology. Βοήθεια " is applied to all conceivable objects " (Harnack, p. 181) by others than the doctors. In fact, both words have a wide range of usage.

(2) In Luke's revision of Mark's stories of miracles, Harnack finds significance in the following (pp. 182-188):

(a) 'Ρίψαν (Luke iv. 35) for σπαράξαν (Mark i. 26).

(b) Συνεχομένη πυρετῷ μεγάλῳ (Luke iv. 38) for κατέκειτο πυρέσσουσα (Mark i. 30).

(c) Πλήρης λέπρας (Luke v. 12) for λεπρός (Mark i. 40).

(d) Παραλελυμένος (Luke v. 18) for παραλυτικός (Mark ii. 3).

(g) Ἔστη ἡ ῥύσις (Luke viii. 44) for ἐξηράνθη ἡ πηγή (Mark v. 29).

(i) Ἐπιβλέψαι (Luke ix. 38).

Of these words, ῥίπτειν and παραλελυμένος are, according even to Harnack, improvements in style. Συνέχεσθαι means 'to be afflicted' in good classical Greek. It would be unsafe to put much stress on the adjectives μέγας and πλήρης; they are not very rare in any Greek writers, and are favourite words with the author in many other connections. 'Ρύσις is taken by Luke from the Marcan context (v. 25), while ἔστη, to judge from the examples given, was used by the doctors transitively in the sense 'to staunch' and not intransitively as in Luke.[1] Granting that ἐπιβλέπειν may be " used technically for a physician's examination of the patient," ἐλέησον in the parallel in Matthew (xvii. 15) suggests that here Luke uses it as he does elsewhere (i. 48) in the sense common in the LXX. of 'pity.'

(3) The examples in Harnack's third class of passages are

---

[1] Perhaps I may here correct the oversight through which all reference to the intransitive use of ἵστημι in the LXX. was omitted in my earlier discussion, *Style and Literary Method of Luke*, both on p. 44 and on p. 57 note 43. In the sense 'cease flowing' the verb is used, as in Plutarch, of a river (Joshua iii. 13, 16), of oil (2 Kg. iv. 6 καὶ ἔστη τὸ ἔλαιον, "And the oil stayed "), and even, as in Luke, *l.c.*, of blood (Exod. iv. 25, 26 LXX., not Heb. or Eng. : ἔστη τὸ αἷμα τῆς περιτομῆς τοῦ παιδίου μου).—H. J. C.

SUBSIDIARY POINTS 353

(pp. 188-194) : Luke vii. 15 ἀνακαθίζειν ; xiii. 11-13 ἀνακύπτειν, ἀνορθοῦν, ἀπολύειν ; xiv. 2 ὑδρωπικός ; x. 30 ἡμιθανής ; xvi. 21-26 ἕλκος, ἑλκοῦσθαι, καταψύχειν, ὀδυνᾶσθαι, χάσμα, στηρίζειν ; Acts iii. 8 σφύδρον ; ix. 18 ἀποπίπτειν, λεπίς ; xiii. 11 ἀχλύς, σκότος ; xiv. 8 ἀδύνατος ; v. 5-10 ἐκψύχειν, συστέλλειν ; x. 10 ἔκστασις.

Of these words, σφύδρον and ἡμιθανής are both quite rare. Hobart gives no example of either from the doctors, though Harnack has emended one of his quotations from Galen (*Medicus*, 10) to read σφύδρα with Luke. The synonymous forms σφύρα and ἡμιθνής which are cited by Hobart from the doctors are neither of them unusual among lay writers. Of ἀνακαθίζειν Harnack says : " This word in the intransitive sense seems to be met with only in medical writers, who use it to signify ' to sit up again in bed.' " But Plutarch uses it in exactly the same way (*Philopoem.* 368 A, *Alex.* 671 D). Of ἐκψύχειν Harnack says that it "seems to be confined to medical literature. Before Luke (*loc. cit.* and Acts xii. 23) instances of its use are found only in Hippocrates, and then in Aretaeus and Galen." But not only is the word used by the doctors in a different sense, ' to cool off,' but its occurrence in Ezek. xxi. 7, Herondas iv. 29, Babrius 115, 11, in the sense ' to expire ' shows that Luke is using a popular expression. Similarly συστέλλειν used in Acts of wrapping a corpse, though it is quite unusual, is better illustrated by such passages as Euripides, *Troades*, 378, or Lucian, *Imagines*, 7, than by medical passages on the bandaging of limbs or contraction of organs. The remaining words are none of them rare in ordinary Greek ; each can be paralleled in the sense in which Luke uses it from at least two or three lay writings in Hellenistic Greek, such as the Greek Old Testament, the papyri, or the works of writers like Josephus, Philo, Polybius, Lucian, and Plutarch.

(5) Omitting for the moment Harnack's fourth point, for it contains no arguments from vocabulary, we come to his last list of " medical terms " (pp. 196-198). Excluding repetitions, these are παραχρῆμα, προσδοκᾶν, ἀνάπειρος, ὁλοκληρία, ἀποψύχειν,

ἀνάψυξις, πνοή, ἐνπνέειν, ἐκπνέειν, ζωογονεῖν, εἰς μανίαν περιτρέπειν, κραιπάλη, χρῶς, οὐκ ἄσημος πόλις, βελόνη, τρῆμα, ἀρχαί.

These examples are in general of the same character as those already considered. None of them is confined in use to the medical writers. Many of them are of frequent occurrence in Greek literature, as any Greek scholar will know at sight or can prove by consulting a lexicon. Several of the parallels are far from happy. Thus ζωογονεῖν is used by Luke in a sense common in the LXX. but never found in the Greek doctors. Hobart himself confesses that περιτρέπειν does not occur in the medical writings in the same sense as in Acts (p. 268), and that ὁλοκληρία is not used at all (p. 193); but he calls remarkable a parallel to Luke's οὐκ ἄσημος πόλις in the obscure, probably late and spurious *Letters* of Hippocrates, though the litotes, and even the identical expression, can be abundantly paralleled from other writers.

The verbal arguments in Harnack's evidence are unconvincing. In confining his attention to the medical and the Lucan writings and their resemblances, he has failed to observe the differences between them or their agreements with other Greek writers. Some of his examples are not found in the medical writers at all, others are used by them in a sense different from that in which they are employed in Luke and Acts. Even those which really do occur in the same sense in the medical and Lucan writings are not confined to them. This use of "medical terms" by laymen allows of only two alternative explanations: (a) either technical medical language was the common property of unprofessional writers, or (b) the words cited are not really technical terms at all. Whichever explanation be accepted, the use of such words in any book does not prove that its author was a physician. For if medical terms are so loosely defined it is possible to find them in great quantity in many a writer never suspected of medical knowledge.[1]

[1] *E.g.* Lucian or Josephus. The short letter of Aristeas uses 80 of Hobart's words in nearly 200 places in all.

SUBSIDIARY POINTS

Even Matthew and Mark do not fall so far behind Luke in 'medical interest' as Harnack would have us believe. Many terms quite as well attested in the doctors occur in their writings though not in Luke's. Even in the stories of miracles they contain details which Luke omits, including the diagnosis of the centurion's boy as suffering from paralysis (Matt. viii. 6, contrast Luke vii. 2), many significant symptoms in the epileptic (Mark ix. 14-27, cf. Luke ix. 37-43), and at least two entire stories of cures told with much detail (Mark vii. 31-37, viii. 22-26). And also in the summaries of the activity of Jesus and the disciples —and this is Harnack's fourth point (pp. 195, 196)—Matthew no less than Luke emphasises healing and distinguishes different kinds of cases. Thus he even substitutes healing for teaching in his source (Matt. xiv. 14 = Mark vi. 34, Matt. xix. 2 = Mark x. 1, Matt. xxi. 14 = Mark xi. 18), and enumerates much more fully than the parallel passages various diseases (Matt. iv. 23-24 = Mark i. 32-34, 39; Matt. x. 8 = Luke x. 9; Matt. xv. 29-31).

One can but be attracted in the study of Acts by Harnack's argument, especially as to medical language. It is only slowly that a study of the facts convinces the scholar that the whole of the contention as to the medical language of Luke is an immense fallacy. Neither Harnack nor Hobart sufficiently considered the use of the phrases which they call 'medical.' The fact that a word is found in a medical book proves nothing as to the profession of another writer who uses it, if it be also used elsewhere.[1]

The material for a discussion of the relation of Josephus to the Lucan writings was given in the eighteenth century by J. B. Ott, *Spicilegium sive excerpta ex Flavio Josepho ad Novi Testa-*

Luke's indebtedness to Josephus.

---

[1] Of course the real solution of the problem is that neither the doctors nor the laymen used a technical vocabulary in antiquity, and the whole assumption of 'medical language' in any ancient writer is a mare's nest. See G. F. Moore in Cadbury, *Style and Literary Method of Luke*, pp. 53 f., and the statement of Galen in his treatise *On the Natural Faculties* that he used ordinary language. Galen makes a similar claim for Hippocrates, *Comm. Hipp. de epidemiis*, iii. 32 (Kuhn xvii. A. 678) ὁ γάρ τοι τοῦ Ἡρακλείδου υἱὸς Ἱπποκράτης . . . φαίνεται συνηθεστάτοις τε καὶ διὰ τοῦτο σαφέσι τοῖς ὀνόμασι κεχρημένος, ἃ καλεῖν ἔθος ἐστὶ τοῖς ῥητορικοῖς πολιτικά.

menti illustrationem, 1741, and by J. P. Krebs's *Observationes in Novum Testamentum e Flavio Josepho*, 1755. This material was worked over in the nineteenth century, and the theory evolved that Luke was dependent on Josephus. Keim[1] and others adopted this view, but it was most fully stated by Krenkel in his *Josephus und Lucas*, 1894. In some ways, indeed, it was even too fully stated, and a far better impression of the weight of the argument can be gained from F. C. Burkitt's *Gospel History and its Transmission*, pp. 105 ff.

The case will always rest on three passages, and it is safe to say that they can never be completely explained away, yet will never convince every one. They are given here in the order of importance.

Theudas.   (1) In Acts v. 36 f., Gamaliel is represented as referring to the rebellion of Theudas which took place several years after the time when he was speaking. Moreover, he is made to say—that Theudas rebelled before Judas of Galilee. No attempt to discover some other Theudas has succeeded, and it is possible that Luke was misled by an inaccurate memory of Josephus, *Ant.* xx. 5. 1 f. In this passage Josephus describes the insurrection of Theudas in the procuratorship of Fadus, and goes on to tell how the sons of Judas of Galilee, who had raised a rebellion in the time of Quirinius, were executed by Alexander, the successor of Fadus.

It will be seen that here Theudas comes before the mention of Judas, and if any one overlooked the fact that it was the children of Judas, not himself, that were executed, he might easily produce Luke's erroneous combination.

Lysanias.   (2) In Luke iii. 1, Lysanias is represented as the Tetrarch of Abilene about 28 A.D. But the only Lysanias known to history as ruling in Abila died in 36 B.C. Attempts have been made to show that there was another Lysanias at the time mentioned by Luke, but they have not been successful,[2] and it

---

[1] *Aus dem Urchristentum*, 1878, i. 1-27. See also H. Holtzmann's notable articles in the *Z.W.Th.* in 1873, 1877, and 1880.

[2] The most ingenious are those of E. Schürer, *G.J.V.*

SUBSIDIARY POINTS 357

is hardly too much to say that no one would have dreamt of a second Lysanias as ruler of Abila had it not been for this isolated passage in Luke.¹ It is therefore worth noting that when Josephus relates how in 53 A.D., Agrippa II. obtained Abila he adds that this had been (γεγόνει) the tetrarchy of Lysanias. The whole evidence is most conveniently to be found in the article on Lysanias in the *Encyclopaedia Biblica*. It is clear that an inaccurate knowledge of Josephus would adequately account for the error in Luke.

(3) The question of the Tribune to Paul in Acts xxi. 38, "Art thou not the Egyptian who before these days revolted and led out in the desert four thousand men of the Sicarii?" seems a curious combination of three passages in Josephus. In *B.J.* ii. 13. 3, he describes the Sicarii; in the next paragraph the false prophets who led men into the desert, and were destroyed by the cavalry of Felix; finally in the next paragraph comes the story of the Egyptian who led 30,000 men out of (not into) the desert, and the destruction of many by the Roman soldiers.

The Egyptian.

These three examples of Lucan errors explained by Josephus are certainly very persuasive. But they fall just short of demonstration. The case of Theudas is the strongest, but even here there is always the possibility that Luke and Josephus were using a common source, in which the events were arranged in the order given by Josephus.² The case of Lysanias is adequately met by the probability that the district was always known as the 'Tetrarchy (or kingdom) of Lysanias' long after his death, and that Luke, influenced by this, merely made an error in chronology. Finally, the case for dependence on Josephus in the reference to the Egyptian is weakened by the fact that Josephus says that he led 30,000, while Luke says only 4000. The number of rebels grows in tradition more often than it decreases, and Luke's figure is surely the more probable.

Thus the argument that Luke used Josephus is not quite

¹ There were no doubt other persons named Lysanias belonging to the family of Lysanias the Tetrarch; cf. *C.I.G.* 4521 and 4523.
² See, however, the warning of F. C. Burkitt, *Gospel Transmission*, p. 108.

358 IDENTITY OF EDITOR OF LUKE AND ACTS

conclusive. If it were, it would fix the date of Luke and Acts as at the earliest the very end of the first century, for the *Antiquities* of Josephus are not earlier than 93 A.D.

The date of Acts. Is there any other method by which the date of the Gospel and Acts can be fixed? Probably not. At least none has yet been discovered. The extreme limits within which the composition of the two books must fall are c. 60 A.D. or a little earlier, when Paul reached Rome, and c. 150 A.D., when Marcion made use of the Gospel. The two extremes are improbable; but just as there is no decisive proof that Luke was not written before the fall of Jerusalem, there is also none that it was used by any writer before Marcion. Nevertheless, most students think that the rewriting of the Marcan eschatological discourse (Mark xiii.) implies the influence of the last days of Jerusalem. On the other hand, it seems extremely unlikely that the Gospel would ever have been canonised had it not been generally known before the time of Marcion. In other words, Marcion more probably took the Gospel from the Church than did the Church from Marcion. These two arguments may be held to make the probable limits 70-115 rather than 60-150.

Any closer dating depends entirely on the opinion as to the arguments set out above. If Acts was written by a companion of Paul, each year after 80 A.D. becomes increasingly improbable. But if Acts was merely based on a document written by Luke, a later date is easily acceptable.

There is no direct evidence; neither authorship nor date is susceptible of demonstration. No one, however, can study the Lucan writings without forming some opinion, even while acknowledging its precariousness, and it seems right for the Editors of this volume to express their own view. Ten years ago both of them felt reasonably sure that Acts was actually written by Luke, the companion of Paul. Slowly, however, they have come to feel the weight of the argument derived from the comparison with the Pauline epistles, and at present they incline to the view that Luke, the companion of Paul, wrote the 'we-sections,' and probably the narrative adhering to them, but that the combination of this document with the rest of Acts, and the composition of the Gospel, were the work of a later writer, who probably lived in the Flavian period. If they were obliged to choose a more specific date they would take the last five years of the first century, thus leaving room for the probability that Luke was acquainted with Josephus. Nevertheless, they would conclude by repeating that this view is based on a general balance of probabilities, on which wide difference of opinion is possible and even desirable. Its truth cannot be demonstrated; but neither can that of any other view; the only wise course is, whenever a question is at issue involving the authorship or date of Acts, to leave a wide margin for possible error.

III

THE HISTORY OF CRITICISM

I

THE HISTORICAL CRITICISM OF ACTS IN GERMANY

By A. C. McGiffert

ACCORDING to the traditional view, generally accepted both by Catholics and Protestants, the book of Acts was written in Rome, while Paul was still a prisoner there, by his companion Luke, 'the beloved physician,' who drew his materials partly from his own personal observation, partly from Paul and other eye-witnesses of the events recorded. The purpose of the book was wholly historical, to recount the achievements of the apostles, or the history of the early Church, as the gospels had recounted the words and works of Christ, and its trustworthiness was beyond question. <small>The traditional view of Acts.</small>

The traditional view remained unchanged until the close of the eighteenth century, when the Acts began to come under the same scrutiny that was given to the gospels and other writings of the New Testament by the awakening historical criticism of the day. It was evident at once to the critical eye that the book fulfilled in a very imperfect way the historical purpose which had been ascribed to it by tradition. Instead of recording the acts of the apostles it confined itself almost exclusively to Peter and Paul, and even Peter received but scant attention. Moreover, the fragmentary nature of the account, the many omissions evident to any one acquainted with Paul's Epistles, the frequent repetitions, the extreme sketchiness of some parts and the minute detail of others, the marked emphasis upon certain matters, <small>Objections felt.</small>

and the brief and casual reference to others of equal importance all seemed to demand some explanation. If the author was familiar with the period he was writing about, as had been commonly taken for granted, he must have had some other than a purely historical motive, or if not, then his knowledge of the period must have been very limited and fragmentary.[1]

J. D. Michaelis.

Among those who adopted the former alternative and attempted to find an explanation of the peculiarities of Acts in the purpose for which it was written was J. D. Michaelis,[2] who rejected the idea that the Acts was intended to be a history of the Church or a biography of Paul and maintained that it had a double purpose: first, "to record in a trustworthy way the initial outpouring of the Holy Spirit, together with the first miracles for the confirmation of the truth of the Christian religion"; and second, "to report those circumstances that proved the right of the heathen in the Church of Christ, a right opposed by the Jews especially at the time when Luke wrote. Paul himself, whose companion Luke was, was at that time a prisoner in Rome as a consequence of the accusations of the Jews who were hostile to him on the ground that he admitted heathen to the church."[3]

Griesbach and Paulus.

Griesbach of Jena, in an essay published in 1798,[4] is said to

[1] Compare the words of Schwanbeck, writing in 1847: "There were two ways of explaining the fragmentary character of Acts. Either the author would not tell more or he could not. In the former case the general historical purpose of the Acts must be given up or modified; besides the historical aim another more particular aim must be assumed, nullifying the former or pushing it into the background. In the latter case the ignorance of the author concerning many matters is accounted for by the limitations of his sources whether oral or written. The former path was much broader than the latter, and could be travelled more easily without stopping to prove every step in detail. As a consequence it was for a long time exclusively followed, and is still the favourite path" (*Über die Quellen der Schriften des Lukas*, p. 74).

[2] *Einleitung in die göttlichen Schriften des neuen Bundes*, third edition, 1777; Th. ii. § 154.

[3] *Op. cit.* p. 995.

[4] Program de consilio quo scriptor in Actibus Apostolicis concinnandis ductus fuerit (*Jenäer Osterprogram* for 1798). I have not myself seen Griesbach's essay, which is ascribed by some (*e.g.* by Lechler in his *Apostolisches und nachapostolisches Zeitalter*, third edition, p. 7) to Griesbach's colleague Paulus. Compare the remark of Semler, referring to the silence of Acts touching Peter and Paul's dispute at Antioch: "Lucas igitur prudenter omisit eas historiae veteris partes,

have maintained that Acts was written to defend the Apostle Paul against the attacks of the Judaising Christians of the day. He was followed the next year by his colleague Paulus.[1] So far as I am aware neither Griesbach nor Paulus discussed the authenticity of Acts, but the tendency of their theory was, of course, to throw discredit upon its trustworthiness.

Luke's many omissions were explained by Eckermann [2] as due to his purpose to select from the events known to him only such as showed most clearly the miraculous co-operation of God in the establishment of his kingdom on earth.

According to Hänlein,[3] the Acts had the aim of showing God's aid in the spread of Christianity, of promoting the reputation of the Apostles by recording their miracles, and of indicating the claim of the Gentiles to equal rights with the Jews in the blessings of Christianity.[4]

Eichhorn[5] held that the aim of Acts was not to give a history of the Church or of the apostles but of Christian missions. In his New Testament Introduction (§ 148) he discussed at considerable length and repudiated the theory that the book was written to defend Paul's preaching to the Gentiles and his doctrine of the abrogation of the Jewish law.

On the other hand, S. G. Frisch[6] accepted the defence of Paul and his apostleship as one, though not the only purpose of the Acts. "To me," he says, "as I have proved at length, it is evident that Luke while he wished to defend the cause of Paul against adversaries and detractors and to

---

quae ad continuandam divisionem et separationem utriusque familiae converti potuissent, isto tempore " (*Paraphrasis epistolae ad Galatas*, 1779, p. 56).

[1] *Introductionis in Novum Testamentum capita selectiora*, 1799, p. 281 ff.
[2] *Erklärung aller dunkeln Stellen des Neuen Testaments* (1807), vol. ii. p. 164 ff.
[3] *Einleitung in die Schriften des Neuen Testaments* (second edition, 1809).
[4] Th. iii. p. 156 f.
[5] *Einleitung in das Neue Testament*, 1810, vol. ii. § 147.
[6] In his dissertation, " Utrumque Lucae commentarium de vita, dictis factisque Jesu et apostolorum non tam historicae simplicitatis, quam artificiosae tractationis indolem habere " (1817).

vindicate for him among the Christians the highest apostolic authority, and also to remove the doubts and scruples which were troubling the Christian communities, had always another end in mind not only in his second work but also in his first: this, namely, to persuade the Jews and the Jewish Christians who were still in doubt whether they should receive or reject, or whether they should cling to or abandon the Christian religion, that the dignity of Jesus the Messiah was greater than Moses enjoyed, that the origin of the new covenant was divine, and that it was the will of God and of Jesus the Messiah that all men whatsoever should be partakers of Christian salvation. Luke therefore strove, though in a different way, to accomplish the same object as the author of the Epistle to the Hebrews." [1]

Mayerhoff. According to Mayerhoff,[2] the purpose of Acts was to set forth " first, the extensive as well as intensive spread of the Christian Church from its origin in Jerusalem, the centre of Judaism, to Rome, the centre of heathenism; secondly, the opposition to it, which became always the means to a wider spread; and thirdly, the inner confirmation of it." [3]

Credner. Credner [4] explained the peculiar character of Acts by the author's Paulinism. " The selection from primitive Christian history made by the author of Acts is to be explained alone by the fact that he was a Paulinist. He picks out only what is of significance for Pauline doctrine, as the entire work is but an historical commentary on the Pauline sentences: ' The Gospel is the power of God unto salvation to every one that believeth, to the Jew first and also to the Greek.' ' Both Jews and Greeks are all under sin.' ' There is no difference between Jew and Greek.' " [5]

Credner concludes also from the silence of the Book of Acts

[1] *Op. cit.* p. 53 f.
[2] *Einleitung in die petrinischen Schriften nebst einer Abhandlung über den Verfasser der Apostelgeschichte,* 1835.
[3] *Op. cit.* p. 5.
[4] *Einleitung in das Neue Testament,* 1836.   [5] *Op. cit.* I. 1, p. 269.

concerning Paul's death that the author planned to write a third work,[1] an opinion that has been adopted by some modern scholars, *e.g.* by Spitta [2] and Ramsay.[3]

Others, while maintaining the general historical purpose of the book, explained its peculiar character by appealing to the needs of Theophilus, which though unknown to us were known to the author and led him to omit many things already familiar, and to emphasise others because of particular interest to his reader.[4]

In 1836 a new epoch in the criticism of Acts was opened by the revival of the suggestion made nearly forty years before by Griesbach and Paulus that the purpose of the Acts was to defend Paul and Paulinism against the Judaisers. The suggestion was taken up both by Karl Schrader and by Ferdinand Christian Baur, the great Tübingen critic. *[Schrader and F. C. Baur.]*

Up to this time, the omissions and repetitions in the book of Acts were chiefly responsible for the conviction that it was written with a special purpose; but Schrader found the principal difficulty in the difference between the Paul of the Acts and the Paul of the Epistles, thus putting the question, as Baur did too, upon a different level altogether.

In his work on the Apostle Paul [5] Schrader gave a translation of the book of Acts, with brief comments in which he called attention not only to the contrast between the Paul of Acts and the Paul of the Epistles, but also to the author's emphasis upon Paul's dependence on the older apostles, to the evident parallelism in the recorded miracles of Peter and Paul, to the representation of the Roman authorities as uniformly friendly to the latter, and finally, to the omission of any account of his death. *[Schrader's view.]*

"The close of the Acts," Schrader says, "is surprising. Why

[1] *Op. cit.* p. 279.
[2] *Die Apostelgeschichte*, 1891, p. 318.
[3] *St. Paul the Traveller and the Roman Citizen*, 1895, p. 309.
[4] Cf. Hug's *Introduction to the New Testament*, English translation, Andover, 1836, p. 493.
[5] *Der Apostel Paulus*, 1836, Theil v.

does it not relate the death of the Apostle for Christ? The author could not have been ignorant of the terrible fate of the Christians in Rome, their cruel execution as incendiaries by Nero, nor could it have seemed unimportant to him. But in an ecclesiastical book intended to defend the Christians against the Jews, the heathen and the government, in a book which was to be read in public, it was out of place to conclude the experiences of the Apostle with the horrible persecution of Nero. This would have been to nullify all that had been said in Christianity's behalf about the conduct of the government toward the Christians, and to remind their enemies, who were to learn from the book how completely the government had everywhere recognised the innocence of the Christians (for the book was written long after the death of the Apostle), that though they had relied upon the support of the Emperor, they had been put to death by him as the most abandoned criminals. Moreover, it would not have been possible to represent the Emperor in connection with the prosecution as other than a most terrible monster; and this again in a book designed for public use in the Church would have been very dangerous. The Christians could have been accused of embittering their people against the government, of despising it in the person of the Emperor, and of being bad subjects, whereas according to 1 Tim. ii. 1-2 they were to appear as loyal subjects, offering prayers for the government, that they might have peace. Such considerations as these might induce the author of Acts, who sought always to avoid everything offensive, to bring his history to a close not with the obnoxious Neronian persecution but with the edifying assurance that Paul in his imprisonment taught for two whole years free and unhindered." [1]

F. C. Baur's view.

Schrader concluded that the purpose of the author of Acts was controllingly apologetic and that the historical trustworthiness of the book was seriously affected thereby.

In the same year Baur published an essay in which he main-

[1] *Op. cit.* p. 573 f.

HISTORICAL CRITICISM OF ACTS IN GERMANY 369

tained [1] that the book of Acts was written by a Paulinist to defend the Apostle's mission to the Gentiles against the attacks of Jewish Christians by showing that he had everywhere preached first to the Jews and had turned to the Gentiles only after the former had rejected his gospel, so that it was the Jews themselves who were responsible for the existence of a Gentile Christianity. Baur was led to discuss the attitude of the author of Acts in this particular essay on the Epistle to the Romans because of the account of the situation in Rome given in Acts xxviii. 17 ff., which seemed to him a particularly convincing example of the apologetic course of the author of Acts.

In 1838, in an article on the origin of the Episcopate,[2] which also appeared the same year in a separate volume, Baur set forth the well-known Tübingen construction of early Christian history and assigned the book of Acts its place in the group of irenic writings whose purpose was the reconciliation of the two hostile parties, the Jewish Christians and the Paulinists. In this article he summed up the aim of Acts in the following words: "Indeed even the Acts of the Apostles, whatever we may think of its historical trustworthiness, is in its controlling idea and innermost character the apologetic attempt of a Paulinist to initiate and promote the mutual friendliness and union of the two opposing parties by making Paul appear as Petrine and Peter as Pauline as possible, by throwing a veil over differences which, beyond doubt, according to Paul's categorical declaration in the Epistle to the Galatians actually existed between the two apostles, and by leading the Gentile Christians to forget their hostility to Judaism, and the Jewish Christians their hostility to heathenism, in their common enmity to the unbelieving Jews who had made Paul the constant object of their implacable hatred."

The Tübingen theory.

---

[1] "Über Zweck und Veranlassung des Römerbriefs und die damit zusammenhängenden Verhältnisse der römischen Gemeinde," *Tübinger Zeitschrift für Theologie*, 1836, Heft 3, p. 100 ff.

[2] "Über den Ursprung des Episcopats," *Tübinger Zeitschrift für Theologie* for 1838, Heft 3, p. 142 ff.

Schnecken-burger.

Moved by the attacks of Schrader and Baur upon the trustworthiness of Acts, Schneckenburger of Berne took up the study of the purpose of the book, and in 1841 published the first critical and detailed discussion of the matter.[1] Schneckenburger agreed that the purpose of the author of Acts was primarily apologetic, not historical—to defend the Apostle against the attacks of Judaisers and to remove as far as possible the Jewish Christian prejudice against him,—but he maintained that there had been no serious departure from historic fact.

Following Schrader in recognising the wide difference between the Paul of the Epistles and the Paul of Acts, he found the explanation in Luke's desire to make Paul appear in a favourable light to Christians of Jewish birth. Similarly, so he maintained, in reply to the Judaisers' claim of superiority for Peter, Luke emphasised Paul's divine call to apostleship, dwelt upon his heavenly visions, magnified his exploits, minimised the unhappy incidents of his career, and drew a detailed parallel between his achievements and Peter's. Still further, Schneckenburger points out, according to the Acts Paul uniformly keeps the Jewish law with meticulous care, is scrupulous in observing the Jewish feasts, circumcises Timothy, works constantly in harmony with the older apostles upon the occasion of his first visit to Jerusalem, after his conversion wishes to remain there and preach to the Jews, but is compelled by divine command to go to the Gentiles, and throughout his missionary career always addresses the Jews first and turns to the Gentiles only when the former have rejected the gospel. His recorded discourses are such as might have been uttered by any Jewish believer in Jesus' Messiahship and contain no trace of the gospel of freedom from law, which bulks so large in Paul's Epistles. Titus, his uncircumcised Gentile companion, is not mentioned nor is his work in Galatia, where he deviated from his ordinary custom and preached only to the Gentiles. The Antiochian quarrel referred to in Galatians ii. is omitted, as is also all reference to the great

[1] *Über den Zweck der Apostelgeschichte*, 1841.

collection, and the book ends with an account of an interview with the Jews in Rome held in response to Paul's own request. Indeed the whole work is brought to a climax with the final rejection of Christianity by the Jews and Paul's declaration, " Be it known unto you, therefore, that this salvation of God is sent unto the Gentiles ; they will listen."

The interest that dictated Luke's account of Paul's work appears also in the first part of Acts when he is dealing with the Church of Jerusalem and the older apostles. The universalism of the gospel is based on Christ's own command in i. 8, and is symbolised at Pentecost. The high standing of Barnabas in the Christian community at Jerusalem is emphasised because of his subsequent relation to Paul and his help in forwarding Paul's missionary work. Peter's agency in the conversion of Cornelius is given great prominence. He appears as Paul's predecessor in the apostolate to the heathen. He also speaks of Jews and Gentiles as equal in God's sight and declares that the law does not justify, but faith alone. In fact, there is more Paulinism in the first half of the book than in the second, more in the mouths of the early disciples than in Paul's own mouth.

As already said, though Schneckenburger held that the book of Acts was written with an apologetic not an historical purpose, he maintained its substantial accuracy throughout. Luke did not invent or falsify his facts as Schrader and Baur claimed, but simply selected his material in such a way as to produce the desired impression. Had he been inventing freely, of course, he could have made a more complete and consistent defence of Paul, but as it was he felt himself bound by the facts.

Schneckenburger concluded that the work was written by Paul's companion Luke after the death of the Apostle, but before the destruction of Jerusalem, and he explained its limited circulation by the fact that it was meant primarily not for the Church at large and not for the Gentile wing of the Church, but for the Jewish Christians of Rome, who opposed the conversion of the Gentiles not only because of their national exclusiveness, but also because of their fear of the Roman Government which made Jewish propaganda a crime.¹

F. C. Baur's reply to Schneckenburger.

Schneckenburger made a very telling case for his theory, and no one could thenceforth write upon the purpose of the Acts without taking account of his argument. Baur at once recognised its importance, and in his review of Schneckenburger's book ² he appealed to it in support of his own view of the purpose of Acts, which differed very materially from Schneckenburger's. The latter held to the Lucan authorship and trustworthiness of Acts, but his theory of the book's purpose, as Baur abundantly shows, made against both. "It is impossible," so Baur says, "for the author's investigations to stop where he has left them, and one must either turn back or go beyond the point fixed by the author to further studies concerning the historical character of the book as a whole." ³

An admirable summary of Baur's own view is given in his volume on Paul the Apostle which appeared a few years later.⁴ The author of Acts, he says, cannot have been identical with Luke, the friend and companion of the Apostle, "for a writer so large a part of whose account has so little the character of historical objectivity, and who sets the events in such a perspective as to show a definite purpose and tendency, must have been some distance from the facts he records, and can have written only under conditions dominated by interests other than those that can be assumed for the time of the Apostle. This is a necessary conclusion from our discussion, but on the other hand, we must have a care not to draw from the particular aim which controlled the author of a later day too unfavourable a judgment of the historical trustworthiness of the Acts as a whole, for the apologetic interest of the author does not wholly

¹ Schneckenburger argued further for the trustworthiness of Acts and his own interpretation of its purpose in certain notes published after his death in the *Theologische Studien und Kritiken*, 1855, p. 498 f., under the title "Beiträge zur Erklärung und Kritik der Apostelgeschichte."
² *Jahrbücher für wissenschaftliche Kritik*, March 1841 (Nos. 46-48).
³ *Op. cit.* No. 48, p. 381.
⁴ *Der Apostel Paulus*, 1845, p. 12 ff.

exclude the truth, but only limits and modifies it. Unhistorical as its presentation appears at many points where we can test it by Paul's own testimony, it yet agrees in many respects with the history of the times as we know it from other trustworthy witnesses. It therefore remains—even though the common opinion as to its author, its purpose, and its date cannot be accepted—a most important source for the history of the apostolic age, but at the same time a source from which a genuinely historical picture of the persons and events it describes can be gained only after strict historical criticism."

According to Baur, while Luke cannot have been the author of Acts, some of the material may have come from him, and in any case, as the use of the pronoun 'we' shows, he wished to be taken for Luke, the well-known friend and companion of the Apostle.[1]

Baur was followed in his interpretation of the purpose of Acts by Albert Schwegler, another member of the Tübingen School,[2] but Schwegler's judgment of the historicity of the book was even more severe than Baur's. The Acts of the Apostles, he says, "is an apology for the Apostle to the Gentiles and his apostolic work among the heathen, a proposal of peace and an attempt at reconciliation in the form of a history—*in the form of a history*, for even though the first part at any rate, and probably the second as well, are based on older sources and narratives, when we remove the improbable, the impossible, the demonstrably unhistorical, or that which is bound up with it, and especially the freely composed speeches and the countless repetitions, there is extraordinarily little historical reality left. The complete historical trustworthiness of the Acts is impugned even by its numerous purposeful omissions and silences. He who intentionally passes over important events in order to give the matter he deals with another aspect, and intentionally omits characteristic features of a portrait in order to give it a different look,

Albert Schwegler.

---

[1] This had been already suggested by Schrader, *op. cit.* pp. 549, 556, 570.
[2] *Das nachapostolische Zeitalter*, 1846.

cannot be regarded as too upright and conscientious to permit himself positive distortions and unhistorical inventions when it is to his interest to do so. At any rate, we can say this much with certainty concerning our author, that in using and shaping the material given him by tradition, he has proceeded in a most arbitrary and sovereign way. In this connection we have already referred to the Clementine Homilies as affording in many respects a striking parallel. Taking it as a whole, the book of Acts has the worth of an historical document only for the time, the circumstances and the situation which gave it birth." [1]

According to Schwegler, Acts was written in the second century somewhere between the persecution of Trajan and the rise of Marcionism.[2] At the time of its composition Jewish Christianity was still dominant and Jewish Christians were still in the majority. Gradually with the multiplication of Gentile Christians, synchronising with the rise of Gnosticism, conditions changed and the situation which accounted for the book of Acts was outgrown.

Eduard Zeller.

In 1848, still another member of the Tübingen School, Eduard Zeller, son-in-law of Baur and later well known as a historian of philosophy, took a hand in the discussion with an important series of articles in the *Theologische Jahrbücher* (1848–1851),[3] which were revised and published in book form in 1854, under the title *Die Apostelgeschichte nach ihrem Inhalt und Ursprung kritisch untersucht*.[4] Zeller's book is the most elaborate critique

---

[1] *Op. cit.* vol. ii. p. 73 ff.

[2] Schwegler calls attention to the similarity between the Acts and Justin Martyr's *Dialogue with Trypho*, chap. 47, in which the same compromise appears, the recognition, namely, of a circumcised Jewish Christianity in return for the recognition of an uncircumcised Gentile Christianity. "Evidently the situation is essentially the same as in the Acts; the proposition is still that each party shall confine its demands to its own members. Nevertheless, Justin's *Dialogue* indicates that the Gentile party has in the meantime grown stronger, for it concedes what the Acts is still asking for" (ii. p. 118).

[3] An article entitled "Die älteste Überlieferung über die Schriften des Lukas" in the *Jahrbücher* for 1848 was followed in 1849–1851 by a number of articles under the title "Die Apostelgeschichte, ihre Komposition und ihre Charakter."

[4] English translation by Joseph Dare, in two volumes, 1875-6.

of the Acts that has appeared, and his statement of the purpose of the work, while agreeing essentially with Schwegler's, is more careful and discriminating and may be taken as the classic presentation of the Tübingen theory of early Christian history as applied to Acts. Like Baur and Schwegler, Zeller commends Schneckenburger for having proved beyond all doubt the apologetic character of Acts, but criticises him for making too much of its historic trustworthiness. Zeller himself does not doubt its accuracy, so he says, because of its apologetic character, but having discovered its untrustworthiness from a detailed study of its contents, he seeks an explanation and finds it in the apologetic purpose which controlled its composition. This purpose he defines [1] as the attempt to reconcile Jewish Christians and Paulinists by justifying the existence of Paulinism and at the same time sacrificing its extreme claims for the sake of peace. Two points, he says, the author will not sacrifice—the apostolic authority of Paul and the universalism of the gospel. His chief aim is to convince Jewish Christians that a free Gentile Christianity is legitimate. This, of course, implies that its legitimacy was denied, and the book was meant chiefly for those who denied it, to convince them by appealing to history and to conciliate them by conceding the legitimacy of their own Jewish form of Christianity. The book of Acts was thus a mediating work intended not only for Judaisers, but also for Paulinists, for mediation was vain unless the latter accepted the compromise as well as the former. To quote Zeller's own summary of his view: "Accordingly what our author wishes to give is such a delineation of the Apostle Paul in his relation to the Church of Jerusalem and to the Jewish Christian apostles as shall not only justify the person of the Apostle against the accusations and prejudices of the Judaists, but shall also bring about an understanding in reference to Pauline Christianity. With this end, not only are Paul and his cause commended to the Jewish Christians, but on the Pauline side an interpretation of Christianity and a

[1] *Die Apostelgeschichte nach ihrem Inhalt und Ursprung kritisch untersucht*, pp. 316 ff.

conception of the character and doctrine of Paul are promulgated of a sort to fit Paulinism for union with Jewish Christianity by the removal or concealment of its most offensive features. The work is the peace proposal of a Paulinist who wishes to purchase the recognition of Gentile Christianity from Jewish Christians by concessions to Judaism and in this sense desires to influence both parties." [1]

In addition to the author's main purpose of reconciling the Jewish Christian and Pauline parties, Zeller thinks he also desired to conciliate the Roman Government and prove the harmlessness of Christianity from a political point of view by showing that Paul was uniformly acquitted whenever he appeared before the Roman authorities.[2] This points to a time when the Roman Government was hostile to Christianity, say between 110 and 130, and suggests that the work was intended primarily for the Church at Rome, a suggestion confirmed by other arguments already urged by Schneckenburger.[3] The Acts, in fact, according to Zeller, represents Paul as the founder of the Roman Church and his work in Rome as the climax of his career.

Followers of the Tübingen critics.

Baur, Schwegler, and Zeller were followed more or less closely by Hausrath,[4] Samuel Davidson,[5] Hilgenfeld,[6] W. R. Cassels,[7] Scholten,[8] Holtzmann,[9] Havet,[10] Volkmar,[11] and many others.

[1] *Op. cit.* p. 363.
[2] Cf. Schneckenburger, p. 246. For an extreme statement of the theory that Acts was written chiefly or exclusively with a political apologetic purpose, see the articles by the Roman Catholic Aberle in the *Theologische Quartalschrift* for 1855, p. 173 ff., and 1863, p. 84 ff. According to Aberle, the book was written while Paul was still in prison and was intended for use at his trial. Cf. also B. Schäfer's " Studien zur Apostelgeschichte " in the same periodical, 1877, p. 281 ff., 377 ff. [3] Cf. also Frisch, *op. cit.* p. 55 ff.
[4] Cf. *Neutestamentliche Zeitgeschichte*, 1868, vol. iv. p. 236 ff.
[5] *An Introduction to the Study of the New Testament*, 1868, vol. ii. p. 275 ff.
[6] Cf. *Zeitschrift für wissenschaftliche Theologie*, 1871-1872, and *Einleitung in das Neue Testament*, 1875, p. 574 ff.
[7] *Supernatural Religion*, 1874, vol. iii. part 1.
[8] *Das paulinische Evangelium*, German translation from the Dutch, 1881, p. 254 ff.
[9] *Zeitschrift für wissenschaftliche Theologie*, 1882-1883. In his *Handkommentar zum Neuen Testament* (1889) Holtzmann's view is considerably modified. [10] *Le Christianisme et ses origines*, 1884, vol. iv. chap. 4.
[11] *Paulus von Damascus bis zum Galaterbrief*, 1887, p. 22 ff.

On the other hand, Wittichen[1] maintained that Acts was written by a Jewish Christian with the aim of defending the historic rights of Jewish Christianity in the face of the growing preponderance of Gentiles within the Church. " Thus the Third Gospel, together with the Acts of the Apostles, exhibits all the characteristic features of the Jewish Christianity which proceeded from the original apostles in the later phase of its development delineated above. It is distinguished, however, from the writings there described, as for instance from the Gospel of Matthew, by the fact that the Jewish type is even more marked in it than in them."[2] This view found, so far as I am aware, no acceptance.

Among those who supported the traditional position and defended the trustworthiness of Acts over against the Tübingen critics and their followers were Neander,[3] Lechler,[4] Thiersch,[5] Baumgarten,[6] Lange,[7] Lekebusch,[8] and many others. All of them maintained for the most part the traditional theory of Acts, including the authorship of Luke, and after considering in greater or less detail the arguments of the Tübingen School dismissed them as unsound. Lekebusch's discussion is the most careful and thorough of them all, and may be taken as the best and most moderate presentation of the conservative position. He devotes some two hundred pages, or nearly half his book, to the question of the purpose of Acts, summarising his conclusion in the following words : " The Acts is not a Tendenzschrift, either apologetic or conciliatory, still less Judaistic, but a purely historical work, as it claims to be and as, according to the admission even of the

Wittichen.

Upholders of traditional view.

---

[1] *Jahrbücher für deutsche Theologie*, 1866, " Über den historischen Charakter der synoptischen Evangelien," p. 427 ff.
[2] *Op. cit.* p. 480.
[3] *Geschichte der Pflanzung und Leitung der christlichen Kirche durch die Apostel*, fourth edition, 1847.
[4] *Das apostolische und das nachapostolische Zeitalter*, 1851.
[5] *Die Kirche im apostolischen Zeitalter*, 1852. Thiersch recognised the conciliatory aim of Acts, but denied that it had led to any distortion of the facts (p. 119 ff).
[6] *Die Apostelgeschichte, oder der Entwicklungsgang der Kirche von Jerusalem bis Rom*, 1852.   [7] *Das apostolische Zeitalter*, 1853.
[8] *Die Composition und Entstehung der Apostelgeschichte*, 1854.

newer criticism, it appears to be at first sight. It sets forth in unbroken continuity and from the Pauline, universalistic, in a word, Christian point of view, the gradual development of the Church from its rise in Jerusalem to the moment when the great apostle reached Rome, the metropolis of heathenism. The Acts is not a partisan document."[1] "We are not disposed to insist that every story and every reference in Acts is historical because it appears in a canonical book. On the contrary, we admit the perfect right of criticism to test without prejudice the trustworthiness of every item and to declare this or that, as the case may be, unhistorical or mythical. But we cherish the firm conviction that all the exceptions which might rightly be taken to the contents of the work are by no means serious enough to disprove the author's claim to have been a companion of Paul."[2]

Rejection of Tübingen view: (a) by Bruno Bauer;

The Tübingen theory of the purpose of Acts was rejected also on altogether different grounds by Bruno Bauer.[3] Bauer's critical work has been justly condemned because of its extremely subjective character and its sovereign disregard of historical facts, but his book on Acts, though it shares the faults of his other writings, and represents the Acts as a free composition quite devoid of any historical foundation, is very significant because it exposes the weakest point in the Tübingen theory, the notion that the conflict between Judaisers and Paulinists continued long after Paul's death and supplied the occasion for the composition of the Acts and other irenic writings. According to Bauer, at the time the Acts was written, the battle between Judaisers and Paulinists was over and the author knew nothing about it and had no understanding of it. In the days when the strife was still going on, a work like the Acts would have been quite impossible. "When the Acts was written," Bauer says, "the tension of parties had collapsed, the opposition was veiled,

---

[1] *Op. cit.* p. 374.   [2] *Op. cit.* p. 376.
[3] *Die Apostelgeschichte, eine Ausgleichung des Paulinismus und des Judenthums innerhalb der christlichen Kirche*, 1850.

the difference was obliterated and peace had already been concluded. The Acts is not a proposal of peace, but the expression and consummation of peace and toleration."[1]

Bauer's work is also significant because of its interpretation of Catholicism, not as a compromise between Jewish and Gentile Christianity, but as a development of the conservative and legal, or as he calls it, the Jewish spirit in the early Church. " The Acts first brought Judaism to recognition and control within the Church. It helped to fasten the chains that bound the Church to the Jewish world, and the Church clung to the Acts and recognised it as the canonical expression of its own consciousness because it wished this bond with Judaism and this Jewish marriage with the past and with heaven. The author of Acts gave to the Judaism which had neutralised the original differences and put an end to the conflict between them, form, flesh, and blood, and the confirmation of history. The Judaism which was represented in the Acts and was reconciled to Paulinism was naturally not historic Judaism. . . . Nor was it the Jewish Christianity about which recent scholars have so much to say. It did not oppose the freedom of the Gentile Christians, and had no thought of imposing upon them the yoke of the law. On the contrary, where the Judaism of which we are speaking prevailed, the freedom of Gentile Christians and the universality of the Church were taken for indisputable truth, and the earlier hostility between Gentile and Jewish Christians was vanishing. The Judaism of which we speak was rather a power that has asserted its supremacy, even though in changing forms, down to our own time. . . . We mean by Judaism the conservative, conciliatory, anti-revolutionary spirit which, at the same time, conserves the gains of the revolution, and we give it this name because it has received its classical expression in the Old Testament, in its inability to see historic differences, in the Jewish transformation of the historical product of a later time into a divinely given tradition, in brief in Jewish theism which condemns

[1] *Op. cit.* p. 121.

the historical creator to impotence and hands over to heaven the prerogative of revelation. Through the original heritage of the Old Testament received by the new community this Judaism retained its influence in the Church and won for itself a still larger territory." [1]

(b) by Renan.

The French scholar Renan, in his work on *The Apostles*, published in 1866, also rejected the Tübingen theory of the purpose of Acts. At the same time he recognised that the book was far from trustworthy, and that its author, though a companion of Paul, knew very little about the real facts of the period he was describing and wrote with a religious rather than a historical purpose. "The Acts, in a word, is a dogmatic history, written to support the orthodox doctrines of the time or to inculcate the ideas which most appealed to the piety of the author. Let us add that it could not have been otherwise. We know the origin of any religion from the accounts of its believers alone. It is only the sceptic who writes *ad narrandum*." [2] "One of the characteristics of Acts which proves that the author was less concerned to present the historic facts or to satisfy the demands of logic than to edify pious readers is this circumstance, that the question of admitting the uncircumcised is settled over and over again without ever being settled. First by the baptism of the eunuch of Candace, then by the baptism of the centurion Cornelius, both divinely commanded, then by the foundation of the Church at Antioch, then by the pretended council at Jerusalem; in spite of which, in the last pages of the book, the question remains still unsettled." [3]

Overbeck.

The theory of the purpose of Acts maintained by Baur, Schwegler, and Zeller was a part of the Tübingen School's general theory of the development of early Christianity. With the breakdown of the latter the interpretation of Acts as a document of the mediating party in the Church of the second century also broke down, and was ere long generally abandoned. Already

---

[1] *Op. cit.* p. 122 f. [2] *Les Apôtres*, p. xxix.
[3] *Ibid.* p. xxxviii.

in 1870, in the fourth edition of De Wette's *Acts*, Overbeck rejected the Tübingen view, and with the appearance of his commentary a new period opened in the criticism of Acts. Overbeck's work was far and away the most important discussion of the subject that had appeared since Zeller's, and it still remains in many respects the best commentary we have.[1] Overbeck was as drastic in his criticism as either Baur or Zeller, to both of whom he owed much, and he recognised as they did, that the purpose of Acts was apologetic rather than historical, but he interpreted its place and its significance in an entirely different way. It was not written, he maintained, to conciliate the Jewish Christians and promote harmony between the two wings of the Church. When it appeared there was no need of such an effort, for the conflict between Judaisers and Paulinists was altogether a thing of the past, and Gentile Christianity was alone in control.

" From this it is evident that the Acts cannot be understood as a document standing between the primitive Christian parties, original apostolic Jewish Christianity, and Pauline Gentile Christianity. Its Gentile Christianity, to be sure, is not that of Paul. But still less is its Judaism that of the original apostles and to be explained so far as it is Jewish from the desire to put itself at the view-point of the original and genuine Jewish Christianity. Rather the Jewish element in the Acts must have been already a component part of the Gentile Christianity which the book itself represents.

" The book is not to be interpreted as a proposal of peace between the primitive Christian parties, but the attempt of a Gentile Christianity already largely influenced by primitive Christian Judaism to explain its own past, particularly its own origin and its first founder Paul. It is true that Acts has abandoned the essential features of Paulinism with the single exception of universalism. But it has not done this as a

[1] An English translation of Overbeck's Introduction is given in the first volume of the English edition of Zeller's work mentioned on p. 374 above.

concession to a party outside its own circle, but because it shares the interpretation of Paul which, as a result of Judaistic influences at work from the beginning and of the natural inability of Gentile Christianity to comprehend and hold fast to the problems of the original Paulinism, spread among Gentile Christians and finally controlled the old Catholic Church as a whole."[1]

Overbeck recognised also the political motive already pointed out by Schneckenburger, Zeller, and others, and contended that because of it the Book of Acts concluded not with the death of Paul but with the kindly treatment accorded him and the large measure of freedom granted him during his two years in Rome.

Still further, Overbeck agreed with Baur, Schwegler, and Zeller in regarding the Acts as untrustworthy in considerable part. "An historical book which subjects its material to so artificial and arbitrary a scheme as the Acts and modifies it so strongly in the interest of its special aim and its subjective point of view, and which treats its sources so freely, is in general untrustworthy, and must prove its trustworthiness for each single case."[2] At the same time he judged it more favourably than the Tübingen critics, and explained its inaccuracies as due often to mere lack of knowledge rather than deliberate purpose.[3] The author wrote in the second century, so long after the events recorded, that he was largely ignorant of the situation and had lost all sense of the conflicts and controlling interests of the period which he was describing.[4]

Pfleiderer. With Overbeck's work may be compared Pfleiderer's book on

[1] *Op. cit.* p. xxxi f. It is interesting to compare this with the view of Bruno Bauer described on p. 378 ff. above.

[2] *Op. cit.* p. lix.

[3] Similarly Weizsäcker accounts for the frequent untrustworthiness of Acts partly by the author's purpose, partly by his lack of knowledge (*Das apostolische Zeitalter*, 1886, p. 206 ff.).

[4] Cf. Overbeck's article "Über das Verhältniss Justins des Märtyrers zur Apostelgeschichte," in the *Zeitschrift für wissenschaftliche Theologie*, 1872, p. 305 ff., for a further statement of his views concerning the place of Acts in the development of Gentile Christian thought.

Paulinism,[1] which is still more favourable to the Acts. "The analogy of the entire history of Paulinism speaks against rather than for the interpretation of Acts as a Tendenzschrift, which aims to purchase the recognition and friendship of the Jewish Christians by making concessions to them, and which sacrifices the historical Paul to this object. It is certainly much more likely that the author, speaking out of the consciousness of his own time, in which Paulinism was already a changed thing, interpreted the conditions of the apostolic age in good faith and understood and used his sources ingenuously on the assumption that the relation of Jewish and Gentile Christianity could not have been other in the days of primitive Christianity than it seemed in his own, a relation, namely, of mutual approximation and growing understanding and amity on the part of the saner elements in the two parties over against the extremists in both." [2]

As Holtzmann remarks, "Where, according to the Tübingen criticism, the author of Acts *would* not see, according to the newer interpretation, for the most part he *could* not see." [3] This marks the great difference between the critical school of the middle of the nineteenth century and that of a more recent day. While many of the detailed results reached by the earlier critics remain intact, their general attitude toward the Book of Acts has been almost universally abandoned.

Holtzmann.

In this connection mention may be made of the radical Dutch school of Loman and Van Manen.[4] They denied the genuineness of all the Pauline epistles and, while recognising the untrustworthiness of the Acts in many respects, they yet regarded it as a better source for a knowledge of the history of the primitive Church than the epistles from which the Tübingen critics had drawn their principal arguments against it. Van Manen gives a summary of his position in the article on Paul

Van Manen.

---

[1] *Paulinismus*, 1873. English translation in two volumes, 1877.
[2] *Op. cit.* p. 497.
[3] *Handkommentar zum Neuen Testament*, vol. i. p. 308.
[4] See Loman's "Quaestiones Paulinae" in the *Theologisch Tijdschrift*, 1882, 1883, 1886; Steck, *Der Galaterbrief*, 1888; Van Manen, *Paulus*, 1890.

in the *Encyclopaedia Biblica* (1902). "The book bears in part a legendary-historical, in part an edifying and apologetic character. The writer's intention is to instruct Theophilus concerning the old Christian past as that presented itself to his own mind after repeated examination, to increase the regard and affection of his readers for Christianity, and at the same time to set forth how from the first, although hated by the Jews, this religion met with encouragement on the part of the Romans.

"Of a 'tendency' in the strict sense of the word, as understood by the Tübingen School, there is nothing to be seen. The book does not aim at reconciliation of conflicting parties, Petrinists and Paulinists, nor yet at the exaltation of Paul or at casting his Jewish adversaries into the shade, or at placing him on a level with Peter." "The spirit in which Luke set about his work is that of budding Catholicism" (§ 37).

The prevailing state of critical opinion upon Acts in the last decade of the nineteenth century is well represented by Jülicher.[1] According to him Acts contains an ideal picture of the apostolic age, drawn in perfect good faith by a Christian who wished to show the power of God in the apostles, but who was too far from the period described to understand the situation fully and with sources too few and fragmentary to enable him to write a complete and satisfactory history. The book was written not as a defence of Paul and his apostleship, and not as the programme of a mediating party,[2] and the author's inaccuracies and misrepresentations, which have been attributed to set purpose, were due chiefly to ignorance. Acts contains both trustworthy and untrustworthy material, but only the speeches were the free invention of the author. "In the Acts the Gentile Church of the beginning of the second century has codified its best knowledge of the first period of its history."[3]

---

[1] *Einleitung in das Neue Testament*, 1894, p. 259 ff.
[2] "Paul is not Judaised and Peter Paulinised, but both are Lucanised, that is, Catholicised" (p. 263).
[3] *Op. cit.* p. 270. Cf. also Clemen, *Die Apostelgeschichte im Lichte der neueren text-, quellen- und historisch-kritischen Forschungen*, 1905, p. 35 ff., and Knopf in *Die Schriften des Neuen Testaments*, edited by J. Weiss and others, vol. i. p. 529.

HISTORICAL CRITICISM OF ACTS IN GERMANY 385

Up to this point only the history of opinion touching the purpose of Acts has been traced. To the investigation of this subject scholars were led by a desire to explain the book's many omissions, repetitions, and other peculiarities, but there were some who sought the explanation in the character of its sources. So far as I am aware, the first to suggest written sources for Acts was Bernhard Königsmann, who published in 1798 a dissertation on the subject.[1] Königsmann based his assumption of written sources on the prologue of the Third Gospel and on the diversity of style (*orationis varietas et inconstantia*) which marked the various parts of Acts. The author, he maintains, is to be distinguished from the writer of the 'we' passages, for, as shown by the prologue, he was not himself an eye-witness of the events he records and did not wish to be taken for such. Beyond this Königsmann did not attempt to determine the nature or extent of the sources of Acts. His theory that the author of Acts made use of written sources was accepted by Bolten,[2] Ziegler,[3] Heinrichs,[4] Bertholdt,[5] Kuinoel,[6] and others [7]; but the investigation of the question was first taken up seriously

Sources of Acts. Königsmann.

---

[1] *De fontibus commentariorum sacrorum qui Lucae nomen praeferunt deque eorum consilio et aetate*, Altonae, 1798. Reprinted in Pott's *Sylloge Commentationum Theologicarum*, vol. iii., 1802, pp. 215-239.

[2] In his *Geschichte der Apostel von Lukas übersetzt und mit Anmerkungen begleitet*, 1799, p. viii ff. Bolten thinks that Luke used an Aramaic source or sources.

[3] In an article, "Über den Zweck, die Quellen und die Interpolationen der Apostelgeschichte" in Gabler's *Neuestes Theologisches Journal*, vol. vii., 1801, p. 125 ff. Ziegler suggests the Acts of Peter, or the Preaching of Peter, and written accounts of the martyrdom of Stephen and the conversion of Paul as sources for the first part of Acts.

[4] In his *Acta Apostolorum*, i. p. 19 ff. (in Koppe's *Novum Testamentum Graece*, vol. iii., 1809), Heinrichs suggests the Acts of Peter and other possible documents as sources.

[5] In his *Einleitung in sämmtliche kanonische und apokryphische Schriften des Alten und Neuen Testaments*, Theil iii., 1813, p. 1331 ff.

[6] In his *Commentarius in libros Novi Testamenti historicos*, vol. iv., 1818, p. xii ff., Kuinoel by an error refers to Königsmann under the name of Kurzmann, and gives the date of his dissertation wrongly as 1794.

[7] Eichhorn discussed the question in his *Einleitung in das Neue Testament*, 1810, ii. § 149, but rejected the theory of written sources for Acts on the ground of unity of style and manner and uniformity in the use of the LXX.

by J. C. Riehm of Holland, who published in 1821 a book entitled *De fontibus actuum apostolicorum*, in which the subject was dealt with in considerable detail. According to Riehm in the second part of Acts the author made but a sparing use of written sources, being himself an eye-witness of many of the events and a personal friend of Paul and other actors in the history, but the first part of the book was largely based on written sources, many in number, and of a brief and fragmentary character.

Schleiermacher denies the author of the 'we' sections wrote Acts.

Riehm's identification of the author of the 'we' passages with the author of the book as a whole (the traditional position) was disputed by Schleiermacher in his lectures on New Testament Introduction, which were not published until 1845, long after his death, but influenced the course of New Testament criticism some time earlier.[1]

According to Schleiermacher, the author of the 'we' passages (probably Timothy) is to be distinguished from the author of Acts, who made use not only of the travel notes of Timothy but also of other sources in various parts of his book, as is made evident by the frequent repetitions, inconsistencies, and contradictions in his narrative.

Mayerhoff supports identity of authorship.

This opinion was controverted by Mayerhoff,[2] according to whom the identity of style between the 'we' passages and other parts of Acts, which he shows in detail, makes it necessary to assume identity of authorship. But instead of ascribing the work to Luke, Mayerhoff ascribed it, together with

[1] Already in 1817 Schleiermacher published the first volume of a work on the writings of Luke (*Über die Schriften des Lukas, ein kritischer Versuch*), dealing with the Third Gospel and its sources, but the volume on Acts never appeared. Schleiermacher lectured on New Testament Introduction first in 1829–1830, but he must have reached his view about the sources of Acts long before, probably as early as 1817, and it may have been due to his influence that his friend De Wette expressed the opinion that Acts was based in part upon written sources in his introduction to the New Testament, 1826, § 115. In § 113 De Wette says that the Acts may be regarded as "an attempt at a history of the Church which was imperfect and fragmentary, and remained unfinished for lack of information."

[2] *Historisch-critische Einleitung in die petrinischen Schriften; nebst einer Abhandlung über den Verfasser der Apostelgeschichte*, 1835.

the Third Gospel, to Timothy, to whom Schleiermacher had attributed the 'we' passages alone. This novel conclusion was disputed both by Bleek and Ulrich, the former in his review of Mayerhoff's work in the *Studien und Kritiken* for 1836, p. 1021 ff., the latter in an article in the same periodical for 1837, p. 369 ff., entitled "Kommt Lukas wirklich in der Apostelgeschichte vor?"[1]

Like Schleiermacher, Bleek distinguished between Timothy, the author of the 'we' passages, and Luke, the author of the book as a whole. Ulrich took the same position, referring to Schleiermacher's lectures of 1826 as furnishing the starting-point for his own discussion.

With this may be compared the theory of Gfrörer,[2] who made Luke the author of the 'we' passages, but the author of the book as a whole an anonymous writer of the latter part of the first century, an opinion which is still widespread.

The question of the sources was taken up in a still more thorough way by Eugen Schwanbeck, who published in 1847 a detailed study of the subject,[3] going beyond all his predecessors in his discrimination of documents. According to Schwanbeck the author of Acts made use of biographies of Peter and of Barnabas, a rhetorical account of the martyrdom of Stephen, and memoirs of Silas. These memoirs included the 'we' passages, and underlay the second half of the book from the beginning of chapter xv. to the close. At the end of his volume Schwanbeck printed the Greek text of the memoirs of Silas, the biography of Barnabas, and the account of Stephen's death.

Schwanbeck.

[1] Cf. also the same author's article, "Lukas kommt nicht in der Apostelgeschichte vor," in the *Studien und Kritiken*, 1840, p. 1003 ff.

[2] In *Die heilige Sage* (the second part of his *Geschichte des Urchristentums*, 1838), Abtheilung II. p. 245 ff. In I. pp. 383-452, Gfrörer discusses the composition of Acts at great length, concluding that the two parts of the book (i.-xii. and xiii.-xxviii.) come from different hands, and that the first part was largely legendary and its written sources few and fragmentary, while the second part was in the main trustworthy, being written by a companion of Paul and an eye-witness of many of the events recorded. The book of Acts as we have it was subsequently put together by an unknown author of the late first century.

[3] *Über die Quellen der Schriften des Lukas.*

Jacobsen. The discussion of the sources, generally neglected after Schwanbeck's work because of the growing absorption of scholars in the questions raised by the Tübingen School,[1] was taken up again in 1885 by Jacobsen,[2] and in the next ten years there appeared in rapid succession a number of studies of the subject,[3] which it is not necessary to discuss here, as they will be considered in the chapter on the sources.

Johannes Weiss. Ever since, all writers dealing with the Acts have felt themselves compelled to devote a considerable amount of attention to its sources. So much was made during these years of source criticism that the question as to the purpose of the Acts was pushed more or less into the background. From this neglect it was rescued by Johannes Weiss in his brilliant and illuminating book on the Acts,[4] the most important discussion of the purpose of Acts since Overbeck's. Rejecting the idea that Acts was written with either an historical or a religious purpose, Weiss maintained that its controlling aim was to set Christianity right with the Roman Government.[5] " I can understand

---

[1] The question was also discussed at some length by Zeller (*op. cit.* p. 489 ff.), but with mainly negative results. Probably the author had some written documents including the notes or journal of an eye-witness, very likely Luke, from which he took the ' we ' passages. At any rate his work contains many things unrelated to his purpose, or inconsistent with it, which he must have taken either from written sources or from tradition. At the same time the nature and extent of his sources it is impossible to determine. He evidently re-wrote freely, changed things to suit himself, composed speeches and invented situations as need required ; and that he allowed the pronoun ' we ' to stand in certain passages was due to his desire to be taken for the eye-witness whose notes he used. [2] *Die Quellen der Apostelgeschichte.*

[3] *E.g.* among others Wendt in Meyer's *Handbuch zur Apostelgeschichte*, sixth edition, 1888, p. 13 ff. ; Van Manen, " Paulus I." (*De Handelingen der Apostelen*), 1890, p. 58 ff. ; Sorof, *Die Entstehung der Apostelgeschichte*, 1890 ; Spitta, *Die Apostelgeschichte, ihre Quellen und deren geschichtlicher Wert*, 1891 ; Feine, *Eine vorkanonische Überlieferung des Lukas in Evangelium und Apostelgeschichte*, 1891 ; Clemen in his *Chronologie der paulinischen Briefe*, 1893, p. 58 ff. ; Jüngst, *Die Quellen der Apostelgeschichte*, 1895 ; Hilgenfeld, *Zeitschrift für wissenschaftliche Theologie*, 1895-96. Cf. also Krenkel's *Josephus und Lucas*, 1894, in which Luke's dependence on Josephus, both in the Third Gospel and in the Acts, is argued at length.

[4] *Über die Absicht und den literarischen Charakter der Apostelgeschichte*, 1897.

[5] Cf. pp. 177 ff. above. Among others who have seen in Acts a political apologetic purpose, are Weizsäcker, *Das apostolische Zeitalter*, 1886, p. 456 ff. ;

the Acts," he says, "only as an apology for the Christian religion addressed to the heathen and directed against the accusations of the Jews, which shows how it happened that Judaism had been supplanted in its world-mission by Christianity."[1] These accusations were two—that Christians were apostates from Judaism, and that Christianity was dangerous to the State. The author undertakes to meet them by giving an historical account of the way Christianity, though born in Judaism, broke loose from it and supplanted it in its mission to the Roman world. Instead of being apostates from Judaism Christians retained all that was good in the older system and represented the true Judaism which the Roman Government should take under its protection. "No Roman official should lend his support to the Jewish accusations. On the contrary, the State should give the new religion the protection afforded the old, whose place it has taken. To those circles among the Romans, on the other hand, which had hitherto been attracted to Judaism in the hope of finding salvation in it, there is now offered a new and more certain promise of salvation, the teaching, namely, of the resurrection of the dead, guaranteed in the person of the risen one."[2]

The author of Acts made large use of written sources, including the 'we' documents, and his account was often limited and determined thereby, and from them he frequently introduced matters because of their intrinsic interest which had no special bearing on his main thesis. He invented little, confining himself for the most part to the given facts, but interpreting them as a rule in the light of his own interest.

Weiss's is the last elaborate discussion of the purpose of Acts. More recently the question of date and authorship has been chiefly to the front. For this Harnack is in large part

Harnack.

Pfleiderer, *Das Urchristenthum*, 1887, p. 611 ff.; Ramsay, *Paul the Traveller and the Roman Citizen*, 1896, p. 305 ff.; McGiffert, *A History of Christianity in the Apostolic Age*, 1897, p. 345 ff.; and Knopf in *Die Schriften des Neuen Testaments*, edited by J. Weiss and others, vol. i., 1907, p. 530.

[1] *Op. cit.* p. 56.   [2] *Op. cit.* p. 59.

responsible. Practically all historical critics, including Harnack himself, long ago agreed that the traditional view that Acts was written by Luke, the companion of Paul, while the latter was still a prisoner at Rome, was unfounded. But the view has been revived by Harnack in a series of studies on the New Testament.[1]

Harnack gives his general opinion of the criticism of Acts in the following words: "No other New Testament book has had to suffer so much as the Acts, although in spite of its evident weaknesses it is in more than one respect the weightiest and best book in the New Testament. All the mistakes that have been made in New Testament criticism have come to a focus in the criticism of Acts. The book has had to suffer above all because Paul and Paulinism have been understood in a one-sided way and at the same time greatly overrated. It has had to suffer because an incorrect picture has been formed of the nature and relation of Jewish and Gentile Christianity. It has had to suffer because (extraordinary survival of an unjustifiable reverence for the apostolic!) the most extreme demands have been made upon a companion of Paul—a sure understanding of the apostle, congeniality, freedom from every independent tendency, absolute trustworthiness, and an infallible memory."[2]

Lukas der Arzt is devoted to proving that the Third Gospel and Acts were written by Luke, the beloved physician, to whom they are ascribed by tradition. With this in view Harnack gives a considerable part of the volume to a demonstration of the identity of the author of the 'we' sections with the author of the Acts as a whole. In support of it he urges sameness of interest, as for instance, their common interest in miracles and in the power and work of the Spirit, similarity in their

---

[1] *Beiträge zur Einleitung in das Neue Testament*; vol. i. *Lukas der Arzt, der Verfasser des dritten Evangeliums und der Apostelgeschichte*, 1906; vol. iii. *Die Apostelgeschichte*, 1908; vol. iv. *Neue Untersuchungen zur Apostelgeschichte*, 1911, all translated into English.

[2] *Lukas der Arzt*, p. 87.

portraits of Paul, and unity of style and vocabulary. The last point receives the greatest stress, and is regarded as in itself sufficient to prove identity of authorship. After a long discussion of the author's use of sources in other parts of Acts, Harnack concludes: "For the question of the 'we' passages nothing is to be gained from an investigation of the first half of Acts, for it leads at best to the assumption of one or more Aramaic sources. But that is quite irrelevant to the problem of the 'we' sections. As nobody could think of an Aramaic source in this connection, all the observations concerning vocabulary, style, and contents remain in force, and make wholly impossible the separation of the 'we' passages from the rest of the work."[1]

Why one may not think of an Aramaic 'we' document translated by the author, Harnack does not say. There would seem to be no adequate reason why there might not have been such a document, and on Harnack's own showing, if there were, his whole linguistic argument would break down.

Another matter to which considerable attention is given in this volume is the medical language of the author of the third gospel and Acts. Following the Englishman, Hobart, who published a very uncritical book upon the subject in 1882, Harnack goes over the matter afresh and in considerable detail, and concludes with the words: "The proofs are more than sufficient. In my opinion, there can be no doubt that the third gospel and the Acts were written by a physician."[2]

Medical language. Hobart.

Harnack's *Die Apostelgeschichte* has in general the same aim as *Lukas der Arzt*, to prove the Lucan authorship of Acts. It contains a careful study of the characteristics of the book and concludes that, in spite of its many inaccuracies and the author's frequent carelessness as an historian, it is on the whole a work of a very high character, and that there is nothing in it to disprove Lucan authorship, and much on the contrary to support

[1] *Op. cit.* p. 85.
[2] *Op. cit.* p. 137. Compare the strong language of Zahn to the same effect (*Einleitung in das Neue Testament*, vol. ii., 1899, p. 427).

it. The main purpose of the Acts, Harnack thinks, was to show the power of the Spirit as exhibited in the work of the Apostles and in the spread of Christianity. He concedes that the defence of Paul against Jewish accusations was a secondary aim, but denies that the author had any political apologetic motive, though he had admitted such a motive in *Lukas der Arzt* (p. 96).[1] He also thinks it probable that for the first half of his book the author had written sources, but not for the second half.

Harnack's last volume (*Neue Untersuchungen zur Apostelgeschichte*), continues the stylistic argument for the identity of the author of the 'we' passages with the author of Acts, defends Luke's picture of Paul's attitude toward Judaism as contrasted with that contained in Paul's own epistles, and then goes on to prove that Acts was written before the apostle's death while he was still a prisoner in Rome. The argument is brief and all too hasty. All the reasons for a post-Pauline date, some of which Harnack himself had reproduced in the earlier volumes, are dismissed without a word. In favour of the early date he urges the author's omission of a reference to Paul's death;[2] his silence concerning the destruction of Jerusalem and the events leading up to it; his failure to make use of Paul's Epistles; his quotation in xx. 25 of Paul's prophecy that the Ephesian elders would not see his face again (a prophecy falsified, according to Harnack, by Paul's journey to the East after his release from his first Roman imprisonment!); and, finally, a number of primitive traits exhibited in the Acts, in reference to which it may be said that, if they prove anything beyond the use of primitive sources, most of them prove too much, for they make the author of Acts more primitive than Paul, and hence, on Harnack's own principles, require a pre-Pauline date for the book.[3]

---

[1] Compare vol. iv. p. 18 note, where he says: "The long and in part identical speeches of the last quarter of the book must be due to some purpose of the author which we cannot satisfactorily fathom."

[2] Cf. vol. iv. p. 66 ff., with what he says on the other side in vol. iii. p. 48 ff.

[3] *E.g.* a, b, d, e, f, p. 72 ff.

The early date for Acts requires an early date for the Gospel of Luke and a still earlier date for Mark, and Harnack accordingly discusses the origin of these Gospels, reaching the conclusion with surprising ease, considering the general consensus of opinion to the contrary, that there is nothing to prevent the opinion that Luke was written in the early sixties and Mark in the fifties. In all this discussion of the date of Acts Harnack says nothing of the difficulties with which his view is beset because of the inaccuracies of the book and its lack of knowledge of many things one might expect a disciple of Paul to be familiar with. These difficulties, which make it impossible, according to most critics, to think the author a personal companion of Paul, are met in Harnack's first and second volumes by the retort that we must not expect too much of a disciple of Paul writing long after the events described (between 78 and 93, according to volume i. p. 18; about 80, according to volume ii. p. 108). But when the book is pushed back into the lifetime of Paul and is supposed to have been written while Luke was with him in Rome, the difficulties are multiplied many fold. Of this Harnack takes no account whatever, though it is really the crux of the whole situation.[1] It can hardly be imagined that Harnack's treatment of the subject can have any lasting effect upon the course of thought touching the date of the book of Acts and the Synoptic Gospels in spite of the great weight that inevitably attaches to his opinions.

Harnack's volumes have been hailed by many conservative scholars as a confession of defeat on the part of New Testament criticism and an evidence of the bankruptcy of the critical method. This, of course, they were not intended to be, and it must be recognised that in spite of his acceptance of traditional positions touching date and authorship and his rehabilitation of the trustworthiness of Acts at many points where its accuracy has been impugned by the unanimous voice of the critical school, he is yet far from according it his complete

Harnack's verdict as to Luke.

[1] As examples of Harnack's treatment of this matter, cf. pp. 21 ff., 23 ff., 28.

confidence. He ranks it as an historical source higher than many scholars would venture to do, but he is aware of its limitations and does not hesitate to question its facts. One who can speak of the author in the following terms is still far from sharing the traditional opinion touching the infallibility of his work: " Luke is an author who writes smoothly, but as soon as we examine him more closely we find him as a narrator more careless than almost any other New Testament writer. Like a genuine Greek, he pays close attention to his style and observes all the rules. He must be recognised in fact as a literary artist, but when it comes to content he proceeds where he was not himself an eye-witness, in a most negligent fashion, chapter after chapter, and often confuses things completely. This is true both of the Gospel and the Acts." [1]

Supporters and opponents of Harnack. Harnack's conclusions have naturally attracted wide attention. He has found supporters for the theses common to his first and second volumes in Ramsay,[2] Maurenbrecher,[3] and others, and for the early date of Acts in Koch[4] and most recently in Torrey.[5] On the other hand, many have expressed their sharp dissent, for instance, Schürer,[6] Hilgenfeld,[7] Jülicher,[8] Clemen,[9] Bousset,[10] Walter Bauer,[11] P. W. Schmidt,[12] Jean Réville,[13] Loisy,[14] Bacon,[15] and Maurice Jones,[16] who accepts the Lucan authorship but not the early date.

Few who did not already believe in the identity of the

[1] *Lukas der Arzt*, p. 80.
[2] *Expositor*, Dec. 1906 and Feb. 1907.
[3] *Von Jerusalem nach Rom*, 1910.
[4] *Die Abfassungszeit des lukanischen Geschichtswerkes*, 1911.
[5] *The Composition and Date of Acts*, Harvard Theological Studies, i., 1916.
[6] *Theologische Literaturzeitung*, 1906, No. 14 ; and 1908, No. 6.
[7] *Zeitschrift für wissenschaftliche Theologie*, 1906, p. 461 ff.; 1908, p. 176 ff.
[8] *Neue Linien in der Kritik der evangelischen Überlieferung*, 1906, p. 60 ff.
[9] *Theologische Rundschau*, 1907, p. 97 ff.
[10] *Ibid.* 1908, p. 185 ff.   [11] *Ibid.* 1911, p. 277 ff.
[12] *Die Apostelgeschichte bei De Wette-Overbeck und bei Adolf Harnack*, 1910.
[13] *Revue de l'histoire des religions*, 1907, vol. lv. p. 233 ff.
[14] *Revue d'histoire et de littérature religieuses*, 1910, p. 390 ff. ; 1911, p. 476 ff.
[15] *American Journal of Theology*, 1909, p. 59 ff.
[16] *Expositor*, Mar. 1914.

author of the "we" passages with the author of Acts have found Harnack's argument for it convincing, in spite of his proof of identity of style, nor has his attempted demonstration that the author was a physician been generally accepted. Clemen thinks that the evidence makes against rather than for the medical profession of the author. Wellhausen[1] remarks that if Luke is to be found in the 'we' passages of Acts xxvii. he appears to have been by profession a sailor rather than a physician, and Cadbury, in a careful study of the evidence, in his recent volume on *The Style and Literary Method of Luke*,[2] and G. F. Moore in a pungent note in the same volume,[3] seem finally to have demolished the medical argument altogether.[4]

Harnack's discussions have shown that critics are still far from a consensus of opinion touching Acts. In 1889 Holtzmann could say that an agreement seemed possible and imminent,[5] but Wellhausen's words, written in 1907, are nearer the truth—"There is still much to do in Acts."[6]

[1] *Nachrichten von der königlichen Gesellschaft der Wissenschaften zu Göttingen; Philologisch-historische Klasse*, 1907, p. 21.
[2] *Harvard Theological Studies*, vi., 1919.   [3] P. 51 ff.
[4] Cf. also P. W. Schmidt, *op. cit.* p. 9 ff.
[5] *Handcommentar*, vol. i. p. 309.   [6] *Op. cit.* p. 21.

II

BRITISH WORK ON THE ACTS[1]

By J. W. HUNKIN

IN this chapter it is proposed to give a short sketch of the British contribution to the general study of the period covered by the Acts of the Apostles.

It would be easy to amplify the sketch indefinitely along the lines suggested by the references which appear in the footnotes. Books which deal exclusively with textual criticism, and those which are specifically commentaries, are not treated here.

Pelagius. The first British writer, as far as we know, upon any subject whatsoever is Pelagius; and among the earliest of his works is a commentary on the Epistles of St. Paul, published at Rome about 410 A.D.

The Vulgate text of the epistles had been issued in 383–384 A.D. by St. Jerome, and Pelagius based his commentary upon this revised text.

The re-discovery of his work is a problem which has occupied the attention of scholars for some time past.[2] At length Dr. Souter has found in the Grand Ducal Library at Karlsruhe a ninth-century MS. (No. CXIX. of the Reichenau collection) which

---

[1] This chapter has been written along a line suggested by Dr. Foakes Jackson. The writer is greatly indebted to Professor Burkitt for criticism and help.

[2] The chief authorities are: S. Berger, *Hist. de la Vulgate* (Paris, 1893) and *Les Préfaces jointes aux livres de la Bible dans les MSS. de la Vulg.* (Paris, 1902); H. Zimmer, *Pelagius in Irland* (Berlin, 1901); and, latest and most important of all, A. Souter, "The Commentary of Pelagius on the Epistles of Paul: the Problem of its Restoration" (*Proc. Brit. Acad.*, 1905–1906), pp. 409 ff. Dr. Souter is undertaking an edition of the Commentary for the Cambridge Texts and Studies.

is a transcript of an original not later than the middle of the sixth, and probably of the fifth century, and appears to be, if not the sole surviving copy [1] of Pelagius's commentary in its original form, at any rate nearer to the original than any other. It is noteworthy that the commentary is anonymous (as Pelagius's work probably was from the very first), and that its scriptural text agrees closely with that of Codex Amiatinus of the Vulgate.[2] Pelagius's expositions are very brief, as St. Augustine said they were,[3] and most of the epistles are introduced by a short preface. In addition to these there is a general introduction to the epistles, which is also found and again attributed to Pelagius early in the ninth century in the Book of Armagh.

Pelagius's exposition is, as we should expect, above all things clear and logical. But his contribution to the serious study of St. Paul is of the slightest kind. In his general introduction he argues for the Pauline authorship of the Epistle to the Hebrews. That epistle makes, with the other epistles of St. Paul to churches, as distinct from individuals, ten epistles altogether: and this is as it should be, for under the old dispensation there were ten commandments. There are some who say that the epistle does not bear St. Paul's name, and that therefore it cannot be attributed to him. You might as well say, Pelagius replies, that as it bears no name it was written by no one![4] Oddly enough, however, no commentary by Pelagius on the Epistle to the Hebrews survives.

The next British scholar whose work in connection with the Acts calls for our attention is the Venerable Bede. In the list of his published works given at the end of his *Historia Ecclesiastica* we find the following items :

Bede.

(1) Extracts from St. Augustine on the Apostle (*i.e.* St. Paul).
(2) On the Acts, two books.
(3) A book on each of the General Epistles.

---

[1] As Dr. Souter at first seemed to think, but his opinion appears since to have undergone some modification.
[2] And more closely with this codex than with Codex Fuldensis.
[3] Aug. *De pecc. mer.* III. i. 1.
[4] The text of Pelagius's introduction is given in Zimmer, *op. cit.* p. 26.

(4) Chapters for readings in the New Testament (with the exception of the Gospels).

Of the first of these four works no genuine copy appears to be extant. The third [1] is chiefly remarkable for its general preface, now preserved only in the older manuscripts.[2] Bede argues that the first place among the apostles belongs to St. James and not to St. Peter.

The second of the above-mentioned works is of course the most important for our present purpose.

The first book [3] consists of a short commentary in which Bede relies a good deal upon St. Augustine and other Latin fathers, and to some extent makes use of the allegorical method of interpretation. He often quotes from the insipid verses of Arator who had done the Acts into Latin hexameters in two books about 542 A.D.

In the second book,[4] *Liber Retractationis*, or corrections, Bede becomes more critical and gives evidence of having made a careful study of a Greek MS., which indeed was none other than the Codex Laudianus (*Bodl. Laud.* 35), well known to modern textual critics as E^{Acts}.

There is little British work upon subjects connected with the Acts to be recorded for six hundred years after Bede's death.

In the first half of the thirteenth century Robert Grosseteste, equally great as bishop and scholar, is said to have written a short commentary upon the Epistles of St. Paul.[5] In the second half of the fourteenth century a powerful advocate of the studying of the Scriptures in general appeared in the person of John Wycliffe. He maintained that the knowledge of the Scriptures is

Wycliffe. the essence of all knowledge,[6] and in developing his own theory

---

[1] Migne, *Patrologia Latina*, 93, col. 9 f. Dr. Giles, *Bedae omnia opera*, vol. xii. pp. 157 f., in *Patres Ecclesiae Anglicanae*.

[2] *E.g.* B.N. 2366, C.V.L. Ll. 2. 7, Caius 347; see Giles's Preface to vol. xii., by which the statement in *Dict. Nat. Biog.* (Bede) should be corrected.

[3] Migne, *Patrologia*, 92, col. 937 ff.; Giles, *Bedae*, vol. xii.

[4] Migne, *Patrologia*, 92, col. 995 ff.; Giles, *op. cit.* xii. Bede's Commentary on St. Luke is given in Giles, *op. cit.* x. and xi.

[5] S. Pegge, *The Life of Robert Grosseteste* (1793), p. 275.

[6] *De civili dominio*, i. 44 (ed. R. L. Poole for the Wyclif Soc., 1885), p. 402.

of property he appealed especially to the example of the Church as recorded in the first chapters of the Acts. His favourite passage perhaps was Acts iv. (32-35) ending with the words, "And distribution was made unto every man according as he had need" (v. 35).[1]

The disciples were called *Christiani* and not *Jesuani* (Acts xi. 26), he says, "quia Christus est racione *unctus pre regibus et prophetis*, licet Messie authonomatice conveniat qui omnes unguit suos discipulos oleo gracie ut *habitantes fratres in unum* habeant omnia in communi, eciam pilos temporalium usque ad esibilia que sunt *barba* summi pontificis, ut dicitur Ps. cxxxii. 2. Jesu autem est proprium nomen abbatis nostri qui nos non salvat, nisi servemus religionem nostram." [2]

In another chapter in the same work he enumerates eight points in which the early Church is a model of true religion : [3]

1. Its members were all of one mind (Acts iv. 32). 2. They held no property singly. 3. They shared all with others. 4. They preached the Resurrection of Christ. 5. They acted up to their teaching. 6. All lived alike ; there were no rich and poor. 7. They sold their possessions and laid the money at the apostles' feet. 8. They divided to each as he had need.

Again he supports his contention that rulers are to be obeyed by the clergy by quoting Rom. xiii. 1, and reminding his readers of St. Paul's appeal to Caesar (Acts xxv. 10, 11) ; and he calls attention to the fact that it was not for himself but for the saints in Jerusalem that St. Paul collected money (Acts xx. 34 and Rom. xv. 1-3).[4]

But Wycliffe's chief contribution to the study of the New Testament is to be found in the interest he aroused through the translation of the Vulgate into English, which was undertaken by him and completed by his followers. This translation, although

---

[1] See *De civili dominio*, i. 14, p. 97 ; see also iii. 12 (ed. Loserth), p. 196.
[2] *De civili dominio*, iii. 2 (ed. Loserth), p. 15.
[3] *Op. cit.* iii. 6 (ed. Loserth), pp. 77 ff.
[4] *Op. cit.* iii. 9 (p. 143). In the Latin works in which Wycliffe expounds his communistic views we find frequent references to the writings of St. Luke (*e.g. op. cit.* ii. 14, 15).

THE HISTORY OF CRITICISM

it may have had little or no literary effect upon the subsequent translations of the sixteenth and seventeenth centuries, prepared the way for them by creating a demand for the Scriptures in the common language of the people.[1]

English versions.

The genealogy of the later translations of the New Testament in general and of the Acts in particular is indicated in the following table:

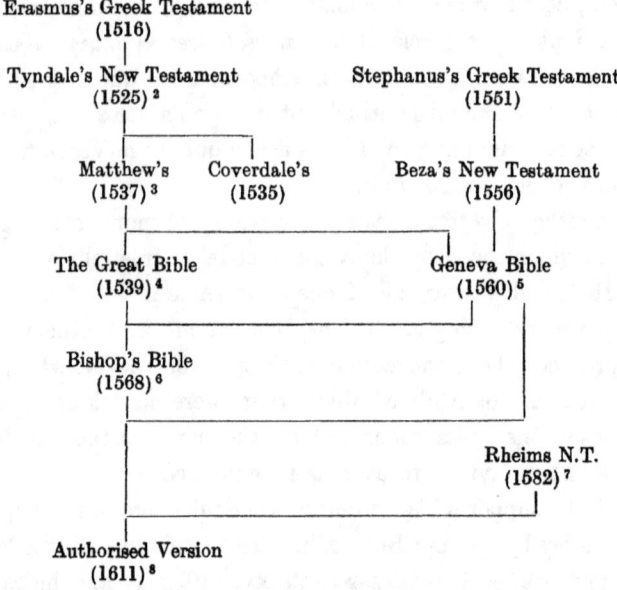

[1] On earlier English translation of parts of the Bible see the introduction to Miss A. C. Paues' edition of a *Fourteenth Century English Biblical Version* (1902). The Acts (i.-xxviii. 28, 30-31, *i.e.* with the omission of xxviii. 29) is contained in four MSS., of which the oldest is in the library of Corpus Christi College, Cambridge (Parker, 434), and the MS. which forms the basis of Miss Paues' edition is at Selwyn College (108, L.1). See also M. Deansley, *The Lollard Bible, and other Medieval Biblical Versions* (1920).

[2] Tyndale also used Erasmus's Latin translation of his text, the Vulgate, and Luther's German translation.

[3] Matthew's New Testament consisted of Tyndale's last revision (1535) which was without marginal notes (of his 1534 edition), but contained headings to the chapters in the Gospels and Acts (though not in the Epistles).

[4] The New Testament in the Great Bible is a revision, by Coverdale, of Matthew's. Coverdale's work shows the influence of the Vulgate and of Erasmus's Latin Version.

[5] The New Testament, 1557: in 1560 the whole Bible, including the N.T.

published in 1557 thoroughly revised. The N.T. had been largely the work of W. Whittingham formerly a Fellow of All Souls and Senior Student of Christ Church. Whittingham had based his text upon Tyndale, and a small translation committee corrected it with the assistance of the Latin translation and commentary of Beza (1556 and 1559).

[6] Another edition, 1569 and another 1572, all under Archbishop Parker's direction. The work is uneven, but is better in the New Testament than in the Old (*A General View of the History of the English Bible* by B. F. Westcott, 3rd ed., W. A. Wright, 1905, p. 231).

[7] Begun at Douai (1568) and finished at Rheims. The translation is made from the Vulgate, but it appears to contain traces of the influence of the Geneva version of 1560 (Westcott, *op. cit.* p. 245 *n.*).

[8] The work was based upon the edition of the Bishops' Bible published in 1602, but the revisers made considerable use both of the Genevan and of the Rhemish version.

It is to William Tyndale more than to any other single translator that the characteristics of the Authorised Version are due.[1] "It is of more cleaner English," said Friar Barons.[2] His translation was the result of a thorough study of the Greek text. The notes in the margin of his 1534 edition are not only homiletical, as *e.g.* Acts xiv. 23, " Prayer and fastynge go to gether"; but reveal a scholar's interest in the narrative itself. For example: Acts xii. 12, " This John is the same Marcke, that wryte the gospel of Marcke": Acts xix. 19, " These syluerlinges which we now and then call pence the Iues call sādes, ād are worth a. x. pēce sterlynge."

William Tyndale.

The Gospels and the Acts in this edition of 1534 were preceded by a table of contents, the items of which are transferred to the separate chapters in the edition of 1536, where the notes [3] are omitted.

[1] It has been calculated that 90 per cent of the words in the Authorised Version come from Tyndale's.

[2] Strype's *Ecclesiastical Memorials* i., App. No. xvii., quoted Westcott, *op. cit.* p. 37. Sir Thomas More's famous criticism of Tyndale's translation is found in his *Dyaloge* (1529). What Sir Thomas objects to more than anything else is Tyndale's substitution of seniours for priestes, congregacion for churche. love for charitye, favour for grace, repentance for penance, and so on (*Dyaloge*, iii. 8).

[3] The chapter headings in the A.V. are not identical with these, nor were they composed by the revision committee. They were apparently left to the various revisers of the various books (see art. by C. Kegan Paul in the *Theological Review*, 1869, p. 102).

Geneva Bible.

The next important advance after Tyndale's was made by the editors of the Geneva Bible (1557 and 1560). This Bible, a moderate quarto in size, printed in Roman letter, with verse divisions, short marginal notes, and maps and plans, was for three-quarters of a century the household Bible of the English people.[1]

Its editors made good use of Beza's Latin translation of the New Testament (1556 and 1559). In several instances, where the Geneva Bible is the first to give a correct translation of the Greek, its accuracy is due to Beza. An example [2] may be taken from Acts xxvii. 9, where Tyndale (followed by the Great Bible) had translated "because also that we (they, G.B.) had overlonge fasted"; and the right rendering, "because also the Fast was now passed," first appears in the Geneva version. This correction no doubt is due to Beza, whose translation reads "quod jam etiam jejunium praeteriisset," and who has a note as follows, "tempus designat Lucas ex more Judaici populi." The earlier translators had been led away by Erasmus, who defends his version in his commentary.[3] Similarly, in Acts xxvii. 13, the Geneva version gets its 'nearer,' instead of 'Asson,' from Beza, while the previous versions follow Erasmus in taking Asson as a place and not as an adverb. Here the Bishops' Bible failed to follow the Geneva correction.

On the other hand, in Acts xxvii. 17, where the older English versions, following Erasmus, rendered $\sigma\kappa\epsilon\hat{v}os$ by 'vessel' and Beza had the more correct translation 'sails,' the Geneva version agrees with the old English versions, and the first sign of Beza's correction appears in the note in the margin of the Bishops' Bible, "some read the sayles."

[1] H. W. Hoare estimates that 160 editions of it were published (*Nineteenth Century*, Ap. 1899).
[2] See Westcott, *op. cit.* p. 227. Westcott also quotes Acts xxiii. 27. Both these examples were originally given by Archbishop Trench (*On the Authorised Version*, p. 113 n.).
[3] *Annotationes*, 1522, p. 276. Wycliffe following the Vulgate had not fallen into this error,—"whanne seylyng thanne was not sikir for that fasting was passid."

BRITISH WORK ON THE ACTS 403

Other notes [1] originate as far as we know with the Geneva version itself. For instance, on Acts xxvii. 17, where its text reads "fearing lest they should have fallen into Syrtes," we find the following note, " ye goulfe Syrtes, which were certaine boyling sandes that swallowed up all that they caught." [2] This note reappears in the margin of the Rheims version in a shorter form —" a place of quicke sandes." Thence apparently it found its way in the A.V. into the text itself as ' quicksands.' [3]

The translators at Geneva had set an example in their committee for translation which was followed years afterwards in England. As a result of the Hampton Court Conference (1604) a large committee was appointed, and, divided into six groups, it worked steadily from 1607 to 1611. The four Gospels and the Acts were allotted to a group of Oxford scholars, of whom the most famous was Sir H. Savile, the Provost of Eton, the most learned classic in England in Elizabeth's reign.[4]

Authorised Version.

Basing their work upon the Bishops' Bible [5] they made full use of all the best preceding versions, both English and Continental, and specially of the Geneva version. It is also clear that they paid considerable attention to the Roman Catholic

---

[1] The headlines at the top of the pages of this version are sometimes very curious : e.g. above Acts xi. 15 ff., " Peter is purged " ; above Acts xii. 18-25, " The plague of tyrantes." But there is nothing in the Acts to come up to the heading of the page containing the account of the beheading of St. John the Baptist (Mk. vi.), " The inconuenience of daunoing." [Ed. of 1582.]

[2] Cf. the similar geographical note upon Salmone (Acts xxvii. 7)—" which was an high hil of Candie bowing to the seaward."

[3] It is a curious fact that Wycliffe's version here has "sondi places." The word Crete (Acts xxvii. 7) came into the A.V. in a somewhat similar way. The Geneva version, followed by the Bishops' Bible, had Candie with Creta in the margin ; in the Rheims version and the A.V. Crete is in the text.

[4] Hallam, *Lit. Hist. of Europe*, ii. 62. His is still the best complete edition of the works of St. Chrysostom.

[5] There seems to have been something lacking in the supervision of this Bible for publication. This fact is illustrated by the curious forms of some of the initial letters. The background of the first letter of the Epistle to the Hebrews is a picture of Leda and the Swan : that of the first letter of the Acts is a picture of Neptune driving in the sea.

version which had been issued from Rheims, and particularly in the matter of vocabulary.¹

It is unnecessary to dwell upon this noble version. Its defects, such as they are, in the Acts are due not so much to carelessness or inaccuracy of translation as to the deficiencies of the Greek text which was before the translators. Erasmus's text which they used had been based on poor MSS. at Basel.

Even from this slight sketch it will be seen that, starting with Erasmus, there had been a succession of students who had broken away from the scholastic tradition and had undertaken fresh studies of the text of the New Testament itself. The movement may indeed be traced back another twenty years to Michaelmas *John Colet.* 1496, when John Colet, having just returned to Oxford from Italy, delivered his famous course of lectures upon St. Paul's Epistles.

Colet began with the Epistle to the Romans and treated it as a whole, bringing out its connection with St. Paul's life and illustrating it by Suetonius's description of the contemporary state of society at Rome.²

Erasmus. A year or two later Erasmus attended some of these lectures when he was at Oxford, and came under the influence of Colet's strong personality. Colet urged him to devote himself to the study of the Scriptures,³ and after some delay, during which he was diligently improving his Greek, Erasmus at length issued his *Novum Instrumentum*, consisting of the Greek text of the New Testament and a Latin version of it, together with Annotations. In these Annotations Erasmus uses the critical method of exposition in much the same way as Colet had done.⁴ He uses it

¹ This is not specially noticeable in the Acts, but examples do occur, *e.g.* xxviii. 11 "sign" (A.V. and Rheims) where the Great Bible, Geneva, and the Bishops' Bible have "badge." For other books see Westcott, *op. cit.* pp. 253 ff., pp. 266 ff.

² A copy of Colet's exposition of this epistle is in Cambridge University Library, MS. Gg 4, 26. It seems to contain corrections in Colet's own handwriting (Seebohm, *The Oxford Reformers*, 3rd ed., 1887, p. 33 *n.*).

³ Seebohm, *op. cit.* p. 128.

⁴ Although in his conversations with Colet Erasmus had to a certain extent defended a manifold sense in Scripture (Seebohm, *op. cit.* p. 124).

cautiously, however, and takes shelter as far as possible behind the Fathers, and especially behind St. Jerome. For example, he points out that St. Jerome had observed the discrepancy between the account of Abraham's doings in St. Stephen's speech (Acts vii.) and the account in the book of Genesis, and simply adds, " Hunc nodum illic nectit Hieronymus nec eum dissolvit." [1]

Erasmus was by this time the writer most admired in Europe, and his publication exerted an immense influence. It may be regarded as the starting-point of modern scientific exegesis.

But we must return to England. The Reformers had appealed from the Church to the Bible, and the Bible came more and more to take the place of the books of the Schoolmen. " The New Testament was locked up again, after a preliminary glance, as an armoury of arguments for or against Protestant bodies." [2] Some of the controversialists were more judicious, some were less, in their use of this armoury. Most judicious of all is Richard Hooker. He instances the decree of Acts xv. 28 to illustrate the fact that laws properly divine may still be mutable,[3]—" this very law . . . is . . . abrogated by decease of the end for which it was given." He points to the case of Matthias (Acts i. 26) to show that the word bishop was not confined in the times of the Apostles to " oversight in respect of a particular Church and congregation. For, I beseech you, of what parish or particular congregation was Matthias bishop ? his office Scripture doth term episcopal." [4] And so on.

Richard Hooker.

A distinct advance had been made at any rate in two

The laity read the Bible.

---

[1] *Annotationes* (Acts vii.), p. 242. And see Seebohm, *op. cit.* pp. 331 f. for other examples. As Professor Burkitt points out (*Encycl. Brit.*, 11th ed., vol. iii. p. 886, Art. "Bible") Erasmus is careful to distinguish between his sources, *e.g.* with regard to St. Paul between (*a*) direct statements in the Acts, (*b*) inferences from the Pauline epistles, and (*c*) the statements of later writers like Dionysius of Corinth (quoted by Eusebius).

[2] Professor Burkitt in one of his lectures in Cambridge in 1910.

[3] *Laws of Ecclesiastical Polity*, III. x. 2 (1594).

[4] Book VII. xi. 3.

respects. In the first place, the laity had begun to be readers of the Bible. A practical man of affairs like William Bradford (1590-1657), the second governor of Plymouth, New England, went so far as to acquire some knowledge of Hebrew as well as Latin and Greek in order " to see with his own eyes the ancient oracles of God in their native beauty." And in the second place, the texts were taken according to their plain literal meaning, and not used as an allegory. This advance was maintained, and more attention paid to historical background, by the writers of the next (the seventeenth) century. Three names may be mentioned, all of them honoured by both sides in the long controversy between Puritan and Churchman, Roundhead and Cavalier. The first was the Roundhead, John Lightfoot, who under the Commonwealth was appointed Master of St. Catharine Hall in Cambridge (1650), and at the Restoration offered to resign, but was confirmed in his mastership by Shelden the Archbishop of Canterbury in recognition of his learning. He is chiefly remembered by his *Horae Hebraicae et Talmudicae*, of which one part deals with the Epistle to the Corinthians (Cambridge, 1664), and another, published posthumously by Richard Kidder in 1678, with the Acts of the Apostles and the Epistle to the Romans. Some years earlier, in 1645, Lightfoot had published a commentary upon the Acts of the Apostles, chapters i.-xii., in the introduction to which he explains that the Acts naturally falls into two sections, the first dealing with the Jews, the second with the Gentiles. His comments are useful and scholarly, and his chief contribution to New Testament study is the light that he throws upon Jewish customs and thought from the Rabbinical writings. "By constant reading of the rabbis," says Gibbon, "he became almost a rabbi himself."

A more popular figure was Henry Hammond, one of Charles I.'s chaplains. His life by Bishop Fell (1661) is one of the most charming of English biographies. During the Commonwealth he found an asylum with Sir John Pakington at Westwood, and there he wrote his *Paraphrase and Annotations upon all the Books of the New Testament* (fol. London, 1653).¹ It is sensibly written, and was much used. Hammond says he purposely abstains "from all doctrinal conclusions and deductions and definitions on one side, and from all Postillary observations, and accommodations, moral, or mystical anagogies on the other side." His plan rather was to weigh the context, to compare one Scripture with another, to study closely the original language and the meaning of Hebrew words as well as Greek, to take "notice of some customes among the Jewes, the Grecians, and Romans," and to add "sometimes the testimonies of the Antients when they appeared most usefull, and when my slender collections enabled me to annex them." In the margin he gives (a translation of) some of the variants from three Greek MSS., one of which is Codex Bezae,—"because this Kingdome of ours hath been enriched with some monuments of Antiquity in this kind, which were probably designed by God for more honourable uses than onely to be laid up in Archives, as dead bodies in vaults and charnel-houses, to converse with dust and worms and rottenness."

This type of scholarship reaches its height in John Pearson, LadyMargaret Professor at Cambridge, Master of Jesus, of Trinity, and finally Bishop of Chester. Pearson again was a royalist, but the Puritans had a great respect for him.² It was in 1659 that he published his great *Exposition of the Creed*. Two years later, when he became Professor at Cambridge, one of the courses of lectures which he delivered was upon the Acts of the Apostles. But his *Lectiones in Acta Apostolorum* were not published till after his death.³ They were accompanied by a short essay entitled "Annales Paulini." ⁴ Pearson makes good use of Roman

Bishop Pearson.

---

¹ Hearne tells us (*Diary*, Bliss, vol. i. p. 352) that he was the first man in England that had copy-money. "He was paid such a some of money (I know not how much) by Mr. Royston, the King's printer, for his Annotationes on the Testament."
² He was apparently the only Episcopalian at the Savoy Conference (1661) who impressed Baxter.
³ By Dodwell in 1688.
⁴ These are both translated from the Latin and edited by J. R. Crowfoot, Cambridge, 1851. The lectures are incomplete (Crowfoot, *op. cit.* p. 50 *n.*).

authors, of Josephus, and of the patristic writings.[1] But he does not allow his pages to be overburdened. One quotation will be sufficient to illustrate the care with which he consulted his authorities. "It may be collected," he says, "from Acts xi. 28, where the Cambridge MS. has 'While *we* were assembled together,' that Luke was before with Paul at Antioch, and had now come up with him at Troas."[2]

The rise of Deism. Thomas Hobbes.

But we are now at the dawn of a new era in the world of thought. In 1651, Thomas Hobbes, a friend of Galileo and Mersenne, published his *Leviathan*. The purpose of this brilliantly written book was to advocate the entire subordination of the ecclesiastical to the secular authority, but incidentally it contained[3] some acute criticism of the Old Testament. His attitude to the New Testament may be summed up in his own words: "At which time,[4] though ambition had so far prevailed on the great doctors of the Church, as no more to esteem Emperours, though Christian, for the Shepherds of the people, but for Sheep; and Emperours not Christian, for Wolves; and endeavoured to passe their Doctrine, not for Counsell, and Information, as Preachers; but for Laws, as absolute Governours; and thought such frauds as tended to make the people the more obedient to Christian Doctrine, to be pious; yet I am perswaded they did not therefore falsifie the Scriptures, though the copies of the Books of the New Testament were in the hands only of the Ecclesiasticks; because if they had an intention so to doe, they would surely have made them more favorable to their power over Christian Princes, and Civill Soveraignty, than they are."

Matthew Tindal.

The rise of Deism has begun. It reaches its summit in Matthew Tindal's *Christianity as Old as the Creation* (1730).

A few quotations will show the new attitude to the Bible: "In things tending to the Honour of God, and the Good of Mankind, the *dernier* Resort is to Reason; whose Dictates, as

---

[1] Cf. M. Poole's massive *Synopsis Criticorum* (1669–76).
[2] *Annals of S. Paul*, ed. Crowfoot, p. 93.   [3] Chapter xxxiii.
[4] *I.e.* at the time of the Council of Laodicea, A.D. 364, p. 281, ed. A. R. Waller (Cambridge, 1904).

they need no Miracles for their Support, so all Doctrines inconsistent with them, tho' they plead endless Miracles, must be look'd upon as diabolical Impostures." [1]

" Had there been but one Language, and a Book writ in that Language, in indelible characters (so that there cou'd be none of these thirty thousand various Readings, which are own'd to be crept into the New Testament) and all cou'd have access to it; yet even then, considering how uncertain the meaning of Words are, and the interest of designing Men to put a wrong sense on them; it must be morally impossible this Religion could long continue the same." [2]

In another passage Tindal quotes from Scripture (*e.g.* Gal. ii. 13, Acts xv. 39, and Rom. vii. 19, 23): " Do not these instances, tho' many more might be added, plainly show that inspir'd Persons, whether Prophets or Apostles, are subject to the same Passions, even to dissembling and lying, as other Men? And that we sin against that Reason, which was given us to distinguish between Good and Evil; Religion and Superstition; if we do not by it examine all Doctrines whatsoever, and by whomsoever deliver'd?" [3]

One more quotation will be sufficient: " And as to those Prophecies, if they may be so call'd, in the New Testament, relating to the *second Coming of Christ*, and *the End of the World*, the best Interpreters and Commentators own, the Apostles themselves were grossly mistaken; there scarce being an Epistle, but where they foretel that those Times they wrote in, were *Tempora novissima*." [4]

---

[1] Chap. xii., 3rd ed. (1732), p. 181. Tindal (p. 249) quotes with approval Nye's explanation of the sun standing still, Josh. x. 12, 13, viz. that the words come from a Poem, written by one Jasher, and are to be taken as " an elegant Fiction, and very proper in a Poem that was written on such an Occasion." Conyers Middleton, another of the Deists, left behind him at his death, 1750, a paper on miracles so heterodox that Bolingbroke advised that it should not be published (*Dict. Nat. Biography*, art. " Middleton," vol. xxxvii. p. 347).

[2] Chap. xiii. p. 260.

[3] *Op. cit.* p. 221.

[4] *Op. cit.* p. 233. And then Tindal refers to more than a dozen passages in the Epistles.

John Toland.

All this, it will be seen, involved a fresh study of the New Testament itself. Indeed some years previously (1696) Toland had contended that his thesis that Christianity was not mysterious but " intended a Rational and Intelligible Religion " was " prov'd from the Miracles, Method and Stile of the New Testament." [1] In his later paper, *Nazarenus* (1718), Toland lays down that " it will not be enough barely to quote our Gospels, Epistles, and the Acts of the Apostles, but their genuineness and integrity must be likewise establish'd by those arguments of which every good Christian may and ought to be appriz'd." [2]

Replies to Deism. John Locke.

Toland had claimed to base his general position upon a philosophy similar to that of John Locke, and Locke was not unnaturally annoyed at having his name bracketed with Toland's by Stillingfleet, Bishop of Worcester, and wrote three replies to the Bishop's charges (1696, 1697, and 1699). Locke had himself in 1695 published *The Reasonableness of Christianity as Delivered in the Scriptures*, which consisted of a careful study of the New Testament itself; [3] and before his death he had prepared a paraphrase and notes on the Epistles of St. Paul to the Galatians, Corinthians, Romans, Ephesians, " to which is prefixed an essay for the understanding of St. Paul's epistles by consulting St. Paul himself." [4]

[1] The heading of Section II. chapter iii. In Sect. III. chapter vi. he discusses the question, " When, why, and by whom were Mysteries brought into Christianity ? " and concludes (§ 91) that " Mystery prevail'd very little in the first Hundred or Century of Years after Christ; but in the second and third it began to establish it self by Ceremonies."

[2] *Nazarenus*, chapter xx. In this paper Toland lays stress on the differences between St. Paul and the other Apostles (especially St. Peter and St. James). See chapters viii. ff.

[3] One of the most striking passages in this book is that (10th ed. vol. vii. pp. 140 f.) in which he shows : " Though yet, if any one should think, that out of the sayings of the wise heathens before our Saviour's time, there might be a collection made of all those rules of morality, which are to be found in the Christian religion ; yet this would not at all hinder, but that the world, nevertheless, stood as much in need of our Saviour, and the morality delivered by him."

[4] In this masterly essay he complains of the chopping and mincing of the text into chapters and verses (Locke, *Works*, 10th ed., vol. viii. p. vii) and maintains that the epistles must be read as wholes. He also contends that " he

The greatest classic of the age, Richard Bentley, also entered the lists, and his reply to Anthony Collins's [1] discourse of Freethinking is characteristic of his vast learning and ready wit. He has no difficulty in exposing the deficiencies of Collins's scholarship and his remarks on Acts xix. 32, xx. 28, vii. 59,[2] xxvii. 14 [3] are good examples of his acute criticism.[4] The whole essay is written in the same spirit which prompted his famous note in the margin of his copy of John Malalas where the chronicler had made a gross blunder in geography: " Euge vero, ὦ 'Ιωαννίδιον " (" Good indeed, Johnny ").

Richard Bentley.

This sketch of the Deistic controversy will serve as an introduction to Paley's *Horae Paulinae* (1790). The purpose of this book was definitely apologetical, and it is, as it was intended to be, a companion to the author's still more famous *Evidences of Christianity*. The Deists had challenged the Church to an unprejudiced examination of the origins of Christianity and had even thrown out insinuations of imposture. The Boyle lecture had been founded in 1692 for the purpose of combating their allegations. One of the early lecturers on this foundation, R. Biscoe, had taken as his subject the Acts of the Apostles [5] (1736-

William Paley.

---

that would understand St. Paul right, must understand his terms in the sense he uses them, and not as they are appropriated by each man's particular philosophy to conceptions that never entered the mind of the apostle " (*Ibid.* p. xxi).

[1] Published 1713. In 1724 Collins published an examination of an essay by W. Whiston (now chiefly remembered as a translator of Josephus) on the fulfilment of the prophecies of the Old Testament in the New Testament, in which he showed that in many cases this fulfilment can only be maintained in the sense in which Whiston maintained it by giving an allegorical interpretation to the Old Testament passages. Whether intentionally or not, Collins made nonsense of the whole subject. Incidentally he threw out the brilliant conjecture that the book of Daniel was a forgery of the age of Antiochus Epiphanes. (See F. C. Conybeare, *The History of New Testament Criticism*, 1910, p. 47.)

[2] 8th ed., 1743, pp. 133 ff.   [3] *Ibid.* pp. 97 ff.

[4] Especially the last, a discussion of the relative value of the readings εὐροκλύδων and εὐρακύλων. We may notice also Bentley's remarks, p. 141, about the " postscripts " to 2 Tim. and Titus—"nobody yet either believ'd or affirm'd that these were underwritten by St. Paul himself. They are nothing but Memorandums or Endorsements written by others long after the death of the Apostle."

[5] 1736, the year in which Butler's *Analogy* was published.

1738). He had shown how various facts stated by St. Luke are confirmed by other writers such as Josephus, Philo, the Rabbis in the Talmud, Roman and Greek writers, and St. Paul in his epistles. Indeed Paley had behind him a century of controversy, and his *Evidences* are a compendium of the most striking arguments against the Deists [1] during that period as they had been absorbed by him in his reading. The *Horae Paulinae* is a much more original work, and illustrates not only the extraordinary clearness of the writer's style, but his great power of observation of details. If a few of his conclusions [2] have to be modified in the light of further research, Jowett's commendation is not undeserved. " The ingenuity of his arguments, the minuteness of the intimations discovered by him, the remoteness and complexity of his combinations leave the impression on the mind of absolute certainty in reference to the great Epistles to the Romans and Corinthians, and of high probability in reference to most of the others." [3]

Paley does not embark upon any criticism of the text itself except in his appendix, where he gives his reasons for rejecting the Euthalian colophons to Galatians, 1 Cor., 1 and 2 Thess., 1 Tim. and Titus: and all the Epistles and every part of the Acts were placed by him upon the same level of authenticity and genuineness.

At the opening of the nineteenth century, then, the New Testament had again been unlocked through the combined efforts of the Deists and their opponents. The Deists had suggested problems: through their lack of scholarship they could do little more.

Advance in textual criticism. The next advance took place in the field of textual criticism. As long ago as 1707, Dr. John Mill [4] had published a careful

---

[1] *E.g.* Paley's argument from the contempt, ridicule, and sufferings undergone by the early professors of Christianity is found in a shortened form on pp. 22 ff. of Biscoe's book (ed. 1742).

[2] *E.g.* with regard to 1 and 2 Thess. For other instances see Dean Howson's edition, 1877. [3] *Commentary* (see below), vol. i. p. 204.

[4] Dr. Mill continued the work of Bishop Fell, who in 1675 had published a collection of more than 100 MSS., one of which was the Codex of the Acts

collation of a number of MSS., but he had not ventured to intrude any of their readings into the received text itself. It was Karl Lachmann, the great authority on Lucretius, who in 1831 produced the first modern critical edition of the New Testament.

The first English scholar to avail himself of this work and to develop it was Henry Alford, the versatile [1] Dean of Canterbury. He began his monumental edition of the New Testament in Greek [2] while Vicar of Wymeswold in Leicestershire, and he struck a new line both by his good use of the researches of the best Continental scholars of his day,[3] and also by making his commentary philological rather than homiletical. Scholars were now beginning to have more help from works of reference such, for example, as Winer's *Grammatik des neutestamentlichen Sprachidioms*.[4]

<small>Henry Alford.</small>

The German writers to whom Alford is most indebted are those who, like de Wette, are typical of the exegesis of the period immediately before Baur.[5] Neander's *Geschichte der Pflanzung und Leitung der christlichen Kirche durch die Apostel* [6]; Wieseler, *Chronologie des apostolischen Zeitalters* [7]; and the commentaries of H. A. W. Meyer are other examples of the German writings used by Alford.

Alford also refers to the commentary of Professor B. Jowett upon St. Paul's Epistles to the Thessalonians, Galatians, and Romans [8]; who likewise acknowledges his indebtedness to some of these and other Continental scholars, notably to the Swiss

<small>Benjamin Jowett.</small>

---

mentioned above as used by Bede, which had recently been presented to the Bodleian Library by Archbishop Laud. It was Mill who first called attention to the connection between Codex E and Bede (*Prol.* p. clvii, col. 1).

[1] It will be remembered that he is the author of several popular hymns, *e.g.* "Come, ye thankful people, come," "Ten thousand times ten thousand."

[2] Four volumes, 1841–1861.

[3] He had spent three months in Bonn, 1847, in order to learn German.

[4] Published in 1821. The first edition of Liddell and Scott's *Greek Lexicon* appeared in 1843: the first edition of C. L. W. Grimm's in 1862–1868. Older works were Surenhusius's *Mischna* (1698–1703); Schoettgen's Rabbinical studies (1733–1742); Bingham's *Origenes Ecclesiasticae* (1708–1722); Mangey's *Philo* (1742); J. J. Wettstein's *Greek Test.* (1751–1752); Holmes and Parsons' *Septuagint* (1798–1827).

[5] A. Schweitzer, *Paul and his Interpreters*, p. 10 *n.*

[6] 1st ed., 1832–1833.   [7] 1848.   [8] 1st ed., 1855.

theologian Usteri, whose *Development of the Pauline System of Doctrine* may be regarded as one of the starting-points of the modern historical study of Paulinism,[1] and to Gfrörer, whom he follows very closely in his treatment of Philo.

Professor Jowett, as we should expect, deals with his subject in a forceful and independent manner. His excursus upon Philo is one of the first attempts in English to estimate the importance of this writer's works for the illustration of the philosophical atmosphere in which the New Testament writers lived, and of the language which they had in common. In another essay Jowett identifies the visit to Jerusalem mentioned in Gal. ii. with that described in Acts xv. and says that "it cannot be denied that these discrepancies are important."[2] At the same time he admits that "they are of a kind which would be likely to arise in two authorities so different," and he makes no attempt to overpress them. He rejects the identification of the Galatians with the barbarous people of Lycaonia.[3] He takes them rather to be Gauls, or at any rate the Phrygians or Greeks associated with them, and suggests that the fickleness of which the Apostle complains "may lead us to conjecture that he is addressing a people subject to violent religious impulses."[4] Bishop Lightfoot speaks of Jowett's work with respect,[5] and brackets with it that of Bishop Ellicott, whose commentaries on the epistles were the standard commentaries in English until Lightfoot's own appeared.

Bishop Ellicott.

Ellicott is a temperamental conservative: he does not approve of Jowett's work, clever as he acknowledges it to be; even Alford is a little too dependent upon the Germans. He himself uses German work, but very cautiously. We should not expect him to take much notice of Baur; Hilgenfeld he finds very useful in

---

[1] 1st ed., 1824. See Schweitzer, *op. cit.* p. 9 *n.*
[2] 2nd ed., vol. i. p. 308.
[3] *Ibid.* p. 237. A foretaste of the South Galatian hypothesis. The hypothesis was expounded a little later by Perrot (*De Galatia provincia Romana*, 1867, pp. 43 ff.).
[4] *Ibid.* p. 238.
[5] In his *Commentary on Galatians* (1865). He had subjected Jowett's commentaries to a searching examination in 1856 (see below).

historical questions, but the tone of his exegesis he thinks bad; while he finds that Fritzsche often treats the Greek Fathers with unjust levity. The chief merit of Ellicott's work is due to his "minute and careful scrutiny" of the Apostle's language, and his commentaries are to be classed with those of Christopher Wordsworth (1856–1860), Godet, the Swiss theologian (1879–1887), E. H. Gifford and T. S. Evans (in the *Speaker's Commentary*, 1881), as monuments of painstaking exegesis.

While all this exegetical work was going on there appeared side by side with it a series of studies illustrative of St. Paul's travels. The first of the series is the essay published in 1848 by a Fellow of the Royal Society, James Smith of Jordanhill, on "The Voyage and Shipwreck of St. Paul." Smith was an enthusiastic yachtsman as well as an eminent geologist, and his work is of permanent value as a demonstration that the twenty-seventh chapter of the Acts was written by an eye-witness and a landsman. He also proved conclusively that the scene of the shipwreck was St. Paul's Bay, Malta, and not the island of Meleda in the Adriatic as had been suggested by some. The acuteness of Smith's critical faculty was made still more evident by the publication in 1853 of his *Dissertation on the Origin and Connection of the Gospels*. He maintained that the correspondence between the synoptic gospels was too close for them to be in literary independence. He illustrated his contention by placing in parallel columns narratives of the same incidents in the Peninsular War written by Alison, Napier, and Suchet, and showed that there was no close verbal agreement between them except when one authority was using another, or two were using common sources. His conclusion was that St. Luke made use of the first and second gospels;[1] and although this particular result has since required modification, the acuteness of Smith's criticism will be recognised at once.

Illustrative studies.

James Smith of Jordanhill.

---

[1] Or rather of the original memoir written by St. Peter in Aramaic (of which the second gospel as we have it now is a translation by St. Mark) and of the Greek Gospel of St. Matthew. See especially pp. 261 ff., 302 ff.

T. Lewin.   The next illustrative work of this kind is found in T. Lewin's *Life and Epistles of St. Paul* (1851). Lewin was a barrister who had travelled a good deal in the Nearer East and made a study of St. Paul's life for upwards of forty years.[1] He paid special attention to chronology and finally published his results in *Fasti Sacri, or a Key to the Chronology of the New Testament* (1865).[2]

Conybeare and Howson.   There followed the similar and more famous work of Conybeare and Howson, *The Life and Epistles of St. Paul*, published first in parts and then completely in 1852.

A late Master of Trinity, after having heard Dean Howson preach a University sermon, is said to have remarked that he never knew till then what a very clever man the late Mr. Conybeare must have been. As a matter of fact, however, this is merely a *bon mot* of the kind familiar to those who knew the late Master, for the credit of the book belongs principally to Howson.[3] It was he who contributed the geographical and historical sections which are its chief merit. Conybeare's work was less important and the translations for which he was responsible were the "least happily executed portion"[4] of the book. Howson continued his work on St. Paul in several other publications, as, for example, his Bohlen lectures on the *Evidential Value of the Acts*, delivered at Philadelphia in 1880. In the same succession and of a still more popular character are A. P. Stanley's *The Epistles of St. Paul to the Corinthians*,[5] a work lively and picturesque rather than scholarly or accurate; and the voluminous writings of F. W.

---

[1] His second edition, 1874, contains above 370 engravings—views of places, maps, plans, and coins—many of them sketches of his own.

[2] A work still found to be very useful on account of its array of collateral evidence by a modern writer like Dr. D. Smith, *Life and Letters of St. Paul*, 1919, p. xi.

[3] Howson, moreover, is said (*Dict. Nat. Biogr.*) to have been an interesting preacher.

[4] Bp. Ellicott. *The Life and Epistles of St. Paul* not only had a large circulation but was widely used in such works as *The Footsteps of St. Paul*, by the author of *The Morning and Night Watches*, written (1855) for youths ("say from ten to seventeen years of age . . . to attract them to a more careful and devout study of the Word of God").

[5] Published in 1855, while Stanley was a Canon of Canterbury.

Farrar. Farrar had made his reputation while Headmaster of Marlborough by his *Life of Christ*, twelve editions of which were exhausted in a single year.[1] Popular and uncritical though this book was it was founded on a wide if old-fashioned scholarship. Farrar followed it up with the *Life and Work of St. Paul*, published in 1879,[2] the ablest and most thorough of all his works. Three years later a third work appeared on *The Early Days of Christianity*.[3]

F. W. Farrar.

Such was the general character of English work about the 'sixties; painstaking exegesis, and illustration by means of travel and a certain amount of archaeology. Meanwhile in Germany renewed interest in Pauline study had been awakened by the startling suggestions of F. C. Baur, which involved the authenticity of a number of the books of the New Testament. Many years before an English divine of the name of Evanson had written a book[4] in which, after accusing the four gospels of gross irreconcilable contradictions, he denied the authenticity of the Epistles to the Romans, Ephesians, and Colossians, and left those to Titus, Philippians, and Philemon doubtful. The Epistle to the Romans he rejected, because he argued from the Acts that "when St. Paul arrived at Rome, for the first time, in the reign of Nero, there was no Christian Church there, as indeed it is not at all probable there should have been. . . ."[5] In the Acts and in the third Gospel he had every confidence: "We have here, then," he says after reviewing and comparing the two works of St. Luke,[6] "every kind of evidence, whereof the nature of the case admits, to convince us of the genuine authenticity and veracity of both these histories; and with these, for my own part, I am

Evanson.

---

[1] And thirty editions were issued in the author's lifetime.

[2] 10th ed., 1904. A long review of the work appeared in the *Church Quarterly Review*, Jan. 1880, where it is objected that Farrar gives a clear and consistent conception of the *man* Paul rather than of the *Apostle* (p. 429).

[3] 1882. The work passed through five editions. Farrar then went on from the New Testament to the History of the Early Church in the first six centuries and published his *Lives of the Fathers: Church History in Biography*, in 1889.

[4] *The Dissonance of the four generally received Evangelists, and the Evidence of their respective authenticity examined* (1792).

[5] P. 258.   [6] Whom he identifies with Silas, p. 111.

abundantly satisfied." For him Prophecy "is by far the most satisfactory, and the only lasting, supernatural evidence of the truth of any Revelation."[1]

Evanson was evidently an acute observer if he was not a great scholar, but he scarcely had sufficient weight to compel the attention of his generation. He was, however, answered not only by a Bampton lecturer,[2] but by Joseph Priestley the scientist, who in his *Letters to a Young Man* (1792-1793) pointed out that "the books called the Gospels were not the cause, but the effect, of the belief of Christianity in the first ages. For Christianity had been propagated with great success long before those books were written; nor had the publication of them any particular effect in adding to the number of Christian converts. Christians received the books because they knew beforehand that the contents of them were true."[3]

F. C. Baur. But Baur was a man of great ability, already famous as a Pauline scholar. Like Strauss[4] he viewed history from the standpoint of a Hegelian philosopher. The early Catholic Church, according to his view, was the synthesis of the two rival forces of Jewish and Gentile Christianity, the first centring in St. Peter and the second in St. Paul. In St. Paul's genuine epistles, which for him were only those to the Galatians, Romans, and the two to the Corinthians, he detected distinct traces of the primitive antagonism. The rest of the epistles attributed to St. Paul, together with the Acts, Baur held to be the result of the effort in the second century to reconcile the two parties in order that the Church might present a united front to the Gnosticism which was then threatening its very existence.[5]

The book[6] in which Baur embodied these ideas was published in 1845, was written with great force and ability, and immediately

---

[1] P. 6.   [2] T. Falconer, 1810.
[3] See F. C. Conybeare, *op. cit.*, 1910, p. 95.
[4] D. F. Strauss, who had been a pupil of Baur's, had published his *Leben Jesu* in 1835-6.
[5] See J. A. M'Clymont, *New Testament Criticism*, p. 231.
[6] *Paulus der Apostel Jesu Christi*.

attracted the attention of the German theologians. The cleverness of his work was also recognised in England, but its importance was not generally realised until W. R. Cassels adopted Baur's dates for the books of the New Testament in two volumes entitled *Supernatural Religion, An Inquiry into the Reality of Divine Revelation*, which he published anonymously in 1874. To this book an answer at once appeared in a series of nine articles in the *Contemporary Review*,[1] by Bishop (then Professor) J. B. Lightfoot. They were followed later by another in the same journal [2] on "Discoveries Illustrating the Acts of the Apostles." Cassels, whose identity was entirely unknown to Lightfoot, replied in the *Fortnightly Review* [3] and elsewhere. Meanwhile his book had passed through six editions by 1875.[4] But the author, acute as he was, was no match for one of the greatest Biblical scholars of the time.

Supernatural Religion.

The best sketch of Lightfoot's life and work is that by F. J. A. Hort in the *Dictionary of National Biography*.[5] After being elected Fellow of Trinity in 1852, he lectured both on the Classics and upon the Greek Testament, and laid the foundations of his future work on St. Paul. He won his spurs as a Biblical critic by an article in the *Journal of Classical and Sacred Philology* for March 1856 [6] upon "Recent Editions of St. Paul's Epistles." The article is chiefly remarkable for its writer's faithful dealing with the recently published editions of St. Paul's Epistles by A. P. Stanley and B. Jowett. A. P. Stanley was convinced by Lightfoot's criticism that it was not his vocation to be a commentator upon the New Testament; he forthwith became a personal friend of his reviewer and produced commentaries no more. As against Jowett, Lightfoot maintained that though every allowance should be made for the difference between the Greek of the New Testament and Attic Greek, there was no sufficient reason "for

J. B. Lightfoot.

---

[1] Dec. 1874 to May 1877.   [2] May 1878.   [3] Jan. 1875.
[4] The only other English theological writer at this date who appears to follow Baur to any great extent is S. Davidson, whose *Introduction to the New Testament* in three volumes was first published in 1848–51.
[5] Vol. xxxiii.   [6] Vol. iii. pp. 81-121.

imputing a want of precision to Greek in this later stage "; [1] and further that there was no evidence that St. Paul's knowledge of the language was imperfect.

Lightfoot's commentaries. Lightfoot's own commentaries are accordingly based upon an exact investigation of the grammar and vocabulary of St. Paul. The first to be published was his commentary on the Epistle to the Galatians [2] (1865); the second, three years later (1868), was upon the Epistle to the Philippians; [3] the third in 1875 was upon the Epistles to the Colossians and to Philemon. These commentaries are strictly scientific in that they attempt to set forth the natural meaning of the original, verse by verse, without any ulterior polemical purpose; and it has been remarked by a very competent observer that the writer's judgment and scholarship show an ever-increasing maturity.

The first of the three works mentioned above contains the celebrated dissertations on "The Brethren of the Lord," and on "St. Paul and the Three"; the third, the exhaustive dissertation on the Essenes; the second, the most famous of all, on the Christian Ministry.

Lightfoot's answer to the Tübingen School. The dissertations appended to the Epistle to the Galatians contain Lightfoot's answer to the Tübingen School. By tracing, step by step, "the progressive history of the relations between the Jewish and Gentile converts in the early ages of the Church as gathered from the Apostolic writings, aided by such scanty information as can be got together from other sources," Lightfoot made use of the historical method of Baur with still greater effect. By a more thorough exegesis, and by a more faithful adherence to the actual sources, Lightfoot constructed a picture of the development of the early Church which was plainly more reliable than anything the Tübingen school had been able to produce.

It was the great merit of Lightfoot not to isolate the New Testament from the remaining documents of the early Church. Along with the New Testament he was studying Clement of

---

[1] *Op. cit.* p. 107.   [2] 10th ed., 1890.   [3] 9th ed., 1888.

Rome,[1] Ignatius,[2] Polycarp,[2] the early Roman succession of Bishops,[3] Hippolytus of Pontus,[3] Eusebius of Caesarea,[4] Roman Archaeology,[5] and Greek and Latin inscriptions of all kinds.

The result was that Lightfoot's work rested on a solid foundation and provided a firm basis upon which subsequent investigators could build.[6] A better illustration of the permanence of his achievements could scarcely be found than the third of the dissertations mentioned above, that on the development of the Christian ministry. Fifty years later, in the *Essays on the Early History of the Church and the Ministry*, edited by the late Professor Swete (1918), Lightfoot's account is reaffirmed.[7]

Another example of a different kind may be quoted from the edition of the Epistle to the Galatians. In the very difficult passage in the second chapter, verses 17, 18, and 19, Lightfoot's interpretation still holds the field.

The chief advances that have been made since Lightfoot's death have taken place along three main lines; the first in Archaeology, the second in Philology, the third in Comparative Religion. With the first, British students associate the name of Sir William Ramsay; with the second, Dr. Grenfell, Dr. Hunt, Professor Deissmann, and the late Professor Moulton; with the third Professor Kirsopp Lake and Professor Percy Gardner.

Advances since Lightfoot.

I. It will be convenient to consider the second of these departments first, because its effect upon the specific study of the Acts is the least. The discovery, the decipherment, and the interpretation of great numbers of papyri and ostraka dating from 300 B.C. to A.D. 300 hidden in various places in Egypt has thrown new light upon the Greek κοινή of the first century A.D., the

I. Philology.

---

[1] Of whose works he published an edition in 1869.   [2] Edited in 1885.
[3] Essays not issued till 1890 in the second edition of *Clement*, published posthumously.
[4] On whom he published an article in the *Dictionary of Christian Biography* (1880).
[5] Especially De Rossi's work on *Subterranean Rome*.
[6] Harnack in the *Theol. Literaturzg.* (June 14, 1890) spoke of Lightfoot's work as of imperishable value, and said that the considerations which he brings forward were never to be neglected.   [7] *Op. cit.* pp. xiii, 87 f.

language in which the New Testament was actually written. Lightfoot himself had almost anticipated this development. In a lecture as early as 1863 he had said with reference to a New Testament word which had its only classical authority in Herodotus, "You are not to suppose that the word had fallen out of use in the interval, only that it had not been used in the books which remain to us: probably it had been part of the common speech all along. I will go further, and say that if we could only recover letters that ordinary people wrote to each other without any thought of being literary, we should have the greatest possible help for the understanding of the language of the New Testament generally."[1] Among the pioneers in the work were Dr. Grenfell and Dr. Hunt, whose series begun in 1898 is happily still continuing.

Grenfell and Hunt.

Upon these and other similar discoveries, as well as upon a study of the ever-increasing number of Greek inscriptions, philologists like Dr. Moulton have been able to construct grammars and lexicons of Hellenistic Greek.[2]

J. H. Moulton.

From these it appears that the language had in some respects lost its old precision. Εἰς and ἐν are almost interchangeable; the optative has almost dropped out of use; verbs are compounded with various prepositions with little or no particular force; and so on. In spite of all subsequent additions to our knowledge, however, such studies as that of Lightfoot on the meaning of κρίνειν and its compounds,[3] based on a close examination of the actual usage of the New Testament writers, still retain their value.[4] On the other hand, one has only to read the

[1] Quoted from the lecture notes of the Rev. J. Pulliblank by Moulton, *Gramm. N.T. Greek*, vol. i. 2nd ed. p. 242 (additional notes).

[2] Part I. of vol. ii. of the late Professor Moulton's *Grammar* was published by his pupil W. F. Howard in 1919; *The Vocabulary of the Greek Testament*, compiled by J. H. Moulton and G. Milligan (1914), is still in the course of publication; A. T. Robertson's *Grammar of New Testament Greek in the Light of Historical Research* (3rd ed., 1919) runs to over 1500 pages.

[3] *On a Fresh Revision of the New Testament* (2nd ed., 1872), pp. 62 ff.

[4] A good introduction to the whole subject will be found in *Cambridge Biblical Essays* (1909), No. 14, "New Testament Greek in the Light of Modern Discovery," pp. 461-505.

translations of W. G. Rutherford to realise what a new light can be thrown upon the interpretation of the New Testament by a real familiarity with the κοινή (*Romans*, 1900; *Thessalonians and Corinthians*, 1908). St. Paul's language is "vigorous and effective but neither correct nor elegant."[1]

W. G. Rutherford.

II. Turning now to Archaeology we fall at once upon *The Historical Geography of Asia Minor*, published by Professor W. M. Ramsay the year after Lightfoot's death.[2] This was at once recognised both in England and on the Continent as a work of extraordinary importance. Mommsen himself explained its "ungewöhnliche Bedeutung" to the Archaeological Institute of Berlin.[3] Sanday declared that "Professor Ramsay's explorations in Asia Minor are among the three or four best things done by Englishmen in the field of scientific scholarship in this generation."[4] Certainly such an array of facts with regard to the historical geography of Asia Minor had never till then been displayed. Inscriptions, coins, ancient and modern literature of all kinds had been searched out and brought to light and laid under contribution in a thoroughly workmanlike manner. The result was a more exact delimitation of the Roman provinces,[5] a more complete definition of the network of roads, a surer identification of the ancient sites of Lystra[6] and Derbe[7] and other places than had ever been achieved by modern scholarship before.

II. Archaeology.

W. M. Ramsay.

Ramsay on Asia Minor.

It was in connection with his work upon Asia Minor that Professor Ramsay turned to the study of the Acts of the Apostles. He tells us[8] that he started with the confident assumption that the book was fabricated in the middle of the second century, and

Ramsay on the Acts.

---

[1] Dean Inge in *Outspoken Essays* (1919), pp. 220 f.   [2] 1890.
[3] *Beiblatt zum Jahrbuch des kaiserlich deutschen archäologischen Instituts*, 1891, p. 37.
[4] See *Expositor*, Series IV. No. 3, 1891, pp. 232 ff.
[5] Bingham in his *Origines Ecclesiasticae* (1708–1722) had studied the state and division of the Roman Empire with a view to its effect upon the organisation of the Church (ix. 1).
[6] At Khatyn Serai.   [7] At Zosta. See Sanday, *op. cit.* p. 240.
[8] *Pauline and other Studies in Early Christian History* (1906), p. 199.

that it was with a view to seeing what light it could throw on the state of Asia Minor at that period that he began to study it at all. He was, however, "gradually driven to the conclusion that it must have been written in the first century and with admirable knowledge." He began, therefore, to work at the second part of the Acts of the Apostles and at St. Paul's Epistles, and some years later he published the first of his studies in the life of St. Paul, *The Church in the Roman Empire before A.D. 170*,[1] followed two years later by *St. Paul the Traveller and the Roman Citizen*.[2] These books, written as they are in a popular style and containing several novel and interesting theories, were at once a great success.

In the first Ramsay pronounced the 'Travel Document' as unquestionably of the first century, but reserved his opinion as to the earlier chapters of the Acts; in the second he confidently ascribed the authorship of the whole book to St. Luke, the companion of St. Paul. Professor Ramsay's main thesis is that St. Paul wrote from the Roman standpoint, and like St. Luke dreamed of the subjugation of the Empire " by the new provincial power of life and truth, the vitalising influence first for the Roman state and later for the world." [3]

The South Galatian theory.

Lightfoot.

Some of Professor Ramsay's minor theories were based on facts already observed by Lightfoot, who had prepared for Smith's *Dictionary of the Bible* an article on the Acts which was not published till 1893.[4] Lightfoot, for instance, had pointed out that the writer of the Acts had close relations with Philippi: [5] Professor Ramsay opined that St. Luke himself was a native of the place. Again, to take a more famous and a more important case, Lightfoot had recognised that "Galatia, as a Roman province, would include, beside the country properly so called,

[1] London, 1893 (now in its 10th edition), of which Part I. is devoted to St. Paul's travels in Asia Minor.
[2] London, 1895 (now in its 14th edition).
[3] *Pauline and other Studies*, p. 200.
[4] Smith's *Dictionary of the Bible*, i. pp. 25-43.
[5] *Ibid.* i. p. 25.

Lycaonia, Isauria, the south-eastern district of Phrygia, and a portion of Pisidia. Lycaonia is especially mentioned as belonging to it, and there is evidence that the cities of Derbe and Lystra in particular were included within its boundaries."[1] But Lightfoot definitely rejected the view that the Galatian churches of the epistle comprise Derbe and Lystra, Iconium and the Pisidian Antioch, largely on the ground that in the Acts " Mysia, Phrygia, Pisidia are all 'geographical expressions' destitute of any political significance " ;[2] that " St. Luke distinctly calls Lystra and Derbe cities of Lycaonia, while he no less distinctly assigns Antioch to Pisidia ; a convincing proof that in the language of the day they were not regarded as Galatian towns " ; and that " the expression used in the Acts of St. Paul's visit to these parts " —the Phrygian and Galatian country—" shows that the district intended was not Lycaonia and Pisidia, but some region which might be said to belong either to Phrygia or Galatia, or the parts of each contiguous to the other."[3]

Ramsay, however, both here and still more fully in *A Historical Commentary on St. Paul's Epistle to the Galatians*,[4] insists that the Acts and the Epistles " plunge him into the movements and forces acting in Asia Minor during the first century when the Roman sphere of duty called Galatia was the great political fact,"[5] and when the most suitable if not the only title a writer could use to cover the inhabitants of all the four cities mentioned would have been ' Galatians.'

Ramsay.

The question can hardly yet be regarded as settled, although the ' South Galatian ' theory has found an increasing number of advocates during recent years.[6] Most if not all of the minor arguments in its favour may be countered without difficulty from the opposite side. The whole question is further involved in that of the relation between St. Paul's own account of his visits to Jerusalem in the second chapter of the Epistle to the Galatians

[1] *Galatians*, 10th ed. p. 7. [2] *Ibid.* p. 19. [3] *Ibid.* p. 20.
[4] London, 1899. [5] *Pauline Studies*, p. 200.
[6] A very convenient summary of the arguments on both sides is given by Moffatt, *Introduction to the Literature of the New Testament* (1911), pp. 90 ff.

and the narrative of the visits in the Acts. From the earliest times the later of the two visits recorded in the Epistle has been identified with the visit recorded in Acts xv.; and the discrepancies between the two accounts are no greater than might be expected if they are really independent.[1] But to this Professor Ramsay demurs. For he has become the champion of St. Luke's accuracy,[2] one might almost say of his immunity from mistakes. He is ready with all kinds of suggestions to defend him.[3] Many of these suggestions are fresh and striking, but some of them seem to rest on a rather slight foundation. Nor are we prepared to adventure with him when he stakes his whole argument on some particular interpretation of a phrase that plainly allows of a certain degree of indefiniteness. Dr. M. Jones [4] has called attention to an example of this procedure in the case of Professor Ramsay's determination of a fixed date in the life of St. Paul from Acts xx. 6.[5] Here the whole argument rests on the assumption that the sentence "And we sailed away from Philippi after the days of unleavened bread" can only mean that St. Paul started on his journey to Jerusalem on the very first morning after "the days of unleavened bread." St. Paul may very well have had to wait at least a day or two for a ship.

In adventures of this kind Sir William is hardly a safe guide. But when he keeps close to some clue which his wide research into the life of the Roman Empire has put into his hands, we could not wish for more skilful leadership. Reference may be made to the essay on the "Supposed Trial of St. Paul in Rome" contributed by Professor Ramsay to the *Expositor* in 1913 as an

Ramsay on St. Luke.

---

[1] This is in general the conclusion to which Lightfoot comes, *Galatians*, pp. 123 ff.

[2] See *The Bearing of Recent Discovery on the Trustworthiness of the New Testament* (1915), pp. 89, 96.

[3] Ingenious examples will be found in *Was Christ born at Bethlehem ?* (1898). It must be granted that Ramsay has shown that most of the case against St. Luke's accuracy in Lk. ii. 1-3 falls to the ground. The governorship of Quirinius is still a doubtful point (T. Nicklin, *Classical Review*, Dec. 1899, p. 460). Mommsen came to the conclusion that Quirinius governed Syria for the first time 3-2 B.C. (*Bearing of Recent Discovery on the Trustworthiness of the N.T.* p. 229).

[4] *Expositor*, 1919 (No. 17), p. 365.   [5] *Ibid.* Ser. V. No. 3, pp. 336 ff.

example,[1] an essay which sheds quite a fresh light upon the twenty-eighth chapter of the Acts.[2]

III. The third advance in the study of primitive Christianity has come from the field of comparative religion. The researches of classical archaeologists and anthropologists have been utilised by Professor Loisy, Professor Kirsopp Lake, and Professor Percy Gardner in painting a livelier picture of the religious milieu in which the infant Christian society found itself.[3] The best introduction to the subject is probably Professor Gardner's *The Religious Experience of St. Paul.*[4] For an account of the mystery religions themselves we still have to rely chiefly upon Continental writers. H. A. A. Kennedy's *St. Paul and the Mystery Religions* (1913) is useful until a more satisfactory account appears; but Dr. Kennedy puts the cards on the table in such a way that it is very difficult to see whether they are all there and still more difficult to pick out the aces. No English work on the subject has yet been published which is complete enough to be quite satisfactory. A *Zeitgeist* is an elusive thing, and is not likely to be caught at the first attempt. Great caution is needed, a caution not sufficiently exercised by pioneers like Reitzenstein;[5] and the clearing of the situation due to their not unnatural extravagances is one of the present tasks of New Testament scholarship.

III. Comparative Religion.

---

[1] *Expositor,* Ser. VIII. No. 5, pp. 264-284.

[2] Outside his own particular province Ramsay is sometimes a little careless; *e.g.* in *Luke the Physician,* p. 58, he quotes as an example of the changes in Mark's narrative which may be attributed to St. Luke's medical interest, Lk. viii. 55, in the following words : " 3. In Luke viii. 55 the physician mentions that Jairus's daughter called for food (cf. Mk. v. 42)." But it is not the daughter but our Lord who calls for food ; and the only difference here between the third gospel and the second is that in St. Luke the request for food follows immediately upon the healing, while in St. Mark it comes after the injunction to secrecy. St. Matthew (ix. 26) omits both. Even in connection with Asia Minor some loose writing will be found in *The Bearing of Recent Discovery on the Trustworthiness of the N.T., e.g.* pp. 193 ff.

[3] A suggestive and widely read book on this subject is Dr. T. R. Glover's *The Conflict of Religions in the Early Roman Empire*; 1909 (now in its eighth edition).

[4] London, 1911. See also *The Growth of Christianity,* 1907 (especially Lecture V.).

[5] *Poimandres* (1904) ; *Die hellenistischen Mysterienreligionen* (1910).

More recent publications.

Here it is only possible to glance at the chief publications which, appearing since 1890,[1] have made more or less use of the new material which has been produced. We may begin with the articles in Dictionaries. Lightfoot's article on the Acts in Smith's *Bible Dictionary* (1893), to which reference has already been made, found a not unworthy successor along the same lines in the article on the same subject which Professor A. C. Headlam contributed to Hastings's *Dictionary of the Bible* (1898).[2] A rival to it appeared in the next year (1899) in Schmiedel's article on the Acts in the *Encyclopaedia Biblica*. Schmiedel adopted to a great extent the position of the Tübingen School, a position which was becoming more and more untenable, as a reviewer of Schmiedel's article pointed out.[3]

The articles on St. Paul in the two Dictionaries present a similar contrast. That in Hastings's by Professor G. G. Findlay is a well-balanced and conservative summary of the Apostle's life and works; that in the *Encyclopaedia Biblica*, on the other hand, in so far as it is by Dr. Hatch, is scholarly and suggestive, but in so far as it is by Professor W. C. van Manen it follows the ultra-Tübingen School[4] on a wild-goose chase.

Chronology.

Another article of great importance for the study of the New Testament is Professor C. H. Turner's article on "Chronology" in Hastings's *Dictionary*. His masterly discussion of the available data leads to a system of chronology intermediate between that

[1] For a long list of older works on the Acts see C. Wordsworth's *Greek Test.* vol. i. part 2, pp. 32-34, (in the ed. of 1872).

[2] That is, three years after the publication of the well-known Commentary upon the Epistle to the Romans (in the International Critical Series), the joint work of Professor W. Sanday and Professor Headlam, and the most notable English commentary of the decade.

[3] In the *Church Quarterly Review*, 1901.

[4] The Dutch school to which van Manen belonged push Baur's theories to still more extravagant lengths. Oddly enough, they "stand Baur's theory on its head" (H. S. Nash, *The Hist. of the Higher Criticism*, 1900, p. 159) and use the Acts to prove that the Epistle to the Galatians is not genuine. Hilgenfeld, on the other hand, Baur's longest-lived disciple, reacts from his teacher's theories to a considerable extent and recognises the genuineness of 1 Thess., Philippians, and Philemon.

of Lightfoot on the one hand and Harnack on the other, and this system has been widely accepted in England as at any rate a provisional standard of dating. The only important addition to the evidence, a votive inscription found at Delphi and published in 1905 which throws light upon the date of Gallio's proconsulship, does not involve any alteration in Professor Turner's table of dates.[1]

The title *Horae Synopticae* (1899) does not suggest the Acts, but in his book Sir John Hawkins has tabulated linguistic facts which have been widely recognised as forming a valid basis for the thesis that the author of the 'we sections' of the Acts is the editor of the whole book.[2] This is by far the simplest and most natural explanation of the data presented by Sir John. It has been advocated with great force by Harnack, whose three books, *Luke the Physician*,[3] *The Acts of the Apostles*,[4] and *The Date of the Acts and Synoptic Gospels*,[5] are indispensable for the study of these works. In these three volumes Harnack's dating of the Acts becomes progressively earlier: in the first the date suggested is A.D. 80; in the second, 65; in the third, 62 at the latest.

Sir John Hawkins and Harnack.

The last date is that which is adopted in one of the three best commentaries in English upon the Acts, that of R. B. Rackham in the Westminster Series, published 1902. Of the other two, T. E. Page's was published long before Harnack's work appeared,[6] and suggests a date somewhat later than A.D. 70; and Professor Knowling's in the *Expositor's Greek Testament*[7] leaves the question open but apparently[8] inclines to agree with Harnack and Rackham. Dr. A. C. McGiffert of New York, formerly a pupil

Date.

---

[1] Professor Turner discusses this inscription in his inaugural lecture as Dean Ireland's Professor, *The Study of the New Testament, 1883 and 1920*, Oxford, 1920, pp. 15 f. The inscription survives only in fragments. The largest of them was published by A. Nikitsky in 1894–95, and was re-published together with three smaller fragments by E. Bourguet, *De rebus Delphicis*, 1905, pp. 63 f. See Deissmann, *St. Paul* (Eng. transl. Appendix I. pp. 235 ff.).

[2] *Op. cit.* 2nd ed. pp. 182 ff.   [3] English translation, 1907.
[4] English translation, 1909.   [5] English translation, 1911.
[6] 1886. It was reprinted nine times between 1886 and 1906.   [7] 1900.
[8] P. 35. Professor Salmon, the most accomplished all-round scholar of his day, took the same view (*Introduction to the N.T.*, 1885).

of Professor Harnack's, in his careful and independent study of the Apostolic Age decides that the indications point to the reign of Domitian as the time when the Acts was composed.[1] Professor Burkitt, on the other hand, agrees with Schmiedel in thinking that the author of the Acts used the *Antiquities* of Josephus,[2] and he therefore dates his work between A.D. 95 and 105.

Monographs.

Passing on now to useful monographs upon various points we shall find it impossible to do justice to them all. We can merely call attention to a few of the more influential.

St. Luke the physician.

As long ago as 1882[3] Hobart of Dublin published his researches on *The Medical Language of St. Luke*. On linguistic grounds he sought to prove "that the gospel according to St. Luke and the Acts of the Apostles were written by the same person, and that the writer was a medical man." It has been recently shown[4] by Professor H. J. Cadbury and Professor G. F. Moore that his argument from a comparison of St. Luke's vocabulary with that of Galen and other medical writers breaks down, although a large number of scholars, including such great names as Harnack and Zahn, had been considerably impressed by it. The early tradition, however, that St. Luke was a physician still remains, and some of the details observed by Hobart and others, *e.g.* in their comparisons of St. Luke's account with that of the other two synoptists, are still not without significance in connection with it.

The organisation of the early Church.

The subject of the organisation of the early Church has called

[1] *A History of Christianity in the Apostolic Age* (1897), pp. 437 f.

[2] See *The Gospel History and its Transmission* (1907), pp. 105 ff. Professor A. S. Peake apparently holds the same opinion (*A Critical Introduction to the New Testament*, 1909, pp. 133 ff.). For a statement of the case against St. Luke's use of Josephus, see *C.Q.R.*, April 1919, pp. 89 ff.

[3] Hobart was by no means the first to work along this line. James Smith, of Jordanhill, in his *Dissertation on the Gospels* notices details in St. Luke's account "which it was natural for a medical man to inquire into" (p. 269), and refers to an article by Walker in the *Gentleman's Magazine* of June 1841.

[4] *Harvard Studies*, vi. Part I., 1919. In Part II. (1920) Professor Cadbury goes on to a similar detailed study of St. Luke's treatment of his sources.

forth several interesting studies. We have Hatch's *Organisation of the Early Church* (1880), maintaining that the Bishop was connected more with administration than with worship;[1] followed by Gore's *Ministry of the Christian Church* (1888);[2] later by Hort's *Christian Ecclesia* (1897); later still by H. F. Hamilton's suggestive study in *The People of God* (1912); finally by the *Essays on the Early History of the Church and the Ministry*, edited by Dr. Swete (1918), which is likely to be the starting point of any further inquiries into the subject which may be made in England.

On the Jewish side of the early Church we have Hort's *Judaistic Christianity* (1894) and H. St. J. Thackeray's *Relation of St. Paul to Contemporary Jewish Thought* (1900).

With regard to the important literary question of the sources of the first part of the Acts we have Professor K. Lake's article in Hastings's *Dictionary of the Apostolic Church*,[3] which builds upon Professor Harnack's above-mentioned *Acts of the Apostles*; and we have also Professor Torrey's impressive attempt to prove that an Aramaic document[4] lies behind Acts i.-xv.;[5] but Professor Burkitt's trenchant criticisms in the *Journal of Theological Studies*[6] will probably restore most students to their former lack of conviction upon the subject.

The sources of the first part of Acts.

Professor Burkitt's work on the Western Text[7] and Dr. Rendel Harris's study of Codex Bezae[8] have an important

Miscellaneous works.

[1] The book gave considerable offence, *e.g.* to the reviewer in the *C.Q.R.* (July 1881, pp. 409 ff.), who felt that Hatch had done no more than discover "external connections which make the bishop an almoner, and the Eucharist a charity supper."

[2] Which was much more favourably received by the *C.Q.R.* (April 1889).

[3] 1916, vol. i. p. 23.

[4] Dr. J. H. Bernard once expressed his opinion with regard to the early chapters of the Acts, that "the hypothesis of an underlying Semitic document affords at once the readiest and the most complete explanation of the fact." (*St. Margaret's Lectures on the Criticism of the New Testament*, 1902, p. 227).

[5] C. C. Torrey, "The Composition and Date of Acts" (*Harvard Theological Studies*, i., 1916).

[6] *J.T.S.* vol. xx., 1918-1919, pp. 320-329. See also J. W. Falconer in the *Expositor*, 1920 (Series VIII. vol. xix. pp. 271 ff.).

[7] *Texts and Studies*, iv. 3.   [8] *Ibid.* ii. 1.

bearing on other problems [1] in the Acts beside the textual one, but we can do no more than name them here.

Bishop Chase's Hulsean lectures on *The Credibility of the Acts* (1902) may be mentioned for their convenient summary of fairly familiar evidence; Mr. C. W. Emmet's *Commentary upon the Epistle to the Galatians* (1912) for the freshness of its treatment of well-worn subjects; and Dr. R. St. J. Parry's edition of the *Pastoral Epistles* (1920) for its notable defence of their much-disputed authenticity. A regiment of worthy successors to Conybeare and Howson may serve to bring up the rear of this straggling review: first, Mr. Baring-Gould's *Study of St. Paul, his Character and Opinions* (1897), in which Mr. Baring-Gould appears to be a little perverse; next, Dr. B. W. Bacon's *Story of St. Paul* (1904), in which Dr. Bacon is very much on his guard against being deceived by the author of the Acts. We may then group together Mr. J. R. Cohu's *St. Paul in the Light of Modern Research* (1911); Dr. David Smith's *The Life and Letters of St. Paul* (1920), an attractive work in which the author shows that he keeps in close touch with the prevailing currents of the best accredited criticism; and Professor A. H. M'Neile's *St. Paul, his Life, Letters and Christian Doctrine* (1920). All three are eminently readable and may be recommended as useful introductions to the subject. Last of all, and in a class by itself, we may put the remarkable essay on St. Paul published by Dean Inge in his *Outspoken Essays*.[2] There has been nothing like it since Matthew Arnold's *St. Paul and Protestantism*.[3] As we read it we can scarcely fail to be struck with the advance that has been made since the days when Dean Farrar's *Life* was criticised as giving a picture of the man rather than of the apostle.

Looking back now over the two centuries which have elapsed since British scholarship began to learn from the Deists to treat the books of the Bible as books, we see that the knowledge of the period covered by the Acts has been pushed forward

---

[1] The most familiar example is that of the Apostolic Decree (Acts xv.). See (*e.g.*) C. H. Turner, *The Study of the New Testament, 1883 and 1920*, p. 30.
[2] 1919, pp. 205-229.   [3] 1870.

steadily if somewhat slowly. British scholarship has shown little tendency to originate startling hypotheses like those of Baur,[1] although it has generally learned something from them. It has rather devoted itself to the more concrete problems of textual criticism and archaeology, and its general temper has been conservative.

British scholarship conservative.

At the present time it is probably true to say that propositions such as the following would be accepted by the great majority of British scholars :

Results generally accepted.

(i.) That the Acts is a product not of the second century but of the first :

(ii.) That there is a very strong probability that the author of the 'we sections' is the author both of the Acts and of the third gospel :

(iii.) That he possesses a great deal of accurate information with regard to St. Paul's journeys, some of it being first-hand :

(iv.) That whatever be his sources for the early chapters of the Acts these "Scenes from Early Days"[2] are well chosen and consistent, and give a picture of the march of events which is at any rate, on the whole, correct in outline.

It is also widely recognised that further advance can only take place through close and exact study, not only of the Apostolic Church itself, but also of its milieu and of the Church of the succeeding age.[3] Such study makes ever-increasing demands upon the equipment of the scholar and can only be carried forward by the combined efforts of the whole company of faithful students throughout the world.

---

[1] Cf. the present attitude of caution with regard to the work of such scholars as Loisy, which nevertheless has already exerted a very considerable influence (see G. Tyrrel, *Christianity at the Cross Roads*, 1909, p. 44).

[2] The phrase is Professor Burkitt's.

[3] See Professor C. H. Turner's inaugural lecture as Dean Ireland's Professor of Exegesis in the University of Oxford (1920—already referred to above), especially pp. 8 and 20. It is very interesting to compare this lecture with that delivered by the late Dr. Sanday on his appointment to the same Professorship in 1883.

APPENDICES

APPENDIX A

TWO LITERARY ANALOGIES

THE preface has explained the purpose of this appendix, of which the first part is by Mr. G. G. Coulton, and the second by the Editors. It is intended to throw some light on two cognate problems of psychology. How far does tradition create, rather than commemorate, in its description of great personalities? How far can writers be trusted, even when they wish to be truthful in their treatment of non-literary sources? A book dealing with this subject by a specialist in psychology would greatly advance the understanding of history, and would render much ignorant criticism impossible. The examples of the Saint of Assisi or the Servant Maid of Suffolk may be taken as indications of what is needed in a more complete collection of narratives necessary to elucidate the problem of the way in which tradition almost unconsciously alters facts in the process of its development.

THE STORY OF ST. FRANCIS OF ASSISI

By G. G. Coulton

When Professor Barzellotti, in 1885, published his brief history of the movement connected with David Lazzaretti of Arcidosso, he called this book "a contribution to the embryology of religious phenomena." Early Franciscan history presents a far wider, and even more interesting, field for this study.

It is only in comparatively recent times that due importance has been given, by conservative students who are in no sense extremists, to the twenty or more years which elapsed between the death of Christ and the very earliest of existing records. Even those who have recognised the extreme probability of a considerable development during those years have often been too ready to assume that this movement had been all along in harmony with the course of later developments, so that the Christianity of Ignatius might safely be described as Primitive Christianity writ large. They have taken for granted a general unity of direction, and have unduly ignored the possibility that this blank in Christian history may conceal very considerable deflections from the original Christian orientation—nay, more, even the impossibility of its concealing an actual *volte-face*. Here it is that the analogy of Franciscan history is so valuable. In those records we can trace, first, how easily the written story of a whole generation might have perished, and, secondly, how grievously we should have erred, in that case, by inferring Francis's actual doctrines too confidently from the actual state of his Order a generation after his death.

The first of these points may be most clearly grasped, perhaps, if we marshal the earliest Christian records, and their Franciscan analogues, side by side. Amidst all our uncertainties as to the former, there is yet sufficient agreement on nearly all hands to render such a comparison possible and profitable; and it seems safest, as an automatic corrective of possible bias, to choose the dates given by Professor C. H. Turner in his article on "Chronology" in Hastings's *Dictionary of the Bible* and in his *Inaugural Lecture* (Oxford, 1921). The uncertainties of date, great as they are in many cases, will not render such a schematic representation entirely valueless, so long as we bear steadily in mind that its truth can only be approximative.

THE STORY OF ST. FRANCIS OF ASSISI

A.D.		Years from Death of Founder	A.D.	
				[St. F.'s own writings.]
				[1216–21. Jacques de Vitry, two letters and *Historia Occidentalis*.]
29.	*CRUCIFIXION.*	0	1226.	*DEATH OF ST. FRANCIS*, and CIRCULAR LETTER OF ELIAS.
				Gap of **2** *years.*
	Gap of **20** *years.*	2	1228–29.	CELANO, VITA PRIOR.
		4	1230.	Bull, " Quo Elongati."
				Gap of **14** *years.*
		18	[1244].	ROTULI LEONIS.
49	**Galatians** and other **Pauline Epistles;** also perhaps the PETRINE REMINISCENCES and Q (LOGIA).	20		*Gap of* **3** *years.*
to		21	1247.	CELANO, VITA SECUNDA.
64.				*Gap of* **8** *years.*
		29	[1255].	TRACTATUS DE MIRACULIS.
				Gap of **5** *years.*
		34	1260.	*DECREE OF UNIFORMITY.* (Narbonne.)
	Gap of **6** *years.*	35	1261.	BONAVENTURA, LEGENDA MAJOR.
				Gap of **5** *years.*
		40	1266.	*DECREE OF DESTRUCTION.*
70.	MARK.	41		
	Gap of **5** *years.*			*Gap of* **14** *years.*
75.	LUKE and ACTS.	46		
	Gap of **15** *years.*	54	[1280].	**Liber de Laudibus.**
90.	MATTHEW.	61		
	Gap of **10** *years.*			*Gap of* **38** *years.*
100 to 120.	**Most other books of the New Testament.**	71 to 91		
		92	1318.	SPECULUM PERFECTIONIS.
				Gap of **4** *years.*
		96	[1322–28].	**Fac Secundum Exemplar.**
				Gap of **4** *years.*
		100	[1326].	**Fioretti.**

Starting from this table, let us note the differences and analogies. (1) The first and greatest difference, that of the personalities of the two Founders, will be present to every reader's mind; it is

Differences and analogies: (1) personality.

indeed often pleaded as a bar to any serious comparison whatever. The present writer feels, on the contrary, that our only way of getting at the true Christ is to deal with him as the man; to recognise the actual recorded limitations of his knowledge, and therefore of his pre-knowledge; and to assume, in default of evidence to the contrary, that as Christianity was preached by human tongues, so also it was left to carry on by human methods its struggle for survival against other religions. On no other supposition can we account for what unfriendly critics call the present bankruptcy of Christianity —a bankruptcy which (if such indeed it be) the historian can trace almost from its earliest recorded history. On the other hand, to admit the claim for Francis as the most Christ-like man since Christ, is, in the judgment of the present writer, to emphasise the enormous gulf between the two persons.

(2) Franciscans not persecuted.

(2) The second difference, almost equally important from our present point of view, is that Francis never resisted unto blood; and that he and the vast majority of his disciples lived and died in favour with the Church of their birth. Not from any tinge of personal timidity, but from pure kindness of heart and sense of solidarity, he shrank from conflict with a hierarchy and a priesthood which needed reform quite as much as the Jewish Church needed it at the Christian era. We possess, therefore, an official biography written only a few months after his death by command of the Pope himself; indeed we can see much of his history through a succession of official documents which have no parallel in early Christian history until we come to the Pliny-Trajan correspondence of 112 A.D.

(3) Actual writings of Francis survive.

(3) Partly for this same reason, partly because those later times have drifted far more documentary wreckage down to us than has survived from an age twelve centuries farther removed from our own, we have actual writings of St. Francis, with such contemporary and subcontemporary descriptions of him and his Order as are almost altogether lacking for the study of Christian origins. These, in the foregoing conspectus, are printed in thick brackets [ ].

(4) Need felt of historical standardisation.

(4) These circumstances have to some extent directly affected the comparison which is our chief interest in this present essay. We are mainly concerned with studying, in the Franciscan legend, the natural action and reaction of centrifugal and centripetal forces. In the earlier days, literary individualism breeds frequent divergences, and even discrepancies, in the story. Then, by more or less conscious reaction, the organised society feels the necessity of historical standardisation. In proportion as the Founder's immediate personal influence is withdrawn, in proportion as his ideal becomes diluted by contamination with other ideals and practices, his official successors are compelled to supply that which is lacking in unity of the spirit by tightening the bonds of disciplinary

THE STORY OF ST. FRANCIS OF ASSISI 441

uniformity. We can find few better illustrations of this, in all religious history, than an anecdote of Francis himself which has been preserved by Wadding under the year 1258, but has received too little attention.

In that year died brother Stephen, who had lived with St. Francis, and cooked for him, in one of those little mountain hermitages to which he loved to retire in the later days of his life, and who solemnly deposed as follows before the Provincial Minister of Tuscany: "I, brother Stephen, dwelt for a few months in a certain hermitage with St. Francis and other brethren, to care for their beds and their kitchen; and this was our manner of life by command of the Founder. We spent the forenoon hours in prayer and silence, until the sound of a board [struck with a mallet, like a gong] called us to dinner. Now the Holy Master was wont to leave his cell about the third hour; and, if he saw no fire in the kitchen, he would go down into the garden and pluck a handful of herbs, which he brought home, saying, 'Cook these, and it will be well with the Brethren.' And whereas at times I was wont to set before him eggs and milk food which the faithful had sent us, with some sort of gravy-stew (*cum aliquo jusculento*), then he would eat cheerfully with the rest and say, 'Thou hast done too much, Brother; I will that thou prepare nought for the morrow, nor do aught in my kitchen.' So I, following his precepts absolutely, in all points, cared for nothing so much as to obey that most holy man; when, therefore, he came and saw the table laid with divers crusts of bread, he would begin to eat gaily thereof, but presently he would chide me that I brought no more, asking me why I had cooked nought, whereto I answered, 'For that thou, Father, badest me cook none.' But he would say, 'Dear son, discretion is a noble virtue, nor shouldst thou always fulfil all that thy superior biddeth thee, especially when he is troubled by any passion.'"

A story of the real Francis.

The very human interest of this story, and the very charm that it adds to the Saint's personality, makes us realise more fully the almost insoluble problem which he set to himself and his Order. Within the walls of that hermitage, or anywhere else where his immediate influence was felt, it was possible to live not only without thought for the morrow, but even without consistency from hour to hour; whithersoever the Saint's impulse led him, the rest followed without effort. But no Order could exist on such a basis; missionary success at one end involved, of necessity, some corresponding failure at the other end, and the mere multiplication of disciples compelled Franciscanism to become partly untrue to the original Francis.

A similar phenomenon is clearly traceable in the earlier Christian records; but we must expect to find peculiarities in Franciscanism corresponding to the differences detailed here above. The knowledge which official outsiders had of the Order would tend to retard Franciscan disintegration; Gregory IX., first as Cardinal-Protector and then as Pope, helped to fix certain points which remained stable amid many uncertainties. Far weaker, yet not altogether negligible, would be the influence of public opinion as shown by contemporary chroniclers. Roger of Wendover's description shows general outside ignorance on many important points; indeed, the friars themselves were very secretive in their dealings with outsiders.[1] The Rules of the Order and St. Francis's Testament (even after Gregory IX. had deprived this document of all legally binding force in his bull *Quo Elongati* of 1230[2]) supplied definite points which, however the friars might neglect them in practice or try to circumvent them in theory, had always to be reckoned with. Moreover, as will presently be seen, Church politics rendered it more important to keep dissidents within the Franciscan Order than to cast them forth as heretics. We must bear in mind, therefore, that the Franciscan historical tradition was, from the first, a rudimentary vertebrate. When, on the other hand, we turn to the Christian historical tradition, the evidence seems to point to an organism comparatively invertebrate at its birth and in its early stages. To adopt a slightly different metaphor, there were certain mechanical checks upon Franciscan variations which we cannot trace in early Christianity.

(5) Difference between the ideal and the actual.

(5) While this earlier vertebration of Franciscanism, if we may so term it, must certainly have worked to a considerable extent against change, yet it was far from preventing change altogether, even upon essential points. We have, therefore, in Franciscan history, a clearly traceable contrast between the ideal and the actual; between what the Order aimed at and what it actually became. It is here that the story is of such importance by reason of the analogies which it will suggest. Though we must beware of the easy *a priori* assumption that every stage of Franciscan evolution implies a similar stage in early Christianity, yet we may most legitimately infer that every such stage may possibly have had its primitive analogue; and we may scientifically exploit this possibility in all cases where it is not ruled out, or at least rendered highly improbable, by the difference of attendant circumstances in the two movements which we are comparing. When we see how flatly men argued, while claiming to be orthodox Franciscans, against certain doctrines of Francis, we may legitimately look very closely, at least, for the

[1] I have brought this out in *From St. Francis to Dante*, chap. xxv. (p. 319 of the first edition).

[2] The *Testament* is printed by Böhmer and translated in Fr. Cuthbert's *Life*; the bull *Quo Elongati* is printed in the appendix to Sabatier's *Spec. Perf.*

THE STORY OF ST. FRANCIS OF ASSISI 443

possibility of similar distortions of Christ's tenets by even the earliest Christians.

With this preface, let us now go through the Franciscan documents in such summary detail as our space will permit. In early Franciscan literary history, as in early Christian, many points are still doubtful. In those cases there is no room for discussion here; but enough references will be given to enable the reader to follow up all important debatable points.

Franciscan documents.

Francis's own writings are in harmony with the other evidence; but, by themselves, they would certainly not have enabled us to reconstruct his unique personality.[1] Much the same may be said of what we learn from Cardinal Jacques de Vitry and other contemporaries. Their testimony is of the utmost corroborative value; but, if Francis had quarrelled with the Church and had been extinguished as Peter Waldo was extinguished, we should have been left with almost as vague an impression of his personality. Elias's circular letter, on the other hand, is a document almost unique in earlier church history; it contains the description of a miracle (the Stigmata) by a person of high responsibility, written within a few hours of its actual observation, and under circumstances which might easily have provoked protest if the writer had indulged in glaring inaccuracies.

Francis's writings, &c.

Celano's *Vita Prior* is a work of very great value. Celano himself had not seen much of Francis personally; his rhetorical skill probably recommended him more than anything else for this particular task; and the papal choice would, of necessity, bring him implicitly under certain official restrictions. We must not exaggerate the contrast on this point between the first and second *Lives*, but it would be still more misleading to ignore it altogether.

Celano's Vita Prior.

Half a generation later, the officials of the Order felt the incompleteness of this first sketch. Great changes had taken place in the interval, with struggles comparable in bitterness and importance (though not in any other way analogous) to the struggle between Early Christianity and Gnosticism. The rule of Frate Elia, and the revolt by which his domination was overthrown, were not only symptoms, but also causes of considerable changes of direction. Those who had known Francis personally were fast dying off. Therefore the General Chapter of 1244, under Crescenzio da Jesi, appealed for fresh first-hand evidence, which was supplied mainly by three intimate companions of the Saint, Leo, Angelo, and Ruffino. From this material, with their approval, and from other sources also, a

The Three Companions.

---

[1] This is true, I think, even of the three *Rules*, the *Testament*, and the *Epistola ad quemdam Ministrum*. Moreover, it must be remembered that, if Francis had broken away from the Church, he would probably not have lived to write any of these, except, perhaps, the first Rule.

Vita Secunda was compiled by Celano, who had again been chosen as the official biographer.[1] Goetz is probably right in contending that this *Vita Secunda* marks far less of a conscious reaction against the tendencies of the *Vita Prior* than Sabatier had assumed, and that, in the main, it holds faithfully to its professed purpose of supplementing, not correcting, its predecessor. At the same time, even apart from the contributions by Leo and his companions, Celano's own share in this *Vita Secunda* shows a noticeable change of attitude towards Elias and his policy.

The Leo-papers. But the main historical interest centres now in the Leo-group; in the contributions of these early companions who had steadily resisted the de-Franciscanisation of the Order. Leo had come into collision with Elias soon after Francis's death, by protesting in word and deed against the collection of vast sums of money to build that magnificent convent and basilica which still commands the city of Assisi; Elias had caused him to be scourged and expelled from the city.[2] That Elias's hand lay heavy on all dissidents, we learn not only from Salimbene (pp. 104, 158), but from a letter quoted by Wadding (an. 1239), in which the General asks the Pope's approval for strong measures against those who resist him in the name of strict observance, "men who, on account of their discipleship and intimacy with our holy father Francis, are held in high esteem both within and without the Order." It is evident, therefore, that the testimony of this group must have a very special historical value. Let us begin by summing up what now seems practically certain with regard to these Leo-papers, as we may call them for brevity's sake.[3]

The writings thus furnished to the General Chapter were not all utilised by Celano.[4] The originals, in whole or in part, were kept for some time at the convent of San Damiano, where Clare and her nuns were friendly to the Spirituals. After a while, some at least

---

[1] This transpires from the following sources: *Leg. 3 Soc.*, Prefatory Epistle; 2 Celano, Preface and last chapter; Salimbene, p. 176; *Analecta Franciscana*, iii. p. 262. Even if we deny the authenticity of the Prefatory Epistle, for which I can see no valid reason, the other evidence is explicit enough on this point.

[2] Glassberger's Chronicle (*Ana. Frs.* ii. 45). Angelo Clareno, in his *Hist. Sept. Trib.*, tells us how St. Antony of Padua was scourged also, and Caesarius of Speyer, who had helped Francis to compose the Rule of 1221, was imprisoned and finally killed by the brutality of his gaoler. Tocco (p. 440) doubts the truth of this, but there is no great intrinsic improbability in the story.

[3] For the evidence as to these *Rotuli Leonis* (otherwise called *Cedulae, Dicta, Verba, Scripta Leonis*), see Goetz, pp. 151-57, and Little, *Guide*, pp. 17-21.

[4] Celano utilised a little more than half the material which was collected later into the *Speculum Perfectionis*. This latter compilation contains 124 chapters, of which 85 furnish the materials for 77 of the 167 chapters in the second part of the *Vita Secunda*.

THE STORY OF ST. FRANCIS OF ASSISI 445

of these notes came into the possession of Ubertino da Casale, the great Spiritual leader, who refers also to an autograph volume of Leo's writings in the friars' library at Assisi. These Leo-papers are appealed to, as against the growing relaxations of the Order, by a whole series of zealous friars, from Petrus Johannis Olivi in about 1280 to Alvarus Pelagius about 1330. In 1318, a Spiritual compiled from them a little book called *Speculum Perfectionis*.[1] This contains, with the seventy-five chapters utilised by Celano, thirty-nine more which Celano has neglected, but which are often of the highest importance. Goetz (p. 216), who goes as far as is reasonably possible in contradiction to Sabatier, decides that, of the one hundred and twenty-four chapters in the *Speculum*, ten can claim with reasonable certainty to be prior to Celano, five seem posterior, and "about fifty" cases must remain doubtful for lack of conclusive evidence. Minocchi reckons that eighty chapters of the book stand practically as they were written in 1246; and I cannot help thinking that later critics will agree more nearly with this conclusion. Many of Goetz's detailed arguments seem captious and unconvincing, and once at least his facts need correction;[2] I cannot help thinking that subsequent criticism will rate the priority of the *Speculum* considerably higher than he does. For the present, however, it is sufficient to point out that the *Speculum* contains a mass of first-hand evidence from some of the Saint's earliest companions, sometimes evidently retouched;[3] retouched also, perhaps, in other places where no evidence has survived to betray the alterations; but, on the whole, bringing us nearer to the real Francis than anything else written since his death.

The Speculum Perfectionis.

Side by side with the *Speculum* we must consider the so-called *Legend of the Three Companions*, around which controversy still rages. Earlier critics, including Sabatier, had taken it to be what its prefatory letter professes—a book composed by three of the Saint's earliest intimates, Leo, Angelo, and Ruffino, in 1246. But Fr. Van Ortroy, in *Analecta Bollandiana*, vol. xix. (1900), undertook to show that it is "une pièce apocryphe, dont les parties sont assez habilement agencées, mais qui n'a aucun rapport avec les premiers disciples de S. François" (p. 138). This thesis was combated by Sabatier in vol. 75 of the *Revue Historique* (1901); by Minocchi in *Archivio Storico Italiano*, fifth series, vols. xxiv. and xxvi. (1899 and 1900);[4] and by Tilemann in his

---

[1] Which Sabatier, misled by a false date in one of his MSS., attributed at first to 1227.

[2] P. 178, where his generalisations about the term *generalis minister* are contradicted by Francis's *Letter to the General Chapter* (Böhmer, pp. 61. 15, and 62. 3).

[3] *E.g.* it is difficult to explain the mistakes as to St. Francis's age and the year of his death in chap. cxxiv.

[4] He maintains the priority of *3 Soc.* to *2 Cel.*, and attributes *3 Soc.* to John of Ceperano.

Speculum Perfectionis u.s.w., especially pp. 109-119. The discussion is far too complicated for this place; here we can only note : (*a*) Even those who doubt the genuineness of the prefatory letter are unable to point out a motive for the forgery. Van Ortroy admits that the supposed forger " n'a pas l'air d'avoir agi dans un but polémique quelconque," and that we may possibly have here a genuine letter " qui se rattache à quelque document franciscain aujourd'hui perdu " (p. 120). (*b*) His elaborate parallel extracts from the *3 Socii*, side by side with 1 and 2 Celano, Julian of Speyer, Bonaventura, Bernard of Bessa, and others whom he supposes the " forger " to have pillaged, have given to others besides Sabatier the impression that this " forger " is really the prior author in most, if not all, these cases. On the other hand, (*c*) the warmest defenders of *3 Socii* are compelled to admit that the prefatory letter, promising a large number of new details and apologising for the want of sequence in this material, stands in flat contradiction to the rest of the book, which is more remarkable for consecutive order than for novelty. The truth may perhaps be found in a conclusion, borne out to some extent by Tilemann's arguments, that this prefatory letter of Leo and his friends was originally attached to the material contributed in answer to the appeal of 1244—in other words, to those papers which we now know mainly through 2 Celano and the *Speculum*. With regard to the body of *3 Socii*, I should venture to suggest that it may represent an earlier sketch begun by Leo immediately after St. Francis's death, and left incomplete because Celano's official life rendered it superfluous. Such a book might conceivably be referred to by the portion here italicised in Ubertino da Casale's assertion that all his own tenets could be proved to be those of the real Francis, since " omnia . . . patent per sua [Francisci] verba expressa, *quae per sanctum virum Leonem ejus socium tam de mandato sancti patris quam etiam de devotione predicti fratris* [*Leonis*] *fuerunt solemniter conscripta in libro qui habetur in armario fratrum de Assisio*, et in rotulis ejus, quas apud me habeo, manu ejusdem fratris Leonis conscriptis, in quibus optime beati Francisci intentio quoad paupertatem regulae declaratur contra omnes abusiones et transgressiones." [1] Such a book—kept in the official library at Assisi, and not only, like the other Leo-papers, preserved by such Spirituals as the nuns of St. Damian's or Ubertino himself—would naturally be exploited by all biographers, from Celano to Bernard of Bessa; and this would account for the apparent priority of the *3 Socii*: the compiler of this book, as we now have it, used the Leo-original more faithfully than Celano or the rest.

But our decision on this point need not greatly affect our parallel between the Franciscan and New Testament records. The acceptance of Van Ortroy's theory would only strengthen two of our main points—the ease with which these early records become contaminated and almost

---

[1] See Goetz, p. 155. Goetz convinces himself, like Van Ortroy, that the *3 Socii* forms of the stories are not prior but posterior; but he ignores the telltale differences of style, and his arguments are, to me, most unconvincing.

THE STORY OF ST. FRANCIS OF ASSISI 447

inextricably intermingled,[1] and the superior chances of survival enjoyed by documents in which the dominant majority recognises its own point of view. This will be most painfully apparent if we admit Van Ortroy's contentions to the full, and decide that there is nothing in the *3 Socii* or the *Speculum* which was not already in the official Celano, to whom, therefore, all other biographers go back, from Julian of Speyer to the author of the *Golden Legend*. " De quelque manière que l'on envisage la filiation des anciennes Vies de S. François d'Assise . . . c'est toujours à Celano que l'on aboutit, directement ou indirectement, comme au premier anneau de la chaîne. . . . L'influence si notoire et si profonde de Celano se manifeste pareillement dans le domaine liturgique " (pp. 136-7).

If all this be indeed true, then the Franciscan legend has been even more thoroughly "officialised" than we have judged it to be on other grounds. Such, in brief, is Franciscan literary history until 1260, thirty-four years after the Saint's death. In that year the General Chapter met at Narbonne, under the generalate of St. Bonaventura, who had been elected three years earlier. This election had great political significance; John of Parma, the previous General (1247-57), had strongly supported the Spiritual minority;[2] there had thus been a decade of great friction between these and the Conventuals, and St. Bonaventura had been chosen not only on account of his intellectual distinction, but even mainly, perhaps, as a moderate who would work hard to reconcile the two extremes.[3] The Chapter of 1260 recognised that the Spirituals found their strongest documentary support in the Leo-papers and the early biographies of St. Francis; therefore it decreed a standardisation of the legend in the interests of uniformity, which (it was hoped) might be also the interests of peace. It was decided " that the variety of many legends should be removed, and that he [Bonaventura] should compose a harmonious, weighty, and genuine history from those different fragments of histories which were current concerning St. Francis."[4] This was aimed not only at the more definitely spiritual

Official Life by St. Bonaventura.

---

[1] For this multiplicity of documents, in different combinations, see Van Ortroy, *l.c.* pp. 119-123; Little, *Guide*, pp. 15, 19-22; Fr. Cuthbert, *Life*, pp. 435-39; and the prefaces to Sabatier's editions of the *Speculum Perfectionis* and the *Actus*. Besides those mentioned in my text, the most important of these is the so-called *Anonymus Perusinus*, closely akin to the *3 Socii*.

[2] The Spirituals (or Zelanti) clung to the original simplicity of the Franciscan ideal, and, in their zeal, tended even to exaggerate this. They dwelt mainly in hermitages : hence the relaxed majority of the Order were termed Conventuals, in contradistinction to mere solitaries.

[3] He met with the usual fate of the moderates; Angelo Clareno (*A.L.K.G.* ii. 280) shows us that he is the unnamed villain of chapter xlviii. in the *Fioretti*; this was the light in which he appeared to the Spirituals.

[4] Wadding, an. 1260, § 18.

writings, but even at Celano, concerning whom Wadding has preserved a notice under the year 1256 (§ 4), that a good many friars were scandalised in these days at the public reading of his *Vita Secunda*. Bonaventura, thus commissioned, produced a *Legenda Major* and a *Legenda Minor*, both of which were submitted to the General Chapter of 1263, and formally approved. The next step was even more significant. The General Chapter of 1266 decreed the destruction of all the pre-Bonaventuran legends, even, so far as possible, all copies found outside the Franciscan Order.[1] It fortunately proved impossible to enforce this in all its strictness; yet the decree was so far successful that "it took just six hundred and thirty-two years to recover all the scattered fragments of Celano's legends of St. Francis,"[2] and that the Leo-papers survived only under protest, and in a disconnected fragmentary condition.[3]

Early friars, if of a literary turn, often made up little commonplace-books of their own.[4] It was natural that such collections should most frequently deal with the life and sayings of the Founder; again, the fullest and best-arranged of such collections would naturally be copied from pen to pen, until they sometimes rivalled even the official publications in popularity. They were anonymous, not only because nothing had any legal right to exist side by side with Bonaventura's two Legends, but also because nobody cared much who had compiled them; their aim was edificatory rather than historical in the modern sense. The same causes which conditioned their birth controlled their growth also; each possessor or transcriber dealt with them as he pleased, adding or omitting or altering according to his own taste. Thus, though the MSS. fall into definite groups,

[1] Van Ortroy has attempted to prove that this refers only to the liturgical legends; but this view is irreconcilable with the actual evidence, and is dismissed as untenable by such moderate conservatives as D'Alençon (Celano, Introd. p. xliii) and Father Cuthbert (*Life of St. F.* p. 430).

[2] Fr. Paschal Robinson, *Short Introduction*, p. 10. Cf. D'Alençon (Celano, Introd. p. xlv). Only twelve MSS. of the *Vita Prior* are known to have come down to modern times; of the *Vita Secunda* two only; of the *Tractatus miraculorum*, a single MS. The author of the *Golden Legend*, who wrote less than thirty years after 1266, did not know the *Vita Secunda*, nor did the author of the *Chron. xxiv. generalium*, writing two generations later. It is difficult to follow Father D'Alençon in his contention that the decree had not much to do with these disappearances.

[3] A similar policy was pursued with regard to the official records of the General Chapter; cf. Statutes of Narbonne (1260; *diffinitio 1*) and Father Ehrle's comments thereon (*A.L.K.G.* vi. pp. 11, 33). D'Alençon points out that the Dominican Order pursued a similar policy, though less brutally thorough, against unofficial lives of St. Dominic (*l.c.* p. xliii, n. 4).

[4] Cf. in quite a different style, the commonplace book of Fr. Giovanni da Camerino, published by Count Monaldo Leopardi in 1833, and MS. Harl. 913, apparently compiled by Fr. Michael of Kildare in the early fourteenth century.

THE STORY OF ST. FRANCIS OF ASSISI 449

they are often contaminated by other groups, and they have sometimes survived in a longer and a briefer redaction, of which it is not always easy to decide which comes nearer to the original.[1] Of these compilations the most important is the *Speculum Perfectionis*, which thus describes itself : " This work was compiled as a biography [*per modum legendae*] from certain ancient materials which the companions of St. Francis wrote and caused to be written in diverse places." [2] Without professing to reproduce the Leo-papers in their entirety, this compilation evidently represents the most complete surviving collection from those documents.

Next in importance I should reckon the *Legend of the Three Companions*, in spite of the adverse judgments of Fr. van Ortroy and Goetz. But, as explained above, there is so little agreement on this point, and the evidence which this book supplies, if genuine, is so nearly consonant with the rest, that we may leave it aside for the present.

With the *Liber de laudibus* we come again to a semi-official The *De* publication. Bonaventura died in 1274, and in 1277 the General *laudibus*. Chapter of Padua appealed for information supplementary to his two *Legendae*. Bernard of Bessa, who had been his secretary, was thus encouraged to write a new biography of St. Francis ; but this throws no fresh light on the Saint himself, and its main significance from our point of view is that its very inception, in connection with the General Chapter decree, testifies to the fact that the Order could not for ever content itself with the limitations which Bonaventura had tried to impose.

It is in this light, then, that we must consider the *Fioretti*, the The *Fioretti*. last, and in some ways the most remarkable phenomenon in early Franciscan literature. It is the least strictly historical, yet by no means the least Franciscan, of all these records. We have it only in an early Italian version ; its exact Latin original has not been found, but a derivative from that original survives in the compilation called *Actus S. Francisci et sociorum ejus*.[3] This forms part of a much larger and more miscellaneous collection called *Fac secundum*

---

[1] Compare the *Speculum Perfectionis*, as edited by Sabatier, with the Roman MS. published at a very low price at Quaracchi by Fr. Lemmens (*Documenta antiqua Franciscana*, i. and ii.). It is probable that this MS. represents " a series of extracts [from the Leo-papers] based on an earlier text than that of Sabatier's *Spec. Perf.*" (Little, *Guide*, p. 21). "A similar, but smaller, compilation from the same materials [as the *Spec. Perf.*] was made or copied by a friar at Avignon a few years later " (*ibid*. p. 19).

[2] Sabatier, *Spec. Perf.* Introd. p. xlvi. Sabatier, misled by his mistake as to the date, removed this note from its proper place, treating it as a matter of minor importance.

[3] A provisional edition of this book was printed in 1902 by Sabatier, who promises soon to give us a critical edition.

exemplar, which again contains the whole or part of six smaller collections. This *Fac secundum exemplar*, which was probably compiled between 1322 and 1328, is found in a large number of MSS., which differ a good deal from each other; all its constituent parts seem to be based on authentic earlier documents of the kind which the Decree of 1266 had attempted to destroy; one of its sections, in fact, consists of eighty-one chapters from the *Speculum Perfectionis*, though not always in identical form. The tendency of the collection is definitely Spiritual.[1] For part of the *Actus*, at any rate, we have for once an author's name; a certain Fr. Ugo da Brunforte had something to do with it. This was a Spiritual friar, nephew to the two brothers Pellegrino and Jacopo da Fallerone who are mentioned in the book (chaps. xxvii., li.). The whole book records the traditions of a particular group, the Spirituals of the Mark of Ancona, where large convents were few, and the majority of the brethren dwelt by twos and threes in mountain hermitages. These, with their similar homes in the Umbrian hills, formed the headquarters of the Spirituals in Italy. The *Fioretti*, therefore, embody a genuine and living tradition of the Saint, primarily, in all likelihood, oral, but passed down continuously from the lips of those who had known him familiarly. Even as a record of historical facts, its reputation has rather revived in recent years.[2] If we were to attempt to characterise it in terms of early Christian documents, it corresponds roughly to the Fourth Gospel, and probably Renan was mainly thinking of the *Fioretti* when he wrote: "Nous avons la preuve que, sauf les circonstances miraculeuses, le caractère réel de François d'Assise répond exactement au portrait qui est resté de lui. François d'Assise a toujours été une des raisons les plus fortes qui m'ont fait croire que Jésus fut à peu près tel que les évangélistes synoptiques nous le dépeignent."[3]

Franciscan and Christian literary tradition.

We are now in a position to consider what light is cast by the Franciscan upon the Christian literary tradition. The significance of the comparison will best be brought out if we begin by eliminating those Franciscan documents which, in the nature of the case, could scarcely have had their parallel in the other period. If St. Francis, like Christ, had died as a condemned felon and rebel against the

[1] For the whole of this complicated question see Sabatier, *Spec. Perf.* Introd. pp. clxxvi-cc, and *Opuscules*, tom. i. fasc. 1, 3. The first thirty-eight chapters of the *Fioretti* are earlier than the rest; the "Considerations on the Stigmata" and the sections dealing with Juniper and Giles do not really belong to the *Fioretti* at all, though they are added to that book in most of the MSS. and all the printed editions.

[2] See Sabatier (*Actus*, Introd. p. xiii), who, however, seems rather to exaggerate the importance of this particular instance.

[3] *Nouvelles Études d'histoire religieuse*, 1884, p. 326.

Church of his birth, all absolutely contemporary notices would have been reduced, at most, to a few unfriendly sentences, possibly altogether mendacious. We should have had none of his own writings, since the little he might have written in those early days of his mission would almost certainly have been destroyed. There would have been no Circular Letter from his official successor; no *Vita Prior*, officially commanded by the head of his Church. The *Tractatus de miraculis*, the two Bonaventura lives, and the *Liber de laudibus* would not have existed, at least in anything like their present form. Of the Leo-papers, and of those sources, whatever they may have been, which underlie the *Three Companions*, the *Anonymus Perusinus*, the *Fioretti*, and *Fac secundum exemplar*, we should probably have had only a small fraction, handed down orally during the early days when it was perilous to be a Franciscan, committed to writing when the generation of first disciples was fast dying out, and "edited" by some later follower who had far less personal knowledge of the master than even Celano had. We should have been, therefore, by so much farther from our present knowledge of early Franciscan history, though not necessarily from that of the essential Francis. His originality, his charm, and his magnetic force might have shone out as clearly from those more fragmentary documents as from these that we now possess; the *Vita Prior*, which would have been by far our most serious loss, supplies little or nothing which might not have been inferred from other sources; these latter, in conjunction with the facts of the growth of the Order and its missionary spirit, would still have shown us something like the true and complete Francis. But there are two or three currents in the early history of the Order of capital importance for the study of religious embryology, for which we should have had no conclusive documentary evidence if the Franciscan had been as meagre as the Gospel records. Some critics would doubtless have inferred, but others would steadily have denied, things which are now admitted on all sides only because they rest upon the most unexceptionable documentary evidence.

(1) *The Three Rules.*—In 1209 or 1210 St. Francis wrote his first Rule, which was confirmed after some hesitation by Innocent III., but only verbally. In 1221, Francis drew up a fresh and fuller Rule; in 1223 a third, which was formally ratified and sealed by Honorius III. If Francis, like Christ, had suffered for his faith, he would never have lived to draw up the Rules of 1221 and 1223; this gives great importance to the differences between these three Rules, which may be summarised here in the words of a writer who will not be suspected of anti-Franciscan bias:

The Rules.

"The Rule of the Friars Minor" (writes Father Cuthbert, *Life*, p. 86) "underwent many changes and modifications before it was finally sealed with the solemn and written approbation of Pope Honorius III. in 1223. That final Rule reflects many issues and experiences in the development of the fraternity, which Francis in these earlier years never contemplated, and in it the fine idealism of his aspiration is somewhat tempered by the exigencies of the world, as pure gold is mixed with harder metal to serve the uses of men. It was indeed necessary to beat out the finer, heroic spirit of the founder of the fraternity with an admixture of more earthly wisdom for the multitude which gathered to him after the first enthusiasm had begun to wane. So only do the idealists retain a following, whether in the Church or outside it." And again (p. 394): " Any one conversant with the life and character of Francis would expect of the Primitive Rule that it would be almost exclusively an expression of principles rather than a code of practical regulations or of ' constitutions.' Francis was from beginning to end an idealist and a poet. In the practical application of his ideals he waited on circumstance ; he made a practical regulation only when a situation arose which demanded a practical decision, and then his decision was formulated by the occasion ; he never seems to have run ahead of the occasion, but he waited until the actual demand for a decision came to him."

Two instances of this process of development may be quoted, one general and one particular. (*a*) The First Rule, by the general agreement of critics of all schools, consisted of little more than a collection of Gospel texts, with a few practical precepts of detail.[1] Many prescriptions of the other two, therefore, are in the nature of afterthoughts ; in other words, the Franciscans began, even in their Founder's lifetime, to run that course of hierarchical evolution which Christianity ran after the Founder's death. (*b*) The Third Rule deliberately omitted one of the most important clauses of the First and Second (chap. xiv.): " When the brethren go through the world, let them carry nothing by the way, neither scrip, nor wallet, nor bread, nor money, nor staff. And into whatsoever house they shall enter, let them first say : Peace be to this house. And in that same house let them remain eating and drinking such things as are set before them. Let them not resist him that is evil ; but whosoever smiteth them on the cheek, let them turn to him the other also ; and if any man take away their coat, let him have their cloak also. Let them give to every one that asketh them ; and of him that taketh away their goods let them not ask them again." [2] This omission was made (says the *Speculum*, c. iii.) by the

[1] It was reconstituted by Karl Müller in his *Anfänge u.s.w.* pp. 14 ff., a reconstitution which Father Cuthbert accepts with a few small changes (*Life*, pp. 87 ff., and 395 ff.). I here use the latter, as more accessible to English readers, and excluding all suspicion of anti-Franciscan partiality.

[2] The texts are from Luke ix. 3, x. 4-8, vi. 29-30, and Matt. v. 39, with slight verbal alterations.

influence of those who "thought they would thus not be bound to the observation of evangelical perfection"; it was bitterly resented by St. Francis, but the officials of the Order carried their point. For, already in Francis's lifetime, the Order had an official hierarchy, which naturally laid increasing stress upon mechanical discipline; the steady pressure of institutionalism upon individualism, which can only be surmised from scattered glimpses in Apostolic history, is clearly recorded in these Franciscan documents. The earliest group of brethren had actually lived up to these few Bible texts; but no Order, in the medieval sense of that word, could live up to them.

(2) This comes out still more clearly in the story of the *Testament*. Francis, in the last months of his life, dictated this document, which is at the same time a spiritual autobiography and a passionate protest against the degradation of the early ideal.[1] "Let not the brethren say, 'This is another Rule,' for this is a reminder, an admonition, and an exhortation; it is my Testament, which I, brother Francis, in my littleness make unto you, my blessed brethren, in order that we may keep more catholically that Rule which we have promised unto the Lord. . . . And in all Chapter meetings, when they read the Rule, let them read these words also. . . . And whosoever shall keep these things, let him be filled in heaven with the blessing of God Most High, and on earth let him be filled with the blessing of His beloved Son, with the most holy Spirit, the Comforter, and all the Powers of heaven and all the Saints." Yet the later history of this document was conditioned not by the emphasis Francis laid on it, nor by the intrinsic importance of the precepts repeated in it, but by its relation to the increasingly bitter contest between individualism and institutionalism within the Order. The *Testament* became the Magna Carta of the Spirituals, since it justified all their main contentions; it is recorded how certain Conventual persecutors burned the *Testament* upon the head of a too persistent Spiritual, in mockery of his protests.[2] But the question, so far as a Pope's

The Testament.

[1] "This was the Testament which St. Francis dictated in these last days at the Porziuncola, to be a memorial to his brethren to the end of time. . . . You who read it may see therein, as in a mirror, the soul of this long story of Francis's life" (Fr. Cuthbert, *Life*, pp. 378-9). "It is more important than any other of [St. F.'s] writings, and its genuineness seems better attested than that of any other" (Goetz, p. 11).

[2] Angelo Clareno, in "Hist. Septem Tribulationum," *A.L.K.G.* iii. 168. The action will be better understood if Ubertino da Casale's words are given in full: "Quin ymo (quod nephas est cogitare) in provintia Marchie et in pluribus aliis locis [prelati Ordinis] testamentum beati Francisci mandaverunt districte per obedientiam ab omnibus auferi et comburi. Et uni fratri devoto et sancto, cuius nomen est N. de Reconoto, combuxerunt dictum testamentum super caput suum. Et toto conatu fuerunt soliciti annullare scripta beati patris nostri Francisci, in quibus sua intentio de observantia regule declaratur."

voice could decide it, was settled very early. Gregory IX., who had been Cardinal Protector of the Order during Francis's lifetime, published in 1230 the bull *Quo Elongati*, which laid down that the brethren were not bound by the *Testament*, and that (although Francis had most explicitly forbidden them to gloss the actual words of his Rule) the brethren were not bound to obey literally that chapter of the Rule which forbids " that the brethren receive money or coin in any way whatsoever, whether directly or through other persons." The Pope annulled in this same bull Francis's prescription in the *Testament* " that the brethren should in no wise seek for letters [1] from the Holy See "; and he spoke of the Founder as having " inserted [in his *Testament*] certain other things which cannot be kept without much difficulty." [2]

The Stigmata.

(3) *The Stigmata.*—Although there is a great deal of miracle even in the earliest Franciscan records, yet these, on the whole, will be found conformable to the general law that the miraculous grows with every fresh step which separates us from the original source.

(*a*) We may trace this in the description of the appearance presented by these marks on Francis's body. In the Circular Letter of brother Elias—a document perhaps unique at that early period, since it gives an absolutely contemporary description of a miracle, drawn up by an eye-witness under circumstances which would probably have left room for criticism from other eye-witnesses— the description is comparatively simple. " *His hands and feet had, as it were, the punctures of nails imprinted on both sides, keeping their scars and showing the blackness of the nails* ; his side, again, seemed lanced, and often oozed blood." This, taken strictly, amounts only to a proof of the existence of wounds somewhat blackened in the centre, from which the beholders might naturally conjecture the stains of rusty iron ; and I believe no early pictorial representation of the Stigmata goes any farther than this. But in literature this simple description was soon outdone. Celano's *Vita Prior*, only two or three years later, tells us (§ 95) : " His hands and feet seemed pierced in the midst by nails, the heads of the nails appearing in the inner part of the hands and in the upper part of the feet, and their points over against them. Now those marks were round in the inner side of the hands and elongated on the outer side ; and certain small pieces of flesh were seen like the ends of nails bent and driven back, projecting from the rest of the flesh. So also the marks of nails were imprinted in his feet, and raised above the rest of the flesh." [3] Bonaventura, in his *Legenda Major*, follows this description ;

---

[1] *I.e.* letters of protection or privilege.

[2] J. H. Sbaralea, *Bullarium Franciscanum*, vol. i. (1759), pp. 68 ff.

[3] *Quasi puncturas clavorum habuerunt ex utraque parte confixas, reservantes cicatrices et clavorum nigredinem ostendentes* (Böhmer, p. 91). If we conjecture

THE STORY OF ST. FRANCIS OF ASSISI 455

and his *Legenda Minor*, written a little later, takes the miracle one step further.[1] " Moreover, the bending of the nails under his feet was so prominent and so far extended that it not only suffered him not to plant his soles freely on the ground, but even a finger could easily be inserted between the bow-like bend of these ends [of the nails], as I myself have heard from those who saw the thing with their own eyes." There is a similar crescendo of the marvellous, from 1 Celano onwards, in the descriptions of the manner in which these marks were imprinted on the Saint by a seraph; and the Treatise on the Stigmata, which became a sort of appendix to the *Fioretti*, betrays, by the frequency with which it records revelations made on the subject to enquiring brethren, how strongly the Order desiderated fresh and confirmatory marvels.[2] But the story of the Stigmata has one other lesson for us which is perhaps even more important than this.

Elias's letter distinctly implies that the wounds were impressed upon the Saint shortly before his death, *non diu ante mortem*.[3] Other contemporary authors say the same; *e.g.* Jacques de Vitry, in a sermon preached before a Franciscan congregation perhaps even before the composition of 1 Celano, says *in morte ejus*. Several testimonies come to us indirectly through Brother Leo, who might be expected to lay most emphasis on an earlier date if such were true; yet, with one exception, which will presently be noticed, Leo's words tell, so far as they tell at all, slightly in favour of the later date. Meanwhile, however, the official Franciscan tradition had taken a line incompatible with Elias's contemporary statement. Celano, in his *Vita Prior*, first records this (§ 94); according to him, and to all later biographies, Francis received the Stigmata during his retreat on Monte Alverno two years before his death. Now, Leo had been with the Saint on that retreat, and all Leo's testimonies but one are either neutral or slightly unfavourable

When the Stigmata were bestowed.

---

reserantes ("disclosing") for *reservantes*, the sense will not be appreciably altered. The letter is printed in Böhmer's *Analecten* and by Amoni at the end of his *Legenda Trium Sociorum*.

[1] *De stigmatibus sacris*, lect. iii.

[2] This same tendency is general in Franciscan historiography; the miracles in 1 and 2 Celano were not considered numerous enough, and his third volume, the *Tractatus de miraculis*, was therefore composed at the express command of the Minister General somewhere about 1250.

[3] Amoni, it is true, prints instead " *nam* diu ante mortem " (p. 106 of his edition of the *3 Socii*, Rome, 1880). But Amoni was a thoroughly unconscientious editor, and he produced no MS. authority for this change, which must therefore be taken only as an index of the anxiety of extreme conservatives to reconcile contradictions in this story. For full discussion of these variations of time, see J. Merkt, *Die Wundmale des hl. F. v. Assisi* (Leipzig, 1910), pp. 34-52.

to that earlier date. Yet, in his autograph note on the back of the autograph blessing which Francis wrote for him, he distinctly falls in with the official tradition, and dates the Stigmata from two years before Francis's death. He makes no claim, however, to have seen the marks during those two years; and the evidence, taken as a whole, points to a very natural process of legendary growth. Leo, though a very honest man, was no historical critic; his own personal experience contained nothing absolutely irreconcilable with the official tradition; his natural and innocent bias was here in the direction of conformity; and therefore he accepted the story, though without vouching for it as a first-hand witness.

The nuns of St. Clare. (4) The early history of the *Second Order* (nuns of St. Clare) shows a great change of front, which we could never have traced if the surviving Franciscan documents had been as scanty as their Apostolic parallels. In this case, the Franciscan ideal of poverty was abandoned even earlier, and more officially, than in the case of the First Order. Though it is almost certain that Francis drew up an early " Form of Life " (*i.e.* Rule) for them, yet this has perished almost without traces, and it probably consisted, like the first Friars' Rule, mainly of Gospel texts. How the Clarisses lived under it at first, we know from Cardinal Jacques de Vitry: " These women live in community just outside the walls of towns, in different dwellings; they accept nothing, but live by the labour of their hands."[1] We know also that St. Francis, and his very earliest disciples, associated for a short time with these nuns in a spirit of freedom which contrasted with the monastic ideals of his day. Yet this latter point is carefully obscured by the official biographers; St. Francis himself, in later life, enjoined a policy of separation upon his brethren; and, in the matter of poverty, the change came even more definitely during his lifetime, though not by his will. As early as 1218-19, we find the Cardinal Protector giving to at least five convents a form of life practically identical with that of the Benedictine nuns, admitting corporate property; and in 1219 he drew up, for the whole Order, a Rule which is astoundingly un-Franciscan, frankly abandoning the ideal of corporate poverty and trying to make up for this by what Clement IV. described as " grievous and intolerable austerities " in other directions. In a bull promulgated when Ugolino had become Gregory IX., he assures us that St. Francis " accepted " this Rule; but this cannot be pressed further than passive acceptance; if St. Francis had been whole-heartedly in its favour, Gregory could hardly have failed to say so. The rest of this tangled story is too long for recapitulation here; it may be read in E. Wauer's *Entstehung und Ausbreitung d. Clarissenordens*, or, better still, in the *De origine regularum O.S.C.* of Father Ligarius

[1] Sabatier, *Speculum*, p. 299; Böhmer, p. 98; Oliger, p. [14].

Oliger, reprinted from vol. v. of the *Archivum Franciscanum historicum*.[1] If our first documents concerning the Second Order had begun some thirty years after Francis's death, it would have been absolutely impossible to recover what we now know to have been the real facts.

(5) The history of *Learning* brings out an even more striking contrast between the first ideal and the official attitude of thirty years later. Here, not only the enormous numerical majority, but the whole hierarchy of the Order and (almost as a matter of course) all its intellectual forces championed the relaxed ideal. It is impossible to reconcile Francis's strict ideal of poverty with that of a student Order. The Saint's only pronouncements as to books and study are most discouraging in their tone; this is brought out all the more strongly by Father Hilarin Felder's attempts to gloss them in favour of his own theory.[2] The most that Father Felder could be said to have proved (and we cannot legitimately insist on reading even this much into the documents) is that Francis would have wished his disciples to know their Bible in the sense in which the tinker Bunyan, and thousands of other popular preachers, have known it. But no great apparatus of books was necessary for this ideal; the Waldensians, by a simple process of memorising, had attained to a knowledge of the Scriptures which extorted the unwilling admiration even of their persecutors.[3] Yet, by 1260 at least, St. Bonaventura was leading the Order along a path of higher study, linked up with actual residence at the universities, which was frankly incompatible with "the extreme and strictest poverty." From that time onwards, the only protests came from those despised and persecuted Spirituals who would have been cast forth altogether from the Order if their elimination had not been even more dangerous, for political reasons, than their presence.[4] All the weight, not only of numbers, but of

Learning in the Franciscan Order.

---

[1] Father Oliger shows no bias, except an occasional over-anxiety to diminish the Benedictine rôle in this story. Father Cuthbert, on the other hand, and Jörgensen betray an astounding ignorance of the actual documents, dismissing the story as a victory for St. Clare's ideal of poverty at the very conjuncture when the final defeat of that ideal was becoming obvious, and making no attempt to pursue the subject to the end. E. Gilliat-Smith's *St. Clare of Assisi* (1914) is a pretentious but confused and unhistorical book.

[2] *Gesch. d. wissenschaftlichen Studien im Franziskanerorden*, Freiburg, 1904. This is a really learned book; its logic is therefore all the more instructive for our present purpose. Fr. Cuthbert (*Romanticism of St. Francis*, pp. 166 ff.) is entirely dependent upon Felder for all that is of any value on this subject.

[3] Étienne de Bourbon, *Anecdotes historiques*, p. 308. Bourbon, who was himself a friar, adds: "This I say on account of their diligence in evil [*i.e.* in learning these forbidden Scriptures] and the negligence of the Catholics in good."

[4] Compare the words of Angelo Clareno, who complains that, even under Crescenzio da Jesi (1244–47) there grew up, to the shame of the Order, "a certain

all other ponderable factors, was against these men; under St. Bonaventura the Franciscans were unquestionably—it may almost be said, essentially—a student Order; and when, about 1270, Roger Bacon speaks of the *duos ordines studentes*, par excellence, it is to the Franciscans and Dominicans that he refers. Indeed the Dominicans, with whom study was from the first a paramount and essential factor in their ideal, can hardly be more definitely characterised as a learned Order than the Franciscans already were at that distance from their Founder's death at which, if the documentary survivals had been exactly parallel with those of early Christian history, our first fairly definite information with regard to the constitution of the Order would begin.

Franciscanism and Apostolic succession in Ignatius. We find here, indeed, a startling crosslight on the theory of Apostolic succession, if we compare the rôle played by Ignatius's evidence with that of Bonaventura. With Ignatius, two short generations after the Founder's death, we are on firm ground; whether Christianity had started in individualism or not, Ignatian Christianity is now definitely collectivist and institutional. With Bonaventura, thirty-four years after Francis's death, or forty-one after the date when Francis began to lose disciplinary hold over his own Order, we are on equally firm ground. Under his Generalate, in 1260, the Chapter of Narbonne decided that learning was definitely included in that " work " which St. Francis had laid as a duty upon all his followers; and Father Felder would therefore have us believe that this construction had been certainly in the Saint's own mind in 1221–23, and almost certainly from the days of the first Rule of 1209 (p. 99). But here, fortunately, we can check the theory by a document of which the analogue in Christian origins would be priceless—by St. Francis's own *Testament* of about 1226. There the Saint writes of his own beginnings with his earliest companions (§§ 4, 5): " We were unlearned and subject unto all men . . . and I used to work with my hands, and I wish to work, and it is my firm wish also that all the other brethren should work at labour [*laboritio*] which pertains to honesty." Those who maintain that a student Order, even in a rudimentary form, was implicit in Francis's ideal are obliged to argue against all the evidence, until they come to a period when the theory of corporate poverty was explained away by the friars and not even held in theory by the nuns; a period

---

insatiable lust of knowledge and show and possessing and getting, changing the poor solitary settlements and building sumptuous edifices " (*A.L.K.G.* ii. 257). Father Felder (p. 95) tries to weaken this by quoting from the Spiritual teacher, Ubertino da Casale: " We have no intention of blaming the holy and orderly study of *theology* "; but here, and a few lines farther down, where Father Felder uses the same word, the original has *sanctae scripturae*, *sanctarum litterarum*, and it is obvious that his whole argument falls with these mistranslations.

when the authority of the *Testament* was officially repudiated, when more than one Spiritual had paid with his life for strict loyalty to the first ideal; when the Stigmata had become something very different from the actual marks seen by Elias and Leo upon the Saint's corpse; when the very memory of that first Franciscan freedom of Clare and her nuns had almost perished; and when the officials were already contemplating that Decree of Destruction which, six years later, fell upon nearly all the most authentic and illuminating of the original documents.[1] At this, which may be called the Ignatian period in Franciscan history, the Order was clearly organised, maintained its general direction, and fixed in a consistent policy which, through succeeding generations, decided it steadily in that same direction.[2] But that direction, as we know from documents which the hierarchy would fain have destroyed, was in some most important respects not only different from, but almost contrary to Founder's mind.

From this brief survey we may draw certain deductions which have a very definite bearing upon the study of Christian origins.

Bearing of the study on Christian origins.

(a) A movement so real and so living as this can keep a great deal of its essential value even while it loses, or even falsifies, values of detail. When all room has been made for legitimate scepticism, students may justify their conviction that the true mind of St. Francis can be known more intimately, if not described more exactly, than the inner mind of any man who lived so long ago. Tamassia's attempt to undermine the whole basis of Franciscan biography is a lamentable exhibition of limited and undigested reading and of perverse logic.

(b) Yet, with all the force which the original impulse exerts even to-day—and the revival of Franciscan interest, especially in Protestant countries, is one of the most striking movements in contemporary thought—it remains undeniable that this impulse was perverted very early in certain directions, and that the majority, while claiming to speak for the Saint, violated his principles so deliberately and consistently that such violation became almost a test of orthodoxy. The more faithful minority were partly driven into heresy, but were mainly retained by force within the Order, since nothing could have exposed the bankruptcy of the ideal more clearly than to permit a few handfuls of Zelanti to form an independent Order based upon the real observance of that Rule which

---

[1] Cf. Wadding's evidence, quoted above, that the movement for suppressing even Celano dates from as early as 1256.

[2] Among the many later reforms in the Second Order, none, I believe, has ever really gone back to the strict observance even of the Rule of 1223, at any rate for any appreciable time.

even the Conventuals professed with their lips.[1] The facts so clearly traceable in this movement may well make us hesitate to decide that an overwhelming majority, claiming to speak for the Founder and anathematising all dissidents, necessarily represents the Founder's mind more truly than the dissidents do.

(c) At the same time, they justify a great deal of Loisy's apologetics for the Catholic Church. Auguste Sabatier has pointed out that there were in Christ's teaching two separate potentialities not easy to reconcile in practice;[2] and the same may be said of Francis. In religion, as in all social movements, even accuracy of detail is less important (if choose we must) than breadth of proportion and the sense of human solidarity. Franciscanism as the Spirituals understood it could not have spread as the Conventuals spread; the Church of Paul could not have become the Church of Constantine; it is not enough for non-Catholics to show the way to Catholics in biblical and historical criticism unless they can rival them also in social solidarity. There is much to be said for the argument of *L'Évangile et l'Église* if only the author had carried his argument down to the present day, thus admitting the possibility that non-Catholic Christianity may be a no less legitimate development, as it certainly is not a less living and widespread development, than Catholic. But this, however logically it may follow from the considerations set forward in the preceding pages, would take us too far afield.

The briefest conclusion would seem to be this, that, while certain Franciscan developments cannot in themselves prove similar developments in early Christianity, yet at least they prove the possibility that the admitted gaps in our earliest Christian evidence may conceal surprises no less startling than those revealed by the Franciscan records. The theory of Apostolical Succession may always hold its ground as a working theory, but only as one working theory among others which have at least as much historical likelihood in their favour. To make Apostolical Succession fundamental is to base ourselves on the assumption that what we know to have actually happened in the thirteenth century could not possibly have happened in the first. And, as that assumption claims sometimes to base itself on one fundamental truth, a few concluding lines may here be devoted to it.

Christ differed so immeasurably from St. Francis (it is argued), that deviations which were possible and natural in early Franciscanism were impossible in early Christianity. We may apply to this

[1] The best accounts of this quarrel are in Tocco, *l.c.*; H. C. Lea, *Inquis. in Middle Ages*, vol. iii.; A. G. Ferrers Howell, *St. Bernardino of Siena*, introductory chapters.

[2] *Esquisse d'une philosophie de la religion*, 1903, pp. 223 ff.

THE STORY OF ST. FRANCIS OF ASSISI

one simple test—the tradition of the words of institution at the Last Supper. Here we have some thirty words, spoken by Christ at a moment which all his hearers knew to be supremely fateful, and sealed with that solemn final warning : " This do in remembrance of Me." The actual hearers had all the receptive memory of illiterate folk absolutely devoted to their Master ; others, to whom the sacred words were passed on, had the same virgin memory, and an even more overwhelming sense of the incomparable solemnity of that occasion. Yet we do not know what those thirty words were ; four times they are recorded in the New Testament, and in four different forms. No one speech of Christ, perhaps, has been so much emphasised as this in every single syllable ; yet there are only six words common to the four records which have come down to us. In the face of this simple fact (which, after all, is only one out of many), can we seriously attribute unparalleled and unapproachable accuracy to that oral tradition upon which, at bottom, the whole Gospel history rests ? Can we reasonably, here, rule out even the possibility of such deflections during the first years of obscurity as we can prove by irrefragable documentary evidence in the first years of Franciscanism ?

BIBLIOGRAPHY

A. GENERAL

There are two cheap and admirable bibliographies: (*a*) A. G. Little, *Guide to Franciscan Studies* (S.P.C.K., 1920, 1s. 6d.), and (*b*) Father Paschal Robinson, *A Short Introduction to Franciscan Literature* (New York, 1907).

B. SPECIAL

A.L.K.G.   *Archiv für Litteratur- und Kirchengeschichte des Mittelalters.* Ed. Denifle and Ehrle. (Freiburg i/B.)

BARZELLOTTI, G.   *David Lazzaretti.* (Bologna, 1855.) The author, a Spencerian philosopher, happened to come into personal contact with this Italian Messiah of the nineteenth century, and made a scientific study of the phenomenon.

BESSA, BERNARD OF.   "Liber de laudibus S. Francisci," printed in *Analecta Franciscana* (Quaracchi), vol. iii.

BÖHMER, H.   *Analekten z. Geschichte d. Franz. v. Assisi.* (Tübingen, 1904.) A cheap and admirable collection of the Saint's writings, with a few extraneous documents of great value.

BONAVENTURA.   *Legenda Major* and *Legenda Minor.* Excellent cheap edition by the friars of Quaracchi near Florence. English translation in Temple Classics by E. G. Salter.

CELANO, THOMAS OF.   *Vita Prior, Vita Secunda,* and *Tractatus de miraculis.* Ed. D'Alençon. (Rome, 1906.) There is another very inaccurate edition of the Latin text by Rosedale; on the other hand, an admirable and most scholarly English version has been published by A. G. Ferrers Howell. (Methuen, 1908.)

CUTHBERT, FATHER.   *Life of St. F. of Assisi,* 1912. In research, the author adds practically nothing; but he is a conscientious compiler from the best modern sources, and his book is valuable as reflecting the mind of a modern Franciscan, who tries to do justice to Sabatier's point of view.

Fioretti di San Francesco. Published in the original Italian by Sansoni, Florence. English translation in Temple Classics by Prof. T. W. Arnold.

THE STORY OF ST. FRANCIS OF ASSISI 463

FRANCISCI S. *Opuscula.* (Quaracchi, 1904.) An excellent and very cheap edition, though the editors have unfortunately omitted the *Canticle of the Sun*, and do not print the valuable supplementary documents which Böhmer supplies.

GOETZ, W. *Die Quellen z. Geschichte d. hl. F. v. Assisi.* (Gotha, 1904.) The fullest work of its kind, valuable for its thoroughness, but often lacking in judgment.

Legenda trium sociorum. Ed. Amoni, 1880, with old Italian translation. An excellent English version by E. Gurney Salter (Temple Classics).

MÜLLER, K. *Anfänge d. Minoritenordens, u.s.w.* (Freiburg i/B., 1885.) A very valuable book, forestalling even Sabatier in many of his most important conclusions.

SABATIER, P. *Vie de St. François d'Assise.* (Paris, 1894.) Translated into English. A new edition, much revised, is promised shortly. By far the best biography of St. Francis.

Speculum Perfectionis. Ed. Sabatier. (Paris, 1898.) Good and cheap translations by Sebastian Evans (Nutt) and Prof. T. Okey (Dent).

TAMASSIA, N. *St. F. of Assisi and his Legend.* Translated by Lonsdale Ragg. (Fisher Unwin, 1910.) The author, a law-professor, tries to analyse Celano and the other legends in the spirit of the Tübingen school, but lacks the necessary historical learning.

TILEMANN, H. *Speculum Perfectionis und Legenda Trium Sociorum.* (Leipzig, 1902.)

TOCCO, F. *L' Eresia nel medio evo.* (Florence, 1884.)

VITRY, JACQUES DE. The most important passages from his two letters and his *Historia Orientalis* are printed by Böhmer, *Analekten*, pp. 94 ff.

WADDING, L. *Annales Minorum.* (Lyons, 1625, etc.)

THE STORY OF MARGARET CATCHPOLE

By The Editors

<small>Not a novel, but professes to be a true story.</small>
Margaret Catchpole professes to be, not a novel, but a true story of a Suffolk maid-servant, who, after an extraordinary career in England, was transported to Australia where she was believed to have married and to have become the founder of a highly respected family in the colony. It was written by a clergyman, the son of the girl's mistress and benefactress, with the distinctly moral object of showing what misery follows surrender to temptation, however strong, and how a return to a right course of life can be rewarded by an old age crowned by felicity. The book attained an enduring popularity, and after a lapse of more than seventy years is still widely read, owing to the interest of the story and the fidelity with which the condition of East Anglia at the beginning of the nineteenth century is presented. From its first appearance, moreover, it gave rise to an animated controversy, first between the author and the editor of the *Bury and Suffolk Post*, then one of the leading Suffolk newspapers, and next with a family in New South Wales, the children of an elderly lady, who was generally, but falsely, believed to be the heroine of the story. The historians and literary men in Australia took a deep interest in the story, and have been generally inclined to question the accuracy, if not the good faith of the author.

<small>Story outlined.</small>
The facts are briefly as follows. Margaret Catchpole, a Suffolk peasant girl, was from childhood conspicuous for her courage and resourcefulness, and her skill in managing horses. She was entirely uneducated, and could neither read nor write. At the age of fourteen she went out to service, and distinguished herself by riding to the doctor in Ipswich to summon him to attend her mistress who had had a fit. She never even stopped

THE STORY OF MARGARET CATCHPOLE 465

to bridle a spirited pony of her master's, but rode him bareback, guided only by a halter, for several miles, and through the narrow streets of the town crowded with carts on market day. This exploit procured her the position of nursemaid to Mr. Cobbold's mother. She was so clever that she managed to educate herself with the children of the household, and rose to the position of cook and almost housekeeper in the large establishment. She had two lovers, the rejected, a virtuous young farmer, and the favoured, a bold and adventurous smuggler, named William Laud. Laud's too-frequent attentions caused her mistress to dismiss her, and after various adventures Margaret was induced to steal a horse belonging to her late master and ride him to London. She was arrested, brought back to Suffolk, tried and condemned to death. Considerable interest was brought to bear in her favour, and she was with difficulty reprieved and committed to gaol at Ipswich. She escaped from prison, joined Laud, and was captured on the sea coast, again tried, and again sentenced to death. Once more the death penalty was commuted and she was transported to Australia for life. She wrote several letters to her mistress from the colony, where she won her pardon by her heroic conduct in rescuing people in a flood, and ultimately married the virtuous lover whom she had in youth rejected. She lived the rest of her life in great prosperity, and her son was believed to have revisited the county of Suffolk and to have tried to purchase a very important estate. Margaret was believed to have died September 10, 1841, at the age of sixty-eight, four years before Mr. Cobbold published his book.

It must be premised that he fully believed that his story was literally true as the following words, taken from the preface, testify:

> The public may depend on the truth of the main feature of this narrative: indeed most of the facts recorded were matters of public notoriety at the time of their occurrence. The author who here details them is a son of the lady with whom this extraordinary female lived, and from whose hands he received the letters and the facts here given.

He had, moreover, every opportunity of ascertaining the facts. He was born at the time they took place, in 1799, and his mother, who played a conspicuous part, lived till 1824. He had access to documents bearing on the case, and knew many people concerned in it.

Truth of narrative severely criticised.
For various reasons Mr. Cobbold exposed himself to a criticism almost as relentless as that which Biblical writers have received in modern days. The publication of his book in 1845 gave rise to misunderstanding and caused pain, though without any intention on the part of the narrator. The result was that his tale, which he solemnly declared to be a true one, was pronounced a pure fiction, which owed its widespread popularity to the belief of its readers that it was a relation of sober fact. Investigation proved that there were certain erroneous statements; but the criticism was on the whole subjective, and could not be substantiated by documentary evidence.

Based on authentic tradition and documents.
The controversies, which lasted long after the appearance of the book—which were not wholly academic, but were inspired by those who had family credit at stake—gave rise to a strong suspicion that in the correspondence which he had published as genuine the author had trusted entirely to his imagination or powers of invention. By the kindness of his lineal descendants we have discovered the authentic documents which were used in the compilation of the book, and, so far, we have been enabled to establish the credit of the author. There are also other documents, including a book of sketches made of the scenes in the novel by Mr. Cobbold, with notes made in 1874, proving that in old age he firmly believed that he had related absolute facts. Even where he may be rightly charged with falsifying certain details, which he might well have done for the sake of heightening the interest of the story, this may be due to his lack of accuracy and critical discernment.

Family tradition.
The materials which were at Mr. Cobbold's disposal were numerous and different in character. First there was the family tradition. His father had an enormous family: twice in his life there were twenty-two children living. His elder brothers and sisters could remember Margaret Catchpole when she was a servant in the family. Her letters from Australia used to come to his mother when he was a growing boy. He knew and conversed with many of those who had played a prominent part in the transactions he relates, and he had an intimate knowledge of the scenes which he describes.

THE STORY OF MARGARET CATCHPOLE 467

When he wrote his book many eye-witnesses of the incidents were alive, and he had abundant opportunity of inquiring into the facts, as he lived all his life near the scene of the early adventures of his heroine, though he had no personal knowledge of her. He was also describing a state of affairs widely different from those of his own time, using the method, employed by some ancient and modern writers, of making some of his actors tell their own story, and, as will be shown, he had before him the documents which he professes to quote. *[Testimony of eye-witnesses. Use of first person in parts of narrative.]*

The documentary evidence in possession of Mr. Cobbold when he wrote the book was discovered in his grand-daughter's possession, in an old bundle of papers, and has been catalogued.

There is a letter, quoted below, from Mr. Charles Cobbold, curator of the Zoological Gardens at Edinburgh, to his brother Richard, in which he describes an interview with Mr. David Hope. The result was that both gentlemen were equally perplexed as to the identity of Margaret and his relative the lady in question, as this extract shows : " When he had gone over his history of her, I went over *mine*, or in other words, Margaret Catchpole's ; at which he was very much interested and astonished ; and expressed himself perfectly satisfied that she must be the Margaret Catchpole whom he had all his life been led to believe was the original Mary Haddock " (dated June 21, 1846).

The disappearance of Margaret from the scene and the uncertainty as to whether she died or married and lived prosperously have a parallel in the mystery which hangs over the death of Paul. There was good evidence for the tradition that Margaret married and lived to be old ; and even the copies made of the registry of her death exhibit discrepancies (see below). It is the same with Paul ; there is a good tradition that he was martyred at Rome, but did the writer of Acts know of his death ? Renan thinks Paul simply disappears from history.

The notes in Mr. Cobbold's sketch-book " Illustrations of Margaret Catchpole. Sketched by the Author of Margaret Catchpole " though made in 1874 when the author was in his seventy-seventh year—the sketches are of course much earlier —show how he relied on oral tradition. *[Notes made by author.]*

(*a*) Sketch III.—" Thomas Colson, alias Robinson Crusoe, the ancient fisherman of the Orwell." Very few are alive now

(1874) who will remember the old fisherman of the Orwell. In his day almost the only real fisherman on the river. He was well read in a book of deep horoscopic literature Saducismus Triumphans (*sic*). The history of this poor man will be found in the *Suffolk Garland*.

(*b*) Sketch II.—" The Priory Farm." My informant was Dr. Stebbing, who was the first to commend M C to my mother.

(*c*) Sketch XXI.—" Carrying Master William Home." The author of M C treasured up in his memory all that fell from the lips of his father and mother concerning all the family events. . . . In such a spirit of love are many things collected and done by many a good old author.

(*d*) Sketch XXV.—" The gaoler and Preventive service men going to take Will Laud and Margaret from the North Vere."

The public records of the County at that period before the employment of stenographic reporters were very meagre, and the evidences given in a Court of Justice but very scant. We are therefore dependent upon Mrs. Cobbold's letter for the facts of how Margaret was taken.

(*e*) Sketch XXVII.—" Will Laud defending the body of Margaret." Concerning this we could only go upon her own account of it, and Ripshaw's evidence. The death of many smugglers and lawless men was little thought of in that day. Margaret had very little pity except from her mistress.

(*f*) Sketch XXIX.—" Margaret's Cottage, Richmond Hill." It is astonishing with what avidity I used to hear my mother read all Margaret's communications from Botany Bay. I have all her letters labelled and dated by my dear father. . . . As to me I remembered all things with gusto.

(*g*) Sketch XXXIII.—" Margaret as last seen at Sydney!" Margaret herself outlived her husband a few years, and died in the same year her dear mistress did.

Criticism of story: (*a*) that the author fabricated the letters.

The criticism of Mr. Cobbold's book began with its first appearance and has continued down to the present day. He has preserved a fragment of a correspondence with Mr. Johnson Gedge, editor of the *Bury Post*, the letter being dated October 20, 1847. Mr. Gedge's words are:

I am well aware that the broad outline of the Narrative, so far as regards her stealing of the horse, conviction, escape, recapture, condemnation, reprieve, transportation, and subsequent rise to wealth, and the arrival of her son in Suffolk for the purpose of buying an estate in the county, is true; and the last fact I imagine to be that for which I am described by the Editor of the *Herald* as your authority, it having been communicated to me, if my memory serve me, by the late Mr. Toplyn of Sproughton. But for the other (or the greater part of the other) incidents—the *romance* of the story,—and for the language and sentiments put into the mouth of the heroine, I have been assured by respectable persons of Ipswich there was no better warrant than your own imagination, and for this reason I abandoned my design of calling especial attention to the book on its appearance, considering that, as an exemplification of human character, it was rather deceptive than instructive. . . . If I have been misinformed—if the motives and circumstances of the offence of Margaret Catchpole, and her preceding and subsequent history, be truly set forth—and if the letters and conversations ascribed to her be indeed true representations of her mind and character—I shall not only be ready to retract and apologize for my remarks, but shall greatly rejoice at being the instrument of setting right a large portion of the public, who are under the same impression as myself, on what may in that case be truly described as a most interesting " *psychological curiosity*."

As has been shown, the style of the letters supposed to be written by Margaret Catchpole warranted Mr. Gedge's assumption that they were fabrications; and his remark toward the end " if the letters and conversations ascribed to her be indeed true representations of her mind and character " indicates, as was indeed the fact, that many who had known Margaret in Suffolk regarded her as no heroine, but as a disreputable person.[1]

The literary defect of *Margaret Catchpole* is that almost every character talks and writes in the same rather pompous language. Suffolk peasants, sailors, smugglers, criminals, judges, Mrs. Cobbold, Margaret, and every character in the book speak to one another in Mr. Cobbold's literary style. On the rare occasions when the author makes people write as he supposes they might have done, his artifice is transparent to the most casual reader. No one would believe that a habitual criminal would forge a letter of Laud, the smuggler, in such terms as these :

Uniformity of style.

DOG AND BONE, LAMBETH, *May* 9, 1797.

DEAR JACK,

Hurrah, my boy! Safely anchored, though I had cut my cable, and run; but I have got into a friendly port, and my pursuers

---

[1] One of the most venerable and respected men in the county wrote in 1915 : " No doubt it was the publication of Mr. Cobbold's story that raised my mother's indignation. I fancy Mr. Cobbold knew little about the character he was dealing with."

shan't easily find me. Precious hard, though, Jack, after just finding out my girl, to have to tack and leave her. You might lend a hand now, just to serve an old friend. Margaret would make my present dull time a little lighter, if you could but find her up, and put her on the right road to find me. I think she would forgive me, if you could explain matters a little to her. Tell her we could get married here, and after a time all would be well. But, Jack, mum must be the order of the day. Don't you fire a volley at me until she's off to London. She must come incog, Jack; ay, in man's clothes, if she can : you know why. A thought strikes me, which if you put it into her head, will just suit her, and me too. Persuade her to borrow the old pony of her master's, from the pasture on the Woodbridge road, or to take it with French leave. It is worth nothing, and will never be inquired after ; and if disposed of, will scarcely be missed. And if she was found out, it would only be treated as a good spree ! So, Jack, try her ; she has a spirit equal to the work, and we shall then be no more parted. Now, do this for

Your old friend,

WILL LAUD.

When, therefore, Margaret is represented as writing the following paragraphs in a letter announcing the arrival of the convict ship at Sydney harbour, one is tempted offhand to say that she could not possibly have written at all, and that such an effusion is entirely due to the inventive genius of the author :

SYDNEY, *Jan.* 21, 1802.

HONOURED MADAM,

With pleasure I cannot describe, I am permitted to take up my pen and write to you, to acquaint you with my arrival in safety at Port Jackson, Sydney, New South Wales, on December 20, 1801. As I left the ship, and was about to be landed, the shore, as I approached it, put me very much in mind of the Cliff on the banks of the river Orwell. The houses, backed by the hills, so much resembled that happy spot, that it put me in good spirits ; and had I but seen your smile to welcome me, I should have been happy indeed. But I thought of you, of your prayers, your advice, your kindness and consolation ; and when I saw land so much like my own dear native home, I really felt as if I was not entirely banished from old England.

Again :

I assure you, my dear lady, that, in taking a ramble through them with my mistress and some of the elder orphans, I felt just as

I imagine your own dear children used to feel when they walked with me to the Grove near Hog Island, I was so pleased with the birds, and trees, and flowers. I only wish I could send you one of the beautiful parrots of this country, but I have no means of so doing at present, as my money is all laid out for my future benefit. I have no money given to me for wages. I have board and lodging; and, if I conduct myself well, Mrs. Palmer says she will lay up a little store against the day of my emancipation or my marriage. With God's help, in whom I trust, I am determined to be independent of all men. I have no desire to be married and settled, as some people say I shall be. I have no wish of the kind, neither do I now nor do I hope to desire any better situation than that I now enjoy, unless it were a return to England.

I grieve to say, my dear lady, that this is one of the wickedest places in the world. I never heard of one, excepting those of Sodom and Gomorrah, which could come up to it in evil practices. People are so bold, so shameless, and so sinful, that even crime is as familiar as fashion in England. . . .

Or this :

The wheat harvest was almost over when I landed. Wheat is here eight shillings per bushel at this time. There are two crops, I understand, each summer, one of wheat and another of Indian corn. I am told that the winter is very short ; I cannot give you any certain information yet, as I have been only one month in the country. This letter, for the same reason will be but a poor one ; my next will, I hope, be more worthy of your perusal. I will make minutes, according to your wishes, of all things which come under my observation. Never, never, my dearest lady, shall I forget your goodness to me, and especially on the last day before I left Ipswich.

Even more incredible is it that a peasant woman who had grown up completely uneducated should have written in another letter in such a strain as this : '

. . . You will find two large, magnificent birds, called here the mountain pheasant ; they are only like our English bird in size. The plume of feathers in the tail of the cock bird would form the most graceful ornament for a queen's head-dress. Two noble feathers, somewhat like a peacock's, only more brilliant and various in their colours, surrounded by the most glittering silver lines of curving feathers, fine as the prairie grass, and sparkling like the waves of the ocean, ornament the tail of the male bird, whilst the female is only remarkable for the elegance of her shape, and not for the beauty of her plumage.

In my opinion, this bird is the peafowl of this country, and not a pheasant. Early in the morning, I have seen him spring from the thickest brushwood, and wing his arrow-like flight to the tallest tree, and there he appears to mimic the notes of the various songsters around him. But the most beautiful attitude that I once saw him in beats every thing I ever beheld of what men term politeness. I have heard and have read of delicate attentions paid to our sex by men of noble and generous dispositions; but I scarcely ever heard of such devoted attention as I one day witnessed in this noble bird toward his mate. I saw her sitting in the heat of the meridian sun upon her nest, and the cock bird seated near her, with his tail expanded, like a bower overshadowing her; and as the sun moved, so did he turn his elegant parasol to guard her from his rays. Now and then he turned his bright eye to see if she was comfortable, and she answered his inquiry with a gentle note and rustle of her feathers.

Was not this a sight calculated to teach us all gentleness? Dear lady, as I looked upon it, the tears came warmly down my cheeks, as I thought of your good husband and yourself; and I dreamed of your writing a poem upon this subject, and reading it to the young ladies in the school-room. I had often wondered what use the tail of this bird could be to him. If this be one of its general uses, surely it is truly ornamental and useful. I hope these birds will come safe to hand. Captain Brooks, of the Buffalo, promised me faithfully that he would himself forward them into Suffolk. The thought that they may reach you and give you pleasure will make me happy for many a long day. Owing to the late floods, everything is become very dear: pork, 2s.; beef and mutton, 2s. 3d.; soft sugar, 6s. and 8s.; tea, 1l. 10s. per pound; a bushel of wheat, 1l. 5s.; printed cotton, 10s. to 12s. per yard; shoes, for females, 13s. per pair. Scarcely any linen cloth to be had. Newspapers, of any date, 1s. apiece.

But a perusal of the two letters which are given *in extenso* will convince the reader that Mr. Cobbold had authentic documents, which he interpreted in his own fashion:

Jan
sedney Dednen th 21 1802
December

honred maddam

Genuine letters of Margaret Catchpole.

with grat plesher i take up my penn to a Quaint you my good Ladday of my saf a rived at new port Jackson new South Wales sedney on the 20 Day of Desember 1801 and as i was a Going to be Landedon on the Left hand of me it put me in mind of the Cleeff Both the housen and Lik wise the hills so as it put me in very Good spirites seeing a places

so much Like my owen nativ home it is grat Deel moor Lik englent then ever i Did expet to a seen for hear is Gardden stuff of all koind excpt gosbres an Cur^rnes and appelle₃ the garddenes are very Buttefull in ded all planted with g^erames and thay run up 7 and 8 foot hy it is a very wooden Cuntre_y for if i goo out aney ^a Distences hear is going throw woodes for miles But thay are very B Buttefull and very prettey B^eardes i oneley wich my Good Ladday i Could send you one of thes parrotes for thay are very Buttefuell But i se so maney Dy on Bord it mak me so very unwilling to send you one But if i should Continner Long in this Countrey i suarteneley will send you sumth_ing out of this wicked Countrey for i must say this is the wickedes places i ever was in all my Life the ^wat harvest was all most over just as i Landded hear weat is 8 suillenes pear Busshell at this time hear is 2 Cropes in the summer one with weat and one w with indey Corn the winter is But very short as thay tell me madam i Cannot give you not much a Count of the Countrey not in this Letter But i will Giv you moor in the next for i niver shorll for Git your Godness my Good Ladday you sheow to me Befor i Left englent and i took every thing over with me safe and thay are a grat sarves to me in Deed Not that i am in such grat trobell at present But God oneley know how it m^ay Be for hear is maney one that hav Been hear for maney year and thay hav thar poor head shaved and sent up to the Coole river and thear Carrey Cooles from Day Light in the morning till Dark at knight and half starved But i hear that is a Going to Be put By and so it hav need for it is a very crouell in ded norfolk islent is a Bad places a nof to send aney poor Cratuer with steel Corler on thear poor neekes But i will tak good keear of my self from that i am prettey well of at present for i was taken of the stores 2 Days after i Landed so i have no govment work to do nor thay hav nothing to do with me oneley when hear Be a gerenel mustter then i must a pe^ear to Leet them know i am hear and if i hav a mind i goo up to paroronato or to towen Gabbey or to
                                   20 miles   30 mile
oxberrey i hav to git a pass or elces i should Be taken up
fortey mile
and put into prisson for a very Lettell will do that hear my Dear Good Ladday wont to say a grat Deel moor But time will not permit for i expet the ship to to saill every Day and i hav Benn very Bad sinces i Com on shor i thought i shold a Lorst my Life But Bless Be to the Lord i am a grat Deel Better and i was Charmenley all my passeg Considren we Com over the Beay of Beskey and wee Crost the Line very well in ded But i tossed a Bout very much in Ded But i should not mind it if i was But a Coming to old englent onces moor for i Cannot say that i Lik this this Contrey no n^or niver shorll the governor hav a Good maney Cowes and a nothen gentelman hear is a good maney horses

and very smart wiskes and Leetell shay Cartes and passeg Bootes my Dear madam i must con Clud and send you moor acount the next time

from your unfortuned searvent

margaret Catchpole

madam pray Be so koind as to Leet Do^{c}t Docter stebbenes ^{hav} that sid of the Letter i hop thes few scroules find you and all your good famley ^{well} and i hop my good Ladey you writ to the fust transport ship that do Come out for i shold Be very to hear from
you
you

. . . . . .

honred madam

sydney october th 18 1807

with the grates of plesher i taik ever opertunetey of wrighten you as it is my Dutey so to do as you are my only Dear frind that i hav and sencly do i p^{r}ay to God for your health and happness and all your good Dear family and hop in God to hear from you soon for that is the only Comfort that i Can find in a foren Land a monkest so maney wicked Creaturs for thay robed me of all my Collectshon a Corden to your wich then in rea^{d}nd$_{ess}$ to a sent to for you my good Laday wich i dear venter to say would a Binn valuable to you as every think was so parfect and in good oder But i will endaver for But sorrey am i w^{h}een i had so Good Convayencencs But i will so^{o}n Be a Bout it a Gain for it is the grates plesher that i hav of waiten on you my Dear Good Laday whot wold my Life Be hear to me was it not for you honread madam you ar niver of my thoughtes Dear madam when i think of the dethes and trobeles you hav had i wonder hoow you Can think on me and sencer do i turn you thankes for the stat of your good family and hop i shorll all wayes Be stated with the same i sencer wich to now hoow m^{iss} ann and miss harit and soifier do and and all your owen Dear family do and if you hav aney knowleg of Gorner Bligh and Can Bertishon to him thear is no dought But somthing wold Be don for me as i Behav so well niver git in to no trobell i hav Binn to Liv with mrs palmer sinces i rot to you my Good Laday By the Bufflow wich i hop you hav receved a smorll Caces with 2 mounten Cookes and a hen fessent and newes papers By the faver of Capt· Brookes on Bord the Bufflow every thing is very Deear pork 2 shillenes mutton and Be^{e}ff 2 and 3 pences par pound soft suger 6 and 8 shillenes par pound tea 30 shillones par pound wheat 25 shillenes par Buchell prented Cotton 10 to 12 shillenes par yard shose 10 and 13 shillenes par pear no Linnen Cloth of no sort to Be got every thing very Deear inded no

paper to Be got for newes papers threed at this time is 1 shillen par Cain But i hay a Leettell Left of that you sent me in that vary nices Box for that was a grat Comfort to me as i had Binn so very ill at that time and under docter massones heear and a Bout 8 monthes ago to oblig mrs p^almer i tock a very Long wolk of 30 miles and over heat my self and Come out with Blesters on my Back as if i had Binn Burnt By smorlles Coles of fier and swelled so Bad that i thought i should a Binn dead very soon But Bless Be to God to i did recover But not well a nof i to stop with mrs palmer for i am
very wak ever sences and afraid of taken Could as ther is so maney heates and Couldes to be taken in Caken.¹

So far we have a proof from the authentic documents that Mr. Cobbold adapted Margaret's letters, though there are some in the book that cannot be traced to any source, and are probably pure inventions. Besides the letters, however, there are the facts, about which there has been no small difficulty.

In Australia the controversy took a personal tone. A lady in New South Wales, who, it is true, had been sentenced to transportation in extreme youth but under cruel circumstances not in the least discreditable to her moral character, was pointed out as the real Margaret Catchpole, the associate of smugglers and criminals in Ipswich. This caused no small pain to herself and her descendants, children, and grandchildren, and on receiving the prospectus of the book from a clergyman in the colony, the Rev. H. D. D. Sparling, the Bishop of Australia wrote recommending that the book should, if possible, not appear, as it would wound the feelings of some of the most loyal supporters of the Church in his diocese. A Mr. Hope of Glasgow remonstrated with Mr. Cobbold for introducing the story of his relative into a novel, and he had some difficulty in appeasing the family.

(b) Discrepancies as to facts.

It was clearly proved that Mr. Cobbold had made some

¹ No one reading these two letters can doubt that Margaret herself wrote far better letters than Mr. Cobbold credited her with. They are, of course, illiterate; but they are natural, unaffected, and contain interesting news. Her editor is like Josephus in his treatment of the Old Testament, unable to see beauty in a simple story told in language which appears barbarous. It will be remembered that there was no more admiration for the Bible as literature in antiquity than there was for uncultivated nature. Even in the eighteenth century the Highlands of Scotland were thought hideous, and Dutch scenery delightful.

serious mistakes regarding her career in Australia. In the first place, the registers of the Church contain a notice of the death of a Margaret Catchpole who came over as a convict in 1801 and died May 13, 1819, aged fifty-eight, a single woman.

This is strictly in accordance with all the documentary evidence. The handbill offering a reward for her capture after her escape from prison describes her in 1800 as about thirty-eight years of age. In a letter dated September 2, 1811, she says, " I am all mos fiftey year old," and in the postscript she adds, " On March the fort^eenth is my barth Day then I am fifety years." This would make the date of her birth 1762. But this conflicts with all Mr. Cobbold tells us of her. He says, " The heroine of this romantic but perfectly true narrative was born in the year 1773." She entered the service of his mother, Mrs. Cobbold, recommended by Dr. Stebbing as " a good strong girl," on May 24, 1793. Her last letter to Mrs. Cobbold, of which no copy exists, is dated June 25, 1812, and announces that she is married and about to have a child. According to Mr. Cobbold, she would have been thirty when she married, and it would have been quite possible for her to have had a family, as he asserts and as was generally believed in Suffolk. Mr. Cobbold is, of course, open to the charge of having deliberately made his heroine ten years younger than she actually was in order to make her more interesting to his readers. Certainly there is a glaring discrepancy between the handbill issued when she escaped from prison and the one Mr. Cobbold prints.

(c) Discrepancy between handbill in book and the authentic document.

The authentic one reads :

May 26 1800

Escaped

From the county gaol at Ipswich last Night, or early this morning :—

MARGARET CATCHPOLE

a convict

Under sentence of transportation for
Felony, and Horse Stealing

She is about 38 years of age, Swarthy complexion, very dark eyes & hair, hard favoured. About 5 Feet 2 Inches high, and

THE STORY OF MARGARET CATCHPOLE

escaped in a convict dress, which she has probably changed, and may be disguised in Men's apparel

Whoever shall apprehend the said

MARGARET CATCHPOLE

so as she may be brought to Justice will be entitled to

a reward of TWENTY POUNDS

Granted by Act of Parliament

Printed by John Bush bookseller binder & stationer at his circulating library Tavern Street.

A copy of this is preserved in the Ipswich Museum. This is Mr. Cobbold's version :

FIFTY POUNDS REWARD

Whereas, on Tuesday night, the 25th of March, or early on Wednesday morning, Margaret Catchpole, a female convict, confined in the Ipswich gaol, made her escape therefrom, either by scaling the wall, or by the connivance of the turnkey, this is to give notice, that the above reward shall be given to any person or persons who will bring the said Margaret Catchpole to Mr. Ripshaw, the gaoler; and one-half that sum to any person or persons furnishing such information as shall lead to her apprehension. And notice is hereby given, that any person concealing or harbouring the said Margaret Catchpole shall, after this notice, if detected, be, by order of the magistrates, punished as the law directs.

N.B.—The prisoner is a tall and dark person, with short hair, black eyes, and of intelligent countenance. She had on the gaol dress, and took away with her the two sheets belonging to her bed.

IPSWICH GAOL, *March* 28, 1800.

As regards another handbill, light is thrown on the subject by a letter found among the author's papers, written by his brother Frederick Cobbold, Esq., late of the 1st Dragoon Guards, on February 18, 1861. It begins : *[margin: Another handbill.]*

"Dear Richard, In consequence of having seen the letter in the Chronicle addressed to you as regards the history of Margaret Catchpole by "Silverpen," I think I can give you some information as to where his information comes from ; he says he did not make his remarks without good proofs before which is all very true he speaks about Margarets Confession and her mark X and our father witnessing of all of which is true and about the advertisement of five pounds & not twenty and Bush being the printer, all true; it is curious how I came by my information—it may be more than two years whilst in conversation with the late Mr. Ross . . . he shewed me the *original* printed hand bill of 24th May 1797."[1]

This refers not to the escape from prison but to the stealing of the horse; but it is especially interesting as showing how the author could alter or write from memory what he could doubtless have copied. His inveterate habit of inaccuracy is shown in the statement that the handbill was printed by Mr. Jackson of the *County Press*, he being proprietor of the *Ipswich Journal*, whereas the bill is printed by " I. Bush Bookseller."

A true copy from the original printed Advertisement :

IPSWICH, May 24, 1797.

STOLEN

Out of the Stable of John Cobbold Esqr on St. Margarets Green in this Town late last night or early this morning, with a Saddle and Bridle a

Strawberry Roan Crop Coach Gelding
Six or Seven Years Old

with a black Main and Nag tail; about 16 hands and an half high; his near hinder leg white a little above the Footlock joint; has a swelling on the Upper part of his tongue, and has the appearance of being a Capital Hunter. A Man was seen riding a Horse answering to the above description about Three oClock this morning on the Road toward London two miles this Side Colchester : ALSO Stolen or Strayed from the lands of the said John Cobbold at the Clift near this Town on Saturday afternoon last

A Stone Bay Colt

about 15 hands high with a black Main and Tail and had been newly shoed. Whoever will give Information of the Person or Persons who stole either the Said Horse or Colt, Shall on Conviction of the Offender or Offenders be paid the Sum of FIVE POUNDS by applying to the said John Cobbold; and also the further Sum of Five Pounds by applying to Mr Brame Attorney at Law at Ipswich, Agent to the Ipswich Association. And if the said Colt is strayed, Any Person giving Information of the Same to the Said John Cobbold,

---

[1] Frederick Cobbold was born in 1789, and his life was saved from a falling wall by the foresight of Margaret.

Shall be Rewarded for their trouble, and all reasonable expenses paid.

Printed by I. BUSH, Bookseller.

fo 176

Mr. Cobbold renders this as follows :

TWENTY GUINEAS REWARD

Whereas, last night, or this morning, May 24th, a fine strawberry roan grey gelding was stolen out of the stable of John Cobbold, Esq. of St. Margaret's Green, Ipswich, together with a new saddle and bridle, and the coachman's stable-dress. Whoever shall give information of the robber, so as to lead to the recovery of the horse, or the conviction of the offender, shall receive the above reward at the hands of the owner.

N.B.—The horse is sixteen hands high, has cropped ears, is six years old, has a cut tail, and is very strong and very fast.

IPSWICH, *May* 24, 1797.[1]

But Mr. Cobbold had a good excuse for saying that Margaret was born in 1773. He prints a letter in the later editions of his book from his old tutor, the Reverend William Tilney Spurdens, headmaster of the Grammar School, North Waltham, Norfolk, who says that he knew Margaret as a child ; for her aunt was a maid in his uncle's house. He recollected particularly that for spelling out an account of the loss of the *Royal George* at Spithead (1780) his uncle gave him sixpence, and " I laid it out in figs, of which Peggy and her swain ate so many as to make themselves ill." If they were both children at this time it points to Margaret's having been born about 1773. When she was in Ipswich Gaol Mr. Spurdens made an effort to see her and wished to give her money, " but she would not know anything of me—in fact *cut me* : and so I kept my money." As one of her original letters, written from the gaol to Mr. Cobbold, shows Margaret was not indifferent to money, is

Discrepancy as to age accounted for.

---

[1] This example is the more interesting because there was no conceivable motive in making the alteration. It is possible that Mr. Cobbold did not in either instance trouble to search for the original, but composed what he thought would have been the sort of notice likely to have been issued. This bears on the question of an official document such as Acts xxiii. 27-30 (Claudius Lysias' letter to Felix).

it possible that Mr. Spurdens's Margaret Catchpole was another person of the same name ?

<small>Confusion of Margaret Catchpole with another person in Australia.</small>

Such, then, are the difficulties in arriving at any definite conclusions on very simple points, and what has been done in Australia to elucidate the truth makes the mystery even deeper. The tendency there is to accept the Suffolk part of the story as substantially true, but to pronounce the relation of Margaret's doings in Australia, including the letters, to be pure fiction. The main interest of the colonial investigators is to discover how the name of Margaret Catchpole came to be so inextricably confused with that of Mary Haydock, afterwards Mrs. Reiby, one of the largest landowners in New South Wales, who died at the age of seventy-eight in 1855.[1]

[1] The writer has been in communication with three authorities on the subject of Margaret Catchpole in New South Wales : the late Mr. James Padley of Lithgow, Mr. George C. Johnson, and Mr. A. G. Foster.

In a long letter dated August 9, 1917, Mr. Johnson writes :

"And not alone have I been engaged in this 'labour of love,'—as it has been to all of us engaged therein ; and just here I may give the names of my principal colleagues, and who they are :—James Padley, I may say, was the pioneer in this good work, in that he led the way prior to the late G. B. Barton —our first Government historian, and brother of Edmund Barton, one of the Supreme Court Judges of the Australian Commonwealth—taking the matter in hand ; J. C. L. Fitzpatrick, now a member of the present Government of New South Wales ; William G. H. Freame, J.P., who is also a member of the Australian Historical Society ; G. A. Foster, another member ; R. W. Farlow, J.P. (a Richmond man, and born within a mile or so of 'Bronte,' where Margaret died) and myself—and we have been designated by irreverent jokers, 'The Catchpoleans.'"

Mr. Padley writes, July 10, 1916 :

"A Copy of the entry in St. Peter's Church of England Register, at Richmond, as follows : 'Margaret Catchpole, aged 51 years, came prisoner in the Nile in the year 1801. Died May 13th, was buried May 14th, 1819.—HENRY FULTON.'"

This proves that she died a single woman.

A former resident of the Richmond District, the late Mr. George Matcham Pitt, descendant of the first free settlers at Richmond, a family of high standing in S.W.S., descendants of Lord Nelson, wrote the following letter some years ago, in the Sydney *Evening News*. He was the son of Thomas Matcham Pitt, the only son of the 'old Mrs. Pitt' who was very fond of Margaret, as she told her friends. A copy of the letter appears in Fitzpatrick's *Good Old Days*.

"HOW SHE DIED"

"To the Editor. Sir,—As you have been making inquiries of Margaret Catchpole, who was buried in Richmond Churchyard in the year 1819, she was a nurse to my mother previous to her death. My father had a flock of sheep at Bronte (Mrs. Pitt's residence), shepherded by a man named Tom who died,

From the correspondence in possession of Mr. Cobbold's family, Mrs. Reiby was to the day of her death extremely sensi-

through catching a heavy cold, from diarrhoea. Margaret attended him, and she caught the same complaint, and it carried her off. I believe this same woman to be the veritable Margaret who was transported from England for horse-stealing; and she never was married. That other Margaret Catchpole, spoken of by the Rev. Mr. Cobbold, had no connection with my mother's nurse. I was quite young in the year 1819, and I, therefore, cannot give you any more information.—Yours, etc., GEO. M. PITT, Holbrook (North Sydney), Dec. 2, 1890."

This is corrected by Mr. Johnson in his letter:

"I called at St. Peter's parsonage, and was shown the entry in the Register, which is as follows:—'36. Margaret Catchpole, aged 58 years. Came prisoner in the ship Nile in the year 1801, died May 13th, was buried May 14th, 1819, by me   HENRY FULTON.'

"You will note the difference between the two—the Rev. Stanley Best gives Margaret's age as fifty-two, and does not mention the year. The present Rector of St. Peter's certifies as above, and writes (to me) as follows:

'The following is an exact record taken from Church records in connection with St. Peter's, Richmond, N.S.W., re Margaret Catchpole. Signed G. J. DILLON, Rector, St. Peter's.'

"Mr. Farlow also says: 'This certifieth that I have on several occasions seen the entry, No. 36, in the Register of St. Peter's Church (C. of E.), Richmond, New South Wales, Australia, relating to the burial of Margaret Catchpole, and vouch for the accuracy of the wording of the entry. . . .
Signed ROBERT WILLIAM FARLOW, J.P.'

"Singular to say, no less than three rectors of St. Peter's have given incorrect copies of the Register. A former Rector (not now a clergyman), R. E. Kemp, gave Margaret's age as fifty-one; the Rev. John Boardman, in 1911, gave me (in a letter) her age as fifty-three years, and now the Rev. Stanley G. Best affirms that her age was fifty-two. The Rev. William Woolls, Ph.D., F.L.S., and Rector of St. Peter's for seven or eight years (during my residence in the district, and the whole time we were personal friends), gave her age as fifty-eight, so also did an earlier Rector, the Rev. —— Ewing; also the Rev. J. Howell Price, who came after Kemp, and now Mr. Dillon. I have by me a tracing of the entry, kindly taken by Mr. Farlow, so that there can be no doubt whatever as to Margaret's age."

Thus the trail of inaccuracy seems to be over the problem both at home and in the colonies. One sentence in Mr. Johnson's letter shows, however, that he is keenly alive to the absurdity of some subjective criticism. Mary Haydock became Mrs. Raby, Reiby, or Rieby. Mr. Cobbold calls Margaret's husband, whose name she begs may be concealed, 'Barry.' It was easy for quidnuncs and malicious people to say when they read Cobbold's book, "Why, that's Mrs. Raby! See, you have only to transpose the letters of the name and add an 'r' and there you are." But it is strange that nobody should have told Mrs. Reiby about the entry in the registry of St. Peter's Church, Richmond, which would once for all have proved that Margaret had been long dead.

tive to the imputation that she was Margaret Catchpole; and Mr. Charles Cobbold in a letter to his brother Richard, given below, was evidently convinced that "Mary Haydock" and "Margaret Catchpole" were the same person.

<small>Letter from the author's brother.</small>

My dear Richard,

Curious things are always happening, & I cannot delay to send the particulars of what has recently transpired, in relation to Margaret :—I think I mentioned to you, that about 2 years ago, I saw a Daughter of (*the supposed*) Margarets, & sent by her, a Note & a Copy of our Mothers poems, directed to Mrs. Raby, at Sydney ; I think I also told you, that this Mrs. Thomson, in conversation with me about her Mother *distinctly admitted*, that her Mothers *maiden name, as she had always understood,* was *Catchpole*, but that I was wrong as to *her Christian name being Margaret*, for her Mothers name was *Mary*; her anxiety to ellicit from me something of her Mothers history, was *great*, beyond everything, I ever before witnessed in life ; & her importunings were so great, that she got from me, that her Mother was from the County of Suffolk, & *that when I was a Child I knew her*; beyond this I said nothing. Now I am inclined to think this has led to the following.—last Thursday week, 4th inst. Wife & I were out for a Walk, & while so, a Gent^{n.} called, & exprefsed himself *very anxious to see me*; he said he was from Glasgow ; Our Servant told him that We were going to Glasgow on the following Monday ; when he requested pen, & Ink, & wrote the enclosed Note.—Accordingly We went on Monday last, to Glasgow ; it was My Wifes birthday ; & she never does, if she can help it, keep it at home, but gets out somewhere. Well, as soon as We arrived in Glasgow, Dannaley & myself, went to see this Mr. Hope, who is an extensive, East, & West India Merchant. He very soon open'ed the budget, by shewing me a Letter, (*I believe*) in Margarets hand writing, in which, (a postscript) she says, " make my best respects to Mr. Cobbold, thank him for the Book but he is mistaken as to his ever having known me."—this, of course, led to a long conversation, & a very interesting one too.—Mr. Hope stated what he had always heard of Mrs. *Reiby's* history, *from his Father*, who was *a Cousin of hers*, & knew *all the particulars of* her *conviction transportation*, &c. his Father (who is dead) always told him that her maiden name was *Mary Haddock* ; that as a Girl, she was a romping, lively, Girl, & very fond of riding ; & would always take advantage of a ride, whenever she could ; that her Father was a small Farmer, living in Lancashire ; (I forget the name of the place tho' he mentioned it ;) that she was one day walking along the road, when a Gent.^{n.} came up to her & asked her to ride his Horse to the Village,

THE STORY OF MARGARET CATCHPOLE 483

(*a little distance off*), to which she readily consented & whilst in the act of so doing, she was taken into custody, & carried away to Lancaster Jail, & in due time, "TRIED AT BURY" in Lancashire ; & convicted, & sentenced to 7 years transportation ; that on her pafsage out, the Captain (Reiby) of the Vefsel, was so taken with her, that on her arrival at Sydney he married her, & settled in Sydney ; that at one time she kept a Spirit Shop there ; and a general Store ; that in course of time, he died, & left her all his property, which was very large ; & that she had 3 Daughters & 2 Sons ; that about *25 years* ago she was over at Glasgow, with two of her Daughters, & that she left them *there*, whilst *she went to London* ; & that at the end of ab^t *3 Weeks* she returned, & took her Daughters away ; that he never knew of her return to Sydney, *'till many months afterwards* when she wrote upon businefs ; that she negotiates businefs, to this day, in a very extensive way, & that he is *her Agent* & (as I said) she addrefses him as " My dear Cousin."— M^r· Hope mentioned very many coincidences corroborative of her being *the very individual* ; & when he had gone over his history of her, I went over *mine*, or in other words *Margaret Catchpoles* ; at which he was very much interested & astonished ; & exprefsed himself perfectly satisfied that she must be *the Margaret Catchpole*, whom *he* has all his life been led to believe Was the original *Mary Haddock* ; he has never seen the "Book" ; but is determined to get it.—he says that her Son was over a few Years since for the purpose of purchasing an Estate in England, but he could not make out where. It is just about 25 years ago that Our poor dear Mother one day, when riding in the Town, threw herself back in the Carriage & exclaimed, " *Good God, there is Margaret Catchpole, if ever I saw her in my life.*"—Grace was with her & well remembers my Mothers anxiety at the conviction of its being Margaret ; She was riding in a Carriage ; & about that time there was some very singular occurrence took place at M^{rs}· *Shorts of Bouldge but* Grace says that it was supposed at the time that *no one else than Margaret*, could have been a party to it—However, there is something very extraordinary in the coincidences & I really still believe her to be the person & that She has for a series of years done all in her power to conceal from her Family her real history & that in consequence a part of it having transpired to elude them, she has from time to time countenanced & adopted M^r· Hopes edition to me—M^r· Hope is extremely anxious to see one of her Letters to my Mother, & has begged of me to ask you to lend *me one of her latest* that he may see if the hand & false spellings at all correspond ; I told him I w^d· try & get the loan of one, but I was quite sure it w^d· be on condition of my taking the most especial care of it ; so if you can let me have one for a little while pray do & I will guarrantee its safe return.

I have been looking very anxiously for *Mary Ann Wellington*; I hope it is coming out; *let me know.*

I am happy to say that We are all quite well as the late hot weather would allow us to be; such a run of heat the Scotch people have never been accustomed to; the thermometer has been in the Shade as high as 86—& in the Sun 130—

Accept for Yr'self, Wife & Boys, the united Love of my Wife, My Son & Your Affectionate Brother

CHARLES COBBOLD.

BROUGHTON PARK, EDINH.,
June 21, 1846.

Let me have Mr. Hopes Note again.

<small>The problem similar to that in Acts.</small>

The object, however, of this paper is not to offer a solution of the intricate problem of Margaret Catchpole, but to give an example of the difficulty of writing true history on the basis of tradition, or even of authentic documents. What has been written bears very closely on the problem of Acts and of other composite documents in early Christian literature. It shows how an author may adapt " We " sections to his purpose and colour them by his own literary style. It illustrates the methods of reporting official documents, and of amplifying narrative. It is on the one hand a warning against subjective criticism, and against placing reliance upon theories, however acute, based on no sufficient evidence, and on the other it shows how good and sincere men may fall into serious errors in relating what they believe to be simple facts, even when they have no motive in misrepresenting them. It is a convincing proof that accuracy in topographical and other detail does not always guarantee the historic truth of every other statement. And, as human nature remains much the same, it justifies treating an ancient document by the guidance of a modern experience.

APPENDIX B

VESTIGIA CHRISTI ACCORDING TO LUKE

By F. C. Burkitt

THE essay on pp. 106-20 indicates the main lines of the thesis that (1) Luke has given us a not misleading impression of the personality and the general career of our Lord, but (2) he has so rewritten and arranged the material taken from his sources that we cannot disentangle them, much less reconstruct them from a consideration of his text alone; and, further, (3) he has done his work so skilfully that it is very difficult to construct out of the Lucan writings a picture of Jesus or his Ministry from any other point of view than Luke's own. It follows from this that the general story of Acts may be accepted with some confidence as a substantially historical account of the Early Days of Christianity, but that we cannot reconstruct the sources used; and, further, that we cannot hope to discover much material for another view of the subject by " reading between the lines " of the Lucan Acts of the Apostles.

This volume of Essays is mainly concerned with Acts, but in view of the importance of the conclusions here stated, I have thought it not out of place to make a reconstruction of the external events of our Lord's Ministry, as far as they can be gathered from Luke alone, so as to learn how much or how little we can expect to control the march of events from what Luke has told us in Acts.

It is advisable, perhaps, to begin with a Note on καθεξῆς (Luke i. 3). Luke claims to write "in order," having followed out everything from the beginning (ἄνωθεν). This certainly does imply, in a general way, chronological order. But it does not necessarily imply a claim of superior chronological order to other " Gospels," or even to Mark. Rather is it a claim to present a chronological order, as contrasted with a systematic or doctrinal one. Luke begins not with a doctrine about God, or with " righteousness and temperance and judgment to come," but with John the Baptist and the birth and infancy of Jesus. He goes on to give a picture of the public career of Jesus, and then, in a second volume, traces the course of the Christian Movement from Jerusalem to Rome, the latter part of his narrative taking the form of scenes from the life of the great missionary, St. Paul. The word καθεξῆς, "in order," is justified by this generally historical treatment of the subject.

An historical presentation of the public life of Jesus necessarily begins with the Baptism by John, and goes on to the final visit to Jerusalem and the incidents of the Passion. But what precisely is it that Luke tells us? The following *précis* exhibits the march of events, according to Luke, up to the arrival in Jerusalem.

[1] Lk. iii. 1, 21. Jesus, having been baptized by John (about A.D. 29)[1] and
[2] iv. 1 ff. subsequently 'tempted' in the desert,[2] returns to Galilee[3]
[3] iv. 14.
[4] iv. 15. and teaches in the synagogues.[4] At 'Nazara,' his own home,
[5] iv. 16 ff. he is rejected,[5] but has more success at Capernaum.[6] Start-
[6] iv. 31 ff. ing from Capernaum, he goes about preaching in " the syna-
[7] iv. 43, 44. gogues of Judaea" (*i.e.* Palestine generally, cf. Luke i. 5).[7]
We next hear of the call of Simon Peter by the Lake of
[8] v. 1 ff. Gennesaret,[8] after which comes a series of anecdotes without
[9] v. 12 ff. any definite indications of place or sequence of time,[9] but in
[10] vii. 1. the story of the Centurion Jesus is again at Capernaum,[10]
[11] vii. 11. and 'afterwards' (or, "on the next day") he is at Nain.[11]
'Afterwards' Jesus with the Twelve and certain women are
[12] viii. 1. journeying about,[12] and Jesus speaks to the crowd in parables.[13]
[13] viii. 4 ff. One day he crosses over the Lake to the country of the
[14] viii. 26. Gerasenes, opposite Galilee,[14] but returns immediately. The
[15] ix. 1 ff. Twelve soon afterwards are sent preaching in the villages,[15]
[16] ix. 10. and on their return Jesus goes away secretly to Bethsaida,[16]
where the crowds follow and the 5000 are fed. One day,
[17] ix. 18. when Jesus is alone praying—no place or time is indicated[17]
—Peter comes with the disciples and declares him to be the
Christ; about eight days after, Peter and John and James
[18] ix. 28 ff. witness the Transfiguration "in the mountain."[18] The de-
[19] ix. 37. moniac boy is healed "on the next day."[19]

[20] ix. 51 ff.
[21] x. 1, 17. Jesus now sets His face to go to Jerusalem, and is conse-
[22] x. 38. quently not received at a Samaritan village.[20] The seventy-
[23] xi. 14, 27, two are sent out and return.[21] On the way Jesus is received
29; xii. 1, 13, by Martha and Mary at a certain village.[22] A number of
54; xiv. 25.
[24] xi. 37, 53; incidents follow, several of which involve the presence of
xiii. 31; xiv. 1; crowds,[23] Pharisees,[24] and a synagogue,[25] all on the way to
xv. 2; xvi. 14.
[25] xiii. 10. Jerusalem.[26] Presently Jesus is "journeying through the
[26] xiii. 22. midst of Samaria and Galilee,"[27] and so arrives at Jericho,[28]
[27] xvii. 11.
[28] xviii. 35. from whence he goes up to Jerusalem.[29]
[29] xix. 28.

It will be clear from this *précis* that had we not the far more detailed, if puzzling, notes of place and time given by Mark, we should be totally unable to make out the course of events in order from the meagre indications furnished by Luke.

This is often forgotten, or not realised at all, by readers of the Third Gospel, for we mentally supply the missing links of time and place from Mark. Why do modern investigators of the Synoptic Problem tend to call Luke ix. 51-xviii. 14 the " Peraean Section " ? The other side of Jordan is never indicated in Luke : the section is only thought of as " Peraean " because it seems to correspond to a journey through Peraea mentioned in Mark x. 1.

But in the Acts Mark fails us. I venture to think we must beware of expecting a higher standard of topographical and chronological exactitude in Acts than in the Third Gospel.

Ἐπειδήπερ πολλοὶ ἐπεχείρησαν ἀνατάξασθαι διήγησιν περὶ τῶν πεπληροφορημένων ἐν ἡμῖν πραγμάτων, καθὼς παρέδοσαν ἡμῖν οἱ ἀπ' ἀρχῆς αὐτόπται καὶ ὑπηρέται γενόμενοι τοῦ λόγου, ἔδοξε κἀμοὶ παρηκολουθηκότι ἄνωθεν πᾶσιν ἀκριβῶς καθεξῆς σοι γράψαι, κράτιστε Θεόφιλε, ἵνα ἐπιγνῷς περὶ ὧν κατηχήθης λόγων τὴν ἀσφάλειαν.

APPENDIX C

COMMENTARY ON THE PREFACE OF LUKE

By HENRY J. CADBURY

IN the study of the earliest Christian history no passage has had more emphasis laid upon it than the brief preface of Luke. It is the only place in the synoptic gospels where the consciousness of authorship is expressed, containing as it does the only reference outside the gospel of John [1] to the origin or purpose of the evangelic record. It has naturally been repeatedly treated in special monographs,[2] as well as in introductions and commentaries, and has been cited in connection with every problem of early Christian literature. This importance, together with the difficulties which its terse and ambiguous language raises, justifies a somewhat extended commentary, especially in connection with a work like Acts which is written by the same author and addressed to the same person.

The following commentary is intended not to repeat all that has been well said before, nor to refute all that has been ill said, but to consider primarily the actual meaning of the words in the light of fresh inquiry into new lexical material, and into the grade of literary culture which the words seem to suggest. Particular stress is laid on parallels from Luke's own usage as forming the best com-

---

[1] John xix. 35; xx. 30, 31; xxi. 24, 25.

[2] See especially W. Grimm, in *Jahrbücher für deutsche Theologie*, xvi. (1871), pp. 33-78 with the list of earlier discussions given there; and add C. A. Heumann and Th. Hase, *Bibliotheca Bremensis*, Class iv. Fasc. 3 (1721), pp. 484-531; Belser, *Theol. Quartalschrift*, Tübingen (1893); W. M. Ramsay, *Was Christ Born at Bethlehem?* (1898), chapter i.; Fr. Blass, *Philology of the Gospels* (1898), chapter ii. and review of same by P. Corssen in *Göttingische Gelehrten Anzeigen* (1899), pp. 313 ff.; A. Beck, *Der Prolog des Lukas-Evangeliums* (Progr. Amberg, 1900); A. T. Robertson, *Luke the Historian in the Light of Research* (1920), chapter iv. (=*Biblical Review*, v. (1920), pp. 171-195); G. H. Whitaker, "The Philology of Luke's Preface," in the *Expositor* for October and November 1920 and March 1921; E. Meyer, *Ursprung und Anfänge des Christentums*, i. (1921), pp. 5-11.

mentary, and the most suggestive solution of obscurities, but it has been thought essential often to present more than one alternative.

The form of the preface should be considered in the light of contemporary Hellenistic literature.[1] Its adoption at once suggests a certain flavour of conventionality on the part of the author as consciously presenting his book to the public. The dedication to Theophilus [2] means this, rather than that the book is intended for a limited circle. Even the specific purpose expressed in the preface —apparently that of defending Christianity from possible misunderstanding and odium on the part of the secular authorities [3]— must not be applied too seriously to the work as a whole. The subjects discussed in prefaces were limited both naturally and by tradition,[4] and several of the conventional *motifs* appear in this brief one. Thus again we are reminded not to lay too great stress on the selection of ideas contained in it. Its very brevity is an admirable illustration of obedience to ancient maxims on preface writing.[5] Its rhetorical balance and periodic construction, contrasting so markedly with the Semitic or Biblical style that follows in Luke i. 5 ff., show that the preface is the work of an artist, rather than that the nativity stories are that of a translator.[6]

[1] On ancient prefaces see H. Lieberich, *Studien zu den Proömien in der griechischen und byzantinischen Geschichtsschreibung* (Munich, 1898, 1900); G. Engel, *De antiquorum epicorum didacticorum historicorum prooemiis* (Diss. Inaug., Marburg, 1910).

[2] On the dedicating of books in antiquity see Rud. Gräfenhain, *De more libros dedicandi apud scriptores Graecos et Romanos obvio* (Marburg, 1892), and J. Ruppert, *Quaestiones ad historiam dedicationis librorum pertinentes* (Diss. Inaug., Leipzig, 1911).

[3] See my article in *The Expositor*, June 1921, "The Purpose expressed in Luke's Preface," and the discussion in the same periodical between D. Plooij (December 1914, February 1917) and Maurice Jones (March 1915); also the argument made two centuries ago by C. A. Heumann (cited above, p. 489 *note*) to the effect that Luke's work is an *apologia*.

[4] See Engel, *op. cit.* pp. 6, 7, 42. This limitation of subject matter is responsible for the close similarity between prefaces. It led in antiquity to frequent charges of plagiarism in prefaces and in modern times to theories of Luke's literary dependence upon Josephus (Krenkel, *Josephus und Lucas*, 1894, pp. 50 ff.), or upon Greek medical writers (references in Moffatt, *Introduction to the Literature of the N.T.* p. 263; and Galen, *De typis* (Kuhn vii. 463) πολλῶν πλατυτέρω . . . πεπραγματευμένων, ἀνάγκαιον ἡγησάμην αὐτός, *De tremore* (ibid. 584) ἐπειδὴ Πυθαγόρας . . . οὐκ ὀρθῶς . . . διὰ τοῦτο ἔδοξέ μοι.

[5] Lucian, *De hist. conscrib.* 23, cf. 55. Compare 2 Macc. ii. 32 ἐντεῦθεν οὖν ἀρξώμεθα τῆς διηγήσεως, τοῖς προειρημένοις τοσοῦτον ἐπιζεύξαντες· εὔηθες γὰρ τὸ μὲν πρὸ τῆς ἱστορίας πλεονάζειν, τὴν δὲ ἱστορίαν ἐπιτέμνειν.

[6] I may content myself here with a reference to my remarks on this subject in the *American Journal of Theology*, xxiv. (1920), pp. 438 f., but as Norden says in a note to the passage there quoted, a study of the contrast in style between ancient works and their prefaces is greatly to be desired.

It is necessary once more to remind the reader that it was the custom in antiquity, on account of the purely physical conditions of writing, to divide works into volumes, to prefix to the first a preface for the whole, and to add secondary prefaces to the beginning of each later one. The impression made on the English reader by Acts i. 1, that the author is making a new start or at least preparing a kind of sequel to his gospel, would not occur to an early reader. The book of Acts is no afterthought. The word "treatise" implies a more complete work than does λόγος. The reference to the preceding book, and the renewed address to the patron, are typical of these secondary prefaces in Greek and Latin literature,[1] and

---

[1] For examples of ἀνακεφαλαίωσις see Norden, *Agnostos Theos* (1913), pp. 311-13, and above pp. 133 ff. But too much stress must not be laid on the single passage there cited from Polybius, nor can it be assumed that προγραφή and προέκθεσις were fixed terms for fixed literary devices. The passage in question is preserved only through the medium of an epitomator, and the statement made cannot be interpreted by observing the actual practice of Polybius, since his work has come down to us in very mutilated form, and possibly was repeatedly revised by the author himself (R. Laqueur, *Polybius*, Berlin, 1913). Beside the references given above, p. 134 *note*, see the discussion by Engel, *op. cit.* pp. 55-57.

The προέκθεσις, more accurately προέκθεσις τῶν πράξεων (or τῆς πραγματείας), mentioned elsewhere also by Polybius, was a synopsis or *argumentum* giving the principal subjects to be discussed. He used it at the beginning of his main narrative (iii. 1. 7) and also at the beginning of each Olympiad. In the passage cited (cf. also xiv. *prooem.*) he explains this custom (cf. the advice of Lucian, *De hist. conscrib.* 53 εὐμαθῆ δὲ καὶ σαφῆ τὰ ὕστερον ποιήσει, τὰς αἰτίας προεκτιθέμενος καὶ περιορίζων τὰ κεφάλαια τῶν γεγενημένων), and compares it with the προγραφή which other writers and Polybius himself (in Books I.-VI.) used at the beginning of each volume instead of (in addition to ?) the προέκθεσις. What was the προγραφή? Is it possible that it is the ordinary preface which was used by Hellenistic historians like Ephorus (Diodorus Sic. xvi. 76) at the beginning of each volume, and sometimes by Polybius himself? It dealt with the same subject matter as a προέκθεσις, but also with the purposes, methods, and value of history, the vices of other historians, and other general subjects. It was therefore often remote from the actual content of the work or individual volume to which it was attached, and in time, under the influence of rhetoric, became an interruptive, excursive, and ridiculous appendage to the narrative.

For the student of Acts the important thing is not the meaning of these words nor the difference between them. Strictly speaking, the present text of Acts has neither προγραφή nor προέκθεσις, whether these terms mean a detached label, a table of contents, or a preface. But aside from these types of prefatory composition it was also a custom among ancient writers, as we know by numerous examples, to make the transition to a succeeding volume by summarizing in a few words the contents of the preceding one. It is this convention—whether it had a technical name or not makes little difference—which is followed by the author in beginning the Book of Acts.

492 COMMENTARY ON THE PREFACE OF LUKE

are intended to recall the original preface to the reader. Luke i. 1-4 therefore is not merely of indirect value to the student of Acts as an introduction to another work written by the same author and addressed to the same patron. It is the real preface to Acts as well as to the Gospel, written by the author when he contemplated not merely one but both volumes.[1] Possibly it was written when the second volume was completed, and therefore applies more especially to that which had more recently been in his thought.[2] It is as necessary to apply the phraseology of the preface to Acts as to the Gospel; and to recognise that references to previous writers, to "eye-witnesses and ministers of the word," to the author's own intimate knowledge of the subjects treated, are equally applicable to both books, as are also such phrases as περὶ τῶν πεπληροφορημένων ἐν ἡμῖν πραγμάτων and περὶ ὧν κατηχήθης λόγων.[3]

ἐπειδήπερ] This form, found here only in the Greek Bible, is not uncommon in Attic prose or in the literary writings of the Hellenistic age, e.g. Philo. It occurs also in the papyri of iii./A.D. Usually, however, like some other relatives in -περ, it occurs when it does not precede the main clause.[4] Perhaps Luke adopts it here to give a formal and literary flavour to his preface without observing the delicate nuance which makes it appropriate for post-positive clauses.

πολλοί] This word is apparently frequent in rhetorical prefaces, as Schwartz, "Zur Chronologie des Paulus" in *Nachrichten von der königl. Gesellschaft der Wissenschaften zu Göttingen*, philol.-histor. Klasse (1907), p. 294, has suggested. Each of the addresses made before Felix in Acts xxiv. begins with it: Tertullus πολλῆς εἰρήνης τυγχάνοντες διὰ σοῦ, Paul ἐκ πολλῶν ἐτῶν ὄντα σε κριτὴν τῷ ἔθνει τούτῳ ἐπιστάμενος. The first sentence in the Epistle to the Hebrews, which vies with Luke's preface for the honour of being the most carefully constructed period in the New Testament, begins with the alliteration: πολυμερῶς καὶ πολυτρόπως πάλαι ὁ θεὸς λαλήσας τοῖς πατράσιν ἐν τοῖς προφήταις κτλ. The Greek prose prologue of the

---

[1] For the possibility that a third volume was intended see the commentary on Acts i. 1 and xxviii. 31.

[2] Cf. *Expositor*, June 1921, p. 439 and note 14.

[3] That the preface applies to Luke only and not to Acts was argued by Grimm, *loc. cit.* pp. 54-58, as by others before him whom he mentions. But the other position is well presented by Zahn, *Introduction*, § 60 note 10, and is naturally accepted by non-theological scholars like Norden and Eduard Meyer (*Die Evangelien*, 1921, pp. 10 f.).

[4] For example, in the Prooemium of Josephus, *Bellum* 6 ἀρχαιολογεῖν μὲν δὴ τὰ Ἰουδαίων ... νῦν τε ἄκαιρον ᾠήθην εἶναι καὶ ἄλλως περιττόν, ἐπειδήπερ καὶ Ἰουδαίων πολλοὶ πρὸ ἐμοῦ τὰ τῶν προγόνων συνετάξαντο μετ' ἀκριβείας.

translator of the poetic Wisdom of ben Sira [1] begins πολλῶν καὶ μεγάλων ἡμῖν διὰ τοῦ νόμου καὶ τῶν προφητῶν καὶ τῶν ἄλλων τῶν κατ' αὐτοὺς ἠκολουθηκότων δεδομένων. So also the editorial epilogue of John's Gospel (xx. 30, 31; cf. the colophon in xxi. 25) begins πολλὰ μὲν οὖν καὶ ἄλλα σημεῖα ἐποίησεν ὁ Ἰησοῦς. Classical students will recall the opening sentence of Xenophon's *Memorabilia* : πολλάκις ἐθαύμασα τίσι ποτὲ λόγοις κτλ. The illustrations given by Schwartz from medical works and from Cicero can be supplemented by many of the opening sentences in the Attic orators. In Dionysius of Halicarnassus see the opening of his *De oratoribus antiquis* : πολλὴν χάριν ἦν εἰδέναι τῷ καθ' ἡμᾶς χρόνῳ δίκαιον, ὦ κράτιστε Ἀμμαῖε (πολλὴν χάριν again opens a speech in *Ant. Rom.* vi. 43) and of his *Epist. I. ad Ammaeum* πολλῶν μετ' ἄλλων ξένων τε καὶ παραδόξων ἀκουσμάτων. In Josephus the long speech of Jeshua, the high priest, in *B.J.* iv. 4. 3 begins : πολλῶν καὶ ποικίλων τὴν πόλιν κατεσχηκότων θορύβων κτλ. Cf. *Ant.* xv. 5. 3 ; xix. 1. 12 ; xix. 2. 2. The decree in Lucian's *Menippus* 20 begins : ἐπειδὴ πολλὰ καὶ παράνομα. From the published papyri one does not gather that this literary form was also a legal one. Possibly the mutilated letter of a sightseer in P Lond. 854 (i./A.D.) offered a parallel, but in any case it is more literary than legal.

In view of the formal nature of the preface as a whole and of this usage in particular one must not press the πολλοί here to mean *very many* predecessors in gospel authorship. There are strong reasons for discounting the force of πολύς in the two instances of its initial use in Acts xxiv. cited above.

ἐπεχείρησαν] This is a good classical word, though it occurs in the Greek Bible chiefly in Luke and in 2 Maccabees, which so often show affinities in vocabulary and style (see above, pp. 73 ff., and Cadbury, *Style and Literary Method of Luke*, pp. 6 ff.). In the other instances it is applied to hostile (Acts ix. 29) or presumptuous (Acts xix. 13) undertakings. For this reason many early interpreters of this preface understood this passage as a reference to imperfect or heretical gospels. But ἐπιχειρέω often has a much more neutral meaning, and by itself it cannot prove that Luke is making odious comparisons, though such comparisons are not unusual in the prefaces of ancient historians. If the earlier accounts were unsatisfactory to Luke, the best proof of that fact is his desire to write another account and the claims he makes for his own composition. The other writers are mentioned as precedents rather than as failures.

---

[1] On this prologue see J. H. A. Hart, *Ecclesiasticus in Greek* (1909), pp. 231-271. He says (p. 235), " The sonorous Genitive Absolute πολλῶν . . . δεδομένων, with its pendant, is a proper opening for such a composition," and compares the Preface of Luke. He thinks this preface influenced the Exordium of the Epistle to the Hebrews (p. 238), as well as Philo and " Aristeas."

COMMENTARY ON THE PREFACE OF LUKE

As Loisy (*Évan. Synop.* p. 271) says, Luke justifies his undertaking by the example of those who had preceded and had no more reason to try than himself. In the κἀμοί he associates himself with the πολλοί rather than dissociates himself: "since many have tried . . . it seemed good to me *also*."

It is true that Josephus uses ἐπιχειρέω of the presumptuous efforts of his rivals to write Jewish history (*Vita* 9 θαρρῶν ἐπεχείρησεν καὶ τὴν ἱστορίαν τῶν πραγμάτων τούτων ἀναγράφειν, 65 Ἰοῦστος γοῦν συγγράφειν τὰς περὶ τούτων ἐπιχειρήσας πράξεις, cf. *B.J.* i. *prooem.* 3 ἱστορίας αὐτὰς ἐπιγράφειν τολμῶσιν), but he also uses it without any criticism of the early Greek historians (*Contra Apion.* i. 2 οἱ μέντοι τὰς ἱστορίας ἐπιχειρήσαντες συγγράφειν παρ' αὐτοῖς), and Polybius uses it of himself (iii. 1. 4; if. 37. 4) and of the ideal historians (xii. 28. 3 ὅταν οἱ πραγματικοὶ τῶν ἀνδρῶν γράφειν ἐπιχειρήσωσι τὰς ἱστορίας).

The use of ἐπεχείρησαν ἀνατάξασθαι for the simple ἀνετάξαντο may be due merely to the desire for rhetorical fulness,[1] as Casaubon suggested, but it is very likely due to the modest periphrases with πειράσομαι with which ancient writers were wont in their prefaces to refer to their own work, *e.g.* Xenophon, *Cyropaedia, prooem. sub fin.* ὅσα οὖν καὶ ἐπυθόμεθα καὶ ᾐσθῆσθαι δοκοῦμεν περὶ αὐτοῦ, ταῦτα πειρασόμεθα διηγήσασθαι, Archimedes, *Arenarius, prooem.* πειράσομαί τοι δεικνύειν δι' ἀποδείξιων γεωμετρικῶν, αἷς παρακολουθήσεις κτλ., 2 Macc. ii. 19-23 τὰ δὲ κατὰ τὸν Ἰούδαν τὸν Μακκαβαῖον . . . ὑπὸ Ἰάσωνος τοῦ Κυρηναίου δεδηλωμένα διὰ πέντε βιβλίων, πειρασόμεθα δι' ἑνὸς συντάγματος ἐπιτεμεῖν.

ἀνατάξασθαι] This word has received a considerable amount of discussion, in which it is often forgotten that it is applied to Luke's predecessors rather than to Luke himself. Its meaning is therefore not of great importance for an understanding of his own composition. This is fortunate, since the word is not very common, and is used in very different senses. It is neither a fixed term, as Wendland, *Die urchristliche Literaturformen*, 2nd edit. p. 325, declares, nor can it be clearly distinguished from συντάξασθαι as meaning "restore from memory" on the basis of the two passages, Plutarch, *De sollertia animalium* 968 C D and Irenaeus iii. 21. 2. It is read by some MSS. in Eccles. ii. 20 ἐπέστρεψα ἐγὼ τοῦ ἀνατάξασθαι τῇ καρδίᾳ μου (vv. ll. ἀποτάξασθαι, τὴν καρδίαν), where the Hebrew יאש is said to mean "to cause to despair"[2]). The word also occurs

---

[1] As a similar expletive, though more Semitic than Greek, may be explained the phrase in the secondary preface, Acts i. 1 ἤρξατο Ἰησοῦς ποιεῖν τε καὶ διδάσκειν.

[2] The commentaries and dictionaries seem to have generally overlooked the compound in Ps. cxxxvi. (cxxxvii.) 6 ἐὰν μὴ προανατάξωμαι τὴν Ἰερουσαλὴμ ἐν ἀρχῇ τῆς εὐφροσύνης μου, where the parallel with ἐὰν μή σου μνησθῶ could be pressed as confirming the interpretation "from memory."

in Aristeas 144 of the establishment of laws by Moses (the form ἀνατέτακται may be either passive or middle, cf. διατέτακται in 147), in the active in Marcus Aurelius iii. 5. 2 ἀνατεταχότος ἑαυτόν, and in the passive in Cassius Dio lxxviii. 18. 5 (ἀνετάγη = " were rehearsed "—Foster ; other translators and editors appear to adopt Reiske's conjecture of ἀνετράπη). The lexica interpret this form as εὐτρεπίσασθαι (Hesychius, Suidas) and later add συντάξαι, ἀναγράψασθαι (Zonaras), but they are evidently thinking principally of this passage.

Probably the emphasis in the word is on the verb rather than on the preposition. Possibly Luke has chosen it as a somewhat scarce (choice) substitute for the usual συντάξασθαι of written composition. But it is very doubtful whether, as Corssen suggests, the thought of literary arrangement (τάξις, the rhetorical *terminus technicus*) is uppermost.[1]

διήγησιν] This word, like ἐπειδήπερ and ἀνατάξασθαι, occurs here only in the New Testament, but unlike them it occurs several times in the Old Testament, including an occurrence in the preface of 2 Maccabees. It is not an unusual word. The verb διηγέομαι occurs in Luke and Acts as well as in Mark and Hebrews.[2] There is no reason to distinguish διήγησις as the name for a writing from what Luke might have called his own work, e.g. λόγος (Acts i. 1). It is rather for the sake of variety than to express a difference that Luke does not repeat of himself in verses 3 and 4 the exact words applied to others in verses 1 and 2. καθεξῆς γράψαι may mean no more and no less than ἀνατάξασθαι διήγησιν.

πεπληροφορημένων] This word occurs in various early Christian writings but rarely if ever in pre-Christian Greek literature. See the instances listed in Lietzmann, *Handbuch zum N.T.* on Rom. iv. 21 and add *Test. XII. Patr.*, Gad, 2. 4 ; Vettius Valens (edit. Kroll) 43. 18 ; 226. 20. In the papyri, however, it is used frequently in the sense of paying off debts, settling legal matters, etc. (Deissmann, *Licht vom Osten*, Eng. trans. pp. 82 f.). The use in the papyri and the probable course of the semasiological history of the word are fully discussed by Lagrange, *Bulletin d'ancienne littérature et d'archéologie chrétiennes*, ii. (1912), pp. 96-100.

The verb and its noun πληροφορία are used by Paul and other early Christian writers in the sense of " conviction." This meaning is still accepted by some scholars here, but there is a real difficulty

---

[1] See Lucian, *De hist. conscrib.* 48, quoted above, p. 12. Cf. F. H. Colson, " τάξει in Papias : the Gospels and the Rhetorical Schools," *Journal of Theological Studies*, xiv. (1912), pp. 62-69.

[2] Hebrews xi. 32, but in ii. 12 διηγήσομαι of the LXX. becomes ἀπαγγελῶ ; see the same interchange in Mark and Luke, in Cadbury, *Style and Literary Method of Luke*, p. 184.

in applying to things the passive of a verb meaning "convince," in the sense of things of which one is convinced. The simpler meaning of the word is " complete." This is well attested and is preferable here. It is supported by the early versions, whose spontaneous testimony, based upon a knowledge of the every-day use of Greek, is, as Lagrange correctly argues, more trustworthy in an instance like this than the learned tradition of patristic *curiositas* descending from Origen.

Perhaps for a second time in this preface Luke has chosen a longer and more sonorous word when a simple πληρόω would have served his purpose as it has done elsewhere, *e.g.* Acts xix. 21 ὡς δὲ ἐπληρώθη ταῦτα, xii. 25 πληρώσαντες τὴν διακονίαν (cf. 2 Tim. iv. 5 τὴν διακονίαν σου πληροφόρησον = Col. iv. 17 βλέπε τὴν διακονίαν ἣν παρέλαβες ἐν κυρίῳ ἵνα αὐτὴν πληροῖς and the combination in Col. iv. 12 τέλειοι καὶ πεπληροφορημένοι).

The suggestion that the fulfilment of Scripture is what Luke means need hardly be taken seriously, though of course πληρόω is so used. Nor does the agricultural force of -φορέω remain as in some other compounds used by Luke : τελεσφορέω (Luke viii. 14, cf. Mark iv. 19 ἄκαρπος), καρποφορέω (Luke viii. 15 = Mark iv. 20), εὐφορέω (Luke xii. 16), καρποφόρος (Acts xiv. 17). We may rather compare the colourless τὸ γεγονός, τὰ γενόμενα (*e.g.* Luke ii. 15 ; xxiv. 18).

πραγμάτων] πρᾶγμα occurs again in Acts v. 4 of the purposed crime of Ananias, and it is not an uncommon word. As used here in the plural it has a somewhat more literary flavour (it occurs in the Greek Bible elsewhere, chiefly in 2 Maccabees and Hebrews) than the Semitic ῥήματα, which usually takes its place in the LXX. and Luke, *e.g.* Luke i. 37 ; ii. 15, 51 ; Acts v. 32 ἡμεῖς ἐσμὲν μάρτυρες τῶν ῥημάτων τούτων. But we are particularly interested to know the scope of the matters on which the predecessors of Luke had written, especially whether they covered the matter now treated in Acts. Certainly neither of the two antecedent phrases can be understood under any interpretation as excluding it. Indeed ἐν ἡμῖν suits better the more recent events of Acts than the events of the Gospel now at least a generation old. Similarly it is possible to see a fitness in the application to the contents of Acts of the word πεπληροφορημένων on the part of a writer who speaks of the Gospel as an " account of all that Jesus began (ἤρξατο) to do and to teach " (Acts i. 1).

καθώς] Here is at least one word that the strictest Atticism condemns. But Luke, even in his best sentence, was not sensitive to this objection,[1] nor did many of his contemporaries share it. Codex Bezae and Eusebius (*H.E.* iii. 4. 6 ; *Demon. Evang.* p. 120)

[1] See, on Luke's uses of this word, Cadbury, *ibid.* p. 142.

COMMENTARY ON THE PREFACE OF LUKE 497

correct it here to καθά, another post-classical word,[1] which the Atticists recommend in its place (Phrynichus, edit. Rutherford, p. 495).

παρέδοσαν] The literary flavour of this form is unmistakable, for while in Attic Greek the aorist in κ for δίδωμι, ἵημι and τίθημι is used in the singular only, in the New Testament it supplies the plural also, with this single exception.[2] Contrast Luke's own -εδώκατε, -έδωκαν in Luke xxiv. 20, 42; Acts i. 26; iii 13; xv. 30.

The word has sometimes been said to exclude written transmission, and thereby to indicate either that Luke did not use written sources or that the written records which preceded Luke's or which he used as sources were not written by apostles. But beside the doubt one feels about dividing rigidly the πολλοί from the αὐτόπται καὶ ὑπηρέται (see next note), there is the fact that παραδίδωμι sometimes means written transmission. See Acts vi. 14 τὰ ἔθη ἃ παρέδωκεν ἡμῖν Μωυσῆς (cf. Aristeas 148); Justin, *Apol.* i. 66 οἱ ἀπόστολοι ἐν τοῖς γενομένοις ὑπ' αὐτῶν ἀπομνημονεύμασιν, ἃ καλεῖται εὐαγγέλια, οὕτως παρέδωκαν. See Eusebius, *H.E.* (edit. Schwartz, Index *s.v.*). The word, therefore, provides no objection to attributing an important written source of the first volume to John Mark (called in Acts xiii. 5 ὑπηρέτην) and an important written source of the second volume to an αὐτόπτης.

ἡμῖν] There seems at first sight little doubt that the writer distinguishes his own group from the αὐτόπται καὶ ὑπηρέται, and that both he and the earlier writers are definitely excluded from the category of eye-witnesses. This is generally conceded for his gospel, and on the authority of Papias it is also conceded for Mark as one of the πολλοί, but not for Acts, where the we-passages are understood to point to αὐτοψία on the part either of the author of Acts or of one of the sources which he used. Without doubt this is one of the reasons why it is customary to limit the preface to the Gospel and to agree with the Fathers[3] that the first volume was written by hearsay, the second from αὐτοψία. But there are three objections to this conventional arrangement: (1) Mark, even if not an eye-witness, was declared by this very writer to be a ὑπηρέτης (Acts xiii. 5) λόγου (note κατήγγελλον τὸν λόγον Acts, *loc. cit.* and xv. 36). (2) If we accept the probable meaning of πεπληροφορημένων, ἡμῖν at its earlier occurrence cannot possibly exclude eye-witnesses

---

[1] The isolated instances of each of these words in classical writers are probably due to defective MS. tradition.

[2] W alone reads παρέδοτε at Mk. vii. 13; see Moulton, *Grammar of N.T. Greek*, ii. p. 209, *note* 3.

[3] See above, p. 258 *n.* 2. The Canon of Muratori says of the Gospel: "ex opinione conscripsit, dominum tamen nec ipse vidit"; of Acts: "conprendit quia sub praesentia eius singula gerebantur."

and so we cannot insist on such an exclusion here. (3) παρηκολουθηκότι may mean precisely that the writer was a witness or actor in the scenes described (see below, *s.v.*).

ἀπ' ἀρχῆς] Compare the qualifications of the "witness of the resurrection"—for it was as such rather than as a member of the twelve that Matthias was chosen—described in Acts i. 21 f. τῶν συνελθόντων ἡμῖν ἀνδρῶν ἐν παντὶ χρόνῳ ᾧ εἰσῆλθεν καὶ ἐξῆλθεν ἐφ' ἡμᾶς ὁ κύριος Ἰησοῦς, ἀρξάμενος ἀπὸ τοῦ βαπτίσματος Ἰωάνου ἕως τῆς ἡμέρας ἧς ἀνελήφθη ἀφ' ἡμῶν, and the similar description in Acts x. 36 ff., especially 37 ἀρξάμενος ἀπὸ τῆς Γαλιλαίας μετὰ τὸ βάπτισμα ὃ ἐκήρυξεν Ἰωάνης, 39 ἡμεῖς μάρτυρες, 41 μάρτυσιν . . . ἡμῖν. Commentators usually cite also Mark i. 1 ἀρχή and Luke iii. 23 ἀρχόμενος as confirming the identification of the ἀρχή here with the baptism of John, but it is doubtful whether Luke read the first or so understood the second. Note, however, that in Luke iii. 1, 2 the era of John is emphasised by an elaborate synchronism.

With the phrase here should be compared the term for Mnason in Acts xxi. 16 ἀρχαῖος μαθητής. See further on ἄνωθεν below, p. 502.

αὐτόπται καὶ ὑπηρέται] Many questions may be raised concerning the grammatical arrangement of these words which cannot be answered, since they imply a clear-cut distinction which the author did not express and may not have felt. For example, we may ask, Are these two classes of persons or one? And do ἀπ' ἀρχῆς, γενόμενοι and τοῦ λόγου go with both nouns or only with the nearest noun respectively? The nearest parallel to the pair of nouns is Acts xxvi. 16 προχειρίσασθαί σε ὑπηρέτην καὶ μάρτυρα ὧν τε εἶδές με ὧν τε ὀφθήσομαί σοι. This suggests that in our passage one group of persons filling two functions is in the writer's mind, but that the dependent genitives go more naturally with the nearest nouns, *i.e.* with μάρτυρα in Acts and with ὑπηρέται in Luke (hence the inversion of order), and only by a kind of zeugma can be applied to the other nouns. The fact that γίνεσθαι is almost invariably used in Greek writers with αὐτόπτης favours assigning the participle to both nouns rather than merely to the nearest. ἀπ' ἀρχῆς perhaps should be connected with the participle rather than with the nouns, since in the parallel in Acts xxvi. 4 (see below, p. 503) it is emphatically connected with γενομένην by being placed between it and the repeated article. The whole would then read, as in the English versions, "they who from the beginning were eye-witnesses and ministers of the word."

The close association of αὐτόπται and ὑπηρέται is further justified when we appreciate that Luke is following a convention of historians in urging the intimate connection of himself and his associates with the facts themselves. The ancient historians like to begin their story ike Vergil's Aeneas with the claim: "ipse vidi et'. . . pars magna

COMMENTARY ON THE PREFACE OF LUKE 499

fui." Two illustrations will suffice: Polybius iii. 4. 13 τὸ δὲ μέγιστον, διὰ τὸ τῶν πλείστων μὴ μόνον αὐτόπτης ἀλλ' ὧν μὲν συνεργός, ὧν δὲ καὶ χειριστὴς γεγονέναι, Josephus, *Contra Apion*. i. 10 δεῖ τὸν ἄλλοις παράδοσιν πράξεων ἀληθινῶν ὑπισχνούμενον αὐτὸν ἐπίστασθαι ταύτας πρότερον ἀκριβῶς ἢ παρηκολουθηκότα τοῖς γεγονόσιν ἢ παρὰ τῶν εἰδότων πυνθανόμενον . . . τοῦ δὲ πολέμου τὴν ἱστορίαν ἔγραψα πολλῶν μὲν αὐτουργὸς πράξεων, πλείστων δ' αὐτόπτης γενόμενος. The opening verses of the first Epistle of John are perhaps a free treatment of the same *motif*. The Canon of Muratori applies them to the origin of the Fourth Gospel: "sic enim non solum visorem sed auditorem se et scriptorem omnium mirabilium domini per ordinem profitetur." In later Christian writers the problem of αὐτοψία continues to be important. The lost Λογίων κυριακῶν ἐξηγήσεις of Papias, perhaps the next oldest Christian work after Luke to contain both preface and dedication, dealt, according to Eusebius, *H.E.* iii. 39, with this subject in its preface; αὐτός γε μὴν ὁ Παπίας κατὰ τὸ προοίμιον τῶν αὐτοῦ λόγων ἀκροατὴν μὲν καὶ αὐτόπτην οὐδαμῶς ἑαυτὸν γενέσθαι τῶν ἱερῶν ἀποστόλων ἐμφαίνει.

The use of αὐτόπτης here in place of μάρτυς, the word used in Acts xxvi. 16 as well as in the cases cited under ἀπ' ἀρχῆς above (p. 498, see also Luke xxiv. 48; Acts i. 8; ii. 32; iii. 15; v. 32; xiii. 31; xxii. 15) is due in part to the difference of meaning (the words are combined in Josephus, *B.J.* vi. 2. 5). μάρτυς emphasises the evidence to be borne, αὐτόπτης the actual presence of the person testifying. But there was evidently among Greek historians a habitual emphasis upon αὐτοψία which led to frequent reference to it in any formal preface [1] as well as throughout historical works. Historians often claimed it for themselves. For examples see Peter, *Wahrheit und Kunst*, pp. 89 (Herodotus), 156 (Ephorus), 227 (Timaeus), 249 (Polybius).

Conversely the rivals of the historian are accused of ἀορασία, as Timaeus is accused by Polybius (xii. 25g, 3; 27). But the claim of eyewitness-ship became a commonplace of rhetoric (Peter, *op. cit.* pp. 226f.) and even in the case of Polybius is evidently exaggerated (*ibid.* p. 260; did he really cross the Alps?). With Diodorus, Josephus, Aelian, and Philostratus the claim is still more suspicious (*ibid.* p. 426). Lucian, *De hist. conscrib.* 29, represents

---

[1] Norden, *Agnostos Theos*, p. 316, says: "Das . . . Motiv autoptischer und referierender Berichterstattung hat nachweislich zum festen Inventare von Proömien gehört. Der τόπος war seit Thukydides (i. 22. 2) so beliebt, dass Lukian ihn in seinen 'wahrhaftigen Erzählungen' sogar parodieren konnte, (i. 4) γράφω τοίνυν περὶ ὧν μήτε εἶδον μήτε ἔπαθον μήτε παρ' ἄλλων ἐπυθόμην." For similar claims see Vettius Valens, vi. 9 (edit. Kroll, p. 260) ἐγὼ δὲ οὐ λόγῳ καλῷ χρησάμενος πολλὰ δὲ καμὼν καὶ παθὼν αὐτόπτης γενόμενος τῶν πραγμάτων δοκιμάσας συνέγραψα.

the extreme romancer as making the same conventional claim: γράφω τοίνυν ἃ εἶδον, οὐχ ἃ ἤκουσα. See further the strictures on stay-at-home historians mentioned above, pp. 9 f.

This conventional emphasis upon αὐτοψία and the use of αὐτόπται in the preface must partly explain the use of " we " in Acts, but it does not determine whether that awkward phenomenon is to be explained as retained from a source or as inserted to mark the personal presence of the writer himself.

γενόμενοι] With the names of officials this aorist participle signifies in the papyri positions no longer held, e.g. ἐπιστράτηγος γενόμενος = ex-epistrategus. Similarly Harnack, *Chronologie der altchristlichen Litteratur*, i. 248 *note*, argued from this word that the αὐτόπται καὶ ὑπηρέται must already have died when Luke wrote. In this case we should translate it " who had been." But the tense cannot be pressed, especially in view of the unofficial nature of the term ὑπηρέτης and the regular use of γενόμενος with αὐτόπτης.[1] The events witnessed are indeed past but not necessarily the testimony. With his change to a date for Luke and Acts prior to 70 A.D. Harnack himself would doubtless withdraw this argument.[2]

τοῦ λόγου] A general term applicable to the story of Christian origins. If connected especially with ὑπηρέται (see above), it can be taken in the more active sense of the preaching of Christianity. See the passages in Acts quoted above, p. 496, and for λόγος without a dependent genitive as here see Acts viii. 4 ; xi. 19 ; xiv. 25 ; xvi. 6 ; xviii. 5. With the phrase ὑπηρέται τοῦ λόγου note especially Acts vi. 4 τῇ διακονίᾳ τοῦ λόγου, xiv. 12 ὁ ἡγούμενος τοῦ λόγου and Gal. vi. 6 ὁ κατηχούμενος τὸν λόγον τῷ κατηχοῦντι. It was natural that under the influence of the Logos doctrine and of the prologue of John both τοῦ λόγου here and τοῦ λόγου τῆς ζωῆς in 1 John i. 1 should have been taken by early Christian interpreters personally of Jesus, the Word of God, cf. 1 Cor. iv. 1 ὑπηρέτας χριστοῦ. So even Corssen, *loc. cit.*

ἔδοξε] This form occurs in Acts xv. 22, 25, 28, [34] but not impersonally elsewhere in Luke or Acts. In xv. 25 it is preceded by ἐπειδή (compare ἐπειδήπερ here). As noted above, p. 492, it is possible that Luke, like some other writers, composed his preface after his work was finished, but the aorist would be equally appropriate before the work was written as a reference merely to

---

[1] See above, p. 499, for some examples. A similar problem is raised by the participle in Papias in Eus. iii. 39. 15 Μᾶρκος μὲν ἑρμηνευτὴς Πέτρου γενόμενος, ὅσα ἐμνημόνευσεν, ἀκριβῶς ἔγραψεν. Probably Papias means to say that Mark wrote after his connection was severed (by Peter's death ?).

[2] He does not seem to mention it in his *Date of the Acts and of the Synoptic Gospels*, though he touches on the associated argument for a late date from the πολλοί of the prologue in a note, p. 125.

the decision to write. A reference to such a decision, with the reason, is a natural commonplace of prefaces.

παρηκολουθηκότι] This word occurs here only in Luke's writings; in the LXX. it occurs only in 2 Maccabees. But it is not an unusual word; cf. [Mk. xvi. 17]; 1 Tim. iv. 6; 2 Tim. iii. 10. Literally it means simply "follow," a sense which some early Christian fathers assigned it here (see below, s.v. πᾶσιν), but the figurative meaning evidently prevailed, and is to be preferred. This still leaves several shades of meaning among which to choose.

(1) The word is used of following what is read or said, e.g. in prefaces (of the reader, not the author); see prefaces of Archimedes (quoted p. 494); of Artemidorus (cited in Wettstein ad loc.); of Theophrastus, *Characteres*, *Prooem.* σὸν δὲ παρακολουθῆσαι καὶ εἰδῆσαι, and [Demos.] Περὶ τοῦ Ἁγνίου κλήρου, ad init. (pp. 1050 f.) ἐπειδὴ ... ἀνάγκη ἴσως ἐστὶν τὰ πραχθέντα ἐξ ἀρχῆς διηγήσασθαι. ὑμεῖς τε γάρ, ὦ ἄνδρες δικασταί, ῥᾷον παρακολουθήσετε ... ἀκροάσασθαι τῶν λεγομένων καὶ παρακολουθεῖν προσέχοντας τὸν νοῦν. πειράσομαι δὲ κἀγώ κτλ. Cf. Vettius Valens vii. 5 (ed. Kroll, p. 276. 23). So Josephus (*Contra Apion.* i. 23) writes of pagan authors of Jewish history whose errors must be excused, οὐ γὰρ ἐνῆν αὐτοῖς μετὰ πάσης ἀκριβείας τοῖς ἡμετέροις γράμμασι παρακολουθεῖν (=ὅτι μὴ ταῖς ἱεραῖς ἡμῶν βίβλοις ἐνέτυχον a few lines above). If this interpretation is adopted here, Luke is claiming to have read the διηγήσεις which the preceding writers had composed.[1] πᾶσιν, neuter, in place of πάσαις, feminine, is not an insuperable objection (cf. Mk. xii. 28 ἐντολὴ πρώτη πάντων), since the antecedent is the distributive singular διήγησις and since the masculine or neuter adjective can be referred to the authors or contents respectively of the διηγήσεις.

(2) Of keeping in touch with things done, with a course of events. This broad meaning is probably to be accepted here as in the familiar parallel, Demosthenes, *De corona* 53 παρηκολουθηκότα τοῖς πράγμασιν ἐξ ἀρχῆς, and other passages cited in Wettstein where the verb often occurs in the perfect participle and is accompanied by ἐξ ἀρχῆς, πράγμασιν or ἅπασιν. It may include reliance upon written information, as is well shown by cases where a letter is said to be written in order that the recipient may keep in touch with events, e.g. P.S.I. 411. 3 ff. (iii./B.C.) ὅπως οὖν παρακολουθῶν καὶ σὺ πρὸς ταῦτα ἐξαγάγῃς τοὺς λόγους γέγραφα, P Lond. 23. 54 ff. (158-7 B.C.) τῆς ... ἐπιστολῆς τ(ὸ) ἀντίγραμφον ὑποτετάχαμεν ὅπως παρακολλούθῃς. P Par. 46. 19 f. (153 B.C.) παρακολουθήσαντά σε τῇ ἀληθείᾳ.

[1] This interpretation is slightly confirmed by the frequency with which a διήγησις is described by Hellenistic historians as εὐπαρακολούθητος (Joseph. B.J. vii. 3. 2; Polyb. iv. 28. 6; v. 31. 4) and δυσπαρακολούθητος (Joseph. Ant. xi. 3. 10). See the occurrences of both adjectives listed by Roberts, *Dionysius of Halicarnassus; the Three Literary Letters*, Glossary, p. 189.

(3) But more intimate contact with events is not excluded by the word, and in the following passages it seems almost to require the meaning of actual presence or participation in the events (cf. Raphel, *Annotationes in sacram scripturam*, ad loc.) : Josephus, *Contra Apion*. i. 10 cited above (p. 499), where παρηκολουθηκότα τοῖς γεγονόσιν seems to be contrasted with παρὰ τῶν εἰδότων πυνθανόμενον and to refer directly to Josephus' own presence and participation at the events recorded by him in his Jewish War ; Lucian, *Symposium* 1, referring to one who had brought a report about a quarrel, οὐ μὴν ἐξ ἀρχῆς γε οὐδ' αὐτὸς ἅπασιν παρεγένετο, ἀλλὰ ὀψὲ μεσούσης σχεδὸν ἤδη τῆς μάχης ἐπέστη ὀλίγον πρὸ τῶν τραυμάτων. ὥστε θαυμάζω εἴ τι σαφὲς εἰπεῖν ἐδύνατο μὴ παρακολουθήσας ἐκείνοις ἀφ' ὧν ἀρξαμένη ἐς τὸ αἷμα ἐτελεύτησεν αὐτοῖς ἡ φιλονεικία. I am inclined to add as examples of this use of the verb Philo, *De decalogo* 18 (196 M.), where he says how foolish it would be to ask a man to bear false witness, saying to him ὦ οὗτος, ἃ μήτ' εἶδες μήτ' ἤκουσας, ὡς ἰδών, ὡς ἀκούσας, ὡς παρηκολουθηκὼς ἅπασιν, ἀφικόμενός μοι μαρτύρησον, and Josephus, *Vita* 65, where he again ridicules Justus' claim of accuracy compared with the knowledge of a participant like himself, μήτε τὰ πραχθέντα κατὰ τὴν Γαλιλαίαν ἐπιστάμενος, ἧς γὰρ ἐν Βηρυτῷ τότε παρὰ βασιλεῖ, μήθ' ὅσα ἔπαθον Ῥωμαῖοι ἐπὶ τῆς Ἰωταπάτων πολιορκίας ἢ ἔδρασαν ἡμᾶς παρακολουθήσας, μήθ' ὅσα κατ' ἐμαυτὸν ἔπραξα πολιορκούμενος δυνηθεὶς πυθέσθαι (cf. a few lines below οὔτε γὰρ τῷ πολέμῳ παρέτυχες). We must therefore leave the possibility open that the author is claiming for himself actual presence and participation in the events described, and that this participle is a paraphrase of αὐτόπται καὶ ὑπηρέται γενόμενοι.

There appears to be no warrant for assigning to the word the sense of deliberate investigation, although Luke's apologists love thus to modernise it. The writer's information had (notice the perfect tense) come to him as the events took place ; it was not the result of special reading and study. His acquaintance with the subject, whatever its degree of intimacy, was something already in his possession. The perfect tense is often thus used of this verb and this is its meaning. See *e.g.* Reiske, *Lexicon to Demosthenes*, *s.v.* The knowledge implied exists in advance,—note πρότερον in the passage quoted from Josephus *Contra Apion*. and προγινώσκοντες in the parallel to ἄνωθεν in Acts xxvi. 4 (quoted in the next note).

ἄνωθεν] Apparently practically synonymous with ἀπ' ἀρχῆς. These synonyms recur in Luke's writings only at Acts xxvi. 4, 5, where they are used in successive and parallel clauses [1] much as they

---

[1] This recurrence of old combinations in new situations is characteristic of this writer. Note how three other words of the preface recur in Acts xviii. 23-25 καθεξῆς, κατηχημένος and ἀκριβῶς.

COMMENTARY ON THE PREFACE OF LUKE 503

are employed here [1]: τὴν μὲν οὖν βίωσίν μου ἐκ νεότητος τὴν ἀπ' ἀρχῆς γενομένην ἐν τῷ ἔθνει μου ἔν τε Ἱεροσολύμοις, ἴσασι πάντες Ἰουδαῖοι, προγινώσκοντές με ἄνωθεν, κτλ.[1] This parallelism between ἄνωθεν and ἀπ' ἀρχῆς confirms the suggestion (3) of the last note that the expressions which they respectively modify are not far from synonymous. On the other hand, if ἀπ' ἀρχῆς points back to John's ministry, ἄνωθεν is not to be differentiated from it so as to suggest the earlier events recorded in Luke i. and ii.

πᾶσιν] If neuter, this adjective refers to πραγμάτων, or more likely is used without antecedent but in much the same sense. It also suggests the object for γράψαι. It is used very freely by Luke (see my *Style and Literary Method of Luke*, p. 115) and cannot be pressed here as indicating superior fulness of contents. Compare again Acts i. 1 περὶ πάντων.

With less probability this form may be taken as masculine, referring either to the many writers or to the eye-witnesses. A decision on the gender depends in part on the meaning given παρηκολουθηκότι. When the latter is translated "read" or "study," its object may be the earlier writers. This agrees well with the prevailing solution of the synoptic problem by means of written sources. But, as has been already noted, many early Christian writers understood the verb of literal accompaniment and thus referred πᾶσιν to αὐτόπται καὶ ὑπηρέται. Perhaps Justin Martyr already bears witness to this interpretation when he quotes [Luke] xxii. 44 as found ἐν τοῖς ἀπομνημονεύμασι, ἅ φημι ὑπὸ τῶν ἀποστόλων αὐτοῦ καὶ τῶν ἐκείνοις παρακολουθησάντων συντετάχθαι (*Dial.* 103; even Papias uses the verb twice of "following" the eye-witnesses in the quotations given in Eus. *H.E.* iii. 39). Irenaeus (iii. 14. 2) evidently understands οἱ ἀπ' ἀρχῆς αὐτόπται καὶ ὑπηρέται γενόμενοι τοῦ λόγου of the apostles, and he speaks of Luke as "sectator et discipulus apostolorum" (iii. 10. 1, cf. i. 23. 1) and "cooperarius apostolorum maxime autem Pauli" (iii. 14. 1). So understood πᾶσιν influenced that body of early speculation commonly known as external tradition, and no doubt helped in the establishment of the Book of Acts as "Acta omnium apostolorum," as the Canon of Muratori calls it. Not only in competition with other books giving separately the Acta of individual apostles,—the Canon continues "sub uno libro scripta sunt,"—but to secure apostolic authority for this anomalous member of the canon of the New Testament (the only canonical book to which could be applied the kind of charge that Tertullian makes of Marcion's Gospel that it does not bear the author's *titulus* on its brow) it was necessary to stress its representativeness of the

---

[1] This is another literary passage; cf. with the unique παρέδοσαν the equally unique ἴσασι here in place of οἴδασιν as Luke xi. 44. Moeris (edit. Pierson, p. 205) says ἴσασι· Ἀττικῶς: οἴδασι· κοινῶς.

apostolic college. See Harnack, *Die Entstehung des N.T.* (1914), pp. 43-46, 66.

ἀκριβῶς] In Acts the adverb is used again (xviii. 25), but usually in the comparative (xviii. 26 ; xxiii. 15 ; xxiv. 22). The adjective and the noun are also used in Acts in two parallel passages (xxii. 3 ; xxvi. 5) but in the sense of strict religious observance.

This common adverb, together with its noun ἀκρίβεια, is especially frequent in prefaces or other passages where the writing of history is discussed. In English it may be rendered either "accurately" or "carefully," depending in part on whether it refers to the acquisition or the presentation of information. (Note the two words in the English and the American Revised Version of Acts xviii. 25 and the corresponding divergence represented by the Greek variants of word order in Ephesians v. 15.) Here also either translation is possible, since on account of its amphibolous position the word may be applied to either παρηκολουθηκότι or γράψαι. Perhaps it goes partly with each since Luke is apparently fond of these constructions. Plummer in his commentary mentions at least twenty-five such cases in the Gospel. If, however, a choice must be made the meaning adopted for παρακολουθέω makes a difference. For instance the Fathers who understood πᾶσιν . . . παρακολουθηκότι of association with the apostles found it difficult to connect ἀκριβῶς with that phrase. οὐ παρέργως is apparently one effort to do so by paraphrase. The same difficulty is met if παρακολουθέω means actual presence at the events, and it may seem best in that case to take ἀκριβῶς with γράψαι and to translate it "accurately." This is natural enough. If, on the other hand, παρακολουθέω means "keep in touch with," "read," or "investigate," then it can take the adverb in the sense "carefully." See the passage from Josephus *Contra Apion.* i. 10 quoted above, p. 499, and other cases where ἀκριβῶς and παρακολουθέω seem to be associated, given in Wettstein *ad loc.* and Hobart, *Medical Language of St. Luke,* p. 90.

καθεξῆς] Another word peculiar to this writer in the Greek Bible, though it is found in kindred writings (*Test. XII. Patr.,* Jud. 25. 1 ; Aristeas 193 Cod. M. ; 1 Clem. 37. 3). It is also used occasionally by later pagan writers (Hero i. 220, edit. A. Schmidt ; Plutarch, *Symposium,* i. 1. 5 ; Aelian, *Var. Hist.* viii. 7) and Christians. Apparently it has not yet been found in papyri. It is formed from ἑξῆς, another Lucan word, just as ἐφεξῆς is formed by the use of another preposition, and can scarcely differ in meaning from these two commoner forms. Thus Luke vii. 11 ἐν τῷ (v.l.) ἑξῆς = Luke viii. 1 ἐν τῷ καθεξῆς. ἐφεξῆς is used by Plutarch as a synonym for καθεξῆς in the context of the passage already cited. ἑξῆς is substituted for καθεξῆς by Athanasius in his paraphrase of Luke's preface (*Festal Epistle* 39).

COMMENTARY ON THE PREFACE OF LUKE 505

The composition of adverbs with prepositions is very common in Hellenistic Greek (Schmid, *Atticismus*, iv. 625 *al.*). Usually the preposition only strengthens the force of the simple adverb, *e.g.* ἐφάπαξ, καθάπαξ. If an etymological sense is retained by the preposition in καθεξῆς it is probably the distributive force, a favourite use of κατά in Luke. " One by one " represents the rendering here of at least two early versions, the Sinaitic Syriac (Burkitt) and the Sahidic (Horner). Cf. *singula* in Canon Muratori, line 36, a passage dealing with Acts, but reminiscent of the preface of Luke as *optime* shows. With καί and an article καθεξῆς, like ἑξῆς, means " et cetera (ceteri)," as Acts iii. 24, 1 Clem. 37. 3. But here and in Acts xi. 4, xviii. 23 the word is perhaps best represented in English by " successively " or " continuously." It need not therefore imply accordance with some fixed order, either chronological, geographical, or literary. The question of order in the gospel narratives is no more raised by this word than by ἀνατάξασθαι (see above). The early Christians, in spite of their interest, from Papias down, in the divergences in order of events in the Gospels, do not appeal in connection with this subject to either of these words in the preface.

The use of the word here is not improbably due to the frequent use of its synonyms ἑξῆς and ἐφεξῆς in reference to the contents of the following writing. In this way, especially between volumes of a many volume work, it is used frequently in reference to the following volume, *e.g.* Thucydides, ii. *ad init.*, Theophrastus, *Hist. Plant.* i. *sub fin.*, iii. *sub fin.*, Dion. Hal. *Ant. Rom.* i. *sub fin.*, iv. *sub fin.*, v. *ad init.*, vi. *ad init.*; Galen, *De usu partium*, vi. *sub fin.*, viii. *ad init.*, etc. In these cases the adverb means " next," " hereafter." So ἑξῆς is used in the papyri in reference to a document subjoined " below." Perhaps in Luke's preface the English " hereinafter " would reproduce this formal suggestion of καθεξῆς. καθεξῆς like ἀκριβῶς may be amphibolous. If the latter is taken with παρηκολουθηκότι it seems more natural to let the clause end with that word than to add καθεξῆς as a third adverb to the participle. The new colon scarcely begins with the enclitic σοί. The position of the word in the English versions is a little unfortunate: " to write unto thee in order, most excellent Theophilus.; that thou mightest know," etc., since, in spite of the semicolon of R.V., it is too easily misunderstood as merely introducing a purpose clause with " in order that " and thus loses all meaning. This would be avoided by rendering " to write in order unto thee, etc."

κράτιστε] This is what the grammarians call an elative superlative. It is found in the N.T. again only in Acts xxiii. 26; xxiv. 3; xxvi. 25, where it is used in address to officials. It is very commonly so used in documents and inscriptions of the Roman empire, equivalent to the Latin *egregius*. In the third century it is

506 COMMENTARY ON THE PREFACE OF LUKE

applied only to men of equestrian rank, but in earlier times senatorial officials also are addressed thus. (See Friedländer, *Sittengeschichte Roms* i.[8] 403 ff. = Eng. trans. iv. 74 ff.) About the history of the use of the word at different dates in Egypt, the papyri give us very full information, which has been summarised (as far as publication in 1912 permitted) by A. Stein, *Wiener Studien*, xxxiv. (1912) 160-170, P. Meyer in note to Hirschfeld, *Die Rangtitel der römische Kaiserzeit* (Kleine Schriften, p. 651 note 5), and most fully by A. Zehetmair, *De appellationibus honorificis in papyris Graecis obviis*, Marburg, 1912. It is used of the prefects of Egypt as early as the reign of Nero.[1] But for other officials it is relatively scarce until the middle of the second century A.D. For a hundred years or more after that it is used freely of the ἐπίτροπος and ἐπιστράτηγος and other principal officials, mostly of equestrian rank. It is used also of the religious officials ἀρχιερεύς and ἀρχιπροφήτης, of the members of the council collectively, and of the council (βουλή) itself.[2] It is natural therefore to conclude that here also Luke is addressing an official of high position.

But the word is used in other dedications, *e.g.* Dionys. Hal. *Ep. ad Ammiaeum*, *praef.* κράτιστε Ἀμμαῖε, cf. *De adm. vi dic.*, *sub fin.* Josephus, *Contra Apion.* i. 1 κράτιστε ἀνδρῶν Ἐπαφρόδιτε, cf. *Vita*, *sub fin.* Hermogenes, *De inventione* iii. 1 (Walz, *Rhet. Graeci*, iii. 98) ὦ κράτιστε Ἰούλιε Μάρικε, *Epist. ad Diognetum* 1 κράτιστε Διόγνητε. While the exact standing of none of the individuals addressed in these prefaces is really known, it seems unlikely that the κράτιστε is always used in an official sense. Epaphroditus, who is called κράτιστε ἀνδρῶν, is a government official (see R. Laqueur, *Der judische Historiker Flavius Josephus*, pp. 23 ff.). Elsewhere he is called τιμιώτατέ μοι Ἐπαφρόδιτε (*Contra Apion.* ii. 1) or simply Ἐπαφρόδιτε (ii. 41). Similarly Ammaeus, who is quite unknown, is elsewhere addressed by Dionysius as φίλε, φίλτατε, βέλτιστε (W. Rhys Roberts, *Classical Review*, xiv. (1900), p. 440), as Theophilus is named without epithet in Acts i. 1. For this usage the Latin equivalent is not *egregius* but *optimus* (so Vulgate and *Canon of Muratori* of Theophilus) and is used freely in dedications of Latin works evidently with no official sense. While therefore the usage of Luke and of other writings generally would seem to make an

---

[1] To the earlier example from that reign add now from P Ryl. 119. 3 τοῦ κρατίστου ἡγημόνος Γαίου Καικίνα Τούσκου.

[2] Stein, *op. cit.* p. 169 f., summarises the evidence as follows: "So sehen wir, dass in Ägypten seit der Mitte des I. Jahrh. nur der Präfekt als κράτιστος bezeichnet wird, in der ersten Hälfte des II. Jahrh. ausserdem noch der Epistrateg und andere Prokuratoren, dass dann seit der Mitte des II. Jahrh. der Präfekt durch den Rang eines λαμπρότατος über die andere Reichsbeamten emporgehoben wird."

COMMENTARY ON THE PREFACE OF LUKE 507

official position for Theophilus quite likely, the peculiar habits of prefaces throw doubt on such an inference. The word may be merely an illustration of conventionally formal, friendly, or flattering speech (cf. Theophrastus, *Characteres* 5).[1]

Θεόφιλε] Cf. Acts i. 1. As a proper name this word occurs frequently from iii./B.C. For instances see Fabricius, *Bibliotheca Graeca*, lib. V. cap. 1, § 20; Heumann, *loc. cit.*, supplemented by Hase, *ibid.* Cf. more recently Moulton and Milligan, *Vocabulary of the Greek Testament*, *s.v.*, and add among other instances a Pisidian (P Lille 27) and a Thessalian (P Petrie I. 19 [30]), both from iii./B.C., a πολιτάρχης (cf. Acts xvii. 6) in Egypt in the time of Augustus (P Oxy. 745), and an ἐπίτροπος in Lycaonia (*Bulletin de correspondance hellénique*, x. (1886) 502). F. Bechtel, *Die historische Personennamen des Griechische bis zur Kaiserzeit* (Halle, 1917), cites from *I.G.* II[2] 788. 8 (iii./B.C.) Θεόφιλος Φιλοθέου Λαμπτρεύς, which suggests that the etymology of the name was not forgotten when the name was given. The name is of Greek origin but is used as early as iii./B.C. of Jews (spelt sometimes Τεύφιλος; see Moulton and Milligan, *loc. cit.* and *B.G.U.* iii. 715 [i. 4] (101-2 A.D.) Ἰωσῆς ὁ καὶ Τεύφιλος). One of the high priests in i./A.D. was so named (Josephus, *Ant.* xviii. 5. 3 *al.*). Among Christians a bishop of Antioch about the end of the second century bore the name (Eus. *H.E.* iv.' 24). Perhaps the rich Theophilus of Antioch in *Clem. Recog.* x. 71 is the same individual and not an independent reference to the addressee of Luke's two books. On Christian legends about Theophilus see further, Lake, *Hastings' Dictionary of the Apostolic Church*, ii. 568 f. But the difficulty in supposing that Theophilus was a Roman citizen, felt by Lake and Ramsay, is easily met (see *Expositor*, June 1921, p. 438, *note* 10).

θεοφιλής is a not uncommon adjective (in the superlative it too became a title in the Roman empire, see Zehetmair, *op. cit.*) and some have supposed that θεόφιλος is used as an adjective here or at least as a name symbolical of the devout reader. Philo explains at the beginning of his *De opificio mundi* that in spite of the greatness and awfulness of his theme he must have the courage to speak of it ἕνεκα τοῦ θεοφιλοῦς. See the same word in Aristeas 287 and in the secondary preface to Ecclus. Prior to the Byzantine period the adjective scarcely appears in the form θεόφιλος. In *B.G.U.* iii. 924. 1 (iii./A.D.) there is one exception (in close connection with κράτιστος according to a probable restoration of a lacuna), Ἡρακλέους πόλεως

---

[1] The omission of the epithet in Acts i. 1 is not significant even if it be understood to imply a high government position, since this title is not constant or compulsory. Least of all does the omission indicate that Theophilus had become a Christian since Luke i. 3 was written.

ἀρχαίας καὶ θεοφίλου ἡ [κρατίστη] βουλή. Perhaps this is an error for θεοφιλοῦς, but unfortunately the two other passages where the same honorary term for Heracleopolis occurred (*B.G.U.* iii. 937. 4 ; *C.P.R.* 205 frg. 2, *v.* 6) are both defective at the point where the ending of the second adjective was written.

In view of the prevalence of the name Theophilus there seems little reason to accept the suggestion that Theophilus here is the typical lover of God. The custom of dedicating books to individuals, real persons more or less intimately known by the author, is also against this explanation. The early Christian Fathers, who were used to the word-play on personal names from the Old Testament, with their own delight in allegory, found in this name an irresistible temptation to draw a moral instead of acknowledging their ignorance about the identity of Theophilus. But their example is not one for modern students to follow.

ἐπιγνῷς] The meaning of this word is fully discussed by Robinson, *Ephesians*, pp. 248 ff., and Moulton and Milligan, *Vocabulary*, p. 236. In Luke it is used of recognising an object or a fact, or of learning something by investigation or inquiry. The latter meaning is to be preferred here, as in Acts xix. 34 ; xxii. 24 ; xxiii. 28 ; xxiv. 8, 11. The simplex is used in the same sense, *e.g.* Acts xxi. 34 = xxii. 30 γνῶναι τὸ ἀσφαλές.

περὶ ὧν κατηχήθης λόγων] The absorption of the antecedent into the relative clause is good classical idiom and not infrequent in the N.T. The four words may be resolved in several ways without much difference of meaning :

(*a*) περὶ τῶν λόγων οὓς κατηχήθης.
(*b*) τῶν λόγων περὶ ὧν κατηχήθης.
(*c*) περὶ τῶν λόγων περὶ ὧν κατηχήθης.

Possibly the first is preferable in view of the accusatives dependent on κατηχέω in the passive in Acts xviii. 25 and xxi. 24 (ὧν, really accusative attracted as here to the case of the antecedent). περί is used with κατηχέω of the personal object in Acts xxi. 21 and 24, and also with τὸ ἀσφαλές (= ἀσφάλειαν here) in Acts xxv. 26. Perhaps, however, the περί should be construed closely with ἐπιγνῷς as in Acts xxiv. 8 παρ' οὗ δυνήσῃ αὐτὸς ἀνακρίνας περὶ πάντων τούτων ἐπιγνῶναι ὧν ἡμεῖς κατηγοροῦμεν αὐτοῦ, a passage which probably provides a close parallel in thought as well as construction.

κατηχήθης] A verb found occasionally in Hellenistic Greek in the sense of oral information, whether accurate or inaccurate. The word apparently does not occur in the LXX. or Plutarch (except the spurious *De fluminibus*). One instance each is cited from Philo (*De leg. ad Gaium* 30), Josephus (*Vita* 65), and the papyri (P Strass. i. 41. 37 = P Lips. i. 32. 1, A.D. 250). The other citations from secular writers are from Lucian and later writers. In the N.T. it is limited,

COMMENTARY ON THE PREFACE OF LUKE 509

like πληροφορέω, to the Lucan and Pauline writings, but it does not occur so often in sub-apostolic literature (2 Clem. 17. 1). By the time of Clement of Alexandria it was a technical term along with φωτίζειν and ἀναγεννάω, all of which he says were used similarly among apparently barbarian philosophers (*Strom.* v. p. 551). In Paul and Christian writers generally it is applied to religious instruction, see Burton, *I.C.C. Galatians*, pp. 336 f. In Acts xviii. 25 it is used of Apollos' accurate but incomplete information about the "way of the Lord." In Acts xxi. 21 and 24 it is used of false information against Paul. Which sense the word has here or whether it must be left neutral depends on whether the clause and the preface as a whole betray the purpose of the writer or the circumstances of the addressee. Probably a neutral translation—" heard "—is safest.

λόγων] A very general word, common in Luke and Acts and in many senses. Cf. λόγου in verse 2 and λόγον in Acts i. 1. Perhaps here περὶ λόγων is used for variety much as περὶ πραγμάτων in verse 1, but of course λόγοι are events reported rather than events fulfilled. In connection with περὶ ὧν κατηχήθης λόγων note the equation Lk. iv. 37 καὶ ἐξεπορεύετο ἦχος περὶ αὐτοῦ εἰς πάντα τόπον τῆς περιχώρου = vii. 17 καὶ ἐξῆλθεν ὁ λόγος οὗτος ἐν ὅλῃ τῇ Ἰουδαίᾳ περὶ αὐτοῦ καὶ πάσῃ τῇ περιχώρῳ (cf. iv. 14 φήμη ... περὶ αὐτοῦ, Mk. i. 28 ἀκοὴ αὐτοῦ).

τὴν ἀσφάλειαν] Used of physical safety by Greek writers of all periods and grades of culture and then of security of status (cf Acts v. 23). In the papyri it has become a concrete noun for a document that serves as security. Here it is used by Luke in the same sense as τὸ ἀσφαλές in Acts xxi. 34; xxii. 30; xxv. 26, and means "the truth" or "the facts" about some matters reported or discussed. An admirable illustration from P Giss. i. 27 may be cited here (time of Trajan or Hadrian). The writer had learned indirectly from a παιδαρίῳ τοῦ κυρίου Ἀπολλωνίου ἀπὸ Μέμφεως ἐρχομένῳ εὐαγγελίζοντι τὰ τῆς νείκης αὐτοῦ καὶ προκοπῆς. οὗ ἔνεκα ἐπιτηδὲς (?) πρός σε ἔπεμψα ἵνα τὸ ἀσφαλὲς ἐπιγνῶ καὶ στεφανηφορίαν ἄξω καὶ τοῖς θεοῖς τὰς ὀφειλομένας σπονδὰς ἀποδῶ. Moulton and Milligan, *s.v.*, do not mention this transference of meaning from "safe" to "certain" as confirmed by the papyri, nor do Grenfell and Hunt recognise it in translating in the Amherst Papyri two letters of a certain Sarapion of about the same date as the preceding: 131. 3 ff. ἕως ἂν ἐπιγνῶ τὸ ἀσφαλὲς τοῦ πράγματος περὶ οὗ κατέπλευσα ἐπιμενῶ, ἐλπίζω δὲ θεῶν θελόντων ἐκ τῶν λαλουμένων διαφεύξεσθαι; 132. 5 ff. (in reply to his son's question how much to pay the workmen) ἐπίγνωθι οὖν τὸ ἀσφαλὲς τί Πολεῖς διδοῖ τοῖς αὑτοῦ καὶ σὺ δός. In Luke i. 4 τὴν ἀσφάλειαν is emphatically placed at the end of the period and is used instead of the synonymous adjective because of its emphatic position. But the selection of the word, as well as the order of the words (see Leipoldt, *Urchristentum und Gegenwart* 1920, p. 24) is perhaps affected by the unconscious rhythm of clausula.[1] It is this verse which specially suggests that the author's avowed purpose in Luke-Acts is the defence of Christianity. The several words of this clause, when considered independently, appear quite indefinite or ambiguous, but similar passages in Acts deal with accusations of Christians due to misrepresentation or ignorance, and make it likely that here also they have an apologetic connotation. If so, Theophilus was not a catechumen but an influential non-Christian (cf. above on κράτιστος), to whom this work is nominally dedicated or addressed with the intention of meeting incriminating reports or impressions by the presentation of exonerating facts (see also *Expositor*, June 1921).

A study of the language of the preface reveals the ambiguity and uncertainty of many words and phrases in it. Clear and precise deductions, such as those made by Zahn in his *Introduction* (especially § 60), throw much more weight upon the sentence than it was designed to bear. It is therefore well to summarise the bearing of the foregoing details on the question of authorship.

The first person is used three times: ἡμῖν . . . ἡμῖν . . . κἀμοί. The first of these has probably no personal meaning: τῶν ἐν ἡμῖν πεπληροφορημένων πραγμάτων could be almost rendered "the Christian story." But the second and third are strictly personal: ἡμῖν means "we Christians who have received the tradition" as opposed to the Christian "eye-witnesses and ministers of the word" who handed on the tradition. The καί in κἀμοί classes the "me," referring to the author, with the πολλοί who had made attempts to construct a narrative, not with the givers of the tradition.

Such seems clearly the natural grammatical conclusion. At the same time it is possible that no particular contrasts are implied between the eye-witnesses and the author but rather an association between them, so that he is giving us not contrasting or even successive stages but rather parallel sentences concerning his story. "Many have recorded it; eye-witnesses and participants have transmitted it; I also, as one well informed, will narrate it." Even so it seems unlikely that he means to identify himself with the eye-witnesses, but in the mist which surrounds the exact meaning of παρηκολουθηκότι no certainty can be reached.

[1] So also the order γενόμενοι τοῦ λόγου of verse 2. Cf. Wilamowitz-Moellendorf, "Die griechische und lateinische Literatur und Sprache" (*Kultur der Gegenwart*, I. viii.) p. 111: "An der Wortstellung und an der Wortwahl, namentlich zwischen Synonymen und den verschiedenen Periphrasen, lässt sich allein hier und da erkennen, was der Rhythmus suchte oder mied; das meiste hat unbewusstes Gefühl so geschaffen, und wir können zufrieden sein, wenn wir unser Gefühl dazu erziehen, die entsprechende Resonanz zu geben."

INDEX I

NAMES AND SUBJECTS

Abbot, E. A., 68, 257
——, T. K., 67
Aberle, M. von, 310, 376
Abila, 357
Abilene, 356
Abraham, 27, 98
Absalom, 104
Achaia, 249, 288
Achmetha, 19
Acta Sanctorum, 247
Adamantius, 240-242, 247
Aelian, 37, 38, 499, 504
Africanus, 248
Agabus, 279
Agincourt, 120
Ahasuerus, 25
Alcamenes, 11
Alcimus, 27
Alexander the Great, 26
——, the Procurator, 356
Alexandria, 31, 262
Alford, Henry, 413
Allard, P., 179
Amelli, A., 247
Amos, 85
Ananias, 146, 268, 284, 318
——, High Priest, 186
Andrew, 249, 259
Anna, 250
Annunciation, 180
Antioch, 24, 98, 128, 147, 152, 154, 168, 173, 174, 248, 269, 271, 272, 278, 282, 292, 295, 304, 305, 325, 326, 327, 328, 329, 337, 341, 342, 347, 380
—— in Pisidia, 195, 337, 425
Antiochene Source. (*See* Source)
Antiochus Epiphanes, 16, 24, 28, 411
Apelleus, 28
Apharsachites, the, 18
Apocrypha, 16, 25, 73

Apollonius, 23, 313, 330
—— of Tyana, 346
Apollos, 179, 288, 290
Aquila, 288, 290, 335
Arabia, 269, 270, 280
Aramaic language, 131
—— Sources. (*See* Source)
Aramaism, 44
Aratus, 12
Archimedes, 494, 501
Aretaeus, 353
Aretas, 269
Aristarchus, 185, 261, 290
Aristeas, 354, 493, 495, 497, 504
Aristides, 37, 38, 180, 248
Aristotle, x, 37, 351
Armagh, Book of, 397
Arnold, Matthew, 432
Artaxerxes, 18, 19, 20, 25, 26
Artemidorus, 501
Artemis, 185
Asia, 262
—— Minor, 119, 174, 327, 328
Asiarchs, 185
Assideans, 23, 27
Athanasius, 504
Athens, vii, 189, 287, 288, 330
Attharates, 22
Atticists, 497
Augustine, 248, 397
Augustus, Life of, 9

Babylon, 19
Bacchides, 24, 27
Bacon, B. W., 177, 248, 394, 432
Bakhuijzen, W. H. van de Sande, 344
Baring-Gould, S., 432
Barnabas, 40, 147, 154, 155, 157, 173, 174, 187, 188, 276, 278, 284, 286, 307, 318, 319, 339, 371, 387
——, the Gnosis, 307

511

Basel, 404
Basilides, 248
Bauer, Bruno, 378, 379, 382
——, W., 394
Baumgarten, M., 377
Baur, F. Ch., 298, 299, 302, 304, 324, 367, 368, 369, 370, 371, 372, 373, 375, 376, 380, 381, 382, 414, 417, 418, 420, 428, 433
Bechtel, F., 507
Beck, A., 489
Bede, the Venerable, 397, 398, 413
Belser, J., 310, 489
Benedictus, 181
Bentley, Richard, 411
Berger, S., 396
Bergh van Eysinga, G. A. van den, 303, 311, 312
Bernard, J. H., 431
Beroea, 287
Bertholdt, L., 385
Bethhoron, 24
Bethlehem, 180
Bethsaida, 116, 117
Bethsura, 24
Beza, T., 402
Bible, Authorised Version, 400
——, Bishop's, 402, 403
——, Geneva, 400, 402, 403
——, the Great, 400
——, Matthew's, 400
——, Tyndale's, 402
Bingham, J., 413, 423
Birt, T., 134, 313
Biscoe, R., 411, 412
Blass, F., 35, 60, 169, 324, 489
Blass-Debrunner, 34, 35, 41
Bleek, F., 387
Boccaccio, 32
Boeotia, 249
Bolten, J. A., 385
Bourguet, E., 429
Bousset, W., 4, 267, 278, 301, 311, 342, 394
Bradford, William, 406
Briggs, C. A., 3
Brückner, M., 307
——, W., 301, 308, 321, 345
Buchanan, E. S., 210
Budge, E. A. W., 250
Burkitt, F. C., 106-120, 141, 143, 144, 171, 172, 196, 313, 356, 357, 396, 405, 430, 431, 433, 485-489, 505
Burton, E. de W., 33
Butler, J., 411

Cadbury, H. J., 36, 38, 49, 50, 55, 69, 74, 140, 161-166, 209-264, 347, 349, 430, 485-511, 489, 493, 496
Cadoux, C. J., 177
Caesar, 399
——, Julius, 14
Caesarea, 127, 157, 168, 185, 342
—— Philippi, 107
Caleb, 27
Callisthenes, 24
Cambyses, 25
Capernaum, 117
Caphar Salama, 28
Captivity, 17
Cassels, W. R., 376, 419
Catchpole, Margaret, 464-484
Cephas, 270, 292, 319
Cerdo, 248
Chapman, Dom J., 242
Charles, R. H., 76, 77, 79, 80, 102
Chase, F. H., 77, 432
Children, the Three, 27
Chorazin, 117
Christianity, Catholic, 195
Chronicles, Books of the, 17, 18
Chrysostom, St. John, 403
Church, the, 187, 191, 194
Cilicia, 271, 273, 322, 325, 337
Circumcision, 274, 276
Clark, W. K. L., 66-105
Claudius, 335
—— Lysias, 178, 185
Clemen, C., 39, 306, 347, 384, 388, 394, 395
Clement of Alexandria, 75, 220-221, 252, 255, 259, 504, 509
—— of Rome, 421
Codex Amiatinus, 397
—— Bezae, 80, 248, 431, 496
—— Fuldensis, 397
Cohn, J. R., 432
Colenso, J. W., 3
Colet, John, 404.
Collins, Anthony, 411
Colossians, Epistle to, 346
Colson, F. H., 495
Commentarii, 9
Conference, Savoy, 407
Connolly, R. H., 203
Constantine, vii
Conybeare, F. C., 411, 418
——, W. J., 416, 432
Cook, S. A., 55
Copticisms, 30

INDEX 513

Corinth, 174, 176, 185, 202, 284, 287, 288, 292, 327, 331
Corinthians, First Epistle to, 153, 274, 277, 283, 331, 412
——, Second Epistle to, 175, 283
Cornelius, 176, 195, 323, 340-342
Corssen, P., 242, 313, 489, 495, 500
Coulton, G. G., 437-463
Council, Apostolic, 24, 153-157, 174, 271-286, 321-328
—— of Laodicea. (*See* Laodicea)
—— of Nicea. (*See* Nicea)
Coverdale, 400
Credner, K., 366
Creed, Apostles', 199, 200
——, Nicene, 200
Crescens, 261
Crispus, 288
Criticism, modern, x
Critics, Higher, 3
Crönert, W., 43
Crowfoot, J. R., 407
Crucifixion, 198
Cureton, W., 246
Cuthaeans, 26
Cyprian, 257
Cyprus, 153, 154
Cyrus, 18, 19, 25

Dalman, G., 44, 47, 143
Dalmatia, 249
Damascus, 153, 168, 170, 173, 266, 269, 270, 280
Damis, 313, 330
Daniel, 27
Dante, 32
Dare, J., 374
Darius, 18, 19, 21, 25, 26
David, 16, 17, 22, 27, 104, 181
Davidson, S., 376, 419
Deanesly, M., 400
Decrees, Apostolic, 274, 326, 328, 432
Deissmann, G. A., 37, 67, 247, 421, 429, 495
Deists, 412
Delphi, 429
Demas, 261
Demetrius, 289
Democracy, Athenian, vii
Demosthenes, 501
Der-Balyzeh, papyrus of, 202, 203
Derbe, 41, 154, 155, 283, 423, 425
Diaspora, 195
Diehl, H., 325
Dio Cassius, 14

Dio Chrysostom, 37, 38
Diodorus, 135, 351, 499
Dionysius, 11, 14
—— of Halicarnassus, 8, 10, 12, 15, 178, 493, 499, 505, 506
Dittmar, W., 84
Dobschütz, von E., 288
Domitian, 255, 430
Driver, W. R., 4
Duris, 12
Dutch School of criticism, 302, 307, 308

Eckermann, J. C. R., 365
Editor of Acts, purpose of the, 177
Egypt, 30
Eichhorn, J. G., 365, 385
Elders, Ephesian, 189
Eleazar, 23, 24
Elijah, 27
Ellicott, Bishop, 414, 415, 416
Emmaus, 24
Emmet, C. W., 265-297, 322, 432
Empire, Roman, x
Engel, G., 490
Epaphras, 261
Ephesians, Epistle to, 201, 306
Ephesus, 175, 176, 185, 201, 202, 288, 297
Ephorus, 491
Ephrem Syrus, 248, 249
Epiphanius, 249
Epistola Apostolorum, 202, 203
Erasmus, 400, 404
Erastus, 246
Esdras, First Book of, 18, 20, 21, 22, 25, 26
Eunuch, Ethiopian, 101
Eupolemus, 28
Euripides, 353
Eusebius, vii, 156, 232-235, 248, 252, 257, 258, 259, 262, 400, 421, 496, 499, 503
Evans, T. S., 415
Evanson, E., 417, 418
Exodus, 188
Ezekiel, 195
Ezra, 19, 188
——, Book of, 17, 18, 20, 21
——, relation of, to 1 Esdras, 22

Fabricius, 507
Fadus, 356
Falconer, J. W., 431
Farrar, F. W., 417, 432

Feine, P., 149, 150, 388
Felix, 178, 185, 186, 196, 334, 357, 491
Fell, Bishop, 406, 412
Festus, 50, 178, 186
Field, F., 35
Findlay, G. G., 428
Forgiveness of sins, 195
Francis, St., of Assisi, 437-463
Friedländer, L., 506
Frisch, S. G., 365
Fritzsche, C. F., 415

Gabler, J. P., 385
Gaius, 185
—— of Derbe, 290
Galatia, 51, 153, 154, 176, 273, 424, 425
Galatians, Epistle to, 119, 153, 155, 173, 174, 175, 277, 283, 291, 292, 317, 323, 412
——, date of Epistle to, 281
Galen, 32, 38, 353, 355, 430, 490, 505
Galilee, 116, 170, 171, 286
Galileo, 408
Gallia, 249
Gallio, 185
Gamaliel, 146, 183, 267, 343, 356
Gardner, Percy, 421, 427
Gaul, 262
Gaza, 101
Geden, A. S., 69, 70, 74
Generation, divine, 190
Genesis, 3, 188
Gennep, A. van, 59
Gercke, A., 305, 327, 345
Gerizim, 28
Gfrörer, A. F., 122, 123, 387, 414
Gibbon, ix, 406
Gifford, E. H., 415
Glossolalia, 194, 340
Glover, T. R., 427
Godet, F., 415
Goliath, 22
Goodwin, W. W., 33
Gore, C., 431
Gorgias, 23, 24
Gospels, the, 17
Gräfenhain, Rud., 490
Greece, 174, 327
Greek language, 30-65
——, Attic, 32, 37
——, Hellenistic, 132
——, Ionic, 33
——, dative in, 43
——, genitive absolute, 42

Greek, historic present, 41
——, infinitive passive, 40
——, present and aorist imperatives, 40
——, Semitic constructions, 42, 46, 47
—— translation, 33, 47, 53
Gregory, C. R., 322
—— Nazianzenus, 249
Grenfell, B. P., 421, 422, 509
Griesbach, J. J., 364, 367
Grimm, W., 489
Grinfield, E. W., 49, 51
Grosseteste, Robert, 398
Guerin, L., 179
Guillemard, W. H., 48

Hachaliah, 19
Haggai, 18
Haiqâr, 79
Halbfas, F., 7
Hallam, H., 403
Hamilton, H. F., 431
Hammond, Henry, 406, 407
Hänlein, K. A., 365
Hannah, 181
Hardy, E. G., 179
Harnack, A. von, 36, 38, 68, 74, 82, 84, 107, 125, 126, 128, 129, 139, 141, 145-147, 151, 153, 161-164, 202, 248, 267, 289, 291, 294, 296, 301, 304, 305, 310, 313, 315, 324, 347, 349, 350, 352-355, 389, 390-395, 421, 429, 431, 500, 504
Harris, J. Rendel, 76, 94, 431
Hart, J. H. A., 493
Harvey, W. W., 314
Hase, Th., 489
Hatch, E., 66, 69, 81, 82, 428, 431
Hauck, A., 321
Hausrath, A., 309, 312, 376
Havet, E., 376
Hawkins, Sir John, 36, 41, 70, 71, 72, 73, 75, 81, 112, 163, 305, 429
Headlam, A. C., 283, 428
Hearne, T., 407
Hebrews, Epistle to, 188, 252, 262, 397, 496
Heinrichs, J. H., 385
Heitmüller, W., 125, 278
Hempel, J., 313
Heracleopolis, 508
Hermas, 192, 251, 255
Hermes, 287
Hermogenes, 506
Herod Antipas, 183

INDEX 515

Herod Antipas, marriage of, 281
—— the Great, 14
—— Agrippa I., 156, 157, 195, 279, 280, 294
—— II., 183, 189, 357
Herodian, 11
Herodias, 281
Herodotus, vii, 422
Heumann, C. A., 489, 490
Hexateuch, 3, 5
Hilgenfeld, A., 124, 310, 344, 376, 388, 394, 414, 428
Hippocrates, 353, 354, 355
Hippolytus, 202, 421
Hoare, H. W., 402
Hobart, W. K., 36, 38, 82, 83, 84, 315, 347, 349, 350, 351, 353, 354, 355, 390, 400, 503
Hobbes, Thomas, 408
Hoennicke, G., 301
Holl, K., 200
Holmes, R., 413
Holtzmann, H. J., 202, 306, 308, 319, 321, 344, 356, 376, 383
Holy Week, chronology of, 108
Homer, 35
Hort, F. J. A., 35, 80, 82, 95, 108, 188, 190, 419, 431
Howard, W. F., 422
Howson, J. S., 416, 432
Hug, J. L., 367
Hunkin, J. W., 396-433
Hunt, A. S., 421, 422, 509
——, W., 398

Iconium, 425
Ignatius, 257, 309, 421
Ilberg, J., 304
Inge, W. R., 423, 432
Inscriptions, 30
Irenaeus, 212-220, 255, 256, 314, 503
Isaiah, 181, 199
Isauria, 425
Israel, 23, 187
Italy, 249

Jacob, 98
Jäger, W., 313
James, 158, 187, 270, 276, 299, 319, 320, 323, 398
——, M. R., 79
Jasher, book of, 16
Jason, son of Eleazar, 28
—— of Cyrene, 23

Jason of Thessalonica, 184, 185
Jeremiah, Book of, 22
Jericho, 69, 116
Jerome, 234-239, 248, 249, 257, 258, 396, 405
Jerusalem, 19, 20, 26, 98, 107-112, 126, 127, 129, 145-147, 154, 168, 170, 173-176, 181, 185, 201, 267, 271-274, 279, 280, 282, 285, 286, 289, 290, 304, 305, 320, 321, 332, 334, 380, 426
——, Council at, 281, 285, 320, 321-323, 324, 336
——, famine in, 156, 279
——, Paul at, 269, 293
—— -Caesarean Source. (*See* Source)
Jeshua, the High Priest, 493
Jesus, 52, 180, 187, 190, 194, 196
—— ascended, 99
——, baptism of, 116, 190, 197
——, death of, 181
——, ministry of, 106
——, speeches of, 121
——, trial of, 184
—— Justus, 261
Joannan, 23
Joel, 85
John, 140, 256, 259, 276, 286, 323
——, Epistle of, 499
——, Gospel of, 161, 190
—— the Baptist, 111, 116, 180
—— Mark, 146, 152, 497
Jonathan, 23, 24
Jones, M., 284, 310, 394, 426, 490
Joppa, 157
Joseph, 23, 24, 27
Josephus, v, 10, 14-16, 20, 24, 26, 28, 29, 39, 41, 55, 63, 80, 121, 156, 294, 310-312, 346, 351, 353, 354, 356, 357, 359, 388, 408, 412, 490, 492-494, 499, 501, 502, 504, 506
—— and Luke. (*See* Luke and Josephus)
——, *Antiquities* of, 16, 345, 358, 430
Joshua, 3, 16, 27, 68
Josiah, 5
Jowett, B., 412, 413, 414, 419
Jozadak, 18
Judaisers, 285
Judas of Galilee, 356
—— Maccabaeus, 16, 22, 24, 29
Judges, Book of, xi, 22, 62
Judith, Book of, 76
Jülicher, A., 291, 296, 301, 304, 341, 344, 384, 394

Julius Africanus, 201, 247
—— Caesar, 9, 14
Justin, 59, 374, 497, 503

Keim, T., 356
Kennedy, H. A. A., 67, 427
Kidder, Richard, 406
Kingdom of God, 116, 194
Klostermann, A., 161
Knopf, R., 384, 389
Knowling, R. J., 429
Koch, H., 394
Königsmann, B. L., 122, 385
Krapp, F., 61
Krebs, J. P., 356
Krenkel, M., 81, 102, 103, 312, 356, 388, 490
Kroll, W., 36, 65
Kuenen, A., 5
Kuinoel, C. G., 385

Lagrange, M. T., 495
Lange, J. P., 377
Language, Medical, 349-355
Laodicea, 408
Laqueur, R., 29, 134, 491, 506
Last Supper, 108
Latinisms, 43
Laud, Archbishop, 413
Law, The, 292, 321, 334
——, Paul and the. (*See* Paul)
Lechler, G. V., 377
Leipoldt, J., 510
Lekebusch, E., 377
Leviticus, 188
Lewin, T., 416
Lieberich, H., 490
Liers, H., 7, 14
Lietzmann, H., 202, 495
Lightfoot, J. B., 5, 276, 414, 419, 420, 421, 424, 425, 428, 429
——, John, 406
Linsenmayer, A., 179
Lipsius, R. A., 246
Livy, 8, 13, 14
Locke, John, 410
Logos, 190
Loisy, A., 107, 278, 394, 427, 433, 494
Loman, A. D., 383
Longinus, 36
Lord (Kyrios), 191, 192
Lucian, 8, 9, 11, 12, 15, 37, 38, 39, 351, 353, 354, 490, 493, 502
Lucius of Cyrene, 201, 247

Luke, 4, 41, 56, 80, 138, 162, 163, 166, 169, 173, 197, 261, 286, 290, 298, 337, 347, 350, 399, 415
——, linguistic character of, 30-65, 161-166
——, medical language in, 349-355
——, preface of, 133-137, 489-510
——, use of Josephus in, 355-358
——, use of Mark in, 106-120
——, use of LXX. in, 66-105
Luther, 292
Lycaonia, 425
Lydda, 157
Lysanias, 356, 357
Lysias, 24. (*See also* Claudius Lysias)
Lystra, 41, 154, 155, 182, 189, 246, 329, 423, 425

1 Maccabees, 22, 23, 26-28
2 Maccabees, 16, 23, 24, 27, 62, 73, 74, 76, 495, 496, 501
3 Maccabees, 73, 74
Macedonia, 68, 119, 249, 288, 327, 329, 336
M'Clymont, J. A., 418
McGiffert, A. C., 272, 363-395, 429
McLachlan, H., 65
M'Neile, A. H., 432
Malalas, John, 411
Malta, 415
Manen, W. C. van, 302, 303, 305, 311, 312, 383, 388, 428
Mangey, T., 413
Marcellus of Ancyra, 202
Marcion, 248, 252, 253, 307, 314, 358, 503
Marcus Aurelius, 495
Mark, 4, 39, 41, 170, 197, 198, 252, 258, 261, 355, 500
——, Gospel of, 15, 19, 29, 37, 70, 72, 106, 129, 133, 137, 138, 147, 155, 157, 161, 163, 173, 175, 184, 189, 190, 194, 195, 286, 393
—— in the Third Gospel, 106-120
Maspha, 24
Mattathias, 23-27, 405
Matthew, 4, 72, 107, 138, 161, 162, 180, 183, 189, 194, 195, 197, 198, 286, 355, 377
Matthias, 405
Maurenbrecher, M., 394
Mayerhoff, E. T., 366, 386
Menaus, 246
Mentz, M., 322
Mesopotamia, 98

INDEX 517

Messiah, 190, 196, 197, 199, 307
Meyboom, H. U., 344
Meyer, E., 489, 492
——, H. A. W., 413
——, P. M., 506
Meyerhoff, E. T., 366, 386
Michael, 58, 79
Michaelis, J. D., 364
Middleton, Conyers, 409
Miletus, 189, 331
Mill, John, 412
Milligan, G., 49, 58, 59, 65, 422, 507, 508
Misch, G., 9
Mishna, 182
Mithredath, 18
Moeris, 503
Moffatt, J., 38, 75, 94, 177, 272, 277, 297, 305, 312, 314, 315, 425, 490
Mommsen, Th., 179, 423
Montefiore, C., 267, 307
Moore, G. F., 355, 395, 430
More, Sir Thomas, 401
Moses, 3, 5, 495
Mosiman, E., 340
Moulton, J. H., 34, 36, 37, 40, 41, 42, 49, 57, 58, 59, 61, 62, 63, 67, 69, 70, 74, 279, 421, 422, 497, 507, 508
Mount of Olives, 109
Muratori, Canon of, 209, 210, 211, 255, 256, 257, 259, 260, 497, 499, 503, 506

Naber, S. A., 303
Nadad, 79
Nash, H. S., 428
Nazara, 118
Nazarenes, 185
Nazareth, 184
Nazarites, 294
Neander, A., 377, 413
Nehemiah, 9, 16, 17, 19-21, 26, 188
Nero, 246, 250, 417, 506
Neumann, K. J., 179
Nicanor, 23, 24, 28
Nicea, 200
Niceta, 248
Nikitsky, A., 429
Norden, E., 7-9, 40, 62, 134, 135, 196, 295, 305, 313, 330, 345, 490-492, 499
Numbers, Book of, 188

Obscurantism, x
Olympiads, 28

Onkelos, 143
Oort, H., 325
Optative, 33
Oracles, Sibylline, 195
Origen, 159, 224-232, 247, 252, 255, 257, 260, 262
Otho, 14
Ott, J. B., 355
Overbeck, F., 298, 318, 319, 324, 381, 382

Page, T. E., 429
Pakington, Sir John, 406
Palestine, 158, 176, 183
——, famine in, 157
——, Martyrs of, viii
Paley, William, 411, 412
Pallis, A., 30
Pamphylia, 154
Papias, 253, 257, 262, 497, 499, 500
Papyri, 30, 33, 34, 40, 42, 47-49, 51, 58, 62, 351, 509
Parker, Archbishop, 400
Parousia, 287, 309
Parry, R. St. J., 432
Parsons, J., 413
Passion, accounts of, 137
Passover, 26
Paues, A. C., 400
Paul, 4, 23, 40, 50, 68, 98, 99, 112, 119, 147, 153-161, 166-170, 173-187, 198, 200, 207, 208, 252, 253, 260, 265, 267, 272, 273, 276, 278, 283-289, 293, 296, 298, 299, 304, 307, 315, 318, 321, 326-329, 334, 337, 338-348, 358, 363, 369-373, 376, 393, 397, 399, 405, 415, 417, 433
——, character of, 296
——, conversion of, 152
—— on idol meats, 326
——, the Jews at Rome, and, 334
——, journeys of, 433
——, the Law, and, 291
——, legality of position of, 181
—— the Pharisee, 307
——, the Pharisees, and, 295
Paul, C. K., 401
Paulus, 365, 367
Peake, A. S., 430
Pearson, John, 407
Pegge, S., 398
Pelagius, 396, 397
Pentecost, 102, 340, 341
Perrot, G., 414

Perry, A. M., 140
Peter, 97, 103, 107, 116, 140, 146, 147, 152, 156, 172, 174, 176, 187, 195, 258, 260, 280, 286, 299, 323, 326, 337, 339, 341, 342, 343, 369, 370, 387, 398
Peter, H., 7, 14
Petrarch, 32
Pfleiderer, O., 272, 291, 294, 308, 321, 331, 382, 389
Pharisees, 295, 296
Phidias, 11
Philarces, 24
Philemon, Epistle to, 346
Philip, 23, 101, 103, 147, 152
Philippi, 158, 249, 287, 327, 336, 348, 424, 426
Philo, 10, 39, 98, 353, 412, 414, 493, 502, 507, 508
Philostratus, 37, 38, 313, 499
Phineas, 27
Phrynichus, 64, 497
Phrynichus, New, 42
Pierson, A., 302
Pilate, 183
Pius I., Pope, 255
Plato, 31
Pliny, 309
—— the Elder, x
Plooij, D., 310, 490
Plummer, A., 292
Plutarch, 12, 13, 14, 39, 59, 65, 351, 353, 494, 504, 508
Polybius, 8, 9, 11, 13, 14, 32, 134, 135, 353, 491, 499, 501
Polycarp, 309, 421
Poole, R. L., 398
Postscripts, 411
Pott, D. J., 385
Pounds, parable of, 108
Praxiteles, 11
Pre-existence, 190
Prefaces, ancient, 133-137, 490-492
Preuschen, E., 56
Priestley, Joseph, 418
Priscilla, 288, 290, 335
Priscillian, 242-245
Problem, Synoptic, 4
Psichari, J., 54
Ptolemy, 24
Pulliblank, J., 422

Q, 106, 162, 194
Quirinius, 146, 356

Rackham, R. B., 429
Radermacher, L., 32, 34, 35, 39, 43, 61
Ramsay, Sir W. M., 34, 35, 41, 57, 62, 179, 281, 308, 311, 322, 348, 367, 389, 394, 423-426, 489
Raphel, 502
Redpath, H. A., 69, 81, 82
Reichardt, W., 248
Reiske, J. J., 502
Reitzenstein, R., 268, 304, 313, 344, 427
Religion, lawful in Roman Empire, 179
Renan, E., 380
Resch, G., 324
Resurrection, 137, 182, 196, 296
Réville, J., 394
Riehm, J. C., 122, 386
Roberts, W. R., 501, 506
Robertson, A. T., 33, 41, 422, 489
Robinson, Armitage, 57, 508
Romans, Epistle to, 283, 289, 406
Rome, 174, 175, 176, 183, 186, 195, 201, 202, 204, 258, 261, 262, 289, 336, 363, 376, 393, 417
Rossi, G. B., 421
Round, D., 282, 322
Rufinus, 202, 232, 259
Ruppert, J., 490
Rutherford, W. G., 33, 62, 64, 423, 497
Ryle, H. E., 79

Sabatier, A., 308
Sadducees, 196
Sallust, 14
Salmon, G., 429
Samaria, 147
Samaritans, 26
Samuel, 181
——, Books of, 16, 22, 62
Sanabassar, 20
Sanballat, 26
Sandan, 58
Sanday, W., 93, 274, 283, 325, 423, 428, 433
Sanhedrin, 146, 149, 150, 172, 183
Sapphira, 146, 284
Sathrabuzanes, 25
Saul, 98
Savile, Sir H., 403
Scaeva, 167
Scheller, P., 7
Schermann, T., 202, 246
Schlageter, J., 32

Schleiermacher, F., 122, 123, 386, 387
Schmid, W., 37, 505
Schmidt, C., 202
———, K., 321
———, P. W., 301, 324, 345, 347, 394, 395
———, W., 63
Schmiedel, P. W., 312, 321, 340, 428, 430
Schneckenburger, M., 298, 370-372, 376, 382
Schoettgen, C., 413
Scholten, J. H., 306, 376
Schrader, K., 367, 368, 369, 370, 371
Schulze, H., 308
Schürer, E., 324, 356, 394
Schwanbeck, E., 122, 123, 128, 387
Schwartz, E., 125, 126, 129, 153-155, 203, 311, 322, 492, 497
Schwegler, A., 298, 344, 373, 375, 376, 380, 382
Schweitzer, A., 413
Sea, Black, 31
—— voyage by Luke, 164
Secundus, 290
Seebohm, F., 404
Selwyn, E. C., 68, 76, 103
Semitisms, 30, 44
———, negative, 54
———, positive, 54
———, primary, 54
———, secondary, 55
Septuagint, 6, 29, 33, 37, 47, 49, 51, 52, 53, 57, 58, 59, 60, 61, 62, 64, 121, 143, 188, 352, 495, 496, 501, 508
—— use of, in Acts, 66-105
Seron, 24
Servant of the Lord, 199
Shealtiel, 18
Shema', 109
Sheshbazzar, 18, 20
Shethar-boznai, 18
Sichem, 98
Sicily, 41
Silas, 123, 158, 184, 287, 288, 290, 329, 387, 417
Simcox, W. H., 62
Simon, 23, 24, 28, 246
—— Magus, 152
—— the Leper, 108
Simpson, D. C., 76
Sirach. (*See* Ecclesiasticus)
Sisinnes, 25

Smith, D., 416, 432
———, Henry Preserved, 3
———, James, 415, 430
———, W. Robertson, 3, 4, 5
Soden, H. von, 178, 247
Solomon, 16, 17
Soltzau, W., 308, 345
Son of God, 190, 192
Son of Man, 189, 190
Sopater, 290
Sorof, M., 388
Sosipater, 290
Sosthenes, 288
Source, Antiochian, 127, 128, 152-154
———, Aramaic, 125, 129, 133, 145, 147
———, Jerusalem-Caesarean, 126-128, 152
———, Pauline, 127, 128, 152
Souter, A., 396, 397
Spain, 258, 260
Sparta, vii
Spirit, Holy, 172, 187, 192, 193
Spitta, F., 125, 128, 150, 248, 304, 305, 345, 367, 388
Stählin, O., 312
Stanley, A. P., 416, 419
Steck, R., 302, 308, 344
Stein, A., 506
Stemplinger, E., 7, 10
Stephen, 23, 98, 123, 147, 148, 149, 150, 151, 176, 183, 267, 343, 387
———, speech of, 149
Stillingfleet, Bishop, 410
Strabo, 13
Strauss, D. F., 299, 418
Strype, J., 401
Suetonius, 289, 335
Surenhusius, W., 413
Swete, H. B., 69, 74, 82, 83, 84, 85, 93, 94, 98, 163, 431
Synagogue, 23
Syria, 271, 273, 325, 337

Tabernacles, Feast of, 19
Tacitus, x, 8, 13, 14
Targums, 143
Tarsus, 58, 147, 168, 271
Tattenai, 18
Temple, the, 24, 26, 109, 111, 114, 180, 185
———, cleansing of the, 108
Tertullian, 192, 222, 223, 252, 253, 255, 503
Tertullus, 178, 185, 246, 492
Testimonies, Books of, 49

Testament of the XII. Patriarchs, 77
Testament, Greek, of Erasmus, 400
——, Greek, of Stephanus, 400
——, New, of Beza, 400, 402
——, New, of Rheims, 400, 403
——, New, of Tyndale, 400
——, Old, 16-29, 66-105
Testimonia to Acts, 209-245
Text, Western, 143
——, XII. Patriarchs, 77, 78
Thackeray, H. St. J., 105, 431
Thebes, 249
Theodotion, 20, 98
Theophilus, 15, 111, 116, 117, 133, 136, 159, 169, 178, 179, 183, 207, 248, 310, 314, 329, 384, 490, 507
—— of Antioch, 507
Theophrastus, 501, 505
Theopompus, 11
Thessalonians, Epistles to, 295, 412
Thessalonica, 184, 284, 287
Theudas, 146, 312, 356
Thiersch, H. W. J., 377
Thucydides, vii, 8, 13, 14, 351
Thumb, A., 32, 63
Timaeus, 8
Timotheus, 24
Timothy, 246, 261, 287, 288, 290, 293, 320, 329, 387
——, circumcision of, 293
——, Epistles to, 411, 412
Tindal, Matthew, 408, 409
Tischendorf, C., 85
Titus, 261, 290, 293, 320
——, Epistle to, 411, 412
Tobit, Book of, 76
Toland, John, 410
Torrey, C. C., 17, 18, 41, 44, 46, 49, 51, 55, 60, 125, 129, 132, 138, 139, 145, 147, 148, 173, 394, 411
Tradition of the authorship of Acts, the, 209-245
—— of the Resurrection, the Galilean, 137, 138, 146, 170, 171
—— of writing history, the Greek, 7-15
—— of writing history, the Jewish, 16-29
Traditions in Acts—
  Antiochian, 127, 128, 152, 153, 154
  Caesarean, 126, 128
  Jerusalem, 126, 128, 145, 154, 156
  Pauline, 127, 128, 152
Transfiguration, 197
Translation, style in, 131

Tree (used of the Cross), 295
Troas, 158, 201, 336
Trophimus, 290
Tübingen, School of, 124, 298-300, 306, 307, 317-319, 321, 348, 369, 376, 377, 378, 380, 383, 384, 420, 428
Turner, C. H., 176, 177, 283, 322, 428, 429, 432, 433
Twelve, the, 182, 183
Tychicus, 290
Tyndale, William, 400, 401
Tyrrell, G., 433

Ulrich, M., 387
Usteri, L., 414

Vazakas, A. A., 144
Vergil, 65, 498
Vettius Valens, 499, 501
Virgin Mary, 190, 192
Vogel, T., 36, 62
Volkmar, G., 376
Vulgate Text, 396, 397, 506

Walker, J. K., 430
Waller, A. P., 408
Watkins, C., 268, 276, 317, 322, 325
We-passages, 158, 160, 161, 166, 167, 207, 300, 305, 314, 327, 329, 330, 331, 343, 348, 392
Weis, J. E., 179
Weiss, B., 124
——, J., 4, 171, 172, 175, 271, 304, 305, 310, 311, 321, 384, 388, 389
Weizsäcker, C. H., 290, 382, 388
Wellhausen, J., 4, 5, 56, 125, 126, 129, 191, 322, 325, 332, 395
Wendland, P., 301, 325, 344, 347, 494
Wendt, H. H., 272-274, 288, 290, 301, 304, 305, 308, 312, 325, 345, 348, 388
Westcott, B. F., 80, 83, 95, 108, 400, 401
Wette, W. M. de, 298, 318, 324, 381, 386
Wetter, G. P. son, 60
Wettstein, J. J., 351, 413, 504
Whiston, W., 411
Whitaker, G. H., 489
Wilamowitz-Moellendorf, U. von, 510
Wilcken, U., 9
Williams, C. B., 35, 36, 42
Windisch, H., 196, 298-348
Winer, G. B., 413

INDEX 521

Wisdom, Book of, 77
Wittichen, C., 377
Wordsworth, Christopher, 415, 428
Wrede, W., 4
Wright, W. H., 400
Wycliffe, John, 398, 401, 402, 403

Xenophon, 42, 62, 494
Xerxes, 26

Zacchaeus, 108, 110
Zacharias, 180
Zahn, Th., 36, 38, 169, 247, 248, 250, 256, 275, 304-306, 308, 311, 312, 314-316, 324, 347, 391, 430, 492, 510
Zebedee, 146
Zechariah, 18
Zehetmair, A., 506, 507
Zeller, E., 124, 298, 299, 305, 306, 324, 374-376, 381, 382
Zephaniah, 101, 103
Zerubbabel, 18-21, 25, 26
Zeus Hellenius, 28
Ziegler, W. K. L., 385
Zimmer, H., 396
Zwaan, J. de, 30-65, 310

INDEX II

BIBLICAL REFERENCES, INCLUDING THE APOCRYPHA AND PSEUDEPIGRAPHA

Reference	Page	Reference	Page
Genesis xii. 1	90	Deuteronomy (*contd.*)—	
xii. 3	94	x. 22	96
xii. 7	96	xii. 12	99
xii. 14	143	xv. 4	102
xv. 13, 14	90, 94	xviii. 15	87, 89
xvii. 8	96	xviii. 15, 16, 19	94
xviii.	103	xxix. 18	99
xviii. 2, 3-8, 16	103	xxix. 28	51
xix. 2	103	xxxiii. 3, 4	100
xx. 8	59	xxxiii. 8	98
xxii. 18	90, 94, 95	Joshua iii. 13, 16	352
xxvi. 24	100	vii. 1	102
xxxix. 4, 21	96	x. 12, 13	409
xli. 40, 41	96	Judges iii.-xvi.	viii
xlvi. 27	96	iv. 21	97
Exodus i. 5	96	v. 5	77
i. 10	77	v. 11	77
ii. 1	99	v. 27	97
ii. 13, 14	86	vi. 34	59
ii. 22	94	xv. 19	84
ii. 24	94	xvi. 26	76
iii. 2	96	1 Samuel iii. 4	102
iii. 5, 7-10	90, 94	xiii. 14	94
iii. 6	90	xxviii. 7, 21, 23	103
iii. 12	94	2 Samuel iii. 12	59
xx. 11	96, 98	xv. 14	104
xx. 28	93	xv. 20	104
xxii. 23	87	xv. 20, 21	104
xxiv. 18	102	xxii. 6	97
xxxii. 28	102	1 Kings x. 6	59
Leviticus xvii. 11	325	xvii. 21	84
xxii. 29	89	xvii. 23	103
xxiii. 29	94	xviii. 12	101, 102
Numbers v. 21-27	351	xviii. 36	96
xxii. 5-41	102	2 Kings ii. 16	101, 102
xxii. 20	102	iv. 6	352
xxii. 28	103	iv. 34	103
Deuteronomy ii. 5	96	iv. 35	103

523

524 THE BEGINNINGS OF CHRISTIANITY

2 Kings (contd.)—	PAGE
vi. 20	103
xix. 16	103
xix. 35	75, 103
1 Chronicles xvi. 35	100
2 Chronicles xxxvi. 22, 23	18
Ezra i.	21
i. 1-4	18
i. 5-11	18
ii.	21
ii. 1-70	18, 19
iii.	21
iii. 1-13	18
iv. 1-3	21
iv. 1-6	18
iv. 4-24	21
iv. 7	21
iv. 7-16	18
iv. 17-24	18
iv. 21	18
iv. 24	18
v. 1	18
v. 1-2	21
v. 3-vi. 12	21
v. 6-17	19
vi. 1-5	19
vi. 3-5	19
vi. 6-22	19
vi. 13-22	21
vi. 14	18
vii. 1	19
vii. 1-26	19
vii. 6	19
vii. 11	19
vii. 24	19
vii. 27-viii. 34	343
vii. 27 to ix. 15	19
x. 1	19
x. 10	19
Nehemiah i.-vii. 5	19, 343
vii. 6-73	19
viii.	26
viii. 1.	19
viii. 1-12	21
xii. 8	74
xii. 31	343
xiii. 6	26
xiii. 6-31	343
Job iii. 24	84
x. 1	84
xxxix. 2	96, 97
Psalm ii. 1, 2	86
ii. 7	87
vii. 7	56
ix. 9	98

Psalm (contd.)—	PAGE
xiv. 2	96
xv. 8-11	85
xv. 10	88
xvii. 5	96, 97
xxi. 28	94, 95
li. 7	59
lxviii. 26	88
lxxvii. 26	64
lxxvii. 36	64
lxxvii. 37	99
lxxxviii. 21	92
lxxxix. 21	94
ci. (cii.)	56
civ. 21	96
cvi. 20	96
cviii. 8	87
cix. 1	87
cxiv. 3	97
cxvii. 22	97
cxxxi. 11	97
cxxxvi. (cxxxvii.) 6	494
Eccles. ii. 20	494
Isaiah ii. 2	94
iv. 3	92
v. 9	59
vi.	333
vi. 9, 10	88
xiv. 13	75
xxviii. 11	102
xxviii. 13	234
xxviii. 16	64
xxix. 6	102
xxxv. 6	102
xlii. 5	96, 98
xlii. 6	99, 102
xlii. 7	96, 100
xliv. 28	94
xlix. 6	92
liii. 7	96
liii. 7, 8	87
liii. 13	96
lxv. 16	58
lxvi. 1	95
lxvi. 1, 2	91
Jeremiah i. 7	100
i. 8	100
i. 10	100
iii. 16	58
viii. 6	59, 99
xii. 6	64
xii. 15	94
xxviii. 1	227
xxxii. 37	51
xli. 19	101

INDEX 525

Jeremiah (contd.)—	PAGE	Judith (contd.)—	PAGE
xliv. 21	58	x. 19	77
li. 50	58	xii. 15	77
Ezekiel iii. 12	101, 102	Wisdom i. 18	77
iv. 14	99	iv. 19	77
viii. 3	101, 102	vii. 26	81
viii. 10	58	xii. 2	64
xxi. 7	84, 353	Ecclesiasticus i. 1	493
xlvii.	58	i. 28	51
Daniel iii. 95	98	xx. 7	84
iv. 27	45	Baruch ii. 17	103
ix. 18	103	Bel 36	102
Hosea xiii. 14	50	1 Maccabees ii. 25	28
Joel ii. 28-32	88	ii. 42	23
Amos v. 19	78	ii. 49-70	23
v. 25, 27	91	ii. 50-68	27
viii. 11	272	iii.-vii.	23
ix. 11, 12	92, 94, 323	iii. 1-9	23
Habakkuk i. 5	92, 94	iii. 50-53	23
Zephaniah ii. 4	101, 102	iv. 42 ff.	28
ii. 11, 12	101	vi. 29 f.	23
iii. 4	101, 102	vii. 13	23, 27
iii. 10	101	vii. 31, 32	29
Haggai ii. 18	51	viii. 1-32	28
Malachi iii. 1, 2	59	x. 20, 21	28
1 Esdras ii. 1-15	21	2 Maccabees i. 4	75
ii. 16-30	21	ii. 19-23	494
iii. 1	26	ii. 23	23
iii. 1-v. 6	21, 22	ii. 25	10
iv. 45	25	ii. 32	490
v. 6	26	iii. 14	75
v. 7-55	21	iii. 29	81
v. 47	26	iv. 6	75
v. 56-65	21	vi. 19, 28	75
v. 66-73	21	viii.-xv.	23
vi. 1-2	21	viii. 1-7	23
vi. 3-34	21	viii. 24	75
vii. 1-15	21	ix. 4	75, 76
vii. 9	26	ix. 5	75
vii. 10-15	26	ix. 5, 9	103
ix. 38-55	21	ix. 9	76
ix. 49	22	ix. 10	75
2 Esdras xviii.	26	ix. 15	76
xxiii. 6	26	ix. 29	76
Tobit ii. 10	84	xiv. 21	75
iii. 17	76	3 Maccabees iii. 8	77
v. 6	75	v. 28	81
x. 7	81	4 Maccabees iv. 11	84, 351
xi. 7	103	v. 4	247
xi. 9	76, 105	Ahikar vii. 35	105
xi. 13	76, 102	viii. 34	105
xi. 16	76	viii. 246	105
xii. 19	102	Apoc. Moses xxxiii. 2	79
Judith v. 20, 21	77	xlii. 8	79
x. 18	77	Aristeas 144	495

Aristeas (contd.)—	PAGE
148	497
193	504
287	507
Ass. Moses iii. 11	78
1 Enoch lvi. 5	79
2 Enoch lxvii. 1-3	104
Jubilees i. 27	79
ii. 1	79
xi. 7	80
Od. Sal. vi.	58
xi.	58
xxx.	58
xlii. 15	50
Ps. Sol. viii. 16	79
Testament of 12 Patriarchs—	
Gad ii. 4	495
Joseph ii. 3	78
vii. 3	78
viii. 4	77
viii. 5	78
ix. 4	78
Judah xxv. 1	504
Matthew i. 21	105
iv. 23, 24	355
ix. 26	427
x.	182
x. 5	141
x. 8	355
xi. 2	140
xiv. 14	355
xv. 29-31	355
xvii. 15	352
xix. 2	355
xx. 33	103
xxi. 14	355
xxi. 42	97
xxviii. 9	171
Mark i. 1	498
i. 9 ff.	190
i. 26	84, 352
i. 28	509
i. 29-39	117
i. 30	84, 352
i. 32-34, 39	355
i. 40	352
i. 40-iii. 19	117
ii. 3	84
iii. 31-ix. 50	117
iv. 19	496
iv. 20	496
iv. 35-39	165
v. 29	352
v. 42	84, 427
vi. 1-6	118, 119

Mark (contd.)—	PAGE
vi. 7	140
vi. 34	355
vi. 45-viii. 26	117
vii. 31-37	355
viii. 15	28
viii. 22-26	355
viii. 26	107
ix. 2-7	332
ix. 14-27	355
x. 1	355, 487
x. 13-52	117
x. 32	107
x. 32-xiii.	108
xi. 1-xiv. 17	117
xi. 11	109
xi. 18	355
xii. 10	97
xii. 28	501
xii. 38	110
xiii.	114
xiii. 3-37	108, 113
xiii. 4-37	115
xiii. 11	145
xiii. 14	114
xiii. 35	33
xv. 10	43
xvi. 5	140
xvi. 7	171
xvi. 8	19, 118
xvi. 17	501
Luke i.	105, 162
i. ii.	163
i. 1-4	316, 346, 489-511
i. 2	254
i. 3	233, 485, 507
i. 4	105, 509
i. 5 ff.	490
i. 7	105
i. 11	105
i. 13	105
i. 15	105
i. 22	35
i. 31	105
i. 35	190
i. 37	496
i. 45	105
i. 54	181
i. 66	113
ii.	105, 162
ii. 1-3	426
ii. 15, 51	496
ii. 23	105
ii. 37	250
iii. 1	356

INDEX

Luke (*contd.*)—	PAGE	Luke (*contd.*)—	PAGE
iii. 1, 2	498	xv. 18	105
iii. 16	337	xv. 19	105
iii. 23	498	xv. 20	76, 105
iv. 14	509	xvi. 2-26	353
iv. 16-30	118	xvii. 11	116
iv. 28-30	184	xvii. 15	353
iv. 31-44	117	xvii. 35	116, 143
iv. 35	84, 352	xviii. 15-43	117
iv. 37	509	xix.-xxi.	108
iv. 38	352	xix.-xxiii.	118, 119
iv. 39	84	xix. 29-xxii. 14	117
v. 12	352	xix. 38	110
v. 12-vi. 19	117	xix. 42-44	110
v. 19	35	xix. 45, 46	110
vi. 17	182	xix. 47	108
vii. 2	355	xx. 1	108
vii. 9	140	xx. 17	97
vii. 11	504	xx. 37	94
vii. 14	35	xxi.	114
vii. 17	509	xxi. 7 ff.	108
vii. 27	35	xxi. 7-36	112-115
viii. 1	504	xxi. 12-19	113
viii. 4-ix. 50	117	xxi. 16	112, 498
viii. 5	84	xxi. 20	113
viii. 14	496	xxi. 22	112
viii. 15	496	xxi. 24	110
viii. 22-24	165	xxi. 29	112
viii. 44	352	xxi. 33	112
viii. 55	427	xxi. 36	35
ix. 31, 44, 51	116	xxi. 37, 38	109
ix. 37-43	355	xxi. 38	113
ix. 38	352	xxii. 32	104
ix. 51-xviii. 14	487	xxii. 32, 33	104
ix. 52 f.	116	xxii. 37	104
x.	247	xxii. 41	43
x. 1	241	xxii. 44	503
x. 2	140	xxii. 47	104
x. 9	355	xxiii. 13	337
x. 21	35	xxiv. 4	140
x. 30	353	xxiv. 18	496
x. 34, 35	351	xxiv. 20, 42	497
xi. 5	33	xxiv. 23	35
xi. 44	503	xxiv. 48	499
xii. 1	28	John i. 13	190
xii. 8	35	vii. 53-viii. 10	70
xii. 16	496	ix. 10 ff.	103
xiii. 7, 9	105	x. 21	103
xiii. 11-13	353	xi. 37	103
xiii. 22	116	xiv. 31	104
xiv. 2	353	xix. 35	489
xiv. 27	35	xx. 30, 31	489, 493
xv. 8	351	xxi. 24	259, 260
xv. 15	105	xxi. 24, 25	489
xv. 17	97	Acts i. and ii.	147, 171

528　THE BEGINNINGS OF CHRISTIANITY

Acts (contd.)—
i.-v.	139, 147, 148, 150, 152
i.-vi. 7	123
i.-vii.	102
i.-xii.	118, 122, 123, 162, 340
i.-xv.	159, 166, 175
i. 1	46, 56, 136, 139, 145, 207, 306, 491, 492, 494, 495, 506, 507, 509
i. 1-v. 16	48, 55, 126
i. 1-v. 42	127, 171
i. 1-xv. 35	44
i. 2	340
i. 3	102, 194, 195
i. 4	50
i. 5	43
i. 6-v. 16	50
i. 6	194
i. 8	79, 341, 499
i. 10	45, 50, 140
i. 12	102
i. 13	140
i. 14-16	139
i. 15	50, 143
i. 16	272
i. 18	79, 272
i. 19	45
i. 20	87, 88, 94
i. 21	272, 498
i. 22	50
i. 25	79
i. 26	405, 497
i. 37-41	139
ii.	45, 46, 50, 102, 139, 141, 195
ii.-iv.	139
ii. 1	46, 50, 143, 272
ii. 1-13	139
ii. 1-47	128
ii. 1, 44, 47	50
ii. 2	102
ii. 4	102
ii. 7	50
ii. 8	79
ii. 10	289
ii. 14	45
ii. 14-16	139
ii. 14-36	115
ii. 17	35, 93, 94, 95
ii. 17, 18	51
ii. 17-21	88
ii. 18	95
ii. 19	93
ii. 22	50
ii. 23	45, 50, 62
ii. 24	50, 96, 97, 177

Acts (contd.)—
ii. 25-28	85
ii. 25-32, 38	337
ii. 30	97
ii. 32	337, 499
ii. 33	51, 192
ii. 34, 35	87
ii. 38	140
ii. 41	102
ii. 44	143
ii. 47	143, 145, 177
iii.	141, 145
iii.-iv. 35	147, 171
iii. 1	80
iii. 1-v. 16	128
iii. 2	51
iii. 3-iv. 6	333
iii. 8	80, 102, 353
iii. 11	80
iii. 11-26	139
iii. 12	45, 49, 51, 102
iii. 13	96, 497
iii. 13, 26	140
iii. 14	80
iii. 15	499
iii. 16	45, 50, 51, 141
iii. 20	33, 51
iii. 22, 23	89, 94
iii. 24	51, 98, 505
iii. 25	90, 94, 95, 98
iii. 26	98
iii. 31	98
iv.	23, 145
iv. 1-23	146
iv. 1-31	172
iv. 2	195
iv. 4	139
iv. 10	62
iv. 11	97
iv. 12	50, 63
iv. 16	45, 51
iv. 18	45
iv. 20	44
iv. 24	80, 96
iv. 25	81
iv. 25, 26	86
iv. 26	143
iv. 27, 30	140
iv. 30	45, 51
iv. 31	139, 280
iv. 32	80, 399
iv. 32-35	399
iv. 34	102
iv. 36	50, 123, 146
iv. 36-v. 16	172

INDEX

Acts (contd.)—

	PAGE
v. 1-11	146
v. 1-16	127
v. 2	102
v. 4	46, 51, 96, 97
v. 5-10	353
v. 8	45, 51
v. 10	35, 96
v. 12	81
v. 14	64
v. 16	48, 56
v. 17	41, 57, 333
v. 17-ix. 30	56
v. 17-42	127, 128, 146, 147, 172
v. 18	49
v. 23	80, 509
v. 24	33, 45
v. 25	50
v. 28	57
v. 32	496, 499
v. 35	80
v. 36	312, 356
v. 38	39, 80
v. 38, 39	77, 80
v. 41	57
vi.	125, 146, 151, 280
vi.-viii. 3	147
vi.-xv.	173
vi. 1-viii. 4	128
vi. 1-xv. 35	127
vi. 1	77
vi. 4	500
vi. 5	45, 57, 316
vi. 6	127
vi. 6-viii. 4	127
vi. 7	176
vi. 8	176
vi. 8-11	150
vi. 8-viii. 3	147
vi. 9-11	148, 149
vi. 12-14	148, 149
vi. 12-vii. 53	150
vi. 14	497
vii.	23, 55, 123
vii. 2	98
vii. 2-21	149
vii. 3	90, 93
vii. 5	96
vii. 6	40
vii. 6, 7	90, 94
vii. 10	96
vii. 13	57
vii. 16	98
vii. 19	77
vii. 21	42, 61

Acts (contd.)—

	PAGE
vii. 22-28	149
vii. 23	45, 58
vii. 23, 30	98
vii. 24	80
vii. 26	40
vii. 27, 28	86
vii. 29	80
vii. 29-34	149
vii. 30	96
vii. 32	90, 93, 94
vii. 33, 34	90, 94
vii. 34	94
vii. 35	62, 86, 102
vii. 35-43	149
vii. 36	78
vii. 37	87
vii. 38	58, 79, 147
vii. 40	62, 87, 95
vii. 42	95
vii. 42, 43	91
vii. 43	94
vii. 44-50	149
vii. 49	95
vii. 49, 50	91
vii. 50	94
vii. 51-56	149
vii. 52	58
vii. 53	58, 63, 148
vii. 54-58a	150
vii. 54-viii. 1	150
vii. 55	79
vii. 57-58	149
vii. 58	35, 266
vii. 58-60	149, 150
vii. 59	411
vii. 59, 60	79, 149
vii. 60	43
viii.	56, 58, 103, 123
viii.-xii.	103
viii. 1a-3	149
viii. 1b-2	149
viii. 2-4	127
viii. 4	151, 500
viii. 4-25	147
viii. 5-40	127, 128
viii. 6	45, 58
viii. 7	58
viii. 10	58, 80
viii. 12	64, 194, 195
viii. 14	140
viii. 16	286
viii. 21	99
viii. 22	99
viii. 23	99

Acts (contd.)—	PAGE
viii. 24	80, 81
viii. 25-40	147
viii. 26 f.	101
viii. 26, 27	102
viii. 26, 29, 39	192
viii. 27	33
viii. 31	33
viii. 32	95
viii. 32, 33	87, 93
viii. 35	64
viii. 36	45
viii. 39	101, 102
viii. 40	126
ix.	153, 167, 268, 336
ix. 1-21	332
ix. 1-30	58, 123, 127, 128
ix. 2	45, 58, 63, 266
ix. 3	45, 58
ix. 10	318
ix. 10, 12	102
ix. 11	327
ix. 15	100, 332
ix. 18	102, 353
ix. 19	270
ix. 19-xiv. 28	59
ix. 21	59, 266
ix. 22	58, 59
ix. 23	45, 270, 318
ix. 26 ff.	319
ix. 26-29	269
ix. 27	270
ix. 29	127, 493
ix. 30	271
ix. 31	50, 176
ix. 31-43	103
ix. 31-48	147
ix. 31-xi. 18	48, 50, 55, 128
ix. 32	50, 156, 174, 176
ix. 38	40, 102
ix. 40	43, 103
ix. 42	45, 64
x. 1.-xi. 18	103, 341
x. 7, 17, 25	45
x. 10	35
x. 14	35, 99
x. 15	40, 50, 57
x. 17	33
x. 17, 19, 23, 25	103
x. 19-20	102
x. 21	102
x. 25	80
x. 28	80
x. 30	50
x. 33	34, 102

Acts (contd.)—	PAGE
x. 34	103
x. 35, 36	96
x. 36	498
x. 37	63
x. 43	195
x. 45	51
x. 46	340
xi.	126, 153, 155, 156, 157, 271, 278, 279, 285
xi. 1	80
xi. 1-13	123
xi. 4	505
xi. 6	451
xi. 8	99
xi. 9	57
xi. 14	102
xi. 17	64
xi. 18	48, 127, 403
xi. 19	127, 151, 316, 500
xi. 19-24	127
xi. 19-30	123, 128, 153
xi. 19-xv. 36	56
xi. 20	159
xi. 21	177
xi. 22	57, 333
xi. 25	127
xi. 26	271, 278
xi. 27	248
xi. 27-30	312
xi. 28	33, 200, 249, 408
xi. 30	127, 279, 322
xii.	103, 156
xii. 1	59
xii. 1-17	156
xii. 1-24	127, 128
xii. 3	63, 80, 95
xii. 6	35
xii. 7	80
xii. 10	59, 80
xii. 11	59, 98
xii. 11	59, 98
xii. 12 ff.	316
xii. 13 ff.	119
xii. 15	80
xii. 16	80
xii. 17	174, 280
xii. 18	34, 44
xii. 18-25	403
xii. 20	59, 75
xii. 22	75
xii. 23	75, 84, 96, 103
xii. 24	176
xii. 25	127, 176, 316, 322, 496
xii. 25-xiv. 28	153

INDEX

Acts (contd.)—	PAGE
xii. 25-xv. 35	128
xii. 35	127
xiii.	123, 155, 337
xiii.-xxviii.	122
xiii. 1	41, 56, 59, 76, 311, 316
xiii. 5	497
xiii. 8	80
xiii. 11	59, 353
xiii. 12	59
xiii. 13	316
xiii. 13-14	41
xiii. 15-41	337
xiii. 16-41	23
xiii. 21	98
xiii. 22	92, 94
xiii. 22-47	61
xiii. 23, 32	295
xiii. 24	59
xiii. 25	59, 60, 337
xiii. 25, 29	45
xiii. 27, 33	295
xiii. 28	337
xiii. 29	80, 295
xiii. 31	499
xiii. 33	87
xiii. 34	92, 94
xiii. 34-37	337
xiii. 35	80, 88
xiii. 38	195, 295, 337, 344
xiii. 41	92, 94, 95
xiii. 46	319
xiii. 47	92, 95
xiv.	123
xiv. 2	60
xiv. 3	60
xiv. 5	45
xiv. 7	62
xiv. 8	60, 84, 353
xiv. 10	80
xiv. 11	287
xiv. 12	500
xiv. 13	35, 41, 57, 80
xiv. 14	286
xiv. 15	60, 96
xiv. 17	44, 60, 496
xiv. 19	80
xiv. 21	41
xiv. 22	194, 195
xiv. 23	64, 402
xiv. 25	500
xiv. 27	49, 60
xiv. 28	34, 44
xiv. 32	411
xv.	52, 122, 126, 153-157,

Acts (contd.)—	PAGE
	162, 167, 174, 175, 271, 272, 273, 275-277, 279, 285, 297, 322, 327, 328, 339, 414, 426, 432
xv.-xvi. 5	153
xv. 1 f.	279
xv. 1-36	56
xv. 2	34, 44, 323
xv. 2-4	123, 323
xv. 2, 23, 35	316
xv. 3	49, 50, 284
xv. 3-13	123
xv. 4	49, 60, 80
xv. 6	35, 323
xv. 7	49, 80, 323
xv. 7-9	341, 342
xv. 7-11	323
xv. 11	344
xv. 13	45, 49, 51
xv. 14	123
xv. 14-21	323
xv. 16	95
xv. 16-18	92, 94
xv. 17	33, 56, 62, 95
xv. 18	49
xv. 22, 25, 28	500
xv. 23	49, 289, 337
xv. 24-26	34
xv. 25	500
xv. 27	34
xv. 28	49, 324, 405
xv. 30	497
xv. 33	49, 50, 52
xv. 35	126
xv. 36	497
xv. 37	40, 297, 316
xv. 39	51, 409
xv. 40	51
xvi.	155, 184, 327, 329, 348
xvi.-xxviii.	44, 159, 339
xvi. 1	50, 51, 158
xvi. 1-3	320
xvi. 1-6	282
xvi. 2	51
xvi. 3	37, 51, 293
xvi. 4, 10.	51
xvi. 4	325
xvi. 5	126, 176
xvi. 6	51, 176, 282, 500
xvi. 7	192
xvi. 9	348
xvi. 10	249
xvi. 10-17	36, 304
xvi. 12	62, 288

Acts (contd.)—	PAGE
xvi. 14	75
xvi. 14, 16	103
xvi. 16	351
xvi. 16, 17	51
xvi. 17	45, 100, 158, 288
xvi. 18	100, 293
xvi. 19	51, 80, 330
xvi. 22	75
xvi. 23	77
xvi. 24	78
xvi. 25	33, 78
xvi. 28	40, 43
xvi. 29	78
xvi. 31	64
xvi. 34	35, 64, 78
xvi. 35	80
xvi. 36	52
xvi. 37	80, 184
xvi. 39	80
xvi. 40	52
xvii.	98
xvii. 1	41
xvii. 2	287
xvii. 4	287
xvii. 4-12	34, 44
xvii. 5	185, 287
xvii. 6	507
xvii. 7	52, 287
xvii. 8	64
xvii. 9	43
xvii. 13	52, 80
xvii. 14	52, 287, 330
xvii. 15	34
xvii. 16	52
xvii. 17	52, 56
xvii. 18	33
xvii. 19	52
xvii. 20	44, 52, 59
xvii. 23	80
xvii. 25	45, 50, 52, 96
xvii. 26	57
xvii. 27	33, 44
xvii. 30	80, 331
xvii. 31	52
xvii. 33	52
xviii.	45, 399
xviii. 1-21	41
xviii. 2	335
xviii. 2, 3	52
xviii. 3	288
xviii. 4	52, 80
xviii. 5	52, 330, 500
xviii. 6	52, 319
xviii. 7	62

Acts (contd.)—	PAGE
xviii. 8	64, 288
xviii. 9	40, 100, 288
xviii. 10	52
xviii. 13	80
xviii. 15	43
xviii. 17	35
xviii. 18	288
xviii. 20	60
xviii. 21	52
xviii. 22	35, 41
xviii. 23	51, 52, 316, 505
xviii. 23-25	502
xviii. 25	45, 52, 80, 179, 504, 508, 509
xviii. 26	52, 80, 504
xviii. 25-26	45, 63, 80
xviii. 27	52, 288
xviii. 43	64
xix.	58, 289
xix. 1	45, 51
xix. 2, 16, 18, 19	45
xix. 4	64
xix. 5	51, 58, 286
xix. 6	340
xix. 8	194, 195
xix. 8, 9, 16, 18, 19	51
xix. 8-20	338
xix. 9	50
xix. 9, 19	57
xix. 9, 23	45, 63
xix. 11	44
xix. 11, 26	50
xix. 11, 36	45
xix. 12	80
xix. 13	493
xix. 14	62, 80
xix. 15	49, 51
xix. 16	80
xix. 17	45, 51
xix. 19	45
xix. 21	50, 51, 176, 189, 311, 496
xix. 23-24	34
xix. 24	44
xix. 25	80
xix. 26, 27	34
xix. 28	80
xix. 29	290
xix. 32	80
xix. 34	508
xix. 35	35, 57
xix. 38	43
xx.	290, 327
xx.-xxviii.	52

INDEX 533

Acts (contd.)—	PAGE
xx. 1	288
xx. 3	288
xx. 4	158, 290, 291, 327
xx. 4-16	304
xx. 5	348
xx. 5-16	36, 329
xx. 6	41, 80, 426
xx. 7	33, 286
xx. 8	80
xx. 9	35, 49, 52, 351
xx. 10	40, 103
xx. 12	34, 44
xx. 13	41
xx. 13-17	41
xx. 14	41
xx. 17-38	338
xx. 18	39, 80, 331
xx. 19	80, 84
xx. 22, 25	50, 52
xx, 24	290
xx. 25	80, 194, 327, 392
xx. 27	52
xx. 28	52, 411
xx. 29	309, 339
xx. 30	53
xx. 31	43
xx. 34	288, 399
xx. 35	331
xx. 36	43
xxi. 1	53
xxi. 1-3	41
xxi. 1-18	36, 304, 329
xxi. 3	41, 62
xxi. 5	43, 53
xxi. 7	41, 63
xxi. 10, 31	42
xxi. 11	45, 50, 80
xxi. 11, 12, 13	53
xxi. 13	34
xxi. 14-xxvi. 32	185
xxi. 16	498
xxi. 17	49, 53, 294, 335
xxi. 17, 34	42
xxi. 20	114
xxi. 21, 24	179, 508, 509
xxi. 24	508
xxi. 25	273, 277, 327, 328
xxi. 27	158
xxi. 29	290
xxi. 30	77
xxi. 31	58
xxi. 34	179, 508, 509
xxi. 39	34, 44
xxii.	45, 98, 153, 167, 268

Acts (contd.)—	PAGE
xxii. 3	266, 504
xxii. 3-21	332
xxii. 4	63
xxii. 4, 14, 22	45
xxii. 6, 17	45, 51, 58
xxii. 10	35
xxii. 11	76
xxii. 12	51, 318
xxii. 14	58
xxii. 15	499
xxii. 17	42, 43
xxii. 17-21	332
xxii. 19	62, 64
xxii. 22, 25	59
xxii. 24	80, 508
xxii. 26	178
xxii. 30	179, 508, 509
xxiii.	123
xxiii. 1-9	333
xxiii. 5	93, 94, 95
xxiii. 6	196, 266, 295
xxiii. 11	311
xxiii. 14	57
xxiii. 15	504
xxiii. 17	35
xxiii. 21	40
xxiii. 26	505
xxiii. 27	402
xxiii. 28	508
xxiii. 30	33
xxiii. 32	41
xxiii. 32-33	41
xxiv.	492, 493
xxiv. 3	75, 178, 505
xxiv. 5, 6	185
xxiv. 7	45, 50
xxiv. 8	508
xxiv. 8, 11	508
xxiv. 11, 27	33
xxiv. 14	64, 334
xxiv. [14] 22	63
xxiv. 15	33
xxiv. 15, 21	196
xxiv. 17	290, 291, 332
xxiv. 19	33, 185
xxiv. 21	295
xxiv. 22	504
xxiv. 27	43
xxv. 10	63
xxv. 10, 11	399
xxv. 12	186
xxv. 13	34
xxv. 16	33
xxv. 16	57

THE BEGINNINGS OF CHRISTIANITY

Acts (contd.)—

	PAGE
xxv. 17	42
xxv. 21	42
xxv. 23	57
xxv. 26	508, 509
xxvi.	40, 99, 153, 195, 268
xxvi. 4	273, 498
xxvi. 4, 5	502
xxvi. 5	266, 295, 504
xxvi. 6	335
xxvi. 9-20	332
xxvi. 11	309
xxvi. 15	99
xxvi. 16	99, 498, 499
xxvi. 16-18	333
xxvi. 17	96
xxvi. 18	103
xxvi. 19	34, 44
xxvi. 20	270
xxvi. 23	49
xxvi. 24	50
xxvi. 25	178, 505
xxvi. 26	34, 44, 50, 108
xxvi. 27	64
xxvi. 29	33, 34
xxvii.	395
xxvii. 1-xxviii. 16	304, 330
xxvii. 1	36, 158
xxvii. 1-3	164
xxvii. 2	290
xxvii. 3	351
xxvii. 3, 17	351
xxvii. 7	403
xxvii. 9-11, 21-26	330
xxvii. 10	33, 34
xxvii. 12, 39	33
xxvii. 14	411
xxvii. 17	402, 403
xxvii. 19	34
xxvii. 24	50
xxvii. 27	33
xxvii. 33	42
xxvii. 34	34, 113
xxvii. 35	45, 286
xxvii. 39	57
xxvii. 41	35
xxviii. 1-7	351
xxviii. 2	44
xxviii. 6	84
xxviii. 8	84
xxviii. 8, 17	45, 51, 58
xxviii. 10	43
xxviii. 11	404
xxviii. 12	41
xxviii. 13	41

Acts (contd.)—

	PAGE
xxviii. 14	41, 311
xxviii. 15	61, 289, 335, 336
xxviii. 16	36, 41, 57, 113, 186, 304
xxviii. 17	41, 45, 50, 57, 158
xxviii. 17-20	335
xxviii. 20	335
xxviii. 21	289
xxviii. 22	45, 335
xxviii. 23	75, 194, 195
xxviii. 23, 31	195
xxviii. 25-28	319
xxviii. 26, 27	88
xxviii. 28	45, 195
xxviii. 30	43
xxviii. 30-31	186
xxviii. 31	176, 194, 492
Romans i. 13	289
i. 18	331
ii. 1 ff.	336
ii. 16	254
vii.	334
vii. 19-23	409
ix., x.	291
x. 4	334
xiii. 1	56, 399
xiv.	321
xiv. 5	294
xv. 1-3	399
xv. 6	35
xv. 23-25	289
xv. 25	290
xv. 25-28	332
xv. 30-32	339
xvi.	290
xvi. 21	247, 290
xvi. 23	290
xvi. 25	254
1 Corinthians i.-iv.	339
i. 1	288
i. 12	288
i. 14	286, 288
i. 26	316
ii. 3	288
iv. 1	500
v. 11	325
vii. 18	292
viii.-x.	326
viii. 1 f.	321
ix. 1	332
ix. 15	288
ix. 20	291, 321
x. 16	286
x. 23	321
xi. 23	268, 286

INDEX 535

1 Corinthians (contd.)—	PAGE	Galatians (contd.)—	PAGE
xiv. 16	. 286	ii. 7 f.	. 319
xiv. 21	. 102	ii. 10	. 279
xv. 1	. 254	ii. 11	292, 323, 326
xv. 3	. 268	ii. 11-13	. 341
xv. 8	. 332	ii. 13	. 409
xv. 9	. 266	iii. 4	. 286
xv. 30	. 35	iii. 5	. 286
xv. 32	. 288	iii. 13	. 295
xv. 55	. 50	iii. 15-25	. 334
xvi. 1	. 290	iv. 4	. 295
xvi. 1-4	. 332	iv. 10	. 294
xvi. 2	. 294	iv. 13	. 283
xvi. 3	. 291	iv. 14	. 287
xvi. 5	. 288	iv. 20	. 282
xvi. 19	. 288	v. 3	. 292
2 Corinthians i. 8	. 289	v. 11	. 286
i. 15 ff.	. 288	v. 20	. 325
i. 16	. 288	vi. 6	. 500
i. 19	. 290	vi. 12	. 286
ii. 12	. 288	Ephesians iv. 28	. 325
ii. 22	. 266	v. 15	. 504
iii. 17	52, 142	vi. 21	. 290
viii., ix.	290, 332	Philippians iii.	. 307
viii. 18 ff.	247, 291	iii. 2	327, 333, 339
x.-xiii.	. 339	iii. 5	. 266
xi.	. 269	iii. 6	. 266
xi. 10	. 249	Colossians iv. 7	. 290
xi. 23	289, 338	iv. 10	. 290
xii. 1	. 34	iv. 10, 11	. 261
xii. 20	. 325	iv. 10, 14	. 316
Galatians i. and ii.	. 269	iv. 11	. 261
i.	. 268	iv. 12	261, 496
i. 6	. 282	iv. 14	. 315
i. 11	. 254	iv. 17	. 496
i. 13	266, 326	1 Thessalonians i. 1	. 290
i. 14	. 266	i. 9	. 287
i. 15	. 296	ii. 9	. 288
i. 15-17	. 268	ii. 12	. 287
i. 16	272, 319	ii. 14	287, 330
i. 17	. 268	iii. 1	287, 330
i. 18	272, 280, 318, 319	iv. 6	. 325
i. 18-24	. 269	2 Thessalonians i. 1	. 290
i. 19	. 270	i. 5	. 287
i. 20	. 271	iii. 8	. 288
i. 21	271, 272	1 Timothy i. 13	. 266
i. 21-24	. 272	iv. 6	. 501
i. 22	267, 278	2 Timothy i. 5	. 320
i. 23	266, 267	ii. 8	. 254
ii. 153, 156, 157, 271, 273, 275, 277, 278, 285, 322, 414		iii. 10	. 501
		iii. 11	. 286
ii. 1	279, 286	iv. 9-12	. 261
ii. 2	. 323	iv. 10	235, 249
ii. 3	. 320	iv. 11	261, 315, 316
ii. 6	. 325	iv. 12	. 290

2 Timothy (contd.)— PAGE
   iv. 20 290
Titus iii. 12 290
Philemon 23, 24 261
   24 . . . 290, 315, 316
Hebrews i. 1 492
   ii. 12 495
   iii. 102
   iv. 12 58
   vi. 1, 2 111
   x. 20 58

Hebrews (contd.)— PAGE
   xi. 32 495
   xi. 34 . . . . 75, 76
1 Peter i. 23 58
2 Peter 251
   ii. 7 97
   iii. 15 f. 309
1 John i. 1 500
Revelation ii. 9 311
   iii. 9 311

INDEX III

GREEK AND LATIN WRITERS

	PAGE
Adamantius, De recta fide, iv. 8	240
Aelian, Var. Hist. viii. 7	504
Antiphon, Frag. iii. 67	62
Archimedes, Arenarius, prooem.	494
Aristophanes, Acharnae, 484	62
Athanasius, Festal Epistle, 39	504
Babrius 115. 11	353
Barnabas vi. 4	97
Caesar, Bellum Gallicum, i. 40	14
Cassius, Dio, xxxviii. 36-46	14
lxxviii. 18. 5	495
Cicero, Ad Atticum, ii. 1 f.	12
Brutus, 262	12
De legibus, i. 2, 5	12
i. 5	11
Clement of Alexandria—	
Adumbr. in 1 Peter	220, 221
Strom. v. 12	220, 221
Strom. v. p. 551	509
Apud Eusebius, H.E. v. 14	75, 259
1 Clement xviii.	94
xxxvii. 3	504, 505
lv.	76
2 Clement xvii. 1	509
Clement. Recog. x. 71	507
Cyprian, De exhort. martyr. 11	257
Testim. adv. Jud. i. 20	257
Demosthenes, De corona	501
Diodorus Siculus, ii. 1	135
xvi. 76	491
Diognetus, Epistle to, i.	506
Dionysius of Halicarnassus, Ad Amm., praef.	493, 506
Ad Pomp. iii. 12	14
Antiq. Rom. i. praef.	505
vi. 43	493
De admir. vi dic., sub fin.	506
De orator. antiq. i. 1	493
De Thucyd. 5, 6	11
9	12
34	13

	PAGE
Euripides, Troades, 378	353
Eusebius, Demon. Evang. p. 120.	496
H.E. ii. 15	254, 259
ii. 22	261
iii. 4	232, 233, 254, 258
iii. 4. 6	318, 496
iii. 4. 7	247
iii. 23	259
iii. 24	254
iii. 24. 15	234, 235
iii. 39	254, 499, 500, 503
iv. 23	257
vi. 14	252, 254, 259
vi. 25	252, 254, 262
Galen, Comm. Hipp. de Epidemiis, iii. 32	355
De fac. nat. i.	39, 353
De tremore, i.	490
De typis, i.	490
De usu partium, vi. sub fin.	505
vi. 584. 12 (Kuhn)	32
vi. 633. 4	32
Hermogenes, De inventione, iii. 1	506
Hero i. 220 (Schmidt)	504
Herodian i. l. 1	11
Herodotus ii. 7	59
Herondas iv. 29	353
Inscriptions—	
C.I.G. xiv. 607	61
C.I.G. 4521	357
C.I.G. 4523	357
I.G. ii. 788. 8	507
Irenaeus i. 23. 1	503
ii. 22	259
iii. 1	254, 212, 213, 254
iii. 10. 1	212, 503
iii. 11. 7	259
iii. 11. 11	256
iii. 14	212, 254
iii. 14. 1	503
iii. 14. 2	503

Irenaeus (contd.)—	PAGE		Longinus, On the Sublime, i. 4	PAGE 36
iii. 15. 1		220	xii. 5	36
iii. 21. 2		494	Lucian, De hist. conscrib. 23	490
v. 20. 2		257	29	499
Epideixis, xliii.		259	37	9
Jerome, Ep. ii. ad Paulinum		254, 257	48	12, 495
xx. 4, ad Damasum,		65, 236, 237	53	491
			55	490
liii. ad Paulinum		236, 237	58	13
Ad. Hedib. ii..		254	60	11
Comment. on Isaiah, iii. 6		234, 235	Imagines, 7	353
Comment. on Matthew, Praef.		238, 239, 259	Menippus, 20	493
			Symposium, 1	502
De vir. ill. 5		252	Marcus Aurelius iii. 5. 2	495
7		236, 237, 254, 258	Moeris, p. 205 (Pierson)	503
8		254	Monarchian Prologue	242
Quaest. hebr. in Gen.		234	Origen, Apud Eus. H.E. vi. 25	224-226
Josephus, Antiq. i. 84. 1.		11		
ii. 61. 1.		11	Hom. on Josh. 7	257
viii., xiii., xiv., xv.		135	Hom. in Luc.	226, 227
xi. 3. 19		501	Papyri—	
xi. 6-8		26	P. Am. 131. 3 ff.	509
xii. 5. 5.		28	132. 5 ff.	509
xii. 6. 2		28	B.G.U. i. 362	61
xii. 6. 3		27	iii. 715. 14	507
xii. 7. 6		28	iii. 924	507
xii. 7, 7		28	iii. 937. 4	508
xii. 10. 2		27	Fay. 109	61
xii. 10. 4		29	P. Giss. i. 27	509
xii. 10. 6		28	P. Lille, 27	507
xv. 5. 3		14, 493	P. Lips. i. 32	508
xviii. 5. 3		507	P. Lond. 23. 54 ff.	501
xix. 1. 12		493	854	493
xix. 2. 2		493	P. Oxy. 745	507
xix. 6. 1		294	P. Par. 46. 19 f.	501
xx. 5. 1		312, 356	P. Petrie, i. 19. 30	507
Contra Apion. i. 2		494	P.R. 205	508
i. 9		41	P. Ryl. 119. 3	506
i. 10		502, 504	P.S.I. 411. 3 ff.	501
i. 23		501	P. Strass. i. 41. 37	508
ii. 1. or i. 1.		506	P. Tebt. 43	61
ii. 1		506	Philo, De decalogo, 18	502
ii. 41		506	Legatio ad Gaium, 30	508
B.J. i. prooem. 3		494	De opificio mundi, praef.	507
i. 1. 6		492	De vita Mosis, i. sub fin..	505
i. 19. 4		14	ii. 8	10
ii. 13. 3		357	Phrynichus, p. 126 (Rutherford edit.)	33
iv. 4. 3		493	pp. 342 f.	42
vi. 2. 5		499	p. 495	497
vii. 3. 2		501	Pliny, Epist. x. 96	309
Vita, 9		494	Plutarch, Alex. 671 D	353
65		502, 508	Aratus, 3	12
Justin, i. Apol. 66		497	Coriolanus, 26	10

INDEX

Plutarch (contd.)—
- De defectu oracul. 414 E . 351
- De glor. Athen. 347 A . . 36
- De sollertia animalium, 968 C D 494
- Philopoem. 368 A . . . 353
- Symposium, i. 1. 5 . . 504

Polybius i. 1 10
- i. 14 8
- ii. 56 . . . . 8, 14
- ii. 37. 4 494
- iii. 1. 4 494
- iii. 1. 7 491
- iii. 4 10
- iv. 28. 6 501
- v. 31. 4 501
- v. 75 10
- ix. 2 10
- xi. 1. 5 134
- xii. 4 c 9
- xii. 25 . . . . 8, 9
- xii. 25 a 14
- xii. 25 e 9
- xii. 25 g, 3 . . . 8, 499
- 27 499
- xii. 28. 3 494
- xiv. proem. 491

Polybius (contd.)—
- xvi. 12 11
- xvi. 17. 9 f 8
- xxxvi. 1 14
- Polycarp i. 2 97
- Quintilian x. 1. 31 . . . 11
- Sallust, Catiline, 31 . . . 14
- Suetonius, Claudius, xxv. . . 335
- Tacitus, Annales, xv. 63 . . 14
- Historiae, ii. 47 . . . 14
- Tertullian, Adv. Marc. iv. 2 222, 223, 252, 253
- iv. 5 . . . 252, 254

Theophrastus, Characteres,
- prooem. 501
- Hist. Plant. i. . . . 505

Thucydides ii. ad init. . . . 505
- iv., v., viii. 13
- iv. 54 62

Vettius Valens 43. 18 (Kroll) . 495
- 226. 20 495
- 276. 23 501

Victorinus Petavius, in Apoc. i. 20 256

Xenophon, Agesilaus, 4. 4 . . 62
- Cyropaed. prooem. . . 494
- Symposium, viii. 33 . . 62

www.ingramcontent.com/pod-product-compliance
Lightning Source LLC
Chambersburg PA
CBHW052044290426
44111CB00011B/1612